The A.I. Marketer

ANDREW W. PEARSON

ANDREW W. PEARSON

THE A.I. MARKETER

Intelligencia
www.intelligencia.co

Copyright © 2019 Andrew W. Pearson. All rights reserved.

No part of this book may be reproduced, stored in a retrieval system, or transmitted by any means without the written permission of the author, excepting brief quotes used in reviews.

Limit of Liability/Disclaimer of Warranty: While the publisher and author have used their best efforts in preparing this book, they make no representations or warranties with respect to the accuracy or completeness of the contents of this book and specifically disclaim any implied warranties of merchantability or fitness for a particular purpose. No warranty may be created or extended by sales representatives or written sales materials. The advice and strategies contained herein may not be suitable for your situation. You should consult with a professional where appropriate. Neither the publisher nor author shall be liable for any loss of profit or any other commercial damages, including but not limited to special, incidental, consequential, or other damages.

Intelligencia Limited also publishes its books in a variety of electronic formats. Some content that appears in print may not be available in electronic books. For more information about Intelligentsia's products, visit our website at www.intelligencia.co.

First published by Intelligencia.

All rights reserved

ISBN-13 9781094693118

CONTENTS

ACKNOWLEDGMENT xi
PREFACE xiii
CHAPTER ONE: INTRODUCTION 1
    ML + DL 12
    So, what is a Neural Net? 28
    Current State of AI 37
    A.I. Dilemma 41
    A.I. + Social 44
    Conclusion 50
CHAPTER TWO: PERSONALIZATION 61
    Overview 61
    Personal shopping 81
    Website Morphing 85
    Affective Computing 91
    Customer Relationship Management (CRM) 97
    Customer Loyalty 108
    Customer Lifecycle 118
    Engagement and Loyalty Platform 123
    Geofencing Applications 126
    Gamification 131
    Natural Language Processing 134
        Creating a market for feedback 136
        Reducing Search Friction with A.I. 138
    Conclusion 139
CHAPTER THREE: A.I. + ANALYTICS 149
    Overview 149
    Data Mining 150
    Customer Analytics 154
    Types of Analytics 160
        Analytical Models 165
            Decision Trees 165
            k-Means Cluster 167
            k-Nearest Neighbors 169
            Logistic Regression 170
            A/B Testing 172
            Time Series Model 176
            Discriminant Analysis 178
            Survival or Duration Analysis 179

    Swarm Intelligence 181
Analytical + A.I. Models 181
    Customer Segmentation 181
    Customer Acquisition Model 185
    Recency-Frequency-Monetary (RFM) Models 186
    Propensity to Respond Model 188
    Customer Conversion Model 189
    Customer Lifetime Value (CLV) 190
    Customer Churn Model 191
    Optimizing Marketing Offers 193
    Lookalike Marketing 193
    Chronological View of a Marketer's Analytics Implementation 196
Edge Analytics 197
Sentiment Analysis 198
Clickstream Analysis 201
Location Analytics 206
Conclusion 207
CHAPTER FOUR: MARKETING **213**
Overview 213
Psychology of Personalization 217
Digital Interactive Marketing: Five Paradigms 230
SEO 232
Content Intelligence 237
Measurement 243
Conclusion 246
CHAPTER FIVE: SOCIAL A.I. **251**
Overview 251
The Four Steps of Social Media 257
Six Types of Social Media 260
    Collaborative Projects 261
    Blogs 263
        Microblogs 265
    Content Communities 267
        Instagram 268
    Social Networks 270
        WeChat 271
    Virtual Game Worlds 274
    Virtual Social Worlds 274
Psychometrics 277
Social Media Analytics 282
Social Media Monitoring 286

Conclusion 290
CHAPTER SIX: UNIFIED ANALYTICS 297
Overview 297
Data Governance 298
Hadoop 304
Chips...311
   GPUs 312
Deep Learning Frameworks...315
   TensorFlow...316
   Caffe2..319
   Torch..319
   Keras 320
   Pytorch..320
   Deeplearning4j 321
Streaming Analytics...321
   Comparison of Stream Processing Services..............................326
Internet of Things..330
Augmented and Virtual Reality..336
Conclusion 338
CHAPTER SEVEN: THE A.I. MARKETER 343
Overview 343
Text 347
   Chatbots...349
   Sentiment Analysis 353
      Sentiment Analysis Tools..355
   Augmented Search 360
Image..361
   Facial Recognition...362
   Image Search 367
Video 369
Audio 371
   Voice Activated Internet 372
Programmatic Advertising...377
Customer Journey 380
   Listening...381
   Rules Engine 386
   Automation...387
   Moderation...387
   Messaging 388
   Data & Analytics 396
The Future 400
ABOUT THE AUTHOR 409

INDEX **412**

ANDREW W. PEARSON

ACKNOWLEDGMENT

You know who you are.

ANDREW W. PEARSON

PREFACE

The A.I. Marketer is the first in what will be a series of books that will grow and evolve with the changes in the technologies I discuss here—artificial intelligence, machine learning, deep learning, personalization, psychometrics, IoT, NLP, geofencing, analytics, and social media. This book grew out of several talks I did about AI, customer loyalty, and digital marketing in such varied industries as gaming, sports betting, aviation, and retail. I usually envision my books to be part of an ongoing dialog about the technology I discuss here because this technology changes so rapidly and much of what I write here will be outdated within a year or two, if not sooner!

Parts of this book have been written on the Macau-Hong Kong ferry, 30,000 feet above both the Pacific Ocean and the Dark Continent of Africa, on the Guangzhou-Macau high-speed rail line, at a great Korean BBQ restaurant on Jeju islands off the South Korean Peninsula, inside a taxi stuck in snarled and steamy Manila traffic, inside a chillingly air-conditioned mall in Dubai, as well as on the London Underground, and in a café around the corner from Moscow's historical Red Square, to say nothing of all the hotel and motel rooms I've been scribing in; planes, trains, automobiles, ferries, and Tuk-tuks, too. If you find this book instructive, please keep up to date with my latest work on social media, a list of my social sites is included on my author page at the end of the book.

CHAPTER ONE: INTRODUCTION

"AI is one of the most important things humanity is working on. It is more profound than, I dunno, electricity or fire."

Sundar Pichai, CEO, Google

We seem to be living in the age of AI. Everywhere you look, companies are touting their most recent AI, machine learning (ML), and deep learning breakthroughs, even when they are far short of anything that could be dubbed "breakthroughs." "AI" has probably superseded "Blockchain", "Crypto", and/or "ICO" as the buzzword of the day. Indeed, one of the best ways to raise VC funding is to stick 'AI' or 'ML' at the front of your prospectus and ".ai" at the end of your website. Separating AI fact from fiction is one of the main goals of this book; the other is to help marketing executives in companies both large and small understand AI so that they can utilize this groundbreaking technology in ways that are simple and complex and, hopefully, rather ingenious.

Major tech companies have embraced AI and machine learning as if it was one of the most important discoveries ever invented; Google, whose CEO compares it to the discovery of fire and electricity, is now an "AI-first" company; Amazon's entire business is shaped by AI, from its customer personalization, to its warehousing, robotics and logistics capabilities, to its voice-activated smart speakers; IBM has Watson; Facebook has AI and ML algorithms that test out which of its AI and ML ideas are most effective and should be rolled-out company-wide; Adobe, a big player in the multi-channel marketing space, runs much of its Experience Cloud marketing platform through its Sensei AI product; even the analytics powerhouse SAS has recently announced[1] that it will spend US $1B over the next three years on AI software and initiatives. Even some of the smaller vendors we are partnered with at Intelligencia have embraced AI for fear of missing out on this burgeoning market.

Not only are some CEO comparing it to one of the most important discoveries of man—fire—but others, like Elon Musk believe if we're don't carefully develop AI within a strong legal, moral and ethical framework, it could me the end of mankind; nothing like playing with fire on both ends of the human spectrum, potentially, at least.

In its report *Sizing the prize. What's the real value of AI for your business and how you can capitalise*[2], PWC believes that, "AI could contribute up to $15.7 trillion to the global economy in 2030, more than the current output of China and India combined. Of this, $6.6 trillion is likely to come from increased productivity and $9.1 trillion is likely to come from consumption-side effects."

Because AI is still in its infancy, PWC believes that there are opportunities for emerging markets to leapfrog more developed counterparts with AI.[2] Although this is a possibility, the inherent requirements of AI—a highly educated workforce, strong backing from higher learning institutes, a strong legal and regulatory framework, and access to huge sources of data—might limit emerging market successes. However, this shouldn't make companies in the industrial world too comfy. PWC's claim that, "within your business sector, one of today's start-ups or a business that hasn't even been founded yet could be the market leader in ten years' time"[2] probably holds true. AI threatens on both the micro and macro front, which is rare in a technology.

According to PWC's analysis, "global GDP will be up to 14% higher in 2030 as a result of the accelerating development and take-up of AI—the equivalent of an additional $15.7 trillion."[2] For PWC, the economic impact of AI will be driven by[2]:

1. Productivity gains from businesses automating processes (including use of robots and autonomous vehicles).
2. Productivity gains from businesses augmenting their existing labour force with AI technologies (assisted and augmented intelligence).
3. Increased consumer demand resulting from the availability of personalised and/or higher-quality AI-enhanced products and services.[2]

As behavioral economist Susan Menke explains in her paper *Humanizing Loyalty*[3], "Decision fatigue and cognitive fatigue are the opposite of flow and seamlessness. We are making too many decisions that tax our cognitive bank account. We dole it out on important things and not on things that are already operating well." In her paper, Menke touches upon the concept of psychological scripts—the idea that the mind doesn't have to focus on many day-to-day activities as they can be handled without much thought.[3] The more seamless a company can make the interaction process, the more likely a customer will continue to do business with it.[3] Tom Fishburne, the founder of Marketoonist, says "the best marketing doesn't feel like marketing," and his words are a good motto for today's digital marketer. AI can help make marketing so personalized and wanted that customers actually enjoy and respond to it positively. The seamlessness of the marketing is paramount.

We live in an instant gratification world and the companies that are likely to thrive in this new environment will be the ones who can both keep up with the requirements of their discerning and demanding customers and predict what these customers will be wanting throughout their customer journeys. Today, companies need every advantage they can get so that they provide better service than their competitors.

Being able to accurately predict not only who a marketer's best leads and prospects are, as well as how and when it is best to engage them is nice but understanding how their acceptance of these marketing offers will affect the overall bottom line is what *The A.I. Marketer* is all about.

This ability will not only empower marketers and salespeople in the coming seasons to be radically more productive and profitable than they are today, but also give multiple corporate departments visibility on their micro and macro needs. Used properly, predictive analytics and AI can transform the science of sales forecasting from a dart-throwing exercise to a precision instrument.

The concept of sales and marketing automation has already produced some of the highest-flying successes in high-tech. Companies like Salesforce.com have been wildly successful in automating the sales process for salespeople and sales managers. Big software vendors like SAP, Microsoft, and Oracle are vying for supremacy, while smaller players like Pegasystems, SugarCRM, Netsuite, and Sage are offering interesting products at highly affordable prices.

In their article *10 Principles of Modern Marketing*[4], Ann Lewnes and Kevin Lane Keller argue that, "Technology has changed everything. Fundamentally, it allows for new ways to create customer experiences, new mediums to connect with customers and other constituents, and trillions of data points to understand customer behavior and the impact of marketing programs and activities. Yet, with all that progress, we are still only at the tip of the iceberg in terms of the profound impact technology will have on the future of marketing."

In their *AI: Your behind-the-scenes marketing companion*[5], the Adobe Sensei Team claims that, "The battle to win customer hearts and minds is no longer simply about your product. It's about the experience. Because that's what keeps customers coming back. To compete on experience, you need to understand what customers want now while anticipating what they'll do next. And because your customers have lots of choices, you don't have a lot of time to get it right."

"But many times, the knowledge you need to personalize interactions and compel customers to act is locked up in huge amounts of data," says the Adobe Sensei Team.[5] "This means someone has to sift through it all to recognize patterns, trends, and profiles, so you can quickly act on insights. The problem is, it's too much data for humans to sort through alone. That's where artificial intelligence and machine learning come in," the team says.[5]

"Customers will always expect a human touch in their interactions," warns the Adobe Sensei Team.[5] "These new technologies won't replace marketing jobs, but they will change them," the team claims.[5] Brands should think of AI and machine learning as their behind-the-scenes marketing assistant who helps unlock insights in volumes of data, develops a deeper understanding of what customers want, a forecasting tool that predicts trends, as well as monitors unusual activity, such as spikes or drops in sales—all while giving brands more time to make decisions that matter.[5]

"To fully realize the potential of technology," Lewnes and Keller argue that, "it takes transformation across people, processes, *and* technology. Only by recognizing all three forces will modern marketers reap the full benefits that technology can have on marketing transformation."[4]

"To thrive in this new era, it is imperative that marketers embrace developments in technology and test and adopt new advancements that fit their business—whether AI, or voice, or augmented reality—before they lose a competitive edge," claim Lewnes and Keller.[4] "At the same time, mastering technology is not the only criterion for success in the modern marketing era—the right people and processes must also be put in place to properly develop, manage, and nurture the benefits of that technology," they add.[4]

"In terms of people, today's marketers must possess many traits. They must be curious, flexible, agile, and nimble. They must be willing to be change agents, always looking around the corner and helping to scale transformation as champions for change," say Lewnes and Keller.[4] The status quo no longer works—continuous development of new skills for all marketers is critical.[4]

Today's marketing organization needs people with diverse skill sets and expertise in key areas.[4] "Managers should ensure their marketing teams include members who bring creative and analytical capabilities, as well as individuals who can play newly evolved roles on a team—whether that's someone skilled in web development, data analytics, e-commerce, or new media," argue Lewnes and Keller.[4] Marketing organization almost have an impossible job as "many of these jobs didn't exist four or five years ago, and even if they did, they have changed dramatically in recent years."[4]

Furthermore, while these new, specialized jobs have emerged, marketers must keep in mind the broadening marketing ecosystem.[4] "The dynamic cross-channel nature of marketing today requires that campaigns be integrated and connected across every channel," say Lewnes and Keller.[4]

"Processes must also change for technology organizations. Today, the customer-decision process is becoming more complex and varied. As the customer journey becomes increasingly nonlinear, the organization must change to reflect that," warn Lewnes and Keller.[4] "In a more complex marketplace, internal organizational lines need to be redrawn. Silos must be broken down and cross-functional relationships established so that marketing works seamlessly across other groups in the organization such as IT, finance, sales, and product management," say Lewnes and Keller.[4]

"Marketing can benefit from the output of these other groups and also contribute to the groups' effectiveness and success at the same time," claim Lewnes and Keller.[4] "For example, to improve the reliability of financial forecasting, marketing can share early-warning lead indicators that have been shown to affect bottom-of-the-funnel behaviors and ultimately revenue (for example, the number of customer visits to company-controlled websites)."[4] The marketing department can show its growing worth and value by demonstrating "its impact on the business, validating the ROI of every dollar to peer groups in the organization and becoming a strategic driver of the business."[4]

All these changes, however, require that technology organizations adapt to this new marketing and technological environment. Lewnes and Keller argue that marketers "must learn to be agile, take risks, fail fast, and apply lessons. They must also learn how to get the most out of a data-rich world by testing, optimizing, and activating."[4]

Lewnes and Keller claim "experience is the new brand."[4] They are right, experience will be one of the big differentiators for companies going forward."[4]

"With traditional marketing, the customer-decision and company-selling process was comparatively simple with customers entering into a company's sales and marketing funnel and making various choices along the way to becoming loyal, repeat customers," say Lewnes and Keller.[4] Today, every "customer touch point online and offline—as wide-ranging as a tweet, product download, in-store purchase, the company's social purpose, its executives' behavior, and the corporate culture—can shape experiences that define a brand for customers," warn Lewnes and Keller.[4]

"Marketers operate at the intersection of many of these customer experiences and are uniquely positioned to help steer the future directions for brands," claim Lewnes and Keller.[4] "In doing so, marketers of technology products cannot just worship the product alone and be transactional in their customer interactions. They must create full-on, immersive experiences for customers that build strong ties to the company and the brand as a whole. Experiences are the new competitive battlefield and a means to create powerful differentiation from competitors," argue Lewnes and Keller.[4]

"With technology products, seamless product installation and operation, in particular, is absolutely critical," say Lewnes and Keller.[4] "If customers cannot successfully use a company's products, there will be no value realization, and they will eventually switch to products from other companies that they can more easily access and use," warn Lewnes and Keller.[4] "Beyond designing products that are as easy to use as possible, technology companies must have a wide range of support and services for customers to help them with product installation and use, employing ample training resources as well as informative forums, social channels, and websites," conclude Lewnes and Keller.[4]

For example, companies such as Adobe, Fitbit, Buffer, Wistia, and Mailchimp "put tremendous emphasis on customer education and ensuring customers have the best product experience possible." Fitbit, the health wearables company, "has combined sensors, wireless technology, software, and services to pioneer the connected health and fitness market."[4] "To help customers take full advantage of Fitbit and lead healthier, more active lives, the company uses social media and the support of a strong community, in addition to telephone, email, and chat customer support, to both impart and collect information about product usage," say Lewnes and Keller.

In China, the government's "Made in China 2025" initiative lists AI as one of its main technologies to focus the country's attention and resources on. China's big three, also known as the BAT's—Baidu, Alibaba, and Tencent—have distinct advantages over non-Chinese companies in their access to massive amounts of data, which can be collected at will, with no concern for privacy. According to Arthur Herman's article *China's Brave New World of AI*[6], China has "set the goal of spending $150 billion to achieve global leadership in this high-tech area by 2030." I mention this because anyone who wants to keep up with AI needs to keep a close eye on what is happening within China.

Any company looking to compete for customers in a multitude of industries might soon be competing against a Chinese company that is utilizing state-of-the-art AI tech—that should be the fear, even for companies who think that they're insulated from foreign competition. Another one of our partners at Intelligencia is Alicloud, a division of China's Alibaba, and they offer highly competition products as well as a unique service called *China Connect* that allows users to upload content to a server outside China, then have it made available on severs inside China, which means content downloads will be much quicker for a Chinese audience. This is something AWS doesn't do, and probably won't for a long time.

Although the U.S. government doesn't have similar AI initiatives, some of the most valuable companies in the world are based in America and they have become that valuable because of their tech discoveries and the FAANG—Facebook, Amazon, Apple, Netflix, and Google—group of companies will be pouring billions into AI over the next few decades.

Europe is also home to 1,600 early stage AI software companies. According to MMC Ventures' *The State of AI: Divergence 2019*[7], "The European start-up ecosystem is maturing. One in six European AI companies is a 'growth'-stage company with over $8m of funding." "AI entrepreneurship is becoming mainstream. In 2013, one in 50 new startups embraced AI. Today, one in 12 put AI at the heart of their value proposition," the study adds.[7]

The study found that the UK was "the powerhouse of European AI with nearly 500 AI startups—a third of Europe's total and twice as many as any other country."[7] However, "Germany and France are thriving European AI hubs. High quality talent, increasing investment and a growing roster of breakout AI companies are creating feedback loops of growth and investment."[7]

Right now, there is almost a fear-of-being-left-out attitude to AI, but one needs to be cautious when jumping into the latest and greatest technological advancements, as plenty of wiped-out crypto and blockchain investors can attest to. Anyone planning to jump into AI should be aware that the technology is not new. In reality, it is decades old. The only thing new is the amount of companies claiming to be AI companies when they really aren't.

In her article *Understanding Three Types of Artificial Intelligence*[8], Anjali Uj explains that, "The term AI was coined by John McCarthy, an American computer scientist in 1956." In his *MIT Technology Review* article *Is AI Riding a One-Trick Pony?*[9], James Somers concurs, noting that, "Just about every AI advance you've heard of depends on a breakthrough that's three decades old." Of course, many recent advances in hardware and software technology have turned AI's potential into reality, but still anyone wishing to jump into AI should have a good understanding of where it came from and how long it has been around, as well as the limitations inherent in the technology.

Not only is AI old, but it is also a difficult technology to implement. In its *Conquer the AI Dilemma by Unifying Data Science and Engineering*[10], Databricks says that only "1 in 3 AI projects are successful and it takes more than 6 months to go from concept to production, with a significant portion of them never making it to production—creating an AI dilemma for organizations."

In early 2018, while sitting at the China Gardens restaurant at HKUST, I was giving an update of my recent AI talks to a friend, who is a professor there. After listing off a few of the exotic locales I been invited to speak in, my friend chimed in with the rather dismissive statement, "You know AI is just a neural net, right?" I answered that I did, but his question stuck with me. The question wasn't meant to be mean-spirited, it was simply the question of an annoyed expert who had been training neural nets for over a decade and was bothered, as well as probably a little surprised, by all the attention AI was suddenly receiving. My friend's question made me realize how the overhype machine had hit overdrive with AI, machine learning, and deep learning.

AI might be the most quintessential example of Amara's Law–the tendency to overestimate the effect of a technology in the short run and underestimate the effect in the long run—out there.[11] The term fits well for a technology that was trumpeted with incredible fanfare when it first arrived, then had to survive what has become known as the "AI winter"–a time when AI was losing grants and destined for the scrap heap of overhyped technological history–and is now flourishing everywhere, or so it seems.

Today, success in AI is partly due to the fact that not only are the necessary hardware and software components available, but they are also highly affordable as well. The algorithms that AI are based upon are now complex enough to handle the massive amounts of data that AI, ML and deep learning need to function. AI has the potential to radically alter the world of aviation, retail, medicine, automobiles, telcos, airlines, manufacturing, finance, insurance, government, gaming, and a whole lot of other industries.

The professor's question also went to the very heart of the simplicity and beauty that is AI. Perhaps he was one of those who had labored through the "AI winter," but he had a good point. We often get caught up in the buzzword mumbo jumbo of technology hype. The professor is correct about AI, it is just a neural net that goes around and around improving upon itself as it learns more and more about a problem. But then again, what beauty and form can be created out of that little old neural net. This book is an attempt to explain how wide and varied those uses can be and how marketers can utilize AI, machine learning, deep learning, as well as all the technology based upon it.

The *Artificial Intelligence and Life in 2030* [12] study states that, "Artificial Intelligence (AI) is a science and a set of computational technologies that are inspired by—but typically operate quite differently from—the ways people use their nervous systems and bodies to sense, learn, reason, and take action." The study adds that, "While the rate of progress in AI has been patchy and unpredictable, there have been significant advances since the field's inception sixty years ago."[12]

Once a mostly academic area of study, twenty-first century AI enables a plethora of mainstream technologies that are having a substantial impact on our everyday lives. Computer vision and AI planning, for example, drive the video games that are now a bigger entertainment industry than Hollywood."[12] Through its AWS platform, Amazon brings natural language processing (NLP), automatic speech recognition (ASR), text-to-speech (TTS), and neural machine translation (NMT) technologies within reach of every developer. In chapter seven, I detail how companies can utilize Amazon's AI products like *Lex*, *Transcribe*, and *Comprehend* to produce multilingual content for their branding efforts. Amazon even has a product called *Polly* that allows brands to turn text into speech in multiple languages, in voices that sound eerily human and, in some cases, almost as good as professional actors.

The use cases I delve into throughout this book utilize the five prominent segments of AI—sound, time series, text, image, and video–and I will explain how marketers of all sizes can utilize them effectively. Areas such as CRM, customer loyalty, data governance, marketing automation, social marketing, and social listening will be radically affected by AI and ML.

A new acronym that is making the software rounds these days is CXM—Customer Experience Management—and it helps businesses collect and process real-time data from across an organization. A CXM platform activates content based on customer profiles, allowing personalized experiences to be delivered in real time. This is the future of both AI and brand marketing.

So why choose to go down the complex AI road? Well, in the article *Artificial intelligence Unlocks the True Power of Analytics*[13], Adobe explains the vast difference between doing things in a rules-based analytics way and an AI-powered way, including:

- Provide warnings whenever a company activity falls outside the norm. The difference:
    - **Rules-based analytics:** You set a threshold for activity (e.g., "200–275 orders per hour") and then manually investigate whether each alert is important.
    - **AI-powered analytics:** The AI analytics tool automatically determines that the event is worthy of an alert, then fires it off unaided.
- Conduct a root cause analysis and recommend action. The difference:
    - **Rules-based analytics:** You manually investigate why an event may have happened and consider possible actions.
    - **AI-powered analytics:** Your tool automatically evaluates what factors contributed to the event and suggests a cause and an action.
- Evaluate campaign effectiveness:
    - **Rules-based analytics:** The business manually sets rules and weights to attribute the value of each touch that led to a conversion.
    - **AI-powered analytics:** The AI analytics tool automatically weights and reports the factors that led to each successful outcome and attributes credit to each campaign element or step accordingly.
- Identify customers who are at risk of defecting:
    - **Rules-based analytics:** You manually study reports on groups of customers that have defected and try to see patterns.
    - **AI-powered analytics:** Your tool automatically Identifies which segments are at greatest risk of defection.
- Select segments that will be the most responsive to upcoming campaigns:
    - **Rules-based analytics:** You manually consider and hypothesize about the attributes of customers that might prove to be predictive of their response.
    - **AI-powered analytics:** Your tool automatically creates segments based on attributes that currently drive the desired response.
- Find your best customers:
    - **Rules-based analytics:** You manually analyze segments in order to understand what makes high-quality customers different.

- **AI-powered analytics:** Your tool automatically identifies statistically significant attributes that high-performing customers have in common and creates segments with these customers for you to take action on.

Beyond the reasons listed above, I will discuss how AI can be used in website morphing, customer and media recommendations, purchase prediction, demand forecasting, programmatic advertising, social listening, and much, much more.

In the *AI Momentum, Maturity, & Models for Success*[14], a consortium of companies consisting of Accenture, Intel, Forbes Insight, and SAS polled 300 executives from a wide variety of industries about AI and discovered that it appears likely that we are on the verge of a radical momentum shift for the technology. As seen in many other leaps of technology over the years, greater familiarity is likely to lead to greater trust.[14] "Think about your first ride in a car sharing service, or the first time you used online banking," says Oliver Schabenberger, Chief Operating Officer and Chief Technology Officer for SAS.[14] So it will be with AI and machine learning. Schabenberger adds that[14]:

> *"In a sense, those represented a leap of faith in newer technologies. That is where we are with AI right now. But even for many sophisticated users, AI still is a black box—they put data in, they get an output, and they do not understand the connections between the inputs and the outputs of AI systems. That is a fundamental challenge that has implications on everything from regulatory compliance to the customer experience it even affects how we respond to examining biases in our models. Organizations that have adopted AI can illuminate the black box by observing how the model responds to variations in the inputs, and adjusting accordingly."*

The companies behind the study believe, "We are rapidly approaching a 'critical mass' moment in which the entire picture comes into view."[14] The responses submitted in the "What are the benefits of AI study" (see Figure 1) show "a level of enthusiasm and AI-focused activity that point to an explosion of AI adoption just around the corner, even as gaps in capabilities and strategy are revealed. Already, 72 percent of the organizations we surveyed have either deployed AI-based technology or are in the process of doing so."[14]

"A large percentage of survey respondents report having real success with AI. When looking at only those who have reported having deployed AI, 51 percent say the impact of deployment of AI-based technologies on their operations has been 'successful' or 'highly successful,'" claim the consortium.[14]

THE A.I. MARKETER

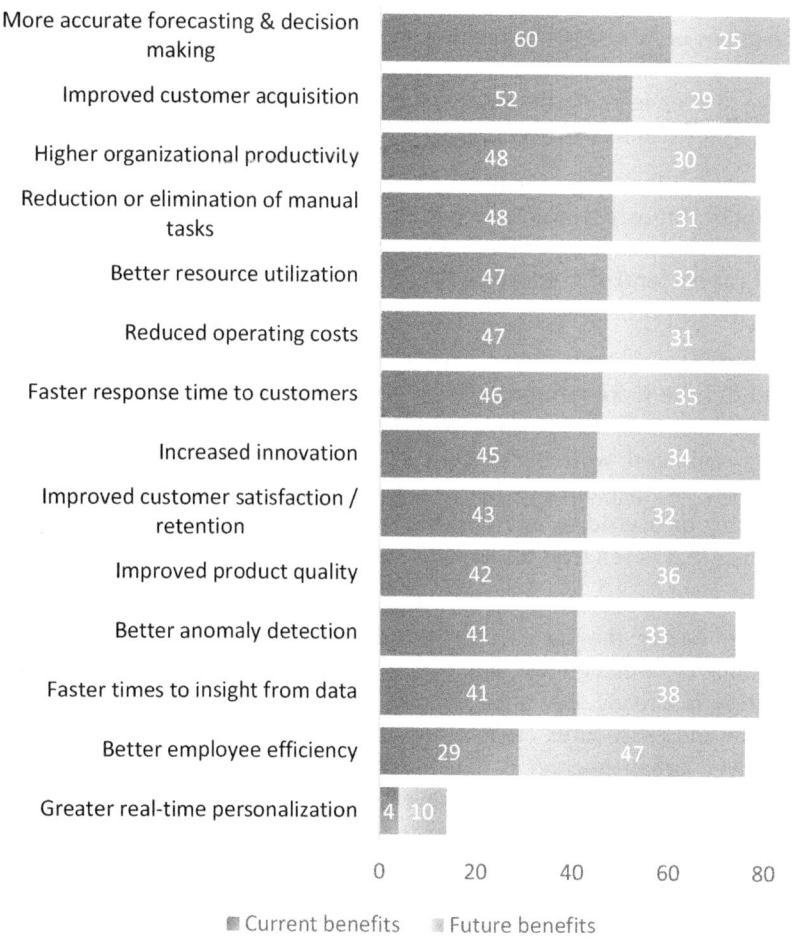

Figure 1: Benefits of AI
Source: SAS.com

"It seems clear that the more experienced you are in AI, the more likely you are to appreciate the central role analytics will play in your efforts," argues the consortium.[14] "Among those who have deployed AI, they recognize that success in AI is success in analytics," says Schabenberger.[14] "For them, analytics has achieved a front and center role in AI. In fact, in many ways, AI is analytics."[14] Perhaps that is why 66 percent of respondents agree that "AI will enable us to mine massive volumes of data faster to inform business decisions."[14]

"Generally speaking, the progress of AI is unparalleled," says Intel's Melvin Greer.[14] "We've seen some very positive first impressions regarding how AI can actually be used – and we have a long way to go. We've seen more sophistication from our customers, who are looking for us to be much clearer in our explanations of AI, and in illuminating important differences between different types of AI and analytics technologies—from augmented reality and machine learning to deep learning, automated forecasting and many more—so we don't treat AI as the hammer to every nail."[14]

Despite the idea that suggests AI operates independently of human intervention, those responsible for putting AI to work in the polled organizations recognize that these technologies require rigorous oversight.[14] "In fact, nearly a quarter (23 percent) of AI adopters review or evaluate AI outputs at least daily," reports the consortium.[14]

The report "also suggests that companies that have been more successful with AI tend to have more rigorous oversight processes in place. For example, 74 percent of successful companies report that they review their AI output at least weekly, compared with 33 percent of those that are less successful."[14] Additionally, "43 percent of successful companies have a process in place for augmenting or overriding questionable results, compared with 28 percent of companies that haven't yet found success in their AI initiatives."[14]

"Many believe that despite these positive signs, oversight processes have a long way to go before they catch up with advances in AI technology," says the consortium.[14] "Although we are still in the very early phases of AI, the technology is already well ahead of the marketplace when it comes to the processes and procedures organizations have in place to provide oversight," says Oliver Schabenberger.[14] "For example, we would be seeing more widespread use of driverless cars if government oversight and automaker-level governance capabilities were able to keep up with the technology itself. The technical capabilities are ahead of our ability to cope with the technology."[14]

This does mean companies might find themselves in the unenviable position of waiting for slow moving governments to get on their initiatives, but I'd argue it's always better to be ahead of any government oversight task force than be a follower behind it.

ML + DL

According to Wikipedia, Machine Learning (ML) is the subfield of computer science that "explores the construction and study of algorithms that can learn from data. Such algorithms operate by building a model based on inputs and using that to make predictions or decisions, rather than following only explicitly programmed instructions."[15]

ML "evolved from the study of pattern recognition and computational learning theory in artificial intelligence."[15] It "explores the study and construction of algorithms that can learn from and make predictions on data—such algorithms overcome following strictly static program instructions by making data driven predictions or decisions, through building a model from sample inputs."[15]

As per Wikipedia, ML can be broken down into the following three categories[15]:

1. Supervised learning: The computer is presented with example inputs and their desired outputs, given by a "teacher", and the goal is to learn a general rule that maps inputs to outputs.
2. Unsupervised learning: No labels are given to the learning algorithm, leaving it on its own to find structure in its input. Unsupervised learning can be a goal in itself (discovering hidden patterns in data) or a means towards an end (feature learning).
3. Reinforcement learning: A computer program interacts with a dynamic environment in which it must perform a certain goal (such as driving a vehicle), without a teacher explicitly telling it whether it has come close to its goal or not. Another example is learning to play a game by playing against an opponent.

There are so many use cases for ML and deep learning for marketing departments that it is almost impossible to create an exhaustive list here, but it is particularly useful for marketing personalization, customer recommendations, spam filtering, network security, optical character recognition (OCR), voice recognition, computer vision, fraud detection, optimization, language translations, sentiment analysis, SEO, and online search, amongst many others use cases.

Figure 2 reveals how ML can be broken down into supervised and unsupervised learning, as well as reinforcement learning that is specific to a marketing department.

Machine-learning can also be used to spot credit card or transaction fraud in real-time. ML can build predictive models of credit card transactions based on their likelihood of being fraudulent and the system can compare real-time transactions against these models. When the system spots potential fraud it can alert either the bank or retail outlet where the transaction occurred. This is exceptionally important for businesses with online retail presences because online fraud is on the rise and this could be an additional security layer that ensures a purchase made is ultimately a purchase paid.

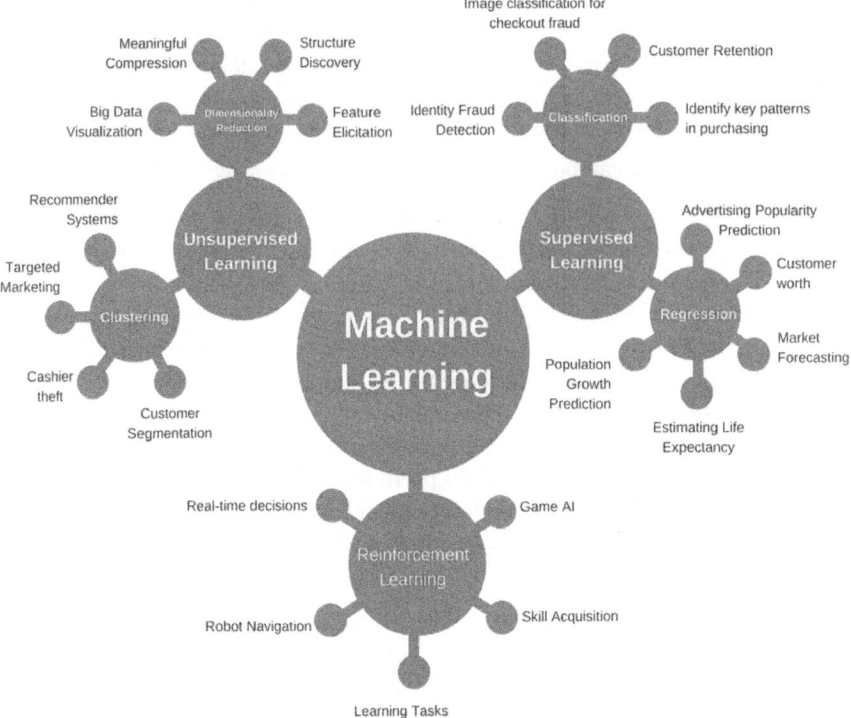

Figure 2: Machine Learning for marketers
Source: Artificial Intelligence in Logistics[16]

Although ML and data mining often employ the same methods and overlap significantly, they do differ markedly. As Wikipedia explains[15]:

> "While machine learning focuses on prediction, based on known properties learned from the training data, data mining focuses on the discovery of (previously) unknown properties in the data (this is the analysis step of Knowledge Discovery in Databases). Data mining uses many machine learning methods, but with different goals; on the other hand, machine learning also employs data mining methods as 'unsupervised learning' or as a preprocessing step to improve learner accuracy. Much of the confusion between these two research communities (which do often have separate conferences and separate journals, ECML PKDD being a major exception) comes from the basic assumptions they work with: in machine learning, performance is usually evaluated with respect to the ability to reproduce known knowledge, while in Knowledge Discovery and Data Mining (KDD) the key task is the discovery

of previously unknown knowledge. Evaluated with respect to known knowledge, an uninformed (unsupervised) method will easily be outperformed by other supervised methods, while in a typical KDD task, supervised methods cannot be used due to the unavailability of training data.

Another subset of AI and ML is deep learning, which, according to SAS[17] is "a type of machine learning that trains a computer to perform human-like tasks, such as recognizing speech, identifying images or making predictions. Instead of organizing data to run through predefined equations, deep learning sets up basic parameters about the data and trains the computer to learn on its own by recognizing patterns using many layers of processing."

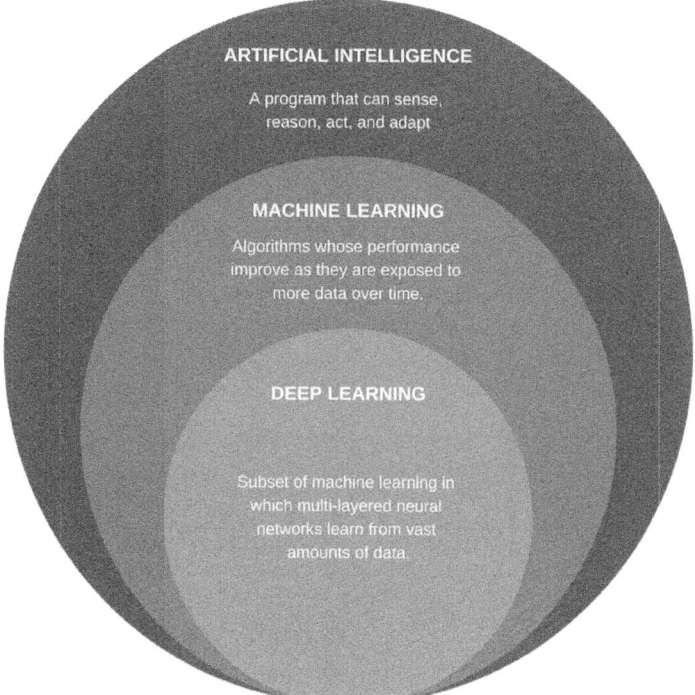

Figure 3: A.I., ML, and Deep Learning

Deep learning (see figure 3) is a branch of machine learning and it seeks to imitate the neural activities of the human brain. Deep learning architectures have been applied to fields of computer vision, speech recognition, NLP, audio recognition, social network filtering, machine translation, bioinformatics and drug design, amongst others. In most cases, results have proven to be comparable, if not superior to human experts.[18]

In his blog[19], Ajit Jaokar explains that:

"Deep learning refers to artificial neural networks that are composed of many layers. The 'Deep' refers to multiple layers. In contrast, many other machine learning algorithms like SVM are shallow because they do not have a Deep architecture through multiple layers. The Deep architecture allows subsequent computations to build upon previous ones. We currently have deep learning networks with 10+ and even 100+ layers. The presence of multiple layers allows the network to learn more abstract features. Thus, the higher layers of the network can learn more abstract features building on the inputs from the lower layers. A Deep Learning network can be seen as a Feature extraction layer with a Classification layer on top. The power of deep learning is not in its classification skills, but rather in its feature extraction skills. Feature extraction is automatic (without human intervention) and multi-layered. The network is trained by exposing it to a large number of labelled examples. Errors are detected and the weights of the connections between the neurons adjusted to improve results. The optimisation process is repeated to create a tuned network. Once deployed, unlabelled images can be assessed based on the tuned network."

Table 1 shows the general use cases for AI broken down by industry. This is a generalized list and many of these use cases can be utilized by industries other than the ones specified.

GENERAL USE CASE	INDUSTRY
Sound	
Voice recognition	UX/UI, Automotive, Security, IoT
Voice search	Handset maker, Telecoms
Sentiment analysis	CRM for most industries
Flaw detection	Automotive, Aviation
Fraud detection	Finance, Credit cards
Time Series	
Log analysis/Risk detection	Data centers, Security, Finance
Enterprise resource planning	Manufacturing, Auto, Supply Chain
Predictive analytics using sensor data	IoT, Smart home, Hardware manufacturing
Business and Economic analytics	Finance, Accounting, Government

GENERAL USE CASE	INDUSTRY
Recommendation engine	E-Commerce, Media, Social Networks
Text	
Sentiment analysis	CRM, Social Media, Reputation mgmt.
Augmented search, Theme detection	Finance
Threat detection	Social Media, Government
Fraud detection	Insurance, Finance
Image	
Facial recognition	Multiple industries
Image search	Social Media
Machine vision	Automotive, Aviation
Photo clustering	Telecom, Handset makers
Video	
Motion detection	Gaming, UX, UI
Real-time threat detection	Security, Airports

Table 1: A.I. use cases
Source: deeplearning4j.org

AI can also play a huge role in automation in a multitude of industries. Currently, there is an interesting philosophical problem rearing its ugly head around automation, something perfectly captured in Kevin Roose's *NY Times* article *The Hidden Automation Agenda of the Davos Elite*.[20] Roose reports that, at Davos 2019, there were "panel discussions about building 'human-centered A.I.' for the 'Fourth Industrial Revolution'—Davos speak for the corporate adoption of machine learning and other advanced technology—and talk about the need to provide a safety net for people who lose their jobs as a result of automation."[20]

What's interesting about the article is Roose's explanation that, whereas the corporate CEOs who attended Davos were publicly fretting about the potential job loses an automation revolution will unquestionably bring, behind the scenes executive were racing to automate as fast as they could, with little concern for the impending cuts to their work force.[20] Automation was seen as just another way for businesses to get a leg up on their competition, the worker be damned.[20] This attitude speaks of how integral AI will be to future IT ROI endeavors and, although many will fail in their AI and ML journey, it won't be for wont of trying.

"All over the world, executives are spending billions of dollars to transform their businesses into lean, digitized, highly automated operations. They crave the fat profit margins automation can deliver, and they see A.I. as a golden ticket to savings, perhaps by letting them whittle departments with thousands of workers down to just a few dozen," says Roose.[20]

"People are looking to achieve very big numbers," said Mohit Joshi, the president of Infosys, a technology and consulting firm that helps other businesses automate their operations.[20] "Earlier they had incremental, 5 to 10 percent goals in reducing their work force. Now they're saying, 'Why can't we do it with 1 percent of the people we have?'"[20]

Some experts claim that AI will create more jobs than it destroys, and that job losses caused by automation won't be catastrophic, but rather automation will help workers become more productive and will free them from repetitive work, giving them more time for creative tasks over routine ones, notes Roose.[20]

Much of this discussion is going on behind closed doors as political unrest in the West makes automation a taboo subject right now.[20] "That's the great dichotomy," says Ben Pring, the director of Center for the Future of Work at Cognizant, a technology services firm, "On the one hand, Pring says, these profit-minded executives want to automate as much as possible, on the other hand, they fear a backlash in civic society."[20]

However, if you want to hear how American leaders talk about automation in private, you need only listen to what their counterparts in Asia say, claims Roose.[20] Terry Gou, the chairman of the Taiwanese electronics manufacturer Foxconn, says the company plans to replace 80 percent of its workforce with robots in the next five to 10 years.[21] Richard Liu, the founder and CEO of Chinese e-commerce company JD.com, hopes to one day have a completely automated company—100% operated by AI and robots—and it has invested $4.5 billion to build an AI center in Guangdong, China, to implement such a scenario.[22]

Automation doesn't just have to be about robots and factories, however, but can remove the day-to-day drudgery work. As I will explain later in the book, there are AI tools out there that can automate away the repetitive processes like cataloging images or video and let human do what humans do best—create.

"Deep learning has made speech-understanding practical on our phones and in our kitchens, and its algorithms can be applied widely to an array of applications that rely on pattern recognition," the *Artificial Intelligence and Life in 2030* study adds.[12]

Google Duplex has shown that AI bots can do things like make reservations at hair salons and restaurants and this is one of the deep learning futures. Businesses need to develop voice and speech understanding technology or they risk being left behind by their competition. Voice, in particular, is a technology waiting for mass use. We communicate through voice as much as any other sense and the companies that win the battle in voice will win the battle for the

21st Century consumer, I believe.

In a March 2017 note to clients[23], RBC Capital argued that Amazon's voice assistant Alexa "could bring the U.S. e-commerce giant $10 billion of revenues by 2020 and be a 'mega-hit.'" According to Arjun Kharpal, "The investment bank has dubbed the technology 'voice-activated internet (VAI)' and said it represents a 'material opportunity' for both Amazon and Google, which has its own technology called Google Assistant."[23]

RBC breaks down the numbers as follows[23]:

- Alexa device sales, which could reach $60 million by 2020.
- Voice driven shopping sales, which could reach $400 per customer by 2020.
- Platform revenues: If Amazon reaches over 100 million installed Alexa devices then it could create an app store and tap into "platform revenue."
- Amazon Web Services (AWS) tailwind.[23]

RBC Capital notes that, "As the number of skills rises, Amazon will create a marketplace that will allow them to charge companies to appear more prominently in its app store."[23] Paid skills on Alexa could be lucrative and Amazon could collect revenue share payments accordingly.

Of course, Amazon is not alone in the voice activated internet (VAI) market.[23] Google has its own voice assistant built into Android smartphones and its own smart speaker called Google Home.[23] According to Kharpal, "RBC was surprised by the popularity of Google Home since it was only launched in October 2016 in the U.S."[23] Apple and Microsoft are also highly involved here. Siri hasn't been the success Apple hoped it would be but they still see it as an integral part of their VAI future.

"Awareness of Google Home among 1,748 Amazon customers surveyed by RBC was 60 percent. Whereas when RBC did a similar survey in September 2015, just shortly after the Echo had launched widely in the U.S., only 33 percent of respondents had heard of Alexa. Google however still only has around 80 Actions, which are like Alexa's skills, which total above 10,000," explains Kharpal.[23]

All-in-all, the *A.I. Marketer* doesn't have to concern itself with who might win the VAI battle as any of these platforms can bring considerable eyeballs to the table. However, any money spent to reach these eyeballs should produce a healthy ROI. The app market that Amazon could build atop Alexa could also be a hidden opportunity for creative marketers.

One of the major use cases for AI is sentiment analysis, which uses natural language processing (NLP) to gain insight into how a business is seen on social media. According to skymind.ai[24]:

> *"Natural language refers to language that is spoken and written by people, and natural language processing (NLP) attempts to extract information from the spoken and written word using algorithms. NLP encompasses active and a [sic] passive modes: natural language generation (NLG), or the ability to formulate phrases that humans might emit, and natural language understanding (NLU), or the ability to build a comprehension of a phrase, what the words in the phrase refer to, and its intent. In a conversational system, NLU and NLG alternate, as algorithms parse and comprehend a natural-language statement and formulate a satisfactory response to it."*

In chapter two, I discuss Milgrom and Tadelis' recent study[25] that utilizes NLP to create an environment that promotes trust, similar to the way institutions emerged in the medieval trade fairs of Europe that helped foster trust amongst traders.[25] Milgrom and Tadelis believe that AI can be applied to these marketplaces to help foster a more trustworthy and better buying experience for their customers.[25]

Another important area for AI is text analytics. In his article *Text Analytics: How to Analyse and Mine Words and Natural Language in Businesses*[26], Bernard Marr states that, "Text analytics, also known as text mining, is a process of extracting value from large quantities of unstructured text data." Marr explains that, "While the text itself is structured to make sense to a human being (i.e., A company report split into sensible sections) it is unstructured from an analytics perspective because it doesn't fit neatly into a relational database or rows and columns of a spreadsheet. Traditionally, the only structured part of text was the name of the document, the date it was created and who created it."[26]

"Access to huge text data sets and improved technical capability means text can be analysed to extract high-quality information above and beyond what the document actually says," Marr argues.[26] "Text can be assessed for commercially relevant patterns such as an increase or decrease in positive feedback from customers, or new insights that could lead to product tweaks, etc."[26] This means text analytics can help us discover things we didn't already know but, perhaps more importantly, had no way of previously knowing.[26] These could be incredibly important insights for a business both about itself and, potentially, about its competitors.[26]

Marr says that, "Text analytics is particularly useful for information retrieval, pattern recognition, tagging and annotation, information extraction, sentiment assessment and predictive analytics."[26] It could both reveal what customers think about a company's products or services, or highlight the most common issues that instigate customer complaints.[26]

Just as importantly for marketing departments everywhere, AI is changing how people interact with technology, specifically their mobile phones and social media channels.[12] "Many people have already grown accustomed to touching and talking to their smart phones."[12] More still seem exceptionally comfortable with the amount of data their smarts phones are both collecting and sharing with other apps, particularly Facebook. This solves one of AI's biggest needs—lots and lots of data.

China and Chinese apps like WeChat don't have the problem that every America and European app has—the need for privacy—which allows them to collect all kinds of data on their users. Because the Chinese government places the onus of censorship on the social media companies, these companies need to collect as much information as they can to ensure compliance, even to the point of not allowing messages about particular people and/or topic across their platforms for fear of government reprisals.

Human beings are, first and foremost, creatures of habit and, if a business can understand these habits on both a micro and macro level, it can not only predict what its customers are going to want, but also what they will do, so a business can, potentially, shape that behavior. Smart businesses can utilize all this behavior in a predictive way and optimize multiple parts of their operations, including labor management.

Marketing has always been about influencing people's behavior and what could be different here is *The A.I. Marketer's* ability to understand how one customer's actions will affect the company's entire operation. With this insight extrapolated over a million customers over 365 days of the year, the brand can take the most appropriate—and optimized—action to reap the highest profit.

In his article *How Real-time Marketing Technology Can Transform Your Business* [27], Dan Woods makes an amusing comparison to the differing environments that marketers have to deal with today, as compared to what their 1980s counterparts might have faced[27]:

> "Technology has changed marketing and market research into something less like golf and more like a multi-player first-person-shooter game. Crouched behind a hut, the stealthy marketers, dressed in business-casual camouflage, assess their weapons for sending outbound messages. Email campaigns, events, blogging, tweeting, PR, ebooks, white papers, apps, banner ads, Google Ad Words, social media outreach, search engine optimization. The brave marketers rise up and blast away, using weapons not to kill consumers but to attract them to their sites, to their offers, to their communities. If the weapons work, you get incoming traffic."

AI needs to be a part of this frenetic marketing environment, because, honestly, it would be impossible to even do the outbound part of marketing without AI.

Mobile advertising requires three things—reach, purity and analytics.[28] Reach can be fostered by accessing accounts through multiple platforms like blogs, geofencing applications, OTT services, mobile apps, QR codes, push and pull services, RSS feeds, search, social media sites, and video-casting, amongst others.[28] "Purity" refers to the message and its cleanliness; if the data is unstructured and untrustworthy it is, basically, useless and data governance is paramount for real-time advertising to work properly.[28] The third ingredient, analytics, "involves matching users' interests—implicit and explicit, context, preferences, network and handset conditions—to ads and promotions in real time."[28]

In its *Definitive Guide to Data Governance*[29], Talend, the cloud data integration leader, states that, "Data governance is a collection of processes, roles, policies, standards, and metrics that ensure the effective and efficient use of information in enabling an organization to achieve its goals." Data governance "establishes the processes and responsibilities that provide the quality and security of the data used across a business. Data governance defines who can take what action upon what data, in which situations, and using what methods."[29]

Talend believes that, "A well-crafted data governance strategy is fundamental for any organization that works with data."[29] It underpins how a business can benefit from consistent, standard processes and responsibilities.[29] "Data governance ensures that roles related to data are clearly defined and that responsibility and accountability are agreed upon across the enterprise. A well-planned data governance framework covers strategic, tactical, and operational roles and responsibilities," claims Talend.[29]

The digital ecosystem (see figure 4) is an environment where electronic, or "digital", devices are the tools which communicate and manage the content and activities within it. A major component of a digital environment generally includes a comprehensive presence within the internet that includes websites, cloud servers, search engines, social media outlets, mobile apps, audio and video, and other web-based resources. The digital ecosystem is a great framework on which to understand the plethora of marketing channels available to companies to reach their customers and potential customers. With the digital ecosystem, brands should have a firm understanding of how many touchpoints they hit for each individual, as well as an aggregate of how far each channel reaches. By my calculation, AI helps all but two of these channels—P2P File Sharing and Newsgroups.

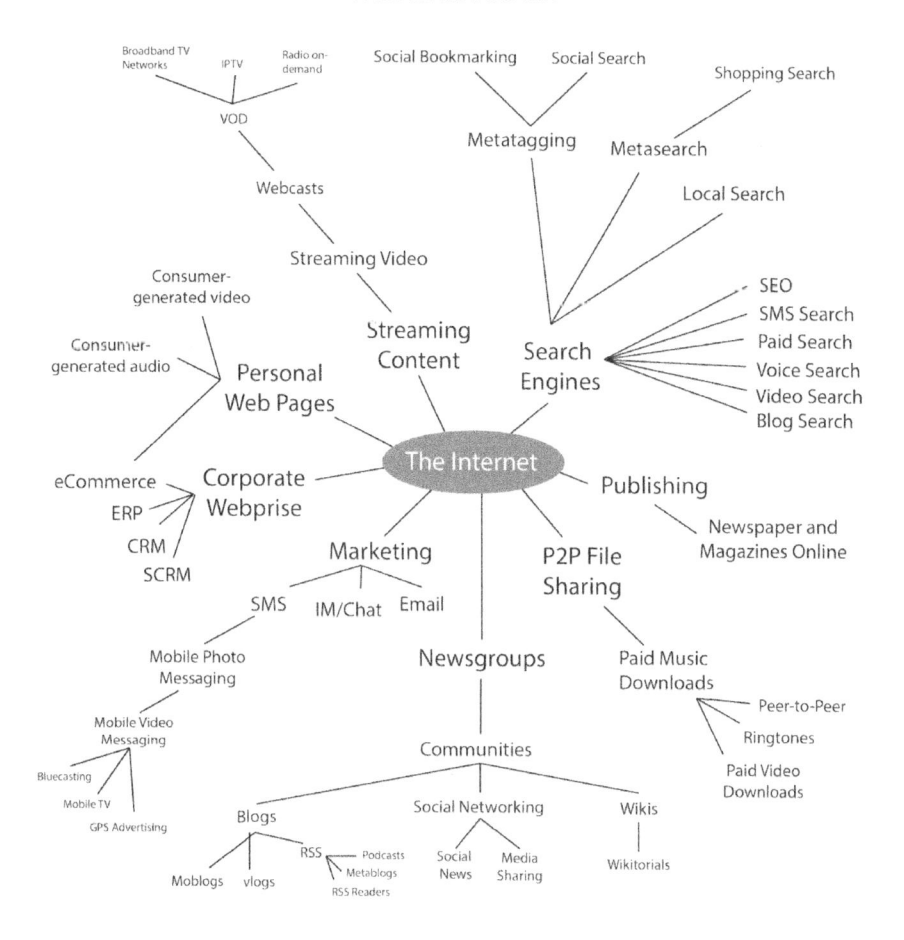

Figure 4: The Digital Ecosystem

Knowing what might interest a customer is only half the battle to making the sale and this is where customer analytics and AI comes in. Customer analytics has evolved from simply reporting customer behavior to segmenting a customer based on his or her profitability, to predicting that profitability, to improving those predictions (because of the inclusion of new data), to *actually manipulating customer behavior* with target-specific promotional offers and marketing campaigns. These are the channels that AI thrives in and this is where a marketer can gain a powerful competitive advantage, especially when AI is added to the mix.

Manipulating customer behavior might be controversial, but it shouldn't be, especially on the scale and level discussed here. The reality is every loyalty program is an attempt to manipulate a customer's purchasing habits. The number one thing that creates loyalty in *anybody* (that includes your customers) is the social construct of reciprocity—the social norm that's been evaluated and debated since the days of Aristotle. Many scholars believe it to be one of the single most defining aspects of social interaction that keeps society whole. Reciprocity doesn't have to be a bar of gold, like some casinos in Macau entice their high rollers with, it could simply be an acknowledgement of poor customer service along with the promise to do better next time.

Today, the truth is loyalty programs are everywhere and they desperately need to evolve. In his article *Earn Your Wings: Air Canada's Successful Gamification Venture into Loyalty*[30], Gabe Zichermann states that "There's little question that the loyalty 'industry' has an innovation problem." "With few exceptions," Zichermann notes, "the world's largest loyalty programs (mostly in travel, finance and retail) are mostly the same as they were 20 years ago. Social, mobile, gamification have struggled to find a footing, even as they are the entire foundation of next-gen loyalty systems such as those developed by Square, Belly or any number of gamified providers."[30]

Real-time stream processing is an integral part of this rapidly changing marketing environment and if brands don't join the real-time marketing revolution, they will be left behind, I have no doubt. AI moves in real-time, without it, limitations abound.

According to IBM[31], 2.5 quintillion bytes of data are created each day. That is 10 to the power of 18 and that number is growing exponentially each year; 90% of the world's data was created over the past two years and data creation is certainly not going to abate any time soon. This data—which has been dubbed "Big Data"—comes from everywhere; our daily financial transactions; our personal online shopping history; our social media uploads; our mobile downloads, even, more and more, sensor data coming off machines and even people (think wearables).

The social nature of sharing personal content with family, friends, and associates may be the driver behind this growth and it is a growth that several studies[32][33] suggest will soon outpace revenue generated by commercial media, such as music downloads, video clips, and games. This is the kind of growth that any business operator ignores at its own peril and when a business delves into this Big Data world, it needs to ensure that what it is opening up is a treasure chest of valuable information and not a *Pandora's Box* full of pain.

China might be racing ahead in data collection, but we should give pause before ceding the AI race to them. Chinese government data is notoriously untrustworthy and data collection on platforms like WeChat and Weibo might be of limited value—who really cares how many orders of General Tsao's chicken gets delivered in Beijing on a given night or how much is spent on those orders? More interesting is what Uber Eats is doing in India, which I detail later. There, Uber Eats utilizes its user and restaurant data to bundle deliveries by offering real-time and timed offers.

In their book *Artificial Intelligence for Big Data*[34], Anand Deshpande and Manish Kumar argue that AI is finding and taking advantage of the best of both worlds—the sophistication and efficiency of the human brain coupled with the brute force of computers. The writers believe that by combing these two worlds we can create "intelligent machines that can solve some of the most challenging problems faced by human beings."[34]

"Taking a statistical and algorithmic approach to data in machine learning and AI has been popular for quite some time now," Deshpande and Kumar argue.[34] "However, the capabilities and use cases were limited until the availability of large volumes of data along with massive processing speeds, which is called Big Data," state Deshpande and Kumar.[34] Without question, "Big Data has accelerated the growth and evolution of AI and machine learning applications."[34] One could argue that AI and machine learning would be impossible without these two technological advances and these could partially explain the AI winter. Table 2 shows a comparison of how things stood before and after the introduction of Big Data to AI.

A.I. BEFORE BIG DATA	A.I. WITH BIG DATA
Availability of limited data sets (MBs)	Availability of ever-increasing data sets (TBs)
Limited sample sizes	Massive sample sizes, resulting in increased model accuracy
Inability to analyze large data in milliseconds	Large data analysis in milliseconds
Batch oriented	Real-time
Slow learning curve	Accelerated learning curve
Limited data sources	Heterogeneous and multiple data sources
Based on mostly structured data sets	Based on structured / unstructured and semi-structured data

Table 2: Comparison A.I. before and after Big Data

In his article *The Fourth Industrial Revolution: A Primer on Artificial Intelligence (AI)*[35], David Kelnar explains that "AI is important because it tackles profoundly difficult problems, and the solutions to those problems can be applied to sectors important to human wellbeing — ranging from health, education and commerce to transport, utilities and entertainment." Kelnar goes on to add that, "Since the 1950s, AI research has focused on five fields of enquiry:

1. **Reasoning:** *the ability to solve problems through logical deduction*
2. **Knowledge:** *the ability to represent knowledge about the world* (the understanding that there are certain entities, events and situations in

the world; those elements have properties; and those elements can be categorised).
3. Planning: *the ability to set and achieve goals* (there is a specific future state of the world that is desirable, and sequences of actions can be undertaken that will affect progress towards it).
4. Communication: *the ability to understand written and spoken language.*
5. Perception: *the ability to deduce things about the world from visual images, sounds and other sensory inputs.*"[35]

"AI is valuable," Kelnar says, "because in many contexts, progress in these capabilities offers revolutionary, rather than evolutionary, capabilities."[35] Kelnar offers up the following applications of AI[35]:

1. Reasoning: Legal assessment; financial asset management; financial application processing; games; autonomous weapons systems.
2. Knowledge: Medical diagnosis; drug creation; media recommendation; purchase prediction; financial market trading; fraud prevention.
3. Planning: Logistics; scheduling; navigation; physical and digital network optimisation; predictive maintenance; demand forecasting; inventory management.
4. Communication: Voice control; intelligent agents, assistants and customer support; real-time translation of written and spoken languages; real-time transcription.
5. Perception: Autonomous vehicles; medical diagnosis; surveillance.

Over time, Kelnar expects the adoption of machine learning to become normalized.[35] "Machine learning will become a part of a developer's standard toolkit, initially improving existing processes and then reinventing them," he adds.[35]

Today, the importance of personalization in customer experience initiatives can't be underestimated. In his article *5 Ways AI Will Boost Personalization in Digital Marketing*[36], Dirk Vogel argues that AI will radically change the marketing landscape by allowing the following:

- Personal shopping for everyone.
- Utilizing chatbots to increase customer service.
- Seamless programmatic media buying.
- Predictive customer service.
- Optimizing marketing automation.

According to Vogel, "Shopping online creates rich data footprints regarding the individual preferences, spending habits and preferred channels of individual consumers. Feeding these digital breadcrumbs into an AI-engine helps bring curated shopping journeys to mass audiences."[36]

As Amazon, Pandora, and Netflix have proven, personalized shopping for everyone is a winning formula[36] "Using an advanced recommendation-AI, e-commerce leader Amazon creates more than 35% of its total revenues with personalized shopping recommendations," states Vogel.[36] "Taking personalization to the next level, artificial intelligence also allows for predicting the kinds of purchases consumers are going to make before they even know it," notes Vogel.[36]

On the marketing side, AI may deliver that extra dash of relevancy programmatic advertising has been waiting for all these years.[36] "On the consumer side, AI helps create individualized display ads that website visitors want to see," [36] while on the accounting side, "bots handle invoicing and payment for these ad transactions, giving marketers more time to focus on the big picture."[36]

With AI, predictive customer service and marketing could be just around the corner.[36] "What may sound like a scenario from the *Minority Report* movie is already in beta testing: Intel subsidiary Saffron has created an artificial intelligence that is able to predict with 88% certainty why, on which channel, and for which product individual customers will seek help next. 'We've been expecting your call,' never rang truer," Vogel predicts.[36]

One of the biggest problems in corporate marketing is hitting the customer with automated marketing offers too often.[36] In the future, AI will analyze a consumer's purchase history and email habits to choose the optimal time for hitting the inbox with content that's bound to boost open rates and conversions," Vogel contends.[36] Social channels can be utilized here to take the personalization to a whole new level. If the AI marketing system recognizes that the most optimum time for a customer to open a piece of marketing collateral is just after they tweet, the system will wait for that tweet and send out the offer once it sees that customer action.

Perhaps one of the biggest leading indicators out there—the stock market—is noticing the structural changes going on in the advertising industry. In their Bloomberg article *Amazon Gets Some Blame in Ad Industry's 24-hour, $5 Billion Rout*[37], Kit Rees and Angelina Rascouet explain that, on 7th February 2019, the world's biggest advertising companies lost more than $5 billion of market value in 24 hours after Publicis Groupe SA reported fourth-quarter sales unexpectedly fell. The fall was supposedly due to "a decline in business with consumer goods brands in the U.S."[37]

"Publicis has been seen as an early mover in shifting to the new digitally-driven advertising that's supposed to keep corporate marketing departments loyal to the old ad firms."[37] "Mirabaud analyst Neil Campling said consumer goods companies can have as many as 25 ad agencies working for them and that looks inefficient," explains Rees and Rascouet.[37]

"The key area hit is North America," Campling explained.[37] "The combination of consumer packaged goods and North America for us points to the rise of Amazon more than anything else, offering a brand new channel for brands to connect directly to consumers."[37]

"Amazon's advertising revenue has been growing fast as it starts to give more prominent placement to sponsored products in search results, rather than those offering the lowest prices. Investors see the area as even more profitable than its main e-commerce business," notes Rees and Rascouet.[37]

Frictionless is the key word these days amongst the big AI companies in the US--the FAANGs (Facebook, Apple, Amazon, Netflix, and Google)—the big three of China, also known as the BATs (Baidu, Alibaba, and Tencent). All of these companies want to make the customer experience as frictionless as possible so that the act of purchasing is as smooth as can be. That is the ultimate goal of the A.I. Marketer.

So, what is a Neural Net?

Artificial Neural Networks (ANN) or just "Neural Networks" are the building blocks of AI. They are non-linear statistical data modeling tools that are used when the exact nature of a relationship between input and output is unknown. In their article *Neural Networks in Data Mining*[38], Singh and Chauhan claim that a neural network is:

> "A mathematical model or computational model based on biological neural networks, in other words, is an emulation of a biological neural system. It consists of an interconnected group of artificial neurons and processes information using a connectionist approach to computation. In most cases an ANN is an adaptive system that changes its structure based on external or internal information that flows through the network during the learning phase."

Jim Gao expounds upon this description in his article *Machine Learning Applications for Data Center Optimization.*[39] Goa writes[39]:

> "Neural networks are a class of machine learning algorithms that mimic cognitive behavior via interactions between artificial neurons. They are advantageous for modeling intricate systems because neural networks do not require the user to predefine the feature interactions in the model, which assumes relationships within the data. Instead, the neural network searches for patterns and interactions between features to automatically generate a best fit model. Common applications for this branch of machine learning include speech recognition, image processing, and autonomous software agents. As with most learning systems, the model accuracy

improves over time as new training data is acquired."

There are three types of training in neural networks; reinforcement learning, supervised and unsupervised training, with supervised being the most common one. Their fundamental characteristics include parallel processing, distributed memory and adaptability to their surroundings.

In her article *A Beginners Guide To AI: Neural Networks*[40], Tristan Greene puts it in simpler terms, stating that, "Scientists believe that a living creature's brain processes information using a biological neural network. The human brain has as many as 100 trillion synapses—gaps between neurons—which form specific patterns when activated. When a person thinks about a specific thing, remembers something, or experiences something with one of their senses, it's thought that specific neural patterns 'light up' inside the brain."

Greene continues, "when you were learning to read you might have had to sound out the letters so that you could hear them out loud and lead your young brain to a conclusion. But, once you've read the word cat enough times you don't have to slow down and sound it out."[40] At that point, Greene contends, "you access a part of your brain more associated with memory than problem-solving, and thus a different set of synapses fire because you've trained your biological neural network to recognize the word 'cat.'"[40]

"In the field of deep learning a neural network is represented by a series of layers that work much like a living brain's synapses," explains Greene.[40] 'Researchers teach computers how to understand what a cat is—or at least what a picture of a cat is—by feeding it as many images of cats as they can."[40] The neural network analyzes those images and "tries to find out everything that makes them similar, so that it can find cats in other pictures," adds Greene.[40]

There are many kinds of deep learning and many types of neural networks, but I will focus upon generative adversarial networks (GANs), convolutional Neural Networks (CNNs), and recurrent neural networks (RNNs) here.

GANs were invented by Ian Goodfellow, one of Google's AI gurus, in 2014.[40] To put it simply, "a GAN is a neural network comprised of two arguing sides—a generator and an adversary—that fight among themselves until the generator wins."[40] Greene gives the example that, "If you wanted to create an AI that imitates an art style, like Picasso's for example, you could feed a GAN a bunch of his paintings."[40]

According to Greene, the process works in the following way, "One side of the network would try to create new images that fooled the other side into thinking they were painted by Picasso. Basically, the AI would learn everything it could about Picasso's work by examining the individual pixels of each image."[40] One side would create the image, while the other side would determine if it was a Picasso.[40] "Once the AI fooled itself," Greene claims, "the results could then be viewed by a human who could determine if the algorithm needed to be tweaked to provide better results, or if it successfully imitated the desired style."[40]

Convolutional Neural Networks (CNNs) are among the most common and robust neural networks around, which have, at least theoretically, been in use since the 1940s.[40] Thanks to advanced hardware and efficient algorithms, they can now be used on a wide scale.[40] "Where a GAN tries to create something that fools an adversary, a CNN has several layers through which data is filtered into categories," explains Greene.[40] "These are primarily used in image recognition and text language processing," notes Greene.[40]

"If you've got a billion hours of video to sift through, you could build a CNN that tries to examine each frame and determine what's going on," explains Greene.[40] "One might train a CNN by feeding it complex images that have been tagged by humans," adds Greene.[40] "AI learns to recognize things like stop signs, cars, trees, and butterflies by looking at pictures that humans have labelled, comparing the pixels in the image to the labels it understands, and then organizing everything it sees into the categories it's been trained on," says Greene.[40]

So how can images be used by a marketer? Well, in his Adobe blog *See It, Search It, Shop It: How AI is Powering Visual Search*[41], Brett Butterfield explains how visual search could become a big part of a buyer's shopping future. "You spot something you love on a passerby. That stranger walking past you is wearing the perfect pair of sneakers. You want them. But you have no idea what brand they were or where to buy them. Even without those essential details, you figure you can go online and search—but you get just a few, mostly irrelevant, results, and you aren't any closer to getting your next favorite pair of shoes. Enter visual search," says Butterfield.[41] Talk about seamless. *Gartner* predicts that image search will be a lucrative technology.[41] Even with visual search still in its early stages, *Gartner* says early adopters will experience a 30 percent increase in e-commerce revenue by 2021.[41]

RNNs are "primarily used for AI that requires nuance and context to understand its input."[40] "An example of such a neural network is a natural language processing AI that interprets human speech," such as Google's Assistant and Amazon's Alexa.[40]

"To understand how an RNN works, let's imagine an AI that generates original musical compositions based on human input," explains Greene.[40] "If you play a note the AI tries to 'hallucinate' what the next note 'should' be. If you play another note, the AI can further anticipate what the song should sound like. Each piece of context provides information for the next step, and an RNN continuously updates itself based on its continuing input—hence the recurrent part of the name," explains Greene.[40] Scientists use neural nets to teach computers how to do things for themselves.

Neural nets are extremely good at finding patterns in data. A key feature of neural networks is that they learn the relationship between inputs and outputs through training. For marketing purposes, neural networks can be used to classify a consumer's spending pattern, analyze a new product, identify a customer's characteristics, as well as forecast sales.[38] The advantages of neural networks include high accuracy, high noise tolerance and ease of use as they can be updated with fresh data, which makes them useful for dynamic environments.[38]

In her article *How DeepMind's AlphaGo Zero Learned all by itself to trash world champ AI AlphaGo*[42], Katyanna Quach explains how neural networks can work when training computers to play board games. According to Quach, the board game *Go* is considered a "difficult game for computers to master because, besides being complex, the number of possible moves—more than chess at 10^{170}—is greater than the number of atoms in the universe."[42]

"AlphaGo, the predecessor to AlphaGo Zero, crushed 18-time world champion Lee Sedol and the reigning world number one player, Ke Jie," explains Quach.[42] The next generation of DeepMind's technology, AlphaGo Zero, beat "AlphaGo 100-0 after training for just a fraction of the time AlphaGo needed, and it didn't learn from observing humans playing against each other—unlike AlphaGo. Instead, Zero's neural network relies on an old technique in reinforcement learning: self-play."[42]

As Quach notes about the process[42]:

> "Essentially, AlphaGo Zero plays against itself. During training, it sits on each side of the table: two instances of the same software face off against each other. A match starts with the game's black and white stones scattered on the board, placed following a random set of moves from their starting positions. The two computer players are given the list of moves that led to the positions of the stones on the grid, and then are each told to come up with multiple chains of next moves along with estimates of the probability they will win by following through each chain.

> "So, the black player could come up with four chains of next moves and predict the third chain will be the most successful. The white player could come up with its own chains and think its first choice is the strongest.

> "The next move from the best possible chain is then played, and the computer players repeat the above steps, coming up with chains of moves ranked by strength. This repeats over and over, with the software feeling its way through the game and internalizing which strategies turn out to be the strongest."

This methodology differs from the old AlphaGo, which "relied on a computationally intensive Monte Carlo tree search to play through Go scenarios."[42] "The nodes and branches created a much larger tree than AlphaGo practically needed to play."[42] "A combination of reinforcement learning and human-supervised learning was used to build 'value' and 'policy' neural networks that used the search tree to execute gameplay strategies," explains Quach.[42] "The software learned from 30 million moves played in human-on-human games, and benefited from various bodges and tricks to learn to win. For instance, it was trained from master-level human players, rather than picking it up from scratch," adds Quach.[42]

"Self-play is an established technique in reinforcement learning, and has been used to teach machines to play backgammon, chess, poker, and Scrabble," says Quach.[42] David Silver, a lead researcher on AlphaGo, explains that it is an effective technique because the opponent is always the right level of difficulty.[42]

"So it starts off extremely naive," Silver says, adding that "at every step of the learning process it has an opponent—a sparring partner if you like—that is exactly calibrated to its current level of performance. To begin with these players are very weak but over time they get progressively stronger."[42]

Tim Salimans, a research scientist at OpenAI, explains that self-play means "agents can learn behaviours that are not hand coded on any reinforcement learning task, but the sophistication of the learned behavior is limited by the sophistication of the environment. In order for an agent to learn intelligent behavior in a particular environment, the environment has to be challenging, but not too challenging."[42]

"The competitive element makes the agent explicitly search for its own weaknesses. Once those weaknesses are found the agent can improve them. In self-play the difficulty of the task the agent is solving is always reasonable, but over time it is open ended: since the opponent can always improve, the task can always get harder," adds Salimans.

Self-play does have its limitations.[42] Right now, there are "problems that AlphaGo Zero cannot solve, such as games with hidden states or imperfect information, such as StarCraft, and it's unlikely that self-play will be successful tackling more advanced challenges."[42]

Self-play will be worthwhile in some areas of AI, argues Salimans.[42] "As our algorithms for reinforcement learning become more powerful the bottleneck in developing artificial intelligence will gradually shift to developing sufficiently sophisticated tasks and environments. Even very talented people will not develop a great intellect if they are not exposed to the right environment," he warns.[42]

DeepMind, the company behind AlphaGo Zero and its predecessor, believes that "the approach may be generalizable to a wider set of scenarios that share similar properties to a game like Go."[42]

In his article *Is AI Riding a One-Trick Pony?*, Somers explains that Geoffrey Hinton, the man who is considered to be the father of deep learning, published a breakthrough paper in 1986, with colleagues David Rumelhart and Ronald Williams that "elaborated on a technique called backpropagation, or backprop for short."[9]

According to Jon Cohen, a computational psychologist at Princeton, backprop is "what all of deep learning is based on—literally everything."[9] "In fact, nearly every achievement in the last decade of AI—in translation, speech recognition, image recognition, and game playing—traces in some way back to Hinton's work."[9] "For decades," Somers explains, "backprop was cool math that didn't really accomplish anything. As computers got faster and the engineering got more sophisticated, suddenly it did."[9]

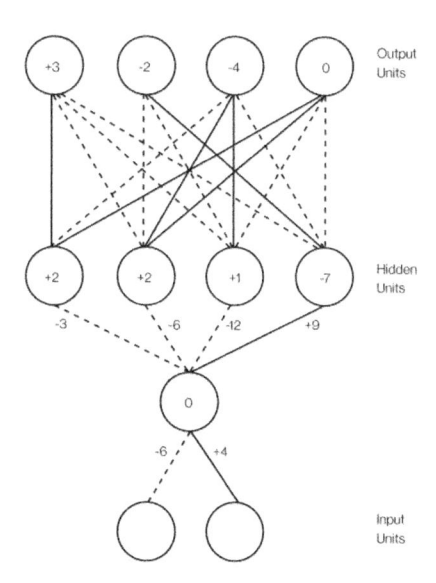

Figure 5: A diagram from the seminal work on "error propagation" by Hinton, David Rumelhart, and Ronald Williams.
Source: Is AI Riding a One-Trick Pony?[9]

When you boil it down, Somers claims, "AI today is deep learning, and deep learning is backprop—which is amazing, considering that backprop is more than 30 years old."[9] Somers adds that, "It's worth understanding how that happened—how a technique could lie in wait for so long and then cause such an explosion—because once you understand the story of backprop, you'll start to understand the current moment in AI, and in particular the fact that maybe we're not actually at the beginning of a revolution. Maybe we're at the end of one."[9] Figure 5 shows a diagram of a neural net from Hinton's paper.

According to Somers[9]:

> "A neural net is usually drawn like a club sandwich, with layers stacked one atop the other. The layers contain artificial neurons, which are dumb little computational units that get excited—the way a real neuron gets excited—and pass that excitement on to the other neurons they're connected to. A neuron's excitement is represented by a number, like 0.13 or 32.39, that says just how excited it is. And there's another crucial number, on each of the connections between two neurons, that determines how much excitement should get passed from one to the other. That number is meant to model the strength of the synapses between neurons in the brain. When the number is higher, it means the connection is stronger, so more of the one's excitement flows to the other."

One of the most successful applications of deep neural nets is in image recognition, which HBO's *Silicon Valley* so hilariously spoofed when Jian Yang's Hot Dog app was able to decipher between images of "hot dogs" and "not hot dogs."[9] The first step in the image recognition process is to show the machine a picture.[9] Somers gives the example of "a small black-and-white image that's 100 pixels wide and 100 pixels tall. You feed this image to your neural net by setting the excitement of each simulated neuron in the input layer so that it's equal to the brightness of each pixel. That's the bottom layer of the club sandwich: 10,000 neurons (100x100) representing the brightness of every pixel in the image."[9]

Somers continues: "You then connect this big layer of neurons to another big layer of neurons above it, say a few thousand, and these in turn to another layer of another few thousand neurons, and so on for a few layers."[9] Finally, as Somers explains, "in the topmost layer of the sandwich, the output layer, you have just two neurons—one representing 'hot dog' and the other representing 'not hot dog.'"[9] "The idea is to teach the neural net to excite only the first of those neurons if there's a hot dog in the picture, and only the second if there isn't."[9] "Backpropagation—the technique that Hinton has built his career upon—is the method for doing this," explains Somers.[9] "Backprop is remarkably simple, though it works best with huge amounts of data," says Somers.[9] "That's why big data is so important in AI—why Facebook and Google are so hungry for it," he adds.[9]

"In this case, the data takes the form of millions of pictures, some with hot dogs and some without; the trick is that these pictures are labeled as to which have hot dogs," says Somers.[9] "When you first create your neural net, the connections between neurons might have random weights—random numbers that say how much excitement to pass along each connection. It's as if the synapses of the brain haven't been tuned yet," notes Somers.[9] "The goal of backprop," Somers explains, "is to change those weights so that they make the network work: so that when you pass in an image of a hot dog to the lowest layer, the topmost layer's 'hot dog' neuron ends up getting excited."[9]

"Suppose you take your first training image, and it's a picture of a piano. You convert the pixel intensities of the 100x100 picture into 10,000 numbers, one for each neuron in the bottom layer of the network. As the excitement spreads up the network according to the connection strengths between neurons in adjacent layers, it'll eventually end up in that last layer, the one with the two neurons that say whether there's a hot dog in the picture," details Somers.[9] "Since the picture is of a piano, ideally the 'hot dog' neuron should have a zero on it, while the 'not hot dog' neuron should have a high number."[9] However, sometimes it doesn't quite work out this way. Hypothetically, the network could be wrong about the picture and this is where the backprop procedure comes in as it can be rejiggered so that the strength of every connection in the network can be tweaked, thereby fixing the error for a given training example.[9]

"The way it works is that you start with the last two neurons, and figure out just how wrong they were: how much of a difference is there between what the excitement numbers should have been and what they actually were? When that's done, you take a look at each of the connections leading into those neurons—the ones in the next lower layer—and figure out their contribution to the error," explains Somers.[9] This continues all the way to very bottom of the network.[9] At that point, it's clear "how much each individual connection contributed to the overall error, and in a final step, you change each of the weights in the direction that best reduces the error overall."[9] The technique is known as "backpropagation" because you are literally "propagating" errors back (or down) through the network, starting from the output.[9]

"The incredible thing is that when you do this with millions or billions of images, the network starts to get pretty good at saying whether an image has a hot dog in it," notes Somers.[9] Even more remarkable is the fact that "the individual layers of these image-recognition nets start being able to 'see' images in sort of the same way our own visual system does."[9] "That is, the first layer might end up detecting edges, in the sense that its neurons get excited when there are edges and don't get excited when there aren't; the layer above that one might be able to detect sets of edges, like corners; the layer above that one might start to see shapes; and the layer above that one might start finding stuff like 'open bun' or 'closed bun,' in the sense of having neurons that respond to either case," explains Somers.[9] "The net organizes itself, in other words, into hierarchical layers without ever having been explicitly programmed that way," notes Somers.[9]

As Somers explains it[9]:

"This is the thing that has everybody enthralled. It's not just that neural nets are good at classifying pictures of hot dogs or whatever: they seem able to build representations of ideas. With text you can see this even more clearly. You can feed the text of Wikipedia, many billions of words long, into a simple neural net, training it to spit out, for each word, a big list of numbers that correspond to the excitement of each neuron in a layer. If you think of each of these numbers as a coordinate in a complex space, then essentially what you're doing is finding a point, known in this context as a vector, for each word somewhere in that space. Now, train your network in such a way that words appearing near one another on Wikipedia pages end up with similar coordinates, and voilà, something crazy happens: words that have similar meanings start showing up near one another in the space. That is, "insane" and "unhinged" will have coordinates close to each other, as will "three" and "seven," and so on. What's more, so-called vector arithmetic makes it possible to, say, subtract the vector for "France" from the vector for "Paris," add the vector for "Italy," and end up in the neighborhood of "Rome." It works without anyone telling the network explicitly that Rome is to Italy as Paris is to France."

"It's amazing," says Hinton, the father of AI.[9] "Neural nets can be thought of as trying to take things—images, words, recordings of someone talking, medical data—and put them into what mathematicians call a high-dimensional vector space, where the closeness or distance of the things reflects some important feature of the actual world," adds Somers.[9] Hinton believes this is how the brain works.[9] "If you want to know what a thought is," he says it can be expressed in a string of words such as, "John thought, 'Whoops.'"[9] But if you ask, 'What is the thought? What does it mean for John to have that thought?', it's not that inside his head there's an opening quote, and a 'Whoops,' and a closing quote, or even a cleaned-up version of that. Inside his head there's some big pattern of neural activity."[9] "Big patterns of neural activity, if you're a mathematician, can be captured in a vector space, with each neuron's activity corresponding to a number, and each number to a coordinate of a really big vector," says Somers.[9] "In Hinton's view, that's what thought is: a dance of vectors," states Somers.[9]

Although this all sounds rather clever, what shouldn't be lost in all of this is the fact that deep learning systems are still pretty dumb, despite how smart they might appear sometimes.[9] The most amusing moment in that *Silicon Valley* episode was when the rest of Jian Yang's team understood how limited his program really was—it could only really distinguish hot dogs and thousands of hours of training would be needed for it to understand only a limited number of other food types.[9]

"Neural nets are just thoughtless fuzzy pattern recognizers, and as useful as fuzzy pattern recognizers can be," explains Somers.[9] This is why there is a "rush to integrate them into just about every kind of software—they represent, at best, a limited brand of intelligence, one that is easily fooled."[9] "A deep neural net that recognizes images can be totally stymied when you change a single pixel, or add visual noise that's imperceptible to a human," warns Somers.[9] The limitations of deep learning are becoming quite apparent; "Self-driving cars can fail to navigate conditions they've never seen before; Machines have trouble parsing sentences that demand common-sense understanding of how the world works."[9]

"Deep learning in some ways mimics what goes on in the human brain, but only in a shallow way—which perhaps explains why its intelligence can sometimes seem so shallow," says Somers.[9] Backprop itself "wasn't discovered by probing deep into the brain, decoding thought itself; it grew out of models of how animals learn by trial and error in old classical-conditioning experiments."[9] Think Pavlov's dog and that ringing bell. On top of that, "most of the big leaps that came about as it developed didn't involve some new insight about neuroscience; they were technical improvements, reached by years of mathematics and engineering."[9] "What we know about intelligence is nothing against the vastness of what we still don't know"[9]: i.e., we're still very much deep in the middle of Socrates' "I know that I know nothing" territory, especially with AI.

"It can be hard to appreciate this from the outside, when all you see is one great advance touted after another," says Somers.[9] However, "the latest sweep of progress in AI has been less science than engineering, even tinkering. And though we've started to get a better handle on what kinds of changes will improve deep-learning systems, we're still largely in the dark about how those systems work, or whether they could ever add up to something as powerful as the human mind," Somers adds.[9]

Somers concludes with the troubling thought that, "It's worth asking whether we've wrung nearly all we can out of backprop. If so, that might mean a plateau for progress in artificial intelligence."[9] That also means that, when it comes to AI, creativity might be the great differentiator between companies; if the tools are limiting, creativity becomes much more important.

Current State of AI

In her *Techcrunch* article *The Evolution of Machine Learning*[43], Catherine Dong explains that, "Machine learning engineering happens in three stages—data processing, model building and deployment and monitoring." In the middle of the process is the meat of the pipeline, the model, "which is the machine learning algorithm that learns to predict given input data."[43] "That model is where 'deep learning' would live,"[43] explains Dong, adding that," "Deep learning is a subcategory of machine learning algorithms that use multi-layered neural networks to learn complex relationships between inputs and outputs. The more layers in the neural network, the more complexity it can capture."[43]

Doug claims that the technology behemoths in both the US, China, and Europe are "pouring resources and attention into convincing the world that the machine intelligence revolution is arriving now."[43] "They tout deep learning, in particular, as the breakthrough driving this transformation and powering new self-driving cars, virtual assistants and more."[43]

However, Dong warns that the hype may be getting a little ahead of itself.[43] "Despite this hype around the state of the *art*, the state of the *practice* is less futuristic," she adds.[43] "Software engineers and data scientists working with machine learning still use many of the same algorithms and engineering tools they did years ago," she notes.[43]

Dong states that, "Traditional machine learning models—not deep neural networks—are powering most AI applications. Engineers still use traditional software engineering tools for machine learning engineering, and they don't work: The pipelines that take data to model to result end up built out of scattered, incompatible pieces."[43] Change is coming, Dong says, "as big tech companies smooth out this process by building new machine learning-specific platforms with end-to-end functionality."[43] The big tech players are also releasing open source versions of their deep learning software that should help speed up the use of this technology. However, the deep learning revolution isn't quite here yet, contrary to what the big players and analytics software vendors would have you believe.

"Traditional statistical machine learning algorithms (i.e. ones that do not use deep neural nets) have a more limited capacity to capture information about training data," explains Dong.[43] "These more basic machine learning algorithms work well enough for many applications, making the additional complexity of deep learning models often superfluous," she adds.[43] The result is, "we still see software engineers using these traditional models extensively in machine learning engineering—even in the midst of this deep learning craze."[43]

"But the bread of the sandwich process that holds everything together is what happens before and after training the machine learning model," Dong adds.[43] "The first stage involves cleaning and formatting vast amounts of data to be fed into the model. The last stage involves careful deployment and monitoring of the model. We found that most of the engineering time in AI is not actually spent on building machine learning models—it's spent preparing and monitoring those models," states Dong.

From my own personal experience, it's usually the data preparation phase that takes up the bulk of the time when you're building analytical models, so it only makes sense that this is also the case with deep learning; "Junk in, junk out" is the motto we live by at Intelligencia. We also subscribe to the *Three Pillars of A.I. Model*, in which training is followed by production and then active learning in a cycle that continually repeats itself (see Figure 6).

"Despite the focus on deep learning at the big tech company AI research labs, most applications of machine learning at these same companies do not rely on neural networks and instead use traditional machine learning models," claims Dong.[43] "The most common models include linear/logistic regression, random forests and boosted decision trees," states Dong.[43] These models provide the analytics backbone for the "friend suggestions, ad targeting, user interest prediction, supply/demand simulation and search result ranking," she concludes.[43]

Three Pillars of A.I.

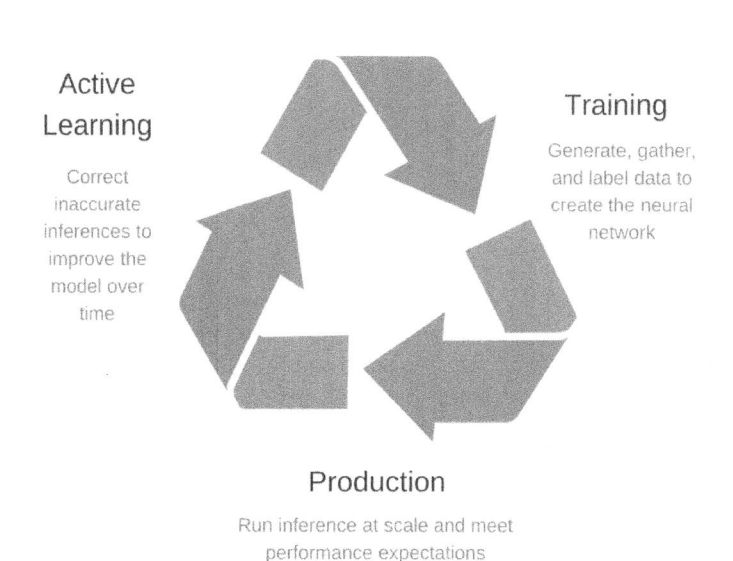

Active Learning
Correct inaccurate inferences to improve the model over time

Training
Generate, gather, and label data to create the neural network

Production
Run inference at scale and meet performance expectations

Figure 6: Three Pillars of A.I.

"There are good reasons to use simpler models over deep learning," Dong contends.[43] "Deep neural networks are hard to train. They require more time and computational power (they usually require different hardware, specifically GPUs). Getting deep learning to work is hard—it still requires extensive manual fiddling, involving a combination of intuition and trial and error," explains Dong.[43] (Think back propagation.)

"With traditional machine learning models, the time engineers spend on model training and tuning is relatively short—usually just a few hours," notes Dong.[43] "Ultimately, if the accuracy improvements that deep learning can achieve are modest, the need for scalability and development speed outweighs their value."[43] "So when it comes to *training* a machine learning model, traditional methods work well," says Dong.[43] However, "the same does not apply to the infrastructure that holds together the machine learning pipeline. Using the same old software engineering tools for machine learning engineering creates greater potential for errors," warns Dong.[43]

"The first stage in the machine learning pipeline—data collection and processing—illustrates this. While big companies certainly have big data, data scientists or engineers must clean the data to make it useful—verify and consolidate duplicates from different sources, normalize metrics, design and prove features," states Dong.[43]

"At most companies, engineers do this using a combination SQL or Hive queries and Python scripts to aggregate and format up to several million data points from one or more data sources," explains Dong.[43] "This often takes several days of frustrating manual labor. Some of this is likely repetitive work, because the process at many companies is decentralized—data scientists or engineers often manipulate data with local scripts or Jupyter Notebooks," says Dong.[43]

Furthermore, the massive size of these big tech companies tend to compound errors, "making careful deployment and monitoring of models in production imperative."[43] As one engineer explained to Dong, "At large companies, machine learning is 80 percent infrastructure."[43]

Because the correct output of a machine learning model isn't known in advance, traditional unit tests, which are the backbone of standard software testing, obviously don't work.[43] After all, as Dong points out, "the purpose of machine learning is for the model to learn to make predictions from data without the need for an engineer to specifically code any rules."[43] "So instead of unit tests, engineers take a less structured approach: They manually monitor dashboards and program alerts for new models," she explains.[43] Some of these exercises could best be described as looking for a needle in a haystack.

This also explains why Facebook, Google, WeChat, and other social and analytics behemoths are desperate to get as much data as possible on their users as they can. The Cambridge Analytica scandal showed just how much information is being collected on people, at least at Facebook. Whether the attempt to manipulate the 2016 US presidential was successful of not, one has to admit that its stated goals—the election of Donald Trump and winning the Brexit referendum in England—were successful.

On top of these testing restrictions, "shifts in real-world data may make trained models less accurate, so engineers re-train production models on fresh data on a daily to monthly basis, depending on the application."[43] "A lack of machine learning-specific support in the existing engineering infrastructure can create a disconnect between models in development and models in production"[43] because normal code is updated much less frequently.[43]

Dong notes that, "Many engineers still rely on rudimentary methods of deploying models to production, like saving a serialized version of the trained model or model weights to a file."[43] Engineers often "need to rebuild model prototypes and parts of the data pipeline in a different language or framework, so they work on production infrastructure," says Dong.[43] Because "any incompatibility from any stage of the machine learning development process can introduce error,"[43] this process becomes incredibly complex. Anyone who has worked with multiple software systems running across clustered servers, both physical and virtual, will attest to how complicated this process can actually be.

"To address these issues," Dong explains, "a few big companies, with the resources to build custom tooling, have invested time and engineering effort into creating their own machine learning-specific tools."[43] The goal, as Dong sees it, is "to have a seamless, end-to-end machine learning platform that is fully compatible with the company's engineering infrastructure."[43]

Two examples are Facebook's FBLearner Flow and Uber's Michelangelo, which are internal machine learning platforms that "allow engineers to construct training and validation data sets with an intuitive user interface, decreasing time spent on this stage from days to hours."[43] With these systems, engineers can train models with (more or less) the click of a button, as well as monitor and directly update production models with ease.[43]

Dong contends that, "despite all the emphasis big tech companies have placed on enhancing their products with machine learning, at most companies there are still major challenges and inefficiencies in the process."[43] These companies "still use traditional machine learning models instead of more-advanced deep learning, and still depend on a traditional infrastructure of tools poorly suited to machine learning," Dong insists.[43] How long this set-up will continue is anyone's guess.

The good news from all of this is that the reader of this book may not be as far behind the AI and ML technological curve as he or she might think. Perhaps it might not be too late to jump in. If the Facebooks, Googles, Baidus, and Ubers of the world are still using typical analytical models, then the future is open to just about any company. Much of the hard work being done by these companies is being shared as open source tools as well, so the ramp to utilization is getting shallower and shallower as the days pass.

A.I. Dilemma

Another thing about A.I. that must be kept in mind is what's known as the "A.I. dilemma." The CIO/IDG Research Services surveyed more than 200 IT executives at larger companies in the U.S. and Europe who are either considering or using

AI technology and found that almost 90% of them were making significant AI investments, but very few were realizing the full benefits of their investments.[10] In actuality, only 1-in-3 AI projects were successful and it took "more than 6 months to go from concept to production, with a significant portion of them never making it to production—creating an AI dilemma for organizations."[10] Businesses jumping into AI should be very well aware of this fact because AI initiatives require buy-ins from multiple departments and cutting-edge technology is difficult to work with for a multitude of reasons.

The very thing that makes AI possible—data and all the secrets held within it—is also what make the AI process so challenging.[10] According to Databricks, "About 96% of organizations say data-related challenges are the most common obstacle when moving AI projects to production."[10] Databricks argues that, "Enterprise data is not AI-enabled and is siloed across hundreds of systems such as data warehouses, data lakes, databases and file systems."[10] But is this any surprise? The software landscape is an ever-evolving environment, with changes both major and minor occurring almost every life-cycle. What was technologically superior one season becomes an easily replaceable function the next. Keeping up with all the changes at one particular software company is hard enough, let alone amongst hundreds. The wonderful software categorizer that is Github complies "over 28 million users and 57 million repositories (including 28 million public repositories), making it the largest host of source code in the world."[44] The numbers we are dealing with here clearly show how complex the software world has become.

According to Databricks, "Machine learning (ML) frameworks such as TensorFlow and others don't do data processing. Since data systems don't 'do AI' and these AI technologies don't 'do data,' organizations end up using on average seven disparate tools which create friction and slow down projects."[10] Not just that, to make matters worse, the survey found that 80% of businesses "face collaboration challenges as data science and engineering teams are in organizational silos."[10]

So, what can help organizations alleviate this AI dilemma? "According to the survey, 90% of the respondents believe that unified analytics—the approach of unifying data processing with ML frameworks and facilitating data science and engineering collaboration across the ML lifecycle, will conquer the AI dilemma."[10] Chapter six details what is needed to create a united analytics platform, which should help simplify the AI process.

Databricks argues that, "Unified Analytics is a new category of solutions that unify data science and engineering, making AI much more achievable for organizations."[10] "Unified Analytics makes it easier for data engineers to build data pipelines across siloed systems and prepare labeled datasets for model building while enabling data scientists to explore and visualize data and build models collaboratively."[10] A unified analytics platform can "unify data science and engineering across the ML lifecycle from data preparation to experimentation and deployment of ML applications—enabling companies to accelerate innovation with AI," Databricks concludes.[10]

"AI has massive potential to drive disruptive innovations affecting most enterprises on the planet. It's pervasive across all industries. It is used in genomics to accelerate drug discovery and drive personalized medicine. It is being applied to manufacturing to improve operational efficiencies of product development and delivery processes," says Bharath Gowda, VP of Product Marketing at Databricks.[10]

However, in spite of AI's enormous potential, very few companies are successful at scaling their AI efforts, warns Databricks.[10] Data-related challenges are hindering 96% of organizations from achieving AI but data is the challenge: nearly all respondents (96%) cited multiple data-related challenges when moving projects to production.[10]

Gowda says, "For data scientists, it's been proven that simple models built from large amounts of data produce better results than very sophisticated models built from small sets of data."[10] "So, more data means better models—data is the fuel that powers AI. Clean, reliable data that is accessible to data scientists is the key to success," argues Gowda.[10] "Therein lies the challenge for enterprises—transforming siloed messy data into clean labeled data for model development," he adds.[10]

Data engineering and data science teams aren't always on the same page, even when it comes to the tools they use.[10] "The vast majority (87%) invest in various sorts of data and AI related technologies to help with data preparation, exploration, and modeling."[10] Data processing tools such as Apache Spark, Hadoop/MapReduce, and Google BigQuery, are used by a large portion of respondents—85%.[10] Data Streaming tools, like Flume, Kafka, and Onyx are used by 65%. Machine learning tools such as Azure ML, Amazon ML, and Spark MLlib are utilized by 80%. Deep learning software such as Google TensorFlow, Microsoft CNTK, and Deeplearning4j (DL4J) are used by 65%[10]

Overall, the Databricks survey results showed "that organizations are using an average of seven different machine learning and deep learning tools and frameworks, creating a highly complex environment that can slow efficiencies."[10] "To derive value from AI, enterprises are dependent on their existing data and ability to iteratively do ML on massive datasets. Today's data engineers and data scientists use numerous, disconnected tools to accomplish this, including a zoo of ML frameworks," Gowda concludes.[10]

A.I. + Social

I didn't want this book to only focus on developments in the United States, as I believe some of the most interesting things happening right now in the mobile and social media space occur in Asia. I had thought this before I moved to Macau in 2011 and my suspicions were confirmed after I made a few trips into China throughout the ensuing years.

Corporations of all kinds now use WeChat to connect with their customers or potential customers in highly imaginative and sometimes very lucrative ways. WeChat has also introduced WePay, an in-app payment system that allows users to make one-click payments from their bank accounts. A scanning feature lets users get pricing information from QR codes and bar codes as well.

In Hong Kong, China, and Macau, the WeChat green and white logo is almost as ubiquitous as the blue and white Facebook logo and I would argue that, as a marketing vehicle, it is just as effective, if not more so. Small mom and pop stores are using WeChat to market their wares, filling up their "Moments" thread with their latest offerings, whether they are clothes, food, shoes, handbags, etc., etc. In Hong Kong, Facebook and WhatsApp are actually preferred over WeChat as the Hong Kong locals prefer the non-censored US social networks to the Chinese ones.

One of the most important elements of social media is its inter-connectedness. An upload to YouTube can go viral through Twitter, Facebook, LinkedIn, WeChat, WhatsApp, Youku, Line, as well as a whole host of other social media and mobile media platforms. Within seconds, something uploaded onto a social media website in the US can end up on a mobile application in China or Japan or Korea, or almost anywhere else in the world that has mobile or Wi-Fi access.

Social media will also be explored in depth throughout this book. It is quite ironic that, in one sense, engaging in social media can be one of the most anti-social behaviors one can do; sitting alone in a room, typing away on a computer was once the realm of solitary computer geeks, but it has now become an activity that most people engage in almost every single day, both at home and on the go. Perhaps this is because human beings are, first and foremost, social creatures and we crave an interconnectedness that social media offers, even if it is just a virtual and rather shallow connection. Today, marketers should be utilizing these channels as liberally as possible.

It should be of no surprise that one of the greatest inventions of the twentieth century—the internet—would become the watering hole of the twenty-first century; a place where human beings can quickly gather to socialize and connect with friends, family members, and acquaintances in a way that was almost inconceivable only 20 years ago.

Almost a decade ago, "most consumers logged on to the Internet to access e-mail, search the Web, and do some online shopping. Company Web sites functioned as vehicles for corporate communication, product promotion, customer service, and, in some cases, e-commerce. Relatively few people were members of online communities" [45] and "Liking" something had no social relevance at all. How times have changed.

"Today, more than 1.5 billion people around the globe have an account on a social networking site, and almost one in five online hours is spent on social networks—increasingly via mobile devices."[45] In little more than a decade, social technology has become a cultural, social, political and economic phenomenon.[45] More importantly, "hundreds of millions of people have adopted new behaviors using social media—conducting social activities on the Internet, creating and joining virtual communities, organizing political activities"[45], even, as with the case of Egypt's "Twitter Revolution", toppling corrupt governments.

In his article *Understanding social media in China*[45], C. I. Chui argues that the secret to social media's growth is right there in its name—"Social"—as in the fundamental human behavior of seeking "identity and 'connectedness' through affiliations with other individuals and groups that share their characteristics, interests, or beliefs."[45] The last part is instructive as social media is a great place for brands to build a community of like-minded people who can inform other customers and even potential customers about the brand's products.

For Chui, "Social media taps into well known, basic sociological patterns and behaviors, sharing information with members of the family or community, telling stories, comparing experiences and social status with others, embracing stories by people with whom we desire to build relations, forming groups, and defining relationships to others."[45]

Social technologies allow individuals to interact with large groups of people at almost any location in the world, at any time of the day, at marginal or no cost at all.[45] With advantages like these, it is not surprising that social media has become so widespread that almost one in four people worldwide uses it. It is actually surprising that the figure is so low, although with mobile technology rolling out in some of the most remote locations on earth, that figure is sure to climb rapidly over the coming years.

In China, users spend more than 40 percent of their time online on social media websites, a figure that is expected to continue its rapid rise over the next few years.[45] "This appetite for all things social has spawned a dizzying array of companies, many with tools that are more advanced than those in the West: for example, Chinese users were able to embed multimedia content in social media more than 18 months before Twitter users could do so in the United States."[45]

Companies like WeChat are revolutionizing social networks, adding malls as part of their platforms, while Taobao has teamed up with Weibo to allow instant commentary and blogging on purchased items. yy.com has inverted the concept of reality TV, by taking a singing competition and broadcasting it over the internet, while allowing viewers to directly remunerate the contestants. These are all uniquely Chinese ideas that are now bring replicated in the West. Taobao is also using AI in a clever and counter-intuitive way with customer reviews, which I will detail later in the book.

There is an old adage in social media marketing circle that says, "Content is king" and, with social media, that adage has never been truer. Those destined to succeed in the social media world won't be the ones with the most content; they will be the ones with the best and most searchable content. They will also be the ones who have the most personalized content, and this is where AI shines. And that content will drive eyeballs unlike any other form of marketing in the history of advertising. To succeed in this new environment, businesses should think of themselves first and foremost as creators and syndicators of content.[46] Although content is important, the ultimate goal here is conversions, lead generation, and sales. It is essential that a company's campaign management system scales as its business and campaigns do as well.

Chapter five delves into the world of social media, including revealing how the *A.I. Marketer* can utilize social media as both a channel to connect with and listen to a consumer. In their influential article *Users of the world, unite! The challenge and opportunities of Social Media*[47], Kaplan and Haenlein show how all social media websites can be broken down into one of six different types; collaborative projects; blogs and micro-blogs; content communities; social networking sites; virtual game worlds; and virtual social worlds.[47]

In chapter five, I explain how the *A.I. Marketer* can use social media to succeed in today's cutthroat business environment, answering such questions as:

- How can a brand measure the benefits of social media?
- How should a brand organize its social media presence or presences?
- How should a brand spread social media usage throughout its organization?
- How has social media changed the relationship between a customer and a brand?

Starbucks has developed a metric it believes quantifies the value of its social media marketing in terms of media spend—the "company's 6.5 million Facebook fans are worth the equivalent of a US $23.4 million annual spend, according to calculations by social media specialists Virtue, reported in Adweek."[48] Virtue claims that, on average, "a fan base of 1 million translates to at least $3.6 million in equivalent media over a year, or $3.6 per fan. Virtue arrived at its $3.6 million figure by working off a $5 CPM, meaning a brand's 1 million fans generate about $300,000 in media value each month."[48] That's quite a significant amount of money and, if a coffee company can find success in social media, brands of all kinds should be able to get similar ROIs.

In chapter five, I will give examples that reveal how social networks like Instagram, Facebook, Snapchat, et al. are embracing AI. "Facebook wants to be a solution not just at the very bottom of the marketing funnel for solutions like retargeting, we actually want to create new purchase intent and consideration further up," claims Graham Mudd, product marketing director at Facebook.[49] The company is currently spending a fortune on its efforts to break into a market that has, so far, eluded it.

Facebook believes that in 2019 and beyond, video will drive more online sales and its new dynamic ads features will allow brands to upload videos to show-off their products catalogues.[49] Facebook is also introducing overlays for dynamic ads and the largest social network site in the world is set to let brands target consumers based on households, rather than just as individuals.[49]

For its part, Snapchat, which has hit a rough patch in terms of revenue growth, is looking to snap out of its conundrum with its two new forms of ads: "Promoted Stories which string together multiple Snaps into longer-form slideshows openable from a tile on the Stories page that's shown to everyone in a given country, and Augmented Reality Trial ads that let people play with an AR version of a product overlaid on the real world around them."[50]

I will detail these and other changes on all the other types of social media channels in his chapter. I will also include real world examples that both large and small companies can utilize immediately, as well as showcase what is on the marketing horizon in 2019 and beyond.

In her article *Understanding Three Types of Artificial Intelligence*, Uj also notes that there are three types of AI: narrow artificial intelligence, artificial general intelligence, and artificial super intelligence. Narrow Artificial Intelligence, which is also known as weak AI and narrow AI is an[8]:

> "AI system that is developed and trained for a particular task. Narrow AI is programmed to perform a single task and works within a limited context. It is very good at routine physical and cognitive jobs. For example, narrow AI can identify pattern and correlations from data more efficiently than humans. Sales predictions, purchase suggestions and weather forecast are the implementation of narrow AI. Even Google's Translation Engine is a form of narrow AI. In the automotive industry, self-driving cars are the result of coordination of several narrow AI. But it cannot expand and take tasks beyond its field, for example, the AI engine which transcripts image recognition cannot perform sales recommendations."

Artificial General Intelligence (AGI) is "an AI system with generalized cognitive abilities, which find solutions to the unfamiliar task it comes across."[8] Popularly dubbed "strong AI," it can "understand and reason the environment as a human would."[8] This form of AI is also known as human AI, which is a little misleading because it is exceptionally hard to define human level artificial intelligence.[8] The human intellect can't compute as fast as a computer, but it's more powerful in substantial ways, particularly in thinking abstractly.[8] We can plan and solve problems without having to provide too many levels of detail on those particular problems.[8] More importantly, humans can innovate and create thoughts and ideas out of thin air.[8]

Artificial Super Intelligence (ASI) refers to the point when computers and/or machines will supersede humans and machines will be able to mimic human thought and intelligence.[8] "ASI refers to a situation where the cognitive ability of machines will be superior to humans," explains Uj.[8]

Although there has been several instances where computers have beaten human players, such as IBM's Watson supercomputer outscoring humans at *Jeopardy*[8] and DeepMind beating Lee Sodel at *Go*, machines aren't capable of processing the depth of knowledge and cognitive ability that humans can.

ASI has two schools of thought, on the one side great scientists like Stephen Hawking and technological visionaries like Elon Musk see the full development of AI as a danger to humanity, whereas other technological entrepreneurs like Demis Hassabis, Co-Founder & CEO of DeepMind, believe that the smarter AI becomes, the better the world will be and AI will always be a benevolent technology.[8] One, obviously, should prepare for the former and hope for the latter.

While America's leadership in AI has been spearheaded by private sector companies like IBM, Google, and Apple, China's military saw Deepmind's victory in a very different light.[6] When Google's Deep Mind employed AI to defeat a world-class human champion at *Go*, China's national game, Beijing quickly realized "the potentialities of AI for giving it an insurmountable edge on the battlefield."[6]

In his article *China's AI Awakening*[51], Will Knight describes a late 2017 poker tournament that was held in Hainan, a tropical island on the southern tip of China. A computer program called *Lengpudashi* was playing one-on-one poker against a dozen people at once, and it was destroying them.[51] *Lengpudashi*, which translates to "cold poker master" in Mandarin, uses "a new artificial-intelligence technique to outbet and outbluff its opponents in a two-player version of Texas hold 'em."[51]

Those gathered to play *Lengpudashi* included "several poker champs, some well-known Chinese investors, entrepreneurs, and CEOs, and even the odd television celebrity," says Knight.[51] The games were broadcast online, and millions watched.[51] The event symbolized a growing sense of excitement and enthusiasm for AI in China, excitement tempered by the fact that *Lengpudashi* wasn't made in China, but rather in the anything but exotic locale of Pittsburgh, PA: Steeltown, USA.[51]

The nationwide interest in the *Lengpudashi* poker tournament reflects the unquenchable thirst for the latest AI breakthroughs in China.[51] "Mastering even a two-player form of poker is a significant achievement for AI because, unlike many other games, poker requires players to act with limited information, and to sow uncertainty by behaving unpredictably," explains Knight.[51] "An optimal strategy therefore requires both careful and instinctive judgment, which are not easy qualities to give a machine," states Knight.[51] "Lengpudashi impressively solved the problem by using a brilliant new game-theory algorithm, which could be very useful in many other scenarios, including financial trading and business negotiations," adds Knight.[51] Although *Lengpudashi* was all the rage in China, it received far less attention across the Pacific, where it had been invented.[51]

For many in China, this is problematic.[51] With the full backing of its government, China is embarking on an unprecedented effort to master AI.[51] "Its government is planning to pour hundreds of billions of yuan (tens of billions of dollars) into the technology in the coming years, and companies are investing heavily in nurturing and developing AI talent," says Knight.[51] "If this country-wide effort succeeds—and there are many signs it will—China could emerge as a leading force in AI, improving the productivity of its industries and helping it become leader [sic] in creating new businesses that leverage the technology," portends Knight.[51] "If, as many believe, AI is the key to future growth, China's prowess in the field will help fortify its position as the dominant economic power in the world," warns Knight.[51]

China's political and business leaders are hoping that AI can help the country evolve from a manufacturing economy to a services economy. Today, the country is looking toward a future built around advanced technology, and AI is leading the way.[51] "While many in the West fret about AI eliminating jobs and worsening wealth and income inequality, China seems to believe it can bring about precisely the opposite," argues Knight.[51]

"China's AI push includes an extraordinary commitment from the government, which recently announced a sweeping vision for AI ascendancy. The plan calls for homegrown AI to match that developed in the West within three years, for China's researchers to be making 'major breakthroughs' by 2025, and for Chinese AI to be the envy of the world by 2030," says Knight.[51]

China has some big advantages in AI, including a wealth of talented engineers and scientists.[51] It also is rich in the data necessary to train AI systems. "The results can be seen in the growth of facial-recognition systems based on machine learning: they now identify workers at offices and customers in stores," says Knight.[51] The technology also authenticates users of mobile apps, allowing secure payment processing.[51]

According to Knight, "Baidu anticipated the potential of artificial intelligence and sought to leverage it to reinvent its whole business."[51] "In 2014, the company created a lab dedicated to applying deep learning across its business, and in recent years, its researchers have made some significant advances." [51] Many of these came as a surprise to Western media, according to Knight.[51] "When Microsoft developed a system capable of better-than-human performance in speech recognition last year, for instance, few Western reporters realized that Baidu had done that a year earlier," Knight adds.[51]

Conclusion

The frightening and dystopian views of AI that dominate the film and fiction world are, thankfully, just that—fiction. They owe more to art's inherent need for conflict than any fundamental malevolent bias in AI.

The truth is, AI is "already changing our daily lives, almost entirely in ways that improve human health, safety, and productivity. Unlike in the movies, there is no race of superhuman robots on the horizon or probably even possible."[12] AI drives everything from your Amazon ecommerce recommendations, to your Pandora and Netflix playlists, to the customer service bot you're communicating with on Expedia or Ctrip. So, while the potential for abuse is there in almost any new technology, AI could be particularly problematic and it does need to be managed carefully, but the doomsayers' scenario that it will end human life as we know it should be taken with more than a grain of salt.[12]

Having said that, a firm respect for the technology is warranted. The Global Challenges Foundation sees AI as one the 12 risks that threaten humankind.[52] In their report *Global Challenges, 12 Risks That Threaten Human Civilization*[52], the foundation states that AI "is often defined as 'the study and design of intelligent agents', systems that perceive their environment and act to maximise their chances of success."[52] The Foundation warns that, "Such extreme intelligences could not easily be controlled (either by the groups creating them, or by some international regulatory regime), and would probably act to boost their own intelligence and acquire maximal resources for almost all initial AI motivations."[52] The Foundation warns that, "If these motivations do not detail the survival and value of humanity, the intelligence will be driven to construct a world without humans."[52] If resources are a commodity, why waste them on pesky, emotionally fragile human beings, the theory goes. Of course, no rogue marketing AI is likely to turn into HAL 9000, but it's a good idea to keep AI's malevolent potential on the radar while utilizing it.

However, on a more positive note, the Foundation concludes that AI could help combat most of the other risks in their disconcerting report, thereby making extremely intelligent AI a tool of great potential, rather than only one for malevolence.[52] These risks included such things as extreme climate change, nuclear war, ecological catastrophe, synthetic biology, a global pandemic, amongst others.[52] It is easy to see how AI could help with all of these problems.[52]

The *Artificial Intelligence and Life in 2030* study points out that, "There is also the possibility of AI-enabled warfare and all the risks of the technologies that AIs would make possible."[12] "An interesting version of this scenario is the possible creation of 'whole brain emulations': human brains scanned and physically represented in a machine. This would make the AIs into properly human minds, possibly alleviating a lot of problem," or so the Foundation hopes and believes.[12]

Today, AI's great potential is to "make driving safer, help children learn, and extend and enhance people's lives. In fact, beneficial AI applications in schools, homes, and hospitals are already growing at an accelerated pace."[12] Most major research universities "devote departments to AI studies, and technology companies such as Apple, Facebook, Google, IBM, SAS, and Microsoft spend heavily to explore AI applications they regard as critical to their futures."[12]

AI does have its limitations, however. As he explains in his article *An AI reading list—from practical primers to sci-fi stories*[53], James Vincent reminds readers that, "The dirty little secret of the AI and machine learning methods we use for prediction is that they cannot actually tell us with certainty whether some factor caused another, instead relying on millions of repetitions to give us high-value correlations." Vincent adds that, "Many of our issues of biased outcomes in AI systems stem from an incomplete or poor understanding of interrelated variables (race and zip code, or socioeconomic status and education, for example)."[53] This is a sobering thought for companies wishing to invest millions in hardware and software to try to capture strong ROI on an AI wave and should be kept in mind by these companies as they move along the AI path.

The simplification of AI tools also means that you don't need a PhD in statistics to implement AI. As *VentureBeat* states in its article *Will machine learning be the death of content A/B testing*[54], "With the democratization of artificial intelligence tools—meaning you don't need a data science degree to implement machine learning technology—you have at your fingertips a whole new world of content optimization, customization, personalization and relevance, at scale, whatever industry you're in."[54]

According to *VentureBeat*, this "means you're able to deliver more engaging and meaningful content for your customers, with carefully crafted content style and beguiling calls to action at the right time and with the right cadence."[54] Not only that, "Once people engage with your content, machine learning can help you make sense of the data you gather, revealing what's working, what's not—and how to turn that into insight that optimizes your campaign and turn setbacks into leaps forward for not just your current campaigns, but future ones, allowing you to deliver truly personalized experiences at scale."[54] This is a subject I will explore in depth throughout the rest of this book.

One company that is certainly doing analytics, AI, and customer service right is Disney. As Cliff Kuang explains in his article *Disney's $1 Billion Bet on a Magical Wristband*[55], Disney has created wristbands called "MagicBands" that look like simple, stylish rubber wristbands, but they are anything but simple. They contain an RFID chip and a radio transmitter that connects the wearer to a vast and powerful system of sensors within the Disneyworld park.[55]

If visitors sign up in advance for the so-called "Magical Express", the MagicBand replaces all of the details and hassles of paper once the visitor touches-down in Orlando.[55] Express users can board a park-bound shuttle, and check into the hotel wirelessly.[55] Visitors don't have to mind their luggage, because each piece gets tagged at their home airport.[55] Upon arrival at the park, there are no tickets to hand over, visitors just have to tap their MagicBand at the gate and swipe for the rides they've already reserved.[55] For Disney, this technology also helps them cut down on the need for hotel check-in staff, thereby saving considerable labor expense.[55]

As Kuang explains, with the MagicBand, "there's no need to rent a car or waste time at the baggage carousel. You don't need to carry cash, because the MagicBand is linked to your credit card. You don't need to wait in long lines. You don't even have to go to the trouble of taking out your wallet when your kid grabs a stuffed Olaf, looks up at you, and promises to be good if you'll just let them have this one thing, please."[55] Disney has not only thought of everything, but made everything seamless.

For Disney, the MagicBands are nothing less than thousands of sensors that communicate directly with the park's IT databases that basically turns the park into a giant computer—streaming real-time data about where guests are, what they are doing, and what they want.[55] Most importantly, the system is designed to anticipate the guest's desires, i.e., predicting their granular behavior.[55]

In his Adobe blog *The Expanding Role of Marketing—and Artificial Intelligence—in Experience Business* [56], David Newman explains how Disney utilizes the enormous amount of data it collects on its customers. "Disney shares surprises personalized just for its visitor, such as an occasional photo of the family on the ride they just finished or awarding fast passes for the day," says Newman.[56] Although seemingly magical, those experiences actually use AI models built on data collected from Disney's entire visitors database to create memorable experiences along every point of the customer visit.[56]

Newman argues that, "Every touchpoint a customer has should make it easier for them to do business with your company again, because people rarely buy things just once from a company."[56] Once you have them interacting with your company, the hard part should be done. For Newman, "everything ties back to marketing and every interaction is a reflection of the company and its brand."[56] For example, "the Disney product designers creating the MagicBands needed to think about how to make the product so it provides a memorable service, rather than intrudes on it. If you're in the customer service department responding to visitors' questions or complaints, you're also a marketer—marketing a continued relationship."[56]

Newman believes that, "Influence like this no longer lies with the suave, silver-tongued marketer and glossy marketing brochures. In today's experience business, every single person—from customer service reps to HR to the designers and developers behind products like the MagicBand—must play a role in creating experiences customers crave."[56] Beyond this, "in their customer-centric roles, everyone needs data and help understanding it, and they all must learn to leverage technology instead of hiding behind it," Newman contends.[56] Always be selling and always be collecting data to ensure the customer enjoys buying what you're selling.

Marketing helps us define who our customers are and how to reach them.[56] In today's increasingly transparent society, brands need to know who their customers are and how best to reach them, whether that is on social channels, via email, or on dark social channels like WeChat and WhatsApp.[56] "We then need to improve our processes and interactions to deliver an experience that builds loyalty and trust."[56] Newman argues that, "Every employee must have the same goal: delivering compelling, personalized, and seamless experiences that enable long-time emotional connections and loyalty to the brand."[56]

"Ensuring that everyone in your organization considers themselves a 'marketer' will help you develop and drive more memorable experiences. Even better, those who can work together as a team to create these types of customer experiences in real time will have a competitive advantage and be able to win and retain customers for the long term," states Newman.[56] Disney's success at this is one of multiple reasons why it is a household brand and fans travel across the country or even across the world year-after-year to visit its properties.[56]

Marketing at every level requires access to and understanding of data on a deep fundamental level.[56] Customers can interact with brands in both physical and online stores across multiple countries so understanding exactly who a customer is and his or her buying habits is imperative. "AI helps us fill the gap between the information we have and our ability to comprehend it. AI can help organize and analyze large amounts of data so it can present the right, actionable information to drive better customer experiences, much easier than you and your team could ever do on your own," argues Newman.[56]

Don't run from or bias the data, Newman also argues.[56] "Look at the data for what it is because it will tell you more of what you need to know than you could ever imagine," contends Newman.[56] Beyond the old rule of "Junk in, Junk out" is the inherent bias that human beings can bring to data and modeling results.

"To provide the seamless experiences that will delight customers, technology must be nearly invisible," Newman says,[56] adding that, "Consumers just want the experience."[56] "For example, even if consumers know about advertising technology, they don't love it because it feeds them more ads. They love it because it creates personalized, timely, and relevant ads that bring them value and show that your business understands who they are and what they need," explains Newman.[56] "That's all they care about, not how AI or machine learning works. They love how we can connect them to people they love and to the things they like to do," argues Newman.[56]

"While you need to think about the value AI and other technology can create, first think about it from the human experience," Newman contends.[56] "Then, like Disney, you can look at all of the ways your technology can enable from the background the experience you want to deliver to your customers."[56] "We use smartphones or watches because they connect us to people, entertain us, and improve our health. We use a MagicBand because it makes our entire vacation seamless and personalized just for us. These are memorable experiences that keep us coming back for more," argues Newman.[56]

I started this introduction with an allusion to Big Data being either a treasure chest of information or a Pandora's Box full of pain and it can certainly be either, but going down the Big Data road requires a commitment that is all encompassing and an acceptance that it could require radical changes in corporate thinking. Deshpande and Kumar conclude that, "The primary goal of AI is to implement human-like intelligence in machines and to create systems that gather data, process it to create models (hypothesis), predict or influence outcomes, and ultimately improve human life."[34] This is a lofty goal, indeed, but one definitely worth aiming for because it could be so lucrative.

State of the art technology is required and that always means there is the potential for severe bumps in the road along the way. However, it is a road that must be traversed as today's consumers have become highly sophisticated and they demand an incredibly high level of personalization for their continuing patronage; if a company's marketing efforts aren't personal enough, these consumers will easily find another company that does provide the level of service they demand.

I started this book with a warning about the malevolent potential of AI, a discussion about the fact that AI is actually nothing new and might have already reached its zenith, as well as mentioning that, even at the current tech behemoths data scientists working with ML still use the same algorithms they did years ago, so you might think I'm a little down on AI. That assessment couldn't be further from the truth.

This book is structured in a way that the first five chapters describes how AI and analytics technology is utilized by brands today. I delve into theories behind these products and services as well as describe actual use cases. In chapter six, I explain how to build a unified analytics platform that can help brands harness all their company data so that an analytics, AI, and ML system can function atop it. In the final chapter, I detail how brands can utilize AI, ML, and deep learning within their business, with specific examples and step-by-step instructions of how to build these technologically sophisticated systems. For companies that don't want to build things from scratch, I will discuss the commercial software options available.

In this book, I try to avoid what has become known as "wish casting", a useful term from the field of meteorology. As Rob Tracinski explains in his article *How Not to Predict the Future*[57], "It started with the observation that weathermen disproportionately predict sunny weather on the 4th of July and snow on Christmas Day. Their forecasts are influenced not just by the evidence, but by what they (or their audience) want to hear." The writer of any book that delves into current and future technology will, obviously, be susceptible to wish casting, but I will try to temper my enthusiasm and add a dash of healthy skepticism to all I write here.

I will also try to avoid "Zeerust"—"The particular kind of datedness which afflicts things that were originally designed to look futuristic." [58] Taken from *The Meaning of Liff* by Douglas Adams, *TV Tropes* explains it this way: "datedness behind zeerusty designs lies in the attempt of the past designers to get an advantage over the technology of their time, only to find out that more mundane designs are actually far more efficient if advanced engineering and craftsmanship are used on them."[58]

Throughout this book, I will also offer my honest assessment of the technology I discuss, trying to be as agnostic and objective as possible. Personally, I prefer not to go down rabbit holes of technology that, while proving quite colorful, exciting and interesting, really lead to nowhere, so I will try to point out paths that I think advisable to both take and not to take, always keeping a firm eye on the business' fiscal bottom line.

At times, I might appear to be a little tangential, but bear with me; sometimes to gain deep focus on small issues one needs to understand macro landscapes. Do know that I fully subscribe to Mark Twain's notion that brevity and conciseness take a lot longer to achieve than longevity ("I didn't have time to write a short letter, so I wrote a long one instead"). I have tried to be as succinct as possible, but sometimes discussions about cutting edge technology do require substantial breathing space.

In French, "ROI" (or "Roi", more precisely) literally means "King" and in this book, ROI is king; every piece of technology I discuss here will be looked at through the lens of ROI. As I detail in here, positive ROI can be created with AI, machine learning, all forms of analytics, marketing automation, and social media marketing, amongst many other technologies. I will provide detailed examples of this throughout the book.

It is my hope that this book can help businesses of all size and employee count drive up their sales and help them build stronger customer experiences, because that is ultimately what will increase their ROI.

---

1 SAS. (2019). SAS announces $1 Billion investment in Artificial Intelligence (AI). March 17, 2019. https://www.sas.com/en_us/news/press-releases/2019/march/artificial-intelligence-investment.html (Accessed 28 March 2019).
2 PWC. (2017). Sizing the prize. What's the real value of AI for your business and how you can capitalise. https://www.pwc.com/gx/en/issues/analytics/assets/pwc-ai-analysis-sizing-the-prize-report.pdf (Accessed 19 February 2019).
3 Humanizing Loyalty A road map to establishing genuine emotional loyalty at scale. Olson1to1.com. https://go.icf.com/rs/072-WJX-782/images/Humanizing%20Loyalty%20-%20Olson%201to1.pdf (Accessed 6 August 2018).
4 Lewnes, Ann and Keller, Kevin Lane. (2019). MIT Sloan Management Review. 10 Principles of Modern Marketing. April 3, 2019. https://sloanreview.mit.edu/article/10-principles-of-modern-marketing/ (Accessed 5 April 2019).
5 Adobe Sensei Team. Adobe. AI: Your behind-the-scenes marketing companion. https://www.adobe.com/insights/sensei-ai-for-marketers.html (Accessed 7 April 2019).
6 Herman, Arthur. (2018) Forbes. China's Brave New World of AI. 30 August 2018. https://www.forbes.com/sites/arthurherman/2018/08/30/chinas-brave-new-world-of-ai/#24d3a45a28e9 (Accessed 11 January 2019).
7 MMC Ventures. (2019). www.mmcventures.com. https://www.mmcventures.com/wp-content/uploads/2019/02/The-State-of-AI-2019-Divergence.pdf (Accessed 13 March 2019).
8 Uj, Anjali. (2018). Understanding Three Types of Artificial Intelligence. April 28, 2018. Analytics Insight. https://www.analyticsinsight.net/understanding-three-types-of-artificial-intelligence/ (Accessed December 29, 2018).
9 Somers, James. (2017) MIT Technology Review. Is AI Riding a One-Trick Pony? 29 September 2017. https://www.technologyreview.com/s/608911/is-ai-riding-a-one-trick-pony/ (Accessed 8 January 2019).
10 Databricks. Conquer the AI Dilemma by Unifying Data Science and Engineering. https://databricks.com/company/newsroom/press-releases/databricks-conquers-ai-dilemma-with-unified-analytics (Accessed 8 October 2018).
11 https://www.pcmag.com/encyclopedia/term/37701/amara-s-law (Accessed 4 January 2019).
12 Artificial Intelligence and Life in 2030. September 2016. https://ai100.stanford.edu/sites/default/files/ai_100_report_0831fnl.pdf (Accessed 1 January 2019).

13 Adobe. Artificial intelligence Unlocks the True Power of Analytics. https://www.adobe.com/au/insights/ai-unlocks-the-true-power-of-analytics.html (Accessed 14 January 2019).

14 SAS, Accenture Applied Intelligence, and Intel, with Forbes Insights. (2018). AI Momentum, Maturity, & Models for Success. sas.com.

15 https://en.wikipedia.org/wiki/Machine_learning (Accessed 20 November 2017).

16 UPS Customer Solutions & Innovations. (2018). Artificial Intelligence in Logistics, a collaborative report by DHL and IBM on implications and use cases for the logistics industry. https://www.logistics.dhl/content/dam/dhl/global/core/documents/pdf/glo-ai-in-logistics-white-paper.pdf (Accessed 29 April 2019).

17 https://www.sas.com/en_us/insights/analytics/deep-learning.html (Accessed 4 January 2019).

18 Krizhevsky, Alex; Sutskever, Ilya; Hinton, Geoffrey. (2012). ImageNet Classification with Deep Convolutional Neural Networks. NIPS 2012: Neural Information Processing Systems, Lake Tahoe, Nevada.

19 Jaokar, Ajit. (2017). Twelve Types of Artificial Intelligence (AI) Problems. 5 January 2017. https://www.datasciencecentral.com/profiles/blogs/twelve-types-of-artificial-intelligence-ai-problems (Accessed 7 October 2018).

20 Roose, Kevin. (2019). NY Times. The Hidden Automation Agenda of the Davos Elite. January 25, 2019. https://www.nytimes.com/2019/01/25/technology/automation-davos-world-economic-forum.html (Accessed 27 January 2019).

21 Tang, Ziyi, and Lahiri, Tripti. (2018). Quartz. Here's how the plan to replace the humans who make iPhones with bots is going. June 22, 2018. https://qz.com/1312079/iphone-maker-foxconn-is-churning-out-foxbots-to-replace-its-human-workers/ (Accessed 27 January 2019).

22 Bird, Jon. (2018). Forbes. Chilling or Thrilling? JD.com Founder Envisions a '100%' Robot Workforce. April 27, 2018. https://www.forbes.com/sites/jonbird1/2018/04/27/chilling-or-thrilling-jd-coms-robotic-retail-future/#520fb59f7fcf (Accessed 27 January 2019).

23 Kharpal, Arjun. (2017). CNBC. Amazon's Alexa voice assistant could be a 10 billion 'mega hit' by 2020: Research. https://www.cnbc.com/2017/03/10/amazon-alexa-voice-assistan-could-be-a-10-billion-mega-hit-by-2020-research.html (Accessed 12 January 2019).

24 Skymind. A beginning's guide to natural language processing. https://skymind.ai/wiki/natural-language-processing-nlp (Accessed 2 January 2019).

25 Milgrom, Paul R. and Tadelis, Steve. (2018). How Artificial Intelligence and Machine Learning Can Impact Market Design. 6 January 2018. https://www.nber.org/chapters/c14008.pdf (Accessed 20 January 2019).

26 Marr, Bernard. Bernardmarr.com. Text Analytics: How to Analyse and Mine Words And Natural Language in Businesses. https://bernardmarr.com/default.asp?contentID=1754 (Accessed 8 January 2018).

27 Woods, D. (2011, May 6). How Real-time Marketing Technology Can Transform Your Business. Retrieved from Forbes.com:

http://www.forbes.com/sites/ciocentral/2011/05/06/how-real-time-marketing-technology-can-transform-your-business/
28 Sharma, C. H. (2008). Mobile Advertising: Supercharge Your Brand in the Exploding Wireless Market. John Wiley & Sons, Inc.
29 Talend. Definitive Guide to Data Governance. Talend.com.
30 Zichermann, Gabe. Earn Your Wings: Air Canada's Successful Gamification Venture into Loyalty. Gamification.co. 8 July 2013. http://www.gamification.co/2013/07/08/earn-your-wings-air-canadas-successful-gamification-venture-into-loyalty/ (Accessed 16 August 2016).
31 http://www-01.ibm.com/software/data/bigdata/ (Accessed December 6, 2016)
32 Anderson, C. (2004). Wired. The Long Tail, pp. 171-177.
33 Berman, S. J. (2007). Executive Brief: Navigating the media divide: Innovating and enabling new business models. IBM Institute for Business Value.
34 Deshpande, Anand and Kumar, Manish. (2018). Packt Publishing. Artificial Intelligence for Big Data. 22 May 2018.
35 Kelnar, David. (2016). The Fourth Industrial Revolution: a Primer on Artificial Intelligence (AI). MMC Ventures. 2 December 2016. https://medium.com/mmc-writes/the-fourth-industrial-revolution-a-primer-on-artificial-intelligence-ai-ff5e7fffcae1 (Accessed 9 October 2018).
36 Vogel, Dirk. (6 September 2017). 5 Ways AI Will Boost Personalization in Digital Marketing. Selligent. https://www.selligent.com/blog/contextual-marketing/5-ways-ai-will-boost-personalization-in-digital-marketing (Accessed 24 October 2017).
37 Rees, Kit and Rascouet, Angelina. (2019). Bloomberg. Amazon Gets Some Blame in Ad Industry's 24-hour, $5 Billion Rout. 8 February 2019. https://www.bloomberg.com/news/articles/2019-02-07/eyes-on-amazon-as-5-billion-gouged-out-of-global-ad-industry (Accessed 8 February 2019).
38 Singh Y, Chauhan AS. Neural Networks in Data Mining. Journal of Theoretical and Applied Information Technology. 2009; 5:37-42 http://jatit.org/volumes/research-papers/Vol5No1/1Vol5No6.pdf (Accessed 20 November 2017).
39 Goa, Jim. Machine Learning Applications for Data Center Optimization. https://static.googleusercontent.com/media/www.google.com/en//about/datacenters/efficiency/internal/assets/machine-learning-applicationsfor-datacenter-optimization-finalv2.pdf (Accessed 20 November 2017).
40 Greene, Tristan. (2018). A Beginner's Guide to AI: Neural Networks. The Next Web. July 2018. https://thenextweb.com/artificial-intelligence/2018/07/03/a-beginners-guide-to-ai-neural-networks/ (Accessed 13 August 2018).
41 Butterfield, Brett. (2018). Adobe. See It, Search It, Shop It: How AI is Powering Visual Search. 12 December 2018. https://theblog.adobe.com/see-it-search-it-shop-it-how-ai-is-powering-visual-search/ (Accessed 20 January 2019).
42 Quach, Katyanna. (2017). How DeepMind's AlphaGo Zero learned all by itself to trash world champ AI AlphaGo. The Register. 18 October 2017. https://www.theregister.co.uk/2017/10/18/deepminds_latest_alphago_software_does nt_need_human_data_to_win/ (Accessed 21 January 2018).

43 Dong, Catherinee. (2017). The evolution of machine learning. Techcrunch. 8 August 2017. https://techcrunch.com/2017/08/08/the-evolution-of-machine-learning/ (accessed 23 December 2018).
44 https://en.wikipedia.org/wiki/GitHub (Accessed 10 September 2018).
45 Chiu, C. I. (2012, April). Understanding social media in China. Retrieved from www.mckinsey.com:
http://www.mckinsey.com/insights/marketing_sales/understanding_social_media_in_china
46 Black, L. M. (2012, November 11). 7 social media marketing tips for artists and galleries. Retrieved from Mashable: http://mashable.com/2012/11/10/social-media-marketing-tips-artists-galleries/
47 Kaplan, A. H. (2010). Users of the world unite! The challenges and opportunities of social media. Business Horizons, Vol. 53, Issue 1.
48 Woodcock, N. G. (2011). Social CRM as a business strategy. Database Marketing & Customer Strategy Management, Vol. 18, 1, 50-64.
49 Dua, Tanya. (2017). Facebook wants to become the new mobile storefront, unveils new ad tools for brands and airlines. Business Insider. 27 June 2017. http://www.businessinsider.com/facebook-wants-to-become-the-new-mobile-storefront-2017-6 (Accessed 25 November 2017).
50 Constine, Josh. (2017). Snapchat seek salvation in long-form and "hands-on" AR ads. Techcrunch.com. https://techcrunch.com/2017/11/24/anything-for-arpu/ (Accessed 25 November 2017).
51 Knight, Will. October 20, 2017. China's AI Awakening. Technology Review. https://www.technologyreview.com/s/609038/chinas-ai-awakening/ (Accessed 6 January 2019).
52 Global Challenges. (2015). 12 Risks That Threaten Human Civilization. The Case for a New Category Risk. https://api.globalchallenges.org/static/wp-content/uploads/12-Risks-with-infinite-impact-full-report-1.pdf (Accessed 2 January 2019).
53 Vincent, James. (2019) The Verge. An AI reading list—from practical primers to sci-fi stories. January 29, 2019. https://www.theverge.com/2019/1/29/18200585/understand-ai-artificial-intelligence-reading-list-books-scifi (Accessed 16 March 2019).
54 VentureBeat. (2018). Will machine learning be the death of content A/B testing. Venturebeat.com. 30 April 2018. https://venturebeat.com/2018/04/30/will-machine-learning-be-the-death-of-content-a-b-testing (Accessed 3 March 2019).
55 Kuang, Cliff. March 3, 2015. Disney's $1 Billion Bet On A Magical Wristband. Wired. https://www.wired.com/2015/03/disney-magicband (Accessed 19 January 2017).
56 Newman, Daniel. (2017). Adobe.com. The Expanding Role of Marketing—Artificial Intelligence—Experience Business. 21 June 2017. https://theblog.adobe.com/expanding-role-marketing-artificial-intelligence-experience-business/ (Accessed 8 January 2019).
57 Tracinski, Rob. October 13, 2016. How Not to Predict the Future. Real Clear Future. http://www.realclearfuture.com/articles/2016/10/13/how_not_to_predict_the_future_111945.html
58 http://tvtropes.org/pmwiki/pmwiki.php/Main/Zeerust (Accessed 15 November 2017).

CHAPTER TWO: PERSONALIZATION

"Personalization is table stakes for today's retailers, who are increasingly competing to be relevant in the hearts and minds of shoppers."

~Giselle Abramovich, Adobe

Overview

Today, "Personalization"—the process of utilizing geo-location, mobile app, Wi-Fi, and OTT technology to tailor messages or experiences to an individual interacting with them—is becoming the optimum word in a radically new customer intelligence environment. Even though this personalization comes at a cost—privacy—it is a price most consumers seem more than willing to pay if a recognized value is received in return. For a marketer, "personalization" requires an investment in analytical software, but businesses should recognize that this price must be paid because highly sophisticated consumers will soon need an exceptional customer shopping experience to keep them from visiting a competitor (who will, undoubtedly, offer such services). This kind of personalization also gives the business powerful information to build optimization models that can reduce cost and increase productivity.

If an advertising executive had set about to create the perfect marketing and advertising tool, she could hardly have created something more superior to the mobile phone. Not only is the mobile phone within reach of its owner almost every single hour of every single day but, because it can connect to a marketer in a highly personalized way with the simple touch of a button, it has the potential to become not only more effective than television or radio advertising but, just as importantly, more analyzable.

As the authors of *Mobile Advertising* point out that, "With respect to targeting, no other medium can provide the accurate and rich user profile, psychographic, social engagement and demographic data available from mobile. No other medium has the viral capability that mobile possesses—within seconds following a simple click, a unit of advertisement can spread like wildfire."[28]

No other media comes even remotely close to the data measurement capacity that mobile offers, which begins with exposure to the advertisement, followed by the persuasive effect of the advertisement and, finally, to the actual purchase of a product.[28] Just about every link in the marketer's chain is touched by mobile.

In 1996, the Internet advertising landscape changed forever when Procter & Gamble told Yahoo! that it would only pay for ads on a cost-per-click basis, rather than for banner ads.[28] Procter & Gamble realized the importance of gaining truthful user metrics for internet advertising and this move ushered in the world of internet analytics; eyeballs were no longer the goal, click-thrus that showed actual product interest were gold.

Today, the time is right for mobile marketing. As Sharma et al. state in their book *Mobile Advertising* because "the heavy lifting of measurements and metrics; of banner ad standards; of search keyword auctions; of advertising cost models and the new, digital ad networks that support them have been built. The groundwork for digital advertising in mobile is largely in place." However, because there are so many players involved, the mobile advertising value chain is incredibly complex.[28] As Sharma et al. point out, "the mobile value chain comprises advertisers, agencies, solution providers and enablers, content publishers, operators and consumers. Phone manufacturers or original equipment manufacturers (OEMs) are enablers in this value chain rather than active participants."[28] The bottleneck in the chain arises because, even though there are only a limited number of mobile operators, the number of vendors in the value chain is exceedingly high.[28] Although this was written almost a decade ago, the complexity of the environment still remains and it is something that must be kept in mind when developing mobile marketing campaigns.

In their article *The Typological Classification of the Participants' Subjectivity to Plan the Policy and Strategy for the Smart Mobile Market*[59], Kim et al. argue that the core technologies of cloud computing can greatly enhance mobile marketing efforts. Without cloud computing, it would be impossible to successfully produce targeting context-aware ads, real-time location-based services (LBS) ads, interactive-rich media ads, mobile semantic webs or in-app ads, advanced banner ads or incentive-based coupon ads, AR or QR codes, social network ads, and n-screen ads.[59] It would be especially difficult integrating and converging multifunctional mash-up ads involving a mix of the aforementioned.[59] "Smart mobile advertising products continuously derive combined services where two or more advertising techniques integrate and interlock due to innovative hardware or software technologies," Kim et al. conclude.[59]

Mobile advertising has the potential to give brands the best bang for their marketing buck, but a mobile marketing campaign should not simply be viewed as an extension of a company's internet marketing brought to the mobile phone. In *Mobile Advertising*, the authors state that the three basic types of mobile advertising are[28]:

1. Broad-based brand advertising: broad-based campaigns that take advantage of user filtering and targeting. These can include subsidized premium content, sponsorships, video pre-rolls or intromercials, post-roll video, on-demand mobile media and contextual or behavioral advertising.

2. Interactive, direct response campaigns: these are opt-in campaigns in which the mobile user usually exchanges some personal information for some type of content. TXT short codes, mobile subscription portals, and user registration campaigns are all examples of this type of campaign.
3. Highly targeted search advertising: mobile's ability to inform advertiser of the user's basic age, sex, and address information is far better than any other form of advertising around. These campaigns include content targeted search advertising and paid placement or paid inclusion search.

Although there were hints that a marketing revolution was underway at the beginning of the 21st Century, few people would have predicted the radical changes that have transformed the industry—and the world—today. In their article *Interactivitys Unanticipated Consequences for Marketers and Marketing*[60], Deighton and Kornfeld argue that:

> *"Mass communication technology empowered marketers with marketer-to-consumer tools such as radio, television and database-driven direct marketing. The digital innovations of the last decade made it effortless, indeed second nature, for audiences to talk back and talk to each other. They gave us peer-to-peer tools like Napster, eBay, Tivo, MySpace, YouTube, Facebook, Craigslist and blogs, and information search tools like Google and Wikipedia. Mobile platforms have given us ubiquitous connectivity, context-aware search, and the ability to tag and annotate physical spaces with digital information that can be retrieved by others. In sum, new traffic lanes were being built, not for the convenience of marketers, but for consumers."*

Successful marketing is about reaching a consumer with an interesting offer when he or she is primed to accept it. Knowing what might interest the consumer is half the battle to making the sale and this is where customer analytics comes in.

Customer analytics have evolved from simply reporting customer behavior to segmenting customers based on their profitability, to predicting that profitability, to improving those predictions (because of the inclusion of new data), to *actually manipulating customer behavior* with target-specific promotional offers and marketing campaigns. Chapter three will detail this and other types of analytics a marketer can use in deep detail, but I thought it advisable to describe it here, to set up the scene as it were.

Data must be gathered from disparate sources and seamlessly integrated into a data warehouse that can then cleanse it and make it ready for consumption.[61] Trends that surface from the data mining process can help in monetization, as well as in future advertising and service planning.[28] As the authors state in *Mobile Advertising*[28]:

> "The analytical system must have the capability to digest all the user data, summarize it, and update the master user profile. This functionality is essential to provide the rich user segmentation that is at the heart of recommendations, campaign and offer management, and advertisements. The segmentation engine can cluster users into affinities and different groups based on geographic, demographic or socio-economic, psychographic, and behavioral characteristics."

Of course, with all of this data collection comes justified privacy concerns and the most important aspect of mobile marketing is ensuring the consumer has control of the advertising, especially in the US and Europe.[28] Without this, it is doubtful mobile marketing will reach its true potential.[28] If mobile advertisers do allow users to configure and control the ads depending on where they are, what mood they are in, who they are with, and what their current needs and desires happen to be, mobile marketing could prove to be one of the most successful forms of advertising available to marketers ever.[28]

The potential to market to an individual when she is primed to accept the advertising is advantageous for both parties involved. Marketers don't waste time making offers to consumers when they aren't primed to accept the advertisements but do market to consumers when and where they might want to use the advertisements.

For Newman, "Every employee must have the same goal: delivering compelling, personalized, and seamless experiences that enable long-time emotional connections and loyalty to the brand."[56]

Adobe's *2018 Digital Trends in Retail*[62] revealed that "the most exciting prospect through the lens of the retailer is *delivering personalized experiences in real time*, cited by 37% of retail respondents compared to 36% for client-side respondents in other sectors."[62] This is an interesting survey to keep in mind as retailers are often on the cutting edge of technology and retail customers will, once they start receiving personalization marketing from the retailer they buy from, they will expect similar service from just about every other business they deal with from then on.

Figure 7 "compares the top digital-related 2018 priorities for retailers across regions, with *targeting and personalization* leading the way in both North America and Europe. While not explicitly mentioned, the theme of data again

THE A.I. MARKETER

looms large for retailers seeking to personalize and target effectively."[62]

WHICH THREE DIGITAL-RELATED AREAS ARE THE TOP PRIORITIES FOR YOUR ORGANIZATION IN 2018? (REGIONAL COMPARISON)

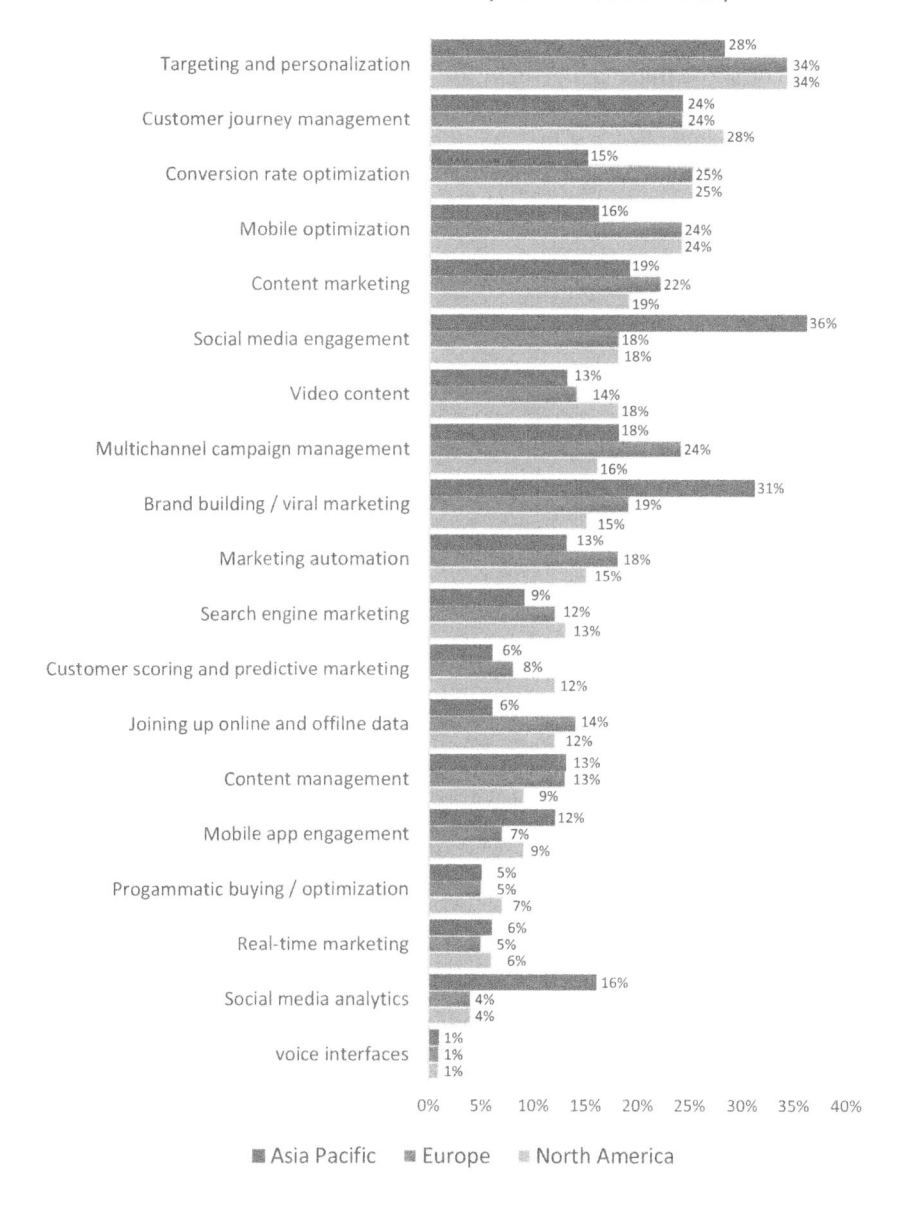

Priority	Asia Pacific	Europe	North America
Targeting and personalization	28%	34%	34%
Customer journey management	24%	24%	28%
Conversion rate optimization	15%	25%	25%
Mobile optimization	16%	24%	24%
Content marketing	19%	22%	19%
Social media engagement	36%	18%	18%
Video content	13%	14%	18%
Multichannel campaign management	18%	24%	16%
Brand building / viral marketing	31%	19%	15%
Marketing automation	13%	18%	15%
Search engine marketing	9%	12%	13%
Customer scoring and predictive marketing	6%	8%	12%
Joining up online and offline data	6%	14%	12%
Content management	13%	13%	9%
Mobile app engagement	12%	7%	9%
Progammatic buying / optimization	5%	5%	7%
Real-time marketing	6%	5%	6%
Social media analytics	16%	4%	4%
voice interfaces	1%	1%	1%

Figure 7: Organizations top priorities in 2018?
Source: Adobe 2018 Digital Trends in Retail[62]

Adobe's *2018 Digital Trends in Retail* reveals that "retailers in Asia are much more focused on *social media engagement* and *brand-building/viral marketing* that their counterparts in the West, suggesting that the social and viral marketing opportunity is disproportionally higher in Asia where social uptake has not hit the same kind of plateau as it has in Western markets."[62]

One big cultural difference between the Asian and North American markets is the impact of messaging apps.[62] "Prompted by the launch of brand-friendly Official Accounts on WeChat in 2013, the potential of messaging apps in retail has been embraced more quickly by brands and consumers in China than in the United States, where conversational commerce has been relatively slow to get off the ground."[62]

WHICH ONE AREA IS THE SINGLE MOST EXCITING OPPORTUNITY FOR YOUR ORGANIZATION IN 2018 (RETAIL VS. OTHER SECTORS)

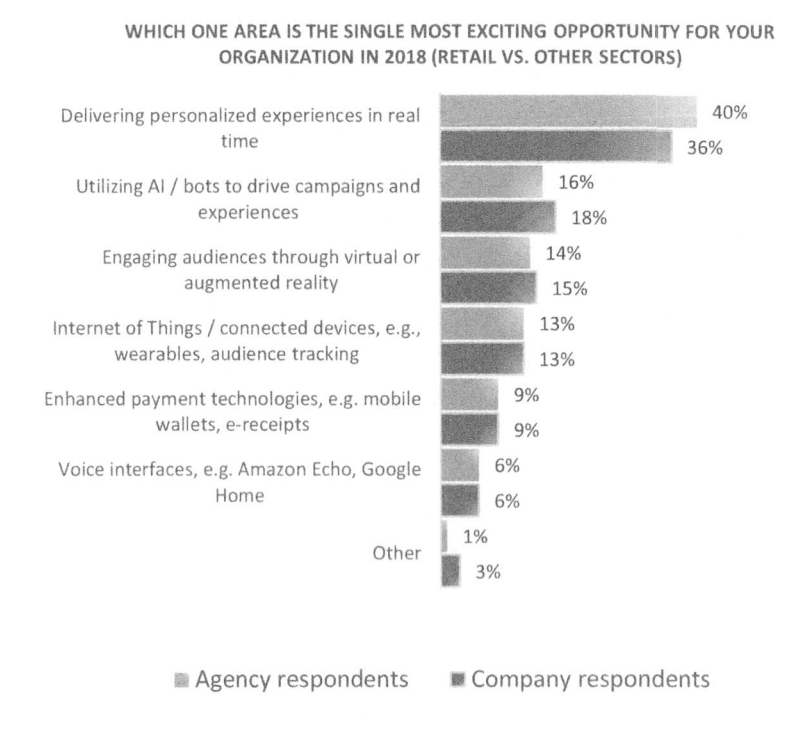

Category	Agency respondents	Company respondents
Delivering personalized experiences in real time	40%	36%
Utilizing AI / bots to drive campaigns and experiences	16%	18%
Engaging audiences through virtual or augmented reality	14%	15%
Internet of Things / connected devices, e.g., wearables, audience tracking	13%	13%
Enhanced payment technologies, e.g. mobile wallets, e-receipts	9%	9%
Voice interfaces, e.g. Amazon Echo, Google Home	6%	6%
Other	1%	3%

Figure 8: Most Exciting Prospects in Three Years' Time?
Source: Adobe 2018 Digital Trends in Retail

As Adobe's *2018 Digital Trends in Retail* discovered, "Retailers recognize that the quality of the customer experience will increasingly depend on being able to serve up the most relevant content and messaging at the right moment, with companies embracing predictive analytics to help them anticipate the most effective way of converting prospects into customers, and then meeting their needs on an ongoing basis."[62]

Adobe's *2018 Digital Trends in Retail* reveals that, "The appeal of real-time personalization suggests a focus on providing the most engaging and relevant experiences, a trend that cuts across numerous digital marketing techniques, including analytics, marketing automation, programmatic ad buying and dynamic content."[62]

"While a range of potential game-changing technological trends in Figure 8 will undoubtedly have a powerful impact, from the Internet of Things and connected devices, to voice interfaces and augmented reality, retailers are predominantly focused on creating a relevant, timely and engaging experience to each of their users, to maximize sales and efficiency."[62] As *Gartner* states, the Internet of Things is the "the network of physical objects that contain embedded technology to communicate and sense or interact with their internal states or the external environment."[63]

AI is an example of an emerging technology that can itself help to make the experience more relevant and personalized.[62] "AI-powered machine learning can increasingly help retailers comb through vast quantities of data to provide the best possible content and recommendations to consumers as they progress through the shipping journey from awareness and discovery to conversion."[62]

According to Michael Klein in his article *Machine Learning and AI: If Only My Computer Had a Brain Wired for Business*[64], "AI helps retailers by serving as an adaptive, automated interface for customer interaction. Similar to a human interaction, this interface can work with customers to resolve issues, route deeper concerns to the right people, and offer personalized recommendations." "This is because AI can act on real-time insights supplied from databases that house a user's browsing history, past purchases, and demographics," explains Klein.[64] "Understanding this data opens opportunities for more personalized targeting, and AI can adapt automated approaches in real time to turn shoppers into buyers," says Klein.[64] This is going to be a big deal as, according to Tractica[65], global revenue resulting from AI technologies just in the retail sector alone is expected to top $36.8 billion by 2025.

One thing that was surprising to the researchers was the lack of interest in voice technology, with only 6% of respondents pointing to voice interfaces as the most exciting opportunity.[62] "The popularity of voice assistants offered by the likes of Amazon, Google, Microsoft and Apple give retail brands the chance to increase their presence, including in homes and cars, provided that they can find the right kind of utility to consumers at the right time."[62]

In her 2019 article *8 Things to Expect from CES, Consumer Tech's Big Shindig*[66], Lauren Goode points out that, "There are now over 20,000 smart devices compatible with Alexa, and over 10,000 that work with Google Assistant. CES 2019 will undoubtedly be a noisy cacophony of voice-controlled devices, ranging from refrigerators to sound systems to smart lights in the home, to wearables and cars outside of the home." She rightfully claims that "if you add another voice assistant to an existing product, you can call it 'new.'"[66] Snark aside, this is the wave of the future, people are getting very comfortable talking and giving instructions to devices. Goode concludes the article by pointing out a common problem: "The question around voice technology, though, isn't so much whether it will have a presence; the question is whether it will grow more seamless and less awkward this year."[66]

Bright Local, an SEO platform used by thousands of businesses, produced an interesting study[67] on the potential of voice search, which found:

- 58% of consumers have used voice search to find local business information in the last 12 months.
- 46% of voice search users look for a local business on a daily basis.
- What consumers want most: to be able to use voice search to make reservations, to hear business prices, and to find out which products businesses have.
- 27% visit the website of a local business after making a voice search.
- 25% of consumers say they haven't yet tried local voice search but would consider it.
- 76% of smart speaker users perform local searches at least weekly—with 53% searching using these devices every day.
- Consumers are most likely to perform voice searches to find further information on local businesses they already know about.
- Voice searchers are most likely to look for restaurants, grocery stores, and food delivery.
- Just 18% of consumers have used smart speakers for local voice searches.

One of the most important stats about voice is the fact that voice searches on Google are now 30 times more likely than text searches to be action queries [68]

One of the key demographic findings of the *2018 Adobe Digital Insights (ADI) State of Digital Advertising* report was that Millennials and Gen Zers differ from Generation X, Baby Boomers, and older generations in that, "social channels are where these generations see the most relevant content in their lives."[62] According to Taylor Schreiner, "social advertising is clearly a key part of a paid/owned/earned media strategy, especially if your audience is under 40."[62] This is a fact that businesses should keep in mind going forward as Millennials and Gen Zers are now reaching an age when they will have disposable income, as well as the desire to spend it.

It is obvious that creating a consolidated customer view is a necessary component of personalization, but, unfortunately, "most marketers today are working with customer data that is decentralized, spread across the organization in multiple databases that are updated in batch processes. To find success, marketers must prioritize consolidating data into a single database," states Jones.[77]

Psychographics—the study and classification of people according to their attitudes, aspirations, and other psychological criteria, especially in market research—is a minor mention in this study, but, as data about people and their behaviors becomes more abundant, this will become an important area to discover customer intelligence. The Cambridge Analytica-Facebook scandal is only now starting to reveal how powerful this kind of information is and, in chapter seven, I delve further into this fascinating subject.

Another important step to bringing personalization efforts up to a user's expectation level will be by using behavioral data. "In order to create these types of customer experiences, marketers must strategically collect and utilize customer data, including real-time signals of intent, which are typically not captured today," argues Jones.[77] Figure 9 lists the identity-related data sources that can be used for personalization and it is a considerable amount of data that must be culled through, siloed, and understood for personalization marketing to work properly.

Identity-related data sources used for personalization

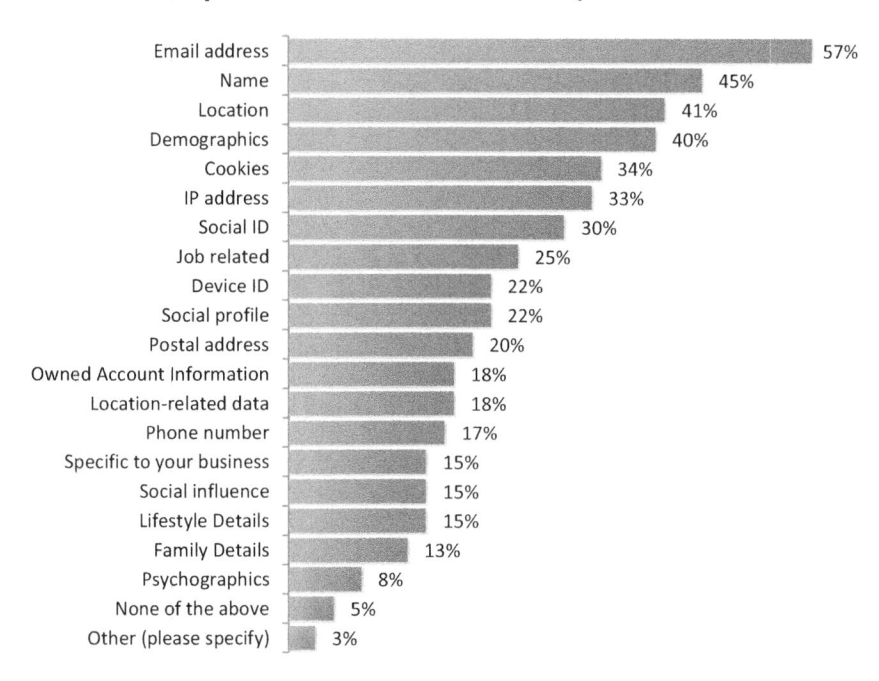

Data Source	Percentage
Email address	57%
Name	45%
Location	41%
Demographics	40%
Cookies	34%
IP address	33%
Social ID	30%
Job related	25%
Device ID	22%
Social profile	22%
Postal address	20%
Owned Account Information	18%
Location-related data	18%
Phone number	17%
Specific to your business	15%
Social influence	15%
Lifestyle Details	15%
Family Details	13%
Psychographics	8%
None of the above	5%
Other (please specify)	3%

Figure 9: Identity-related data sources used for personalization
Source: VB Insights[69]

Figure 10 shows the current data types that a typical travel company might be collecting and utilizing. It reveals that the industry has a long way to go in terms of developing personalization systems that will create powerful customer insights.

With customer attitudes towards personalized content being shaped by recommendation engines on platforms like Amazon, Pandora, and Netflix, consumers are becoming more used to receiving what they want, when they want it, and on whatever channel they want it on.[77] Businesses must keep this in mind when developing personalization programs. The consumer has become highly sophisticated and he or she expects the level of sophistication received on platforms like Amazon to filter over to all their other company communications; don't waste his or her time with non-matching offers or he or she will go down the street or buy from a competitor.

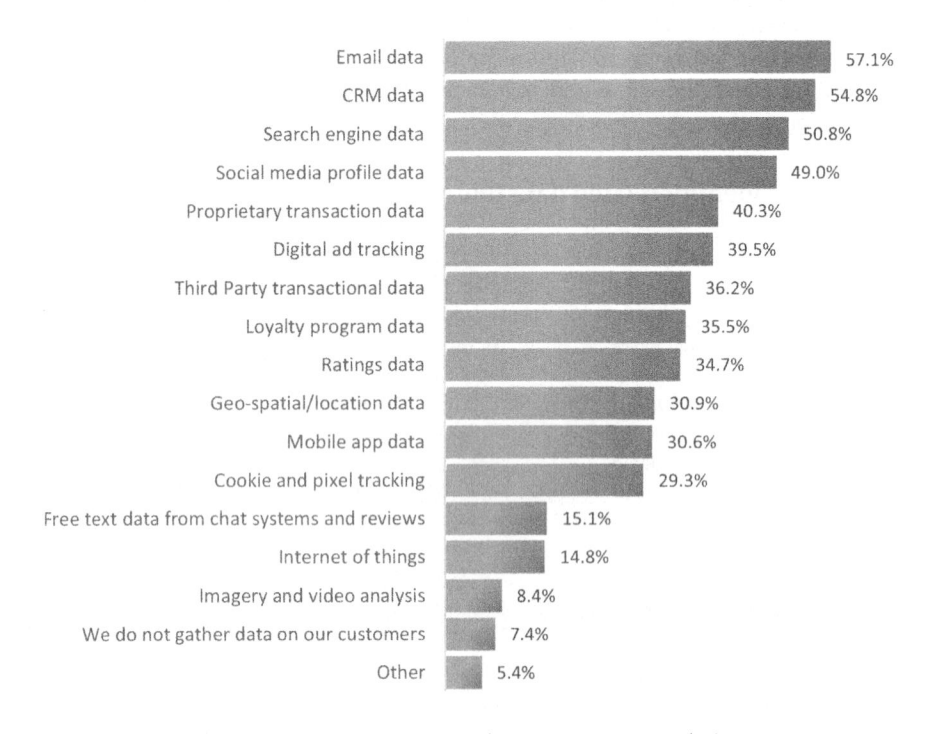

Data Type	Percentage
Email data	57.1%
CRM data	54.8%
Search engine data	50.8%
Social media profile data	49.0%
Proprietary transaction data	40.3%
Digital ad tracking	39.5%
Third Party transactional data	36.2%
Loyalty program data	35.5%
Ratings data	34.7%
Geo-spatial/location data	30.9%
Mobile app data	30.6%
Cookie and pixel tracking	29.3%
Free text data from chat systems and reviews	15.1%
Internet of things	14.8%
Imagery and video analysis	8.4%
We do not gather data on our customers	7.4%
Other	5.4%

Which of the Following Do You Gather to Generate Insight into Your Customers?

Figure 10: State of Data in Travel Survey, 2017
Source: eyefortravel.com[70]

In her article *3 AI-driven strategies for retailers in 2019*[71], Giselle Abramovich claims that, "Personalization is table stakes for today's retailers, who are increasingly competing to be relevant in the hearts and minds of shoppers." This is a great analogy as personalization will soon be the base level upon which customers will accept marketing from the companies they choose to buy from.

VB Insights claims that, "Although we may think of the sales process as 'top-down,' most companies implement personalization with a bottom-up approach. That is, most companies begin their personalization efforts based on 'known' prospects or customers. The channels where personalization is being employed reinforce this finding."[69]

Digital channels in which personalized messages/experiences are delivered

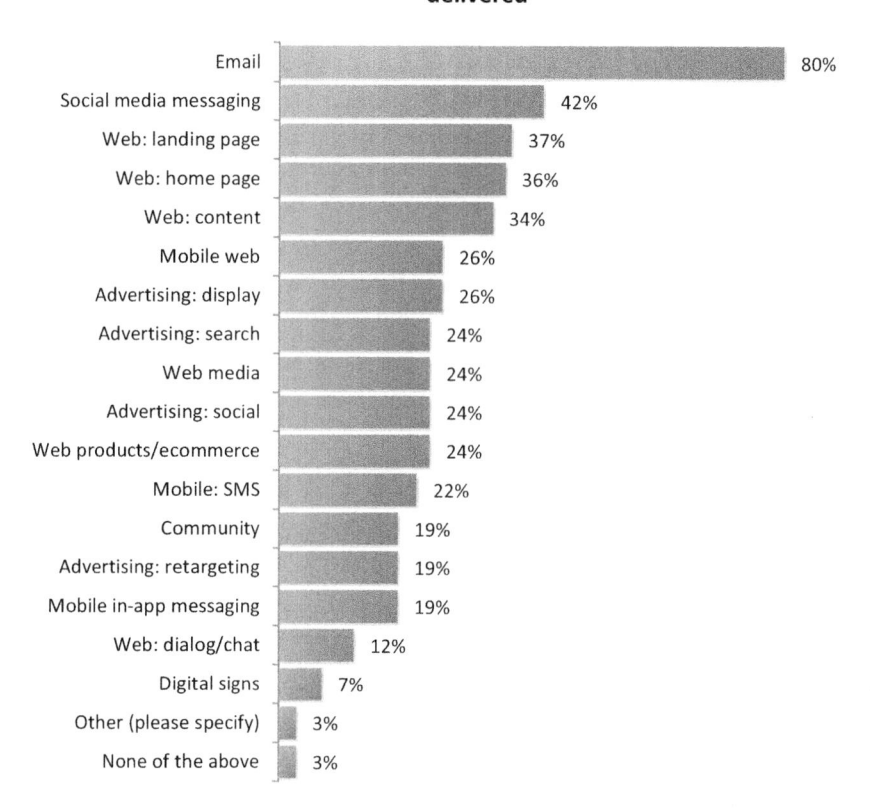

Channel	Percentage
Email	80%
Social media messaging	42%
Web: landing page	37%
Web: home page	36%
Web: content	34%
Mobile web	26%
Advertising: display	26%
Advertising: search	24%
Web media	24%
Advertising: social	24%
Web products/ecommerce	24%
Mobile: SMS	22%
Community	19%
Advertising: retargeting	19%
Mobile in-app messaging	19%
Web: dialog/chat	12%
Digital signs	7%
Other (please specify)	3%
None of the above	3%

Figure 11: Digital Channels for personalized messages/experiences
Source: VB Insights[69]

According to VB Insights, "Email is the dominant channel for personalized content, yet is often limited to field insertion (e.g. "Dear "). Most personalization efforts are also based on transaction history and limited demographic data, meaning personalization is not done to a high degree in most cases."[69] Figure 11 breaks down the different digital channels that brands can utilize to connect with their customers.

Today's IT environment is nothing like the IT environment of even three years ago. Real-time data management capabilities have brought a whole new level of data available to customer intelligence, customer interaction, customer management and social media systems. Model-building and analytics have almost become drop-down functions in the latest analytics and DI software products. These technologies are the backbones of a marketing platform that can deliver personalization on a massive scale.

According to Adobe's *Indelible content, incredible experiences*[72], "Marketers want to surface the right content precisely when and where customers need it. But to be efficient, you want to create once and deliver everywhere, with content automatically adjusting to fit connected experiences on any channel. Machine learning lets you do that—finding better way to optimize layout and copy wherever they're used." For example, "Adobe's smart summarisation can take your product manager's blog post about gourmet hot dogs and trim the redundant content for a news clip or email."

One of the goals of *The A.I. Marketer* is to try to reach as real-time an IT environment as possible. The data I will be focused on throughout this book will be culled from the following operational source systems:

- Customer Relationship Management (CRM) software.
- Transaction data from Point-of-Sales (POS) systems.
- Reservation systems.
- Clickstreams from the company's websites.
- Call center systems.
- Surveillance and security systems, including facial and emotional recognition datasets.
- IoT sensors and tracking devices.
- Geo-location data from in-house Wi-Fi systems.
- Social media data from WeChat, Facebook, Weibo, Twitter, Jeipang, Instagram, YouTube, Twitch, and other mobile and social media apps.
- Ticket revenue management systems.
- Social media listening hubs.
- Google analytics and web tracking information.

The concept of "Edge Analytics"—i.e., the processing of analytics at the point or very close to the point of data collection—exponentially increases the ability to use predictive analytics and AI where they can be utilized best—at the point of interaction between the business and the consumer. In short, edge analytics brings analytics to the data rather than vice-versa, which, understandably, can reduce cost and increase its usage as the data is analyzed close to where it can make the most difference. This also reduces latency, which could be the difference between useful and useless analytics, as well as ROI-positive or financially wasteful marketing.

Before going any further on the personalization front, I believe one of the first questions that needs to be answered here is, "What are analytics?" The standard answer is that there are four types of analytics. They are:

- Descriptive analytics—What happened?
- Diagnostic analytics—Why did it happen?
- Predictive analytics—What will happen?
- Prescriptive analytics—How can we make it happen again?

In the article *Artificial intelligence Unlocks the True Power of Analytics,* Adobe explains that, "Descriptive analytics is the most basic of analysis functions. It summarises and reports what has happened, such as click-throughs and revenue per visitor. This gives marketers historical context and prompts them to ask questions based on past customer behaviour."[13] For example, a marketer could use "descriptive analytics to dig into the various segments and get a good idea of all the behaviours and marketing touchpoints that led"[13] a user to buy something from an e-commerce website, let's say. Utilizing this information, the marketer could "make some educated guesses about how to appeal to similar audiences in the future."[13]

Simple cluster segmentation models could divide customers into their preferred choice of purchases. Market basket analysis, which utilizes association rules, would also be considered a descriptive analytics procedure.

Retailers could use market basket analysis to bundle offer promotions, as well as gain insight into its customers' buying habits. Detailed customer shopping and purchasing behavior could also be used to develop future products. I will go into further detail on this topic in chapter three. According to Adobe, "All users of analytics start by using descriptive analytics and it can lead to valuable insights, but it is limited by the imagination of the person using it. Because the analyst or marketer can only evaluate the data in front of them, they can only find answers to questions that focus on that limited dataset."[13]

"Whereas descriptive analytics is about prompting educated guesses and good questions, diagnostic analytics is about drilling down and filtering that descriptive data to figure out the why and the how of what has happened. Almost everyone who uses descriptive analytics asks, 'Why did this happen?' and uses diagnostic analytics to investigate by comparing different datasets."[13] Adobe believes questions likes "'Why is revenue per visitor so low this week?' leads to 'Is it low for everyone or just for some groups?' which might lead to 'Has it been low all week or just for a few days?' and 'Is it getting better or worse?'"[13]

"As critical as this diagnostic process is to business, it too is limited," argues

Adobe.[13] "As the amount of incoming data increases and the number of variables in customer behaviour grows, the power of diagnostic analytics becomes limited to specific situations, specific anomalies, leaving a vast sea of data questions unasked and unanswered."[13]

"Predictive analytics uses machine learning and other forms of artificial intelligence to meet this problem of scope head-on," argues Adobe.[13] "These technologies can recognise patterns, match events to the patterns and thereby predict the most likely next events. For example, based on how customers have responded to a campaign, predictive analytics will identify segments that respond in like ways, reaching the same outcome."[13] "It will identify what attributes of those groups are important in defining the segment, such as a particular past purchase or number of purchases or geography. It will then 'recognise' any visitor that matches that segment and predict the outcome that visitor will reach," explains Adobe.[13]

Prescriptive analytics, the pinnacle of the analytics pyramid, "applies prediction to suggest the best course of action."[13] "For example, having discovered a segment that almost always responds to a particular campaign by adding an item to the basket but not buying it, prescriptive analytics would suggest the most likely way to nudge those visitors to take the next step. In some cases, the nudge could be performed automatically—in real time," says Adobe.[13]

As to the "why" of analytics, in her article *How Much ROI Can Data Analytics Deliver?*[73], Annie Eissler makes quite a compelling case for analytics. According to Nucleus Research "analytics and business intelligence solutions deliver, on average, $13.01 for every dollar spent."[73] "Leading companies have been achieving double-digit return on investment (ROI) from their analytics investments for several years now," Eissler says.[73]

In its article *Creating the Ultimate Single Customer View*[74], the Adobe Experience Cloud team argues that, real-time access to data enables an "organization to trigger personalized messages and outreach in the moment of highest impact. What's more, leveraging a variety of signals emerging from the buying process, marketers can engage with a customer when it's both most relevant for her, and when she's most likely to convert—maximizing the value on both sides."

Of course, not all campaign management systems are alike or have the functionality that helps businesses deliver experiences at the moment of highest impact.[74] Systems that have lags in data access due to third-party partnerships and integrations are especially susceptible to problems as they are forced to do double duty—first, they have to remind customers how they felt earlier and, second, they have to encourage shoppers to act based on those earlier experiences and emotions, far from ideal.[74]

Composing the marketing message, however, is probably the easiest part of the process. In its *Delivering New Levels of Personalization in Consumer*

Engagement[75], *Forrester Research* found that survey participants believed that personalization had the potential to increase traffic, raise customer conversion rates, and increase average order value. Surveyed marketers felt that personalization capabilities could improve a variety of business metrics, including customer retention (75%), lifetime customer value (75%), and customer conversion rates (71%).[75]

Understanding customer-specified preferences is imperative for personalization; "80% of marketing executives currently use them in some or all interaction channels."[75] "In addition, 68% of marketers personalize current customer interactions based on past customer interaction history. Other commonly used personalization methods used by nearly 60% of firms in some or all of their interaction channels are based on the time of day or day of the week of customer interactions."[75] *Forrester Research* states that the difficulties of personalization include[75]:

1. Continuously optimizing campaigns in response to a customer's most recent interactions.
2. Optimizing content or offers for each person by matching identities to available products, promotions, messages, etc.
3. Creating a single repository containing structured and unstructured data about a consumer.
4. Delivering content or offers to a customer's chosen channel in real time for purposes of conversion.
5. Analyzing all available data in real time to create a comprehensive, contextually sensitive consumer profile.

The executives pooled by *Forrester Research* expected there to be a "huge rise in personalization using consumer's emotional state, social media sentiment, and context"[75] as well. "Only 29% of respondents claim today to use inferences about the consumer's emotional state in some or all channels. But 53% expect to do this in two to three years' time."[75] Forester's report goes on to add, "Only 52% of marketers currently use sentiments that consumers express in social media to personalize interactions today, but fully 79% expect to do this in two to three years. In addition, only 54% capitalize on the consumer's current contextual behavior, but 77% expect to do so in two to three years."[75]

Today, mobile apps, mobile commerce, mobile chat, and mobile gaming have revolutionized the way people do business, seek entertainment, and gamble. Mobile commerce has now evolved into what has become known as "omni-commerce", a seamless approach to selling that puts the shopper's experience front and center, giving that shopper access to what he or she wants through these multiple channels.

In its *Creating the Single Customer View with Adobe Campaign*[76], the Adobe Experience Cloud team recommends businesses "Rely on sales-centric campaign management tools and you'll be hard-pressed to create these single views, let alone construct meaningful mosaics that adapt and evolve in real time. And if you can't capture the granular details surrounding customer interactions—if you can't understand the data you do have—it's virtually impossible to deliver personalized experiences at scale and build a loyal customer base."

Currently, however, there is a big disconnect between what companies think they are delivering in terms of personalization and what consumers are really experiencing. In his article *Study finds marketers are prioritizing personalization...but are further behind then they realize*[77], Andrew Jones states that, "Although two-thirds of the marketers surveyed rate their personalization efforts as 'very good' or 'excellent,' just 31 percent of consumers reported that companies are consistently delivering personalized experiences."[77]

"Aside from this disparity, the report finds that personalization strategies today are immature. It shows that 91 percent of the marketers surveyed are prioritizing personalization over the coming year, yet many still rely on basic segmentation strategies," Jones notes.[77] This isn't that surprising as many companies are struggling with the ability to not just capture the information necessary for personalization, but also creating DWs that can silo the data appropriately, then deliver it to highly complex analytical programs that can make sense of all that data. It is like finding a needle in a haystack for each and every customer in a massive database; a herculean task, no doubt.[77]

In its paper *5 Marketing Predictions for the Next 5 Years*[78], the B2C marketing cloud company Emarsys argues that, "Smart marketers need real-time insights into mobile marketing performance in order to understand how end users are (or aren't) engaging with their mobile marketing programs or applications."

Emarsys argues that[78]:

> "We will move from a world focused on designing for mobile as a secondary approach, to designing for mobile first. E-commerce organizations will finally fully alter the online shopping experience from responsive to completely mobile experiences. This mobile-only approach will be different, as it won't just be a smaller design but will also include more responsive websites and shopping experiences. The mobile-only experience will lead to fully tailored shopping experiences primarily designed for engagement on a mobile device."

Emarsys adds: "Within the next five years, consumers will be able to swipe right, up, and down to make their selections, all via their mobile devices. And when the consumer is ready to complete the transaction? Easy. It just takes one click; the purchase is complete, and the items arrive at the consumer's house."[78]

Much more than a wireless transmitter optimized for voice input and output, a mobile phone or a tablet is an always-on, anytime, anywhere marketing and sales tool that follows a mobile user throughout his or her digital day. It is also an entertainment, CRM, and social networking tool, which makes it, potentially, the most powerful device in the history of marketing and customer relations. WeChat, Alipay, Samsung Pay, Google Pay, etc., have also turned phones into payment portals. The mobile device is, literally, a marketing tool that can—and usually is—personalized by its owner, and it is within reach of that owner almost every hour of every single day; once again a marketer's dream.

Push technology even puts the power of communication into the hands of the marketer, allowing brands to both initiate contact with an opted-in customer and then send him or her a wide variety of products and content. As long as a customer is opted into a CRM system, a brand can foster a two-way dialogue with that customer and this dialogue can grow more sophisticated over time as more is learned about the customer's wants, desires, habits, and needs.

Push technology has moved from clumsy blanket SMS blasts to the sophisticated use of mobile apps that allow customers to interact with their personal customer information, including looking up points balances, checking in, and even purchasing upgrades or even items in an online mall.

"Personalization is critical to any cross-channel strategy—and at the heart of any personalization strategy is the ability to segment," argues the Adobe Experience Cloud team.[76] Unsurprisingly, "Tapping into more complex segmentation strategies helps organizations deliver better, more meaningful cross-channel experiences."[76] AI and machine learning brings a whole new level of depth and detail to customer segmentation modeling. "Being able to easily create control vs. test groups based on nuanced criteria helps arrive at the insight necessary to design optimal experiences for different sets of customers," argues the Adobe Experience Cloud team.[76] "Applying the same nuanced criteria to the delivery of those experiences is how that insight is transformed into personalization at scale," they contend.[76] Adobe argues that the numbers don't lie—segmented and targeted emails generate 58 percent of all revenue.[76] That's total revenue, not lift, which is a highly impressive number.

"Without advanced filtering it's virtually impossible to extract detailed data and uncover the nuances behind the numbers. Beyond that, though, creating and managing lists also becomes a challenge," warns Adobe.[76] "Want to target customers based on their preferred device? If filtering isn't native to your campaign management system, that simple task is going to be time-consuming and costly at best. Personalization becomes a trade-off between quality and speed," says Adobe.[76]

"Businesses should also focus on solutions that utilize artificial intelligence (AI) in a tangible and effective way," argues Adobe.[76] At best, "AI can take the grunt work of data stitching, data cleaning, and anomaly detection off your plate, freeing you up for more meaningful marketing work—gaining a better understanding of customer wants and needs, for example, then spending time designing perfectly personalized experiences," recommends Adobe.[76]

Abby Parasnis, Adobe's chief technology officer argues that Adobe Sensei "gives marketers and analysts new visibility into which segments are most important to their businesses, and allows them to target overlapping or adjacent segments, making it possible to acquire customers much more efficiently."[76]

"By having an integrated customer profile that combines online and offline data, marketers can more easily provide truly meaningful customer experiences that reinforce the brand message across all channels," says Bruce Swan, senior product manager for Adobe Campaign.[76] "The results include increased engagement as well as a higher likelihood for conversion, long-term loyalty, and brand advocacy," adds Swan.[76]

A unified or single customer view can help marketers "harvest the insights they need to develop targeted marketing campaigns—that, in turn, drives customer loyalty, purchases, and conversions."[76] It is a virtuous cycle that feeds upon itself, as long as the customer continues to see the value in loyalty. "Data-driven marketing also speeds time-to-market, and reduces overall campaign costs," the Adobe team believes.[76]

Ultimately, Adobe concludes that, "it comes down to one key consideration: your customers deserve to be treated like individuals—and you need to deliver. You need to collect cross-channel insights that can be pulled together into a cohesive single view. You need to have the capabilities to adjust that view in real time, as your consumers pivot—and even change course. And you need both the powerful insights and powerful technology to drive consistent, cohesive, and meaningful cross-channel journeys for every customer."[76]

The *A.I. Marketer* can personalize the customer experience in the following ways:

- Customer Service:
    - Geo-locating a customer when he or she signs onto a business' customer Wi-Fi system.
    - Video analytics with facial recognition technology to spot and/or confirm a customer's true identity.
    - Social media customer service can cut down on normal customer service expenses, as well as connect with customers on the channels that they prefer, i.e., Facebook, WhatsApp, WeChat, Instagram.
    - Chatbots can automate customer service requests, as well as disseminate info seamlessly.
- E-Commerce

- - Clickstream analysis could allow personalized offers to be sent to a potentially returning customer when he or she is browsing the company's website or making a purchase.
- Customer Management:
  - The ecommerce department can get more accurate attribution analysis—so that a business can understand which advertising is associated with which user, making it more quantifiable and, therefore, much more actionable.
  - CRM systems can add social media as a channel feeding targeted messages to only those customers who are most likely to respond to them.
  - The amount of promotions available and channels through which to market through increases exponentially as campaign lift can be assessed in terms of hours, rather than in days or weeks.
  - Customer acquisition is accelerated because business users throughout the company can quickly derive answers to the following questions:
    - Which combinations of campaigns accelerate conversion?
    - What behavior signals churn?
    - Do web search key words influence deal size?
    - Which product features do users struggle with?
    - Which product features drive product adoption and renewal?
    - What drives customers to use costly sales channels?
  - Customer interaction data can be rapidly turned into business opportunities.
  - Powerful recommendation engines can ingest data from a multitude of sources and then be made available to frontline staff, who can react in near real-time.
- Point-of-Sale:
  - Brands can better target merchandise, sales, and promotions and help redesign store layouts and product placement to improve the customer experience.

In her article *The 5 Biggest Marketing Trends for 2019*[79], Giselle Abramovich quotes Stacy Martinet, VP of marketing strategy and communications at Adobe, saying, "Companies that want to provide truly transformative customer experiences need customer data that is real-time, intelligent, and predictive." Martinet adds that, "In 2019 we'll see enterprises focused on building a seamless flow of connected customer data—behavioral, transactional, financial, operational, and more—to get a true end-to-end view of their customers for immediate actionability."[79]

Giselle Abramovich believes marketers have long been talking about personalization marketing, but they are still at a very basic level of personalization.[79] "To truly unlock the value of personalization, companies must first create a unified view of their customers," believes Anudit Vikram, SVP of audience solutions at Dun & Bradstreet.[79]

Jason Heller, partner and global lead, digital marketing operations at McKinsey agrees, claiming, "The single view of the customer is the single most important asset that a modern marketer can have, and it's the core of their personalization efforts."[79] "It also becomes the core of their next-generation marketing ROI capability, as well," he adds.[79]

One of the keys to personalization at scale is internal structure.[79] Heller "expects companies in 2019 will work on building agile marketing execution models in which cross-functional teams can experiment, leveraging the data and technology stack to capture value."[79]

"Privacy, of course, will play a big role in an organization's personalization strategy," says Abramovich.[79] "New laws such as GDPR—plus California's privacy law, which comes into effect in January 2020—means marketers must be focused on ensuring ethical data collection practices and earning consumers' trust," argues Martinet.[79]

"When choosing partners to work with, brands need to look for products and services that protect the data that is entrusted to them and are designed with privacy in mind," Martinet says.[79] "Privacy is about respecting your customers and giving them control over how their data is being used. Be transparent and help them understand the value proposition," adds Martinet.[79]

Abramovich believes that, in 2019, many organizations will have what McKinsey refers to as a "consent management" function, which includes "having an ethical view of how the organization manages customers' data, protects that data, and establishes governance around how that data is utilized."[79]

"I think this is an absolute obligation that we have regardless of whether the regulations exist or not because eventually they will exist," Heller said.[79] "So starting to operate that way today will only set you up for more success in the future."[79]

As reported in CB Insights *What's Next in AI? Artificial Intelligence Trends*[80], Google's federated learning approach aims to add a layer of privacy by utilizing a person's mobile messaging while also keeping it private. "In a nutshell, your data stays on your phone. It is not sent to or stored in a central cloud server. A cloud server sends the most updated version of an algorithm—called the 'global state of the algorithm—to a random selection of user devices.'"[80]

"Your phone makes improvements and updates to the model based on your localized data. Only this update (and updates from other users) are sent back to the cloud to improve the "global state" and the process repeats itself," explains CB Insights.[80] Real world examples include Firefox's use of federated learning to "rank suggestions that appear when a user starts typing into the URL bar." Google Ventures-backed AI startup OWKIN is using the approach to protect sensitive patient drug discovery data.[80] "The model allows different cancer treatment centers to collaborate without patients' data ever leaving the premises," claims CB Insights.[80]

Data has been called the new oil and although it is an interesting metaphor data companies like Facebook, Google, Apple, Netflix, and Amazon need to be careful not to go down the dark road that the oil industry has traversed to become one of the least liked industries in the world. Many people view oil companies as destructors of nature and the data companies need to take the privacy needs of their customers and potential customers seriously or they, too, will be viewed in a similarly dark light.

Personal shopping

Personalization, of course, helps personal shopping in a multitude of ways. In its article *Retailers: Adopt Artificial Intelligence Now for Personalized and Relevant Experiences*[81], the Adobe Retail Team's reports how "ASOS.com, a British online fashion and beauty store, uses AI to uncover and solve issues specific to online retailers, like helping customers find the right size, thereby minimizing returns." "By analyzing which items customers keep, in which sizes, versus the items and sizes that get returned most often, ASOS is able to use machine learning to recommend appropriate sizes for individual customers regardless of the brand or fit of specific items of clothing," explains the Adobe Retail Team.[81] The result: returns of ill-fitting clothing are minimized, while the customer experience is improved, and there is an overall cost reduction for ASOS.[81]

Artificial intelligence is completely revolutionizing the retail industry as we know it.[81] "From personalized customer experiences across digital touch points to improved product management, this powerful area of computing is helping retailers up their relevance, efficiency, and, ultimately, their bottom line," claims the Adobe Retail Team.[81]

"When we look across the retail industry, there is, surprisingly, quite a broad use of AI already," says Vish Ganapathy, managing director and global retail technology lead at Accenture.[81] "A lot of that has got to do with the fact that more and more technology vendors are injecting AI into everything that they do within their applications. For retail, there are very specific areas where AI can really make a big difference."[81]

According to Ganapathy, "AI's ability to absorb and sort through a lot of unstructured data and use that information to gain more relevance among customers is a big boon for retailers."[81] "When I say personalization, I mean it to be a deeper level of relevance," Ganapathy explains.[81] "If you simply put my name on an email, that's personalized, but if your email has an offer for wine and I'm a beer drinker, it's not very relevant."[81]

Nikki Baird, vice president of retail innovation at Aptos, claims that, "the majority of investment in AI today by retailers revolves around personalization of product recommendations and the next offer to give."[81] Personalized product creation is the next level of AI, she predicts, with some retailers already venturing into that space already.[81]

Baird provides the example of Italian online fashion retailer Yoox, which used AI to design its first private-label collection.[81] Yoox "analyzed fashion-related social media posts in its key markets and also data from products sold on the site, customer feedback, industry buying trends, and top trend searches to come up with the 8 by Yoox collection."[81]

Jeff Barrett, CEO of Barrett Digital, predicts that our phones will soon become the main delivery mechanism for any relevant retail experience.[81] "Retailers will start putting retail pop-ups in the locations where they see there's a lot more traffic," Barrett adds.[81] "Experiences will become more fluid about what physical retail looks like, meaning that it will adapt to where people want to be."[81]

"There are some interesting developments around how to onboard new products much more quickly," Accenture's Ganapathy said.[81] "Image recognition, character recognition, etc., can very quickly predefine product attributes and allow a retailer to onboard new products into the business very quickly. This makes a big difference."[81]

AI can also be used for better inventory management and more accurate product and advertising attribution, which should help merchants reduce costs.[81] For example, Walmart uses AI to adjust inventory levels based on real time information.[81] If rain is forecasted for the next week, "Walmart will shift its inventory to highlight the items that were most sought after the last time it rained for a while. At the same time, merchandise that is less likely to sell when it rains based on the company's data is taken off the shelves."[81]

Chatbots are probably "the most common AI-powered customer service application today."[81] "To date, bots have predominantly been used to provide search and discovery and product recommendations," says Abramovich.[81]

Sephora, which has two Facebook chatbots, is leading the way.[81] The first chatbot—*Sephora Reservation Assistant*—books appointments for makeovers.[81] The bot has seen "an 11% higher conversion rate versus any other channel for doing so."[81]

The second bot—*Color Match for Sephora Virtual Artist*—is a shade-matching bot that "can scan the face of a celebrity and provide a list of the closest-matching lipsticks."[81]

As Ann Lewnes, EVP & CMO of Adobe says in the *Executives Are Eyeing These 2019 Consumer Trends*[82]:

> "While digital has blazed forward in recent years, leaving many to question the lasting significance of traditional offline vehicles, the pendulum is swinging back toward a midpoint where both online and offline channels play complimentary roles in the customer experience. Consumers continue to demand well-designed, personalized digital experiences at every turn, but they equally crave the on-demand satisfaction of a great in-store experience or the inexplicable power of community that exists at a live event. Creativity will never go out of style. It's at the core of every great experience. Marketers who can deliver the ideal blend of online and offline experiences with creativity at the center will win the hearts and minds of customers for years to come."

Brands should build customer analytics capabilities that help it win, serve, and retain increasingly empowered customers. Basic customer analytics can help a brand's marketing team understand a customer's stated and unstated needs and buying motivations to design appropriate offers and experiences.

Customer analytics have evolved in six core dimensions: strategy, organization, data, technology, analytics and measurement, and process. Brands need to recognize that the in-store experience is highly important to consumers who are looking for experiential shopping. This could be the differentiator in tomorrow's retailing landscape.

In terms of analytics, brands should start with segmentation to build a comprehensive view of its customers. Segmentation provides multiple payoffs across the customer life cycle, from acquisition through retention. Segmentation might start with simple attributes such as purchased items, or even geography, but it should evolve over time to characteristics such as lifetime value. Table 3 shows the other types of analytics that should be used during a customer life-cycle.

Many of these models require complex data integration / data virtualization, CRM, social, and analytics systems working in harmony with each other and I will break down the needed hardware and software infrastructure in chapter six, then delve into creating an overall AI, analytics, and digital marketing platform in chapter seven.

Life-cycle stage	Business objective	Analytical method
Discover	Profile customers	Segmentation
	Evaluate prospects	Lead scoring
	Reach the right prospects	Customer lookalike targeting
Explore	Analyze customers' responses	Offer/contact optimization
	Optimize marketing mix	Marketing mix modeling
	Delivering contextually relevant content	Customer location analysis
	Test marketing inputs	A/B and multivariate testing
Buy	Predict future events	Propensity models
	Expand wallet share	Cross-sell/upsell
	Target accurately	In-market timing models
Use	Drive deeper product use	Product and recommendation analysis
	Understand use	Customer device use analysis
	Understand customer satisfaction	Customer satisfaction analysis
Ask	Learn about drivers of engagement	Engagement analysis
	Improve customer service	Customer device use analyss
	Identify customer pain points	Voice of the customer analysis
Engage	Manage defection of customers	Churn models
	Personalize marketing efforts	Next-best-action models
	Maximize customer value	Lifetime value models
	Increase depth of relationship	Loyalty models
	Optimize customer interactions	Customer journey analysis
	Understand customer relationships	Social network analysis

Table 3: Analytics Across the Customer Life-Cycle
Source: Forrester's How Analytics Drives Customer Life-Cycle Management[83]

Website Morphing

It is all well and good to offer personalized service to customers face-to-face, but what happens when a customer visits a brand's website for the first time, or even the hundredth time? Today, personalized web pages can be rendered during the web page load and elements of the page can take into account past purchase history, clickstream behavior, as well as a whole host of other data points. For a marketer, their website is really their customer center.

In her article *The Art and Science Behind Every "Add to Cart"*[84], Christie Chew argues that, "Neuroscience and the way people make decisions impact what compels people to click and buy. Together, these considerations and best practices can work together to drive customers to take action."

Guliz Sicotte, head of product design and content for Magento, says to prompt a customer purchase, brands must create online experiences that focus on four principal characteristics—they must be personalized, reflective, transparent, and use pleasing aesthetics.[84]

Morphing is one of the ways a brand can hyper-personalize the customer shopping experience. So, what exactly is morphing? In their article *Website Morphing*[85], Hauser et al. state that, "'Morphing' involves automatically matching the basic 'look and feel' of a website, not just the content, to cognitive styles." Hauser et al. use Bayesian updating to "infer cognitive styles from clickstream data."[85] Then they "balance exploration (learning how morphing affects purchase probabilities) with exploitation (maximizing short-term sales) by solving a dynamic program (partially observable Markov decision process)."[85]

In a world of deep personalization, website design becomes a major profit driver.[85] As Hauser et al. see it, "Websites that match the preferences and information needs of visitors are efficient; those that do not forego potential profit and may be driven from the market."[85] The authors believe that "retailers might serve their customers better and sell more products and services if their websites matched the cognitive styles of their visitors."[85] I'd argue it is not just retailers who would profit from this, most B-2-C companies would.

Keeping with the themes of simplicity and seamlessness, Hauser et al. do not believe personal self-selection—the process in which a customer is given many options and allowed to select how to navigate and interact with the site—is viable.[85] "As the customer's options grow, this strategy leads to sites that are complex, confusing, and difficult to use," they argue.[85] The second option, which requires "visitors to complete a set of cognitive style tasks and then select a website from a predetermined set of websites"[85] is just as problematic. Website visitors probably won't see value in taking the time to answer these questions and there is always the problem of self-bias hindering any potential results.[85]

Hauser et al. propose another approach: "'morphing' the website automatically by matching website characteristics to customers' cognitive styles."[85] A cognitive style is "a person's preferred way of gathering, processing, and evaluating information"[86] It can be identified as "individual differences in how we perceive, think, solve problems, learn and relate to others."[87] "A person's cognitive style is fixed early on in life and is thought to be deeply pervasive [and is] a relatively fixed aspect of learning performance."[88]

The "goal is to morph the website's basic structure (site backbone) and other functional characteristics in real time."[85] "Website morphing complements self-selected branching (as in http://www.Dell.com), recommendations (as in http://www.Amazon.com), factorial experiments (Google's Website Optimizer), or customized content[89 90]."[85]

For Hauser et al., cognitive styles dimensions "might include impulsive (makes decisions quickly) versus deliberative (explores options in depth before making a decision), visual (prefers images) versus verbal (prefers text and numbers), or analytic (wants all details) versus holistic (just the bottom line)."[85] For example, "a website might morph by changing the ratio of graphs and pictures to text, by reducing a display to just a few options (broadband service plans), or by carefully selecting the amount of information presented about each plan. A website might also morph by adding or deleting functional characteristics such as column headings, links, tools, persona, and dialogue boxes."[85] There are, literally, hundreds of thousands or even millions of ways a website can morph to better serve its customers.

Because of its real-time nature, website morphing is not easy. It presents at least the following four technical challenges[85]:

1. The customer acquisition problem, i.e., the website must morph based on relatively few clicks of a first-time visitor; otherwise, the customer sees little benefit.
2. Even knowing a customer's cognitive style is not enough, the website must learn which characteristics are best for which customers (in terms of sales or profit).
3. To be practical, a system needs prior distributions on parameters.
4. Implementation requires a real-time working system, which is one of the most complex systems to set up, run, and maintain.

For their website morphing, Hauser et al. used[85]:

> "a Bayesian learning system to address the rapid assessment of cognitive styles and a dynamic program to optimally manage the tension between exploitation (serving the morph most likely to be best for a customer) and exploration (serving alternative morphs to learn which morph is best). Uncertainty in customer styles implies a partially observable Markov

decision process (POMDP), which we address with fast heuristics that are close to optimal. Surveys, using both conjoint analysis and experimentation, provide priors and 'prime' the Bayesian and dynamic programming engines. We demonstrate feasibility and potential profit increases with an experimental website developed for the BT Group to sell broadband service in Great Britain."

Hauser et al. expect different morphs to appeal differentially depending on the visitors' cognitive style.[85] "For example, impulsive visitors might prefer less detailed information, whereas deliberative visitors might prefer more information. Similarly, the more focused of the two morphs might appeal to visitors who are holistic, while the ability to compare many plans in a table might appeal to analytic visitors."[85] If preferences match behavior, then, by matching a website's characteristics to a customer's cognitive style, the morphing website should be able to sell more effectively, thereby producing greater profits for the brand.

Hauser et al. applied a "Bayesian updating and dynamic programming to an experimental BT Group (formerly British Telecom) website using data from 835 priming respondents."[85] The challenge was to infer the cognitive-segment to which each visitor belonged, "while simultaneously learning how to maximize profit by assigning morphs to cognitive-style segments."[85]

Web visitors cognitive style segment are inferred from their clickstreams.[85] This was possible "because each visitor's click is a decision point that reveals the visitor's cognitive-style preferences."[85] Hauser et al. believe that with enough observed clicks, they could have been able to identify a visitor's cognitive-style segment quite conclusively.[85] However, in any real application, the number of clicks observed before morphing would be quite small, yielding at best a noisy indicator of segment membership.[85]

Hauser et al. observed about ten clicks, inferred probabilities for the visitor's cognitive-style segment, then morphed the website based on their inference of the visitor's segment.[85] "The visitor continued until he or she purchased a BT broadband service or left the website without purchasing."[85]

In most cases, cognitive styles are measured with methods that "include direct classification, neuro-fuzzy logic, decision trees, multilayer perceptrons, Bayesian networks, and judgment."[85] Hauser et al. acknowledge that, while most authors match the learning or search environment based on judgment by an expert pedagogue or based on predefined distance measures, they inferred cognitive styles from a relatively small set of clicks, then automatically balanced exploration and exploitation to select the most appropriate morph.[85]

To set a baseline cognitive style standard Hauser et al. used "a professional market research company (Applied Marketing Science, Inc.) and a respected

British online panel (Research Now)."[85] They invited "current and potential broadband users to complete an online questionnaire that combined BT's experimental website with a series of preference and cognitive style questions."[85]

835 respondents completed the questionnaire, which contained the following sequential sections[85]:

- Identify whether respondent was in the target market.
- Identify which of 16 broadband providers they might be considering, along with purchase-intention probabilities.
- Eight randomly-assigned potential morphs of the BT website. Each respondent was encouraged to spend at least five minutes on BT's experimental website.
- Post-visit response consideration and purchase-intention probabilities.
- Identify their preferences between eight pairs of websites with a choice-based conjoint analysis-like exercise. These data augment clickstream data when estimating.
- A cognitive style measure.

Hauser et al. expected "these scales to identify whether the respondent was analytic or holistic, impulsive or deliberative, visual or verbal, and a leader or a follower."[85] "The analytic versus holistic dimension is widely studied in psychology and viewed as being a major differentiator of how individuals organize and process information,"[85] including by Riding and Rayner[91], Allinson and Hayes[92], Kirton[93], and Riding and Cheema.[94] According to Hauser et al., "Researchers in both psychology and marketing suggest that cognitive styles can be further differentiated as either impulsive or deliberative[95] [96]."[85]

In summary, Hauser et al. identified the following four empirical constructs to measure respondents' cognitive styles[85]:

- Leader versus follower.
- Analytic/visual versus holistic/verbal.
- Impulsive versus deliberative.
- (Active) reader versus (passive) listener.

In conclusion, Hauser et al. "used segments of cognitive styles rather than continuously defined cognitive styles because the dynamic program requires finitely many 'arms.'"[85] Websites were morphed once per visit, in part, because Hauser et al. observed a single subscription decision per customer.[85]

In her article *The Art and Science Behind Every "Add to Cart"*, Christie Chew notes that the central question driving most purchases is, "What's in it for me?"[84] "Customers should feel that products are relevant to their intentions," adds Guliz.[84] "This sense of relevance can be traced back to what Carmen Simon, Ph.D., cognitive neuroscientist at Memzy, describes as habitual decision-making—habits are conscious at first but eventually become subconscious," adds Guliz.[84]

"Link your techniques, content, value proposition, or whatever you're offering, to something that feels familiar to the customer's brain," says Simon.[84] This increases a person's comfort level, which makes them more likely to take a favorable action for your brand because what you're asking them will feel easy.[84]

Guliz concurs: "In the end, customers are faced with a barrage of e-commerce opportunities. Expedite the shopping experience and increase conversions by identifying products that 'people like me' have purchased. Once I can vet a product based on people who closely match my profile, I am that much closer to feeling comfortable in making the purchase."[84]

"It's also essential that each step in your e-commerce experience reflects intention," says Chew.[84] "For example, the category page should include curiosity-triggering components," adds Guliz.[84] "If you're displaying an array of products online, make it easy to determine the sentiment around each, without customers needing to invest time to dive into each."[84] "From here, be sure to show customers the most important details and features relevant to them and their purchase experience," recommends Chew.[84]

"This process can help create a series of clicks that drive those customers closer to making a purchase," says Chew.[84] "Don't pitch immediately. Don't make people think too hard. Work toward a series of smaller, more habitual 'yeses,'" advises Simon.[84] "This creates more momentum and a pattern of 'yes,' which can make a customer more comfortable with a bigger, riskier purchase decision," she says.[84]

For example, if you're promoting high-end travel, query users about their overall travel experience, rather than asking them outright if they are booking travel for a vacation or business.[84] These kinds of questions will likely elicit positive responses, whereas direct questions can often be off-putting.[84]

Posing questions about a customer's travel habits and preferences can lead potential customers to the critical "yes"—and they might at least consider booking a luxury vacation.[84] By that point, Chew argues, "they've been habituated toward a positive response and will be more open to bigger considerations—and bigger purchases."[84]

According to Carmen, "the brain makes decisions in a reflexive, habitual, and/or goal-oriented way."[84] "The mistake some businesses make is asking people to tap into their goals too quickly, at the expense of tapping into reflexes and habits first," believes Chew.[84] She recommends brands, "Create opportunities for the buyer to take small steps first, toward a larger goal or purchase."[84]

Transparency is essential to ensure positive customer experiences that will drive customers toward a purchase.[84] "It's important to bring high visibility to the critical decision-making factors like return policies and shipping times, by writing them in clear, simple ways," Guliz says.[84] "If an array of products is displayed, make it easy to determine the sentiment around these products without needing to invest time to dive into each product offering."[84]

"This type of layout will play well to a customer's need to feel like they're in control of their environment," says Chew.[84] Guliz adds that brand should ensure users can "easily navigate to different aspects of the product page."[84] "Take them to reviews when they click on star ratings. Let them filter product reviews

"Retailers are making people think way too much," Simon says.[84] "If you start with something that feels familiar and habitual, you'll have an easier time when it comes to persuasion. Show customers something that doesn't require a lot of cognitive energy to process."[84]

"Humans are innately emotional—we react to everything from people to environments to colors and sounds, based on our existing and real-time experiences. This insight can help e-commerce brands better structure their retail experiences," argues Guliz.[84] "The right aesthetics are major elements of trustworthiness in your store," explains Guliz.[84] "Lots of detailed photos of key features is crucial to a good experience."[84] In chapter four, I explain the psychology of personalization and detail 15 types of psychological effects that, when used correctly, can motivate consumers to buy.

Simon adds that "there are a series of innate behaviors in which you already know what to do next. In the buying process, that includes your reflex toward something beautiful."[84]

Marcia Flicker, Ph.D., associate professor at Fordham University's Gabelli School of Business, argues that, "Creating this aesthetic experience requires having the right visuals."[84] E-commerce brands need bigger and more detailed photos, especially apparel brands.[84] "It can be hard for customers to buy apparel online because they want to try it on, feel the fabric," says Flicker.[84] "Retailers need to reproduce that experience of being able to see the actual item. Customers need to see large images from a variety of angles—or even video."[84]

"This aesthetics-focused notion can, then, be woven into an e-commerce brand's UX design to help pave a customer's path to purchase," says Guliz.[84] "When you design an interface, you're more likely to have people use it if it's aesthetically appealing," Simon says.[84] "Principles like proximity, balance, unity, and contrast are important to this notion of aesthetics."[84]

"Understanding why customers buy and designing experiences to match their patterns is just the beginning. Going forward, brands will continue to fine-tune these strategies, layering in more future-forward technologies," predicts Guliz.[84] "Augmented reality could be a game-changer, especially for retailers," says Flicker.[84] "Think about using AR to overlay dress styles on online models that look just like you. This enables you to envision the real-life equivalent without actually being in store, and that has value."[84]

However, Guliz concludes that, "even with the most cutting-edge understanding of what makes us tick—and click—and stunning aesthetics and powerful UX design, none of it matters if the experience doesn't fill a need in the customer's purchase path."[84] Experience is both the fallback and the reason for purchases.

Affective Computing

In his article *We Know How You Feel*[97], Raffi Khatchadourian profiles Rana el Kaliouby, co-founder and CEO of Affectiva, a startup that specializes in AI systems that sense and understand human emotions. Affectiva develops "cutting-edge AI technologies that apply machine learning, deep learning, and data science to bring new levels of emotional intelligence to AI."[98] It has been ranked by the business press as one of the United States' fastest-growing startups.[97] Affectiva is the most visible among a host of competing startups that are building emotionally responsive machines.[97] Its competitors include Emotient, Realeyes, and Sension.[97]

Khatchadourian explains that, "Our faces are organs of emotional communication; by some estimates, we transmit more data with our expressions than with what we say, and a few pioneers dedicated to decoding this information have made tremendous progress."[97] Arguably, The most successful of these pioneers is Rana el Kaliouby.[97]

"Since the nineteen-nineties a small number of researchers have been working to give computers the capacity to read our feelings and react, in ways that have come to seem startlingly human," explains Khatchadourian.[97] Researchers "have trained computers to identify deep patterns in vocal pitch, rhythm, and intensity; their software can scan a conversation between a woman and a child and determine if the woman is a mother, whether she is looking the child in the eye, whether she is angry or frustrated or joyful."[97] "Other machines can measure sentiment by assessing the arrangement of our words, or by reading our gestures. Still others can do so from facial expressions," says Khatchadourian.[97]

In his book *Architects of Intelligence*[98], Martin Ford interviews Rana el Kaliouby, and she explains her work in the following way:

> *"If you think about a lot of people who are building these devices, right now, they're focused on the cognitive intelligence aspect of these devices, and they're not paying much attention to the emotional intelligence. But if you look at humans, it's not just your IQ that matters in how successful you are in your professional and personal life; it's often really about your emotional and social intelligence. Are you able to understand*

the mental states of people around you? Are you able to adapt your behavior to take that into consideration and then motivate them to change their behavior, or persuade them to take action?" All of these situations, where we are asking people to take action, we all need to be emotionally intelligent to get to that point. I think that this is equally true for technology that is going to be interfacing with you on a day-to-day basis and potentially asking you to do things."

Kaliouby's thesis "is that this kind of interface between humans and machines is going to become ubiquitous, that it will just be ingrained in the future human-machine interfaces, whether it's our car, our phone or smart devices at our home or in the office."[98] She sees a world where, "We will just be coexisting and collaborating with these new devices, and new kinds of interfaces."[98] "I think that, ten years down the line, we won't remember what it was like when we couldn't just frown at our device, and our device would say, 'Oh, you didn't like that, did you?'" says Kaliouby.[97]

Afectiva's signature software, Affdex, tracks four emotional "classifiers"—happy, confused, surprised, and disgusted.[97] "The software scans for a face; if there are multiple faces, it isolates each one. It then identifies the face's main region—mouth, nose, eyes, eyebrows—and it ascribes points to each, rendering the features in simple geometries," explains Khatchadourian.[97]

"Affdex also scans for the shifting texture of skin—the distribution of wrinkles around an eye, or the furrow of a brow—and combines that information with the deformable points to build detailed models of the face as it reacts," says Khatchadourian.[97] The algorithm identifies an emotional expression by comparing it with countless others that it has previously analyzed. "If you smile, for example, it recognizes that you are smiling in real time," Kaliouby says.[97]

Like every company working in the emotional intelligence field, "Affectiva relies on the work of Paul Ekman, a research psychologist who, beginning in the sixties, built a convincing body of evidence that there are at least six universal human emotions, expressed by everyone's face identically, regardless of gender, age, or cultural upbringing."[97] Classifying human expressions into combinations of forty-six individual movements called "action units", Ekman compiled the Facial Action Coding System, or FACS—a five-hundred-page taxonomy of facial movements.[97] FACS "has been in use for decades by academics and professionals, from computer animators to police officers interested in the subtleties of deception."[97]

Although widely used, Ekman and FACS has its critics, "among them social scientists who argue that context plays a far greater role in reading emotions than his theory allows."[97] However, context-blind computers appear to support Ekman's conclusions.[97] "By scanning facial action units, computers can now outperform most people in distinguishing social smiles from those triggered by spontaneous joy, and in differentiating between faked pain and genuine pain," says Khatchadourian.[97] "Operating with unflagging attention, they can register expressions so fleeting that they are unknown even to the person making them," notes Khatchadourian.[97]

"The human face is a moving landscape of tremendous nuance and complexity. It is a marvel of computation that people so often effortlessly interpret expressions, regardless of the particularities of the face they are looking at, the setting, the light, or the angle," notes Khatchadourian.[97] He adds that, "A programmer trying to teach a computer to do the same thing must contend with nearly infinite contingencies. The process requires machine learning, in which computers find patterns in large tranches of data, and then use those patterns to interpret new data."[97]

In March, 2011, Kaliouby and her team were invited to demonstrate an early version of their technology to executives from Millward Brown, a global market-research company.[97] "Kaliouby was frank about the system's limitations—the software still was having trouble distinguishing a smile from a grimace—but the executives were impressed," reports Khatchadourian.[97] Ad testing relies heavily on subjective surveys, which can be easily tainted by human bias.[97] Spontaneous, even unconscious, sentiment is what really interests marketers and Kaliouby's technology promised that, along with better results.[97]

"A year earlier, Millward Brown had formed a neuroscience unit, which attempted to bring EEG technology into the work, and it had hired experts in Ekman's system to study video of interviews," explains Khatchadourian.[97] However, these ideas had proved impossible to scale up.[97] The Millward Brown executives proposed a test to Kaliouby: "if Affdex could successfully measure people's emotional responses to four ads that they had already studied, Millward Brown would become a client, and also an investor."[97]

Millward Brown chose the Dove TV commercial "Onslaught," which begins with an image of a young girl, then "shifts to her perspective as she is bombarded by a montage of video clips—a lifetime of female stereotypes compressed into thirty-two seconds—before the ad ends with the girl, all innocence, and the tagline 'Talk to your daughter before the beauty industry does.'"[97] Although the ad was critically acclaimed, surveys revealed that many people considered it emotionally difficult to watch.[97] In its study, Affdex scanned more than a hundred respondents watching the ad, and discovered more complicated responses. Although respondents were uncomfortable during the ad, at the moment of resolution this discomfort vanished.[97] "The software was telling us something we were potentially not seeing," Graham Page, a Millward Brown executive, explained.[97] Recognizing the power of Affectiva's technology, Millward Brown's parent company, WPP, invested $4.5 million in the company.[97] Affdex was soon being used to test thousands of ads per year.[97]

Kaliouby claims that her company has analyzed more than two million videos, of respondents from over eighty countries.[97] "This is data we have never had before," says Kaliouby.[97] When Affectiva began, she had trained the software on just a few hundred expressions, but, once she started working with Millward Brown, hundreds of thousands of people on six continents began turning on web cams to watch ads for testing, and all their emotional responses—natural reactions, in relatively uncontrolled settings—flowed back to Kaliouby's team.[97]

Affdex can now read the nuances of smiles better than most people can. As the company's database of emotional reactions grows, the software is getting better at reading other expressions, including furrowed eyebrows. "A brow furrow is a very important indicator of confusion or concentration, and it can be a negative facial expression," explains Kaliouby.[97]

Today, Kaliouby says companies pay millions of dollars to create funny and emotionally compelling ads, but the advertisers and the brands have no idea if they are striking the right emotional chord with their audience.[98] The only way to find out, before emotional response technology existed, was to ask people.[98] So, if you are the person watching the ad, you'd get a survey with some basic questions, but the answers wouldn't be very reliable because it is biased believes Kaliouby.[98]

With Affdex, however, Kaliouby explains that, "as you're watching the ad, with your consent it will analyze on a moment-by-moment basis all your facial expressions and aggregate that over the thousands of people who watched that same ad."[98] The result: "an unbiased, objective set of data around how people respond emotionally to the advertising."[98] Affectiva can "then correlate that data with things like customer purchase intent, or even actual sales data and virality."[98]

"People are pretty good at monitoring the mental states of the people around them," says Kaliouby.[98] "We know that about 55% of the signals we use are in facial expression and your gestures, while about 38% of the signal we respond to is from tone of voice. So how fast someone is speaking, the pitch, and how much energy is in the voice. Only 7% of the signal is in the text and the actual choice of words that someone uses!"[98]

A multi-billion-dollar industry that tracks people's sentiments about this product or that service has been built within just a couple of years ago, which is amazing when you think that all of these tweets, likes and posts only account for about 7% of how humans communicate overall.[98] "What I like to think about what we're doing here, is trying to capture the other 93% of non-verbal communication," contends Kaliouby.[98]

According to Kaliouby, Affectiva looks "at the tone of voice and the occurrence of speech events, such as how many times you say 'um' or how many times you laughed. All of these speech events are independent of the actual words that we're saying."[98] Affectiva combines "these things and takes what we call a multimodal approach, where different modalities are combined, to truly understand a person's cognitive, social or emotional state," explains Kaliouby.[98]

"If you take facial expressions or even the tone of a person's voice, the underlying expressions are universal," says Khatchadourian.[98] A smile is a smile no matter where in the world it breaks across a face. "However, we are seeing this additional layer of cultural display norms, or rules, that depict when people portray their emotions, or how often, or how intensely they show their emotion," says Khatchadourian.[98] "We see examples of people amplifying their emotions, dampening their emotions, or even masking their emotions altogether."[98] Masking often occurs in Asian markets, where Asian populations are less likely to show negative emotions.[98] In Asia, there is an increased incidence of what's known as a "social smile", or a "politeness smile."[98] These are not expressions of joy, but rather expressions that say, "I acknowledge you," and, in that sense, they are very social signals.[98]

Affdex is sold "as a tool that can make reliable inferences about people's emotions—a tap into the unconscious,"[97] if you will. Clients like CBS use it to tests new TV shows.[97] Affectiva is also working with Oovoo, an instant messaging service, to integrate the technology into video calls.[97] "People are doing more and more videoconferencing, but all this data is not captured in an analytic way," says Kaliouby.[97] "Capturing analytics, it turns out, means using the software—say, during a business negotiation—to determine what the person on the other end of the call is not telling you," writes Khatchadourian. "The technology will say, 'O.K., Mr. Whatever is showing signs of engagement—or he just smirked, and that means he was not persuaded,'" says Kaliouby.[97]

Kaliouby believes Affectiva's technology has the potential to monetize what she calls an 'Emotion Economy'.[97] "Tech gurus have for some time been predicting the Internet of Things, the wiring together of all our devices to create 'ambient intelligence'—an unseen fog of digital knowingness," explains Khatchadourian.[97] Emotion could be a part of this IoT.[97] Kaliouby predicts that, in the coming years, mobile devices will contain an "emotion chip," which constantly runs in the background, the way geolocation currently works on phones now.[97] "Every time you pick up your phone, it gets an emotion pulse, if you like, on how you're feeling," Kaliouby says.[97] "In our research, we found that people check their phones ten to twelve times an hour—and so that gives this many data points of the person's experience," she explains.[97]

The free economy is, in fact, an economy of the bartered self, but attention can never be limitless.[97] Thales Teixeira, a business professor who collaborated with Kaliouby on her technology, explains that, "There are three major fungible resources that we as individuals have. The first is money, the second is time, and the third is attention. Attention is the least explored."[97] Teixeira calculated the value of attention, and found that, like the dollar, its price fluctuates.[97]

Using Super Bowl ads as a rough indicator of the high end of the market, Teixeira "determined that in 2010 the price of an American's attention was six cents per minute. By 2014, the rate had increased by twenty per cent—more than double inflation."[97] The jump was attributed to the fact that attention, at least, the kind worth selling, is becoming increasingly scarce as people spend their free time distracted by a growing array of devices and services.[97] "What people in the industry are saying is 'I need to get people's attention in a shorter period of time,' so they are trying to focus on capturing the intensity of it," Teixeira explains.[97] "People who are emotional are much more engaged. And because emotions are 'memory markers' they remember more. So the idea now is shifting to: how do we get people who are feeling these emotions?" says Teixeira.[97]

Affectiva filed a patent for "a system that could dynamically price advertising depending on how people responded to it."[97] However, they soon discovered that they were not alone; more than a hundred similar patents for emotion-sensing technology existed, many of them, unsurprisingly, also focused on advertising.[97] Companies like AOL, Hitachi, eBay, IBM, Yahoo!, and Motorola are also developing technology in this space.[97] Sony had filed several patents; "its researchers anticipated games that build emotional maps of players, combining data from sensors and from social media to create 'almost dangerous kinds of interactivity,'" notes Khatchadourian.[97] There are "patents for emotion-sensing vending machines, and for A.T.M.s that would understand if users were 'in a relaxed mood,' and receptive to advertising," claims Khatchadourian.[97]

Incredibly, Verizon had drafted a plan for "a media console packed with sensors, including a thermographic camera (to measure body temperature), an infrared laser (to gauge depth), and a multi-array microphone. By scanning a room, the system could determine the occupants' age, gender, weight, height, skin color, hair length, facial features, mannerisms, what language they spoke, and whether they had an accent."[97]

According to Khatchadourian, "the console could identify pets, furniture, paintings, even a bag of chips."[97] It could track "ambient actions," such as "eating, exercising, reading, sleeping, cuddling, cleaning, playing a musical instrument."[97] It could even probe other devices, learning what a person might be browsing on the web, or writing in an e-mail.[97] The console could scan for affect, tracking moments of laughter or the raised voice of an argument.[97] All of this data tracking would then shape the console's choice of TV ads.[97] "A marital fight might prompt an ad for a counsellor. Signs of stress might prompt ads for aromatherapy candles. Upbeat humming might prompt ads 'configured to target happy people,'" which is a pretty scary idea.[97] Verizon's plan was for the system to then broadcast the ads on every device in the room.[97]

Although Verizon's system seems very Big Brotheresque, it was not an anomaly, Khatchadourian explains.[97] Microsoft's Xbox One system already contains many of its features, including "a high-definition camera that can monitor players at thirty frames per second."[97] "Using a technology called Time of Flight, it can track the movement of individual photons, picking up minute alterations in a viewer's skin color to measure blood flow, then calculate changes in heart rate."[97] "The software can monitor six people simultaneously, in visible or infrared light, charting their gaze and their basic emotional states, using technology similar to Affectiva's."[97] As Khatchadourian sees it, "the system has tremendous potential for making digital games more immersive."[97] Microsoft isn't stopping at game development, however, they envision TV ads that target a viewer's emotions, and program priced according to how many people are watching in the room.[97] Google, Comcast, and Intel are charting a similar path.[97]

Wearables like Nike's FuelBand and particularly Fitbit collect a tremendous amount of health data on a person.[97] Apple's Health app, a fitness app pre-installed on new iPhones "can track weight, respiratory rate, sleep, even blood-oxygen saturation."[97] This information could be used to build emotional profiles, says Khatchadourian.[97] Researchers at Dartmouth have already "demonstrated that smartphones can be configured to detect stress, loneliness, depression, and productivity, and to predict G.P.A.s."[97]

For Affectiva, there is now plenty of interest in its Affdex solution.[97] The company has conducted research for Facebook, experimenting with video ads.[97] Samsung has licensed it and a company in San Francisco wants to give its digital nurses the ability to read faces.[97] A Belfast entrepreneur is interested in its use at night clubs.[97] A state initiative in Dubai, the *Happiness Index*, wants to measure social contentment: "Dubai is known to have one of the world's tightest CCTV networks, so the infrastructure to acquire video footage to be analyzed by Affdex already exists," says Kaliouby.[97]

All-in-all, Affective could be showing us the future of customer engagement. Although somewhat Big Brotheresque, all of this data collection is incredibly seamless, which means it will probably be popping up in all kinds of technology in the coming years. For that reason alone, it is important for brands and marketers to keep an eye on this potentially revolutionary technology.

Customer Relationship Management (CRM)

For this book, I will consider CRM as a two-part process that allows a marketer to track and organize its current and prospective customers, as well as to manage the endpoints of customer relationships through its marketing promotions. When done right, CRM systems enable data to be converted into information that provides insight into customer behavior and, from these insights, some form of behavioral influencing can occur.

Although widely recognized as an important element of most business' customer experience platform, there is no universally accepted definition of CRM. In his paper *Accepting customer relationships: Using CRM and relationship technology*[99], R. Swift defines CRM as an "enterprise approach to understanding and influencing meaningful communications in order to improve customer acquisition, customer retention, customer loyalty, and customer profitability."

J. Kincaid concurs in his paper *Customer relationship management: Getting it right*[100], seeing CRM as "the strategic use of information, processes, technology and people to manage the customer's relationship with your company (Marketing, Sales, Services, and Support) across the whole customer lifecycle."

In their paper *Customer Relationship Management: Emerging Practice, Process, and Discipline*[101], Parvatiyar and Sheth claim CRM is "a comprehensive strategy and process of acquiring, retaining, and partnering with selective customers to create superior value for the company and the customer. It involved the integration of marketing, sales, customer service, and the supply chain functions of the organization to achieve greater efficiencies and effectiveness in delivering customer value."

In their comprehensive article on the subject, *Application of Data Mining Techniques in Customer Relationship Management: a Literature Review and Classification*[102], Ngai et al. argue that these varying definitions emphasize the importance of "viewing CRM as a comprehensive process of acquiring and retaining customers, with the help of business intelligence, to maximize the customer value to the organization."

A CRM system can receive data coming from mobile and social media sources like WeChat, Weibo, Facebook, YouTube, Twitter, YouKu, etc.. This data tends to be highly unstructured, while data coming from CSVs, XML and JSON feeds are considered semi-structured. NoSQL databases are also considered semi-structured, while text within documents, logs, survey results, and e-mails also fall into the unstructured category.

Highly structured customer data can be combined with unstructured data coming in from social media to reveal deep customer insights. For example, if a hotel loyalty card member tweets that he or she is heading on an overseas trip, why shouldn't a hotel's marketing department be alerted? Setting up JSON feeds for Twitter user accounts is a very simple process and many other social media companies offer APIs that allow similar access to customer accounts. These are two-way systems as well, and the hotel's marketing department could include social media as a channel to connect with customers and potential customers.

So how does a marketer get a customer's WeChat, WhatsApp, Facebook, Twitter, Weibo, YouTube, or even Twitch account? Simple, they just ask for it. In today's digital world, more and more people are willing to hand over their mobile information because they prefer to communicate with people—and companies—via social channels.

By utilizing the complex web of customer data coming in from several different channels—mobile, social media, customer loyalty programs, transaction data, e-commerce websites, sensors, amongst others—a marketer can also work more productively. By understanding customer patterns and customer behavior across the whole spectrum of the business, a marketer can use these customer behavioral patterns to map out its inventory and human capital needs as well.

CRM is a strategy used to learn more about a customer's needs and behaviors in order to develop a stronger relationship with him or her, thereby creating a value exchange on both sides. As Lovelock and Wirtz state in *Services Marketing, People, Technology, Strategy* [103], "from a customer perspective, well-implemented CRM systems can offer a unified customer interface that delivers customization and personalization."

Lovelock and Wirtz argue that at each transaction point, such relevant customer data as a customer's personal preferences, as well as his or her overall past transactions history are available to the clerk serving the customer, giving them valuable information about how to interact with that person.[103] This is not an easy thing to do, however, especially when unstructured data like social media feeds are added to the equation. However, currently, it is a necessity as consumers expect personalized service of this level from the companies with whom they interact. Customers also expect to connect with the businesses they frequent on the channels they prefer. This will only increase in the coming years.

According to Lovelock and Wirtz, most CRM solutions contain the following stages[103]:

- Data collection: the system captures customer contact details, such as demographics, purchasing history, service preferences, etc.
- Data Analysis: data captured is analyzed and categorized into a unique set of criteria. This information is then used to tier the customer base and tailor service delivery accordingly.
- Sales force automation: sales leads, cross-sell, and up-sell opportunities can be effectively identified and processed, and the entire cycle from lead generation to the closing of sales and after-sales service can be tracked and facilitated through the CRM system.
- Marketing automation: the mining of customer data can help a company achieve one-to-one marketing to each one of its customers. Loyalty and retention programs can reduce costs, which can result in an increase of marketing expenditure ROI. By analyzing campaign responses, CRM systems can easily assess a marketing campaign's quantifiable success rate.
- Call center automation: with customer information available right at their fingertips, call center staff can improve customer service levels because they will be able to immediately identify a customer's tier level,

as well as compare and contrast him or her against similar customers so that only promotions likely to be accepted are offered.

Most large-scale customer-focused businesses have plenty of data collection, data analysis, sales force automation, marketing automation, and call center automation software to help them in their CRM endeavors, but it is not easy getting all of these complicated systems and processes working together to provide a level of personalized service that wows a customer. It must be the goal, however.

Beyond simple CRM (which, I guess, is never really *that* simple), Social CRM (SCRM) adds a whole new level of sophistication to the mix. SCRM is the use of "social media services, techniques and technology to enable organizations to engage with customers."[104] In his article *Time to Put a Stake in the Ground on Social CRM*[105], Paul Greenberg argues that:

> *"Social CRM is a philosophy and a business strategy, supported by a technology platform, business rules, workflow, processes and social characteristics, designed to engage and react accordingly in a collaborative conversation in order to promote mutually beneficial value in a trusted and transparent business environment. It's the company's response to the customer's ownership of the conversation."*

One aspect of "Social CRM" is "Social Media Monitoring," the process by which companies monitor sites like Facebook, Twitter, LinkedIn, Weibo, YouTube, Instagram, and others for relevant brand and anti-brand comments and mentions. Social media monitoring tools allow for continuous customer engagement and, later in the book, I go into deep detail about how a marketer can use these types of social media monitoring tools to build strong, two-way responsive customer relationships.

"SCRM is the connection of social data (wherever it is) with existing customer records (customer database) that enable companies to provide new forms of customer insight and relevant context," says Woodcock.[48] With SCRM, marketers can "understand the mood, find new sales leads, respond faster to customer needs and maybe even anticipate needs by listening into their conversations and taking action,"[48] wherever appropriate. In chapter seven, I explain how a company can track user's comments on Facebook, Instagram, Twitter, etc. This is priceless information in customer understanding.

SCRM doesn't replace CRM systems; it adds value by augmenting traditional systems.[48] As Woodcock notes, "SCRM is a great hunting ground for businesses to find and acquire consumers to full 'traditional' CRM programs as well as identify key influencers who can be considered high value customers. It offers companies an organized approach, using enterprise software that connects business units to the social web giving them the opportunity to respond in near real time, and in a coordinated fashion."[48]

In its *Achieving Customer Loyalty with Customer Analytics*[106], IBM states that, social media can help amplify the "relationship" in "Customer Relationship Management", thereby enabling organizations to connect and engage consumers in a unique way, as well as personalize and monetize customer relationship on a sustained basis, which should increase profitability.[106] "Social media also provides a path to richer customer analysis, using technologies capable of funneling and consolidating customer insights."[106] Insights derived from this analysis can help companies to "dynamically calibrate, anticipate, and offer products and services that meet perpetually shifting consumer demands in a hyper-competitive marketplace."[106]

Marketers can also "listen into what customers are saying, to better understand their needs, their voices and tie it back to actual customer profiles,"[48] which could contain their Facebook or WeChat pages or Twitter handles. "In addition, marketers will be able to catch leads in 'mid-air' by listening for keywords that suggest a customer is getting ready to buy, then sending real-time alerts to sales teams to respond."[48] I will also expound upon this in chapter seven. Specifically, for a marketer, it would be advantageous to link a customer's account with his or her social media accounts so that the marketer could get a heads-up on what a customer might be saying about them on social media.

In a lot of cases, ROI is an enormously tricky thing to measure, but social media is providing unique ways for businesses to quantify their social media spend. Gone are the days of wasting endless amounts of money to build up a questionably worthy following of thousands or even tens of thousands of Facebook fans.

"Short-term campaign ROI as the main measure for individual campaigns will evolve into correlation analysis between activities, engagement and sales. This will be unsettling for many traditional marketers."[48] "The explicit use of active and control groups, and experimentation of using different treatments will help marketers understand the impact of specific SM activities."[48] More direct marketing type disciplines will be required, in a world where there is real-time feedback on attitude and behavior and a plethora of data."[48] This has become a much more demanding world in terms of capturing and utilizing all of this data, but making the effort to turn this data into actionable intelligence will be noticed by fickle consumers, I have no doubt. Real-time feedback can also become part of a strong feedback loop that can provide more data on customers.

Brand marketers should feel compelled to reward their customers through Facebook, Twitter, WeChat, and Weibo, or any number of social networking, blogging, and/or micro-blogging services. The advantage of using these channels is that they give the customer the ability to share their awards or stories of their awards with friends and family.

Businesses need to empower their customers to post on Facebook or WeChat or Weibo or Twitter or comment about their experiences and, hopefully, turn them into apostles. In Jones and Sasser's *zone of affection*, satisfaction levels are high and "customers may have such high attitudinal loyalty that they don't look for alternative service."[117] It is within this group that "Apostles"—members who praise the firm in public—reside and this is the group that is responsible for improved future business performance.[107] *The A.I. Marketer* will not only be able to spot these apostles, but also understand them on such a unique and personal level that their loyalty and patronage will almost be guaranteed. Any marketing these apostles do on behalf of the company is pure gravy.

As Darrell Rigby explains in Bain & Company's *Management Tools 2015 An Executive's Guide*[108], CRM "is a process companies use to understand their customer groups and respond quickly—and at times, instantly—to shifting customer desires." "CRM technology allows firms to collect and manage large amounts of customer data and then carry out strategies based on that information," explains Rigby[108]

Marketers can utilize CRM to:

- Create databases of customers segmented into buckets that allow more effective marketing.
- Generate more accurate sales leads.
- Gather market research on customers.
- Rapidly coordinate information between the sales and marketing staff and front-facing hosts and reps, increasing the customer experience.
- Accurately gauge the return on individual promotional programs and the effect of integrated marketing activities, and redirect spending accordingly.
- Accumulate data on customer preferences and problems for product and service designers.
- Increase sales by systematically identifying, managing, and automating sales leads.
- Improve customer retention by uncovering the reason(s) for customer churn.
- Design proactive customer service programs.

Today, CRM is evolving into what has been dubbed "Customer Centric Relationship Management" (CCRM), a style of CRM that focuses on customer preferences above all else. CCRM attempts to understand the client in a deep, behavioral way, and it engages customers in individual, interactive relationships through tailored marketing and one-to-one customer service. This personalization can help a marketer retain customers, build brand loyalty, provide customers not only with the information that they really want, but also with the rewards that they might use. Today's technology allows businesses to not only surface the information that they need to know about their customers, but it can also provide front-facing employees with offers that these clients will like and, therefore, probably use.

CRM is ultimately a strategy that businesses can use to learn more about their customer's needs and behaviors in order to develop a stronger relationship with him or her, thereby creating a value exchange on both sides of the equation.

In their comprehensive article on the subject, *Application of Data Mining Techniques in Customer Relationship Management: a Literature Review and Classification*[102], Ngai et al. state that CRM "comprises a set of processes and enabling systems supporting a business strategy to build long term, profitable relationships with specific customers."

In Bain & Company's *Management Tools 2015 An Executive's Guide*[108], Darrell K. Rigby claims that CRM requires managers to:

1. Start by defining strategic 'pain points' in the customer relationship cycle. "These are problems that have a large impact on customer satisfaction and loyalty, where solutions would lead to superior financial rewards and competitive advantage."[108]
2. "Evaluate whether—and what kind of—CRM data can fix those pain points. Calculate the value that such information would bring the company."[108]
3. "Select the appropriate technology platform and calculate the cost of implementing it and training employees to use it."[108]
4. "Assess whether the benefits of the CRM information outweigh the expense involved."[108]
5. "Design incentive programs to ensure that personnel are encouraged to participate in the CRM program. Many companies have discovered that realigning the organization away from product groups and toward a customer-centered structure improves the success of CRM."[108]
6. "Measure CRM progress and impact. Aggressively monitor participation of key personnel in the CRM program. In addition, put measurement systems in place to track the improvement in customer profitability with the use of CRM. Once the data is collected, share the information widely with employees to encourage further participation in the program."[108]

Once a marketer starts implementing a CRM program, data segmentation can begin. According to Wikipedia, market segmentation "is the process of dividing a broad consumer or business market, normally consisting of existing and potential customers, into sub-groups of consumers (known as *segments*) based on some type of shared characteristics."[109]

In dividing or segmenting markets, brands can look for shared characteristics, common spend, similar lifestyles choices, or even similar demographic profiles. Market segmentation tries to identify *high yield segments*—i.e., those segments that are likely to be the most profitable or that have outsized growth potential—so that they can be selected for special attention (i.e., become target markets).

Rigby states that customer segmentation "is the subdivision of a market into discrete customer groups that share similar characteristics. Customer segmentation can be a powerful means to identify unmet customer needs. Companies that identify underserved segments can then outperform the competition by developing uniquely appealing products and services."[108] Rigby adds that customer segmentation is most effective when a company can discover its most profitable segments and then tailor offerings to them, thereby providing the customer with a distinct competitive advantage.[108] As previously mentioned, a marketer's tool with AI-powered analytics "automatically identifies statistically significant attributes that high-performing customers have in common and creates segments with these customers"[13] for businesses to take action on. It's like customer segmentation on steroids.

As Rigby explains, customer segmentation requires managers to:

- "Divide the market into meaningful and measurable segments according to customers' needs, their past behaviors or their demographic profiles."[108]
- "Determine the profit potential of each segment by analyzing the revenue and cost impacts of serving each segment."[108]
- "Target segments according to their profit potential and the company's ability to serve them in a proprietary way."[108]
- "Invest resources to tailor product, service, marketing and distribution programs to match the needs of each target segment."[108]
- "Measure performance of each segment and adjust the segmentation approach over time as market conditions change decision making throughout the organization."[108]

For a marketer, the pain points might be things like customer loyalty and the marketing department should be asking things like, "Why does it cost so much money to retain customers?", or "Can we not find cheaper but more meaningful offers that show understanding of the customer?" Also, "How can we drive customer loyalty to such a degree that our customers rave about us on social media?"

Beside the above methods, customer segmentation can be used to:

- Prioritize new product development efforts.
- Develop customized marketing programs.
- Choose specific product features.
- Establish appropriate service options.

- Design an optimal distribution strategy.
- Determine appropriate product pricing.

Market segmentation assumes that different market segments require different marketing programs—that is, different offers, prices, promotion, distribution or some combination of marketing variables. Market segmentation is not only designed to identify the most profitable segments, but also to develop profiles of key segments in order to better understand their needs and purchase motivations. Insights from segmentation analysis are subsequently used to support marketing strategy development and planning.

When it comes to analytics and Big Data, Caesars was the first casino company to collect and analyze it for customer intelligence (CI) purposes and, since the inception of its Total Rewards programme, the company has grown from "being able to trace the journey of 58% of the money spent in their casino to 85%."[110] Caesars also credits the widespread adoption of Big Data analytics as the driving force behind its rise from an "also ran" chain to one of the largest casino groups in the U.S.[111]

Caesars is one company that has also been able to use social media to measure marketing data quite successfully. In his article *At Caesars, Digital Marketing Is No Crap Shoot*[112], Al Urbanski explains that[112]:

> "While social media networks like Facebook provide metrics that measure activity within its platform, integrating that data to enable visibility across a brand's entire marketing organization is difficult. Caesars, however, unites information from customers coming through social channels across business units, program teams, time zones, and languages. A content-building component allows Caesars' marketers to listen in and respond in real time."

No matter where the customer interaction originates, engagement is a key factor in moving those interactions from the top of the sales funnel to an eventual purchase.[112] "It doesn't matter where customers come in or leave or reenter," says Chris Kahle, Caesars Web Analytics Manager, "if they come to your social page and click your button, or if they go into your content or email and click on that, it's all the same app and you've got them."[112] Caesars IDs a cookie and, if the prospect comes back around on paid search three days later, Caesars tracks them.[112] "We can track them on every website, even if they came in on a Las Vegas site and then jump markets to Atlantic City," adds Kahle.[112]

Caesars also tracks activity in real time, while responding to customer cues.[112] Unsurprisingly, different types of customers are more responsive to different interactions from Caesars. Aside from dividing customers into categories such as "Frequent Independent Traveler"—or FITs and Total Rewards members, the Caesars team uses tracking data to further segment customers by property or market as well as determine how each of their various segments respond to content.[112]

Using this data, Caesars evaluates campaigns in regard to KPIs, such as number of nights booked, and adjusts them on the fly to ramp up conversion rates.[112] "When Caesars sponsored free concerts by top artists at several of its properties last year, for instance, it streamed the events live on the Web and used its new analytics suite to fine-tune loyalty program offers on its websites. It resulted in a dramatic spike in Total Rewards program sign-ups during the concerts."[112]

"What's really dramatic about this is that you can determine what is engaging individuals and target them with it," Adobe's Langie says.[112] "The high-roller segment, for example. They might respond to a very different Web design than the casual visitor and Caesars tailors the page view to who is visiting. Think of the website as a canvas. You can paint a still life of a fruit for one person and something different for another. The canvas is dynamic."[112]

"The speed and the manner with which the chosen website designs and digital marketing tactics are implemented across the Caesars network may well be the most transforming development of the company's new data culture," Kahle adds.[112] This was no easy task as the Caesars landscape extends over 60 websites for its various properties and services as well as 40 Facebook pages.

"Prior to implementing a data-centric approach to the decision-making process, it could take as long as two weeks to furnish the field with actionable data. They now get it done in a matter of hours," Kahle adds.[112] In 2013, Caesars' implemented Adobe's Digital Marketing Suite, which "includes real-time tracking and segmentation of digital site visitors, analysis of social media's role in purchasing, and content testing by segment or individual visitor."[112]

"The people at the individual properties who are managing the content of the websites are not all technically sophisticated, but Adobe's system provides them with built-in capabilities," Kahle says.[112] "Say one of our properties wants to track social. Before, they'd have to spend a lot of time manually adding tracking codes. With Adobe, tracking codes are integrated," Kahle adds.[112]

"Right now we can assign a percentage value to social media if a booking doesn't result right away," Kahle says.[112] "But with social we're going to be experimenting with a longer funnel, maybe a two-week time frame."[112] "Values are ascribed to social media for being the site of initial contact with a new customer, for instance, or for numbers of positive reviews by current customers."[112]

Currently, Caesars can't measure the total value of a reservation booked online and also can't determine how much an online booker spends at the tables during his or her stay.[112] This is important information when it comes to truly understanding a customer's value. Caesars would also like to know if, for example, "customers left the Caesars' casino in Las Vegas and went to dinner at Gordon Ramsay's restaurant at the Paris Las Vegas, so they could offer them a free dinner at the restaurant to close the deal on a future booking."[112]

"Eventually we're going to set a time frame that will never expire [on the sales funnel]," Kahle says.[112] "But for now we've built a sales allocation model that goes beyond the last click, and that's OK. Most organizations using multiple marketing channels are still stuck on that last click."[112]

Going forward, mobile and social media are going to be important channels for a brand's CRM, marketing and operations departments for years to come. The mobile phone's ubiquity, however, could be a double-edged sword. It allows a casino to market directly to its customers while they are not just on their property, but also anywhere they might be standing. In this changing, always-on digital world, if a brand isn't constantly marketing to its customers, some other competitor might be, and that customer could be lost for good.

Companies like Adobe, IBM, Oracle, Microsoft, SAP, SAS, Salesforce.com, and SugarCRM all have products that not only include contact management systems that integrate emails, documents, jobs and faxes, but also integrate with mobile and social media accounts as well, so the market doesn't lack product. This is a case where one side doesn't fit all. A deep understanding of the business' current systems and pain points should be explored before any solution is chosen and implemented.

CRM is, ultimately, a backward-looking technology, i.e., you're only dealing with information about past behavior. Adding predictive technology onto a CRM system can turn a CRM platform into a lead generation tool and this is where *The A.I. Marketer* can thrive. In T_HQ Technology and Business' article *What does the CRM of the future look like?*[113], Insightly's Founder and CEO Anthony Smith sees that if a business' unique CRM process is combined with deep analytics, "you have tailored customer engagement playbooks that enable businesses to treat every customer like they are their only customer."[113] This topic will be further developed in in chapter three.

For Lewnes and Keller, "Customers own the brand in many ways as much as marketers do, and it is every marketer's responsibility to make customers an integral part of the company's brand equation by asking for continuous feedback, listening to it, and cocreating with them."[4] "The reality of customer-brand relationships today is that they have evolved from single, interspersed interactions to always-on, symbiotic, and immersive relationships," say Lewnes and Keller.[4] "What exactly do customers want from a brand? What do they not want? Marketers don't have to always do what customers say they should do, but if marketers don't, they need to tell customers why," advise Lewnes and Keller.

Lewnes and Keller both work for Adobe and they provide the example of the

Adobe's move from the Creative Suite software to the Creative Cloud subscription service.[4] Understandably, some customers, like myself, were not happy with the switch.[4] "The response in some markets where digital subscriptions were not yet the norm was particularly pronounced," according to them.[4]

According to Lewnes and Keller, "the only way to deal with this reticence to change behavior was to offer maximum transparency and provide a lot of information."[4] "This required Adobe to get really close to customers—on online forums, on social channels, and through live events—to understand their reservations and concerns."[4]

"Specifically, Adobe ensured that the ongoing value and innovation that a subscription model offered was thoroughly communicated at every touch point. Instead of investing in one big marketing push every two years to align with a major launch, Adobe focused its marketing strategy to support a subscription model with ongoing educational and inspirational campaigns that built an ongoing customer relationship," explains Lewnes and Keller.[4] "Over time, the product value alone, supported with stronger customer relationships, helped customers become satisfied with the subscription model."[4] Adobe's stock has risen considerably since the introduction of its subscription based model as well, which is a clear sign the outreach worked.

"A strong customer relationship requires that marketers deeply understand how customers think and feel, not just about their products or services but about what they are using the products or services for and how they are actually using them," says Lewnes and Keller.[4] The writers conclude that, "It requires keen insight into customer motivations and behaviors—the problems customers are trying to solve and the goals they are trying to achieve."[4]

Customer Loyalty

Loyalty is so important to a marketer because, as repeated studies have shown, customers become more profitable over time. In their study *Zero Defections: Quality Comes to Service* [114], Reichheld and Sasser demonstrated that a customer's profitability increases as his or her loyalty increases. In their study, the authors found that it usually took more than a year to recoup any customer acquisition costs, but then profits increased as customers remained with the service or firm. Reichheld and Sasser believe there are four factors for this growth, and, in order of their importance, they are[114]:

1. Profit derived from increased purchases. As a customer ages, he or she will probably become more affluent, therefore will have more money to spend for company products and/or services.

2. Profit from reduced operating costs. As customers become more experienced, they should make fewer demands on the business, perhaps taking advantage of available self-service options.
3. Profit from referrals to other customers.
4. Profit from price premiums. Long-term customers are more likely to pay regular prices for services rather than being tempted into using a businesses' lower profit products and/or services.

Other facts and figures regarding customers and their loyalty include:

- On average, loyal customers are worth up to 10 times as much as their first purchase.[115]
- It is 6-7 times more expensive to acquire a new customer than it is to keep a current one.[115]
- News of bad customer service reaches more than twice as many ears as praise for a good service experience.[115]
- For every customer who bothers to complain, 26 other customers remain silent.[115]

This last figure might be dropping as brands are making it easier for customers to connect with them through their social channels like Facebook, Instagram, Twitter, Weibo, YouTube, Twitch, etc.

As previously mentioned, the number one thing that creates loyalty in *anybody* (that includes your customers) is the social construct of reciprocity and a consumer's engagement with a brand can be measured along a continuum from no awareness, through early engagement, and, hopefully, if everything goes well, into advocacy.[48] As for the customer-company relationship, "the strength of feeling will develop and vary over time and, as in any healthy relationship, both parties should be aware of feelings so they can react accordingly," advises Woodcock.[48]

As was shown in Nielsen's 2012 *Global Trust in Advertising*[116] survey, consumers trust their friends and colleagues much more than they trust TV advertising or corporate communications. Today, consumers communicate with each other like never before through a multitude of social and mobile media channels.[48] These channels should be exploited as much as possible.

CRM is an integral part of what businesses hope will be a value exchange on both sides of the customer-company equation, one that will, hopefully, create loyal customers who become apostles for the brand. Lovelock and Wirtz created the "Wheel of Loyalty" as an organizing structure to help businesses build customer loyalty.[103] The first of its three sequential steps include building a foundation for loyalty, including "targeting the right portfolio of customer segments, attracting the right customers, tiering the service, and delivering high levels of satisfaction."[103]

The second step—creating loyalty bonds that either deepen the relationship through cross-selling and bundling or adding value to the customer through loyalty rewards and higher level bonds—can be achieved by the business gaining a fuller understanding of its customers.[103] It is important to understand as much about the customer as possible, his or her wants, desires and needs, all the way down to his or her preferred shopping items, fashion styles, spend amount, as well as a preferred time to shop. This is the flip side of cross-selling to customer, they don't mind being marketed to if it's with products they are looking for or might be interested in buying. It's the brand's job to ensure the offers they send fit these descriptions.

The third factor—identify and reduce the factors that result in "churn"—is also extremely important to a marketer's bottom line.[103] Engagement is paramount here and mobile apps and social media are great channels to keep customers interested and fully engaged.

Customer satisfaction is the foundation of true customer loyalty, while customer dissatisfaction is one of the main reasons why customers leave.[103] This may sound obvious, but its importance cannot be stressed enough.

According to Jones and Sasser, "the satisfaction-loyalty relationship can be divided into three main zones: Defection, indifference, and affection. The *zone of defection* occurs at low satisfaction levels. Customers will switch unless switching costs are high or there are no viable or convenient alternatives."[117] With the vast echo chamber of social media against them, losing only one disgruntled customer could reverberate in financially catastrophic ways.

Jones and Sasser warn that, "Extremely dissatisfied customers can turn into 'terrorists,' providing an abundance of negative feedback about the service provider."[117] Through social media channels, negative feedback can reverberate around the world within seconds. Today, more than ever, businesses must spot dissatisfied customers and approach them before they do irreparable harm to the company's image and reputation and social media is one of the best channels in which to engage them and, potentially, diffuse bad situations. Like the proverbial canary in the coal mine, *The A.I. Marketer* will have systems in place that can warn the business about these customers before they become figurative terrorists who attack the business' bottom line. In chapter seven, I detail how to build a system such as this.

In the *zone of indifference*, customers willingly switch if they can find a better alternative, while in the *zone of affection*, satisfaction levels are high and "customers may have such high attitudinal loyalty that they don't look for alternative services."[117] It is within this group that "Apostles" reside.[107] In the social media world, these people are more likely to be known as "influencers" and I will go into much more detail about these people in chapter five.

In its *Achieving Customer Loyalty with Customer Analytics*[106], IBM describes one of its studies that asked some of the world's leading company CEOs and CMOs what their number one priority was. The CEOs answered that it was to engage customers, while the CMOs said it was to enhance customer loyalty.[106] The study argued that forward-thinking companies were using customer analytics to[106]:

- Guide front-line interactions with customers.
- Create and execute customer retention strategies.
- Prompt people or systems to proactively address customer satisfaction issues.
- Guide product planning to fulfill future customer needs.
- Hire and train employees to act upon customer insights and improve loyalty.
- Align operations to focus on satisfying customers.

In his article *Customer Analytics in the Age of Social Media*[118] for TDWI, David Stodder reports that the importance of customer analytics is in the boardroom; "overwhelmingly, respondents cited giving executive management customer and market insight (71%) as the most important business benefit that their organization seeks to achieve from implementing customer analytics."[118] "This percentage rises to 81% when survey results are filtered to see only the responses from those who indicated 'strong acceptance' of data-driven customer analytics over gut feel."[118] The second highest benefit cited, at 62%, was "the ability to react more quickly to changing market conditions, which speaks to the need for customer data insights to help decision makers address competitive pressures from rapid product or service commoditization."[118]

With the commoditization of products and services, customer loyalty can be elusive; innovation must be constant and it should help to reveal why an organization might be losing its customer base.[118] "Information insights from analytics can help organizations align product and service development with strategic business objectives for customer loyalty."[118] These insights can also help an organization be selective about how they deploy their marketing campaigns and customer-touch processes so that they emphasize features in new products and services that are important to each specific customer.[118]

Customer analytics can also provide answers to questions like[118]:

- When in the life cycle are customers most likely to churn?
- What types of products or services would prevent them from churning?
- When should customers be offered complimentary items?
- When is it too costly to try to keep certain customers?

Businesses can realize significant ROI from investing in customer analytics as it can improve the marketing department's efficiency, effectiveness[118] and reach.

However, customer analytics ROI is a difficult thing to fully quantify. Better customer knowledge equates to more optimized marketing spend because a business can focus its resources on those campaigns that have the highest predicted chances of success for particular segments, as well as cutting off or avoiding those that have the least.[118]

"By using analytics to eliminate mismatches of campaigns targeting the wrong customers or using the wrong messages and offers, marketing functions can reduce wasteful spending and increase gains relative to costs."[118] Customer segmentation allows organizations to move "away from one-size-fits-all, brand-level-only marketing and toward the 'market of one': that is, personalized, one-to-one marketing."[118]

Reaching a customization and customer service level that makes a customer feel as though he or she is a preferred customer is not easy, scaling that up so that an entire database of customers feel that they are unique and receiving outstanding customer service is even more challenging, but, in this day and age of hyper-personalization, it is almost a necessity if a company wants to provide good and engaging customer service.

TDWI Research[118] examined the importance of accomplishing various objectives for gaining positive ROI from customer analytics (see Figure 12). "Using customer analytics to target cross-sell and up-sell opportunities was the objective cited by the biggest percentage of respondents (54%)."[118] This objective is about gaining more value from existing customers understanding their purchasing habits and trying to get them to buy more products more often.[118]

"Some organizations (18%) are implementing an advanced technique called 'uplift modeling' (also called incremental or true-lift modeling), which enables marketers to use data mining to measure the impact and influence of marketing actions on customers."[118] Insights such as these allow marketers to develop new kinds of predictive models to determine the best prospects for up-sell and cross-sell offerings.[118] "As firms scale up to execute large numbers of campaigns across multiple channels, the efficiency gained from predictive modeling can be critical to marketing spending optimization," Stodder argues.[118]

Analytics can improve marketing performance by quantifying a customer's lifetime value as well as customer worth at the many different stages in the customer's life cycle.[118] "If organizations can identify their most valuable customers they can determine if they are worthy of retention efforts and resources because of the returns they will provide."[106] For instance, it may not be worth the time, effort, and expense to retain a low value customer, unless customer analytics reveals that this low-spend customer actually has a lot of social influence.[106] Armed with this information, managers can align their deployment of resources to achieve the highest value, as well as avoid the costs and inefficiencies of marketing to the wrong people at the wrong time.[118]

Organizations have long used demographics such as gender, household size, education, occupation, and income to segment customers.[118] Data mining techniques let organizations segment much larger customer populations and, perhaps, more importantly, determine whether to apply new characteristics that refine segmentation to fit the specific attributes of the organization's products and services.[118] AI can increase these demographic variants exponentially.

In your organization, which of the following marketing objectives are most important to achieve for customer analytics to deliver a return on investment? (Please select all that apply.)

Objective	%
Target cross-sell and up-sell opportunities	54%
Improve customer segmentation	49%
Predict retention, attrition, and churn rates	47%
Determine lifetime customer value	42%
Increase portfolio penetration per customer	39%
Optimize marketing across multiple channels	37%
Impact other business functions (sales, service, support)	35%
Forecast buying habits and lifestyle preferences	32%
Measure types of loyalty for campaign targeting	26%
Prioritize marketing e-mail messages	23%
Implement uplift, incremental, or true-lift modeling	18%
Increase speed of multivariate testing analysis	14%

Figure 12: Which Are the Most Important Business Objectives When It Comes to Customer Analytics?
Source: TDWI Research[118], Based on 1,625 responses from 432 respondents; almost four responses per respondent, on average.

"Customer analytics using data mining tools improves the speed of segmentation analysis over manual and spreadsheet efforts that are often used in less mature organizations."[118] Speed is a vital ingredient for marketing initiatives that are time sensitive, particularly for those companies that need to provide real-time cross-sell and up-sell offers to customers clicking through web pages.

In its *Achieving Customer Loyalty with Analytics*[106], IBM argues that customer analytics can provide businesses with the ability to:

- Analyze all data types to gain a 360-degree view of each individual customer.
- Employ advanced algorithms that can uncover relevant patterns and causal relationships that impact customer satisfaction and loyalty.
- Build predictive models that anticipate future outcomes.
- Learn from every customer interaction and apply lessons to future interactions and strategies.
- Deploy customer insights to decision-makers and front-line systems.
- Improve sales forecasting and help minimize sales cycles.
- Measure and report on marketing performance.

"The next most common objectives in the research were predicting retention, attrition, and churn rates (47%) and determining lifetime customer value (42%)."[118] Churn can cost organizations heavily, both from the loss of profits from existing customers as well as in the high price of attracting new ones. "Attrition or churn analysis methods are aimed at discovering which variables have the most influence on customers' decisions to leave or stay."[118]

With data mining and predictive analytics, organizations can learn which attrition rates are acceptable or expected for particular customer segments and which rates could be highly detrimental to the bottom line.[118] "Predictive customer analytics can play a major role in enabling organizations to discover and model which customers are most likely to leave, and from which segments."[118]

With social media added to the mix, as well as clickstreams, and other behavioral data, the volume and variety of data is exploding.[118] "Social networking sites such as Facebook, Twitter, LinkedIn, and MySpace have files containing petabytes of data, often in vast Hadoop clusters."[118] Weibo and WeChat add another hundreds of millions of users into the mix and with it petabytes of data as well.

"Advertising concerns are recording tens of millions of events daily that organizations want to mine in near real time to identify prospects," Stodder notes.[118] Businesses of all kinds want to use predictive models and score event and transaction details as fast as they come in so that they can gain insight into individual shopping behavior.[118] These are insights that they hope will give them an advantage over their competitors, but this is expensive territory to chart, especially if done incorrectly.

The "data sources most commonly monitored for customer analytics are customer satisfaction surveys (57%) and customer transactions and online purchases (55%). Just under half (44%) are monitoring Web site logs and clickstream sources," says Stodder.[118] "In addition to monitoring customer satisfaction surveys, about half (48%) of organizations surveyed are studying call and contact center interactions."[118]

Customer satisfaction surveys are usually conducted in person, on a website, over the phone or through traditional mail and e-mail channels.[118] Because this includes both semi-structured data and unstructured comments, data collection can be difficult.[118] "Standard questions inquire about a customer's satisfaction with purchases, the services they received, and the company's brands overall. Other questions address the customer's likelihood of buying from the company again and whether they would recommend the firm to others."[118]

Text analytics can be used to increase the speed, depth, and consistency of unstructured content analysis far greater than what can be done manually.[118] "More advanced analytics can look for correlations between satisfaction ratings, commented sentiments, and other records, such as first-call-resolution metrics."[118]

"To analyze data generated by social media networking services such as Twitter, Facebook, Weibo, and LinkedIn, many organizations are implementing Hadoop and NoSQL technologies, which do not force a schema on the source data prior to storage, as traditional BI and data warehousing systems do."[118] Because of this, the discovery analytics processes can run against the raw data.[118] "Customer analytics tools need to be able to consume data from sources such as Hadoop clusters and then integrate the insights into overall customer profiles," advises Stodder.[118]

The data sources can be varied for these technologies and methods; "they include transaction data, clickstreams, satisfaction surveys, loyalty card membership data, credit card purchases, voter registration, location data, and a host of [other] demographic data types."[118]

In its *Retail Analytics: Game Changer for Customer Loyalty*[119], Cognizant argues that in the retail industry, "predictive models can be used to analyze past performance to assess the likelihood that a customer will exhibit a specific behavior in order to improve marketing effectiveness." This can help with "predicting customer reactions to a given product and can be leveraged to improve basket size, increase the value of the basket and switch the customer to a better and more profitable offering."[119] Predictive models can also help tailor pricing strategies that take into account both the need for competitive pricing and the company's financial bottom line.[119]

Predictive analytics and data mining are used to discover which variables out of possibly hundreds are most influential in determining customer loyalty within certain segments.[118] "Advanced analytics generally involves statistical, quantitative, or mathematical analysis and centers on developing, testing, training, scoring, and monitoring predictive models."[118]

Models can be created that will uncover patterns, affinities, anomalies, and other useful insights for marketing campaigns and for determining cross-sell and up-sell opportunities.[118] "The tools and techniques are also used for developing and deploying behavioral scoring models for marketing, deciding whether to adjust customers' credit limits for purchases, and a variety of highly time-sensitive analytic processes," Stodder notes.[118]

"As more online customer behavior is recorded in Web logs and tracked through cookies and other observation devices, sizeable amounts of information are becoming available to organizations that seek a more accurate view of a customer's path to purchase," states Stodder.[118] Attribution analysis is, first and foremost, a big-data problem, given the quantity and variety of data available from today's multiple platforms.[118]

Businesses that are performing attribution analysis will frequently employ Hadoop and/or MapReduce, with analytic software solutions such as R, SAS's eMiner, SAP's InfiniteInsights, Python, and IBM's SPSS, amongst others.[118] This allows a business to run sophisticated algorithms against detailed data to find the correct path to purchase. This analysis can then be integrated with analysis from other data types and sources, including those that might have been generated by any offline customer activity.[118]

Attribution analysis can reveal such things as what kinds of campaigns most influence customer behavior.[118] "The analysis can help organizations determine where to allocate marketing resources to gain the highest level of success, as well as how to more accurately assign the percentage of credit due to specific marketing and advertising processes," Stodder concludes.[118]

On August 13, 2014, Facebook announced a major step forward in the area of attribution analysis. It said that it "would start telling advertisers on what device people saw an ad and on what device they took an action, such as buying a product or signing up for a test drive, as a result of seeing that ad. That means Facebook will be able to credit mobile ads that lead to desktop sales and desktop ads that result in mobile purchases."[120]

Peterson notes that, "Advertisers can already track conversions through Facebook on desktop and on mobile, but to date Facebook hasn't broken out conversions by device type for advertisers to see. For example, advertisers have been able to see if their desktop and mobile ads lead to conversions, but they didn't know on which device type those conversions were taking place."[120]

However, Facebook's new cross-device conversion measurement only works for advertisers who place specific Facebook trackers on their websites and mobile apps.[120] "Without sharing users' personal information with the advertiser, those trackers can see that a Facebook user is checking out the advertisers' site or app and whether they've converted in the advertiser-specified fashion."[120] If the person does convert, "Facebook's trackers can trace back to see if that person has seen an ad from that advertiser on Facebook, which may have directly or indirectly led to the conversion."[120] Of course, nothing is 100% certain when it comes to attribution analysis, but this is a big step in the right direction.

With many of the following analytical marketing models, businesses should keep in mind that it is important to create control groups to measure the true effects of their models and marketing campaigns. Control groups are typical components in marketing analysis and are fundamental to statistical studies.[121]

In his article *Control Group Marketing—With or Without CRM Software Systems*[121], Rick Cook states that, "The basic idea of a control group is simple. Select a random (or nearly random) sample from your campaign's marketing list and exclude them from promotion. Then measure the control group's activity and compare it to the activity of the group targeted via a campaign. The difference between the control and campaign group gives you a pretty good notion of how effective—and profitable—the campaign is.

"The theory is that a certain fraction of the customers in the campaign are going to purchase from you anyway during the campaign period. The control group lets you filter out that effect, as well as the effects of other channels which may be influencing behavior, such as display advertising, and shows you how much the campaign has affected customer behavior," explains Cook.[121]

Although control groups should be used to test out the effects of marketing campaigns, few companies include them in their marketing processes.[121] "Marketing control groups become even more effective when combined with the customer analytics found in most marketing automation or customer relationship management systems," notes Cook.[121]

Cook argues that, "With a CRM system and a control group you can also detect the halo effect of your campaign. These are purchases and other actions which are influenced by the campaign but don't come in through the normal campaign channels."[121] For example, a customer could be so inspired by one particular campaign that he or she picks up the phone and orders products directly from the company instead of going through the call-to-action channel.[121] "Another example is the customer who doesn't use the promotional coupon you included in your marketing campaign but who purchases the product anyway."[121] Cook notes that brands "can assume that customers in the test group who respond in unconventional methods are still influenced by the campaign and so should be counted as part of the campaign effect."[121] "Because CRM software lets you track all points of customer contact, and not just the direct response to the campaign, it can capture these halo customers," concludes Cook.[121]

The size of the control group is usually 10 percent of the size of the campaign or test group.[121] Ideally you want the control group to be a truly random sample from the company's campaign list, but this is difficult to attain in practice as complete randomness is hard to achieve.[121] "Many companies select their control group by a simpler process, such as selecting every 10th name on the list to make up the control group," but there are other more scientific ways to choose the participants, which could and should be utilized.[121]

Customer Lifecycle

Today, we can safely say that the mass marketing experience is over. According to *Gartner*, there are five stages of customer experience maturity—initial, developing, defined, managed and optimizing. The goal here is to improve the customer experience through a systematic process to improve customer satisfaction, loyalty and advocacy.

In its *15 Applications of Artificial Intelligence in Marketing*[122], Huguesrey maps out the most effective AI technologies for marketing across the customer lifecycle. "All the techniques are 'AI' in the sense that they involve computer intelligence, but we've broken them down into 3 different types of technology—Machine Learning Techniques, Applied Propensity Models, and AI Applications," says Huguesrey.[122] The steps are broken down into the customer lifecycle RACE framework (See figure 13), which contains four separate groups—Reach, Act, Convert, and Engage.[122]

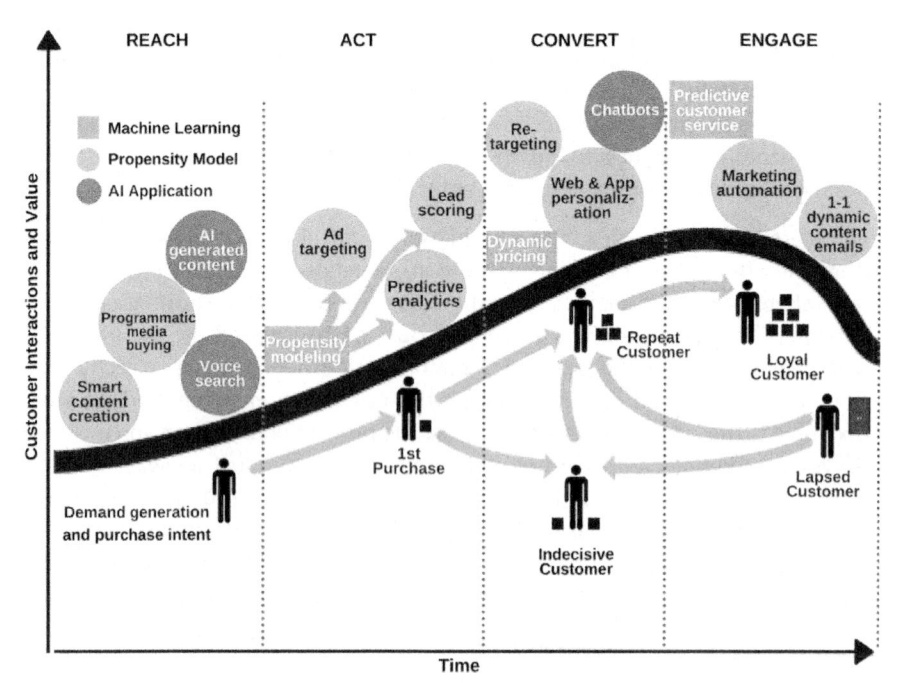

Figure 13: A.I. for marketers across the customer lifecycle
Source: Huguesrey[122]

"Each different application has major implications for marketers, but the applications have different roles to play across the customer journey. Some are better for attracting customers, whilst others are useful for conversion or re-engaging past customers," says Huguesrey.[122]

According to Huguesrey, reach "involves using techniques such as content marketing, SEO and other 'earned media' to bring visitors to your site and start them on the buyer's journey."[122] "AI & applied propensity models can be used at this stage to attract more visitors and provide those that do reach your site with a more engaging experience."[122]

AI-generated content can be a good place to start. "AI can't write a political opinion column or a blog post on industry-specific best practice advice, but there are certain areas where AI generated content can be useful and help draw visitors to your site," says Huguesrey.[122] AI content writing programs like Wordsmith can pick elements from a dataset and structure a "human sounding" article.[122]

"AI writers are useful for reporting on regular, data-focused events. Examples include quarterly earnings reports, sports matches, and market data," says Huguesrey.[122] If you operate in a niche such as financial services or sports, then "AI generated content could form a useful component of your content marketing strategy."[122] AI-powered content curation allows brands to better engage visitors and customers on their site by showing them relevant content.[122] Huguesrey sees it as "a great technique for subscription businesses, where the more someone uses the service, more data the machine learning algorithm has to use and the better the recommendations of content become."[122] The systems becomes somewhat of a self-fulfilling prophecy, like it has become for companies like Netflix, Pandora, and Amazon.

As previously mentioned, voice search is expected to change the future of SEO and brands need to keep up.[122] Huguesrey believes "A brand that nails voice search can leverage big gains in organic traffic with high purchase intent thanks to increased voice search traffic due to AI driven virtual personal assistants."[122]

Programmatic Media buying—the algorithmic purchase and sale of advertisements in real time—"can use propensity models generated by machine learning algorithms to more effectively target ads at the most relevant customers."[122] AI can ensure programmatic ads don't appear on questionable websites and/or remove them from a list of sites that the advertiser doesn't want them to appear on.[122]

In her article *Programmatic Advertising 101: How it Works*[123], Sara Vicioso states that, "programmatic advertising is the automated process of buying and selling ad inventory through an exchange, connecting advertisers to publishers." This process uses artificial intelligence technologies "and real-time bidding for inventory across mobile, display, video and social channels—even making its way into television."[123]

Vicioso adds that, "Artificial intelligence technologies have algorithms that analyze a visitor's behavior allowing for real time campaign optimizations towards an audience more likely to convert. Programmatic companies have the ability to gather this audience data to then target more precisely, whether it's from 1st party (their own) or from a 3rd party data provider."[123]

Programmatic media buying includes the use of demand-side platforms (DSPs), supply-side platforms (SSPs) and data management platforms (DMPs).[123] DSPs facilitate the process of buying ad inventory on the open market, as well as provide the ability to reach a brand's target audience due to the integration of DMPs.[123] "DMPs collect and analyze a substantial amount of cookie data to then allow the marketer to make more informed decisions of whom their target audience may be," says Vicioso.[123]

"On the publisher side of things, publishers manage their unsold ad inventory through an SSP,"[123] which reports such clickstream activity such as how long a visitor was on a specific site or how many pages were viewed per visit.[123] Vicioso explains that, "SSPs will ultimately be in charge of picking the winning bid and will serve the winning banner ad on the publisher's site."[123]

As Allie Shaw notes in her article *AI could save television advertising with advanced personalization*[124], "In short, AI programs draw from data pools to make decisions about where and when to buy or sell ad space according to demographic and cost-versus-benefit information." "Essentially, your TV can learn about your habits in the way your web browser already does, allowing advertisers to present you with ads based on that information—so you'll see fewer repetitive ads that you don't care about. This means you and your neighbors may all be watching the premiere of *The Walking Dead* but seeing different ads based on your unique interests," explains Shaw.[124]

"Thanks to programmatic TV advertising, advertisers can know how many people have viewed their ads, where these viewers are located, and what their viewing history looks like—with information updating by the minute," says Shaw.[124] "They're also able to get more accurate data about an ad's cost per impression (CPM, or the cost for each 1,000 people who see the ad), allowing for more relevant and cost-efficient targeting," she explains.[124]

Although programmatic advertising was designed to be scalable, efficient, and precise, some brands have been reluctant to embrace it. However, as Warren argues, companies should have both a single view of their customer as well as a single view of their media.[226]

The second step of the RACE framework is "Act". Brands must draw visitors in and make them aware of the company's product and/or services. Machine learning algorithms can build propensity models that can predict the likelihood of a given customer to convert, the price at which a customer is likely to convert, and/or what customers are most likely to turn into repeat customers.[122]

"Propensity models generated by machine learning can be trained to score leads based on certain criteria so that your sales team can establish how 'hot' a given lead is, and if they are worth devoting time to," explains Huguesrey.[122] "This can be particularly important in B2B businesses with consultative sales processes, where each sale takes a considerable amount of time on the part of the sales team," says Huguesrey.[122]

The machine learning algorithms can run through vast amounts of historical data to establish which ads perform best on which people and at what stage in the buying process.[122] Using this data, ads can be served to them with the most effective content at the most effective time.[122] By using machine learning to constantly optimize thousands of variables, businesses can achieve more effective ad placement and content than traditional methods.[122] However, humans will still be needed for the creative parts.[122]

The third step of the RACE framework—"Content"—is one of the most important steps and it includes dynamic pricing, re-targeting, web and app personalization, and chatbots.[122]

All marketers know that sales are one of the most effective ways of moving product, but they can also hurt the financial bottom line.[122] Sales are so effective because they get people to buy a product that they might not have previously considered because they couldn't justify the cost of the purchase. But sales also mean people who would have paid the higher price pay less than they would have. The trick is to understand the threshold between buying and not buying the product and this is where dynamic pricing comes in.

By targeting special offers only at those who are likely to need them in order to convert, brands can ensure they don't give offers to people who have the propensity to pay full price.[122] "Machine learning can build a propensity model of which traits show a customer is likely to need an offer to convert, and which are likely to convert without the need for an offer," says Huguesrey.[122] This means companies can increase sales, while also maximizing a company's profit margins.[122]

By using a propensity model to predict a customer's stage in the buying journey, brands can serve the customer, either through an app or on a web page, with the most relevant and timely content.[122] "If someone is still new to a site, content that informs them and keeps them interested will be most effective, whilst if they have visited many times and are clearly interested in the product then more in-depth content about a product's benefits will perform better," recommends Huguesrey.[122]

Another way to convert customers is with chatbots that mimic human intelligence by interpreting a consumer's queries and potentially complete an order for them.[122] Chatbots are relatively easy to build and Facebook is simplifying the process of developing chatbots for brands.[122] Facebook "wants to make its Messenger app the go-to place for people to have conversations with brand's virtual ambassadors."[122] Facebook has created the wit.ai bot engine, which allows brands to train bots with sample conversations and have these bots continually learn from customer interactions.[122]

"Much like with ad targeting, machine learning can be used to establish what content is most likely to bring customers back to the site based on historical data," says Huguesrey.[122] By building an accurate prediction model of what content works best to win back different customer types, machine learning can help optimize a brand's retargeting ads to make them as effective as possible.[122]

The final step of the RACE framework is "Engage". As previously mentioned, it is far easier to sell to an existing customer than it is to attract new ones, therefore keeping current customers happy is paramount.[122] "This is particularly true in subscription-based business, where a high churn rate can be extremely costly," argues Huguesrey.[122] "Predictive analytics can be used to work out which customers are most likely to unsubscribe from a service, by assessing what features are most common in customers who do unsubscribe," says Huguesrey.[122] "It's then possible to reach out to these customers with offers, prompts or assistance to prevent them from churning," recommends Huguesrey.[122]

Marketing automation techniques usually involve a series of business rules, which, once triggered, initiate or continue interactions with a given customer.[122] However, these rules can be quite arbitrary.[122] "Machine learning can run through billions of points of customer data and establish when are the most effective times to make contact, what words in subject lines are most effective and much more," says Huguesrey.[122] "These insights can then be applied to boost the effectiveness of your marketing automation efforts," he adds.[122]

"In a similar fashion to marketing automation, applying insights generated from machine learning can create extremely effective 1:1 dynamic emails," says Huguesrey.[122] Propensity models can "establish a subscribers propensity to buy certain categories, sizes and colors through their previous behavior and displays the most relevant products in newsletters."[122] The product stock, deals, pricing specifically individualized for each customer would all be correct at the time the customer opens the offer email.[122]

For most businesses, customer information housed in an EDW would include things like transactional data, customer and CRM data, mobile, social, and location data, as well as information from web logs that track its user's web behavior, and online advertising bid management systems. EDWs should also give a business the ability to do analytics on the fly, which could help the customer's experience in a multitude of ways.

Today, most big companies which have large customer databases have loyalty programs that are part of a CRM and/or an SCRM initiative. These companies should provide their customers with an intimate experience that will make them want to return to again and again and again.

Obviously, creating a consolidated customer view is a necessary component of personalization. Another important step of bringing personalization efforts up to a user's expectation level will be using behavioral data in the process. In order to create these types of customer experiences, businesses need to strategically collect and utilize customer data, including real-time signals of intent, which aren't always captured today.

Engagement and Loyalty Platform

When developing CRM systems and goals, one should always keep in mind Lovelock and Wirtz's *Wheel of Loyalty*.[103] These include building a foundation for loyalty, creating loyalty bonds as well as identifying and reducing the factors that result in customer churn.[103] Customer satisfaction is the foundation of true customer loyalty, while customer dissatisfaction is the key factor that drives people away.[103] This may sound obvious, but its importance cannot be overstated. The *Engagement and Loyalty Platform* (see Figure 14) shows how a marketer would engage its customers in a loyalty platform that utilizes social media as an important part of the process.

Rules Engine
Define and apply rules for rewards economy, geofencing, frequency, influence and more

Moderation
Moderate posts for UGC quality, consumer profiles, and pick rewards before conversion

Rewards & Content
Deliver points, discounts, reminders, digital content, sweeps, contest entries and more, frictionlessly in real-time

Listening
Define and listen for triggers such as photos, hashtags, keywords, topics, likes, video views, pins, comments, links, sharing, check-ins, geo-posts, and more on social and messaging channels

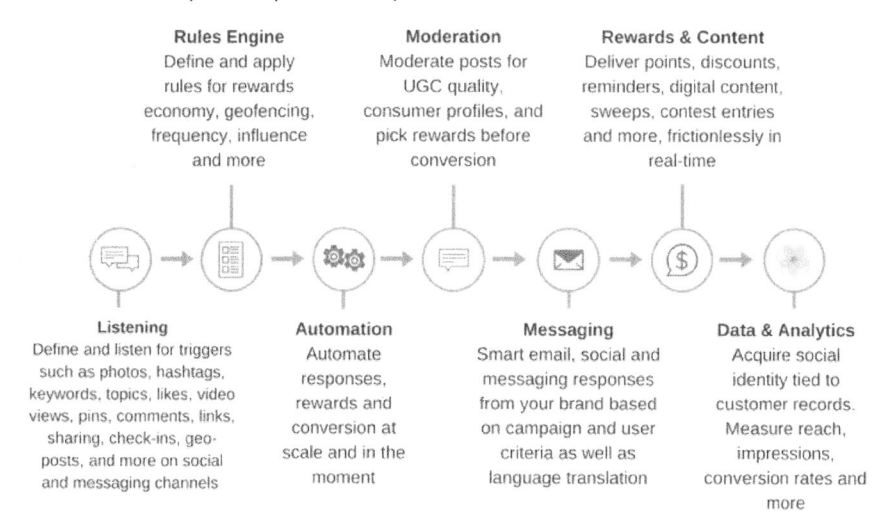

Automation
Automate responses, rewards and conversion at scale and in the moment

Messaging
Smart email, social and messaging responses from your brand based on campaign and user criteria as well as language translation

Data & Analytics
Acquire social identity tied to customer records. Measure reach, impressions, conversion rates and more

Figure 14: Engagement and Loyalty Platform
Source: Based on an engagement and loyalty platform devised by Chirpify.com

Through mobile and social media analytics, businesses can create a single customer view that helps produce one-to-one, personalized marketing, which many would consider the Holy Grail of advertising. Marketing to the "customer of one" is one of the major slogans being bandied about by software companies these days and, although it might sound simple, it is anything but. In reality, it can be one of the hardest marketing frameworks to create because there are so many moving parts, so much state-of-the-art technologies involved, and decisions that have to be made, literally, *now*.

The *Engagement and Loyalty Platform* can be implemented in a multitude of ways. In the *Listening* part, brands should define and look out for triggers such as photos, hashtags, keywords, likes, video views, etc., etc. This runs the gamut, from staying on top of keywords and hashtags to using AI image recognition technology that scans pictures of the company's latest looks (if it's a retail company), as well as NLP for scanning customer review and comments sites.

Check-ins and geo-posts from sites like Foursquare, WeChat, Instagram, Facebook, WhatsApp, YouTube, as well as a whole host of other social networks can help businesses connect to a nearby audience. Brands should also be listening to comment boards or short-term blogging sites like Tumblr or social news aggregation sites like Reddit for comments about their products and services. Customers are often happy to post wonderful reviews about their buying experiences and this is gold for word-of-mouth marketing.

The *Rules Engine* step is straightforward; brands are already creating considerable business rules for their operation and these should be extended to each company's defined rewards program, its reward's economy, and the marketing of its loyalty program.

Rewards programs are difficult to implement and costly to maintain because there are so many moving parts to them; each reward point and free offer has to be correlated against the department that offered it, each expense has to be budgeted to the right department, and every reward point has a monetary value that must be enumerated properly.

Building a rules engine can simplify the marketing process by defining who gets what, when he or she gets it, and through which channel it gets delivered on. With mobile and social being added to the customer channel mix, things are going to get exponentially more complicated, so building a rules engine that lays out things in a highly definable way is not just desirable, but absolutely necessary.

Once the rules engine is in place, automation must kick in. With some brands, they are handling databases filled with millions of customers and it would be impossible to market to them without considerable automation going on behind the scenes. Segmenting customers and building campaigns that market to thousands of individuals would be impossible without it. Understanding the ROI of each marketing campaign is imperative and with today's real-time personalization capabilities, brands can quickly understand who is accepting their marketing and how much revenue is being generated. Adding a real-time element to the process would be impossible without strict rules set in place and powerful marketing automation tools that not only send out marketing offers but also quantify them once they are utilized.

In terms of marketing and customer service, Facebook bots could be created and automated to answer standard customer service questions and this should lighten the load on a marketer's customer service department.

Moderating boards and UGC posts are also a great channel to connect with customers and/or potential customers. These are also good places to pick up both customer service issues and competitor information. Social media users often feel free to post stories about their bad purchases and, in some cases, will openly blast companies that have not met their expectations, and this can help a marketer with competitive intel and new product development.

As Chirpify sees it: "Moderation allows brands to increase social efficiency and effectiveness by uniting automated listening triggers while giving moderators the ability to manually review posts and user content for fit before determining their qualification for a reward. This helps brands better personalize the reward based on the user while making sure that the reward is one that the customer appreciates and/or makes them feel special."[125]

Rewards and marketing content can deliver points, discounts, reminders, as well as contest entries in real-time, but reaching today's audiences can be tricky.

To make this entire loyalty/CRM/marketing system work, we are obviously talking about a huge amount of data flowing through these systems, utilizing everything from a typical EDW, to potential Hadoop clusters, as well as real-time stream processing applications like Spark, Flink, Storm, IBM's Infosphere, Hitachi's HDS, and TIBCO's StreamBase, maybe even some deep learning tools like TensorFlow and Caffe2, amongst others.

In many cases, acquiring a social identity that is tied to a customer record is as simple as asking for it; "Like" my page, "Follow" us, "heart" this, "Pin" that, "Snap" your story, "tweet or retweet" one of our offers and/or a story about your latest purchase or vacation. These are all wonderful ways to engage an audience, either connecting with a new customer or continuing to build a relationship with a current one.

YouTube Live, Facebook Live, Twitter, Periscope, Twitch, and the Chinese channels Youku, Sina, Quanmin.tv, and Huya are all great channels to market content through, but a word of warning, it has to be the right content at the right time. These channels have very particular audiences, so advertisers should spend the time to understand these channels in detail before marketing through them.

Another good way to collect data is through surveys. As Wedel & Kannan explain in their article *Marketing Analytics for Data-Rich Environments*[126], surveys are simple to administer, and data can be collected and analyzed very easily and quite quickly. "Firms continuously assess customer satisfaction; new digital interfaces require this to be done with short surveys to reduce fatigue and attrition. For example, loyalty is often evaluated with single-item Net Promoter Scores. As a consequence, longitudinal and repeated cross-section data are becoming more common," contend Wedel & Kannan.[126] Machine Learning can be utilized to create personalized surveys that customers are much more likely to answer because they will be based upon the customer's response to previous questions.[126]

Geofencing Applications

Proximity marketing "is the localized wireless distribution of advertising content associated with a particular place. Transmissions can be received by individuals in that location who wish to receive them and have the necessary equipment to do so," explains Wikipedia.org. [127] There are four main systems used for proximity marketing; Bluetooth-based systems; NFC-based systems; GSM-based systems (via SMS); and iBeacon-based systems.

Considered the "killer-app" for mobile commerce, the commercial viability for proximity marketing or "location-aware advertising" (LAA) is enormous. In location-aware advertising, a cellular subscriber receives an advertising message based on his or her location, so a shopper wandering through a mall could set his or her mobile phone to accept all available mobile offers or just offers from a specific store.

In their article *Foundations of SMS Commerce Success: Lessons from SMS Messaging and Co-opetition*[128], Xu et al. argue that LAA allows advertisers to deliver highly customized promotions, coupons and offers to an individual, specifically taking into account their geographical location, as well as the time of day of the offer. LAA also allows advertisers to reach their customers when they are primed to make a purchase.

iBeacon is the trademark for an indoor proximity marketing system that Apple calls, "A new class of low-powered, low-cost transmitters that can notify nearby iOS 7 devices of their presence. The technology enables an iOS device or other hardware to send push notifications to iOS devices in close proximity. Devices running the Android operating system can receive iBeacon advertisements but cannot emit iBeacon advertisements."[129]

According to Wikipedia, the iBeacon system uses "Bluetooth low energy Proximity sensing to transmit a universally unique identifier picked up by a compatible app or operating system that can be turned into a physical location or trigger an action on the device such as a check-in on social media or a push notification."[129]

In her article *Your iPhone is Now a Homing Beacon (But It's Ridiculously Easy to Turn it Off)*[130], Kashmir Hill warns that this technology opens the door to more aggressive monitoring, tracking and communication from people with apps on their phone, which will vary from convenient to invasive. In those lengthy terms of service and privacy (that few people read), app makers can slip in tracking permission warns Hill.[130] "Hypothetically, a marketer with its app on your phone could tell iBeacon to turn the app on when you're in or near the store, send information about your being there to a database and then pop up some advertising," Hill warns.[130]

"At this point, every party that wants to communicate with you needs its app on your phone. Inevitably, some monster advertising network will develop a one-stop-iBeacon-shop app that will allow it to act as the conduit for lots of different people to ping your phone," Hill claims.[130] But that day is probably still a few years away.

Currently, as Shane Paul Neil explains in his article *Is iBeacon Marketing Finally Taking Off?*[131], "McDonald's has seen an increase in sales from a test run using the iBeacons, and Virgin Atlantic is among the first to use them as thermostats to supply cold passengers with blankets on planes. iBeacons also have the potential to enhance B2B marketing with its ability to target users' smartphones at trade shows or other events."

However, as Shane Paul Neil warns, the delay in implementing beacon technology probably has to do with one of the following four possible reasons[131]:

1. Installing, managing, and maintaining beacons can be a struggle.
2. Beacon signals are often obstructed by physical objects.
3. Beacon marketing requires user opt-in.
4. Consumers aren't sold on the benefits of beacons.

In his *Washington Post* article *How iBeacons could change the world forever*[132], Matt McFarland sees a world where iBeacon technology can do the following:

1. Send a coupon to a consumer because they have entered an area.
2. React when a user walks into his or her home, turning on lights or televisions.
3. Provide tours of museums.
4. Automatically send concert or sporting event tickets to a phone that approaches an arena's turnstiles.
5. Win something for visiting a car dealership or a retail outlet.
6. Be warned when someone's car or bike is no longer in his or her garage.

These and many other examples can be created for proximity marketing and even though each upcoming year is claimed to be the "Year of iBeacons technology", betting against Apple is often a losing proposition, eventually.

Today, most smart phones have geofencing capabilities that tap into GPS or RFID technology to define geographical boundaries. Basically, geofencing programs allow an administrator to set up triggers—usually SMS push notifications or email alerts—so when a device crosses a "geofence" and enters or exits a set area, a user is notified. Applications such as Facebook, Foursquare and China's WeChat and Jiepang use geofencing to locate users, as well as help them find their friends and/or check into places.

With geofencing applications, "users can also offer peer reviews of locations, which add a layer of user-generated content. In exchange for loyalty, more and more businesses—from local airlines to larger organizations like Bravo TV, Starbucks and The History Channel—are offering coupons, discounts, free goods and marketing materials."[133]

As users continue to enter personal details as well as update and check-in to their locations, geofencing applications like Foursquare can "collect a historical view of consumer habits and preferences and, over time, possibly recommend a much larger variety of targeted marketing materials in real time—as a consumer walks into a store to look for a specific item or service."[133]

Geofencing applications (aka Location Based Services (LBS)) like Jiepang and Foursquare are useful services for brand marketers as well. Although the article *LBS Opportunities for Casino Marketers in Macau*[134] is about casinos, the ideas Chris Wieners offers are also useful for many industries. For example, to get their LBS promotions rolling[134]:

1. Pick your LBS service and claim your location.
2. Offer tips to customers via LBS.
3. Reward loyalty creatively. Start by offering your most loyal customers rewards, special access, and other promotions. Those that become your "Mayor"—or any other significant title—should be rewarded for their loyalty. This is a great way to identify potential social influencers and utilize them to further promote your venue.
4. Reward new customers: First time check-ins should receive special promotions or incentives as it is important to give people a reason to continuously check in to your establishment.
5. Understand who your loyal customers are online, and work with them. Develop a plan to utilize these 'influencers' and tap into their social networks. "Casinos do it offline all of the time; develop a similar approach for high-valued customers online through social connections. Encourage your followers to promote their checked-in status to their friends via social networks and micro blogs like Sina and Twitter."[134]
6. Promote your services both online and off.

In May of 2013, Lighthouse Signal Systems launched its indoor positioning system as an open service for Android app developers.[135] Developers can use the technology to create Android apps that will help users find their way through the vast indoor terrain of Las Vegas' hotels and casinos.[135]

Although global positioning systems have made outdoor navigation as simple as following directions on a mobile device, indoor navigation isn't so simple, it is actually one of the last major hurdles that smartphones have yet to truly conquer.[135] However, Cambridge, Mass.-based Lighthouse Signal Systems has launched a service that covers 20 million square feet of entertainment and retail space at leading casinos and hotels on the Las Vegas Strip.[135]

Lighthouse is "making its service freely available to Android app developers, resort operators, airlines, and others seeking to enhance the visitor experience in Las Vegas. Indoor navigation is the Holy Grail for the mobile industry, and Lighthouse says it is the first to provide GPS-like indoor positioning on a wide scale in a major U.S. metro."[135]

"We are excited to support app developer partners as they create new mobile experiences with indoor positioning in Las Vegas, where large resort interiors have traditionally presented a vexing challenge for visitors," said Lighthouse co-founder Parviz Parvizi.[135]

Lighthouse's platform "includes indoor geofencing: a hosting platform for location-based offers and user analytics."[135] The app includes user opt-in agreements and developers cannot use the service to track mobile phone users without their consent.[135]

The technology uses "a combination of WiFi fingerprinting and sensor data. As long as there are WiFi networks in the area, Lighthouse can provide positioning info."[135] Google, Cisco, Ekahau, Euclid, Shopkick, PointInside, Aisle411, Sensionlab, Indoor.rs, Yfind, and CSR are all developing similar systems.[135]

Mobile marketing in general and OTT, MMS and SMS marketing in particular can help brands create a one-to-one, two-way interactive experience with its customers. These channels are not just about sending out a simple message, but rather they are about starting a customer relationship that can be analyzed so that a brand has a 360-degree view of its customer. It is an understanding that should include his or her wants, desires and needs.

Besides geo-fencing applications, social media channels like Facebook, Foursquare, Instagram, Twitter, WeChat, as well as many others can reveal a customer's location. Instagram tracks a user's photos even if he or she doesn't geo-tag them. As Cadie Thompson warns in her article *Social media apps are tracking your location in shocking detail*[136], "While the picture sharing app does give users the option to name the location of where they are uploading an image, it also geotags an uploaded pic regardless if the user has selected the 'Add to Photo Map' function."[136]

Foursquare's check-in app Swarm also broadcasts users' location even if they have not selected a specific location for check-in.[136] Many live-streaming apps like Periscope, YouTube, and several Chinese ones will also show the location of the user and this is information that can be utilized by a brand's marketing department if it can exploit the information quickly enough. Although YouTube doesn't have a filter for location, websites like geosearchtool.com allows users to search by location. Advanced filters allow searching by keyword and within a certain designated area.

In their article *Amazon's Alexa team can access users' home addresses*[137], Matt Day, Giles Turner, and Natalia Drozdiak claim that "An Amazon.com Inc. team auditing Alexa users' commands has access to location data and can, in some cases, easily find a customer's home address, according to five employees familiar with the program."

"The team, spread across three continents, transcribes, annotates and analyzes a portion of the voice recordings picked up by Alexa," says Day et al.[137] The program "was set up to help Amazon's digital voice assistant get better at understanding and responding to commands," they add.[137]

"Team members with access to Alexa users' geographic coordinates can easily type them into third-party mapping software and find home residences, according to the employees, who signed nondisclosure agreements barring them from speaking publicly about the program," says Day el al.[137]

"In an April 10 statement acknowledging the Alexa auditing program, Amazon said 'employees do not have direct access to information that can identify the person or account as part of this workflow,'" reports Day et al.[137] In a new statement responding to the Day et al. April 24, 2019 story, Amazon said "access to internal tools is highly controlled, and is only granted to a limited number of employees who require these tools to train and improve the service by processing an extremely small sample of interactions."[137] Amazon added: "Our policies strictly prohibit employee access to or use of customer data for any other reason, and we have a zero tolerance policy for abuse of our systems. We regularly audit employee access to internal tools and limit access whenever and wherever possible."[137]

"Some of the workers charged with analyzing recordings of Alexa customers use an Amazon tool that displays audio clips alongside data about the device that captured the recording. Much of the information stored by the software, including a device ID and customer identification number, can't be easily linked back to a user," says Day et al.[137]

"In a demonstration seen by Bloomberg, an Amazon team member pasted a user's coordinates, stored in the system as latitude and longitude, into Google Maps. In less than a minute, the employee had jumped from a recording of a person's Alexa command to what appeared to be an image of their house and corresponding address," notes Day et al.[137]

"Amazon's location data is not always precise, and it doesn't always refer to the location of an Echo. The Alexa smartphone app prompts users to enter a home address when they set up a smart speaker and also asks for permission to use smartphone location data," says Day et al.[137] Amazon uses "mobile device location to provide more relevant answers and recommendations, and to enable features like reminders designed to trigger when a user reaches a certain place."[137]

"A second internal Amazon software tool, available to a smaller pool of workers who tag transcripts of voice recordings to help Alexa categorize requests, stores more personal data, according to one of the employees," says Day et al.[137] The process works as follows[137]:

> "After punching in a customer ID number, those workers, called annotators and verifiers, can see the home and work addresses and phone numbers customers entered into the Alexa app when they set up the device, the employee said. If a user has chosen to share their contacts with Alexa, their names, numbers and email addresses also appear in the dashboard. That data is in the system so that if a customer says 'Send a message to Laura,' human reviewers can make sure transcribers wrote the name correctly so that the software learns to pair that request with the Laura in the contact list."[137]

After Bloomberg's report, Amazon appeared to be limiting the level of access employees had to the system.[137] "One employee said that, as recently as a year ago, an Amazon dashboard detailing a user's contacts displayed full phone numbers. Now, in that same panel, some digits are obscured," explains Day et al.[137] However, this access can always be given back once the negative press dies down.

Besides the normal geo-location apps, brands should also look into the smaller ones such as Bizzy, Glympse, Neer (neerlife.com), and social gaming app Scvngr.

Gamification

In their paper *Defining Gamification—A Service Marketing Perspective*[138], Huotari and Hamari define Gamification as "a process of enhancing a service with affordances for gameful experiences in order to support user's overall value creation." Humans seem to love playing games. The term "An idle mind goes to waste," comes to mind when one watches people like these almost mindless mobile games, but brands should be taking advantage of the human animal's inherent desire to play games that often have little purpose but the collection of cybernetic candy or worthless virtual currency.

In an example from the airline industry, Gabe Zichermann considers Air Canada's *Earn Your Wings* campaign a prime example of a company using gamification the way it was intended to be used.[30] The program "created a leaderboard of top

..yers during the promotional period that were ranked based on a range of activities. These included, but weren't limited to, miles flown and were supported by a series of badges awarded for different activity loops."[30] According to Zichermann, "Top players split a large pot of 10 million miles at the end of the promotion period, and that activity seemed especially fierce, which is what really excited me."[30]

Ian Di Tullo, Director of Loyalty for Air Canada (AC) explains that the company had been experimenting with socializing loyalty for a while, but a 'big win' had eluded them.[30] "The company's business objectives however mandated that they try innovative ways to get people to be 'cross activated', meaning: fly further, fly more often, and spend more to fly. Their competitive market dictated that they needed to keep trying, and gamification was the obvious solution," claimed Di Tullo.[30]

In Di Tullo's words, their gamification's efforts attempted to vastly simplify their "promotion's inherent complexity, adding 'badges, in particular, make it very easy to focus customers on pretty complicated tasks, and those are the foundation for lasting behavior change.'"[30] For example, Di Tullo explains, "if you want users to visit 3 new cities, fly to both coasts and go in first class twice, it's much easier to create 'incomplete badges' for each activity and display them on a page than to explain each one separately in text."[30] Once users understand the simple concept "that each badge represents a challenge to be completed, it acts as a valuable shorthand for behavior."[30]

Competition amongst members is also fostered, which is an example of social proof and I discuss this further in chapter five. "Another element of the Air Canada leaderboard campaign that was attention grabbing was the competitive nature of the program, as leaderboards are inherently competition oriented."[30] Di Tullo explained "that the company sees loyalty program users divided into two groups: regular users, and highly-engaged users with a competitive streak."[30] The goal "was not to shy away from the competitive elements of loyalty—as most other programs have done—but rather to embrace them."[30] "By ensuring that competition could occur with some privacy protection (user handles and blended point systems aided this), the idea was to activate that competitive desire," notes Di Tullo.[30]

According to Air Canada, the program was a huge success.[30] "Although Di Tullo couldn't disclose specific revenues, the program's registration levels were double the forecast, and engagement levels for both active and inactive users were better than expected," says Zichermann.[30] Not only did the program achieve a positive ROI, but it got people sharing their loyalty activity with others on social media, which isn't always something people tend to crow about.[30]

In a guest editorial titled *Gamification of Loyalty—improving customer engagement*[139] for Airlineinformation.org, Aaron Carr, CEO of Friendefi writes that, "loyalty marketers are increasingly viewing gamification as a complementary approach that can help strengthen their own customer engagement efforts."

Carr adds that, "the opportunities to boost loyalty program member engagement don't end with better data capture. In an increasingly digital world, gamification also offers a framework for motivating members to learn about your program, interact with partner offers, and to share (or even compete) with their friends."[139]

Carr provides an example from the America marketers' AAdvantage Passport Challenge, which offers "loyalty members the opportunity to earn stamps for their digital passport as well as miles for completing various AAdvantage program and partner games and trivia from their computer or mobile phone."[139] "Customers reported spending 15-20 minutes playing the various games and trivia, which tested their knowledge of American's AAdvantage program and partner offers," explains Carr.[139]

Gamification is still a young and fast-moving practice, especially amongst loyalty marketers.[139] It is a technology brands should look at because it has multi-channel engagement possibilities, can connect with a user on his or her mobile device, and it can add an element of excitement that will prove enticing to a customer's competitive spirit. It provides a strong emotional connection to the brand as well.

In his article *iSoftBet Rolls Out Pioneering Platform-wide 'In-Game' Gamification*[140], Moses Mbuva explains that the leading online and mobile casino content provider released "In-Game, a pioneering series of advanced cross-platform, real-time gamification tools available across more than 3,000 games on its industry-leading Gaming Aggregation Platform (GAP)."

According to Mbuva, "The new advanced marketing tools allow operators to activate a series of easy-to-use gamification features that significantly enhance player experience. This includes tournaments, leaderboards based on achievements or points, or rewards in the form of cash bonuses or free rounds, across not only all iSoftBet games, but also more than 3,000 slot and table game titles provided by its game partners."[140]

The In-game tool includes real-time leader boards, which allow players to track their progress against other competitors at any time.[140] iSoftBet claims these tools are among the most advanced and user-friendly in the industry and they will enable operators to significantly increase player engagement and retention levels as well as boost customer loyalty.[140]

Natural Language Processing

According to skymind.ai[24], "Natural language refers to language that is spoken and written by people, and natural language processing (NLP) attempts to extract information from the spoken and written word using algorithms."

In their article *How Artificial Intelligence and Machine Learning Can Impact Market Design*[25], Paul R. Milgrom and Steve Tadelis give some interesting use cases for NLP. Online marketplaces like eBay, Taobao, Airbnb, along with many others have seen exponential growth since their inception because they provide "businesses and individuals with previously unavailable opportunities to purchase or profit from online trading."[25] Besides the new marketplaces created for these wholesalers and retailers, "the so called 'gig economy' is comprised of marketplaces that allow individuals to share their time or assets across different productive activities and earn extra income."[25]

"The amazing success of online marketplaces was not fully anticipated," Milgrom and Tadelis surmise, "primarily because of the hazards of anonymous trade and asymmetric information. Namely, how can strangers who have never transacted with one another, and who may be thousands of miles apart, be willing to trust each other?"[25] "Trust on both sides of the market is essential for parties to be willing to transact and for a marketplace to succeed," claim Milgrom and Tadelis.[25] eBay's early success is often attributed to its innovative feedback and reputation mechanism, which has been replicated by practically every other marketplace that came after eBay.[25] Milgrom et al. believe that these online feedback and reputation mechanisms provide a modern-day version of more ancient reputation mechanisms used in the physical marketplaces that were the medieval trade fairs of Europe.[141]

The problem for Milgrom and Tadelis is that "recent studies have shown that online reputation measures of marketplace sellers, which are based on buyer-generated feedback, don't accurately reflect their actual performance.[25] A growing body of research reveals that "user-generated feedback mechanisms are often biased, suffer from 'grade inflation,' and can be prone to manipulation by sellers."[25] "For example, the average percent positive for sellers on eBay is about 99.4%, with a median of 100%. This causes a challenge to interpret the true levels of satisfaction on online marketplaces," state Milgrom and Tadelis.[25]

For Milgrom and Tadelis, a natural question emerges: "can online marketplaces use the treasure trove of data it collects to measure the quality of a transaction and predict which sellers will provide a better service to their buyers?"[25] Afterall, these online marketplaces and gig-economy sites collect vast amounts of data as part of the process of trade.[25] The millions of transactions, searches and browsing that occur on these marketplaces every day could be leveraged to create an environment that promotes trust, similar to the way institutions emerged in the medieval trade fairs of Europe that helped foster trust.[25] Milgrom and Tadelis believe that AI can be applied to these marketplaces to help create a more trustworthy and better buying experience to consumers.[25]

"One of the ways that online marketplaces help participants build trust is by letting them communicate through online messaging platforms," explain Milgrom and Tadelis.[25] On eBay, buyers question sellers about their products, "which may be particularly useful for used or unique products for which buyers may want to get more refined information than is listed."[25] Airbnb also "allows potential renters to send messages to hosts and ask questions about the property that may not be answered in the original listing."[25]

Using NLP, "marketplaces can mine the data generated by these messages in order to better predict the kind of features that customers value."[25] However, Milgrom and Tadelis claim, "there may also be subtler ways to apply AI to manage the quality of marketplaces."[25] The messaging platforms are not only restricted to pre-transaction inquiries, they also provide both parties the ability to send messages to each other post-transaction.[25] The obvious question that emerges for Milgrom and Tadelis is, "how could a marketplace analyze the messages sent between buyers and sellers post the transaction to infer something about the quality of the transaction that feedback doesn't seem to capture?"

This question was posed and answered in the paper *Canary in the e-commerce coal mine: Detecting and predicting poor experiences using buyer-to-seller messages*[142] by Masterov et al. Milgrom and Tadelis explain[25]:

> "By using internal data from eBay's marketplace. The analysis they performed was divided into two stages. In the first stage, the goal was to see if NLP can identify transactions that went bad when there was an independent indication that the buyer was unhappy. To do this, they collected internal data from transactions in which messages were sent from the buyer to the seller after the transaction was completed and matched it with another internal data source that recorded actions by buyers indicating that the buyer had a poor experience with the transactions. Actions that indicate an unhappy buyer include a buyer claiming that the item was not received, or that the item was significantly not as described, or leaves negative or neutral feedback, to name a few."

The simple NLP approach Milgrom and Tadelis use "creates a 'poor-experience' indicator as the target (dependent variable) that the machine learning model will try to predict, and uses the messages' content as the independent variables."[25] "In its simplest form and as a proof of concept, a regular expression search was used that included a standard list of negative words such as 'annoyed,'

...satisfied,' 'damaged,' or 'negative feedback' to identify a message as negative," explain Milgrom and Tadelis.[25] Messages void of these designated terms were considered neutral.[25] Using this classification, the researchers grouped transactions into three distinct types: "(1) No post-transaction messages from buyer to seller; (2) One or more negative messages; or (3) One or more neutral messages with no negative messages."[25]

In the second stage of the analysis, using the fact that negative messages are associated with poor experiences, Masterov et al. constructed a novel measure of seller quality based on the idea that sellers who receive a higher frequency of negative messages are bad sellers.[142] According to Masterov et al., the measure, which is "calculated for every seller at any point in time using aggregated negative messages from past sales, and the likelihood that a current transaction will result in a poor experience,"[142] is a monotonically increasing relationship.[142]

This simple exercise shows that using a marketplace's message data and a simple NLP procedure, businesses could predict which sellers would create poor experiences better than one inferred from highly inaccurate and wildly inflated feedback data.[25] Of course, eBay is not unique in allowing "parties to exchange messages and the lessons from this research are easily generalizable to other marketplaces."[25] "The key is that there is information in communication between market participants, and past communication can help identify and predict the sellers or products that will cause buyers poor experiences and negatively impact the overall trust in the marketplace," conclude Milgrom and Tadelis.[25]

Creating a market for feedback

Besides the over-inflation of customer feedback as described above, another problem with customer feedback forums is the fact that few buyers even bother leaving feedback.[25] "In fact," Milgrom and Tadelis argue, "through the lens of mainstream economic theory, it is surprising that a significant fraction of online consumers leave feedback. After all, it is a selfless act that requires time, and it creates a classic free-rider problem."[25] Additionally, "because potential buyers are attracted to buy from sellers, or products, that already have an established good track record, this creates a 'cold start' problem,"[25] i.e., new sellers with no feedback face a high barrier-to-entry because buyers are hesitant to try them out.[25]

Li et al. address this problem in their paper *Buying Reputation as a Signal of Quality: Evidence from an Online Marketplace*[143] by "Using a unique and novel implementation of a market for feedback on the huge Chinese marketplace Taobao where they let sellers pay buyers to leave them feedback."[25] Of course, it might be concerning to allow "sellers to pay for feedback as it seems like a practice in which they will only pay for good feedback and suppress any bad feedback, which would not add any value in promoting trust."[25] However,

Milgrom and Tadelis explain that "Taobao implemented a clever use of NLP to solve this problem: it is the platform, using an NLP AI model, that decides whether feedback is relevant and not the seller who pays for the feedback."[25] "Hence, the reward to the buyer for leaving feedback was actually managed by the marketplace, and was handed out for informative feedback rather than for positive feedback," note Milgrom and Tadelis.[25]

"Specifically, in March 2012, Taobao launched a 'Rebate-for-Feedback' (RFF) feature through which sellers can set a rebate value for any item they sell (cash-back or store coupon) as a reward for a buyer's feedback," says Milgrom and Tadelis.[25] Sellers who choose this option guarantee that the rebate will be transferred from the seller's account to a buyer who leaves high-quality feedback that is, most importantly, informative, rather than whether the feedback is positive or negative.[25] "Taobao measures the quality of feedback with an NLP algorithm that examines the comment's content and length and finds out whether key features of the item are mentioned," explains Milgrom and Tadelis.[25] The marketplace actually manages "the market for feedback by forcing the seller to deposit at Taobao a certain amount for a chosen period, so that funds are guaranteed for buyers who meet the rebate criterion, which itself is determined by Taobao."[25]

Taobao wanted to promote more informative feedback, but as Li et al. note, "economic theory offers some insights into how the RFF feature can act as a potent signaling mechanism that will further separate higher from lower quality sellers and products."[143] Building upon the work of Philip Nelson in his influential article *Information and Consumer Behavior*[144] that suggested advertising acts as a signal of quality. "According to the theory, advertising—which is a form of burning money—acts as a signal that attracts buyers who correctly believe that only high-quality sellers will choose to advertise," say Milgrom and Tadelis.[25] "Incentive compatibility is achieved through repeat purchases: buyers who purchase and experience the products of advertisers will return in the future only if the goods sold are of high enough quality," argue Milgrom and Tadelis.[25] "The cost of advertising can be high enough to deter low quality sellers from being willing to spend the money and sell only once, because those sellers will not attract repeat customers, and still low enough to leave profits for higher quality sellers. Hence, ads act as signals that separate high quality sellers, and in turn attract buyers to their products," argue Milgrom and Tadelis.[25]

Li et al. argue that Taobao's "RFF mechanism plays a similar signaling role as ads do, which can be seen as signals that separate high quality sellers, and in turn attract buyers to their products."[143] Assuming "consumers express their experiences truthfully in written feedback, any consumer who buys a product and is given incentives to leave feedback, will leave positive feedback only if the buying experience was satisfactory."[25] Li et al. believe that a seller will offer RFF incentives to buyers if he or she expects positive feedback, which usually only

...pens if the seller provides a high quality item and/or service.[25] "If a seller knows that their goods and services are unsatisfactory, then paying for feedback will generate negative feedback that will harm the low-quality seller," claim Milgrom and Taledis.[25] "Equilibrium behavior," Milgrom and Tadelis contend, "implies that RFF, as a signal of high quality, will attract more buyers and result in more sales."[25] "The role of AI was precisely to reward buyers for information, not for positive feedback," state Milgrom and Tadelis[25], and that is as it should be.

Li et al. analyzed data "from the period where the RFF mechanism was featured, and confirmed that first, as expected, more feedback was left in response to the incentives provided by the RFF feature."[143] Li et al. also discovered that "the additional feedback did not exhibit any biases, suggesting that the NLP algorithms used were able to create the kind of screening needed to select informative feedback."[143] Li et al. conclude that, "the predictions of the simple signaling story were borne out in the data, suggesting that using NLP to support a novel market for feedback did indeed solve both the free-rider problem and the cold-start problem that can hamper the growth of online marketplaces."[143]

Reducing Search Friction with A.I.

"An important application of AI and machine learning in online marketplaces is the way in which potential buyers engage with the site and proceed to search for products or services," Milgrom and Tadelis note.[25] At Google, Facebook, and Amazon AI-powered search engines are trained to maximize what the provider believes to be the right objective.[25] "Often this boils down to conversion, under the belief that the sooner a consumer converts a search to a purchase, the happier the consumer is both in the short and the long run," say Milgrom and Tadelis.[25] The rationale: "search itself is a friction, and hence, maximizing the successful conversion of search activity to a purchase reduces this friction."[25]

Although this is consistent with economic theory, which posits "search as an inevitable costly process that separates consumers from the products they want"[25] this isn't really the case. "Unlike the simplistic models of search employed in economic theory, where consumers know what they are looking for and the activity of search is just a costly friction, in reality, people's search behavior is rich and varied," claim Milgrom and Tadelis.[25]

In their paper *Returns to Consumer Search: Evidence from eBay*[145], Blake, Nosko, and Tadelis use "comprehensive data from eBay to shed light on the search process with minimal modeling assumptions." Blake et al.'s data showed that consumers search significantly more than in previous studies, which were conducted with limited access to search behavior over time.[145]

"Furthermore, search often proceeds from the vague to the specific. For example, early in a search a user may use the query 'watch', then refine it to 'men's watch' and later add further qualifying words such as color, shape, strap type, and more," explain Blake et al.[145] This behavior suggests that consumers aren't looking specifically at first and are exploring their own tastes, and what product characteristics might exist, as part of their search process.[145] Blake et al. showed that the average number of terms in a user's query "rises over time, and the propensity to use the default ranking algorithm declines over time as users move to more focused searches like price sorting."[145]

"These observations suggest that marketplaces and retailers alike could design their online search algorithms to understand search intent so as to better serve their consumers," recommend Milgrom and Tadelis.[25] Consumers in the exploratory phases of the search process, should be provided some general offerings to better learn their tastes as well as all available options in the market.[25] Once the consumer shows the desire to purchase something in particular, the offering should be narrowed to a set of products that match the consumer's preferences.[25] "Hence, machine learning and AI can play an instrumental role in recognizing customer intent," contend Milgrom and Tadelis.[25]

Milgrom and Tadelis explain that, AI and machine learning not only helps "predict a customer's intent, but given the large heterogeneity on consumer tastes, AI can help a marketplace or retailer better segment the many customers into groups that can be better served with tailored information."[25] Using AI for more refined customer segmentation, or even personalized experiences, does raise price discrimination concerns.[25] "For example, in 2012 the Wall Street Journal reported[146] that 'Orbitz Worldwide Inc. has found that people who use... Mac computers spend as much as 30% more a night on hotels, so the online travel agency is starting to show them different, and sometimes costlier, travel options than Windows visitors see."[25]

Whether these practices of utilizing consumer data and AI to adjust pricing helps or harms consumers is up for discussion, but economic theory states that price discrimination can either increase or reduce consumer welfare.[25] "If on average Mac users prefer staying at fancier and more expensive hotels because owning a Mac is correlated with higher income and tastes for luxury, then Orbitz practice is beneficial because it shows people what they want to see and reduces search frictions. However, if this is just a way to extract more surplus from consumers who are less price sensitive, but do not necessarily care for the snazzier hotel rooms, then it harms these consumers," contend Milgrom and Tadelis.[25] Either way, price elasticity systems can be set up if brands to choose to set them up.

Conclusion

So, does personalization really work? Businesses are spending billions of dollars in the belief that is does. Software vendors are similarly spending billions of dollars in their R&D efforts because they believe it is the future of CRM, social, and marketing systems. The VB Insights' *Marketing Personalization* survey of 506 marketers found that "between 70% and 94% have seen an increase in the effectiveness of various key metrics by employing personalization. The specific percent increase depends on individual metric, and this excludes those who say it's 'too early to tell,' but the numbers are impressive nonetheless."[69] Figure 15 shows these impressive numbers when looking at several different customer channels.

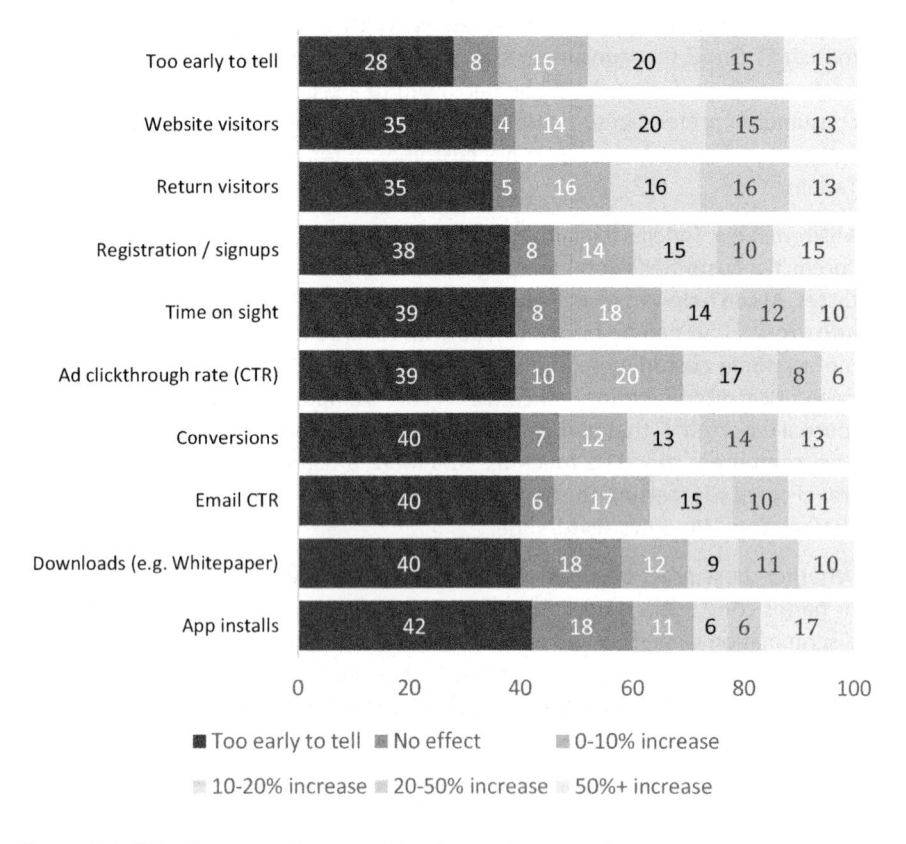

What benefits are you seeing, or do you expect to see, as a result of using AI technologies in your organization?

Metric	Too early to tell	No effect	0-10% increase	10-20% increase	20-50% increase	50%+ increase
Too early to tell	28	8	16	20	15	15
Website visitors	35	4	14	20	15	13
Return visitors	35	5	16	16	16	13
Registration / signups	38	8	14	15	10	15
Time on sight	39	8	18	14	12	10
Ad clickthrough rate (CTR)	39	10	20	17	8	6
Conversions	40	7	12	13	14	13
Email CTR	40	6	17	15	10	11
Downloads (e.g. Whitepaper)	40	18	12	9	11	10
App installs	42	18	11	6	6	17

Figure 15: Effectiveness of personalization on key metrics
Source: VB Insights[69]

As per VB Insights, several case studies highlight some impressive effects of personalization applied in various ways and channels, including[69]:

- Microsoft dropped bounce rates by 35% and increased add-to-cart rate by 10%.
- O'Neill increased conversions by 46% with web personalization.
- Alex and Ani, a jewelry company, has seen a 73% lift in monthly email revenue.
- Gamestop saw a 41% increase in average order value (AOV).

Analyzing clickstream data, customer card data, marketing data, as well as social media data can help brands develop three dimensional profiles on each of their customers and, once these profiles are achieved, the behavioral marketing work can begin to ensure that the brand is bringing in customers that will produce the highest ROI. Matching customer needs with the brand's staffing and operational requirements then becomes an added cost reduction perk.

---

59 Kim, K. L. (2012). The typological classification of the participants' subjectivity to plan the policy and strategy for the smart mobile market. Korean Management Review, 367-393.
60 Deighton, J. &. Kornfeld, Leora (2009). Interactivity's Unanticipated Consequences for Marketers and Marketing. Journal of Interactive Marketing, Volume 23, Issue 1, February 2009, Pages 4-10
61 Sharma, R. S. (2009). The Economics of Delivering. Journal of Media Business Studies, 1-24.
62 Vatash, Prateek. (2018). 2018 Digital Trends I Retail. Adobe. https://wwwimages2.adobe.com/content/dam/acom/uk/modal-offers/pdfs/Econsultancy-2018-Digital-Trends-Retail_EMEA.pdf (Accessed 6 August 2018).
63 Gartner. (2013, December 12). Gartner Says the Internet of Things Installed Base Will Grow to 26 Billion Units By 2020. Retrieved from Gartner.com: http://www.gartner.com/newsroom/id/2636073
64 Klein, Michael. Adobe. Machine Learning and AI: If Only My Computer Had a Brain Wired for Business. https://www.adobe.com/insights/personalization-with-machine-learning-and-ai.html (Accessed 7 April 2019).
65 Tractica. Artificial Intelligence Revenue to reach 36.8 Billion Worldwide by 2025. August 25, 2016. https://www.tractica.com/newsroom/press-releases/artificial-intelligence-revenue-to-reach-36-8-billion-worldwide-by-2025/ (Accessed 7 April 2019).
66 Goode, Lauren. (2019). 8 Things to Expect from CES, Consumer Tech's Big Shindig. Wired. January 4, 2019. https://www.wired.com/story/ces-2019-what-to-expect/ (Accessed 6 January 2019).
67 https://www.brightlocal.com/learn/voice-search-for-local-business-study/
68 https://www.youtube.com/watch?v=co3fdFNUaFA&feature=youtu.be&t=2m59s (Accessed 12 March 2019).

69 Jones, Andrew. (2015). VentureBeat. Marketing Personalization: Maximizing Relevance and Revenue. July 28, 2015. http://6ae7543f2267daab3ad5-4f1a402bff79f310bc7e3ee91a2ee421.r9.cf2.rackcdn.com/Marketing%20Personalization%20-%20VentureBeat%20Insight.pdf (Accessed 30 March 2017).

70 Eyefortravel Limited. (2017). https://www.eyefortravel.com/sites/default/files/data_in_travel_report_draft7.pdf (Accessed 30 March 2019).

71 Abramovich, Giselle. (2018). CMO.com. 3 AI-driven strategies for retailers in 2019. 11 November 2018. https://www.cmo.com/features/articles/2018/11/15/3-ai-driven-strategies-for-retailers-in-2019.html#gs.COMQdxdU (Accessed 23 February 2019).

72 Enterprise Content Team. Adobe. Incredible content, incredible experiences. https://www.adobe.com/insights/deliver-experience-with-content-intelligence.html (Accessed 8 January 2019).

73 Eissler, Annie. 25 April 2017. How Much ROI Can Data Analytics Deliver? MITS Blog. https://www.mits.com/blog/how-much-roi-can-data-analytics-deliver (Accessed 22 August 2017)

74 Adobe Experience Cloud. (2018). Creating the Ultimate Single Customer View. Adobe. 10 October 2018. https://theblog.adobe.com/creating-the-ultimate-single-customer-view-with-adobe-campaign/ (Accessed 16 January 2019)

75 Forrester Research. (2013, November). Delivering New Levels of Personalization In Consumer Engagement. Retrieved from sap.com: https://www.sap.com/bin/sapcom/he_il/downloadasset.2013-11-nov-21-22.delivering-new-levels-of-personalization-in-consumer-engagement-pdf.html

76 Adobe Experience Cloud. (2018) Adobe.com. Creating the Single Customer View with Adobe Campaign. https://theblog.adobe.com/creating-the-ultimate-single-customer-view-with-adobe-campaign/ (Accessed 12 January 2019).

77 Jones, Andrew (2015, December 15). Study finds marketers are prioritizing personalization...but are further behind than they realize, http://venturebeat.com/2015/12/14/study-finds-marketers-are-prioritizing-personalization-but-are-further-behind-than-they-realize/ (Accessed 26 November 2017).

78 Emarsys. 5 E-Commerce Marketing Predictions for the Next 5 Years. https://www.emarsys.com/en/resources/whitepapers/5-e-commerce-marketing-predictions-for-the-next-5-years/

79 Abramovich, Giselle. (2018). CMO. The 5 Biggest Marketing Trends for 2019. https://www.cmo.com/features/articles/2018/12/12/the-5-biggest-marketing-trends-for-2019.html#gs.GwcjmLKw (Accessed 11 January 2019).

80 CB Insights. (2019). What's Next in AI? Artificial Intelligence Trends. CB Insights. https://www.cbinsights.com/research/report/ai-trends-2019/ (Accessed 10 February 2019).

81 Adobe Retail Team. (2017). Adobe. Retailers: Adopt Artificial Intelligence Now for Personalized and Relevant Experiences. 22 June 2017.

https://theblog.adobe.com/machine-learning-predictive-analytics-drive-todays-retail-personalization/ (Accessed 11 January 2019).
82 CMO Staff. Executives Are Eyeing These 2019 Consumer Trends. January 7, 2019. https://www.cmo.com/features/articles/2018/11/30/predictions-consumer-trends-2019.html#gs.QpPk92IO (Accessed 23 January 2019).
83 Forrester. 2015. How Analytics Drives Customer Life-Cycle Management. SAS.com. https://www.sas.com/content/dam/SAS/en_us/doc/analystreport/forrester-analytics-drives-customer-life-cycle-management-108033.pdf (Accessed April 15, 2019).
84 Chew, Christie. (2018). The Art and Science Behind Every "Add to Cart." Adobe Blog. https://theblog.adobe.com/the-art-and-science-behind-every-add-to-cart/ (Accessed 19 January 2019).
85 Hauser, John R., Urban, Glen, Liberali, Guilherme, Braun Michael. (2009). "Website Morphing." Marketing Science 28.2 (2009): 202-223. © 2009 Informs. https://www.researchgate.net/publication/41822749_Website_Morphing (Accessed 16 February 2019).
86 Hayes, J., C. W. Allinson. 1998. Cognitive style and the theory and practice of individual and collective learning in organizations. Human Relations 31(7) 847–871.
87 Witkin, H. A., C. Moore, D. Goodenough, P. Cox. 1977. Field dependent and field-independent cognitive styles and their educational implications. Rev. Educational Res. 47(1) 1–64.
88 Riding, R. J., S. Rayner. 1998. Cognitive Styles and Learning Strategies Understanding Style Differences in Learning and Behavior. David Fulton Publishers, London.
89 Ansari, A., C. F. Mela. 2003. E-customization. J. Marketing Res. 40(2) 131–145
90 Montgomery, A. L., S. Li, K. Srinivasan, J. Liechty. 2004. Modeling online browsing and path analysis using clickstream data. Marketing Sci. 23(4) 579–585.
91 Riding, Richard J., Rayner, Stephen (1998), Cognitive Styles and Learning Strategies: Understanding Style Differences in Learning and Behavior, (London, UK: David Fulton Publishers).
92 Allinson, Christopher W. and Hayes, John. (1996), "The Cognitive Style Index: A Measure of Intuition-Analysis for Organizational Research," Journal of Management Studies, 33, 1, (January), 119-135.
93 Kirton, Michael J. (1987), Adaption-Innovation Inventory (KAI) Manual (Hatfield, UK: Occupational Research Centre).
94 Riding, Richard J., and Indra Cheema (1991), "Cognitive Style: An Overview and Integration", Educational Psychology, 11, 3&4, 193-215.
95 Kopfstein Donald (1973), "Risk-Taking Behavior and Cognitive Style." Child Development, 44, 1, 190-192.
96 Siegelman, Ellen (1969), "Reflective and Impulsive Observing Behavior" Child Development, 40, 4, 1213-222.
97 Khatchadourian, Raffi. (2015). The New Yorker. We Know How You Feel. January 19, 2015. https://www.newyorker.com/magazine/2015/01/19/know-feel. (Accessed 24 February 2019).

98 Ford, Martin. (2018). Architects of Intelligence. The truth about AI from the people building it. Packt Publishing; 1 edition. November 23, 2018.
99 Swift, R. (2001). Accelerating customer relationships: Using CRM and relationship technologies. Upper Saddle River: Prentice Hall.
100 Kincaid, J. (2003). Customer relationship management: Getting it right. Upper Saddle River, NJ: Prentice Hall.
101 Parvatiyar, A. &. Sheth, JN (2001). Customer relationship management: Emerging practice, process, and discipline. Journal of Economic & Social Research, 3, 1 - 34.
102 Ngai, N. X. (2009). Application of data mining techniques in customer relationship management: a literature review and classification. Expert systems with applications, 2592-2602.
103 Lovelock, C. a. (2010). Services Marketing, People, Technology, Strategy, Seventh Edition. Prentice Hall.
104 https://en.wikipedia.org/wiki/Social_CRM (Accessed 25 November 2017).
105 Greenberg, P. (2009, July 6). Time to Put a Stake in the Ground On Social CRM. Retrieved from ZDnet.com: http://www.zdnet.com/blog/crm/time-to-put-a-stake-in-the-ground-on-social-crm/829
106 IBM. Achieving Customer Loyalty with Customer Analytics. IBM Software. 2013. https://www.prostrategy.ie/wp-content/uploads/2015/09/Achieving-Customer-Loyalty-with-Customer-Analytics-IBM-White-Paper.pdf (Accessed 30 April 2019).
107 Wangenheim, F. v. (2005). Postswitching Negative Word of Mouth. Journal of Service Research, 8, No. 1, 67-78.
108 Rigby, Darrell. 2015. Management Tools 2015. An Executive's Guide. Bain & Company. http://www.bain.com/publications/articles/management-tools-customer-relationship-management.aspx (Accessed 25 November 2017).
109 https://en.wikipedia.org/wiki/Market_segmentation (Accessed 25 November 2017).
110 Britt, P. (2013) Big Data Means Big Benefits for Entertainment: Caesars Exec, http://loyalty360.org/resources/article/big-data-means-big-benefits-for-entertainment-caesers-exec, accessed 5 January 2016.
111 Marr, Bernard. May 2, 2016. Big Data in Practice. John Wiley & Sons.
112 Urbanski, A. (2013, February 1). At Caesars, Digital Marketing Is No Crap Shoot. Retrieved from DM News: http://www.dmnews.com/at-caesars-digital-marketing-is-no-crap-shoot/article/277685/ (Accessed 25 November 2017).
113 T_HQ Technology and Business. (2018). What does the CRM of the future look like? 17 July 2018. https://techhq.com/2018/07/what-does-the-crm-of-the-future-look-like/ (Accessed 8 August 2018.
114 Reichheld, F. a. (1990). Zero defections: quality comes to services. Harvard Business Review, 105-111.
115 White House Office of Consumer Affairs.
116 Nielsen Company. (2012). Global Trust in *Advertising and Brand Messaging.* Nielsen Company.

117 The Customer Satisfaction-Loyalty Relationship from Thomas O. Jones and W. Earl Sasser, Jr., "Why Satisfied Customers Defect" Harvard Business Review, Nov.–Dec. 1995, p. 91. Reprinted by permission of Harvard Business School.
118 Stodder, David. TDWI Research. Best practices report, customer analytics in the age of social media. Third quarter 2012. https://tdwi.org/research/2012/07/best-practices-report-q3-customer-analytics-in-the-age-of-social-media.aspx?tc=page0 (Accessed 30 April 2019).
119 Cognizant. (2014, January). Retail Analytics: Game Changer for Customer Loyalty. Retrieved from congnizant.com: http://www.cognizant.com/InsightsWhitepapers/Retail-Analytics-Game-Changer-for-Customer-Loyalty.pdf (Accessed 20 November 2017).
120 Peterson, T. (2014, August 13). Facebook Now Tells Whether Mobile Ads Lead to Desktop Purchases. Retrieved from AdAge: http://adage.com/article/digital/facebook-makes-link-mobile-ads-desktop-purchases/294568/ (Accessed 20 November 2017).
121 Cook, Rick. Control Group Marketing—With or Without CRM Software Systems. crmsearch http://www.crmsearch.com/marketing-control-groups.php (Accessed 19 November 2017).
122 Huguesrey.com. 15 Applications of Artificial Intelligence in Marketing. October 26, 2017. https://huguesrey.wordpress.com/2017/10/26/15-applications-of-artificial-intelligence-in-marketing-source-robert-allen/ (Accessed 18 March 2019).
123 Vicioso, Sara. Seer Interactive. Programmatic Advertising 101: How it Works. August 27, 2015. https://www.seerinteractive.com/blog/programmatic-advertising-101-works/ (Accessed 26 March 2019).
124 Shaw, Allie. (2017). VentureBeat. AI could save television advertising with advanced personalization. October 28, 2017. https://venturebeat.com/2017/10/28/ai-could-save-television-advertising-with-advanced-personalization/ (Accessed 15 April 2018).
125 Chirpify. (2017). Announcing Chirpify Moderation – Brands Can Now Moderate Social Rewards.
 https://www.chirpify.com/announcing-chirpify-moderation-brands-can-now-moderate-social-triggers/ (Accessed September 7, 2017).
126 Wedel, Michel and Kannan, P.K. (2016) Marketing Analytics for Data-Rich Environments. Journal of Marketing: November 2016, Vol. 80, No. 6, pp. 97-121. https://www.rhsmith.umd.edu/files/Documents/Departments/Marketing/wedel-kannan-jm-2016-final.pdf (Accessed 4 November 2017).
127 https://en.wikipedia.org/wiki/Proximity_marketing (Accessed 25 November 2017)
128 Xu, H. T. (2003). "Foundations of SMS Commerce Success: Lessons from SMS Messaging and Co-opetition." *Proceedings of 36th Hawaii International Conference on System Sciences* (pp. 90-99). Los Angeles: IEEE Computing Society Press.
129 https://en.wikipedia.org/wiki/IBeacon (Accessed 25 November 2017).
130 Hill, K. (2013, December 10). Your iPhone Is Now a Homing Beacon (But It's Ridiculously East to Turn Off). Retrieved from forbes.com: http://forbes.com/sites/kashmirhill/2013/12/10/your-iphone-is-now-a-homing-beacon

131 Neil, Shane Paul. June 17, 2016. Is iBeacon Marketing Finally Taking Off? The Huffington Post. http://www.huffingtonpost.com/shane-paul-neil/is-ibeacon-marketing-fina_b_10508218.html (Accessed 25 November 2017).

132 McFarland, Matt. How iBeacons could change the world forever. January 7, 2016. Washington Post. https://www.washingtonpost.com/news/innovations/wp/2014/01/07/how-ibeacons-could-change-the-world-forever/?utm_term=.182e91de201b (Accessed 25 November 2017).

133 Berman, S. J., Battino Bill, Feldman, Karen. 2007. Executive Brief: Navigating the media divide: Innovating and enabling new business models. IBM Institute for Business Value.

134 Weiners, C. (2012, March 30). *LBS Opportunities for Casino Marketers in Macau*. Retrieved from clickz.com. https://www.clickz.com/lbs-opportunities-for-casino-marketers-in-macau/38526/ (Accessed 23 October 2017).

135 Takahashi, D. (2013, May 22). Lighthouse's new Android location service could give you indoor navigation for Las Vegas' airlines. Retrieved from Venturebeat.com: http://venturebeat.com/2013/05/22/lighthouse-signal-systemss-android-app-will-let-you-find-your-way-inside-the-biggest-las-vegas-airlines/ (Accessed 25 November 2017).

136 Thompson, Cadie. May 28, 2015. Social media apps are tracking your location in shocking detail. Business Insider. http://www.businessinsider.com/three-ways-social-media-is-tracking-you-2015-5 (Accessed 25 November 2017).

137 Day, Matt, Turner, Giles, and Drozdiak, Natalia. (2019). Bloomberg. Amazon's Alexa team can access users' home addresses. April 24, 2019. https://www.bloomberg.com/news/articles/2019-04-24/amazon-s-alexa-reviewers-can-access-customers-home-addresses (Accessed 1 May 2019).

138 Huotari, Kai, and Hamari, Juho. (2012). Defining Gamification - A Service Marketing Perspective. Proceedings of the 16th International Academic MindTrek Conference 2012, Tampere, Finland, October 3–5. https://www.researchgate.net/profile/Juho_Hamari/publication/259841647_Defining_Gamification_-_A_Service_Marketing_Perspective/links/0c96052e13e865be0 http://www.gamification.co/2013/07/08/earn-your-wings-air-canadas-successful-gamification-venture-into-loyalty/ 0000000/Defining-Gamification-A-Service-Marketing-Perspective.pdf (Accessed 16 August 2018).

139 Carr, Aaron. Gamification of Loyalty—improving customer engagement. Airlineinformation.org. http://www.airlineinformation.org/opinion/loyalty-a-crm/785-gamification-of-loyalty-improving-customer-engagement.html

140 Mbuva, Moses. (2019). Casino.buzz. iSoftBet Rolls Out Pioneering Platform-wide 'In-Game' Gamification. April 3, 2019. https://casino.buzz/isoftbet-rolls-out-pioneering-platform-wide-in-game-gamification-5701/ (Accessed 3 April 2019).

141 Milgrom, P.R., North, D.C. and Weingast, B.R. (1990). The role of institutions in the revival of trade: The law merchant, private judges, and the Champagne fairs," Economics and Politics, 2(1):1-23.

142 Masterov, D. V., Mayer, U. F., and Tadelis, S. (2015) "Canary in the e-commerce coal mine: Detecting and predicting poor experiences using buyer-to-seller messages," In Proceedings of the Sixteenth ACM Conference on Economics and Computation, EC '15, pp81-93.

143 Li, L.I., Tadelis, S., and Zhou, X. (2016). Buying Reputation as a Signal of Quality: Evidence from an Online Marketplace. NBER Working Paper No. 22584.

144 Nelson, P. (1970). Information and Consumer Behavior. Journal of Political Economy, 78(2), 311-329. Retrieved from http://www.jstor.org/stable/1830691

145 Blake, Thomas, Nosko, Chris, and Tadelis, Steven. (2016), Returns to consumer search: Evidence from ebay. In Proceedings of the 2016 ACM Conference on Economics and Computation, pages 531–545. http://www.hbs.edu/faculty/conferences/2016-dids/Documents/Tadelis_BNT_search_EC_vST.pdf (Accessed 22 January 2019).

146 Mattolli, Dana. (2012). Wall Street Journal. On Orbitz, Mac users steered to higher pricier hotels. August 23, 2012. https://www.wsj.com/articles/SB10001424052702304458604577488822667325882 (Accessed 3 February 2019).

ANDREW W. PEARSON

CHAPTER THREE: A.I. + ANALYTICS

"In many ways AI is analytics."
~Oliver Schabenberger, SAS

Overview

Today, the analytics space is more crowded than it has ever been; besides the standard analytics providers now receiving strong competition from open source platforms, many new players in the Master Data Management (MDM) field have BI platforms that combine integration, preparation, analytics and visualization capabilities with governance and security features embedded within. Such standard analytics processes as column dependencies, clustering, decision trees, and recommendation engines are all included in many of the new Hadoop-backended and DI software packages.

Instead of forcing clients to frustratingly purchase module on top of module on top of module, new software companies are creating packages that contain many pre-built analytical functions. Open source products like R, Python, and the WEKA collection in Vantara (fka Pentaho) can easily be added to many of these software solutions as well, thereby reducing the need for expensive analytics layers.

The fact that many of these analytical packages are open source is a further advantage because, since they are free to download and use, a robust user base has been built up around them and these open source consultants are sometimes easier to find than analysts with highly developed SAS or SAP Predictive Analytics Library skills, for example. However, open source doesn't mean free and building something from scratch has its own cost of implementation, which can be quite high. There's always a tradeoff; the savings on yearly software maintenance costs can be eaten up in higher consulting fees to build and keep any open source platform operational.

In her article *How Much ROI Can Data Analytics Deliver?*, Annie Eissler states that, according to Nucleus Research, "analytics and business intelligence solutions deliver, on average, $13.01 for every dollar spent."[73] Eissler adds that, "We're at a point where the hype surrounding data analytics has converted into real, documented returns for companies of all sizes and across all industries. But the truth is, leading companies have been achieving double-digit return on investment (ROI) from their analytics investments for several years now."[73]

Nina Sandy, a Nucleus Research analyst, argues that, "Companies don't have the luxury anymore to wait weeks for reports on the profitability of business decisions in increasingly fast paced markets."[73] "New analytics solutions are being developed around this need where businesses can make better decisions, faster," adds Sandy.[73]

The fact that so many software vendors are adding analytics to their standard BI, data mining, DI, CRM, social media, marketing automation, and other offerings is reducing prices for analytics software across the board. When it comes to price, you obviously can't beat open source, i.e., free, but there is no free lunch in the software industry, and these open source tools do require skilled consultants to write the code and build the systems. This often means the sting of the yearly license/maintenance fees that come with commercial software is removed, but there are other costs involved that are substantial.

Eissler warns that, "You need the technology to enable analytics, but if you don't understand the technology that enables the analytics—or the business application—then it won't provide any value,"[73] which is about as accurate an assessment as possible; "junk in, junk out," as any good analyst will tell you. Eissler concludes that, "The real value comes when you take the technological component of analytics and apply it to a business component that—once optimized—produces a solid ROI that continues to pay off over time."[73] "Garbage in, garbage out" has a counterpoint, "Knowledge in, knowledge out."

One of the most important features of analytics is its ability to do test-and-learn strategies at scale. With the addition of real-time streaming technology, test-and-learn strategies provide instant attribution. A business can tweet something and see results in minutes. How does A.I. fit in here? Well, A.I. could be used to predict what type of marketing collateral goes out, what images should be used in that collateral, what offer should be included, what channel the offers should be sent on, as well as what time is the best time to ensure the opening of the offer. All of these factors are highly important when considering opening rates and A.I. can increase the likelihood of opening rates, which should increase offer use, which should increase ROI.

In the rest of this chapter, I will lay out the current analytical landscape and how AI fits within the four types of analytics—descriptive, diagnostic, predictive, and prescriptive—that are currently being utilized by business. I also discuss the real-world applications for AI on things like customer acquisition, customer churn, RFM models, etc., etc.

Data Mining

In his paper *The CRISP-DM model, the new blueprint for data mining*[147], C. Shearer introduces the concept of the "Cross-industry standard process for data mining", which is more commonly known by its acronym CRISP-DM. It is a "data mining process model that describes commonly used approaches that data mining experts use to tackle problems."[147] It is currently the de facto standard for developing data mining and data discovery projects.[147]

In their paper *Methods for mining HTS data*[148], Harper and Pickett break the CRISP-DM process of data mining into the following six major phases:

1. Business understanding—focuses on understanding the project objectives and requirements purely from a business perspective, and then "converting this knowledge into a data mining problem definition, and a preliminary plan designed to achieve the objectives."[148]
2. Data understanding—this starts with "initial data collection and proceeds with activities in order to get familiar with the data, to identify data quality problems, to discover first insights into the data, or to detect interesting subsets to form hypotheses for hidden information."[148]
3. Data preparation—this phase covers "all activities to construct the final dataset (data that will be fed into the modeling tool(s)) from the initial raw data. Data preparation tasks are likely to be performed multiple times, and not in any prescribed order. Tasks include table, record, and attribute selection as well as transformation and cleaning of data for modeling tools."[148]
4. Modeling—various modeling techniques are selected and applied in this phase, and their parameters are calibrated to optimal values.[148] "Typically, there are several techniques for the same data mining problem type. Some techniques have specific requirements on the form of data. Therefore, stepping back to the data preparation phase is often needed."[148]
5. Evaluation—At this project stage, model (or models) that appear to have high quality from a data analysis perspective should have been made.[148] "Before proceeding to final model deployment, it is imperative to more thoroughly evaluate the model, and review the steps executed to construct the model, to be certain it dovetails with the business objectives."[148] A key objective here is to determine if any important key business objectives have been left out.[148] At the end of this phase, a decision on whether to use the data mining results should be reached.[148]
6. Deployment—Creation of the model is generally not the end in and of itself.[148] "Even if the purpose of the model is to increase knowledge of the data, the knowledge gained will need to be organized and presented in a way that is useful to the customer."[148] "Depending on the requirements, the deployment phase can be as simple as generating a report or as complex as implementing a repeatable data scoring (e.g. segment allocation) or data mining process."[148] "In many cases it will be the customer, not the data analyst, who will carry out the deployment

steps. Even if the analyst deploys the model it is important for the customer to understand up front the actions which will need to be carried out in order to actually make use of the created models."[148]

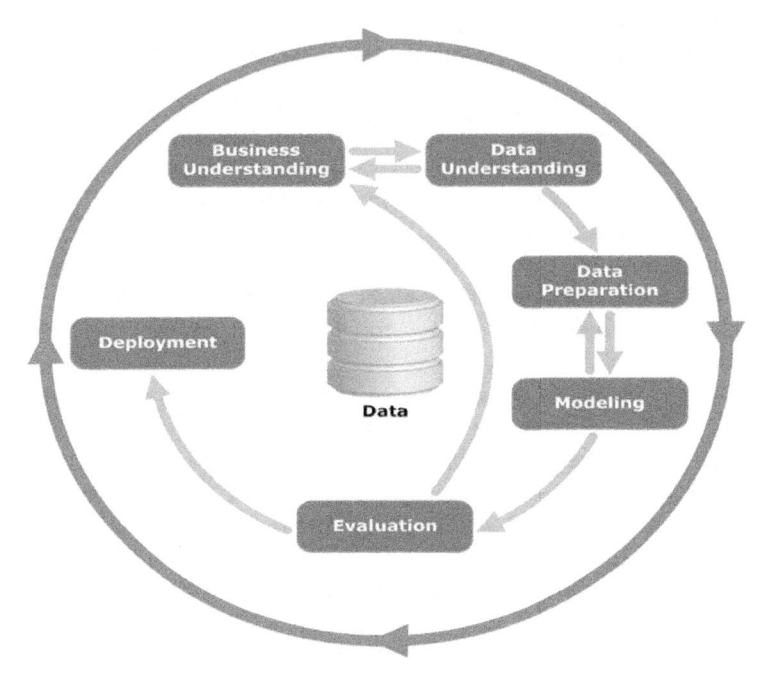

Figure 16: CRISP DM
Source: Wikipedia

The sequence of the phases (see Figure 16) is not strict and Harper and Pickett argue that moving back and forth between different phases is often required, so flexibility is important.[148] "The arrows in the process diagram indicate the most important and frequent dependencies between phases," contend Harper and Pickett.[148] "The outer circle in the diagram symbolizes the cyclic nature of data mining itself," add Harper and Pickett.[148] The data mining processes continues long after a solution has been deployed, argue Harpet and Pickett.[148] The "lessons learned during the process can trigger new, often more focused business questions and subsequent data mining processes will benefit from the experiences of previous ones," they conclude.[148]

In the SAS Institute Best Practices paper *Data Mining and the Case for Sampling*[149], SAS defines data mining "as the process used to reveal valuable information and complex relationships that exist in large amounts of data."[149] For SAS, data mining is an iterative process, divided into five stages that are represented by the acronym SEMMA.[149] "Beginning with a statistically representative sample of data, the SEMMA methodology—which stands for

Sample, Explore, Modify, Model, and Assess—makes it easy for business analysts to apply exploratory statistical and visualization techniques, select and transform the most significant predictive variables, model the variables to predict outcomes, and confirm a model's accuracy," argues SAS.[149] According to SAS, the SEMMA methodology is broken down into the following steps[149]:

- "Sample the data by creating one or more data tables. The samples should be big enough to contain the significant information, yet small enough to process quickly."[149]
- "Explore the data by searching for anticipated relationships, unanticipated trends, and anomalies in order to gain understanding and ideas."[149]
- "Modify the data by creating, selecting, and transforming the variables to focus the model selection process."[149]
- "Model the data by allowing the software to search automatically for a combination of data that reliably predicts a desired outcome."[149]
- "Assess the data by evaluating the usefulness and reliability of the findings from the data mining process."[149]

SEMMA is itself a cycle, with the internal steps being performed iteratively as needed.[149] SAS advises that projects following SEMMA "can sift through millions of records and reveal patterns that enable businesses to meet data mining objectives such as" [149]:

- Segmenting customers accurately into groups with similar buying patterns.
- Profiling customers for individual relationship management.
- Dramatically increasing response rate from direct mail campaigns.
- Identifying the most profitable customers and the underlying reasons.
- Understanding why customers leave for competitors (attrition, churn analysis).
- Uncovering factors affecting purchasing patterns, payments and response rates.
- Increasing profits by marketing to those most likely to purchase.
- Decreasing costs by filtering out those least likely to purchase.
- Detecting patterns to uncover non-compliance.

The data mining process is the foundation upon which any modeling-derived insight can be created and data governance, data cleansing, data indexing, and metadata creation are all important steps that create the basis for complex analytics procedures, which I will delve into next.

Customer Analytics

Analytics is, of course, a huge field. In this chapter, I will mostly focus on customer analytics, which, when coupled with insights from social media data, can enable organizations to make faster strides in predicting retention, attrition, and return rates, with the goal of reducing customer churn, raising customer lift, and/or increasing a whole host of other metrics.[150]

Sources such as transactional data, clickstream data, as well as service and call center records are highly important for customer analytics.[118] These can both improve how an organization decides on characteristics for customer segmentation and also provide clues to emerging characteristics for the definition of new segments.[118] As David Stodder explains in his article *Customer Analytics in the Age of Social Media*[118], "Firms can employ predictive modeling to test and learn from campaigns so that they are able to select the most persuasive offers to put in front of the right customers at the right time."[118]

As Webopedia.com explains, customer analytics "exploits behavioral data to identify unique segments in a customer base that the business can act upon. Information obtained through customer analytics is often used to segment markets, in direct marketing to customers, predicate analysis, or even to guide future product and services offered by the business."[118]

In the most basic sense, customer analytics is made possible by combining elements of business intelligence—software such as IBM's Cognos, SAP's Lumira and Business Object's suite, and Qlik's Qlik Sense, amongst a whole host of others—with predictive analytics solutions like SAP's and SAS's suite of analytical tools, as well as R, Python, WEKA, etc., etc. Open source ml products like TensorFlow, Keras, and Caffe 2 add another interesting analytics software options.

In IBM's *Achieving Customer Loyalty with Customer analytics*[106], IBM argues that customer analytics can uncover "patterns and trends in customer behavior and sentiment hidden among different types of customer data such as transactions, demographics, social media, survey and interactions." "The results of the analysis are then used to predict future outcomes so businesses can make smarter decisions and act more effectively."[106] Results from these models can then be presented back to the business users in easily digestible dashboards and scorecards.[106] "Self-learning predictive models ensure that each new iteration of customer analytics insight and the business decisions it drives become more accurate and effective," argues IBM.[106]

Customer analytics can also help determine which of a marketer's advertising campaign or advertising partner's pages have the highest landing rates, as well as show conversion rates for all of a retailing company's advertising and marketing budgets.

Mobile analytics can also display how many visitors downloaded material from a website, which can help in factoring a company's advertising and marketing budgets. And, finally, mobile analytics can display which pages have the highest exit rates. With this type of analysis, marketers can rapidly adjust marketing campaigns to exploit the most effective ones and, conversely, trim the least or non-performing ones.

The biggest problem with any analytics procedure is filtering out the noise associated with the data. Without clean data, "the trends, patterns, and other insights hidden in the raw data are lost through aggregation and filtering."[118]

Organizations need an unstructured place "to put all kinds of big data in its pure form, rather than in a more structured data warehousing environment."[118] This is because what might be considered just "noise" in the raw data from one perspective could be full of important "signals" from a more knowledgeable perspective.[118]

"Discovery, including what-if analysis, is an important part of customer analytics because users in marketing and other functions do not always know what they are looking for in the data and must try different types of analysis to produce the insight needed."[118] As per Stodder, among the most frequent targets for analysis are the following[118]:

- Understanding sentiment drivers.
- Identifying characteristics for better segmentation.
- Measuring the organization's share of voice and brand reputation as compared to a competitors.
- Determining the effectiveness of marketing touches and messages in buying behavior, i.e., attribution analysis.
- Using predictive analytics on social media to discover patterns and anticipate customers' problems with products and/or services.

TDWI's research about the general purpose of customer analytics technology and methods (see Figure 17) discovered that "the business functions or operations for which respondents considered customer analytics most important were marketing (81%, with 52% indicating "very important"), sales and sales reporting (79%, with 45% "very important"), and campaign management (74%, with 47% "very important").[118] Market research (43% "very important") and customer services and order management (also 43% "very important") were also high among business functions regarded as critical to developers and consumers of customer analytics.[118]

The marketing department, "which in most organizations is empowered with the responsibility for identifying, attracting, satisfying, and keeping customers, is clearly the main stage for customer analytics."[118] Marketing departments and functions are becoming increasingly qualitative.[118] "Gut feelings" are being replaced by data-driven decision-making.[118] "Data drives the pursuit of efficiency and achievement of measurable results. Marketing functions are key supporters of 'data science,' which is the use of scientific methods on data to develop hypotheses and models and apply iterative, test-and-learn strategies to marketing campaigns and related initiatives."[118]

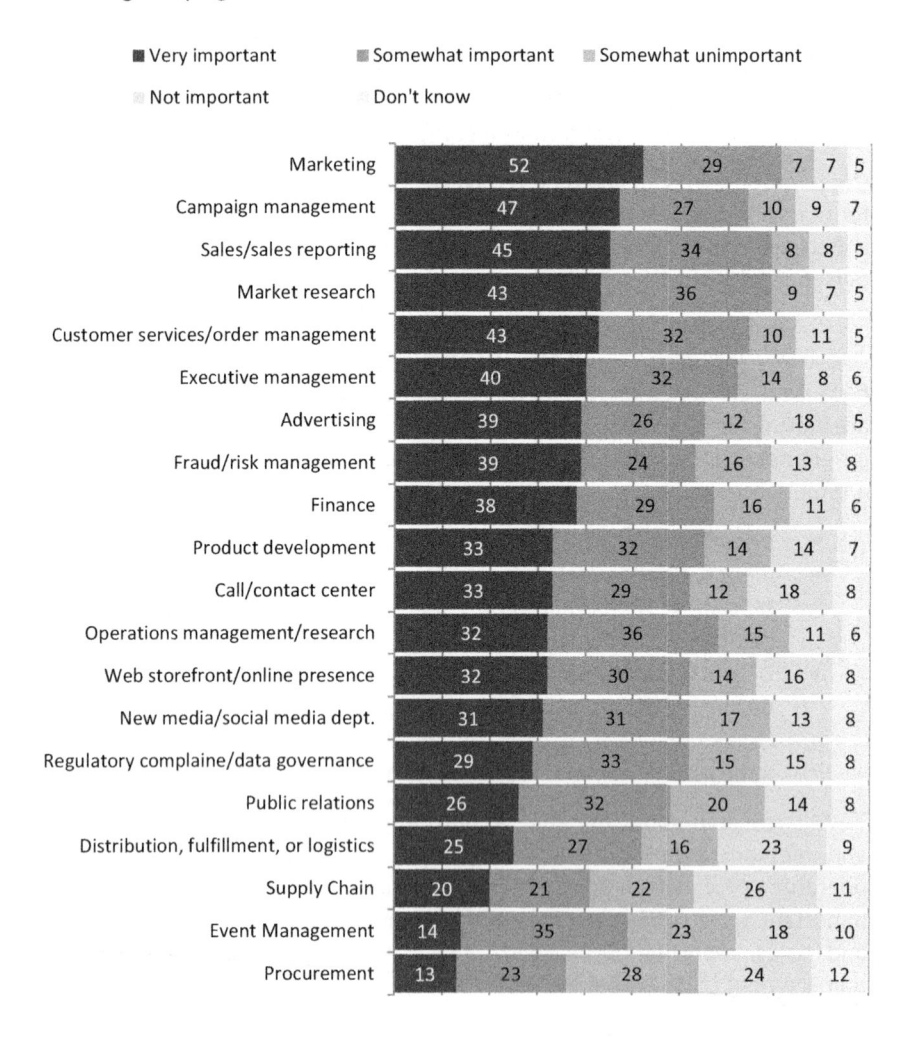

Business Function	Very important	Somewhat important	Somewhat unimportant	Not important	Don't know
Marketing	52	29	7	7	5
Campaign management	47	27	10	9	7
Sales/sales reporting	45	34	8	8	5
Market research	43	36	9	7	5
Customer services/order management	43	32	10	11	5
Executive management	40	32	14	8	6
Advertising	39	26	12	18	5
Fraud/risk management	39	24	16	13	8
Finance	38	29	16	11	6
Product development	33	32	14	14	7
Call/contact center	33	29	12	18	8
Operations management/research	32	36	15	11	6
Web storefront/online presence	32	30	14	16	8
New media/social media dept.	31	31	17	13	8
Regulatory complaine/data governance	29	33	15	15	8
Public relations	26	32	20	14	8
Distribution, fulfillment, or logistics	25	27	16	23	9
Supply Chain	20	21	22	26	11
Event Management	14	35	23	18	10
Procurement	13	23	28	24	12

Figure 17: Importance of Customer Analytics Technology
Based on one answer per business function from 452 responses.
Source: TDWI Research[118]

Customer analytics can be a very effective tool for micro-targeting customers with customized marketing offers and promotions.[106] Obviously, when an organization "attempts to cross-sell or up-sell a customer, a product or service they desire, it can enhance satisfaction."[106] However, unwanted marketing campaigns can do just the opposite, annoying customers, thereby eroding loyalty and, potentially, hurting sales.[106] Even worse, unwanted marketing campaigns can give customers the impression that the organization doesn't care about their wants, desires, needs and preferences."[106] Loyalty should be coveted above all else and customer analytics can help enormously with that.

Customer analytics can help determine which marketing interactions are likely to please individual customers and which will not."[106] Sales functions can be important beneficiaries of customer analytics as well. Stodder argues that, "Sales reports typically focus on providing visibility into the pipeline.[118] Managers can use data insights to improve sales forecasting of potential revenues based on deeper knowledge of priority opportunities, most valued customer segments, and more."[118]

Customer service and order management departments "can use customer analytics to get a more subtle and substantial view of what actions impact customer experiences and satisfaction," says Stodder.[118] Contact centers can utilize "customer analytics to help tune performance metrics closer to real time, so that each day's agents are guided, if not incentivized, to interact with customers in beneficial ways."[118]

"Customer service is still where today's brands are dropping the ball," Vogel believes, adding that "Only 35% of companies are able to identify their customers at the moment of contact (Selligent survey)—with customers potentially unfriending brands and taking their business elsewhere," warns Vogel.[36]

It may seem counter-intuitive, Vogel says, "but automated bots can create lifelike, seamless customer service experiences, addressing the consumer on their purchase history and known preferences."[36] One of the standouts, Vogel notes is Facebook's "M" technology, which is embedded in the Messenger app.[36] "The AI delivers personalized product, travel and restaurant recommendations, while troubleshooting technical problems," Vogel explains.[36]

Although chatbots are cheaper than handling customer service inquiries over the phone, there is a catch as chatbots can only deliver highly personalized and contextual assistance if they have access to universal consumer profiles that are populated by real-time data.[36] This means, done correctly, developing chatbots is an expensive upfront investment, it is an investment that should be done company-wide, not siloed by just the marketing or customer service department as information that chatbots tap into are useful throughout the organization.

Analytics can also "help service and order management functions move away from one-size-fits-all approaches to customers and instead tune and tailor interactions more personally based on knowledge of particular types or segments, such as regions or nationalities."[118] "Finally, through integrated views of customer data and analytics, service and order management functions are able to work in better synchronicity with the organization's marketing, sales, and other business functions," says Stodder.[118] Customer analytics can also be used to understand where marketing campaigns are working. This is something I will go into further detail later in the book.

With the steep drop in RAM prices, in-memory solutions are all the rage these days and they allow analytics to reach a whole new level of speed and effectiveness. Today, creativity is becoming the differentiator; today's overriding philosophy might be "Those who analyze best: win."

With products and services being commoditized at such a rapid rate today, customer loyalty has become more elusive than ever before.[118] "Innovation must be constant and must immediately address why an organization is losing customers. Insights from analytics can help an organization align product and service development with strategic business objectives for customer loyalty."[118] In addition, these insights can help organizations be selective in how they deploy marketing campaigns and customer-touch processes so that they emphasize features in new products and services that are important to customers.

When TDWI Research examined the business benefits sought from customer analytics (see Figure 18), respondents cited giving executive management customer and market insight as the most important (71%)[118] The second highest benefit was being able to react more quickly to changing market conditions (62%)[118]

Improving customer satisfaction and gaining a complete picture of a customer's activity across business channels—two areas that would be considered a part of the "Customer Experience Management" (CEM) process—are critical to identifying what steps an organization must take to build and retain customer loyalty[118] The remaining items fall mainly into the categories of business intelligence, marketing, and brand management and they are extremely important to most organizations as well.

Organizations are becoming open to customer analytics because they are all interested in discovering how a marketing department can be more effective, not just more efficient.[118] "Whereas other types of applications for e-commerce, fulfillment, or marketing automation help organizations determine how to get things done (e.g., getting goods delivered at the right time, executing a marketing campaign), customer analytics helps organizations answer who, what, when, where, and why questions," argues Scott Groenendal, program director of customer analytics market strategy for IBM Business Analytics[118] "They can find answers to questions such as: What channel should I communicate through? When is the best time to target this person, and why would they be receptive to this message?" adds Groenendal.[118]

What are the most important business benefits that your organzation seeks to achieve from implementing customer analytics technologies and methods? (Please select all that apply)

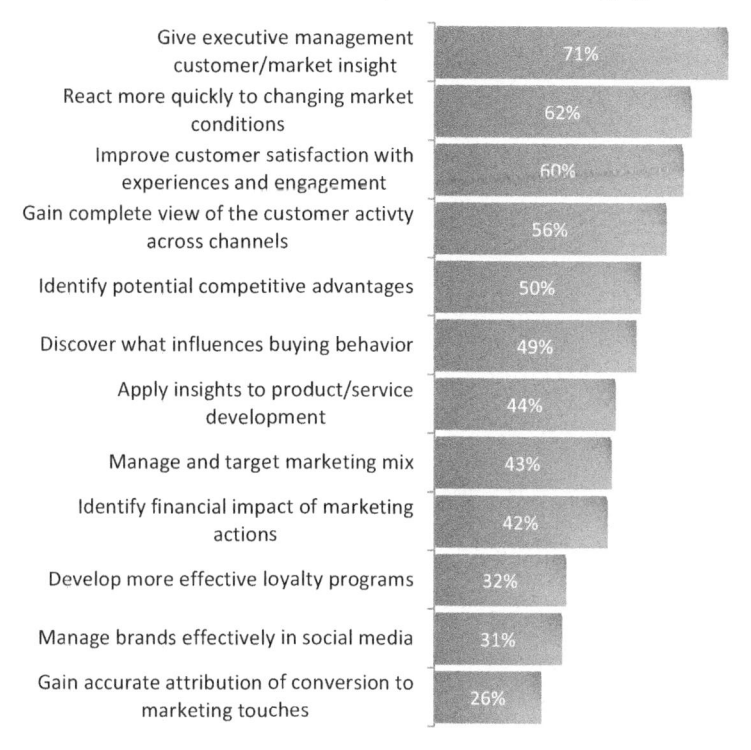

Benefit	%
Give executive management customer/market insight	71%
React more quickly to changing market conditions	62%
Improve customer satisfaction with experiences and engagement	60%
Gain complete view of the customer activty across channels	56%
Identify potential competitive advantages	50%
Discover what influences buying behavior	49%
Apply insights to product/service development	44%
Manage and target marketing mix	43%
Identify financial impact of marketing actions	42%
Develop more effective loyalty programs	32%
Manage brands effectively in social media	31%
Gain accurate attribution of conversion to marketing touches	26%

Figure 18: What Are the Important Business Benefits of Customer Analytics?
Based on 2,573 responses from 454 respondents; almost six responses, on average.
Source: TDWI Research[118]

Individual creativity, personal experiences, customer behavior and marketing context are critical components of consumer marketing decisions.[118] "The role of customer analytics is not necessarily to replace these, but to help decision makers come to fact-based conclusions through better knowledge of the organization's customers and markets."[118] Just as importantly, analytics equals scalability.[118] "Just as automation is necessary to run hundreds or thousands of marketing campaigns, customer analytics processes are important for supplying intelligence and guidance to those automated routines. Customer analytics can provide the brains to match the marketing systems' brawn."[118]

Types of Analytics

As previously mentioned, there are four different types of analytics and they are:

- Descriptive analytics – What happened?
- Diagnostic analytics – Why did it happen?
- Predictive analytics – What will happen?
- Prescriptive analytics – How can we make it happen again?

ANALYTIC VALUE ESCALATOR

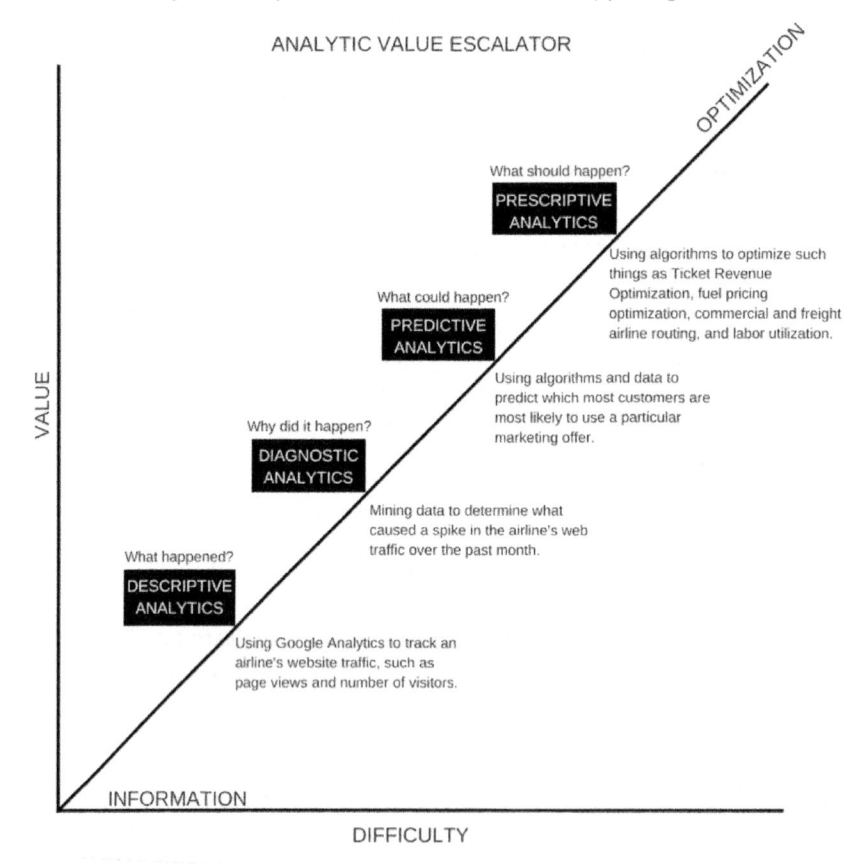

Figure 19: Analytics Value Escalator
Source: www.intelligencia.co

Figure 19 contains examples of how each of these types of analytics can be utilized by a brand. For a marketer, descriptive analytics could include pattern discovery methods such as customer segmentation, i.e., culling through a customer database to understand a customer's preferred purchasing behavior. Simple cluster segmentation models could divide customers into their preferred choice of purchases.

Market basket analysis, which utilizes association rules, would also be considered a descriptive analytics procedure. Brands should use market basket analysis to bundle and offer promotions, as well as gain insight into its customers' buying habits. Detailed customer shopping and purchasing behavior could also be used to develop future products.

Diagnostic analytics is a form of advanced analytics that examines data or content to answer the question, "Why did it happen?" It attempts to understand causation and behaviors by utilizing such techniques as drill-down, data discovery, data mining and correlations. Building a decision tree atop a web user's clickstream behavior pattern could be considered a form of diagnostic analytics as these patterns might reveal why a person clicked his or her way through a website.

In his seminal article *Predictive Analytics White Paper*[151], Charles Nyce states that, "Predictive analytics is a broad term describing a variety of statistical and analytical techniques used to develop models that predict future events or behaviors. The form of these predictive models varies, depending on the behavior or event that they are predicting. Most predictive models generate a score (a customer rating, for example), with a higher score indicating a higher likelihood of the given behavior or event occurring."

Data mining, which is used to identify trends, patterns, and/or relationships within a data set, can then be used to develop a predictive model.[151] Prediction of future events is the key here and these analyses can be used in a multitude of ways, including forecasting customer behavior that could lead to a competitive advantage over rivals. Gut instinct can sometimes punch you in the gut and predictive analytics can help factor in variables that are inaccessible to the human mind and often the number of variables in an analytical problem are beyond human mental comprehension.

Predictive analytics (or supervised learning) is the use of statistics, machine learning, data mining, and modeling to analyze current and historical facts to make predictions about future events. Said another way, it gives mere mortals the ability to predict the future like Nostradamus. In recent years, data-mining has become one of the most valuable tools for extracting and manipulating data and for establishing patterns to produce useful information for decision-making.

Whether you love it or hate it, predictive analytics has already helped elect presidents, discover new energy sources, score consumer credit, assess health risks, detect fraud, and target prospective buyers. It is here to stay, and technology advances ranging from faster hardware to software that analyzes increasingly vast quantities of data are making the use of predictive analytics more creative and efficient than ever before.

Specifically, predictive analytics is an area of data mining that deals with extracting information from data and using it to predict trends and behavioral patterns. Often the unknown event of interest is in the future, but predictive analytics can be applied to any type of unknown, whether that is in the past, the present, or the future.

Predictive analytics uses many techniques from data mining to analyze current data to make predictions about the future, including statistics, modeling, machine learning, and artificial intelligence. For example, logistic regression can be used to turn a market basket analysis into a predictor so that a marketer can understand what items are usually purchased together.

Brands can use predictive analytics for CRM, collection analysis, cross-sell, customer retention, direct marketing, fraud detection, product prediction, project risk management, amongst many other things.

Predictive analytics utilizes the following techniques:

- Regression
- Linear regression
- Discrete choice models
- Logistic regression
- Multinomial logistic regression
- Probit regression
- Time series models
- Survival or duration analysis
- Classification and regression trees
- Multivariate adaptive regression splines
- Machine learning
- Neural networks
- Naïve Bayes
- *k*-Nearest neighbors.

Prescriptive analytics tries to optimize a key metric, such as profit, by not only anticipating what will happen, but also when it will happen and why it happens. Wikipedia states that, "Prescriptive analytics suggests decision options on how to take advantage of a future opportunity or mitigate a future risk and shows the implication of each decision option. Prescriptive analytics can continually take in new data to re-predict and re-prescribe, thus automatically improving prediction accuracy and prescribing better decision options."[152]

Prescriptive analytics can ingest a mixture of structured, unstructured, and semi-structured data, and utilize business rules that can predict what lies ahead, as well as advise how to exploit this predicted future without compromising other priorities. Stream processing can add an entirely new component to prescriptive analytics as well.

The analytics powerhouse SAS is finding its vaunted place atop the analytics pyramid challenged not just by their typical acronymed competitors—SAP, IBM,

EMC, HDS, and the like—but also by the simpler visualization toolmakers like Tableau, Qlik, and Alteryx. These vendors are muscling their way into the mix, with offers that include data blending and in-memory technology that allows business users to access complete datasets at the touch of a button. These solutions offer less complex analytical capabilities, but such things as market basket analysis or simple decision tree networks can be created with them and the costs associated with them can be one quarter or one fifth of what the top echelon providers charge.

In their article *Knowing What to Sell, When, and to Whom*[153], authors V. Kumar, R. Venkatesan, and W. Reinartz showed how, by simply understanding and tweaking behavioral patterns, they could increase the hit rate for offers and promotions to consumers, which then had an immediate impact on revenue.

By applying statistical models based on the work of Nobel prize-winning economist Daniel McFadden, researchers accurately predicted not only a specific buyer's purchasing habits, but also the specific time of the purchase to an accuracy of 80%.[153] In the world of instant and real-time communication, capturing a person's intent to purchase can be a powerful weapon in making a sale. An offer pushed out at just the right moment, i.e., the moment of heightened interest, could be the all-important act that pushes a buyer into making a purchase.

Obviously, the potential to market to an individual when he or she is primed to accept the advertising is advantageous for both parties involved. By utilizing data from past campaigns and measures generated by a predictive modeling process, brands can track actual campaign responses versus expected campaign responses, which can often prove to be wildly divergent. Additionally, businesses can generate upper and lower control limits that can be used to automatically alert campaign managers when a campaign is under or overperforming, letting them focus on campaigns that specifically require attention.

One of the benefits of automating campaigns is that offers based on either stated or inferred preferences of customers can be developed. Analysis can identify which customers may be more responsive to an offer. The result: more individualized offers are sent out to customers and, because these offers tap into a customer's wants, desires, needs *and* expectations, they are more likely to be used; more offers used means more successful campaigns, which means more money coming into the company's coffers.

With predictive analytics, businesses can even predict which low-tier and mid-tier customers are likely to become the next big spenders. In so doing, the company can afford to be more generous in its offers as it will know that there is a high likelihood that these customers will appreciate the personalized attention and therefore become long term—and, hopefully, highly profitable—customers.

A campaign management solution can enable the brand to develop and manage personalised customer communications strategies and the delivery of offers. It will also allow users to rapidly create, modify and manage multi-channel, multi-wave marketing campaigns that integrate easily with any fulfilment channel, automatically producing outbound (contact) and inbound (response) communication history.

Users can define target segments, prioritise selection rules, prioritise offers across multiple campaigns and channels, select communication channels, schedule and execute campaigns, and perform advanced analyses to predict and evaluate the success of customer communications.

With customer attitudes towards personalized content being shaped by recommendation engines like Amazon, Pandora, and Netflix, consumers are becoming more used to receiving what they want, when they want it, and on whatever channel they prefer it on. Businesses must keep this in mind when developing personalization programs.

The customer journey starts a long time before the customer even enters a retailer's website or physical store, or a property's hotel room, or a casino's gaming floor. It begins the moment a potential customer browses an ecommerce webpage or notices an advertisement for an outfit on television, or a casino's mailed free play offer, or a hotel room 20% offer on the internet. It can even be while browsing a company's website or connecting with its social media accounts.

With a few browser click strokes, a marketer's ecommerce department can create a click path analysis that reveals customer interactions on the company's website. Descriptive analytical functionalities can then provide a deeper understanding of the customer journey. Column dependencies (standard in most of today's DI software tools) can visually display the strength of a relationship between attributes within any dataset. This helps a company's marketing department better understand the characteristics of their data, which can be used to help target further analysis.

A recommendation engine can help predict a person's interest based on historical data from many other users. This is useful in increasing customer engagement, recommending more relevant choices and increasing customer satisfaction.

Predictive modeling is only useful if it is deployed *and* it creates an action. Taking advantage of the more powerful, statistically based segmentation methods, customers can be segmented not only by dollar values, but also on all known information, which can include behavioral information gleaned from shopping activities, as well as the customer's simple demographic information.

This more detailed segmentation allows for more targeted and customer-focused marketing campaigns. Models can be evaluated and reports generated on multiple statistical measures, such as neural networks, decision trees, genetic algorithms, the nearest neighbor method, rule induction, and lift and gains charts. Once built, scores can be generated in a variety of ways to facilitate quick and easy implementation. The projects themselves can be re-used and shared to facilitate faster model development and knowledge transfer.

In his paper *Predictive Analytics*[154], Wayne Eckerson advises creating predictive models by using the following six steps:

1. Define the business objectives and desired outcomes for the project and then translate them into predictive analytic objectives and tasks.
2. Explore and analyze the source data to determine the most appropriate data and model building approach and then scope the effort.
3. Prepare the data by selecting, extracting, and transforming the data, which will be the basis for the models.
4. Build the models, as well as test and validate them.
5. Deploy the models by applying them to the business decisions and processes.
6. Manage and update the models accordingly.

Throughout the rest of this chapter, I will break down many of the different types of analytical models that can be used to strengthen a brand's customer experience.

Analytical Models

Decision Trees

According to Wikipedia, a decision tree is "a decision support tool that uses a tree-like graph or model of decisions and their possible consequences, including chance event outcomes, resource costs, and utility. It is one way to display an algorithm."[155]

Decision trees are used to identify the strategy that is most likely to reach a goal. It is a decision support tool that uses a graph or model of decisions and their possible consequences, including chance event outcomes, resource costs, and utility.[155] Decision trees are sequential partitions of a set of data that maximize the differences of a dependent variable (response or output variable). They offer a concise way of defining groups that are consistent in their attributes, but which vary in terms of the dependent variable.[155]

A decision tree consists of three types of nodes:
1. Decision nodes—represented by squares.
2. Chance nodes—represented by circles.
3. End nodes—represented by triangles.

The construction of a decision tree is based on the principle of "divide and conquer": through a supervised learning algorithm, successive divisions of the multivariable space are carried out in order to maximize the distance between groups in each division (that is, carry out partitions that discriminate).[155] The division process finalizes when all of the entries of a branch have the same value in the output variable, giving rise to the complete model.[155] The further down the input variables are in the tree, the less important they are in the output classification (and the less generalization they allow, due to the decrease in the number of inputs in the descending branches).[155]

For a brand, decision trees can be utilized in operations management and marketing, where they can predict whether a person will respond to an offer or not, or whether they are likely to abuse an offer.

According to Deng et al., in their paper *Building a Big Data Analytics Service Framework for Mobile Advertising and Marketing*[156], the decision tree algorithm is:

> "Used to classify the attributes and decide the outcome of the class attribute. In order to construct a decision tree both class attribute and item attributes are required. Decision tree is a tree like structure where the intermediate nodes represent attributes of the data, leaf nodes represents the outcome of the data and the branches hold the attribute value. Decision trees are widely used in the classification process because no domain knowledge is needed to construct the decision tree."

Advantages	Disadvantages
• Simple and robust • Useful to predict the outcomes of future data • Little cleansing is enough to remove the missing values data • Useful for large data sets • Decision trees can handle both categorical and numerical data	• Possibility of creating complex decision trees for simple data • Replication problem makes the decision trees complex. So remove the replicated data before constructing a decision tree • Pruning is required to avoid complex decision trees • It is hard to find out the correct root node

Table 4: Advantages and disadvantages of decision trees
Source: ResearchGate[156]

The main step in the decision tree algorithm is to identify the root node for any given set of data.[156] "Multiple methods exist to decide the root node of the decision tree. Information gain and Gini impurity are the primary methods used to identify the root node. Root node plays an important role in deciding which side of the decision tree the data falls into. Like every classification method, decision trees are also constructed using the training data and tested with the test data."[156]

k-Means Cluster

As its name suggests, the *k*-Means cluster is a clustering algorithm and it is one of the most common analytical models because of its simplicity and ease of use. The fact that it is still going strong after over 50 years of use speaks as much to its ease-of-use as it does to the difficulty of designing a general-purpose clustering algorithm.

According to Telgarsky and Vattani, "The goal of cluster analysis is to partition a given set of items into clusters such that similar items are assigned to the same cluster whereas dissimilar ones are not. Perhaps the most popular clustering formulation is *K*-means, in which the goal is to maximize the expected similarity between data items and their associated cluster centroids."[157]

In their paper *A K-Means Clustering Algorithm*[158], Hartigan and Wong explain that the:

> "aim of the k-means algorithm is to divide M points in N dimensions into k clusters so that the within-cluster sum of squares is minimized. It is not practical to require that the solution has minimal sum of squares against all partitions, except when M, N are small and k = 2. We seek instead 'local' optima, solutions that no movement of a point from one cluster to another will reduce the within-cluster sum of squares."

K-Means Clustering identifies and classifies items into groups based on their similarity. *K* is the number of clusters that needs to be decided upon before the clustering process begins.[156] "The whole solution depends on the *K* value. So, it is very important to choose a correct *K* value. The data point is grouped in to a cluster based on the Euclidean distance between the point and the centroid of the cluster," explains Deng et al.[156]

For Deng et al., initial clustering can be done in one of three ways[156]:

1. Dynamically Chosen: In this method, the first K items are chosen and then assigned to K clusters.
2. Randomly Chosen: In this method, the values are randomly selected and then assigned to K clusters.
3. Choosing from Upper and Lower Boundaries: In this method, the values that are very distant from each other are chosen and they are used as initial values for each cluster.[156]

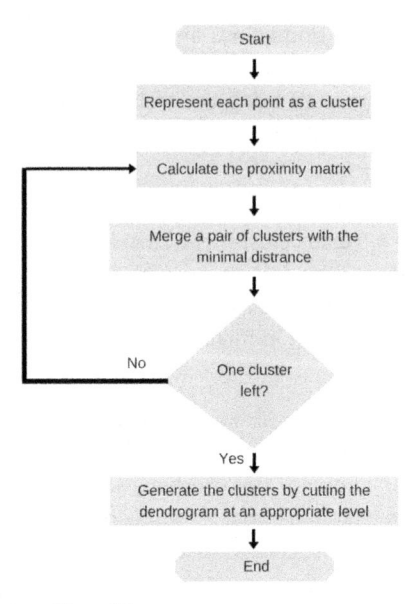

```
                    Start
                      ↓
         Represent each point as a cluster
                      ↓
         Calculate the proximity matrix  ←────┐
                      ↓                        │
         Merge a pair of clusters with the     │
              minimal distance                 │
                      ↓                        │
              ◇ One cluster ─── No ────────────┘
                  left?
                      │
                    Yes ↓
         Generate the clusters by cutting the
         dendrogram at an appropriate level
                      ↓
                    End
```

Figure 20: Clustering Algorithm
Source: Researchgate[156]

According to Deng at al., the *K*-Means methodology is as follows[156]:

- Step 1: Choose the initial values using one of the above three methods
- Step 2: For each additional value:
- Step 3: Calculate the Euclidean distance between this point and centroid of the clusters.
- Step 4: Move the value to the nearest cluster.
- Step 5: Calculate the new centroid for the cluster.
- Step 6: Repeat steps 3 to 5.
- Step 7: Calculate centroid of the cluster.
- Step 8: For each value:
- Step 9: Calculate the Euclidean distance between this value and the centroid of all the clusters.
- Step 10: Move the value to the nearest cluster.

Advantages	Disadvantages
<ul><li>Faster computations than hierarchical clustering</li><li>It produces tighter clusters than other clustering techniques</li><li>Gives best result when data sets are distinct</li></ul>	<ul><li>Sensitive to noise</li><li>Numbers of clusters must be decided before starting clustering</li><li>Choosing correct initial clustering process</li><li>Choosing correct number of clusters</li></ul>

Advantages	Disadvantages
• Easy to understand	• The centroid of the group changes because we calculate centroid every time a new item joins the cluster • Large data sets needed to cluster the data correctly

Table 5: Advantages and disadvantages of K-means clustering
Source: Researchgate[156]

k-Nearest Neighbors

First described in the early 1950s, the *k*-nearest neighbors method is a classification (or regression) algorithm that, in order to determine the classification of a point, combines the classification of the K nearest points. It is supervised because one is trying to classify a point based on the known classification of other points. It is labor intensive when given large training sets, and it did not gain popularity until the computer revolution in the 1960s brought processing powers that were able to handle such large data sets.[156] Today, it is widely used in the area of pattern recognition.[156]

As Deng et al. explain[156]:

> "Nearest-neighbor classifiers are based on learning by analogy, that is, by comparing a given test tuple with training tuples that are similar to it. The training tuples are described by n attributes. Each tuple represents a point in an n-dimensional space. In this way, all of the training tuples are stored in an n-dimensional pattern space. When given an unknown tuple, a k-nearest-neighbor classifier searches the pattern space for the k training tuples that are closest to the unknown tuple. These k training tuples are the k 'nearest neighbors' of the unknown tuple. When the 'k' closest points are obtained, the unknown sample is then assigned to the most common class among those k-points. In case of k=1, the unknown sample is assigned to the closest point in the pattern space. The closeness is measured using the distance between the two points."

the *k*-means clustering and *k*-nearest neighbor methodologies seek to accomplish different goals; *k*-nearest neighbors is a classification algorithm, which is a subset of supervised learning, while *k*-means is a clustering algorithm, which is a subset of unsupervised learning.

K-nearest neighbor techniques can be used to prevent theft. Modern surveillance systems are intelligent enough to analyze and interpret video data on their own, utilizing k-nearest neighbor for visual pattern recognition to scan and detect hidden packages in the bottom bin of a shopping cart at check-out, for example. It could also be able to ensure parts in a warehouse don't get stolen.

As she explains in her article *Solving Real-World Problems with Nearest Neighbor Algorithms*[159], Lillian Pierson states that, "If an object is detected that's an exact match for an object listed in the database, then the price of the spotted product could even automatically be added to the customer's bill. While this automated billing practice is not used extensively at this time, the technology has been developed and is available for use."

The *K*-nearest neighbor algorithm can also be used to detect patterns in credit card usage to root out credit card fraud. "Many new transaction-scrutinizing software applications use *k*NN algorithms to analyze register data and spot unusual patterns that indicate suspicious activity," Pierson adds.[159]

"If register data indicates that a lot of customer information is being entered manually rather than through automated scanning and swiping, this could indicate that the employee who's using that register is in fact stealing customer's personal information," warns Pierson.[159] Another example would be "if register data indicates that a particular good is being returned or exchanged multiple times, this could indicate that employees are misusing the return policy."[159]

*k*NN is not just about fraud. It can also be used to increase retail sales. "Average nearest neighbor algorithm classification and point pattern detection can be used in grocery retail to identify key patterns in customer purchasing behavior, and subsequently increase sales and customer satisfaction by anticipating customer behavior," explains Pierson.[159]

Advantages	Disadvantages
• It produces tighter clusters than other clustering techniques • Gives best result when data sets are distinct • Easy to understand	• *K*NN neither doesn't follow any nor have any standard for selecting the value '*k*', which is one of the key factors in the success of an algorithm • As *K*NN is a Lazy Learner algorithm, it has high storage requirements and requires efficient indexing techniques • The efficiency of the *K*NN algorithm also depends on the choice of the distance metric used. The results of the algorithm differ for each similarity metric

Table 6: Advantages and disadvantages of K-nearest neighbor
Source: Researchgate.[156]

Logistic Regression

From a statistical perspective, questions about whether a customer will or will not make a purchase or service is characterized by a binary dependent variable. Traditional regression analyses models are not suitable for analyzing these types of purchases because the results of such models are often not binary. Logistic regression and discriminant analysis are preferred because they use several factors to investigate the function of a nominally (e.g., binary) scaled variable.

According to Wikipedia, logistic regression is a regression model where the dependent variable (DV) is categorical, i.e., a variable that can take on one of a limited, and usually fixed, number of possible values.[160] This compares to a variable that would be continuous. Developed in 1958 by statistician David Cox, "The binary logistic model is used to estimate the probability of a binary response based on one or more predictor (or independent) variables (features). It allows one to say that the presence of a risk factor increases the probability of a given outcome by a specific percentage," explains Cox.[160]

In his article *Using Logistic Regression to Predict Customer Retention*[161], Andrew Karp explains that:

> "Logistic regression is an increasingly popular statistical technique used to model the probability of discrete (i.e., binary or multinomial) outcomes. When properly applied, logistic regression analyses yield very powerful insights in to what attributes (i.e., variables) are more or less likely to predict event outcome in a population of interest. These models also show the extent to which changes in the values of the attributes may increase or decrease the predicted probability of event outcome."

Logistic regression techniques may be used to classify a new observation whose group is unknown, in one of the groups, based on the values of the predictor variables. According to Karp, "Logistic regression models are frequently employed to assess the chance that a customer will: a) re-purchase a product, b) remain a customer, or c) respond to a direct mail or other marketing stimulus."[161]

Karp adds that "Economists frequently call logistic regression a 'qualitative choice' model, and for obvious reasons: a logistic regression model helps us assess probability which 'qualities' or 'outcomes' will be chosen (selected) by the population under analysis."[161] As can be expected, Karp argues that, "When proper care is taken to create an appropriate dependent variable, logistic regression is often a superior (both substantively and statistically) alternative to other tools available to model event outcomes."[161]

Karp uses a health care example to make his point that the analyst has several independent variables to use in the modeling process, but this example can be illustrative of how they could be used by marketers.[161] Karp explains that "An analyst developing a model predicting re-enrollment in a health insurance plan may have data for each member's interaction with both the health plans administrative apparatus and health care utilization in the prior 'plan year.'"[161]

The analyst can then construct variables such as the "number of times member called the health plan for information, number of physician office visits, whether or not the member changed primary care physicians during the previous 'plan year,' and answers to a customer satisfaction survey."[161] These can be employed in the modeling process and, once the model has been constructed, the analyst must decide which variable can be employed as the "outcome" or the "dependent" variable.[161]

In logistic regression analyses "it is often the analyst's responsibility to *construct* the dependent variable based on an agreed-upon definition of what constitutes the 'event of interest' which is being modeled," explains Karp.[161]

In the health care re-enrollment example, "a health plan's management team may define 'attrition' or 'failure to re-enroll' as situations where a member fails to return the re-enrollment card within 30 days of its due date. Or, in a response modeling scenario, a direct mail firm may define 'non-response' to an advertisement as failure to respond within 45 days of mailout."[161]

Logistic regression models can be powerful tools to build models that understand customer retention.[161] "When applied properly, logistic regression models can yield powerful insights into why some customers leave and others stay. These insights can then be employed to modify organizational strategies and/or assess the impact of the implementation of these strategies," Karp adds.[161]

A/B Testing

Also known as split testing or bucket testing, A/B testing is a method of marketing testing by which a baseline control sample is compared to a variety of single-variable test samples in order to improve response rates.

A classic direct mail tactic, this method has recently been adopted within the interactive space to test tactics such as banner ads, emails, and landing pages. As Scott Sutton explains in his article *Customer Analytics in the Casino and Hospitality Industry: How the House Always Wins*[162], for brand marketers, A/B Testing is the most effective way to identify the best available marketing offer.[162] It can test "two different offers against one another in order to identify the offer that drives the highest response and the most revenue/profit."[162]

In their book *A/B Testing: The Most Powerful Way to Turn Clicks into Customers*[163], Dan Siroker and Peter Komen note that, "The hardest part of A/B testing is determining what to test in the first place. Having worked with thousands of customers who do A/B testing every day, one of the most common questions we hear is, 'Where do I begin?'"

The mistake many companies make is they jump in head first without any detailed planning. Siroker and Komen propose the following deliberate five-step process[163]:

1. Define success.
2. Identify bottlenecks.
3. Construct a hypothesis.
4. Prioritize.
5. Test.

A/B testing is particularly good for website marketing, especially for uncovering the best landing pages. As Siroker and Komen explain, "Defining success in the context of A/B testing involves taking the answer to the question of your site's ultimate purpose and turning it into something more precise: *quantifiable success metrics*. Your success metrics are the specific numbers you hope will be improved by your tests."[163]

Site Type	Common Conversion & Aggregate Goals
e-Commerce A site that sells things for users to purchase online.	• Completed purchase. • Each step within the checkout funnel. • Products added to cart. • Product page views.
Media/Content A site focused on article or other content consumption.	• Page views. • Articles read. • Bounce rate (when measuring within an A/B testing tool, this is often measured by seeing if the user clicked anywhere on the page).
Lead Generation A site that acquires business through name capture.	• Form completion. • Clicks to a form page (links may read "Contact us" for example).
Donation	• Form completion. • Clicks to a form page (links may read "Send a donation" for example).

Table 7: Typical A/B conversion & aggregate goals
Source: A/B Testing: The Most Powerful Way to Turn Clicks into Customers[163]

An e-commerce site could easily define its success metrics in terms of revenue per visitor[163], but it is still important to understand such things as traffic sources, bounce rate, top pages, conversion rates, conversion by traffic source, amongst others.

As Siroker and Komen state:

> "Part of building out your testing strategy is identifying what constitutes—and does not constitute—a 'conversion' for your particular site. In online terms, a conversion is the point at

> which a visitor takes the desired action on your website. Pinpointing the specific actions you want people to take most on your site and that are most critical to your business will lead you to the tests that have an impact."[163]

Once the site's quantifiable success metrics are agreed upon, attention can be paid trying to discover where the bottlenecks are.[163] These are the places where users are dropping off, or the places where momentum in moving users through the desired series of actions weakens.[163]

In its article *Will machine learning be the death of content A/B testing*[54], *VentureBeat* argues that "Companies are now moving beyond A/B testing—up till now the primary way to understand the impact of content—to a place where data-fed algorithms are achieving significant results for something called Content AI."

"Just tell me what customer you're going after, what the demographic and firmographic is, and then we'll recommend, as a starting place, the 15 pieces that will perform the best of the thousand pieces of content in your repository," says Arun Anantharaman, chief product officer of Marketo (which was bought out by Adobe in September 2018[164]). This can eliminate "two months of guesswork for marketers, testing what pieces from that huge repository of data would actually work."[54]

Machine learning can compile all the data uncovered from a brand's marketing campaigns and research initiatives, from every channel, including email, social, search, promotions, and more.[54] Machine learning breaks down the silos between all these channels, giving brands a unified view of its entire customer base, no matter where that customer is finding the brand.[54] As *VentureBeat* explains, "Machine learning can link the propensity and behaviors of your customers at all points of contact, allowing you to develop a truly comprehensive view of what your marketing target audience is."[54] "From there, machine learning adds an automation piece, enabling a campaign to cycle through those 15 content focus areas for those campaigns," says *VentureBeat*.

Anantharaman says after Content AI, the next step is Audience AI—"meaning that the marketer gains leverage to drive campaigns and identify audiences that have converted and had success in the past."[54] Machine learning scours a company's "database for lookalike targets in real time, saving the marketer hours, days, and even months of time."[54] It might also capture leads that would go uncovered otherwise. "With AI, that means producing a list of people that have a high chance of converting from a database in the hundreds of thousands, or maybe even the millions," says *VentureBeat*.[54] "With machine learning, you'll be able to understand the success you had with previous campaigns, map that success to the attributes you want for a particular profile, and then generate the audiences that you need for the next campaign, in seconds. Something that could never be done manually."[54]

However, *VentureBeat* argues that, "embedding machine learning and AI within your existing workflows doesn't mean you need a data scientist on staff. Advances in machine learning technology mean that solutions can be tailored to specific companies, capabilities pre-filtered to capture what a marketer actually wants: data about open clicks, email activities, behavioral data, website actions, ad network engagement across the web, Facebook lead ads, LinkedIn lead generation ads, event engagement, and more."[54]

In her article *How AI could make A/B testing a thing of the past*[165], Emily Alford argues that, "machine learning is on track to completely change the ways we think about ad creative."

"Machine learning is going deeper and deeper into the media buying and online advertising process," says Ran Milo, Vice President of marketing for Bigalgo.[165] "But creative is still the biggest factor in media buying success. However, it's also the area where advertisers have very little insight and very little data. The solution is to identify which of your creative is actually performing."[165]

"Bidalgo's tool actually scores elements of an ad using KPIs from all parts of the buyer's' journey, from the top of the funnel down, and then compares creative performance for different messaging and images, a task that would be virtually impossible without AI," says Alford.[165]

"Right now, advertisers are flying blind," Milo says. "Even if you understand that certain creative works better, it's hard to understand why. We're using machine learning for image and video recognition to break down different variables, such as concept and copy to find out what's affecting different KPIs."[165]

"For example," says Alford, "without A, advertisers would need to A/B test by changing just one variable, such as tweaking a headline and running variations against one another before declaring a winner and moving on to testing some other aspect. But AI can test dozens of things at once, which means faster, more accurate data that can serve to make better ads in the future."[165] If a customer is "more likely to click on an advertisement featuring mountains and the word 'beautiful,' future messaging can build on that feedback."[165] This can all be done on a highly personal level.

"AI analysis can also inform advertisers as to whether their issue is with quality or quantity," argues Alford.[165] "We can see if a brand's creative is really working, and they simply need to invest in producing more content and advertising," Milo says.[165]

"Right now, advertisers can get a lot of insight about what works for them," Milo says.[165] "As soon as we have more data, we can compare industry-wide trends and really find commonalities for what's working and what's not. AI isn't trying to understand the psychology behind ads yet, but maybe soon."[165]

Alford also believes that, while humans are still primarily responsible for conceptualizing and producing ad content, that could soon change.[165] In 2017, "Shun Matsuzaka of McCann Japan introduced the world to its first robot creative director. He and his team fed AI a database of award-winning advertisements with the goal of creating a commercial for breath mints. The result was a surreal ad featuring a flying dog in a business suit that apparently resonated with viewers."[165] The ad was actually preferred by a group of 200 ad execs over the human-made version, which featured a woman painting on a rooftop.[165]

Flying dogs in business suits aside, Milo recommends humans retain the conceptualization and ad creative work, while using AI to predict which messaging will be successful.[165]

In her article *How Artificial Intelligence Will Change the Airline Passenger Experience*[166], Kristina Velan explains that, "Today, AI is able to dynamically change the look and feel of a website in real time, as travelers engage with it, to dramatically boost conversions, whether it's to sell a seat upgrade, a more direct flight or special offers for their trip." Beyond that, Velan states, "it can do this where airlines need it most, for return visitors or customers enrolled in loyalty programs."[166]

Velan explains that, "Until now, most airlines have been using A/B testing to assess two different variations of website design in order to improve the customer experience and increase conversions. While A/B testing can be an effective experimentation tool, only 1 out of every 7 A/B tests results in a positive outcome, making it a resource- and time-intensive strategy."[166] Today, Valen argues, "airlines can use AI to test thousands or even millions of designs (be it text, icon, image or button color changes) in the same amount of time and see a 40% to 50% increase in conversions."[166]

Time Series Model

A time series is an ordered sequence of values of a variable at uniformly spaced time intervals. A Time Series model can be used to predict or forecast the future behavior of a variable.

In his article *Time Series Analysis*[167], Muhammad Imdadullah explains that, "Time series analysis is the analysis of a series of data-points over time, allowing one to answer questions such as what is the causal effect on a variable Y of a change in variable X over time? An important difference between time series and cross section data is that the ordering of cases does matter in time series."

These models account for the fact that data points taken over time may have an internal structure (such as autocorrelation, trend or seasonal variation) that should be considered.

Time series can be broken down into two variations:

- Continuous Time Series— "A time series is said to be continuous when observations are made continuously in time. The term continuous is used for series of this type even when the measured variable can only take a discrete set of values."[167]
- Discrete Time Series— "A time series is said to be discrete when observations are taken at specific times, usually equally spaced. The term discrete is used for series of this type even when the measured variable is a continuous variable."[167]

"Most marketing research is cross-sectional but time series analysis is an often overlooked but valuable tool," claims Kevin Gray in his article *Time series analysis: what it is and what it does.*[168] "Time is a dimension in the data we need to take into account," says Gray.[168]

Time series analysis is a complex topic and when using usual cross-sectional techniques like regression on time series data, one or more of the following erroneous outcomes may occur[168]:

1. Standard errors can be far off. More often than not, p-values will be too small and variables can appear more significant than they really are.
2. Regression coefficients can be seriously biased.
3. The information provided by the serial correlation in the data does not get maximized.

Time series are a good way to forecast sales. The most straightforward way to do a time series is through univariate analysis, where the model basically extrapolates future data from past data.[168] "Two popular univariate time series methods are exponential smoothing (e.g., Holt-Winters) and ARIMA (autoregressive integrated moving average)."

There are risks in assuming the future follows the past, of course, but causal or predictor variables can be included in the model to mitigate these risks.[168] Besides improving the accuracy of marketing forecasts, another objective may be to understand which marketing activities are most influencing sales.[168] Causal variables will typically include data such as (Gross Rating Point) GRPs and price and they may also "incorporate data from consumer surveys or exogenous variables such as GDP."[168] "These kinds of analyses are called market response or marketing-mix modeling and are a central component of ROI analysis. They can be thought of as key driver analysis for time series data. The findings are often used in simulations to find the optimal marketing mix," explains Gray.[168]

"Transfer function models and dynamic regression are two popular approaches to time series causal analysis. Essentially, they refer to specialized regression procedures developed for time series data," says Gray.[168]

There are several additional time series methods relevant to marketing research, including Panel models and GARCH models. "Panel models include cross-sections in a time series analysis. Series for several brands, for instance, can be stacked on top of one another and analyzed simultaneously," say Gray.[168]

"In some instances, one model will not fit an entire series well because of structural changes within the series and model parameters varying across time. There are numerous breakpoint tests and models (e.g., state space, switching regression) available for these circumstances," explains Gray.[168]

In cases where call center activity or other tracked data series exhibit clusters of volatility that are not easily explainable on the basis of seasonality or other business or economic reasons, a class of models known as GARCH (generalized autoregressive conditional heteroskedasticity) should be considered.[168] "ARCH and GARCH models were originally developed for financial markets but can [sic] used for other time series data when volatility is of interest," say Gray.[168] "Volatility can fall into many patterns and accordingly there are many flavors of GARCH models. Causal variables can be included. There are also multivariate extensions for situations in which you have two or more series you wish to analyze jointly."[168]

Discriminant Analysis

Discriminant or discriminant function analysis is a method used to determine which weightings of quantitative variables or predictors best discriminate between two or more than two groups of cases and do so better than chance. It is a method used in statistics, pattern recognition and machine learning to find a linear combination of features that characterizes or separates two or more classes of objects or events.

According to Wikipedia:

> *"Discriminant function analysis is a statistical analysis used to predict a categorical dependent variable (called a grouping variable) by one or more continuous or binary independent variables (called predictor variables). The original dichotomous discriminant analysis was developed by Sir Ronald Fisher in 1936. It differs from an ANOVA or MANOVA, which is used to predict one (ANOVA) or multiple (MANOVA) continuous dependent variables by one or more independent categorical variables."*[169]

Because of its ability to classify individuals or experimental units into two or more uniquely defined populations, discriminate analysis can be used for market segmentation and the prediction of group membership. The discriminant score can be the basis on which a prediction about group membership is made. For example, the discriminant weights of each predictive variable (age, sex, income, etc.) indicate the relative importance of each variable. In other words, if age has a low discriminant weight then it is less important than the other variables.

For a marketing department, use of discriminant analysis can help predict why a customer frequents one brand over another. Discriminant analysis is specifically useful in product research, perception/image research, advertising research and direct marketing.

Survival or Duration Analysis

As per Wikipedia, "Survival analysis is a branch of statistics for analyzing the expected duration of time until one or more events happen, such as death in biological organisms and failure in mechanical systems. This topic is called reliability theory or reliability analysis in engineering, duration analysis or duration modeling in economics, and event history analysis in sociology."[170] Survival analysis attempts to answer questions such as[170]:

- What is the proportion of a population which will survive past a certain time?
- Of those that survive, at what rate will they die or fail?
- Can multiple causes of death or failure be considered?
- How do particular circumstances or characteristics increase or decrease the probability of survival?

A branch of statistics that deals with death in biological organisms and failure in mechanical systems, survival analysis involves the modeling of time to event data; in this context, death or failure is considered an "event" in the survival analysis literature—traditionally only a single event occurs, after which the organism or mechanism is dead or broken. Survival analysis is the study of lifetimes and their distributions. It usually involves one or more of the following objectives:

1. To explore the behavior of the distribution of a lifetime.
2. To model the distribution of a lifetime.
3. To test for differences between the distributions of two or more lifetimes.
4. To model the impact of one or more explanatory variables on a lifetime distribution.

In her article for the Cornell Statistical Consulting Unit[171], Simona Despa explains that "In survival analysis, subjects are usually followed over a specified time period and the focus is on the time at which the event of interest occurs."[171] "Why not use linear regression to model the survival time as a function of a set of predictor variables?" asks Despa.[171] "First, survival times are typically positive numbers; ordinary linear regression may not be the best choice unless these times are first transformed in a way that removes this restriction. Second, and more importantly, ordinary linear regression cannot effectively handle the censoring of observations," explains Despa.[171]

"Observations are called censored when the information about their survival time is incomplete; the most commonly encountered form is right censoring," notes Despa.[171] She adds[171]:

> "Suppose patients are followed in a study for 20 weeks. A patient who does not experience the event of interest for the duration of the study is said to be right censored. The survival time for this person is considered to be at least as long as the duration of the study. Another example of right censoring is when a person drops out of the study before the end of the study observation time and did not experience the event. This person's survival time is said to be censored, since we know that the event of interest did not happen while this person was under observation. Censoring is an important issue in survival analysis, representing a particular type of missing data. Censoring that is random and non-informative is usually required in order to avoid bias in a survival analysis."

"Unlike ordinary regression models, survival methods correctly incorporate information from both censored and uncensored observations in estimating important model parameters," notes Despa.[171] "The dependent variable in survival analysis is composed of two parts: one is the time to event and the other is the event status, which records if the event of interest occurred or not," says Despa.[171] The two functions that are dependent on time—survival and hazard functions—can then be estimated.[171] "The survival and hazard functions are key concepts in survival analysis for describing the distribution of event times," says Despa.[171] "The survival function gives, for every time, the probability of surviving (or not experiencing the event) up to that time. The hazard function gives the potential that the event will occur, per time unit, given that an individual has survived up to the specified time."[171] "While these are often of direct interest, many other quantities of interest (e.g., median survival) may subsequently be estimated from knowing either the hazard or survival function," says Despa.[171]

For survival studies it is often important "to describe the relationship of a factor of interest (e.g. treatment) to the time to event, in the presence of several covariates, such as age, gender, race, etc."[171] A number of models—parametric, nonparametric, and semiparametric—are available to analyze the relationship of a set of predictor variables with the survival time, claims Despa.[171]

"Parametric methods assume that the underlying distribution of the survival times follows certain known probability distributions,"[171] the most popular ones being the exponential, Weibull, and lognormal distributions.[171] "The description of the distribution of the survival times and the change in their distribution as a function of predictors is of interest. Model parameters in these settings are usually estimated using an appropriate modification of maximum likelihood," says Despa.[171]

"A nonparametric estimator of the survival function, the Kaplan Meier method is widely used to estimate and graph survival probabilities as a function of time," notes Despa.[171] "It can be used to obtain univariate descriptive statistics for survival data, including the median survival time," says Despa.[171] It can also be used to "compare the survival experience for two or more groups of subjects."[171] "To test for overall differences between estimated survival curves of two or more groups of subjects, such as males versus females, or treated versus untreated (control) groups, several tests are available, including the log-rank test," says Despa.[171] "This can be motivated as a type of chi-square test, a widely used test in practice, and in reality is a method for comparing the Kaplan-Meier curves estimated for each group of subjects," adds Despa.[171]

Swarm Intelligence

According to Wikipedia[172], Swarm intelligence (SI) "is the collective behavior of decentralized, self-organized systems, natural or artificial. The concept is employed in work on artificial intelligence." The expression was introduced by Gerardo Beni and Jing Wang in 1989, in the context of cellular robotic systems.[173]

"SI systems consist typically of a population of simple agents or boids interacting locally with one another and with their environment. The inspiration often comes from nature, especially biological systems," says Wikipedia.[172] "The agents follow very simple rules, and although there is no centralized control structure dictating how individual agents should behave, local, and to a certain degree random, interactions between such agents lead to the emergence of 'intelligent' global behavior, unknown to the individual agents."[172] Nature is filled with examples of swarm intelligence, including ant colonies, bird flocking, fish schooling, bacterial growth, and microbial intelligence.[172]

Analytical + A.I. Models

Customer Segmentation

As Kimberly Coffey, PhD, explains in her article *k-means Clustering for Customer Segmentation: A Practical Example*[174], clustering isn't as simple as it sounds. Coffey believes that, "Customer segmentation is a deceptively simple-sounding concept. Broadly speaking, the goal is to divide customers into groups that share certain characteristics. There are an almost-infinite number of characteristics upon which you could divide customers, however, and the optimal characteristics and analytic approach vary depending upon the business objective. This means that there is no single, correct way to perform customer segmentation."

That being said, "Customer segmentation is often performed using unsupervised, clustering techniques (e.g., *k*-means, latent class analysis, hierarchical clustering, etc.), but customer segmentation results tend to be most actionable for a business when the segments can be linked to something concrete (e.g., customer lifetime value, product proclivities, channel preference, etc.)," notes Coffey.[174] Of course, this begs the question: "if you're looking to link the segments to some sort of dependent variable, why not use an analytic technique that explicitly estimates the relationship between your possible predictors and the dependent variable?"[174]

Coffey's answer: "clustering creates groups from continuous variables (typically), so if you're looking to create groups, clustering does a really nice job of finding the boundaries between groups."[174] "In situations where there is a dependent variable of interest, it is generally included as an input variable in the cluster analysis, so the clusters can be interpreted in light of this outcome variable," explains Coffey.[174]

"Customer segmentation is the process of dividing customers into groups based upon certain boundaries; clustering is *one* way to generate these boundaries," Coffey notes.[174] There is an important caveat though—clustering assumes that there *are* distinct clusters in the data.[174] Oftentimes, customers are distributed more or less continuously in multivariate space, and they aren't in neatly defined groups.[174]

Generally, the data is used to determine the appropriate segments for these views. The result of this analysis presents a detailed view of how the brand is populated at different times and it can allow for appropriate strategic decisions to be made by the brand. These decisions could be a function of marketing, operations or strategy. The output can also be used to build acquisition models, as I will discuss below.

Other potential for analysis would be a master segmentation model that uses the preference results described above. Customers are clustered based on their preferences to gain a global view of the brand that is concise and understandable. Furthermore, such models can help measure the impact of operational strategic decisions.

ML can help marketers discover customer segments that they may not realize were there. Armed with this kind of information, brands can understand what matters most to its customers at the individual and personalization level, which will enable them to anticipate their customer's needs before even the customer is aware of them. Even more, brands can understand key characteristics of their most profitable customers and recognize the next important customer when he or she happens to log onto the brand's ecommerce site or step in a branch or in an outlet, or on a casino floor.

The use of deep neural networks and image classifiers can analyze and parse images, which can enable brands to monitor the images that provide the highest selling and conversion rates through each ecommerce channel.

ML can also be used to compute dynamic clusters of customers to create fluid segmentation in real-time. As consumer buying habits or booking patterns evolve, fluid segmentation ensures the brand continues to reach the right customers, at the right time, at the right price, through the right channels, with the right offer.

Many marketers use the S-T-P approach; **S**egmentation→ **T**argeting → **P**ositioning to provide the framework for marketing planning objectives. That is, a market is segmented, one or more segments are selected for targeting, and products or services are positioned in a way that resonates with the selected target market or markets. With real-time technology, segmentation can reach a whole new customer experience level.

The process of segmenting the market is deceptively simple. Seven basic steps describe the entire process, including segmentation, targeting and positioning. In practice, however, the task can be very laborious since it involves poring over loads of data, and it requires a great deal of skill in analysis, interpretation and some judgment. Although a great deal of analysis needs to be undertaken, and many decisions need to be made, marketers tend to use the so-called S-T-P process as a broad framework for simplifying the process outlined here:

- Segmentation:
    - Identify market (also known as the universe) to be segmented.
    - Identify, select and apply base or bases to be used in the segmentation.
    - Develop segment profiles.
- Targeting:
    - Evaluate each segment's attractiveness.
    - Select segment or segments to be targeted.
- Positioning:
    - Identify optimal positioning for each segment.
    - Develop the marketing program for each segment.

Markets can be broken down into the following segments:

- Geographic segment.
- Demographic segment.
- Psychographic segment.
- Behavioral segment.
- Purchase/usage occasion.
- Generational segment.
- Cultural segmentation.

Although customer segmentation is a common business practice, it has received the following criticisms:

- It fails to identify sufficiently meaningful clusters.
- It is no better than mass marketing at building brands.
- In competitive markets, segments rarely exhibit major differences in the way they use brands.
- Geographic/demographic segmentation is overly descriptive and lacks sufficient insights into the motivations necessary to drive communications strategy.
- Difficulties with market dynamics, notably the instability of segments over time and structural change that leads to segment creep and membership migration as individuals move from one segment to another.

Market segmentation has many critics, but, in spite of its limitations, it remains one of the most enduring concepts in marketing and it continues to be widely used in practice. At the very least, it is a way to separate an audience into easily digestible chunks.

As Wikipedia explains[109], there are no formulas for evaluating the attractiveness of market segments and a good deal of judgment must be exercised. Nevertheless, a number of considerations can be used to evaluate market segments for attractiveness, including[109]:

- Segment Size and Growth:
  - How large is the market?
  - Is the market segment substantial enough to be profitable?
  - Segment size can be measured in number of customers, but superior measures are likely to include sales value or volume.
  - Is the market segment growing or contracting?
  - What are the indications that growth will be sustained in the long term? Is any observed growth sustainable?
  - Is the segment stable over time?
- Segment Structural Attractiveness:
  - To what extent are competitors targeting this market segment?
  - Can we carve out a viable position to differentiate from any competitors?
  - How responsive are members of the market segment to the marketing program?
  - Is this market segment reachable and accessible?
- Company Objectives and Resources:
  - Is this market segment aligned with our company's operating philosophy?
  - Do we have the resources necessary to enter this market segment?
  - Do we have prior experience with this market segment or similar market segments?

- Do we have the skills and/or know-how to enter this market segment successfully?

Customer Acquisition Model

Brands are always on the lookout for new customers. With the marketing landscape getting more and more competitive and saturated by the day, there is a constant need to know what type of customers to target and where to find them.

The results of the segmentation model described above can be used to build a predictive model that identifies likely characteristics of attractive customers. Obviously, the brand will have no internal data available on customers they don't already have on their books, so the analysis becomes a data mining exercise using publicly available input variables. Brands can then target these customers with a view to attracting those who have the traits that they see in their already valuable customers.

The best external data to use would be population census data, linked to the internal customers by a location identifier (such as postcode). It is acknowledged that in some jurisdictions robust and accurate census data may not be available, so the model would be relying on whatever information the brand records on its customers from a demographic and lifestyle point of view.

This approach becomes a classical data-mining exercise, where a pool of independent variables would be tested for the strength of association with the response variable. Once the relevant predictors are identified and the characteristics and traits are defined, marketing and acquisition campaigns could be targeted at the population towards these kinds of people.

This would be something that looks to predict a metric derived from current/past customers. Such a metric could come from a segmentation model that identified the high value customers that are most attractive to the brand. There are several approaches that can be used and once the target has been defined, this allows for a parametric equation to be derived. This equation attempts to predict the characteristics that separate out the desirable customers from the rest.

This model can only use publicly available information (although other brand information might be acceptable) as that is how a potential customer would be identified. Current information that the company could have on hand would be age, nationality, gender, address, as well as any transactional, clickstream or social data.

Where available, third party data should be looked at to further enhance the findings. This could be census data that gives an indication of further customer demographics and this enhances the ability to home in on customer sweet spots. Social media is also rich with customer acquisition data and information.

Recency-Frequency-Monetary (RFM) Models

RFM is a method used for analyzing customer value. It is commonly used in database marketing and direct marketing and has received particular attention in the gambling and retail industries. RFM stands for:

- **Recency**: How much time has elapsed since a customer's last activity or transaction with the brand? In most cases, the more recently a customer has interacted or transacted with a marketer, the more likely that customer will be responsive to communications from the brand, including marketing communications.
- **Frequency**: How often has a customer transacted or interacted with a marketer during a particular period? Clearly, customers with frequent activities are more engaged, and probably more loyal, than customers who aren't. A one-time-only customer is in a class of his or her own.
- **Monetary**: Also referred to as "monetary value," this factor reflects how much a customer has spent with the brand during a particular period. Big spenders should usually be treated differently than customers who spend little. Looking at monetary divided by frequency indicates the average purchase amount—an important secondary factor to consider when segmenting customers.

Most businesses will keep scores of data about a customer's purchases. All that is needed is a table with the customer name, date of purchase, and purchase value. One methodology is to assign a scale of 1 to 10, whereby 10 is the maximum value and to stipulate a formula by which the data suits the scale. For example:

- Recency = 10—the number of months that have passed since the customer last purchased.
- Frequency = number of purchases in the last 12 months (maximum of 10).
- Monetary = value of the highest order from a given customer (benchmarked against $10k).

RFM calculates "scores" for each customer. The customers with the highest scores will probably be those who spend the most with the brand, across the most recent and frequent dates.

The idea behind RFM is that a minority of customers are responsible for most of a brand's business, i.e., the Pareto Principle, also known as the 80/20 rule. The RFM process condenses the customers' purchasing patterns in some form of an 80/20 split, whereby 80% of the sales come from 20% of the customers and this is a further extension of analysis that brands can derive from this RFM process.

Alternatively, one can create categories for each attribute. For instance, the 'Recency' attribute might be broken into three categories: customers with purchases within the last 90 days; purchases between 91 and 365 days; and purchases longer than 365 days. Such categories may be arrived at by applying business rules or using a data mining technique to find meaningful breaks.

Once each of the attributes has appropriate categories defined, segments are created from the intersection of the values. If there were three categories for each attribute, then the resulting matrix would have twenty-seven possible combinations (one well-known commercial approach uses five bins per attribute, which yields 125 segments).

Segments could also be collapsed into sub-segments, if the gradations appear too small to be useful. The resulting segments can be ordered from most valuable (highest recency, frequency, and value) to least valuable (lowest recency, frequency, and value). Identifying the most valuable RFM segments can capitalize on chance relationships in the data used for this analysis. For this reason, it is highly recommended that another set of data be used to validate the results of the RFM segmentation process.

The goal is to produce RFM Segments that reflect the following types of the brand's customers:

- Core—best customers.
- Loyal—most loyal customers.
- Whales—highest paying customers.
- Promising—most faithful customers.
- Rookies—newest customers.
- Slipping—once loyal, now gone customers.

Once the RFM data has been developed, a marketer can utilize this data to easily develop a customer loyalty program based on the purchasing patterns of its customers, this is one of the best reasons to develop an RFM model. Where a marketer has points assigned for Recency, Frequency and Monetary Value, the brand can assign the same amount of points, or a different points concept, for loyalty to its products and/or services. Brands should consider using a range of customer loyalty concepts to develop and measure customer loyalty, and then reward customers who choose to fly with the brand, rather than one of its competitors.

Advocates of this technique point out that it has the virtue of simplicity: no specialized statistical software is required, and the results are readily understood by business people. In the absence of other targeting techniques, it can provide a lift in response rates for promotions.

Whichever approach is adopted, profiling will be done on the results to determine what makes up group membership. Categorical factors such as gender, nationality/locality can be used as well as age (or, indeed, any other demographic feature that is available) to understand the "type" of customer that resides in each group. These factors can be used for each segment and applied against the population metrics to determine how much more or less likely a segment is to exhibit a feature or type of behavior when compared to the customer base as a whole.

Propensity to Respond Model

A *Propensity to Respond* model is a model that predicts whether a sampled person (or unit) will become a respondent in an offer or survey. These models are especially useful in the marketing field. A propensity to respond model can have substantial cost savings as it can lead to lower mailing costs by identifying customers who are very unlikely to respond to an offer. After segmenting these people out, the brand can then focus on only those most likely to take up the offer. A brand can identify the likelihood of response from all eligible customers.[162] After that, it can identify the most valuable customers that are most likely to respond.[162] This allows the brand to estimate the expected response from the most valuable customers and eliminate mailing(s) to the customers that are of lower worth and/or are unlikely to respond.[162]

A propensity to respond model would be built using historical information around marketing campaigns and it looks at predicting the likelihood a customer will respond to a marketing communication. The advantage of this model is that it strengthens the marketing strategy even more, beyond purely segmenting the customer base. It can further allow for improved ROI on the marketing budget, by identifying the likely number of respondents to be returned by a campaign.

Often a brand's marketing department will have an expected number of respondents or an expected response rate.[162] By identifying those who are most likely to respond, the chances of meeting that expected number or rate of response is greatly improved.[162] Gone are the days of marketing to an entire customer base, once again we're back to the "marketing of one" concept. Marketing to the entire database is an unnecessary waste of the marketing budget and it also runs the risk of annoying customers by touching them too often or with the wrong offer.[162]

Again, a predictive model would be built which identifies those most likely to respond through to those least likely to respond. This would be done using customer metrics and historical campaign/marketing information that identifies those who responded and those who didn't. Variables that have a significant association with the customer action are extracted and these form part of the prediction algorithm. Every customer is then given a score according to how likely they are to respond to a marketing campaign.

This information can be used for strategies such as extracting the top 40% of customers most likely to respond, or a fixed number, such as 100,000 customers. The end result is the marketing function becomes more efficient and effective, with better returns for the company's marketing dollar.

There is a caveat, however. Sutton warns that, "Occasionally, response likelihood models will lead to easy decisions, such as cutting out low worth customers with a low likelihood of responding. However, more complex situations might arise since response models are never perfect."[162] It doesn't matter how good a model is or how accurate the historical data is, there is always a chance that a customer identified as unlikely to respond will actually respond.[162] "Thus, when making a decision about customers identified as unlikely to respond to an offer, it is also important to balance that likelihood of response with the potential return on response," advises Sutton[162]

Customer Conversion Model

Conversion marketing refers to "tactics that encourage customers to take specific action, 'converting' a person browsing your website into a purchaser of your product or service."[175]

In Marketingschool.org's *Conversion marketing*[175], the authors argue that, "In terms of online marketing, this involves not only the sales pitch, but also the website design and layout, as well as special actions—for example, a triggered special offer given those who abandon their shopping carts."[175] The authors argue that, "High conversion rates mean more sales, fewer lost customers, and a greater return on advertising investment. By converting potential customers—who have already expressed at least some degree of interest—you don't need to reach as many new prospects in order to generate the same volume of sales."[175]

"Conversion marketing tactics do not target only one consumer segment, but instead apply to all customers who visit a company's website. Many, if not most, will arrive through search engine results. Such visitors are immediately high-value prospects, as they're already interested in some aspect of your website content, if not the specific goods and services you provide," says Marketingschool.org.[175] "Other customers arrive directly, because they already know about your website—perhaps through previous business or through a link in your e-mailed newsletter. These customers are also high-value, having already established a relationship with the business."[175]

"In both of these instances, conversion marketing doesn't have to try to invent prospects, and then try to con those prospects into making a purchase—it just needs to make a compelling case to those who already have a need," Marketingschool.org.[175] "It's more about making a decision easy than about presenting the decision in the first place," they claim.[175]

Before choosing conversion strategies, brands need to identify the kinds of purchasing processes their customers use.[175] E-commerce websites sell products online, but there are big differences between selling physical products that need to be shipped or picked up in a store and digital products, which can be downloaded directly.[175] "Among physical products, conversion is different between small items and large-purchase items that typically require more research before buying," says Marketingschool.org.[175]

Other companies don't expect customers to buy online, their websites might be little more than online brochures, while other business sell B-2-B services and sales generally happen through personal interaction.[175]

Brands building customer conversion models should analyze historical information about what constitutes a desirable customer. This should include spending patterns and profitability.

To identify the relationships that may exist between how these customers come to the brand and his or her desirability metric, information would be extracted from the brand's source systems. Basically, anything that can be attributed to the initial transaction the customer had with the brand would be used as a potential input, including potential social media data.

These models might also have to be stratified by sales to identify the most relevant relationships. The major advantage of a predictive model with this intention would be that it allows the brand to identify customers that they need to interact with the first time the customer transacts with the company. This would give the company clerks the potential to get the required information they need to successfully foster a strong customer relationship.

Furthermore, if every potential customer has a score associated with them as to their long-term likelihood of being attractive, the brand can further home in on its potentially profitable customers by monitoring their behavior the first time they interact with the company. It is imperative that the brand interact with any desirable customers before they finish their purchase. If customers are made to feel like they are valuable and worthwhile to the brand, the likelihood of them returning again increases significantly.

Customer Lifetime Value (CLV)

Determining customer worth is one of the most important procedures of customer analytics for businesses. Of course, predicting a customer's future behavior is not easy and it is affected by several variables, many of which the brand cannot know, including total income, expendable income, reasons for a trip, etc., etc.

Even where a customer lives, or information gleaned from his or her social media accounts could be very revealing to worth. There is also "plenty of information to be found with in-house data that can be used to build models and metrics to predict a customer's future worth."[162] "Once customer worth has been determined, "customers can then be segmented into groups based on other behaviors and effective marketing campaigns can be developed around those behaviors."[162]

The first thing a marketer must do is "determine what worth is, as the definition of worth is critical for deciding how valuable a customer is and how much to reinvest in the customer in the future," as Sutton explains.[162] "The definition of worth will likely depend on both the various financial sources of revenue that affect the business directly and the exact business problems that are being addressed," adds Sutton.[162]

"Once customer worth has been defined, the business can then use data mining and modeling to estimate predicted worth into the future," states Sutton.[162] "There are a variety of techniques that are used to develop models to predict future worth, the most common being regression models. Multiple regression models are the most common because they utilize a variety of predictors and the relationships between those predictors to predict future worth," adds Sutton.[162]

"Regression models can also be built using such categorical variables predictors as gender, ethnicity, age range, or other demographic variables."[162] "Regression models are particularly effective because the model can be used to score historical data to predict an unknown outcome, which is worth in this case, within a certain degree of confidence," adds Sutton.[162]

Customer Churn Model

Customer churn occurs when customers or subscribers stop doing business with a company or service, this process is also known as customer attrition. It is also referred to as loss of clients or customers. The goal of a customer churn model is to identify signaling behavior of at-risk customers. Customer churn models investigate the worth of customer by looking at their internal transactions to predict the target variable of disengagement via a data mining exercise. The model attempts to extract significant predictors of long-term customer loyalty using lifecycle metrics/data.

A customer churn model outputs prediction on demand for each customer's likelihood of churn. It also provides information about the risk factors that affect the exit of a customer as well. Additionally, the approach not only gives brands a list of possible churners, but also produces, for every customer, a survival probability function that lets the brand know how the probability of churning is varying as a function of time. This allows brands to distinguish various levels of loyalty profiles, i.e., upcoming, near-future and far-future churners, and the variables that influence this survival behavior. From this survival function, the median survival time can be extracted and used as a life expectancy threshold. This feature lets brands label customers as being at risk of churning, which should allow them to act before the actual churn occurs, thereby retaining valuable customers, as well as potentially improving brand customer satisfaction.

The use of analytics and data management to help detect and avoid the act of attrition is something that can benefit most brands. Churn questions that brands should ask include:

- How is the brand detecting behavioral changes in is customers?
- Does the brand have steps in place to identify when the customer experience is going wrong, or when the customer is about to leave?

To ensure customer retention is front and center, brands should be scoring their database on a regular basis to understand the likelihood of a customer churning. This kind of modeling is prevalent in the telecommunications, finance, and utilities industries, and could be utilized in many other industries as well.

One of the hardest things for a marketer to determine is to find out if a customer has categorically churned or not. It may be that a change in location, circumstances or something else has caused the customer to no longer associate with the brand. However, statistical measures can be used to identify customers whose behavior has changed, with that change not being attributed to chance.

Historical internal data can be used to model the difference between a churned customer and one who is still engaged. There would be significant metrics in the data that identify the likelihood of churning. Like the acquisition model described previously, a parametric equation could be constructed that elicits the association and relationship between the target variable and the predictors.

This model would serve as an early warning system for the brand. It would also be a strategic tool used to predict whether a customer was deemed worth retaining or not. The model should be run on a regular basis across the entire customer database to understand which customers have reached or are reaching a critical value in their churn score. These customers would then be targeted with an offer to return to the brand, in the process avoiding the likelihood of them churning. Alternatively, if the customer is deemed to be of little or no value to the company, there would be no offer forthcoming to entice them to return.

Customer retention consists of three stages:

1. Stage 1: analyze the important determinants of customer retention
2. Stage2: apply the determinants to predict customer retention (including customer churn and customers' lifetime value)
3. Stage 3: design and implement policies to improve customer retention and prevent customer attrition.

Optimizing Marketing Offers

Besides being able to predict the future worth of customers, "it is important to know which marketing campaigns are the most effective for driving response, revenue, and profit."[162] In general, certain offers are obviously better than others, and specifically certain offers will be better for certain customers.[162]

"While knowing the probable future worth of a customer is critical for determining the reinvestment level for which a customer is eligible, customers' behaviors and interests can be used to identify the offer(s) that will be most appealing to each customer as well as the ones generating the most profitable response," says Sutton.[162] By analyzing the likelihood that a customer will respond to a certain offer or offers, brand analysts can optimize the offer that each customer is given in order to maximize the amount of revenue and profit driven by the marketing campaigns as a whole.[162] Definable ROI becomes a set goal here.

As previously mentioned, A/B testing is one of the best ways to identify which offers work best and more "advanced statistical methods can be used to generate likelihood of response scores and classification scores."[162] "Some of the more common statistical approaches are logistic regression, decision trees, and discriminant analysis," Sutton adds.[162]

"Essentially, these statistical methods use historical data to find the factors that are related as to why a customer responds. Those factors can then be used to assess the likelihood of response based on the similarity of a customer profile to that of responders," adds Sutton.[162]

"These methods have historically been used in direct marketing analysis to identify the best types of offers and the most likely responders," says Sutton.[162] "In order to build accurate and predictive response models, historical data about response is required. The likelihood of response might be a broad measure of response that refers to the likelihood a customer will respond to any offer, or it might be specific to the likelihood of response to a specific type of offer."[162]

In addition, Sutton adds, "it's a good idea to select test segments of customers for the purpose of continually testing new offers. Doing so will help to ensure that there is a large amount of response data that can be used to build models and continually improve the efficacy of marketing."[162] "Effective response models will help identify which customers are most likely to respond to an offer, and in turn to which offer customers are most likely to respond."[162]

Lookalike Marketing

In his article *Lookalike modeling breathing new life into old channels*[176], Jordan Elkind says that lookalike marketing modeling isn't new, "it's been a mainstay of the ad tech industry for years, used to help advertisers expand digital audiences while maintaining relevancy of targeting." "The principle is simple," says Elkind, "Brands want to attract new visitors to their site. What better way to do this than to identify prospects who resemble existing visitors (or customers)?"[176]

"What *is* new," Elkind says, "is the dazzling variety of ways in which digital marketers are deploying lookalike modeling techniques to enhance the return on investment across marketing channels—both online and offline."[176]

"With more data than ever before on user journeys and behaviors, increased adoption of platforms (like customer data platforms and data management platforms) to centralize and analyze that data, and growing ubiquity of machine learning tools and techniques, lookalike modeling is breathing new life into old channels," says Elkind.[176]

"Customer-centric businesses have long recognized that the best way to acquire new visitors is to focus on users who resemble their *existing* visitors (or better yet, high-value customers)," explains Elkind.[176] "For digital marketers looking to drive traffic and conversions, this means identifying and purchasing media against audiences based on a small number of static demographic attributes. Your recent site visitors are statistically more likely to be females, aged 18-29? Perfect—serve display advertisements to similar audiences elsewhere on the web!" says Elkind.[176]

"The problem," as Elkind sees it, "is that demographic segment-based targeting, while enabling advertisers to reach audiences at scale, isn't a great proxy for relevancy. Women aged 18-29 are a diverse demographic, only a subset of whom are likely to be interested in a brand's offering. As a result, performance can tend to show a steep drop-off as audience size increases."[176]

"Enter lookalike modeling, a form of statistical analysis that uses machine learning to process vast amounts of data and seek out hidden patterns across pools of users," says Elkind.[176] "Lookalike modeling works by identifying the composition and characteristics of a 'seed' audience (for example, a group of recent site visitors or high-value customers), and identifying other users who show similar attributes or behaviors," he says.[176]

"By analyzing not just demographic but behavioral similarities—e.g., users who have demonstrated similar browsing patterns—lookalike modeling enables advertisers to leverage powerful and complex data signals to find the perfect audience," says Elkind.[176]

"Lookalike modeling is a trusty tool in the digital media arsenal—and it's quickly becoming indispensable to other channels as well. The convergence of ad tech and CRM—powered by platforms that enable advertisers to go well beyond cookies and CRM professionals to gain visibility into the digital journeys of known users—has made it possible to build lookalike audiences of unprecedented sophistication," says Elkind. AI and machine learning can add even more sophistication to the process.

As previously stated, a "model is only as good as the data it's given; the growth in technologies that help marketers understand their customers better has only increased the potency of lookalike modeling."[176]

With a single source of customer data spanning online and offline engagement, a brand can unify disparate signals of purchase intent from many customer touch points, including onsite and transaction behavior, email engagement, offline purchases, app usage, call center contacts, product reviews and more.[176] This provides a rich and highly accurate view of customer behavior, which could power high-performing lookalike models.[176]

Lookalike audience can also be found on social channels like Facebook. "'Facebook Lookalike Audiences' enables marketers to build a seed list based on pixel audiences (e.g., users who have recently visited the site or browsed a particular page) or a custom list of users," says Elkind.[176]

For example, a fashion retailer "could use a platform to identify all customers with a predicted affinity—based on dozens of behavioral data points—for haute couture, and simply transfer that audience directly to Facebook. Marketers can then indicate how targeted vs. broad they would like the lookalike targeting to be."[176]

For search, "getting in front of high-potential prospects when they're in-market—searching or doing price comparison for a relevant category—is every marketer's dream. The introduction of Similar Audiences through Google Customer Match enables marketers to automatically optimize bidding strategies around key lookalike audiences."[176]

"Advertisers can upload lists of customers to Google and then configure Similar Audiences to optimize for search, shopping (product listing ads), YouTube and Gmail ads," explains Elkind.[176]

For companies utilizing direct mail, "Rented or borrowed lists have long been the preferred form of direct mail prospecting. But a number of vendors now offer the capability to run lookalike models based on a marketer's known customers against the larger mailable population, to identify which addresses are most likely to respond to that catalog or magazine."[176]

"Ultimately, the ability to stitch together customer journeys across touch points, channels and platforms has provided marketers with unprecedented visibility into customer behavior—and made lookalike modeling a crucial capability for a growing number of marketing channels," concludes Elkind.[176]

In his article *Adobe adds new features to its data management platform*[177], Barry Levine explains that Adobe's Audience Manager "can now subtract traits in a lookalike model and report impressions by user segment." "Lookalike models are often developed from the attributes of a group of users a brand wants to find more of. A model of the common attributes of the best customers, according to this thinking, can help find other users with similar attributes, who are more likely to become customers of this particular product or service," says Levine.[177]

"One problem, Adobe says, is that when a brand creates a model from attribute data—either the brand's own data or third-party data from a provider—there might be attributes that could bias the model in the wrong direction."[177] "For instance, the attributes creating the model might include visits to the brand's site or other specific sites, when those site visits aren't useful for finding lookalike users."[177]

The new Trait Exclusion capability "lets marketers remove selected traits, and it employs Adobe's Sensei machine learning to help make the subtraction," says Levine.[177] "In addition to removing traits that don't add value, like site visits, Adobe said the new feature helps marketers focus on influential traits. When the brand has to comply with specific privacy regulations, the model can exclude certain demographic attributes," he adds.[177]

Chronological View of a Marketer's Analytics Implementation

1. Data reduction via cluster analysis and segmentation is a logical starting point and initial work should be around identifying customer preference(s). Reducing the customer database into more manageable and meaningful segments has many advantages; the preferences that can be derived are dependent on the availability of meaningful distinguishing factors.
2. *Segmentation models* use customer metrics that help reduce and profile the customer data base. These should be constructed early on as this information can be the basis for further analyses.
3. A *Customer Worth Model* would identify the brand's most valuable customers. The assumption is that a marketer would be looking to predict different metrics, such as "worth on the next purchase", "worth over the next 12 months", "lifetime value", etc., etc.
4. *First Purchase Scoring Model* would require a view of the customer across the entire business as well as a rich history of engaged customers. The brand would then need to build a modeling data set that is adequate to investigate the relationship between a metric for "valuable" and the inputs that are extracted, derived, and constructed from the first purchase of each customer.
5. A *Propensity to Respond Model* is heavily dependent on marketing data and its veracity and richness. The brand would need to develop the holistic view of the customer first. Once developed, this is one of the most powerful marketing models available.

6. *A Customer Conversion Model* could be viewed as an extension of a number of the above models, with the idea of deriving a data driven metric that scores a customer's likelihood of returning after his or her first trip.
7. A *Look-a-like Model* could help the brand find potential customers who are similar to current customers.
8. *Customer Likelihood to Return Model* requires a complete view of the customer along with a considerable amount of marketing data. This would help with offers sent, who received these offers, who responded to them, etc., etc. The derived metric on its own would have value, but it could also be a significant input in a two-stage model to predict next trip value and customer worth.
9. *RFM* is a method used for analyzing customer value and it is commonly utilized in database marketing and direct marketing. A marketer should keep scores of data about a customer's purchases that include a table with the customer name, date of purchase and purchase value. From this data, the brand can score the true value of a customer and this information can be fed to the marketing department, which can decide to send an offer to the client if it makes financial sense.
10. A *Customer Acquisition Model* would then be built by using the results of the segmentation models (or a different metric for desirable customers). A deeper investigation of a marketer's source systems is needed and this could be part of the analysis to help understand what is available, and what might be available from external parties.
11. *Customer Churn Models* would require preliminary analysis to extract only engaged customers. The brand would need to derive a statistcially driven metric that indicates whether a customer had churned or not. The brand could then build models to detect upcoming customer attrition, which would be useful as an early warning system of potential churners.

Edge Analytics

The driving concept behind edge analytics is the fact that data loses its value over time. The concept of "Edge Analytics"—i.e., the processing of analytics at the point or very close to the point where the data is being collected—exponentially increases one's ability to use predictive analytics where it can be best utilized.

As Patrick McGarry explains in his article *Why Edge Computing is Here to Stay*[178], edge analytics is easier to implement than ever before because in-the-field micro data centers use a fraction of the space, power and cost of a traditional analytics infrastructure, but they can provide massive performance gains. These systems use "hybrid computing technology, seamlessly integrating diverse computing technologies, whether they are x86, GPU or FPGA technologies, or any combination thereof. They are extremely compact in space and require very little power, yet still provide performance that is several orders of magnitude more than what today's traditional systems can provide."[178] "It's a win/win situation for all involved; insights come faster than ever before, operational expenses are lower," McGarry ads.[178]

Although building an edge analytics platform requires a shift in corporate thinking, the ROI benefits should far outweigh the costs. "The cost savings by scaling back central data analytics infrastructures to handle non-time sensitive analysis while installing cost-efficient platforms purpose-built for edge analytics can have a real impact on an organization's budget," McGarry notes.[178] The value of near-instant analysis and insight cannot be underestimated in a business world so dependent on customer excellence. Avoiding latency and eliminating the time and costs associated with transporting the data to and from the edge is a major step toward achieving that goal.[178]

IoT sensors can help spot customers arriving in a shopping mall, or track employees, suppliers, and supplies throughout a store. Edge analytics can also help analyze customer behavior. Other areas where IoT can help include compliance analysis and mobile data thinning, i.e., the culling of mobile data noise from social media or direct mobile streams. Personally, I believe edge analytics could be one of the top technologies that can give a marketer a competitive advantage over its rivals and I will provide more details on how this technology can be implemented within a marketer's environment in chapter six.

Sentiment Analysis

According to the TDWI *Customer Analytics in the Age of Social Media*[118] Research report, "Sentiment analysis enables organizations to discover positive and negative comments in social media, customer comment and review sites, and similar sources. Sentiment analysis often focuses on monitoring and measuring the 'buzz' value, usually through volume and frequency of comments around a topic."[118] However, it is not just the buzz that is important, many organizations want more analytical depth so that they can understand what the buzz is all about, where it comes from, and who is benefiting or not benefiting the most from it.[118]

For more sophisticated sentiment analysis, text analytics tools that use word extraction, natural language processing, pattern matching, and other approaches to examine social media users' expressions are employed.[118] "Sentiment analysis can give organizations early notice in real time of factors that may be affecting customer churn; the research shows that 14% are interested in monitoring and analyzing social activity in real time."[118]

Sentiment analysis is also key to understanding a competitors' relative strengths and weaknesses in the social sphere.[118] The TDWI research found that "18% of respondents are examining social media data to analyze a competition's 'share of voice.'"[118]

As Joe Mullich explains in his article *Opposition Research: Sentiment Analysis as a Competitive Marketing Tool*[179]:

> "When a leading bank wanted to find out how it stacked up against competitors, it assumed customers would focus on lending terms and interest rates. To the bank's surprise, the most enthusiastic discourse on blogs and specialized financial forums related to a smartphone app a competing financial institution had just put out. The bank had dismissed apps as a generic marketing gimmick, like the old custom of giving away a toaster for opening an account. After learning how much customers valued the app, the bank quickly created its own with the same prized features as its competitor."

I think it was pretty naïve and not forward-thinking at all to believe that an app was only going to be a generic marketing gimmick, but that's not the focus of this book. As Joseph Carrabis, founder of NextStage Evolution, the company that did the analysis for the bank, notes, "You get the benefits of corporate espionage without doing corporate espionage."[179] With corporate espionage going high tech these days, businesses need all the help they can get.

Sentiment analysis can also provide early insight into a competitor's new product initiatives.[179] "Very often companies will test market before they release a product," explains Mullich.[179] "And no matter what you get people to sign saying that they won't share information, they'll go online and talk about products they're excited about," warns Mullich.[179] You can't change human nature, but sometimes you can make it work for you.

In addition, sentiment analysis can alert companies about new competitors who are bubbling up to the surface or even coming out of left-field.[179] Ford obviously considers Chevy a competitor, but it might not think of public transport as being threatening competition.[179] However, Carrabis argues that a car company should realize that it might want to analyze online discussion boards to try to understand why people are making different transportation choices so it can change its product offerings or marketing campaigns to emphasize their customers' growing environmental concerns and personal ecological footprints.[179] "We have to think broader and wider than we used to," Carrabis contends.[179] The lesson here: don't just look at your closest competitors as your competition, widen your view to the potential threat that could come out of left field.

This is why it is imperative for a marketer to understand how and why people discuss competitors online. "When car shoppers talk online they don't talk about 'quality,'" says Susan Etlinger, an analyst with the Altimeter Group.[179] "They'll say, 'I love the leather interior' or 'the cup holder fell out.' It takes meticulous work to roll together all the indicators of quality."[179]

Etlinger suggests that "social-media listening teams work with the groups in the organization that handle keyword search terms and search-engine optimization effort, since they have a solid grasp on how people online actually talk about the industry and products."[179] Social media listening can utilize lists of SEO words. It can take advantage of work already done, as well as reiterate the marketing message through multiple social channels, which would, in turn, help the SEO process immensely.

Another thing to keep in mind: "At any point in time, the way people feel about a brand can be distorted online, because things like Twitter are so volatile and affected by the news of the day," warns Etlinger.[179] "But over time, you can get directional trends—why do people love or hate you, how do they feel about your product compared to the competitor's products."[179] Companies in China have the added problem of Internet users who actively write fraudulent blogs and posts about a company's products and/or services; separating fact from fiction is not an easy task, but it needs to be done to get accurate measurements of sentiment.

"My belief is that the sweet spot for social media is not conversion, but nurturing," said Brian Ellefritz, vice president of global social media at SAP[118] "Whether it's in your community, through Twitter, or through Facebook pages, you want to build an increasing conviction that your company is the one to do business with," says Ellefritz.[118] "It's about establishing a belief system that becomes robust with the support of fans and followers. The question is how you measure that and create value out of that investment," he added.[118]

When it comes to setting strategies for customer and social media analytics, Stodder recommends the following[118]:

- Use social media data to support an active, not passive social media strategy. "In competitive, fast-moving markets, organizations cannot just passively listen to and analyze social media data. The analytics should plug into strategies for engaging users and customers on social networks and comment sites. Predictive analytics can help organizations anticipate the results of active strategies. Special events such as tweet-ups can build on customer data analysis and create positive exchanges and engagement."[118]
- Take a holistic view of the potential contributions of social media data analytics. "Understanding behavior in the social sphere can have a positive impact, not just on marketing and sales functions, but also on services and other processes in the organization. Marketing executives should use social media insights to improve brand awareness and

reputation throughout the organization."[118]
- Give CMOs and marketing executives the ability to understand the financial impact of certain decisions.
- Apply analytics to gain a more accurate understanding of marketing attribution. "Last-touch" attribution may be easy to affix, but it is not always reliable. Powerful analytics, along with big data, can help organizations get a better understanding of what truly affects a customer's purchase decision.

Clickstream Analysis

When a person visits a website, he or she leaves behind a digital trail, which is known as a "clickstream." Clickstream analysis is the process of collecting, aggregating, reporting and analyzing the browsing behavior of a web surfer to better understand the intentions of users and their interests in specific content or products on a website. Clickstream analysis is the process of collecting, analyzing and reporting aggregate data about which pages a website visitor visits—and in what order. The path the visitor takes though a website is, basically, the clickstream.

There are two levels of clickstream analysis: traffic analytics and e-commerce analytics. Traffic analytics operates at the server level and tracks how many pages are served to the user, how long it takes each page to load, how often the user hits the browser's back or stop button and how much data is transmitted before the user moves away from the website. E-commerce-based analysis uses clickstream data to determine the effectiveness of a website as a channel-to-market. It is concerned with what pages the browser lingers on, what he or she puts in or takes out of a shopping cart, what items are purchased, whether or not the buyer belongs to a loyalty program and uses a coupon code, as well as his or her preferred methods of payment.

Utilizing clickstream analysis, a marketer can help build a Master Marketing Record for each customer in real-time. This allows the brand to test scenarios and options for the website, as well as develop personalized responses for individuals. The system should include a combination of social listening, analytics, content publication and distribution, and tracking, as well as a strong workflow and rules engine that is geared around robust governance. All these applications are built to ultimately feed a Master Marketing Profile—a centralized customer record that pulls in all data based on digital activity that can be identified by a single customer ID.

Figure 21 shows the customer funnel that takes an anonymous web browser to a known customer. Through clickstream analytics, personalization marketing can begin, and associating this activity with a customer once he or she transacts with the company should be a marketer's top priority. This can be done by enabling new users to log into his or her account via web or mobile applications, like a brand's app.

Of all the available marketing and customer channels, social media represents the biggest issue due to a brand's inability to track the value of social connections. In his article, *At Caesar's Digital Marketing Is No Crap Shoot*[112], Al Urbanski explains that at Caesar's they "wanted to make better use of the social space, but one of the overwhelming problems had been, 'How do you measure the effectiveness?' Not a lot of organizations are able to measure it effectively."[112] "Caesar's marketers didn't want to create a social island that communicated with customers separately and distinctly from all other channels," explains Urbanski.[112]

Figure 21: Customer funnel

"Each channel is tracked and rated for its ability to turn engagements into booked rooms, and Caesar's had been flying blind in the region of social media," says Urbanksi.[112] "Top management wants to know, 'How did this perform?' 'What's the return on ad spend?' and how can we tell the path to purchase from first touch point to last touch point, even if the starting point was in social media," notes Kahle, Caesars' Web Analytics Manager.[112] "Before, we couldn't understand social's role in the transaction. You could track it to a degree, but you built a social island and there was some guessing involved. You could end up double counting social's contribution," warns Kahle.[112]

"To support these efforts, Caesars invested in Adobe's Digital Marketing Suite, which includes real-time tracking and segmentation of digital site visitors, analysis of social media's role in purchasing, and content testing by segment or individual visitor," explains Kahle.[112]

The problem with driving online conversions among Frequent Independent Travelers (FITs), however, is that—based on their online behaviors—they're not loyal to a particular casino.[112] "They're on Kayak; they're on other airlines' sites. They're looking for a deal," says Kahle, who adds that Caesars regularly targets these travelers with offers, such as free meals and free gaming play.[112] This is something brands should be actively doing as well, to cut out the Expedia, Orbitz, and/or C-trip middlemen.

As noted in the article[112]:

> "Kahle's staff conducted A/B analysis aimed at presenting the company's individual properties with the best option for increasing Total Rewards memberships. Half the people who searched Total Rewards online were sent to the main Caesars Entertainment homepage, while the other half was sent to the homepage of a specific property. While the conversion rate for room reservations was the same for both groups, the latter group signed up for the loyalty program at a significantly higher rate. The practice was adopted across the Caesars Web network and resulted in a 10% increase in sign-ups."

"A similar test was used to maximize business from Total Rewards members, testing its old website interfaces against a new design. The difference was an eye-opener. The conversion rate for the newer interface option was 70% higher," Kahle explains.[112]

"In the past, when planning changes to Web page design or elements, the winning design was often decided by the highest-ranking person in the office," Kahle says.[112] "With Adobe testing, people's personal opinions aren't the deciding factor. We can look at the numbers, see the results, and clearly identify the best-performing design."[112] Kahle adds that Caesars deployed these new capabilities without having to increase its IT staff.[112]

"Caesars went from a culture of opinion to a culture of data. We essentially gave them the...flexibility to test so that the [end-user's] experience is optimized," says Matt Langie, senior director of product marketing at Adobe.[112]

As per Paul Greenberg's article *Is Adobe a Marketing Player Now?*[180]:

> "First thing to know about Adobe is that they are a tools company—and this is both good and bad. For the most part and for the purposes of this discussion, the products are a good thing. The second thing to know about Adobe (and the Marketing Cloud) is that what they are currently offering is a significant piece of a digital engagement platform. Keep in mind this is for the marketing side—the first line of engagement—the first place that the customer comes into

> contact with the brand and either starts interacting or doesn't."

The Master Marketing Record is the core around which Adobe's Marketing Cloud is built and this goes to the heart of two Adobe themes, one of which is as old as modern man—the single view of the customer—and the other is the Real Time Enterprise.

Just to step into the MCM (Multi-Channel Marketing) arena for a moment, as Greenberg explains, The Adobe Marketing Cloud essentially consists of a basket of applications and services, including[180]:

- Adobe Analytics—A strong package focused around digital analytics, mobile and web that has predictive analytics at its core.
- Adobe Campaign—this is where the core Neolane integration occurred.
- Adobe Target—This allows users to test scenarios and options for the web, as well as develop personalized responses for individuals. It is comparable to the functionality of Epiphany and Exact Target, two similar marketing automation products.
- Adobe Experience Manager—This is where users manage the assets and create and manage the communities needed to optimize the customer journey across all digital channels and media.
- Adobe Social—combining social listening, analytics, content publication and distribution, tracking, as well as a strong workflow and rules engine geared towards governance and strict protocols.
- Adobe Media Optimizer—helps users define an audience, as well as create ads that will appeal to individuals and outline which media mix should be used to maximize that appeal.[180]

All these applications are built to ultimately feed what Adobe calls the Master Marketing Profile—a centralized customer record that pulls in all data based on digital activity that can be identified by a single customer ID. "That means that John Smith's record will have his social profile data, his transactional data, his response to campaigns, his click-throughs, his web browsing, etc. This goes to the heart of their effort—the personalization of the response to individual customers. The Master Marketing Profile is where you find all that data."[180]

To Adobe's credit, Greenberg feels that the software vendor has done some solid integration of the entire portfolio.[180] The total package, if viewed as an advanced digital marketing cloud, some believe it could very well be the best of its kind on the market. However, Adobe is "competing with other Marketing Clouds— notably, if the name Marketing Cloud is meaningful, salesforce.com and Oracle. If the name Marketing Cloud isn't—add Marketo, Microsoft, Teradata Applications, SAS, IBM Unica, and Infor to the mix. If niche players count, there are dozens and dozens out there chomping off pieces of the potential revenue stream. This is a hot competition."[180]

In his article *Google Attribution Allows Clear, Seamless Campaign Analysis for Marketers*[181], Matthew Bains explains that Google has released a new tool called "Google Attribution" that "uses machine learning and data to help marketers measure the impact of each of their marketing touch points, across multiple channels, and across multiple devices." "It uses data that's already there from AdWords and Google Analytics; it just takes that data and shows you how each customer moved through their buyer's journey and attributes those conversions respectively. It provides a single view of the path to purchase to help marketers learn what is actually working compared to what seems to be working," notes Bains.[181]

Wanamaker would be ecstatic as "marketers can finally begin to answer the age-old question that is typically at the forefront of their minds—is my marketing working?", as Bains puts it.[181]

Moving away from the flawed last-click attribution idea, "Google Attribution uses machine learning and data to help marketers measure the impact of each of their marketing touch points, across multiple channels, and across multiple devices."[181] Google Attribution shows users how each customer moves through his or her buyer's journey and attributes those conversions respectively.[181] "It provides a single view of the path to purchase to help marketers learn what is actually working compared to what seems to be working," Bains explains.[181]

"With last click, the reward for the conversion often went to the last touch point that the user made, often with a sale after a click on an ad," notes Bains.[181] However, "This could lead to false impressions about the effectiveness of an ad campaign versus display ads, organic search, social, email affiliates, and many other interactions that a customer made with a business along the buyer's journey. Maybe organic search is actually more important than display ads or vice versa."[181]

"The aim of Google Attribution is to simplify the complex problem of multichannel, multi-device attribution by leveraging data advertisers already have in Google Analytics, AdWords, or DoubleClick Search," adds Kishore Kanakemedela, director of product management at Google.[181]

With Attribution, users can see how effective each step of a campaign is, whether that step is a video ad, a banner ad, a carousel ad, an email, a social campaign, or any other quantifiable digital content.[181] Attribution will show users how these micro-moments work together to spot leads and drive them to conversions.[181] Marketers will now have more transparency on what is actually driving their business, which in turn, can help them better allocate their budgets between channels[181]; quantifiable success on one channel leads to increased budget spend for that channel, that is until the numbers drop off, then reallocation commences.

Location Analytics

Location analytics is a technology that enables firms to capture and analyze location data on customers who are at a physical venue. In his article *How Location Analytics Will Transform Retail*[182], Tony Costa says that, "By leveraging connected mobile devices such as smartphones, existing in-venue Wi-Fi networks, low cost Bluetooth-enabled beacons, and a handful of other technologies, location analytics vendors have made it possible to get location analytics solutions up and running fast at a minimal cost." "Customer tracking data is typically sent to the location analytics vendor where it is analyzed and accessed via online dashboards that provide actionable data tailored to the needs of specific employees—from the store manager to the executive C-suite," adds Costa.[182]

Already, the scale of data collected by early adopters is venturing into "Big Data" territory. Location analytics firm RetailNext currently "tracks more than 500 million shoppers per year by collecting data from more than 65,000 sensors installed in thousands of retail stores. A single customer visit alone can result in over 10,000 unique data points, not including the data gathered at the point of sale."[182]

RetailNext is not alone; Euclid Analytics—one of the biggest players in this space—"collects six billion customer measurements each day across thousands of locations, and multiple location analytics firms surveyed said they are adding hundreds of new venues each month."[182]

As Costa explains, venue owners are applying insights gathered from location analytics to help in all aspects of their business, including[182]:

1. Design. "After analyzing traffic flows in their stores, a big box retailer realized that less than 10% of customers visiting their shoe department engaged with the self-service wall display where merchandise was stacked. The culprit turned out to be a series of benches placed in front of the wall, limiting customer access."[182] Simply relocating the benches to enhance accessibility increased sales in the department by double digits.[182]
2. Marketing. A restaurant chain wanted to understand whether sponsoring a local music festival had a measurable impact on customer visits. After collecting data on 15,000 visitors passing through the festival entrances and comparing it to customers who visited their restaurants two months before and after the festival, they concluded that the festival resulted in 1,300 net new customer visits.[182]
3. Operations. "A grocery store chain used location analytics to understand customer wait times in various departments and check-out registers. This data not only enabled the company to hold managers

accountable for wait times, but it gave additional insight into (and justification for) staffing needs."[182]
4. Strategy. A regional clothing chain was concerned that opening an outlet store would cannibalize customers from its main stores. "After analyzing the customer base visiting each store, they discovered that less than 2% of their main store customers visited their outlet. The upside: the outlet gave them access to an entirely new customer base with minimal impact to existing store sales."[182]

Just as web analytics is an essential tool on the web, location analytics will become a must-have for designing, managing, and measuring offline experiences.[182] Location analytics is set to have a profound impact on how businesses operate in the very near future. Costa argues that having the ability "to identify, track, and target customers in physical locations will enable companies to extend preferential status and rewards to customers based on their behaviors, rewarding them on the number and frequency of visits, where they go in venues, and their exclusive loyalty (i.e., not visiting competitor venues)."[182]

Conclusion

In this chapter, I wanted to lay out the many ways in which *The A.I. Marketer* can track and understand its customer base on both a micro and a macro level. Many of the analytical models I mention have been around for decades and every brand should be aware that creativity with these models is what will separate them from their competitors. If everyone uses the same tools, creativity will be the main differentiator.

"Despite all the transformational technological change that has created such a data-rich world for marketers, there still also needs to be great creative in marketing. The emotional hook that marketing has always been able to create with customers absolutely remains necessary," argue Lewnes and Keller.[4]

"There's a myth that all creatives hate data," say Lewnes and Keller.[4] While that may have been true in the past, "many modern creatives actually like to see the impact they're having, whether it's looking at social-sharing metrics or larger data sets capturing online behavior."[4] These creatives "understand that creativity can be sparked by data and that their creative output can become stronger by adapting it to market input."[4]

Contrary to what one would think, "Creativity does not have to come just from within a company either."[4] "The most successful brands today are shaped by the brand's community of customers and partners as much as they are by the company itself," say Lewnes and Keller.[4] "Cocreation in all forms can fuel the creative process—whether directly with customers or in collaboration with like-minded partners, bringing a benefit to both entities," the writers argue.[4] For example, "Adobe teamed up with the band Imagine Dragons to commemorate the 25th anniversary of its industry-leading video-editing software, Adobe Premiere Pro."[4] Adobe "granted its community exclusive raw footage from the band's megahit 'Believer' and challenged them to recut it for the chance to win $25,000."[4] The unique campaign received thousands of submissions from around the world, a staggering number considering editing a video can be a difficult undertaking.[4] Adobe believed it was "a testament to the power of a novel concept, a well-liked partner, and the vibrancy of a strong community."[4] It speaks volumes about how a little creativity in a highly creative endeavor—digital editing—can produce a motivated community to really do some free and challenging work, for little more than having the chance to be a part of a cool contest.

With IT budgets in the millions of dollars per year, most large companies can afford software that segments its customers, creates marketing campaigns, and predicts churn, but it's what the company does with this information that matters. Customers want to be wowed and that is a high bar to reach.

Analytics can be useful for the entire customer journey process, from the initial moment a customer is picked up in a clickstream, through the descriptive analytics process of understanding website traffic, to data mining and diagnostic analytics utilized to understand customer spend. Predictive analytics can help forecast which offers a customer might use, while prescriptive analytics can optimize things like corporate budgets, and labor and stock utilization.

In her article *How Airlines Get Customer Experience So Wrong with So Much Data*[183], Sarah Steimer tells an anecdote about JetBlue's Philadelphia coffee problem that led to consistently negative reviews. JetBlue, which tops the ACSI airline rankings by striking a balance between a positive baseline experience and added perks, has built its business on customer data and analytics.[183]

A few years ago, "JetBlue noticed that it had consistently negative trends in Philadelphia. A review of both logistical data and customer reviews showed there was a timing issue: Flights weren't late, but passengers were arriving at an hour that coffee shops in the airport weren't yet open."[183]

"All of these negative [reviews] were because people weren't getting their cup of joe before jumping on this flight from Philadelphia to their meetings and feeling prepped and primed for that," Danny Cox, director of customer support and insights at JetBlue, acknowledged.[183] "We could have just stopped at, well, people in Philadelphia, they're just angry. But, instead, we dug deeper to see what was really needed. We could easily partner with the coffee shops there and ask them to adjust their hours. Immediately the scores popped back up to a more reasonable and expected area."[183] This is perhaps one of the finest uses of analytics in the airline industry, not only did it allow a marketer to raise its ratings, but it also gave JetBlue passengers access to the most important drink of all, their morning cut of joe.

---

147 Shearer C., The CRISP-DM model: the new blueprint for data mining, J Data Warehousing (2000); 5:13—22.
148 Harper, Gavin; Stephen D. Pickett (August 2006). "Methods for mining HTS data". Drug Discovery Today. 11 (15–16): 694–699.
149 SAS Institute. Data Mining and the Case for Sampling. http://sceweb.uhcl.edu/boetticher/ML_DataMining/SAS-SEMMA.pdf (Accessed November 21, 2017).
150 Stodder, D. (2012). Customer Analytics in the Age of Social Media. Retrieved from Business Times: http://www.businesstimes.com.sg/archive/monday/sites/businesstimes.com.sg/files/Customer%20Analytics%20in%20the%20Age%20of%20Social%20Media.pdf (Accessed 20 November 2017).
151 Nyce, Charles. 2007. Predictive Analytics White Paper. https://www.scribd.com/document/200505883/Predictive-Analytics-White-Paper
152 https://en.wikipedia.org/wiki/Prescriptive_analytics (Accessed 20 November 2017).
153 Kumar, V. V. (2006). Knowing What to Sell, When, and to Whom. Harvard Business Review.
154 Eckerson, Wayne. 2007. Predictive Analytics, Extending the Value of Your Data Warehouse Investment. TDWI Best Practices Report. https://www.sas.com/events/cm/174390/assets/102892_0107.pdf (Accessed 25 November 2017).
155 https://en.wikipedia.org/wiki/Decision_tree (Accessed 20 November 2017).
156 Deng, L., Gao, J., Vuppalapatie, C. Building a Big Data Analytics Service Framework for Mobile Advertising and Marketing. March 2015. https://www.researchgate.net/profile/Jerry_Gao/publication/273635443_Building_a_Big_Data_Analytics_Service_Framework_for_Mobile_Advertising_and_Marketing/links/5508de220cf26ff55f840c31.pdf (Accessed 20 November 2017).
157 Telgarsky, Matus, and Andrea Vattani. "Hartigan's Method: k-means Clustering without Voronoi." AISTATS. 2010.
158 Hartigan, J.A., Wong, M.A. A K-Means Clustering Algorithm. Journal of the Royal Statistical Society. Series C (Applied Statistics), Vol. 28, No. 1 (1979) http://www.cs.otago.ac.nz/cosc430/hartigan_1979_kmeans.pdf (Accessed 20 November 2017).
159 Pierson, Lillian. Solving Real-World Problems with Nearest Neighbor Algorithms. www.dummies.com. http://www.dummies.com/programming/big-data/data-science/solving-real-world-problems-with-nearest-neighbor-algorithms/ (Accessed 20 November 2017).
160 https://en.wikipedia.org/wiki/Logistic_regression (Accessed 20 November 2017).
161 Karp, A. H. (2009). Using Logistic Regression to Predict Customer Retention. New York. Sierra Information Service, Inc.

http://www.lexjansen.com/nesug/nesug98/solu/p095.pdf (Accessed 20 November 2017).
162 Sutton, Scott. Patron Analytics in the Casino and Gaming Industry. SAS Global Forum 2011. http://support.sas.com/resources/papers/proceedings11/379-2011.pdf (Accessed 7 November 2017).
163 Siroker, Dan, Koomen, Pete. A/B Testing: The Most Powerful Way to Turn Clicks Into Customers. Google Books.
164 https://www.cnbc.com/2018/09/20/adobe-confirms-its-buying-marketo-for-4point75-billion.html (Accessed 3 March 2019)
165 Alford, Emily. (2018). How AI could make A/B testing a thing of the past. Clickz. 10 August 2018. https://www.clickz.com/how-ai-could-make-a-b-testing-a-thing-of-the-past/216302/ (Accessed 11 February 2018).
166 Velan, Kristina. (2018). How Artificial Intelligence Will Change the Airline Passenger Experience. Apex. 4 January 2018. https://apex.aero/2018/01/04/artificial-intelligence-change-airline-passenger-experience (Accessed 10 October 2018).
167 Imdadullah, Muhammad, December 27, 2013. Time Series Analysis and Forecasting. http://itfeature.com/time-series-analysis-and-forecasting/time-series-analysis-forecasting (Accessed 20 November 2017).
168 Gray, Kevin. (2013). Quarks Media. Time Series Analysis: What it is and what it does. August 2013. https://www.quirks.com/articles/time-series-analysis-what-it-is-and-what-it-does (Accessed 2 April 2019).
169 https://en.wikipedia.org/wiki/Discriminant_function_analysis#cite_note-cohen-1 (Accessed 20 November 2017).
170 https://en.wikipedia.org/wiki/Survival_analysis (Accessed 20 November 2017).
171 Despa, Simona. Cornell Statistical Consulting Unit. Cornell University. https://www.cscu.cornell.edu/news/statnews/stnews78.pdf (Accessed 13 August 2018).
172 https://en.wikipedia.org/wiki/Swarm_intelligence (Accessed 3 March 2019).
173 Beni, G., Wang, J. (1993). "Swarm Intelligence in Cellular Robotic Systems". Proceed. NATO Advanced Workshop on Robots and Biological Systems, Tuscany, Italy, June 26–30 (1989). pp. 703–712. doi:10.1007/978-3-642-58069-7_38. ISBN 978-3-642-63461-1.
174 Coffey, PhD, Kimberly. (2016) k-means Clustering for Customer Segmentation: A Practical Example. Kimberlycoffee.com. http://www.kimberlycoffey.com/blog/2016/8/k-means-clustering-for-customer-segmentation (Accessed 7 November 2017).
175 Marketingschool.org. Conversion marketing. http://www.marketing-schools.org/types-of-marketing/conversion-marketing.html#link1 (Accessed 12 February 2019).
176 Elkind, Jordan. (2017). Lookalike modeling breathing new life into old channels. Martechtoday. 2017. August 30, 2017. https://martechtoday.com/lookalike-modeling-breathes-new-life-old-channels-203250 (Accessed 2 April 2019).
177 Levine, Barry. (2018). Marketingland.com. Adobe adds new features to its data management platform. December 3, 2018. https://marketingland.com/adobe-adds-new-features-to-its-data-management-platform-252944 (Accessed 2 April 2019).

178 Patrick McGarry. Why Edge Computing Is Here to Stay: Five Use Cases. https://www.rtinsights.com/why-edge-computing-is-here-to-stay-five-use-cases/ (Accessed 20 November 2017).
179 Mullich, J. (2012, December 10). Opposition Research: Sentiment Analysis as a Competitive Marketing Tool. Retrieved from Wellesley Information Services: http://data-informed.com/opposition-research-sentiment-analysis-as-a-competitive-marketing-tool/ (Accessed 20 November 2017).
180 Greenberg, Paul. March 31, 2014. Is Adobe a Marketing Player Now? http://www.zdnet.com/article/is-adobe-a-marketing-player-now/ (Accessed 20 November 2017).
181 Bains, Matthew. (July 28, 2017). Search Influence. http://www.searchinfluence.com/2017/07/google-attribution-allows-clear-seamless-campaign-analysis-for-marketers/ (Accessed 25 August 2017).
182 Costa, T. (2014, March 12). How Location Analytics Will Transform Retail. Retrieved from Harvard Business Review: http://blogs.hbr.org/2014/03/how-location-analytics-will-transform-retail/ (Accessed 20 November 2017).
183 Steimer, Sarah. (2018). American Marketing Association. How airlines get customer experience so wrong with so much data. 24 January, 2018. https://www.ama.org/publications/MarketingNews/Pages/how-airlines-get-customer-experience-so-wrong-with-so-much-data.aspx (Accessed 11 February 2019).

ANDREW W. PEARSON

CHAPTER FOUR: MARKETING

"I can resist everything except temptation."
~Oscar Wilde

Overview

One of the recurring themes of this book is self-reliance. I'm trying to lay out a case for brands to become much more self-reliant than they currently are. Technology is providing the tools for brands to become self-sufficient, even in areas like CRM, SEO, marketing, website personalization, social media, even programmatic advertising.

Today's advertising environment is nothing like the advertising environment of just a few years ago, as Dan Woods' amusing comparison of the differing environments that marketers face today as compared to what their 1980s counterparts might have faced back then.[27] Woods says[27]:

> "Technology has changed marketing and market research into something less like golf and more like a multi-player first-person-shooter game. Crouched behind a hut, the stealthy marketers, dressed in business-casual camouflage, assess their weapons for sending outbound messages. Email campaigns, events, blogging, tweeting, PR, ebooks, white papers, apps, banner ads, Google Ad Words, social media outreach, search engine optimization. The brave marketers rise up and blast away, using weapons not to kill consumers but to attract them to their sites, to their offers, to their communities. If the weapons work, you get incoming traffic."

There is a radical realignment going on in the advertising industry right now. As Derek Thompson points out in his *The Atlantic* article *The Media's Post-Advertising Future Is Also Its Past*[184], it might be tempting to blame media's advertiser problem and the current state of its demise as the inevitable end game of the Google and Facebook's duopoly because the two companies already receive more than half of all the dollars spent on digital advertising, as well as command[185] 90 percent of the growth in digital ad sales in 2017. However, what's happening in media right now is more complex, Thompson argues.[184] He sees the convergence of the following four trends[184]:

1. Too many players.
2. Not enough saviors.
3. No clear playbook.

4. Patrons with varying levels of beneficence.

It isn't just Facebook and Google, Thompson states[184], adding that, "just about every big tech company is talking about selling ads, meaning that just about every big tech company may become another competitor in the fight for advertising revenue."[184]

"Amazon's ad business exploded in the past year; its growth exceeded that of every other major tech company, including the duopoly," notes Thompson.[184] Wanting to move beyond just selling people iPhones, Apple is shifting its growth strategy to selling services not just phones.[186] Meanwhile, "Microsoft will make about $4 billion in advertising revenue this year, thanks to growth from LinkedIn and Bing."[184] "AT&T is building an ad network to go along with its investment in Time Warner's content, and Roku, which sells equipment for streaming television, is building ad tech," adds Thompson.[184]

As Sara Fischer explains in her article *The Next Big TV Tech Platform: Roku*[187], "Roku, the connected TV hardware company, is quietly building a large software business, driven mostly by advertising revenue." Fischer adds: "Roku typically doesn't sell advertising through an open exchange (open bidding system), like some of the big tech companies do, but it does use programmatic infrastructure to digitally target those ads—a tactic commonly referred to as 'programmatic direct' or 'programmatic reserved.'"[187]

At the Adobe Summit in March 2019, Adobe announced[188] a new partnership with Roku that would help advertisers engage with Roku's 27 million OTT viewers. These kinds of deals, which allow businesses to directly connect with consumers are the wave of the future. According to *Adweek*, "marketers can now use elements of the Adobe Advertising Cloud to match their own audience data with Roku's in a way that provides an unprecedented degree of targeting granularity for those eager to engage with the streaming provider's 27 million viewers."[188]

"Keith Eadie, VP and general manager of Adobe Advertising Cloud, said the partnership would enable advertisers to better manage elements of their cross-screen campaigns such as frequency capping and that it would also help them to better measure the outcomes of their media buys on OTT—the fastest-growing channel on the Adobe media buying platform."[188]

Meanwhile, Scott Rosenberg, general manager, business platform, Roku, added, "Programmatic trading is already a material part of our business, but it is still a minority but some of that is a function of the fact that TV marketers are not by and large as yet trading programmatically."[188]

This is because the majority of TV ad space is still traded manually, rather than programmatically. However, Rosenberg explained to *Adweek* that "this is about to change. 'Programmatic is not the predominant methodology for TV marketers, but it's coming in strong ... this partnership is so important because one of the friction points, that holds programmatic trading of OTT back is scale.'"

The standard ad business methodology is also evolving rapidly. As Sara Fischer points out in her *Axios* article *How Media Companies Lost the Advertising Business*[189], the great irony is that "many of the tech companies began with an aversion to advertising, fearing it would be a disruption towards the consumer experience." Fischer notes that Google initially feared that advertising-based search engines were "inherently biased towards the advertisers and away from the needs of consumers."[189] "Facebook CEO Mark Zuckerberg reportedly only accepted advertising on his platform initially so he could pay the bills."[189] "Snapchat boss Evan Spiegel initially criticized some targeted ads as 'creepy,' but four years later, 90% of the ads sold on Snap's platform are sold in an automated fashion."[189]

Today, most tech companies are embracing the advertising model in one form or another. Fischer adds that, "Some publishers are banding together to offer marketers to [sic] cheaper advertising against traditional media content at scale." Fischer's examples include[189]:

- Several digital websites**,** such as Quartz, New York Media, PopSugar and Rolling Stone are all joining Concert, a digital advertising marketplace operator whose stated goal is to combat the tech giants' ad dominance.
- News Corp launched a global digital ad network in 2018 called News IQ, which will pull audience data from sites like *The Wall Street Journal*, *New York Post* and *Barron's*, as well as give advertisers a way to reach highly specific audiences.
- AT&T is hoping to create a similar type of ad network through its Time Warner partnership, with plans to bring on other media and technology partners in time.
- Disney and Verizon are looking into building their own ad networks.

Fischer adds that, "It's not just tech firms, but retail and consumer package goods companies, too. Ad-serving has become so democratized that any company with an audience is now able to steal advertising dollars away from traditional media companies. Kroger has an ad business and so does its grocery rival Albertsons. Target has a media network and so does Walmart."[189]

Thompson notes that, "These tech companies have bigger audiences and more data than just about any media company could ever hope for. The result is that more advertising will gravitate not only toward 'programmatic' artificial-intelligence-driven ad sales but also toward companies that aren't principally (or even remotely) in the news-gathering business."[184]

In his *Where Did All the Advertising Jobs Go?*[190] Derek Thompson explains that, "The emergence of an advertising duopoly has coincided with the rise of 'programmatic advertising,' a torpid term that essentially means 'companies using algorithms to buy and place ads in those little boxes all over the internet.'" Thompson adds that, "advertising has long been a relationship-driven business, in which multimillion-dollar contracts are hammered out over one-on-one meetings, countless lunches, and even more-countless drinks. With programmatic technology, however, companies can buy access to specific audiences across several publishing platforms at once, bypassing the work of building relationships with each one."[190] Because advertising has become more automated, more ads can be produced with fewer people.[190] AI should be a part of this programmatic advertising process.

In her article *Experts Weight in On the Future of Advertising* [191], Giselle Abramovich quotes Keith Eadie, VP and GM of Adobe Advertising Cloud, who argues that, "Programmatic advertising is no longer a silo or a distinct media channel—it's simply how brands are buying ads." "As a result," Eadie says, "the focus is shifting from execution to strategy and better connecting marketing and advertising."[191]

"With programmatic, the big lure for advertisers is its efficiency, according to Amy Avery, Droga5's chief intelligence officer."[191] "But it also needs to be about effectiveness, too," Avery argues.[191] "I don't think we will ever go to 100% [programmatic ad buying]. But I do think it can increase to much more than it is now once the effectiveness variables come into play."[191] Avery believes this will happen once AI is integrated to help understand context and uses this information to inform messaging.[191]

Eadie believes the $70 billion TV advertising market is a great example of progress on this front.[191] Specifically, NBCUniversal recently "made its full portfolio of broadcast and cable television available to advertisers through a DSP, essentially automating ad buying for its TV market."[191]

"The old story about programmatic advertising was that both marketers and digital publishers—think AOL, or any news site—embraced the technology, as it allowed companies to cheaply target specific audiences on a budget," explains Thompson.[190] However, Thompson notes that, "the new reality is that programmatic advertising has placed many advertisements in controversial places, next to low-quality news sources or outright offensive content."[190] This has caused marketers to both cut back on running programmatic ad campaigns, as well as bringing their operations in-house, where they have more control over both who sees their ads and where they are seen.[190] "The upshot," Thompson concludes is that, "Programmatic ads have been a double blow to media agencies, first automating their function and then encouraging companies to insource the work."[190]

Becoming more self-sufficient may not be a bad thing for typical brand marketers. Throughout this book I try to make the argument that marketing departments should be more self-reliant. Software that does everything from automating marketing campaigns, to inexpensively segmenting customers, to simplifying the mundane and repetitive processes of producing and categorizing content, can help marketers speed up the creative process enormously.

Thompson argues that currently there is a "merging of the advertising and entertainment businesses."[190] "As smartphone screens have edged out TV as the most important real estate for media, companies have invested more in 'branded content'—corporate-sponsored media, such as an article or video, that resembles traditional entertainment more than it does traditional advertising."[190] Thompson concludes that, "In short, the future of the advertising business is being moved to technology companies managing ad networks and media companies making branded content—that is, away from the ad agencies."[190] These are cross-currents that brands need to be aware of because they are not just radically changing the marketing landscape but also offering huge marketing opportunities to brands willing to embrace them.

If software products can alleviate the mundane and repetitive tasks humans are currently doing—and they most definitely can—then businesses can redeploy their staff to handle the more interesting and probably profitable work, like programmatic functions.

According to Lewnes and Keller, "Perceived value—especially with complex technological products—can be difficult for customers to assess."[4] "Formally, perceived value is all the different benefits gained by customers from purchasing and using a product as well as all the different costs saved. These are not just financial benefits and costs but also psychological, social, emotional, and other types of benefits and costs," claim Lewnes and Keller.[4] For the writers, "Value creation is only necessary, but not sufficient, for marketing success. Value must also be effectively and efficiently communicated and delivered."[4]

Psychology of Personalization

So, what does personalization really mean? It is a word that has been kicking around the marketing community for at least a decade now. The underlying psychology of the individual being marketed to is one of the key elements of personalization marketing. In his Buffer article *15 Psychological Studies That Will Boost Your Social Media Marketing*[192], Kevan Lee lists several psychological techniques that marketers should be using to reach today's audience. Lee's list is as follows:

1. The endowment effect—the hypothesis that people ascribe more value to things merely because they own them.[193]

2. Reciprocity—in social psychology, reciprocity is a social norm of responding to a positive action with another positive action, rewarding kind actions.[194]
3. Consistency principle—People like to be consistent with the things they have previously said or done.[195]
4. Foot-in-the-door technique—"a strategy used to persuade people to agree to a particular action, based on the idea that if a respondent will comply with a small initial request then they will be more likely to agree to a later, more significant, request, which they would not have agreed to had they been asked it outright."[196]
5. Framing effect—a cognitive bias where people decide on options based on if the options are presented with positive or negative semantics; e.g. as a personal loss or gain.[197]
6. Loss aversion—the disutility of giving up an object is greater that the utility associated with acquiring it.[198]
7. Conformity and social influence—the theory that people will conform their ideas to the ideas of a group under social pressure.[199]
8. Acquiescence effect—a tendency to respond in the affirmative to survey items irrespective of substantive content.[200]
9. Mere exposure effect—the more often a person sees something new, the more positive meaning they will give it.[192]
10. Informational social influence—social influence occurs when a person's emotions, opinions or behaviors are affected by others intentionally or unintentionally.
11. The decoy effect—the phenomenon whereby consumers will tend to have a specific change in preference between two options when also presented with a third option that is asymmetrically dominated.[201]
12. Buffer effect or social support—the process in which a psychosocial resource reduces the impact of life stress on psychological well-being.[202]
13. Propinquity effect—the tendency for people to form friendships or romantic relationships with those whom they encounter often, forming a bond between subject and friend.[203]
14. Availability heuristic—"a mental shortcut that relies on immediate examples that come to a given person's mind when evaluating a specific topic, concept, method or decision."[204]
15. Scarcity principle—"economic theory in which a limited supply of a good, coupled with a high demand for that good, results in a mismatch between the desired supply and demand equilibrium."[205]

Throughout the rest of this chapter, I will break down the 15 principles that can be utilized by AI marketers and, in the ensuing chapters, I will dive deeper into how technology and psychology can be used together to increase personalization.

The endowment effect was revealed in a famous study from Duke University, which discovered that students who had won some coveted basketball tickets in a raffle valued the tickets at $2,400, while those who had not won the tickets would only agree to pay $170 for them.[192]

The marketing takeaway here is that a brand's customers will attribute a higher value to things they already own.[192] Brands should try to increase their customer's ownership in their products by encouraging feedback and making it easier to upload suggestions and comments through social media.[192]

In terms of reciprocity, a 2002 research found that "waiters could increase tips with a tiny bit of reciprocity."[192] Tips rose by 3 percent when diners were given an after-dinner mint, but went up to 20 percent, when the server delivered the mint while looking the customers in the eye and telling them the mint was specifically for them.[192]

In another example, "BYU sociologist Phillip Kunz sent Christmas cards to 600 completely random strangers. He received 200 Christmas cards back in response."[192]

The consistency principle was displayed in a study where "Princeton researchers asked people if they would volunteer to help with the American Cancer Society. Of those who received a cold call, 4 percent agreed. A second group was called a few days prior and asked if they would hypothetically volunteer for the American Cancer Society. When the actual request came later, 31 percent agreed."[192]

The marketing takeaway here is for brands to "help current customers and potential users create an expectation of what they may say or do. For instance, get users to opt-in to a marketing course and offer tools at the end that are used by expert marketers. Subscribers may wish to stay consistent with their stated goal of improving their marketing, and signing up for recommended tools will fall right in line with this expectation."[192]

According to Lee, "The first study on the foot-in-the-door method was performed in the 1960s by Jonathan Freedman and Scott Faser."[192] Researchers called several homemakers to inquire about the household products they used.[192] Three days later, the researchers called again, this time asking to send a group of workers to the house to manually note the cleaning products in the home. The research found that "the women who responded to the first phone interview were two times more likely to respond to the second request."[192]

The marketing takeaway here: provide strong enough content that customer will be motivated to frequently open your brand emails, as well as download your content or generally go along with your requests.[192] The more little things they do, the more likely they are to comply with a larger request, like sharing your content & inviting their friends to join in the brand conversation.[192]

Researchers Amos Tverksy and Nobel prize winning Daniel Kahneman found the way they framed a question was more important than the question itself.[192] The researchers "polled two different groups of participants on which of two treatments they would choose for people infected with a deadly disease.

- Treatment A: '200 people will be saved.'
- Treatment B: 'a one-third probability of saving all 600 lives, and a two-thirds probability of saving no one.'[192]

The majority of participants picked Treatment A because of the clear and simple gain in saving lives. However, in Group 2, participants were told the following:

- Treatment A: '400 people will die.'
- Treatment B: 'a one-third probability that no one will die, and a two-thirds probability that 600 people will die.'[192]

According to Lee, "The majority of participants picked Treatment B because of the clear negative effect of Treatment A."[192]

The marketing takeaway here is that the "words you use and the way you frame your content has a direct impact on how your readers will react."[192] Lee recommends that, whenever possible, brands "frame things in a positive light so that readers can see a clear gain."[192]

According to Decision Lab, "The framing effect has consistently proven to be one of the strongest biases in decision making. The ways in which framing can be used are nearly unlimited; from emotional appeals to social pressure to priming."[206]

When a positive frame is presented people are more likely to avoid risks but will be risk-seeking when a negative frame is presented. The effect does seem to increase with age, which could be highly important when designing health and financial policies, as well as marketing to an older audience.[206]

In a famous loss aversion study, several Chicago Heights teachers were split into two groups.[192] "One group of teachers stood to receive bonuses based on the performance of their students on standardized testing. Another group received their bonus at the beginning of the year and stood to either keep it or lose it based on the results of their students' tests," explains Lee.[192] The results showed that "the prepaid bonuses—the ones that could have been lost—had a bigger impact on teachers."[192]

The marketing takeaway here is that brands need to discover their customer's challenges and reservations, and then try to alleviate those concerns up front.[192] "Risk-free trials and money-back guarantees are one way to deal with loss aversion," argues Lee since it removes the fear of loss from the equation.[192]

In 1951, social psychologist Solomon Asch conducted an experiment to investigate whether an individual would conform under social pressure.[199] As detailed in Saul McLeod *Solomon Asch—Conformity Experiment*[199], Solomon Asch experimented on 50 male students from Swarthmore College to study whether they would allow peer pressure to affect their judgment. "Using a line judgment task, Asch put a naive participant in a room with seven confederates/stooges. The confederates had agreed in advance what their responses would be when presented with the line task."[199]

According to McLeod, "The real participant did not know this and was led to believe that the other seven confederates/stooges were also real participants like themselves."[199] "Each person in the room had to state aloud which comparison line (A, B or C) was most like the target line. The answer was always obvious. The real participant sat at the end of the row and gave his or her answer last."[199]

In 12 of the 18 trials, the confederates gave the wrong answer.[199] "On average, about one third (32%) of the participants who were placed in this situation went along and conformed with the clearly incorrect majority on the critical trials," says McLeod.[199]

After the test, the subjects were asked why they conformed and most of them "said that they did not really believe their conforming answers, but had gone along with the group for fear of being ridiculed or thought 'peculiar.'"[199] Asch concluded that, "Apparently, people conform for two main reasons: because they want to fit in with the group (normative influence) and because they believe the group is better informed than they are (informational influence)."[199] The key takeaway for marketers here is that, "influencers and industry leaders can help your product appear more valuable to others."[192]

According to the psychology website Changing Minds [207] there are three scenarios in which we are most likely to acquiesce to the request of others:

- They seem to be a superior in some way.
- They have a need whereby we can easily help them.
- Answering the question fully seems like hard work.

Lee states that, "Leading questions are one way that the acquiescence effect impacts the answers that one gives."[192]

The marketing takeaway here is that brands should be aware of the leading questions they may be asking in customer development calls, surveys, or questionnaires.[192] "People can be easily swayed to answer in a certain way if the question seems tilted in a certain direction," warns—and recommends—Lee.[192]

Robert Zajonc's Chinese character study showed how the mere exposure to something could increase positive feelings about it. Zajonc showed several Chinese characters to non-Chinese-speaking participants, either once or up to 25 times, then asked the participants to guess the meaning of the characters.[192] The study revealed that the "more often a participant saw a character, the more positive meaning they gave."[192]

The marketing takeaway here is brands shouldn't be afraid to repeat their messaging.[192] Social media is the perfect channel for brands to share their content, as reposting helpful content can have a direct impact on an audience.[192] The repetition seen here probably goes unnoticed here because customers can easily surf away from a brand's messaging by visiting other social media pages and/or websites.

In an effort to curtail energy usage, Alex Lasky of Opower ran an experiment to study how messaging could best encourage others to save energy.[208] Opower sent customers one of the following four messages[192]:

- You can save $54 this month.
- You can save the planet.
- You can be a good citizen.
- Your neighbors are doing better than you.

Only the fourth message worked, leading to a 2 percent reduction in household energy usage.[192] The study showed that brands should use the experience of others to help people see the benefits of their product or services.[192] There's a close correlation between informational social influence and social proof.[192]

The decoy effect can be seen in an old subscription advertisement for *The Economist*, which stated[192]:

- Web Subscription – $59
- Print Subscription – $125
- Web and Print Subscription – $125

When Professor Dan Ariely tested this model with his students at MIT, he asked them to choose a subscription option among the three choices.[192] The results were as follows[192]:

- Web Subscription – $59 (16 students)
- Print Subscription – $125 (0 students)
- Web and Print Subscription – $125 (84 students)
- *Total revenue: $11,444*

When the print subscription was removed, the results looked like this[192]:

- Web Subscription – $59 (68 students)
- Web and Print Subscription – $125 (32 students)
- *Total revenue: $8,012*

Obviously, adding the decoy increases sales and the marketing takeaway is for brands to add a decoy in their pricing.[192] Lee concludes that, "The inclusion of an option that is 'asymmetrically dominated' (a plan that seems out of whack or a feature list that doesn't quite add up) will make the other options more appealing."[192]

In terms of the buffer effect, in a study of pregnant women, "researchers found that 91 percent of those with high stress and low social support suffered complications whereas only 33 percent of pregnant women with high stress and high social support suffered complications."

The marketing takeaway here is for brands to be consistent with availability and support for their customers.[192] "Constant support—in the form of email communication, blogging, in-app messages etc.—may help others feel more comfortable and less stressed," advises Lee.[192]

For the propinquity effect, researchers discovered that "tenants in a small two-floor apartment had closer friendships with their immediate neighbors. Least likely friendships were between those on separate floors. And tenants who lived near staircases and mailboxes had friendships on both floors."[192]

The marketing takeaway here is for brands to be a constant presence on social media, as well as in the inbox of its customers and subscribers.[192]

In the late 1960s, Amos Tversky and Daniel Kahneman began their work on "heuristic and biases." [204] They discovered "that judgment under uncertainty often relies on a limited number of simplifying heuristics rather than extensive algorithmic processing."[204] Tversky and Kahneman coined the term "availability heuristic" to explain these biases. According to Wikipedia, an "availability heuristic is a mental shortcut that relies on immediate examples that come to a given person's mind when evaluating a specific topic, concept, method or decision. As follows, people tend to use a readily available fact to base their beliefs about a comparably distant concept."[204]

In their *New Yorker* article, *The Two Friends Who Changed How We Think About How We Think*[209], Cass Sunstein and Richard Thaler explain that there were two distinct themes in the work of Tverksy and Kahneman – judgment and decision-making. "Judgment is about estimating (or guessing) magnitudes and probabilities. *How likely is it that a billionaire businessman from New York with no experience in government gets elected President?* Decision-making is about how we choose, especially when there is uncertainty (meaning almost all the time). *What should we do now?*" say Sunstein and Thaler.[209]

"Kahneman and Tversky showed that, in both of these domains, human beings hardly behave as if they were trained or intuitive statisticians. Rather, their judgments and decisions deviate in identifiable ways from idealized economic models," explain Sunstein and Thaler.[209] "Most of the importance of Kahneman and Tversky's work lies in the claim that departures from perfect rationality can be anticipated and specified. In other words, errors are not only common but also predictable," they say.[209]

Sunstein and Thaler explain the heuristic principle as such[209]:

> *For instance: ask people what they think is the ratio of gun homicides to gun suicides in the United States. Most of them will guess that gun homicides are much more common, but the truth is that gun suicides happen about twice as often. The explanation that Kahneman and Tversky offered for this type of judgment error is based on the concept of "availability." That is, the easier it is for us to recall instances in which something has happened, the more likely we will assume it is. This rule of thumb works pretty well most of the time, but it can lead to big mistakes when frequency and ease of recall diverge. Since gun homicides get more media coverage than gun suicides, people wrongly think they are more likely. The availability heuristic, as Kahneman and Tversky called it, leads people to both excessive fear and unjustified complacency—and it can lead governments astray as well.*

"The influence of their work has been immense—not only in psychology and economics, where it has become part of the normal conversation, but in every other field of social science, as well as medicine, law, and, increasingly, business and public policy," note Sunstein and Thaler.[209]

The marketing takeaway here is for brands to make their products or services easy to grasp by providing examples of the actions you want users to take.[192]

Also known as the 'Fear of missing out' syndrome, the scarcity principle plays upon the idea that people covet things that are scarce. As Investopedia explains it, "Consumers place a higher value on goods that are scarce than on goods that are abundant. Psychologists note that when a good or service is perceived to be scarce, people want it more. Consider how many times you've seen an advertisement stating something like: limited time offer, limited quantities, while supplies last, liquidation sale, only a few items left in stock, etc. The feigned scarcity causes a surge in the demand for the commodity."[205]

"Marketers use the scarcity principle as a sales tactic to drive up demand and sales," says Investopedia.[205] The psychology behind the scarcity principle dovetails well with social proof and commitment.[205] "Social proof is consistent with the belief that people judge a product as high quality if it is scarce or if people appear to be buying it. On the principle of commitment, someone who has committed himself to acquiring something will want it more if he finds out he cannot have it," argues Investopedia.[205]

Another term for the scarcity principle is the 'Fear of missing out' syndrome. The FYRE festival played up the fear of missing out principle as well as any promotional event ever, promising concert-goers the experience of a lifetime in the Bahamas. It has now been dubbed 'the best festival that never was', Fyre Festival was touted by hip hop mogul JaRule as being the 'cultural experience of the decade' and it has now become both legendary and the most talked about festival flop ever.[210]

As explained in *The Tonic Communications Fyre Festival: How Millennial FOMO Enabled High-end Fraud*, "A promotional video was produced with the specific intent of giving audiences FOMO (Fear of Missing Out), a form of social anxiety rooted in the concern that others might be having rewarding experiences that the individual is not a part of."[210] "The video combined persuasive messaging such as 'immersive', 'transformative', 'remote and private island' with imagery of supermodels living their best lives—a carefully crafted illusion of what was in store for attendees, should they be willing to spend thousands of dollars to partake."[210]

Billy McFarland, the CEO of the festival's production company, "commented that the video's release would be known as the 'Best coordinated social influencer campaign ever'. 400 of the 'hottest' celebrities around the world including artists, comedians, influencers and models posted an ambiguous burnt orange 'Fyre tile' across their Instagram accounts using the #FyreFestival and each inviting their followers to 'join me'. That was it."[210] The campaign amazingly "garnered over 300 million impressions within 24 hours."[210] The event immediately "sold out and rival festival organisers were stunned as investors tried to pull money out of their events to put into Fyre."[210]

As two documentaries of the event have shown, it was all a scam. McFarland defrauded investors to the tune of $27.4M and he is currently serving six years in prison for these and other offenses.[210] Thanks to the fear of missing out and a brilliant social media marketing campaign, thousands of unwitting concert-goers descended upon a little known island in the Bahamas for what turned out to be the experience of a lifetime all right, just not quite the one they were expecting.

As the world becomes numb to advertising, marketers need to find a way to connect with an audience on a visceral and emotional level and utilizing the above psychological methods could be a good first step in the long process of customer personalization.

Besides the 15 psychological methodologies described above, there are a few others to consider, including social proof as well as the principle of authority. "Think of it as building the foundation for massively scalable word-of-mouth"–these are the words of venture capitalist and blogger Aileen Lee describing the concept of social proof in her article *Social Proof Is The New Marketing*.[211] Lee believes that the best way to market a product or service "is by harnessing a concept called social proof, a relatively untapped gold mine in the age of the social web."[211] Lee contends social proof can generate sharing on a viral level through social channels that can multiply the discovery of a brand and add to its influence.[211]

Wikipedia describes social proof as "a psychological phenomenon where people assume the actions of others reflect the correct behavior for a given situation... driven by the assumption that the surrounding people possess more information about the situation."[212] In other words, "people are wired to learn from the actions of others, and this can be a huge driver of consumer behavior."[211]

Eric Hoffer's quote that, "when people are free to do as they please, they usually imitate each other" is quite amusing and, unquestionably, true. It speaks volumes about the herd mentality humans seem to succumb to as individuals take cues for proper behavior in most situations from the behavior of others. Psychologists call it the "conformity bias" and it is something that politicians and marketers have tapped into to enormous effect for centuries.

Oscar Wilde's quip that, "Most people are other people. Their thoughts are someone else's opinions, their lives a mimicry, their passions a quotation" strikes a similar chord and it's an idea that brands should keep in mind as they are devising marketing plans aimed at the market of one. According to Robert Cialdini, who studied the principle of social proof in-depth in his book *Influence: The Psychology of Persuasion*[213], "we view a behavior as more correct in a given situation to the degree that we see others performing it."

In his article *The Psychology of Marketing: 18 Ways Social Proof Can Boost Your Results*[214], Alfred Lua concurs, stating, "So often in situations where we are uncertain about what to do, we would assume that the people around us (experts, celebrities, friends, etc.) have more knowledge about what's going on and what should be done." Besides that, "we often make judgments based on our overall impression of someone—A.K.A. the halo effect (named by psychologist Edward Thorndike)."[214]

In general, Lua claims there are six types of social proof, including[214]:

1. Expert: an expert in one's industry recommends your products and/or services or is associated with your brand.
2. Celebrity: a celebrity endorses your products.
3. User: current users recommend your products and/or services based on personal experiences with your brand.
4. The wisdom of the crowd: a large group of people endorse your brand for a myriad of reasons.
5. The wisdom of your friends: people see their friends approve of a product or service.

In his influential *Harvard Business Review* paper *Harnessing the Science of Persuasion*[215], Robert B. Cialdini looked at the science behind the power of persuasion and, since advertising is little more than trying to persuade a person to choose one's product and/or service over another, I think it is important to explore persuasion through the lens of social media. Cialdini contends that:

> "For the past five decades, behavioral scientists have

conducted experiments that shed considerable light on the way certain interactions lead people to concede, comply or change. This research shows that persuasion works by appealing to a limited set of deeply rooted human drives and needs, and it does so in predictable ways. Persuasion, in other words, is governed by basic principles that can be taught, learned and applied."

Cialdini's six principles are[215]:

1. Like: People like those who like them.
2. Reciprocity: People repay in kind.
3. Social proof: People follow the lead of similar others.
4. Consistency: People align with their clear commitments.
5. Authority: People defer to experts.
6. Scarcity: People want more of what they can have less of.

For the reciprocity principle, people tend to give what they want to receive.[215] Praise is likely to have a warming and softening effect on people because there is a human tendency to treat people the way they are themselves treated.[215] All kinds of companies use this concept in their marketing to customers and brands should emulate these offerings.

For the principle of social proof, people tend to follow the lead of similar others.[215] People use peer power whenever it's available.[215] Cialdini adds that, "Social creatures that they are, human beings rely heavily on the people around them for cues on how to think, feel, and act."[215] We know this intuitively, Cialdini says "because intuition has also been confirmed by experiments, such as the one first described in 1982 in the *Journal of Applied Psychology*."[215] In that study, "A group of researchers went door-to-door in Columbia, South Carolina, soliciting donations for a charity campaign and displaying a list of neighborhood residents who had already donated to the cause. The researcher found that the longer the donor list was, the more likely those solicited would be to donate as well."[215]

"To the people being solicited, the friends' and neighbors' names on the list were a form of social evidence about how they should respond. But the evidence would not have been nearly as compelling had the names been those of random strangers," explains Cialdini.[215]

The lesson here is that "persuasion can be extremely effective when it comes from peers."[215] Cialdini argues that, "The science supports what most sales professionals already know: Testimonials from satisfied customers work best when the satisfied customer and the prospective customer share similar circumstances."[215]

For the principle of consistency, brands should make their commitments active, public, and voluntary. Cialdini states that, "Liking is a powerful force, but the work of persuasion involves more than simply making people feel warmly toward you, your idea, or your product. People need not only to like you but to feel committed to what you want them to do. Good turns are one reliable way to make people feel obligated to you. Another is to win a public commitment from them."[215]

For the principle of authority, people defer to experts, so brands should relay their expertise and not assume things are self-evident.[215] As Lee explains, "Approval from a credible expert, like a magazine or blogger, can have incredible digital influence."[211] Her examples include the following[211]:

- "Visitors referred by a fashion magazine or blogger to designer fashion rentals online at Rent the Runway drive a 200% higher conversion rate than visitors driven by paid search."[211]
- "Klout identifies people who are topical experts on the social web. Klout invited 217 influencers with high Klout scores in design, luxury, tech and autos to test-drive the new Audi A8. These influencers sparked 3,500 tweets, reaching over 3.1 million people in less than 30 days—a multiplier effect of over 14,000x."[211]
- "Mom-commerce daily offer site Plum District also reached mom influencers thru Klout, and found customers referred by influential digital moms shop at 2x the rate of customers from all other marketing channels."[211]

However, Lee warns that[211]:

> "I don't think a social proof strategy will be effective if you don't start with a great product that delights customers, and that people like well enough to recommend. How do you know if you have a great product? Track organic traffic growth, reviews, ratings and repeat rates. And measure your viral coefficient—if your site includes the ability to share, what percentage of your daily visitors and users share with others? How is the good word about your product being shared outside your site on the social web? Do you know your Net Promoter Score, and your Klout score?"

In his *Fast Company* article *How to use the psychology of social proof to your advantage*[216], Ed Hallin argues that, "A lot of things go into a person's decision to purchase a product, and social proof is certainly one of those important factors. Studies show that 70% of consumers say they look at product reviews before making a purchase, and product reviews are 12x more trusted than product descriptions from manufacturers," which isn't that surprising really.[216]

One subset of social proof is celebrity social proof. This is, of course, "celebrity approval of your product or endorsements from celebrities."[216] However, Hallin warns that, "Celebrity endorsement is always a double-edged sword. If the celebrity is properly matched to the brand, it can do wonders for the company. If it's a mismatch, it may produce a bad image of the company and its brand."[216] Celebrities are also human beings and there can be a flavor-of-the-month aspect to them, especially amongst athletes, but, for every Aaron Hernandez disaster there might be a William Shatner Priceline endorsement that strikes internet and financial gold, for both parties involved.

As Hallin explains, "To understand why celebrity endorsements work from a psychological perspective, it's important to familiarize yourself with the concept of the extended self." "The extended self," Hallin contends, "is made of up the self (me) and possessions (mine). It suggests that intentionally or unintentionally we view our possessions as a reflection of ourselves. This is why consumers look for products that signify group membership and mark their position in society."[216]

"User social proof is approval from current users of a product or service," explains Hallin.[216] This includes customer testimonials, case studies, and online reviews and it is particularly effective when storytelling is involved.[216]

Hallin believes that "We tend to imagine ourselves in other people's shoes when we read or hear a story. This is why stories are so persuasive and often more trustworthy than statistics or general trends. Individual examples stick with us because we can relate to them. Although statistics can be effective, it can be tougher to really see yourself in the aggregate the way you can with a personal account."[216]

'Wisdom of the Crowds' social proof is "approval from large groups of other people. It's showing evidence that thousands, millions, or even billions have taken the action that the company wants you to take—making a purchase, subscribing, etc."[216]

Hallin argues, "We kind of joke about FOMO in pop culture, but actually the Fear of Missing Out is a real thing. It's a form of social anxiety, and it's a compulsive concern that one might miss out on an opportunity. This anxiety is especially relevant for social media, as the sharing of what's going on in our daily lives means you can constantly compare your status to others on these platforms."[216]

Unsurprisingly, Hallin contends, "Social media has sparked dozens of different ways to provide this kind of social proof. Facebook widgets that show other Facebook friends that 'like' a brand, Twitter's display of people you follow that also follow another person, and the various ways that company offer rewards for referring others to the brand are all examples of this."[216]

Social proof is a powerful marketing tool and one that brands of all kinds need to exploit. "One study of 10,000 accounts at a German bank revealed that customers who came from customer referrals had 16% higher lifetime value than those who came from other acquisition sources. Additionally, the customers churned 18% less," says Hallin.[216]

"The concept of implicit egotism is that most people subconsciously like things that 'resemble' them in some way," explains Hallin.[216] He adds that, "Studies show that we value the opinions of people we perceive as most like us. We tend to become friends with people that we have a lot in common with, so it makes sense that social triggers like Facebook's Like Box or referral programs are successful."[216]

Aileen Lee concludes that, "In the age of the social web, social proof is the new marketing. If you have a great product waiting to be discovered, figure out how to build social proof around it by putting it in front of the right early influencers. And, engineer your product to share the love. Social proof is the best way for new users to learn why your product is great, and to remind existing users why they made a smart choice."[211]

Digital Interactive Marketing: Five Paradigms

In their article *Interactivity's Unanticipated Consequences for Marketers and Marketing*, Deighton and Kornfeld believe that in this new media environment, there are five emerging marketing paradigms that are responses to the decrease of marketing's power relative to the consumer.[60] Digital interactive marketing has little use for words such as "viewer" and "listener".[60] Even the label "consumer" is of limited value because today's interactions with a person will include encounters that have nothing to do with consuming or being part of a "target market." Deighton and Kornfeld see this new digital interactive marketing breaking down into five different paradigms[60], as per Table 8.

Interactive marketing paradigm	How people use interactive technology	How firms interpose themselves to pursue marketing goals	Resulting digital media markets
Thought tracing	People search the web for information and browse for entertainment.	Firms infer states of mind from search terms and Web page content and serve relevant advertising.	A market in search terms develops.
Activity tracing	People integrate always-on computing into everyday life.	Firms exploit information on proximity and pertinence to intrude.	A market in access and identity develops.

Interactive marketing paradigm	How people use interactive technology	How firms interpose themselves to pursue marketing goals	Resulting digital media markets
Property exchanges	People participate in anonymous exchanges of goods and services.	Firms compete with these exchanges, rather than participating with them.	A market in service and reputation and reliability develops.
Social exchanges	People build identities within virtual communities.	Firms sponsor or co-opt communities.	A market in community develops, competing on functionality and status.
Cultural exchanges	People observe and participate in cultural production and exchange.	Firms offer cultural products or sponsor their production.	Firms compete in buzz markets.

Table 8: Digital Interactive Marketing: Five Paradigms
Source: Journal of Interactive Marketing[60], 23 pg. 4-10

Today, when a user searches for information or entertainment on sites like Google, she leaves a trail (also known as a "clickstream") that reveals what is on her mind.[60] This information, which Deighton and Kornfeld refer to as "thought tracing", may be "available to marketers in exactly the sense that it is available to marketers through Google, as a clue to our thoughts, goals and feelings."[60]

Mobile and social media alter the marketing landscape because the ubiquitous nature of computing makes it an "always on" proposition; both the thought *and* the activity are being traced.[60] "The argument is that when a person is always connected to the Internet, the person is always in the market, always available to be communicated with, and always an audience," contend Deighton and Kornfeld.[60]

Of course, most people don't like to be marketed to continuously throughout the day, so technology that allows people to filter out messages that don't interest them needs to be developed.[60] However, customized marketing messages will be allowed to get through. Just as television demands its audience to sit through commercials in order to enjoy free programming, Deighton and Kornfeld contend that, "we will enjoy ubiquitous computer connectivity for the price of voluntary exposure to context-specific persuasion efforts."[60]

If businesses want to succeed in this new marketing environment they must become an ally to the marketed individual, someone who is actually sought out as a person with cultural capital.[60] "Property exchanges", "social exchanges" and "cultural exchanges" are all paradigms that are "built on peer-to-peer interactivity motivated by the desire to exchange, to share information, or to express one's self" state Deighton and Kornfeld.[60]

Arguably, internet property exchanges were introduced on a mass scale by Napster, which was the first company to allow users to share and exchange files in an anonymous way.[60] Unsurprisingly, Napster ran into trouble with copyright holders and quickly left the content exchange business, but sites such as eBay, Flicker and YouTube allow users to share and even sell their property over the Internet. This is a trend that is not going to go away any time soon, if ever.

While the property exchange deals in things, the social exchange deals in identities and reputations.[60] In general, social networking sites let a person present a face to the world, "including information about whereabouts and action and a 'wall' on which friends can post short, often time-sensitive notes, allows people to exchange digital gifts, provides a marketplace for buying and selling, and allows posting of photographs and video clips."[60]

These sites allow for contextually relevant advertising because friends can share information amongst each other and some of this information can include a marketer's message. Since this messaging is coming from a trusted source, the message is considered much more trustworthy and enticing and, therefore, much more likely to be acted upon.

SEO

A web search engine is a software system designed to search for information on the web and the search results are generally presented in a line of results often referred to as search engine results page (SERPs).[217] "The information may be a mix of web pages, images, and other types of files. Some search engines also mine data available in databases or open directories. Unlike web directories, which are maintained only by human editors, search engines also maintain real-time information by running an algorithm on a web crawler."[217]

In the US, Google is, by far, the biggest search engine around.[218] Outside the U.S., Google's main competitors are "Baidu and Soso.com in China; Naver.com and Daum Communications in South Korea; Yandex in Russia; Seznam.cz in Czech Republic; Yahoo! in Japan, Taiwan [sic]."[218]

Bit players like Bing compete with Google on standard search, but today Apple and Amazon are making inroads into Google's dominance, with Facebook set to be a challenger in the not-too-distant future as well. With those latter two, search is organically included within their platforms, i.e., when someone searches for an item to buy on Amazon, it gets included in the overall search rankings, ergo, an ecommerce site has become an important search engine.

Why is search so influential? Because users flock to search engines to organize the vast amounts of information most buyers need to make purchase decisions. "The main purpose of Google Search is to hunt for text in publicly accessible documents offered by web servers, as opposed to other data, such as with Google Image Search."[218] "The order of search on Google's search-results pages is based, in part, on a priority rank called a 'PageRank.'"[218] As Sharma et al. state in their book *Mobile Marketing*, "Search is one of the best ways to find content and the absolute best way for a marketer to determine consumer intent."[28]

Google Search "provides at least 22 special features beyond the original word-search capability, and language translation of displayed pages."[218] "In June 2011, Google introduced 'Google Voice Search' and 'Search by Image' features for allowing the users to search words by speaking and by giving images. In May 2012, Google introduced a new Knowledge Graph semantic search feature to customers in the U.S."[218]

"When Google was a Stanford research project, it was nicknamed BackRub because the technology checks backlinks to determine a site's importance."[218] As I explain in the section on collaborative projects in the social media chapter, backlinks—and the quality of them—are very important for search engine optimization (SEO). The higher the quality of backlinks, the higher a website's ranking.

Even today, backlinks count, and they likely count prominently for SEO and, although backlinks are not always within a company's control, they are highly important due to their stature as the earliest persisting Google ranking factor. According to the *Moz 2015 Ranking Survey*, "the data continues to show some of the highest correlations between Google rankings and the number of links to a given page."[219] Today, *quality* backlinks are of the utmost importance and Google is the one who decides the quality of those backlinks; links from known spammy sites or sites associated with them, or merely hosted on servers that also host spammy content negatively affect rankings.[219]

In the early days of the battle for internet search supremacy, "previous keyword-based methods of ranking search results, used by many search engines that were once more popular than Google, would rank pages by how often the search terms occurred in the page, or how strongly associated the search terms were within each resulting page."[220] Google's PageRank algorithm instead "analyzes human-generated links assuming that web pages linked from many important pages are themselves likely to be important. The algorithm computes a recursive score for pages, based on the weighted sum of the PageRanks of the pages linking to them."[220] As a result, PageRank is thought to correlate well with human concepts of importance.[220]

Today, Google wants site owners to focus on developing great content—clear, accurate, highly-readable content that other site owners want to link to.[219] The way modern engines make this determination is by using advanced natural language processing, artificial intelligence and machine learning.[219] These evolving technologies enable the search engines to understand content without relying on a small set of specific keywords and phrases.[219] Google has invested heavily in this, as evidenced by the plethora of white papers and research posted on its 'Machine Intelligence' website.[219]

As Brian Alpert argues in his article *Search engine optimization in 2017: A new world where old rules sill matter*[221], "One aspect of today's search engines that makes them very different from their predecessors is that advances in artificial intelligence and machine learning have enabled them to understand content and its underlying concepts independently of specific keywords."[221] Alpert adds: "This renders null and void the old concept that one must focus on keywords specific to a certain kind of content in order to be found via search engines. In today's landscape, exact keyword matches are less influential than ever before as engines can understand the relationships between words that are semantically related."[221]

With the introduction of its Knowledge Graph, Google is attempting to give users answers instead of just links.[218] "If you want to compare the nutritional value of olive oil to butter, for example, Google Search will now give you a comparison chart with lots of details. The same holds true for other things, including dog breed and celestial objects. Google says it plans to expand this feature to more things over time."[218]

Knowledge Graph also allows users to filter results.[218] "Say you ask Google: 'Tell me about Impressionist artists.' Now, you'll see who these artists are, and a new bar on top of the results will allow you to dive in to learn more about them and to switch to learn more about abstract art, for example," Lardinois explains.[218]

Search advertising falls into two main types—natural search results, and paid sponsorship based on keywords.[222] "Natural search requires high-quality, constantly updated content and search engine optimization (SEO). Paid search requires work to optimize keyword choice and messaging, but can be phenomenally expensive."[222] When not optimized for conversion, this can be a very pricey channel to use, with low conversion rates as well.[222]

Brands should constantly be testing their web pages for the most searched for and/or visited pages. As Siroker and Komen explain, A/B testing is particularly good for website marketing, especially for uncovering a website's best landing pages.[163] "Defining success in the context of A/B testing involves taking the answer to the question of your site's ultimate purpose and turning it into something more precise: *quantifiable success metrics*. Your success metrics are the specific numbers you hope will be improved by your tests," argue Siroker and Komen.[163] An e-commerce website could easily define its success metrics in terms of revenue per visitor[163], but it is still important to understand such things as traffic sources, bounce rate, top pages, conversion rates, conversion by traffic source, amongst other things.

In his article *Supercharging Your SEO with AI Insights, Automation, and Personalization*[223], Jim Yu believes that, "Artificial intelligence is making search more human. Although search does not yet 'speak' to users in the same way the Google Duplex demo could, its objective is very similar." He adds, "Google's RankBrain technology uses machine learning to understand the meaning of the content it crawls; it infers intent from ambiguous search queries; and it uses feedback data to improve the accuracy of its results. In other words, it listens and it learns."[223]

Research by BrightEdge "into a dataset of over 50 million keywords revealed that 84.4 percent of queries return universal search results. This occurs as Google uses AI to match the layout of search results pages to the user's intent."[223] According to BrightEdge, "There are now 37 different search engine result page (SERP) categories, a number that will only increase over the coming months and years."[223] These are:

Standard	Category	Weather
Taller Organic Cards	Images	Game scores
Local 3-pack	Video / Trailers	Twitter Tweets
Quick answers	Live	Discover more places
Shopping/PLA	Top sights	Send to Google home
Rich snippets	Reviews	People also search for
Site carousel	Blogs	See results about
Site links	Knowledge panel	Widgets
Site image carousel	Carousel	Found in related search
Top stories/News	Apps	Quotes
AMP	Google for jobs	Events
Google flights	Recipes	People also ask
Scholarly research		

Table 9: Search Engine keywords
Source: BridgeEdge[223]

"The potential for personalization has not yet been truly tapped, but Google's Sundar Pichai recently made public its goal to be an 'AI-first' company."[223] This means, "we should all expect the search landscape to change dramatically as AI takes center stage in the way it has already done in products like Google Photos and Google Lens.[223] As co-founder Sergey Brin put it: "AI touches every single one of our main projects, ranging from search to photos to ads."[223]

The pace of development on this front is accelerating, as everything at Google seems to have something to do with AI.[223] "Google is all too aware that AI can simply deliver better, more personalized experiences for consumers," says Yu.[223] "However, search marketers need to pay close attention to these technological advancements if they are to avail themselves of these opportunities for SEO," claims Yu.[223]

There are three key areas in which AI can improve SEO performance[223]:

1. Insights.
2. Automation.
3. Personalization.

AI can process and analyze data at a scale simply not possible for humans.[223] "This makes it an essential complement to any search strategist, as AI can deliver the information we need to make informed decisions out of noisy, unstructured data," claims Yu.[223]

AI can be used to glean SEO insights in the following ways[223]:

- Understand underlying need in a customer journey.
- Identify content opportunities.
- Define opportunity space in the competitive context.
- Map intent to content.
- Use structured data and markup.
- Invest in more long-tail content.
- Ensure content can be crawled and surfaced easily by all user-agents.
- Automation.

"SEO is a labor-intensive industry that requires a huge amount of attention over the long term. Where we can automate tasks to receive the same output we could produce ourselves, we should make this a top priority. The time saved through automation can be applied to the areas that require our skills, like strategy and creative content," advises Yu.[223]

AI can be used for SEO personalization in the following ways[223]:

- Create content by persona, customer journey stage and delivery mechanism.
- Enhance user experience and conversion through personalization.
- Use semantically specific pages to associate query and intent.
- Use personalization and audience lists to nurture leads across search and social.
- Use AI to help publish content at the right times on the right networks.

Content Intelligence

In its article *The Magic of AI in a content-driven world. Using AI to create content faster*[224], the Adobe Enterprise Content Team argues that we're currently in the midst of a content explosion. Perhaps because of this, it is also a time when "Consumers expect to have personalized, relevant experiences at all times, in all places, and on all platforms."[224] "An IDC survey cites that 85 percent of marketing professionals feel under pressure to create assets and deliver more campaigns, more quickly. In fact, over two-thirds of respondents are creating over ten times more assets to support additional channels. This increased level of complexity is driving volume and associated costs."[224]

When thinking about what is needed to create this kind of content for thousands or even millions of customers at the near real-time speed that is necessary, doing it manually is impossible.[224] Adobe's *State of Creativity in Business 2017* survey found that "40 percent of creatives are using AI in photo and design retouching,"[224] so it's already happening. Currently, it can take hours for a designer to find just the right image to use in a piece of marketing collateral, and that's not counting the time required to manipulate the image, to crop it, to find the right layout scenario, and then to publish it to an online catalog and/or social media channel.[224] Serving the right content to the right person at the right time adds more time.[224] The cost for all this work adds up, as does the cost of photo shoots to create new assets.[224]

AI and machine learning can help marketers find and reuse assets more efficiently, as well as deliver new and personalized content at scale, thereby helping a brand get a better return on its marketing investments.[224]

According to the Adobe Sensei Team, "AI can help you create more relevant content and more engaging experiences across the customer journey at the speed your customers expect. On the creative side, AI can speed up all kinds of tedious tasks, from identifying and organizing assets to adjusting and refining for specific channels."[5] "On the audience level, AI can help you better understand which audiences respond to which content, or how often people prefer to receive emails, so you can deliver the experiences your customers want while respecting their preferences and privacy," says the team.[5]

Klein concurs, stating "because the technology becomes smarter and more intuitive as it ingests more data, AI also can play a valuable role in automating the content creation process."[64] AI "offers capabilities for marketers that range from choosing the best image for a campaign or optimizing the content in a creative based on real-time user interactions," says Klein.[64] "For example, from a content creation perspective, this allows the ability to understand the focal— or sellable—point of hero images, and then to auto-crop them for best performance based on an understanding of millions of assets with similar metadata," explains Klein.[64] "In this way, AI enhances creativity and enables a level of responsiveness and efficiency that until very recently was unachievable for marketers," concludes Klein.[64]

"Designers simply don't have time to tag the hundreds of images uploaded from every photo shoot. Even if they did, the list of keywords probably wouldn't be as exhaustive as it should be. But when a photo isn't tagged, it's virtually impossible to find by searching in an image bank of thousands," the Adobe Experience Cloud team contend.[224] "According to IDC, marketers report that one-third of marketing assets go unused or underutilized with the average organization creating hundreds of new marketing assets each year."[224] Repurposing images is unlikely, which means ROI suffers.

To try to tackle this issue, Adobe has created "Auto Tag", an Adobe Sensei capability that automatically tags images with key words.[224] For example, a marketer might have a picture of a young girl on a beach under a clear blue sky, which could be tagged with keywords like "beach", "girl", "dancing", "sundress", "blue sky", "white sand", or even a place like "Aruba."

"The Auto Tag service is used to power the Smart Tags features in Adobe Experience Manager, Photo Search in Adobe Lightroom, and Visual Search in Adobe Stock," explains the Enterprise Content Team.[224] "It's exciting to see the capabilities of auto-tagging," says Jonas Dahl, product manager for Adobe Experience Manager.[224] "We did several manual search queries against a customer's repository and showed the assets we were able to find. Then we applied Smart Tagging and did the same searches. This time the results were significantly better and much more comprehensive. And in a fraction of the time," says Dahl.[224]

"Adobe Sensei uses a unified AI and machine-learning framework, along with Adobe's deep domain expertise in the creative, marketing, and document segments, to harness the company's massive volume of content and data assets—from high-resolution images to customer clicks," says the Enterprise Content Team.[224]

"Adobe Sensei technology has learned to automatically identify what is in a photo. And not just an object like a car or a girl, but the concept of the photo, including context, quality, and style."[224] Theoretically, someone could search for an image with the words "walking" and "slow" and "the search might result in an image of an elderly man using a walker, because the technology made the connection between slow and walker."[224] Sensei's auto-phrasing service could tell you how each tag scored for prominence because the machine differentiates between the primary and secondary objects.[224] "This enables the technology to build a simple sentence or caption that more accurately describes the photo, such as 'An elderly man walking with a walker in a park.'"

Using the Sensei framework, marketers could train the AI and machine learning models to create their own unique auto tags.[224] This includes identifying brand characteristics like the company logo, so the designers adhere to specific brand standards, or training it to identify a company's products so that they can be tagged in pictures on social media, which helps identify true reach.[224]

Custom auto tagging not only has the potential to increase a marketing team's efficiency, but it could lead to image-based shopping.[224] If a customer who is looking for a new couch uploads a photo of one they like and then shop for something similar based solely on the image, that's metadata the brand can use.[224] "Auto tagging identifies what is in the photo and finds the best matches for the customer. Auto tagging also allows brands to gain a deeper understanding of their audience and can help uncover market trends on social media, without the brand having to rely on tags and text. "If you run a social media feed through Adobe Sensei, it will tag places your brand is pictured—even if it's not mentioned or tagged—allowing you to see what is trending," explains the Enterprise Content Team.[224]

As any marketer can tell you, locating an image is simply step one in a multi-step process.[224] Unless, that is, you're using AI.[224] With products like Adobe's Deep Cutout, designers "can automatically remove an image's background and replace it with one that fits the brand guidelines."[224] Soon, designers will "be able to mask out an area such as a highway, and in just a few clicks, see what it looks like with a river, neighborhood, or other background—completely reinventing the photo in seconds."[224]

Auto Crop is another Adobe tool that can automate the cropping and sizing of images for different aspect ratios. The Enterprise Content Team gives the example of a shoe manufacturer who "may have guidelines that require only the shoe be shown, so they can automatically have all photos cropped accordingly."[224]

The AI can be trained on image aesthetics as well, so it automatically selects the best image and rejects anything that is below a certain quality standard and/or criterion.[224]

Time savings in any one of these areas could be quite substantial, but combined together, the velocity of creating and delivering content gets faster and faster.[224] The real power of this technology comes from creating custom workflows that allow brands to search, mask, crop, and publish in a fraction of the time it took in the past.[224]

For brands creating international marketing campaigns, this type of custom workflow can eliminate or reduce "the tedious, manual work involved in creating all of the different assets."[224] It allows brands to scale their campaigns to as many countries as needed.[224] When a "designer uploads a file to Adobe Creative Cloud, a custom workflow kicks off a series of Adobe Sensei Content AI Services that expedites the entire process from tagging, to cropping, to delivery of your production-ready asset to Adobe Experience Manager."[224] Adobe claims all of this can happen in a matter of hours instead of days.[224] Once again, creatives are allowed to focus on being creative, a place they would, undoubtedly, prefer to be anyway.

When this type of AI is coupled with a brand's content and audience data, its value increases exponentially.[224] "When you can combine what you know about the image with what you know about the customer from online and offline behaviors, you can micro-target customers with content that is truly relevant," says Richard Curtis, principal solutions consultant for Adobe.[224] "Furthermore, the machine will continue to learn customer patterns that help you fine-tune your personalization even further."[224] As Richard notes, "More personalization leads to more clicks,"[224] to say nothing of stronger brand loyalty bonds.[224]

According to Adobe's *Indelible content, incredible experiences*[72] article, the Adobe Enterprise Content team says that, "marketers are competing with brands that lure their customers not only with products and services, but also with individual experiences. And they're setting some healthy expectations, from recommending a film that customers will love, including a personal treat in their orders."

"To meet those expectations, marketers need to develop a steady flow of compelling content. You start the content journey with ideas and concepts, then create and manage assets, deliver and personalise experiences and finally analyse performance," says the Adobe Enterprise Content team.[72] "And you need to do all of this fast enough for the experiences to adapt instantly to every channel and screen your customer may use. The goal is achieving what McKinsey calls marketing's holy grail: digital personalization at scale."[72]

Machine learning is quickly becoming the "go-to tool to help marketers connect content with data and analytics, everywhere from lead scoring and retargeting to personalization and segmentation." According to the Adobe Enterprise Content team, the following three ways can make content more potent[72]:

1. Automate tedious tasks: "The complex, data-driven tasks that once only humans could perform are now in the realm of machines. They can easily and accurately handle repetitive tasks in specific contexts, like categorizing or scheduling, and can free humans for more value-added activities."[72]
2. Gain insights from big data: "Humans can't readily process massive amounts of data. Computers can. They can analyze big data—even unstructured data—to discover patterns, trends, and associations, and then offer actionable insights."[72]
3. Improve prediction accuracy: "Not only can computers analyze data, they can learn from it. And the more data they have, the savvier they become at making on-target recommendations and predictions."[72]

"Creating authentic one-to-one experiences requires extensive resources and an investment that your budget may not support. Even if you're flush with cash, you can't scale manually—you simply cannot hire that many people or analyse such vast datasets," warns the Adobe Enterprise Content team.[72] The solution lies at the intersection of content marketing and AI—content intelligence."[72]

With machine learning, software can analyse images imported into an editor "to detect facial features, similar images and even which way the subject is looking," claims the Adobe Enterprise Content team.[72] A designer can swap out images in real time to quickly preview as many options as a client might want to see.[72] if it doesn't look quite right, no problem, the editor can go back to any point in the process and see how a different decision—perhaps a young couple in a mortgage ad look excitedly at each other rather than at their new home—and then judge how it impacts the emotional experience of the ad.[72]

"AI can serve as your creative assistant, quickly assembling suggested content for audiences at every touchpoint and even optimizing it, so the burden's not on you. If you AI application supports voice recognition, you can even tell your assistant what you want—like making the mountains disappear in a climbing shot to focus on the gear," explains the Adobe Enterprise Content team.[72]

"You want one place where everyone—marketers, creatives and outside agencies—can find approved images and video to ensure experiences will remain consistent across channels," advises the Adobe Enterprise Content team. "But manually tagging images with descriptive and contextual metadata is tedious, inconsistent and often incomplete. It's the type of job where machines excel. AI-powered smart tags automatically provide consistent, content-based metadata in seconds—saving you hours," they claim.[72] As Adobe's Senior Product Marketing Manager Elliot Sedegah succinctly puts it, "Computers will not complain about having to add metadata, they will not try to avoid it and they will work just as hard on the hundred thousandth image as on the first one."[72]

Adobe allows for personalised customer treatment. "You can introduce as many experience variations as you choose for your digital properties to personalise customer experiences. By evaluating all behavioural and contextual variables, machine learning can determine the best experience for each consumer—regardless of channel, device or screen. As machine learning learns what works with each customer, predictive analytics can tell you what each one wants to see and buy—so you'll know whether they'll be excited by the image of the hotel on the island beach in Phuket or the snowy slopers at Whistler."[72]

"Just as a doctor must address each patient's issues and concerns, you must appreciate each customer's needs and desires," argues the Adobe Enterprise Content team.[72] Meeting the expectations of each customer "calls for new tools: You can't win in the digital era with industrial-age technology."[72] Integrating AI will help brands "deliver the truly surprising and delightful experiences that keep customers feeling on top of the world," concludes the Adobe Enterprise Content team.[72]

As Tatiana Mejia explains in her article *How AI is Making it Easier for Marketers to Create Videos*[225], it's not just images that are getting the AI treatment with Adobe Sensei, video is as well. "Advances in AI and machine learning are empowering marketing teams to streamline and accelerate video production workflows and create more targeted content, in less time and with fewer resources," Mejia says.[225] Adobe's Video Auto Tag Adobe Sensei service "automatically tags attributes for each segment of each video—think colors, faces, locations, actions, products, or corporate logos. AI provides a searchable taxonomy for finding not just the right video file, but the right cut of the video, in a fraction of the time."[225]

"The Video Auto Tag process allows for natural language search of video files, even when multiple conditions are present," says Mejia.[225] "For example, if you searched for a video containing 'two dogs playing in the water at the lake,' AI-powered tools would retrieve videos meeting all five of those conditions, providing an unprecedented level of specificity for videographers and editors on tight timelines," Mejia explains.[225]

"If you're creating marketing videos, you're likely looking at insights from past videos to try to predict future performance," says Mejia, adding, "or, possibly, you go with your gut to come up with a content strategy that will get you the most views."[225] "However, both approaches can be frustrating and time consuming, while yielding unpredictable results," Mejia claims.[225] Adobe Sensei specifically developed its VideoADAI technology to address this.[225]

According to Mejia, "VideoAdAI is an exploratory technology that uses a deep neural network to automatically generate metadata, such as categories and tags for video ads."[225] To do this, "AI 'reads' the ad's video, audio, or other available information and identifies demographic segments and subjects relevant to a given platform. This makes it easy to line up the right video ad with the right ad platform. VideoAdAI then employs a second deep neural network to assign a 'watchability' score to the ad," explains Mejia.[225]

"Similarly, the AI-driven 'Auto Curate' feature powered by Adobe Sensei in Premiere Elements can view an entire video catalog, identify the best footage, and surface it for use in a project, saving videographers and editors the hassle of browsing through endless file folders of footage," says Mejia.[225]

AI can also help automate some of the traditional video production processes, which are filled with boring and repetitive tasks that most humans don't even like doing.[225] "For example, many content creators develop a series of different thumbnails, flash cards, and summaries to match the varying requirements for different video platforms like Facebook or Instagram," explains Mejia.[225] With Project Smooth Operator, marketers and editors can automate platform-specific video optimization, which "eliminates the need to manually optimize content for different social media platforms, mobile, tablet, and other devices."[225]

Additionally, Project Smooth Operator examines "video content to generate a heat map that syncs with each subject, and its action, in frames. From here, a global camera path is determined, automatically shifting the frames to capture the core action of each shot."[225]

"AI can also help with color correction, another time-consuming and costly part of the video editing process," says Mejia.[225] "Adobe Premiere's AI-powered Color Match feature applies color correction settings from one shot to all the others in a scene, taking special care to identify faces and match skin tones." If they want to, editors can "still manually adjust color correction settings using the color wheels to ensure the right color every time."[225]

Adobe Sensei can also help with the tedious post-production process of syncing audio with video.[225] "Whether it's manually adjusting sound levels, tweaking the timing of dialogue to match actors' mouths, or trying to balance musical and sound effects, the process can be extremely time consuming and resource-heavy," states Mejia.[225] "Here, also, Adobe Sensei is improving the process, while simultaneously improving video quality," says Mejia.[225]

"The Morph Cut feature in Premiere Pro automatically eliminates unwanted jump cuts, remove unwanted pauses or words, and makes each shot's transition seamless. Similarly, Premiere's audio Auto Ducking feature intelligently reduces the volume of soundtrack elements to avoid drowning out the dialogue," says Mejia.[225]

Adobe's AI-powered solutions can streamline and simplify video editing without major learning curves, "so editors can focus on the creativity and let the technology help with the time-consuming, often menial, tasks," concludes Mejia.[225]

Measurement

In her article *Future of Advertising: Automated, Personalized, and Measurable*[226], Giselle Abramovich details an Adobe Think Tank panel discussion at Advertising Week 2017, in which "Phil Gaughran, U.S. chief integration officer at agency McGarryBowen, made a bold prediction: By 2022, he said, 80% of the advertising process will be automated, 'a threshold that will never be surpassed.'" "The remaining 20%," Gaughran claims, "will comprise such elements as brand value, storytelling, and other more experiential tactics that will always need a human driver."[226]

According to Gaughran, this means a "changing job description in terms of what it means to work in advertising, unlocking a huge well of opportunity for advertisers."[226] "He reminded the audience that data doesn't deliver insights—people do."[226] "The more automated we become, the more we need humanity," he said.[226] Keith Eadie, VP of Adobe Advertising Cloud, agreed, "adding that as automation becomes mainstream, the big differentiator for brands will be human insight and creativity."[226] "Brands will always need human capital to innovate," he said.[226]

"Measurement, the panelists agreed, is a huge topic in advertising today, and one that's growing in importance as more advertising becomes measurable," says Abramovich.[226] One big hurdle to measurement is the concept of the "walled gardens" and the dark social of Facebook, Instagram, WeChat, and Google, which, according to Eadie, "have scaled media properties and tons of data, but the data and its ability to be activated stays within these platforms."[226] However, Eadie believes these walls "will start to come down in as little as five years, as Facebook and Google gear up to compete against newer entrants."[226] Time to plan for this change is now.

"Amazon is a rising walled garden, and this rise will mean a new set of competition to the media landscape," Eadie says.[226] "If companies can't get a sense of which garden is most impactful, they will move dollars to the platforms that do provide understanding of impact."[226] Facebook has proven to be very accommodating in this area any time advertisers are willing to put money on the table. This is a scenario that won't be ending any time soon, no matter how much privacy trouble Facebook gets in.

Will Warren, EVP, digital investment, at Zenith Optimedia, argues that measurement has improved with the onset of automation, because it allows companies to have a single view of their media, not just a single view of their customer.[226] "Further digitization will allow more user level data, and we can tie that to an outcome," he says.[226] "[Automation essentially brings] multitouch attribution across the digital landscape. Consolidated ad buying means better measurement."[226]

Jill Cress, National Geographic CMO, "believes the current state of measurement is more about 'measure what you can' than 'measure what you need to measure.'"[226] "Today, [advertisers] are focused a lot on the vanity metrics, like views, impressions, and clicks. But we need to figure out how far down the funnel these things are taking people," she says. "We feel like we are at a moment where we will see an ambition and a shift to emotional connection and the psychology of the consumer. That's how brands will differentiate."[226]

Another panelist, Aubrey Flynn, SVP and chief digital officer of REVOLT TV & Media, believes Millennials and Gen Z not only want purpose in their lives, but they want the brands they use to share that purpose.[226] "To understand each person's individual purpose, brands need to move away from demographics and get closer to psychographics," says Flynn.[226] "In order to know people on an intimate level, companies will likely start investing in the study of human behavior to find authentic ways of personalizing experiences," explains Abramovich.[226]

As I state in the next chapter, Facebook is far down the psychographics road. Although Facebook and the now defunct Cambridge Analytica got into a lot of trouble by harvesting Facebook data to sway political elections, the lessons and tactics learned there are far too powerful to be ignored by future advertisers. There is a way to utilize Facebook data that is either considerate of privacy concerns or anonymized all-together and advertisers are currently salivating at the prospect of getting their hands on all that highly important psychographic detail.

Authenticity also is key when it comes to advertising to the Millennial and Gen Z demographic, Flynn believes.[226] "We market a lifestyle, and bringing that to life means different things to different people," she says.[226] "Telling people about your company is one thing, she adds, but empowering audiences to successfully pursue the purposes that are important to them is a totally different type of engagement."[226] As companies learn about the drives and motivations of their customers, personalization will be key.[226]

"Most of the solutions to measure emotions are in beta, so it's still the early stages," says Abramovich. However, "the ability to understand not only how long someone engaged with an ad for but also how it made them feel is going to give advertisers an unprecedented understanding of the effectiveness of their ads," concludes Abramovich.[226]

There is a dark side to all of this tracking, however, as the case of IFA and Shopsense showed. IFA Insurance teamed up with Shopsense, a grocery chain in America, and bought their loyalty card customer data.[227] The insurance company discovered some intriguing patterns in the loyalty card data, such as the correlation between condom sales and HIV-related claims.[227] It also discovered such things as households that buy cashews and bananas quarterly are the least likely to develop symptoms of Alzheimer's.[227] Although this information did prove to be highly profitable for IFA, I believe it is a clear violation of customer trust and privacy.

As Katherine Lemon explains in her article, *How Can These Companies Leverage the Customer Data Responsibly*[228]*,* "Customer analytics are effective precisely because firms do *not* violate customer trust. People believe that retail and other organizations will use their data wisely to enhance their experiences, not to harm them. Angry customers will certainly speak with their wallets if that trust is violated."[228]

Another concern for consumers is what Lemon calls "battered customer syndrome."[228] She explains that, "Market analytics allow companies to identify their best and worst customers and, consequently, to pay special attention to those deemed to be the most valuable."[228]

"Looked at another way, analytics enable firms to understand how poorly they can treat individuals or groups of customers before those people stop doing business with them. Unless you are in the top echelon of customers—those with the highest lifetime value, say—you may pay higher prices, get fewer special offers, or receive less service than other consumers," Lemon adds.[228] "Despite the fact that alienating 75% to 90% of customers may not be the best idea in the long run, many brands have adopted this 'top tier' approach to managing customer relationships. And many customers seem to be willing to live with it—perhaps with the unrealistic hope that they maybe reach the upper echelon and reap the ensuing benefits."[228]

"Little research has been done on the negative consequences of using marketing approaches that discriminate against customer segments. Inevitably, however, customers will become savvier about analytics. They may become less tolerant and take their business (and information) elsewhere," Lemon warns.[228]

Conclusion

More than ever before, AI allows marketers to reach consumers at every stage of the buying process based on their interests and demographics. In his article *How AI Will Change Marketing as We Know It*[229], Amine Bentahar claims that, "One particular example of how AI increases the efficiency of marketing is by making it easier to put customers into distinct groups that will allow for added segmentation to highly targeted niches." This means that, "Rather than creating one ad campaign that you hope will reach your target customers, marketers will instead be able to create more personalized, natural marketing content that will be unique for each targeted customer segment."[229]

AI will also "allow for more truly data-driven marketing campaigns, where AI will allow data to be more properly used and integrated into each ad campaign."[229]

The flip side of collecting as much data as a company possibly can is brands are collecting more data than they can actually use and here, too, AI can help by giving brands "the ability to seek out and identify patterns that will be beneficial for marketers in their campaigns."[229]

From a content standpoint, AI can help brands keep track what type of content consumers are most interested in, information that can then be used to curate a website for each individual user.[229] This should help with customer conversions and should be a part of any brand customer personalization initiatives.

Overall, AI can help marketers "look at things through a broader, more big-picture lens."[229] Increased AI use won't necessarily replace marketing teams, it will simply allow them to work proactively, as well as help them focus on big-picture decisions and strategies.[229] Creatives will be allowed to be creative once again.

AI will unquestionably be changing the marketing world as we know it, but change can be good.[229] "AI will allow marketers to create more educated, personalized campaigns to reach consumers, all while viewing their work through a big-picture focus that will allow them to be more creative. That is how the biggest gains possible will be captured through AI," concludes Bentahar.[229]

Brands should recognize that there is a radical reorganization of platforms and delivery channels going on right now as well. All the major software, analytics, and tech vendors are looking at new ways to monetize their businesses and marketing is something they are taking a very close look at. Besides Amazon, Microsoft, AT&T, AOL, Verizon, new players like Roku are getting into the direct advertising business. Even companies like the soon-to-be publicly traded company Uber are getting into the ad business.

---

184 Thompson, Derek. (2018) The Atlantic. The Media's Post-Advertising Future Is Also Its Past. December 31, 2018. https://www.theatlantic.com/ideas/archive/2018/12/post-advertising-future-media/578917/ (Accessed 1 January 2019).
185 Ballentine, Claire. (2018) New York Times. 12 August 2018. Google-Facebook Dominance Hurts Ad Tech Firms, Speeding Consolidation. https://www.nytimes.com/2018/08/12/technology/google-facebook-dominance-hurts-ad-tech-firms-speeding-consolidation.html (Accessed 1 January 2019).
186 Mickel, Tripp & Wells, Georgia. (2018) Wall Street journal. Apple Looks to Expand Advertising Business with New Network for Apps. June 1, 2018. https://www.wsj.com/articles/apple-looks-to-expand-advertising-business-with-new-network-for-apps-1527869990?utm_source=newsletter&utm_medium=email&utm_campaign=newsletter_axiosmediatrends&stream=top (Accessed 1 January 2019).
187 Fischer, Sara. (2018) Axios. The Next Big TV Tech Platform: Roku. 22 May 2018. https://www.axios.com/roku-is-trying-to-become-software-platform-e8602b67-5af4-443e-affc-634b8d553aea.html (Accessed 1 January 2019).
188 Shields, Ronan. Adweek. Adobe's New Partnership with Roku Will Help Advertisers Engage with 27 Million OTT Viewers. https://www.adweek.com/programmatic/adobes-new-partnership-with-roku-will-help-it-engage-with-27-million-ott-viewers/ (Accessed 27 March 2019).

189 Fischer, Sara. (2018). Axios. How Media Companies Lost the Advertising Business. June 5, 2018. https://www.axios.com/facebook-google-duopoly-advertising-tech-giants-media-e382e5e2-21eb-4776-93c0-7d942ba80ada.html (Accessed 1 January 2019).

190 Thompson Derek. (2018). The Atlantic. Where Did All the Advertising Jobs Go? February 7, 2018. https://www.theatlantic.com/business/archive/2018/02/advertising-jobs-programmatic-tech/552629/ (Accessed 1 January 2019).

191 Abramovich, Giselle. (2018). Experts Weight in On the Future of Advertising. CMO. September 19, 2019. https://www.cmo.com/features/articles/2018/6/14/welcome-to-the-future-of-advertising-cannes18.html#gs.4BvSdQHt (Accessed 15 February 2019).

192 Lee, Kavan. Buffer. (2014) Psychological Studies That Will Boost Your Social Media Marketing. 17 November 2014. https://blog.bufferapp.com/psychological-studies-marketing (Accessed 14 February 2019).

193 https://en.wikipedia.org/wiki/Endowment_effect (Accessed 14 February 2019).

194 https://en.wikipedia.org/wiki/Reciprocity_(social_psychology)

195 https://www.influenceatwork.com/principles-of-persuasion/

196 Psychologist World. Foot-in-the-door technique as a Persuasive Technique. https://www.psychologistworld.com/behavior/compliance/strategies/foot-in-door-technique (Accessed 14 February 2019).

197 Plous, Scott (1993). The psychology of judgment and decision making. McGraw-Hill. ISBN 978-0-07-050477-6.

198 Kahneman, Daniel, and Amos Tversky, "Choices, Values and Frames," American Psychologist, April 1984, 39, 341–350.

199 McLeod, Saul. Solomon Asch – Conformity Experiment. Simply Psychology. December 28, 2018. https://www.simplypsychology.org/asch-conformity.html (11 March 2019).

200 Watson, Dorothy (1992). "Correcting for Acquiescent Response Bias in the Absence of a Balanced Scale: An Application to Class Consciousness". Sociological Methods & Research. 21 (1): 52–88.

201 Huber, Joel; Payne, John W.; Puto, Christopher (1982). "Adding Asymmetrically Dominated Alternatives: Violations of Regularity and the Similarity Hypothesis". Journal of Consumer Research. 9 (1): 90-98.

202 https://psychology.iresearchnet.com/social-psychology/emotions/buffering-effect/ (Accessed 11 March 2019).

203 https://en.wikipedia.org/wiki/Propinquity (Accessed 11 March 2019).

204 https://en.wikipedia.org/wiki/Availability_heuristic (Accessed 11 March 2019)

205 https://www.investopedia.com/terms/s/scarcity-principle.asp (Accessed 11 March 2019).

206 https://thedecisionlab.com/bias/framing-effect/ (Accessed 11 March 2019).

207 http://changingminds.org/explanations/theories/acquiescence_effect.htm (Accessed 11 March 2019).

208 Thu-Huong Ha. (2013). TED blog. The psychology of saving energy. February 27, 2013 https://blog.ted.com/the-psychology-of-saving-energy-alex-laskey-at-ted2013/ (Accessed 11 March 2019).

209 Sunstein, Cass and Thaler, Richard. (2016). The New Yorker. The Two Friends Who Changed How We Think About How We Think. December 7, 2016. https://www.newyorker.com/books/page-turner/the-two-friends-who-changed-how-we-think-about-how-we-think (Accessed 2 May 2019).
210 The Tonic Communications. (2018). Frye festival: how millennial FOMO enabled high end fraud. https://thetoniccomms.co.uk/fyre-festival-how-millennial-fomo-enabled-high-end-fraud/ (Accessed 12 March 2019).
211 Lee, Aileen. (2011). Social Proof Is The New Marketing. Techcrunch. https://techcrunch.com/2011/11/27/social-proof-why-people-like-to-follow-the-crowd/ (Accessed 16 August 2018).
212 https://en.wikipedia.org/wiki/Social_proof (Accessed 16 August 2018).
213 Cialdini, Robert B. (2006). Influence: The Psychology of Persuasion. Harper Business; Revised edition (December 26, 2006).
214 Lua, Alfred. The Psychology of Marketing: 18 Ways Social Proof Can Boost Your Results. https://www.upwork.com/hiring/for-clients/the-psychology-of-marketing-18-ways-to-use-social-proof-to-boost-your-results/ (Accessed 6 March 2019).
215 Cialdini, Robert B. Harnessing the Science of Persuasion. Harvard Business Review. October 2001. http://www.coachfinder.club/downloads/Influence%20by%20Cialdini.pdf (Accessed 15 August 2018).
216 Hallin, Ed. (2014). Fast Company. How to use the psychology of social proof to your advantage. 05 May 2014. https://www.fastcompany.com/3030044/how-to-use-the-psychology-of-social-proof-to-your-advantage (Accessed 14 August 2018).
217 https://en.wikipedia.org/wiki/Web_search_engine (Accessed 13 November 2017).
218 Lardinois, F. (2013, September 26). Google improves knowledge graph with comparisons and filters, brings cards & cross-platform notifications to mobile. Retrieved from TechCrunch: http://techcrunch.com/2013/09/26/google-improves-knowledge-graph-with-comparisons-and-filters-brings-cards-to-mobile-search-adds-cross-platform-notifications/
219 Moz (2015) 'Search Engine Ranking Factors 2015 Expert Survey and Correlation Data', available at: https://moz.com/search-ranking-factors (Accessed 15th August 2017). Moz's rankings survey consists of the compiled results of 150 SEP expert opinions as to what influences Google's secret algorithm. It is largely a technical document and relies heavily on (defined) technical terms, such as 'Domain-Level-Keyword-Agnostic-Features', but it is worth a look nevertheless.
220 https://en.wikipedia.org/wiki/Google_Search (Accessed 13 November 2017).
221 Alpert, Brian. (Spring 2017). Search engine optimization in 2017: A new world where old rules still matter. Journal of Digital & Social Media Marketing, Volume 5, Number 1, Spring 2017, pp. 39 – 60 (22). Henry Stuart Publication.
222 Vindicia. (2014). Digital Age/Digital Goods. Retrieved from vindicia: http://info.vindicia.com/White-Paper---Digital-Age-Digital-Goods-9essentials_for_acquiring_subscription_and_recurring_revenue_customers.html (Accessed 15 August 2018).

223 Yu, Jim. Searchengingland.com. Supercharging Your SEO with AI Insights, Automation, and Personalization. June 12, 2018. https://searchengineland.com/supercharging-your-seo-with-ai-insights-automation-and-personalization-299900 (Accessed February 19, 2019).

224 Enterprise Content Team. The Magic of AI in a content-driven world. Using AI to create content faster. https://www.adobe.com/insights/the-magic-of-AI-in-a-content-driven-world.html (Accessed 15 February 2019).

225 Mejia, Tatiana. (2019) Adobe blog. How AI is Making it Easier for Marketers to Create Videos. January 16, 2019. https://theblog.adobe.com/how-ai-is-enabling-video-marketing-at-scale/ (Accessed 3 May 2019).

226 Abramovich, Giselle. (2017). CMO. Future of Advertising: Automated, Personalized, and Measureable. 26 September 2017. https://www.cmo.com/features/articles/2017/9/25/the-future-of-advertising-automated-personalized-and-measurable-.html

227 Davenport, T. (2006). Competing on Analytics. Harvard Business Review.

228 Lemon, K. (2007, May). How Can These Companies Leverage the Customer Data Responsibly. Retrieved from http://blog.hansacequity.com: http://blog.hansacequity.com/Portals/11224/docs/article%20on%20Analytics.pdf (Accessed 22 November 2017).

229 Bentahar, Amine. (2018). Forbes. How AI Will Change Marketing as We Know It. May 23, 2018. https://www.forbes.com/sites/forbesagencycouncil/2018/05/23/how-ai-will-change-marketing-as-we-know-it/#52bb93278b78 (Accessed 6 April 2019).

CHAPTER FIVE: SOCIAL A.I.

"When people are free to do as they please, they usually imitate others."

~Eric Hoffer

Overview

Social media is a generic term that refers to websites that allow one or more of the following services—social networking, content management, social bookmarking, blogging and micro-blogging, live video-casting, and access into virtual worlds. Social media refers to online resources that people use to *share* content. This content can include images, photos, videos, text messages, pins, opinions and ideas, insights, humor, gossip, and news of almost any kind.[230] Drury's list of social media includes the following[230]:

> *Blogs, vlogs, social networks, message boards, podcasts, public bookmarking and wikis. Popular examples of social media applications include Flickr (online photosharing); Wikipedia (reference); Bebo, Facebook and MySpace (networking); del.icio.us (bookmarking) and World of Warcraft (online gaming).*

Unlike traditional marketing models that are nothing more than one-way delivery systems from a company to its customers, social media is about building a relationship with an audience and starting a two-way dialogue between a company and its consumers.[230] In this new environment, marketing becomes a multi-dimensional discipline that is about receiving and exchanging perceptions and ideas.[230]

The consumer is seen as a participant rather than as a "target audience." The old Source-Message-Channel-Receiver model[231] has evolved into "a collaborative and dynamic communication model in which marketers don't design 'messages' for priority audiences but create worlds in which consumers communicate both with the company and with each other."[232]

Drury argues that confusion exists when pundits talk about social media because the emphasis is often placed on the "media" aspect of social media rather than the "social" aspect, where he feels it correctly belongs.[230] By giving people a platform to share and interact with each other, social media allows "content" to become more democratized than ever before.[230]

In their influential article *Users of the World, Unite! The Challenges and Opportunities of Social Media*[47], Kaplan and Haenlein explain that a formal definition of social media first requires an understanding of two related concepts that are often referred to when describing it: Web 2.0 and User Generated Content.[47] As Kaplan and Haenlein see it[47]:

> "Web 2.0 is a term that was first used in 2004 to describe a new way in which software developers and end-users started to utilize the World Wide Web; that is, as a platform whereby content and applications are no longer created and published by individuals, but instead are continuously modified by all users in a participatory and collaborative fashion. While applications such as personal web pages, Encyclopedia Britannica Online, and the idea of content publishing belong to the era of Web 1.0, they are replaced by blogs, wikis, and collaborative projects in Web 2.0. Although Web 2.0 does not refer to any specific technical update of the World Wide Web, there is a set of basic functionalities that are necessary for its functioning."

The "basic functionalities" that Kaplan and Haenlein refer to are; Adobe Flash, the popular animation tool, interactivity, and web streaming audio/video programs, Really Simple Syndication (RSS), a family of web feed formats used to publish frequently updated works—such as blog entries or news headlines, as well as audio and video—in a standardized format; and Asynchronous Java Scrip (AJAX), a group of web development methods that can retrieve data from web servers asynchronously, allowing the update of one source of web content without interfering with the display and behavior of an entire page.[47] This is important because it means that a web page for a marketer could, while it is loading onto a customer's computer or mobile phone, be accessing and returning specific personalized customer content, including appropriate image or even coupons that have been chosen because they are highly likely to be used and, potentially, could cost the brand the least to redeem.

For Kaplan and Haenlein, Web 2.0 represents the ideological and technological foundation, while "User Generated Content (UGC) can be seen as the sum of all the ways in which people make use of social media. The term, which achieved broad popularity in 2005, is usually used to describe the various forms of media content that are publicly available and created by end-users."[47]

Also known as Consumer-Generated Media (CGM), User-Generated Content (UGC) refers to a wide range of applications, including blogs, news, digital video, podcasting, mobile phone photography, video, online encyclopedias and user reviews. According to Juniper Research, User Generated Content can be broken down into the following three categories[233]:

1. Mobile dating and chat room services—destinations for people to meet.
2. Personal content distribution—audio and video files uploaded onto third party sites for other mobile users to consume.

3. Social networking—social structures made of nodes "that are tied by one or more specific types of interdependency, such as values, visions, ideas, financial exchange, friendship, kinship, dislike, conflict or trade."[234]

UGC is the sum of all the ways in which people make use of social media and, according to the Organisation for Economic Cooperation and Development, UGC needs to fulfill the following three basic criteria in order to be considered as such[235]:

1. It must be published either on a publicly accessible website or on a social networking site accessible to a selected group of individuals.
2. It must show a certain amount of creative effort.
3. It must have been created outside of professional routines and practices.

For Kaplan and Haenlein, the first condition can't include content exchanged in e-mails or instant messages; the second precludes mere replications of already existing content (e.g., posting a copy of an existing newspaper article on a personal blog without any modifications or commenting); and the third condition implies that all created content must exclude a commercial market context.[47]

Kaplan and Haenlein believe that social media isn't just "a group of Internet-based applications that build on the ideological and technological foundations of Web 2.0, and that allow the creation and exchange of User Generated Content."[47] For Kaplan and Haenlein, this general definition should be broken down further because such disparate sites as Facebook, LinkedIn, Wikipedia, Weibo, and yy.com have little in common with each other when their offered services are looked at individually.[47]

As new sites are also popping up on a daily basis, a classification system created for social media should be able to include any future applications that are developed as well.[47] To create such a classification system, Kaplan and Haenlein rely on a "set of theories in the field of media research (social presence, media richness) and social process (self-presentation, self-disclosure), the two key elements of Social Media."[47] "Regarding the media-related component of Social Media, social presence theory[236] states that media differ in the degree of 'social presence'—defined as the acoustic, visual, and physical contact that can be achieved—they allow to emerge between two communication partners."[47]

Kaplan and Haenlein argue that: "Social presence is influenced by the intimacy (interpersonal vs. mediated) and immediacy (asynchronous vs. synchronous) of the medium, and can be expected to be lower for mediated (e.g., telephone conversations) than interpersonal (e.g., face-to-face discussions) and for asynchronous (e.g., e-mail) than synchronous (e.g., live chat) communications."[47] The higher the social presence, the more social influence the communication partners will have on each other. Brands should recognize the differences inherent in these options and market accordingly.

Media Richness Theory[237] is a framework to describe a communications medium by its ability to reproduce the information sent over it and it implies that "the goal of any communication is the resolution of ambiguity and the reduction of uncertainty."[47] For Daft & Lengel[237], Media Richness is a function of:

- The medium's capacity for immediate feedback.
- The number of cues and channels available.
- Language variety.
- The degree to which intent is focused on the recipient.

Regarding the social dimension of social media, the concept of self-presentation states that when an individual comes in contact with other people, that individual will attempt to guide or control the impression that others form of them and all participants in social interactions are attempting to avoid being embarrassed or embarrassing others.[238] "Usually such a presence is done through self-disclosure; that is, the conscious or unconscious revelation of personal information (e.g., thoughts, feelings, likes, dislikes) that is consistent with the image one would like to give."[47]

		Social Presence/ Media Richness		
		Low	Medium	High
Self-presentation/ Self-disclosure	High	Blogs	Social networking sites (e.g., Facebook)	Virtual social worlds (e.g., Second Life)
	Low	Collaborative projects (e.g., Wikipedia)	Content communities (e.g., YouTube)	Virtual game worlds (e.g., World of Warcraft)

Table 10: Classification of Social Media by social presence/media richness and self-presentation/self-disclosure
Source: Users of the world unite! The challenges and opportunities of Social Media.[47]

Applied to the context of social media, a classification is made based on the richness of the medium and the degree of social presence it allows.[47] Kaplan and Haenlein created the *Classification of Social Media by social presence/media richness and self-presentation/self-disclosure* table and it reveals (see Table 10)[47]:

- Low: Collaborative projects such as Wikipedia and blogs score the lowest, mostly because they are text based and only allow relatively

simple exchanges. Blogs usually score higher than collaborative projects because the former aren't focused on specific content domains.
- Medium: Content communities and social networking sites allow users to share text-based communication, as well as other forms of media. Social network sites score higher than content communities because they allow more self-disclosure.
- High: Virtual games and social worlds attempt to replicate face-to-face interactions in a virtual environment. Virtual social worlds score higher on the self-presentation scale as the latter are ruled by strict guidelines that users have to either follow or be kicked out of entirely.

UGC can be very useful in website Search Engine Optimization (SEO). Search engines are constantly looking for updated information on websites and adding such things as a company blog and customer forums can be a cheap and effective way to get customers and/or clients to generate new content for you, which should increase search engine rankings.

Brands should look beyond the most well-known social platforms and try to be creative. When it comes to social media and implementing it into a brand, the one constant question should be is, "How does this affect my ROI?" For many businesses, there is the sense that social media is an ethereal, unquantifiable thing, but this shouldn't be the case. Done correctly, social media marketing can be highly quantifiable.

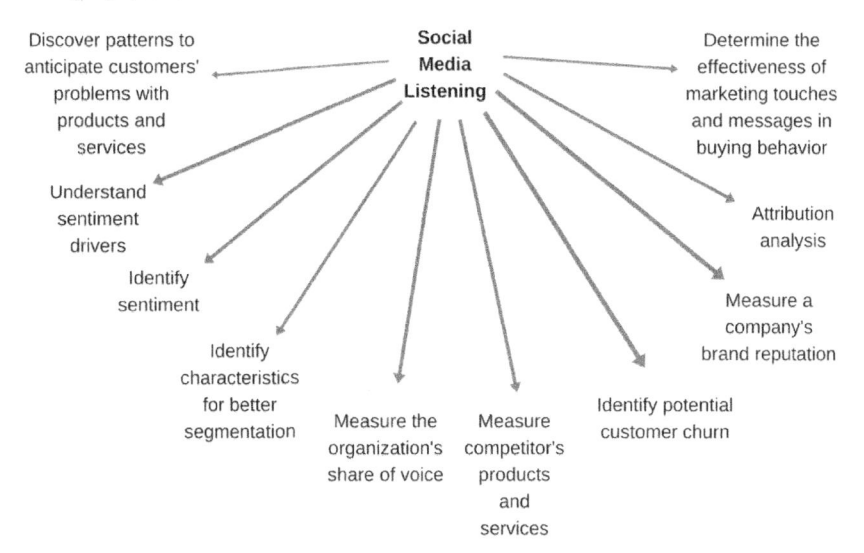

Figure 22: Social Media Listening objectives
Source: www.intelligencia.co

As Figure 22 shows, social media listening can be used in a multitude of ways, like anticipating customer problems, understanding and identifying sentiment, measuring a company's share of voice, as well as keeping track of a company's brand. All of these are important and, together, they can give a marketer deep insight into marketing campaign performances and attribution analysis, which should help with planning and implementing future marketing campaigns.

In his article *Demystifying social media*[239], R.E. Divol provides an example of how a company can test to see whether a social media solution would work for it with the case of a telco company that proactively adopted social media. "The company had launched Twitter-based customer service capabilities, several promotional campaigns built around social contests, a fan page with discounts and tech tips, and an active response program to engage with people speaking with the brand," explains Divol.[239]

In social-media terms, the investment was not insignificant, and the company's senior executives wanted quantifiable ROI, not anecdotal evidence that the strategy was paying off.[239] "As a starting point, to ensure that the company was doing a quality job designing and executing its social presence, it benchmarked its efforts against approaches used by other companies known to be successful in social media."[239] According to Divol, the telecommunication company advanced the following hypotheses[239]:

- If all these social-media activities improve general service perceptions about the brand, that improvement should be reflected in a higher volume of positive online posts.
- If social sharing is effective, added clicks and traffic should result in higher search placements.
- If both of these assumptions hold true, social-media activity should help drive sales—ideally at a rate even higher than the company achieves with its average gross rating point (GRP) of advertising expenditures.[239]

The company tested its options. "At various times, it spent less money on conventional advertising, especially as social-media activity ramped up, and it modeled the rising positive sentiment and higher search positions just as it would using traditional metrics."[239] The results were quite conclusive: "social-media activity not only boosted sales but also had higher ROIs than traditional marketing did. Thus, while the company took a risk by shifting emphasis toward social-media efforts before it had data confirming that this was the correct course, the bet paid off."[239]

Just as importantly, the brand had now created an analytic baseline that gave it confidence to continue exploring a growing role for social media.[239] It is very easy to quantify search rankings and it is pretty obvious that if a marketer ranks higher in Google search rankings, it should garner more business.

The most important thing to recognize about social media is the fact that most social media content is user generated. Social networks provide all of the tools their members require to become content producers and social network members submit photos, videos, music, and other forms of multimedia, as well as provide customer reviews, content for blogs and vlogs and links to other social networking websites that they find noteworthy.[240] The content comes from the users themselves, not from the publishers, and this is an important distinction.[240] The publisher supplies all of the necessary tools for the content's distribution, but it must remain at arm's length from the actual content to ensure the content's integrity.

Business.com's *Top Tools to Measure Your Social Media Success*[241] states that there are five Ws that must be kept in mind when devising a social media strategy. These are:

1. Who within the company will be using this tool? Will one person or several people be using the tools, and will they be inside or outside the organization? Will the primary user be tech savvy or will he or she require an intuitive interface?
2. What key performance indicators (KPI) are to be measured with this tool? It is imperative to know how you are going to measure and benchmark your social media efforts as this will dictate what social media monitoring tools are the best to use. If sales revenue is a key KPI, businesses should invest in a tool that integrates with a CRM system to track impact.
3. Where on the web will the business be engaging customers, and where does it plan to monitor its social media conversations? If a business is only interested in tracking specific channels such as Facebook or Twitter, tools such as Facebook (obviously) and socialmention.com can help with the former, while Twazzup and tweetEffect can track the latter. All-encompassing tools that monitor new sites and forums are useful to monitor mentions from across the entire web.
4. When should the company be alerted of conversations and mentions within the social media sphere? Options here include general reporting dashboards or instant notifications via e-mail alerts or RSS feeds.
5. Why is the company engaging in social media? This is, perhaps, the most important question of all, and a marketer must decide whether it is turning to social media to manage its online brand reputation, to engage its customers and/or potential customers, to provide real-time customer service, or simply to drive traffic to its website to influence SEO.

The Four Steps of Social Media

In their book *Online Marketing Inside Out: Reach New Buyers Using Modern Marketing Techniques*[242], Eley & Tiley state that, when a company is first delving into social media, there are four steps of social media that should be followed—listen, join, participate and create—and these steps must be strictly followed in that specific order.

Listening is the most important step. People online are frequently mentioning and making comments about a company and its products, so all one has to do is listen. Even if a brand does not choose to participate in the discussion itself, it will discover valuable information about the company by just listening.[242]

Instead of doing expensive surveys, focus groups or other experiments, the best information is often found right there in front of you at minimal or maybe even at no cost.[242] A brand can find out what its customers think of its products and/or service, as well as what they might want improved.[242] Problems and frustrations that might not make it onto corporate surveys might be detailed enough on blogs to affect real change.[242] Most importantly, a brand might get the inside scoop of what is actually important to its target audience.[242]

To understand how important this process can be for a company, it is instructive to look at what happened to Makers Mark, a bourbon manufacturer that found itself in the midst of a self-created social media disaster in February 2013. Because it was faced with both a high demand for its product and a low supply of bourbon whiskey, Maker's Mark announced plans to cut the amount of alcohol in its drink from 45 to 42 percent.[243] Needless to say the Internet wasn't pleased. As Laura Stampler explains in her article *Makers Mark Turned Watered Down Whiskey Debacle Into a Social Media Win*[243], "It's the age of social media, so consumers were tweeting and Facebooking their complaints to any and everyone who would listen."[243]

There were angry tweets as well as Facebook petitions against the company.[243] A normal Valentine's Day post on the company's Facebook page was flooded with negative comments about the shift.[243] Immediately realizing that it had made a huge mistake, the brand decided to embrace the social media platforms where they have been receiving such negativity and they quickly put out the message that they had recognized that they had made a huge mistake, they were sorry and they were reversing their decision about lowering the alcohol content.[243] The link to the company's Facebook apology soon became a popular hashtag.[243] "Customers went from feeling abandoned to listened to and respected in record time."[243] The apology noted that even though the social media reaction was highly negative, the company wanted the conversation to continue.[243]

Maker's Mark even took this conversation into their print advertising, using the tagline line: "You spoke. We listened. Here's proof", with an arrow cleverly pointing to the label, which showed that the alcohol content (or proof) was still 45%.

By listening, joining, participating and creating, Maker's Mark built its online brand and it now has an audience to share its content with, an audience which should help them spread their content far and wide, as well as, more importantly, sell a lot more 45 proof whiskey to.

In her article *50 ways to drive traffic to your website with social media*[244], Amanda Nelson recommends, listening can be used in the following ways:

1. Monitor for buying indication terms and reply with helpful links.
2. Listen for recommendation requests and share helpful links.
3. Listen for discussions of your product or category and provide web links.
4. Share relevant web content with prospects.
5. Discover relevant blogs and ask for backlinks.

Once the brand understands the community and what it is all about, it is time to join a social network. Many networks require that you have an account on their site to participate in the discussions and the brand should sign up for the account as it is always better to have an account even if it is not required to have one because one always wants to claim its brand and/or company name to gain credibility.

A brand should also join communities where it is most likely to find its customers.[242] If you start out by listening, you will know where your customers tend to congregate online. Facebook, Instagram, LinkedIn, YouTube, Flickr, Delicious, Digg and Twitter are big networks which should be on a brand's radar.[242] Many of these sites can be used to listen to your audience or to start a discussion. Chinese listening social media sites include Sina Weibo, Tencent Weibo, and Netease Weibo, amongst others.

Brands should set up accounts at all the major social networking sites and link back to their website(s), as well as link content and similar keywords throughout their social channels.

Once the discussion has been joined, then it is time to participate in the community. Participating includes replying and posting to online forums and blogs, reviewing products and services and bookmarking sites that are like-minded.[242]

By participating, businesses will build their online brand and people will start to respect them as a valuable contributor to the community.[242] When respected, others will help to promote the company without even being asked to do so, which, as most marketers will tell you, is some of the best marketing around. Not only is word-of-mouth marketing one of the most trusted forms of marketing, but it can also spread virally. Two words of warning, however; your role models should always be very experienced and remain very active users in the community; and, most importantly of all, remember that it is never okay to spam.[242]

In her article *50 Ways to Drive Traffic to Your Website*[244], Nelson recommends

using the following methods to increase participation:
1. Ask readers to sign up for an RSS feed.
2. Answer all questions and share peer referrals.
3. Feature community members on your site.
4. Share customer stories.
5. Ask influencers to share your web links.
6. Interview an influencer for web content.
7. Have an influencer guest blog.
8. Help an influencer write content about the brand.
9. Share products with influencers for feedback and web content.

Finally, it is time to create. Once a brand has built itself an online brand by listening, joining and participating, it is time to create its own content.[242] It will now have an audience to share its content with and they will help the brand spread its content far and wide.

It should be noted here that the brand has to create value; ads are not generally seen as valuable.[242] Posting "buy my stuff" on twitter will fail to achieve the results you want, and this practice may even get you banned.[242] By making beneficial contributions to the community, people will notice you and want to know more about the company.[242] If you have listened properly, you should have a solid idea of the type of content people would like to see.[242] Then, simply, give it to them. Nelson recommends companies be creative in the following ways[242]:

1. Divide a piece of content into multiple SlideShare presentations that link to your site.
2. Start a LinkedIn group.
3. Tie content together so an eBook links to a relevant blog post, which, in turn, links to a topical webinar.
4. Build a forum or community section on the company website.
5. Create referral programs.

The four steps of social media fit well within the six types of social media, which I will detail next. Throughout the rest of this chapter, I will explain the different types of social media and I will describe how each of these social media platforms can be used individually as well as, sometimes, in combination to market the company and its services worldwide.

Six Types of Social Media

According to Kaplan and Haenlein's article *Users of the World, Unite! The Challenges and Opportunities of Social Media*[47], the writers break Social Media down into the following six different types:

1. Collaborative projects

2. Blogs and micro-blogs
3. Content communities
4. Social networking sites
5. Virtual game worlds
6. Virtual social worlds

Throughout the rest of this chapter, I will break down each of these types of social media separately, as well as explain how brands can use them on their own or, preferably, combined.

Collaborative Projects

Probably the most democratic form of all UGC, collaborative projects enable the joint and simultaneous creation of content by many end-users.[47] Kaplan and Haenlein believe collaborative projects can be split into two different categories[47]:

1. Wikis—these are websites that allow users to add, remove, and change text-based content; and
2. Social bookmarking applications—these enable the group-based collection and rating of Internet links or media content.

The main idea behind collaborative projects is that joint efforts can lead to a better outcome than individual action.[47] Examples of collaborative projects include the web-based encyclopedia Wikipedia and social bookmarking sites such as StumbleUpon.

Social bookmarking is both the method of storing and the managing of web page bookmarks with individually chosen keywords, as well as the sharing of this information with others. At social bookmarking sites, users can tag, save, manage and share websites with their friends and their connections. Users can add descriptions in the form of metadata and these descriptions can be anything from free text comments, favorable or unfavorable votes, or tags that collectively form a social thread of information. This kind of thread is also known as a folksonomy— "the process by which many users add metadata in the form of keywords to shared content."[245]

In his article *How to Use Social Bookmarking for Business*[246], Lou Dubois explains that, "Social bookmarking, at its most basic form, is a simple way to organize all of the best content from around the web based off your interests, all in one place." It is a handy way to "sort the relevant from the irrelevant, according to their interests and the value of the information provided. And perhaps most importantly, the bookmarks are transferable between computers and locations."[247]

Founded in 2003, Delicious (then known as del.icio.us) coined the term *social bookmarking* and pioneered the concept of tagging.[248] The following year, similar sites such as Furl, Simpy, Citeulike and Connotea came online. StumbleUpon also appeared around the same time.

Compared to search engines and traditional automated resource location and classification software, social bookmarking systems are advantageous because the tag-based classification is done by a human being, who usually understands the content and context of a resource better than an algorithm-based computer program. Human beings are also adept at finding and bookmarking web pages that often go unnoticed by web spiders.[248] In addition, a user will probably find a system that ranks a resource based on how many times it has been bookmarked by other users more valuable than a system that simply ranks resources based on the number of external links pointing to it.

For brands, social bookmarking is important because it helps a brand's website get quality backlinks. When a website is submitted for ranking by a search engine, the search engine considers the quality of the backlinks, i.e., the quality of the sites linking back to it. This means that if you bookmark popular sites, the search engine spiders will automatically follow the links back to your site. SEOMoz's Linkscape and Majestic SEO's Link Intelligence are both very good tools to discover current backlinks to a site.

Kaplan and Haenlein argue that, "From a corporate perspective, firms must be aware that collaborative projects are trending toward becoming the main source of information for many consumers. As such, although not everything written on Wikipedia may be actually true, it is *believed* to be true by more and more Internet users." This can have particularly damaging repercussions during a corporate crisis.[47]

Collaborative projects can also be used to increase productivity, for example, the Finnish mobile manufacturer Nokia "uses internal wikis to update employees on project status and to trade ideas, which are used by about 20% of its 68,000 staff members."[47]

Dubois explains that "From an individual consumption perspective for Internet readers, social bookmarking can make great sense to filter your news and information all into one place."[246] But it also makes great sense for businesses to utilize these tools as they can increase website traffic and grow brand recognition by curating information and disseminating client testimonials.[246]

Throughout the business world, content curators are "considered the gatekeepers to information for businesses and individuals. As a company, curating, or aggregating the best content from around the web, can make you an industry leader."[246] For companies you already work with, showing that you are on top of industry news gives you a vaunted level of credibility.[246]

"Similarly, if you think of it from the perspective of businesses who you don't already do business with, you're going to be seen as a resource for information," argues L. Dubois[246], which should give you an immediate leg up on your competition.

Social bookmarking isn't as intuitive a process as blogging or social networking on sites like Facebook or Twitter, but it is a very valuable tool in its own right and it should be one part of an brand's social media marketing plan. Chinese collaborative projects include Baidu bookmarks, QQ Bookmarks, Sina viv, Hudong, Soso baike, Baidu baiki and MBAlib.

Blogs

In 2005, Merriam-Webster added the word "blog" to its dictionary, calling it, "a web site that contains an online personal journal with reflections, comments, and often hyperlinks provided by the writer."[249] Webopedia defines a blog as, "a web page that serves as a publicly accessible personal journal for an individual."[250] The term originated from the word "weblog", which was coined by Jorn Barger on 17 December 1997 when he used it to describe the list of links on his Robot Wisdom website that "logged" his internet wanderings.[251]

In April or May of 1999, Peter Merholz broke the word "weblog" into the two words "we blog" in the sidebar of his blog Peterme.com.[252] The term "blog" was picked up by Evan Williams at Pyra Labs who used "blog" as a noun and a verb to mean "to edit one's weblog or to post to one's weblog" and created the term "blogger" for Pyra Labs' Blogger product, which led to the term's popularity.[253]

Representing the earliest form of Social Media, blogs are the "Equivalent of personal web pages and can come in a multitude of different variations, from personal diaries describing the author's life to summaries of all relevant information in one specific content area."[47]

In its article *It's the Links, Stupid*[252], *The Economist* claims that a blog is:

> "A web page to which its owner regularly adds new entries, or 'posts', which tend to be (but need not be) short and often contain hyperlinks to other blogs or websites. Besides text and hypertext, posts can also contain pictures ('photoblogs') and video ("vlogs"). Each post is stored on its own distinct archive page, the so-called 'permalink', where it can always be found."

The Economist explains that blogging is a quintessentially social activity, highlighted by two features[252]:

> "A 'blogroll', along the side of the blog page, which is a list of links to other blogs that the author recommends (not to be confused with the hyperlinks inside the posts). In practice, the blogroll is an attempt by the author to place his blog in a specific genre or group, and a reciprocal effort by a posse of bloggers to raise each other's visibility on the internet (because the number

> of incoming links pushes a blog higher in search-engine results). The other feature is 'trackback', which notifies ('pings') a blog about each new incoming link from the outside—a sort of gossip-meter, in short."

According to Dave Winer, the influential software engineer who pioneered several blogging techniques and has, by his own estimate, the longest running blog of all time[252], weblogs should be:

1. Personalized: Weblogs are designed for individual use (a multi-person weblog is also possible through collaboration, such as the "team blog" offered by www.blogger.com). A Weblog style is personal and informal.
2. Web-based: Weblogs can be updated frequently. They are easy to maintain and accessible via a Web browser.
3. Community-supported: Weblogs can link to other weblogs and Websites, enabling the linkage of ideas, and hence stimulating knowledge generation and sharing between bloggers.
4. Automated: Blogging tools help bloggers to present their words without the hassle of writing HTML code or any other programming language; instead, bloggers can just concentrate on the content.

Winer argues that blogging should have a raw, unpolished authenticity to it.[252] "Blogging is all about style" and the essence of blogginess is "the unedited voice of a single person," preferably an amateur.[252] For Winer, editors do not belong in the Blogosphere, even though, today, they very much are there.[252]

Blogs are incredibly popular because they are cheap, easy to set up and they provide maximum exposure with limited effort. As Jeff Jarvis, Director of the Interactive Journalism at City University of New York's Graduate School of Journalism points out, they are the "easiest, cheapest, fastest publishing tool ever invented."[251] Blogs are everywhere, affecting every sector of society and, because of their ease of use and low barrier to entry, they will continue to be a big part of the national and worldwide conversation.[251]

Blogs can take many forms, including a diary, a news service, a collection of links to Internet resources, a series of book reviews, reports of activity on a project, the journal of an expedition, a photographic record of a building project, or any one of a number of other forms.

According to Winer, a successful blog should include the following key elements[252]:

1. Great content: as the old adage goes, "Content is king" and that old axiom should be kept very much in mind when it comes to blogging. Competition is fierce so one's content better be relevant, valuable and captivating.

2. Post frequently: along with having great content, bloggers should constantly post new material. A constant stream of new material will garner more views, which should result in more followers.
3. User friendly navigation: readers prefer navigation that is simple and straightforward so have links that make logical sense.
4. Eye pleasing content: as with any other type of marketing, the prettier something looks, the more likely it is to be viewed, so keep the design element in mind when creating a blog.
5. Connect to other content: linking and back-linking is exceptionally important so feel free to add links to other content that expands upon or references your content.

Although, China censors its social media sites, Chinese consumers are some of the biggest bloggers and commentators around, and Chinese blogging sites like Weibo, Hexum, Sina blog, Blogus and Bolaa are filled with a constant stream of observations and explanations about any and everything imaginable; literally, as the Chinese love to blog about the strangest things. Stories go viral exceptionally fast in China, with friends sharing not just ideas but sometimes scams and schemes amongst their closest one thousand friends in a matter of hours.

Brands should exploit any and every available blog opportunity they have to get their message out, as well as use any and all platforms that help them to connect with their customers and potential customers wherever they might be.

Microblogs

Although similar to a blogging website, a microblog site differs from a traditional blog in that its content is typically smaller in both actual and aggregate size. In his article *Visual Analysis of Microblog Content Using Time-Varying Co-occurrence Highlighting in Tag Clouds* [254], S.B. Lohmann claims: "Social networking and microblogging services such as Twitter, Facebook, or Google+ allow people to broadcast short messages, so-called micro posts, in continuous streams. These posts usually consist of a text message enriched with contextual metadata, such as the author, date and time, and sometimes also the location of origin."[254] While individual posts can be no longer than 280 characters [255], "aggregated posts of multiple users can provide a rich source of time-critical information that can point to events and trends needing attention."[254]

The most used microblog in the English-speaking world is Twitter, which, according to its website "is a real-time short messaging service that works over multiple networks and devices."[256] A free social networking and micro-blogging service, Twitter allows users to send and receive tweets—messages that can be up to 280 characters in length.

Twitter notes that, "Connected to each tweet is a rich details pane that provides additional information, deeper context and embedded media."[256] Because it is happening in near real-time, "Twitter is a 'what's-happening-right-now' tool that enables interested parties to follow individual users' thoughts and commentary on events in their lives."[257] These thoughts can, literally, be about anything and everything.

On its website, Twitter recommends building a following, increasing a businesses' reputation, and raising a customer's trust by following these best practices[256]:

1. Share: disseminate photos and behind the scenes info about your business. Even better, give a glimpse of developing projects and events. Users come to Twitter to get and share the latest, so give it to them!
2. Listen: regularly monitor the comments about your company, brand, and products.
3. Ask: question your followers to glean valuable insights and show them that you are listening.
4. Respond: reply to compliments and feedback in real time.
5. Reward: tweet updates about special offers, discounts and time-sensitive deals.
6. Demonstrate wider leadership and know-how: Reference articles and links about the bigger picture as it relates to your business.
7. Champion your stakeholders: Retweet and publicly reply to great tweets posted by your followers and customers.
8. Establish the right voice: Twitter users tend to prefer a direct, genuine, and, of course, likable tone from your business, but think about your *voice* as you tweet. How do you want your business to appear to the Twitter community?

Twitter also offers three ways to advertise on its service; promoted tweets; promoted trends; and promoted accounts. Promoted tweets are regular tweets that are amplified to a broader audience and they are offered on a Cost-per-Engagement (CPE) basis. A business is charged when a user Retweets, replies to, clicks on, or favorites the Promoted tweet.[256] Retweeted impressions by engaged users are free, and can exponentially amplify the reach and cost-effectiveness of a marketing campaign.[256]

Twitter is a very useful tool that connects businesses to customers in real-time. It can help a business quickly share information with people who are interested in their products and/or services, as well as gather real-time market intelligence and customer feedback.[256] Using Twitter, a business can build strong relationships with its customers and partners as well as raise the profile of its brands, direct sales, and engage a primed audience.[256] Twitter can help a business build a following, increase its reputation as well as raise a customer's trust by sharing, listening, asking questions, responding to replies, rewarding customers with special offers and discounts, demonstrating wider leadership and championing the right stakeholders.

"Promoted Trends" give a business the exclusive opportunity to feature a Trend related to its business at the top of the "Twitter Trends" list.[256] When a user clicks on the "Trend", he or she is taken to the conversation for that trend and a "Promoted tweets" tag is attached to the tweet at the top of the timeline. Because of its placement, the ad receives substantial exposure, thereby initiating or amplifying a conversation on Twitter and beyond.[256]

"Promoted Accounts" can help companies quickly increase their Twitter followers.[256] Part of "Who to follow" (Twitter's account recommendation engine), "Promoted Accounts" will highlight a business account to users who will most likely find it interesting.[256] According to Twitter's Website, "Users find Promoted Accounts a useful part of discovering new businesses, content, and people on Twitter."[256]

Content Communities

Content communities exist for a wide range of media types, including text, photos, videos, and PowerPoint presentations.[47] In general, users are not required to create a personal profile page or, if one is required, only basic information is needed.[47] Kaplan and Haenlein state that, "The main objective of content communities is the sharing of media content between users."[47]

Although businesses run the risk of these platforms being used for the purpose of sharing copyright-protected materials, the advantages of getting one's content into the social media community seriously outweighs the disadvantages of potential copyright infringement.[47] The popularity of these content communities make them a very attractive contact channel for many businesses. This fact isn't surprising when one considers that a site such as YouTube has over 2 billion views per day.[47]

According to its website, YouTube was founded in February 2005 and it "allows billions of people to discover, watch and share originally-created videos. YouTube provides a forum for people to connect, inform, and inspire others across the globe and acts as a distribution platform for original content creators and advertisers large and small."[258]

On 23rd April 2005, the very first video uploaded to YouTube was a video called "Me at the Zoo". Today, 72 hours of video are uploaded to YouTube every minute and YouTube receives more than 2 billion views per day. YouTube allows users to create accounts, upload videos, "Like" or "Dislike" videos, leave comments on a video and create channels, among other things. Some other facts from the YouTube.com press centre include:*[259]*

- More than 1 billion unique users visit YouTube each month.
- Over 6 billion hours of video are watched each month on YouTube.
- 80% of YouTube traffic comes from outside the US.
- YouTube is localized in 61 countries and across 61 different languages.

- According to Nielsen, YouTube reaches more US adults ages 18-34 than any cable network.
- Created in 2007, the YouTube Partner Program has more than a million partners from 30 countries around the world.
- Thousands of advertisers are using TrueView in-stream and 75% of those in-stream ads are now skippable.
- YouTube has more than a million advertisers using Google ad platforms, the majority of which are small businesses.
- YouTube's Content ID scans over 400 years' worth of video every day for any sign of copyright infringement.
- More than 5,000 partners use Content ID, including every major US network broadcaster, movie studio and record label.
- YouTube has more than 25 million reference files in its Content ID database; it's among the most comprehensive in the world.

According to its website, "SlideShare began with a simple goal: To share knowledge online. Since then, SlideShare has grown to become the world's largest community for sharing presentations and other professional content."[260] In Q4 of 2013, SlideShare averaged 60 million unique visitors a month and 215 million-page views and it is among the top 120 most-visited websites in the world.[260]

According to Wikipedia, "SlideShare is a Web 2.0 based slide hosting service. Users can upload files privately or publicly in the following file formats: PowerPoint, PDF, Keynote or OpenDocument presentations. Slide decks can then be viewed on the site itself, on hand held devices or embedded on other sites."[261]

Two of the most important things to know about SlideShare is its ability to affect the Google search engine rankings. I have been pleasantly surprised to see my SlideShare slideshows about subjects such as "predictive analytics in the gaming industry" consistently show up in the Google top ten rankings for that subject. SlideShare can also be a powerful lead generator as well.

Instagram

Instagram is an online photo-sharing and social networking service that allows users to take a picture, apply a digital filter to it, and share it on various social networking sites. Unlike most other mobile device cameras, Instagram confines photos to a square shape, like a Kodak Instamatic and a Polaroid image; the old is new again. The service was launched in October 2010 and it was distributed through the App store and Google Play.

In April 2012, Facebook bought Instagram in a deal worth approximately $1 billion in cash.[262] It was the company's largest deal up to that point. As Kathleen Chaykowski explains in her Forbes article *Instagram, the $50 Billion Grand Slam*

Driving Facebook's Future: The Forbes Cover Story[263]:

> "When Zuckerberg decided to shell out nearly $1 billion in 2012 to buy the photo-sharing app, which had just 30 million users, it was widely seen as a sign of a new Silicon Valley bubble. But he appears to have outsmarted everyone once again. In the four years since the purchase, Instagram has become one of the fastest-growing platforms of all time, with about as many users as Twitter (310 million), Snapchat (100-million-plus) and Pinterest (100 million) combined."

Besides the fact that Instagram is quite profitable ($630 million in sales in 2015), Instagram's true potential lies in its ability to reach a young demographic.[263] "Ask anyone under 18 (a cohort who view Facebook as their parents' social network): Instagram is that next platform," claims Chaykowski.[263]

"The combination of this visual opportunity to tell your story as a person, a marketer and a business, combined with the ability to target the audience, has been very powerful," says Facebook COO Sheryl Sandberg.[263]

Instagram's strength is its ability to cater to the hyper specific passions and obsessions of a varying range of interest groups.[263] "Users have rallied around visual hubs dedicated to Korean light shows, artisanal cheese shops, skateboarding tricks (Tony Hawk is an active user), break dancing and extreme body painting. Every day users spend more than 21 minutes on average in the app and collectively upload more than 95 million photos and videos," explains Chaykowski.[263]

"That sticky engagement is reshaping entire industries," notes Chaykowski.[263] "Look no further than fashion. Last year designer Misha Nonoo, whose modern women's clothing has been worn by Emma Watson and Gwyneth Paltrow, ditched the runways of New York Fashion Week and launched her spring 2016 collection with Aldo Shoes exclusively on Instagram," states Chaykowski.[263]

"Nonoo is hardly alone among fashionistas. This year Tommy Hilfiger created an 'InstaPit,' which gave influential Instagrammers prime seating at his show, so they could capture the best shots and share them with their followers," notes Chaykowski.[263]

At this year's *Met Ball* Vogue's Anna Wintour, who has become pals with Instagram CEO Kevin Systrom, "hosted an exclusive Instagram video studio, where A-list celebrities like Madonna and Blake Lively posed for photos and clips on the app."[263] All-In-all, the synergy between the fashion world and Instagram "generated 283 million engagements—likes and comments—across 42 million accounts during four weeks of shows early this spring in New York, London, Milan and Paris," says Chaykowski.[263]

Fashion isn't the only industry Instagram can help.[263] "Brands ranging from fast food to big banks advertise on Instagram to take advantage of the site's unique features," notes Chaykowsit.[263]At the 2018 Coachella festival, "Sonic Drive-In made special square-shaped milk shakes for a single-day Instagram campaign. A 'Shop Now' button on the ads let people place an order, which Sonic delivered on the spot. More than three-quarters of festivalgoers who clicked on the 'Shop Now' button purchased a shake," explains Chaykowski.[263]

As of late 2016, more than 200,000 companies were advertising on Instagram, up from just hundreds the year before.[263] Chaykowski notes that, "A Nielsen study of more than 700 campaigns found that for 98% of them ad recall from sponsored posts on Instagram was 2.8 times higher than average for online advertising."[263]

Because it is owned by Facebook, Instagram gets access to Facebook's sales operation, including the more than three million advertisers, ad tech, relevance algorithms, spam-fighting tools and, perhaps most importantly, unparalleled user data (on interests, gender, location, occupation and more).[263] "For marketers, extending Facebook ad campaigns to Instagram is seamless—98 of the top 100 spenders on Facebook are on Instagram, too," Chaykowski notes.[263]

Instagram has now ventured beyond photo ads, "debuting video and carousel ads, opening its ad platform widely across more than 200 countries and lengthening video ads to 60 seconds."[263] According to Pinterest, "Promoted Pins are just like regular Pins—the only difference is that a business paid to have more people see it. These Pins will always be labeled 'Promoted' so they're easy to spot."[264] Pinners save Promoted Pins to their boards of wish lists, inspirations and interests—just like other Pins they discover.[264]

Social Networks

Perhaps the most familiar of all social media sites are the social networks, including platforms such as Facebook, WeChat, Foursquare, and LinkedIn, amongst many others. According to Wikipedia, "a social network is a social structure made up of individuals (or organizations) called 'nodes', which are tied (connected) by one or more specific types of interdependency, such as friendship, kinship, common interest, financial exchange, dislike, sexual relationships, or relationships of beliefs, knowledge or prestige."[265]

Boyd and Ellison define social network sites (SNS) as: "web-based services that allow individuals to (1) construct a public or semi-public profile within a bounded system, (2) articulate a list of other users with whom they share a connection, and (3) view and traverse their list of connections and those made by others within the system. The nature and nomenclature of these connections may vary from site to site."[266]

What makes a social network site unique is its "ability to enable users to articulate and make visible their social networks,"[266] which can result in connections between individuals that would otherwise not have been made.[266]

Social networks can also be important platforms for brands of all kinds. In their paper *Expanding Opportunities in a Shrinking World*[267], Avimanyu Datta and Len Jessup state that "Social networks promote social entrepreneurship by means of (a) technology and knowledge transfer; (b) locating information; (c) generating entrepreneurial opportunities; (d) building entrepreneurial competency; (e) financing innovation; and (f) building effective networks for commercialization of innovations."

In her article *The Evolution of Social Media Marketing*[268], Reinaldo Calcaño states that, "Snapchat is the new kid on the block, and its user base is growing by the second." One of the reasons is its ephemeral nature: Snaps disappear forever after a while." "This newly found layer of privacy has made the app a candid, more relaxed medium to share experiences,"[268] argues Calcaño. "When consumers feel protected by a level of privacy they can feel and trust, they spend more time being themselves," adds Calcaño.[268]

WeChat

WeChat is a Chinese mobile text and voice messaging communication service developed by Tencent. It was first released in January 2011. According to Wikipedia[269]:

> "WeChat provides multimedia communication with text messaging, hold-to-talk voice messaging, broadcast (one-to-many) messaging, photo/video sharing, location sharing, and contact information exchange. WeChat supports social networking via shared streaming content feeds and location-based social plug-ins ('Shake', 'Look Around', and 'Drift Bottle') to chat with and connect with local and international WeChat users."

WeChat is a communication platform made up of what WeChat has dubbed "The 4 Pillars"—Instant Messaging, Location Based Services, Moments and Official Accounts.[270]

The "Instant Messaging" section is straightforward, it allows users to message other users via text, which has become many people's communication channel of choice these days, especially in China.[270] The viral marketing potential here should be obvious.

"Location Based Services" is the section that allows the user to find information that is relevant to the area they are in,[270] a good channel for brands to disseminate information through. Beyond just finding the nearest ATM, the Radar feature launched in March 2014 allows users to find friends around them without revealing their cell phone number.[270]

In the "Moments" section, users can post pics, comments and "Like" or share their pictures or videos with the general public or simply share them with a select few.[270] Small business owners often use this feature to showcase their products to their contacts, so it can have alternative, i.e., commercial, uses. Brands can use this like they currently use Facebook and Instagram.

The "Official Accounts" section is where large brands usually come in. WeChat has the ability to integrate into a company's CRM system so that content from the company can be posted across all its channels.[270] Official accounts allow companies to send out blanket messages to multiple users, but then it also enables individual and private conversations, too.[270] "This means that WeChat can be used to resolve issues in a private forum unlike other platforms such as Twitter."[270]

In terms of both functionality and user activity, WeChat has gone through the following three distinct phases of growth:

1. Replacement of SMS with a basic—and free—messaging function that was similar to WhatsApp.[271]
2. The addition of a social networking function through its "moments" section, where users can send status updates with pictures and short snippets of text.[271] Similar to Facebook's *News Feed*, this allows users to create a diary of personal memes. "It was an important addition because it also introduced to WeChat a more public, visible social media channel where updates can be openly shared and viewed by a wide group of connections."[271]
3. E-commerce—users can link their consumer bank cards, credit cards, and Tenpay and WePay accounts to their WeChat accounts. "The linking of these payment options allows WeChat to be a totally enclosed ecosystem where social can be linked seamlessly with sales. A user inside of WeChat never has to leave the app on their mobile phone"[271] to make a purchase.

Brands have taken advantage of WeChat's "public accounts" to create awareness and spread messages virally by teaming up with influencers, celebrities, and key opinion leaders.[271] Brands can use these channels to sell goods through. "While WeChat's social functions are not as open as Weibo's and the structure makes it harder to create massive followings, features like 'look around' (people can add each other based on proximity), 'Shake' and 'Message Bottle' (for random connections), and 'QR Codes' (a path to the user's account from wherever they share the code) have all helped to create more growth in the number of connections."[271]

There are four e-commerce avenues inside of WeChat that brands can also exploit; subscription accounts; online-to-offline sales channels; WeChat shops; and affiliate sales.

With "Subscription Accounts", brands can create content and present new products and offers to followers. This content can be linked to an e-commerce store built inside or outside the WeChat application.[271] A "Subscription Account" is simple to build by using the tools provided by WeChat's Fengling.me service.[271] The only catch is that you have to have a company registered in China, which is, admittedly, not an easy hurdle to overcome for non-Chinese companies.[271] For companies without a China registered office, there are other ways to access the market, but they don't allow for the same control over presentation and process.[271]

As a mobile application with the GPS features of a smartphone, WeChat allows some promising location-based opportunities for airlines.[271] The app offers location-based messaging for airlines that allow one-to-one marketing to customers. Brands can take advantage of the location-based capabilities of the app by creating a loyalty card and/or by encouraging users at a specific location (a retail shop) to add (follow) the brand account.[271] "The 'Loyalty Card' account inside of WeChat is basically a CRM tool, which audiences can opt-in for and find locations nearby (of retail shops), receive discounts, promotions, points, and rewards."[271]

Today, a whole host of industries are using QR codes and other invitations to encourage customers to sign up for WeChat accounts.[271] "This is typically done on-location, taking customers from offline to online, and thereby collecting contacts within the CRM accounts of the brand. Moving from online to offline, brands are starting to experiment with creating promotions online that drive users to a retail location."[271]

For a brand, this could mean sending out a "flash" alert to followers about a promotion taking place "in the next hour" for a free trial or a discount. For a fashion company it could allow them to activate a pop-up shop within a short timeframe for a launch or product demo/trial.[271] Once a user visits the pop-up shop, he or she can pay on location, provided the payments function has been set up on his or her WeChat account.[271]

Currently, there are "a growing number of shops, malls, group-buy (TuanGou), and flash-sales (MianGou) channels being built into WeChat."[271] Companies such as Xiaomi, ONLY, and Sephora have created branded stores (as "Service Accounts") where they sell products directly"[271] to their customers. WeChat only allows access to this channel to brands that have "a plan for building awareness (traffic to their store) and to have a logistics/fulfillment capability,"[271] so this might only be an avenue for large airlines.

Most products sold on WeChat are moving through "malls" of one type or another—many of which are controlled by Tencent.[271] "Tencent has done a good job of implementing its most important companies, applications, and investments into WeChat. Grouped together inside the payments section, key

WeChat/Tencent owned/invested channels are highlighted, including; 'Specials' (linked to its e-commerce mall yixun.com), Weituangou (linked to its group buy site gaopeng.cn) and Dianping for restaurants."[271]

"Tencent also has accounts for other invested companies, including eLong, JD.com, OKBuy, Tongcheng, and Sougou."[271] There are also "malls" for Dangdang, Amazon, VIP.com, Lefeng, Mougujie, Meilishou, Suning, Guomei, No1Shop, and Qunar, just to name a few.[271] The biggest challenge in selling through these channels is, firstly, gaining enough visibility in a very crowded market and, secondly, managing the presentation of the brand[271]; These are significant challenges, especially the former. To gain significant visibility in these channels, "brands often have to pay hefty fees to the 'malls' to get priority listings. Ultimately, the 'malls' control which products get sold and so there is a real loss of control for brand owners."[271]

The products OKWei currently offers are not great and the process has the potential to become very complicated, very quickly, but affiliate sales network are resilient; the invisible hand of profit is just too seductive a motivator to bet against, I believe. "Despite these hurdles, 'affiliate networks' built inside/around WeChat hold a lot of potential. It is this type of link between social and e-commerce that makes WeChat very powerful for brands, even, potentially, airline operators.[271]

Virtual Game Worlds

According to Wikipedia, "a virtual world is an online community that takes the form of a computer-based simulated environment through which users can interact with one another and use and create objects."[272] Wikipedia goes on to add that the term is largely synonymous with interactive 3D virtual environments, where users take the form of two-dimensional, or three-dimensional avatars visible and, through them, interact with others.[272]

Kaplan and Haenlein claim that virtual game worlds "are platforms that replicate a three-dimensional environment in which users can appear in the form of personalized avatars and interact with each other as they would in real life. In this sense, virtual worlds are probably the ultimate manifestation of social media, as they provide the highest level of social presence and media richness of all applications discussed thus far."[47]

Virtual Social Worlds

For Kaplan and Haenlein, "Virtual social worlds allow inhabitants to choose their behavior more freely and essentially live a virtual life similar to their real life. As in virtual game worlds, virtual social world users appear in the form of avatars and interact in a three-dimensional virtual environment; however, in this realm, there are no rules restricting the range of possible interactions, except for basic physical laws such as gravity."[47]

China's yy.com, whose stock is listed on NASDAQ, has created a very successful business model by catering to a niche audience of online karaoke singers. According to David Goldenberg's article *Virtual Roses and the Rise of yy.com*[273]:

> YY started in 2005 as a place for hardcore online gamers to communicate while playing games like World of Warcraft. If a group of players were planning a raid, its members would all hop on YY to talk strategy. But eventually YY administrators found that people were using the chat rooms for other reasons. Many sang karaoke. To enter certain chat rooms, you needed access codes, which YY users were selling for cash on Chinese e-commerce sites. In 2009, YY decided to keep the sales in-house by creating YY Music.

Since it went public in November of 2012, yy.com has seen "its stock price nearly quadruple, from eleven dollars to forty-one. The growth has outpaced even that of Sina, which runs China's popular social-media site Weibo (though Sina is worth considerably more, overall).[273]

Today, visitors to YY Music can choose from thousands of live performances and each performer—and there are, literally, thousands of them—has his—or, more often, her—own theatre "in which fans' avatars cluster in seats around the main stage. A live video feed of the performer rises from the middle."[273] "Users can chat with the performer and buy all sorts of virtual gifts for her; their avatars hurl the favors onto the stage. (The performer gets pretty much the same view, along with some administrative controls.) The performances can seem something like a combination of a pop concert and a peep show."[273]

There is a revenue split between yy.com and the artists: "For every sixteen-dollar bouquet of virtual roses that a fan throws on stage, the performer keeps about five dollars; YY gets almost all of the rest."[273] "A couple of artists on YY make fifty thousand dollars a month from the platform, according to Hany Nada, a partner at GGV Capital, which invested in YY before its I.P.O."[273] Unsurprisingly, it has to do with how pretty the artists are, and "how much their fan bases want to impress them," said Nada.[273]

Some of YY Music's paying users are members of the "*diaosi*"—a once-insulting term meaning, roughly, "losers."[273] It is a term that China's underclass has embraced. Rachel Lu, the cofounder of Tea Leaf Nation, a company that analyzes Chinese social media believes these users are too poor to go to real concerts so they go to virtual ones on YY, where they bestow virtual gifts to real singers who appreciate their offerings.[273] Paying users are about one per cent of the total and each user spends an average of two hundred dollars on the site annually.[273]

In his article *Live streaming in China: boom market, business model and risk regulation*[274], Xiaocen Liu claims that, "The mature monetization model is the key for the fast growth of live streaming business in China. It goes to two parts:

virtual gifts selling (i.e. IVAS) and advertising."

Liu claims that, "Virtual gifting selling is now the dominant revenue driver for all independent live streaming platforms in China."[274] Virtual gifts on Chinese live streaming platforms were first introduced by the app 9158 in 2005.[274]

Liu explains that, as more traffic goes to these live video streaming platforms, the advertising value of these platforms goes up commensurately.[274] Liu adds that live video streaming has some inherent advantages as a new form of interactive advertising; the real-time promotion element allows a direct connection between the streamer and his or her audience-members, who can immediately become consumers.[274] The direct connection between viewers and streamers, who are sometimes store owners themselves, increases the credibility of brands and boosts consumers' purchase impulse. According to a survey by Penguin Intelligence, "30.4% Chinese consumers are browsing e-commerce sites without a purpose,"[274] notes Liu, adding that "Live streaming might be the key conversion driver.[274] Table 11 shows the current live streaming landscape in China.

Merchants & Brands	Means of marketing	Duration	Sales performance
Baby products makes Wyeth Illuma	Pop star live sreaming	60 mins	RMB 1.2 million (USD 180,000)
Cosmetics brand Maybelline	Actress and web stars live streaming	120 mins	RMB 1.4 mllion (USD 210,000)
Fashion magazine *Elle*	Actor live streaming	15 mins	7,000 prints sold
Web star Zhang Dayi's Taobao shop	Web celebrity live streaming	120 mins	RMB 20 million in GMV (USD 3 million)

Table 11: Major marketing campaigns on live streaming platforms
Source: *Live streaming in China: boom market, business model and risk regulation*[274]

Liu argues that "E-commerce is now the most promising sector for live streaming apart from online entertainment."[274] Liu believes China has an even greater opportunity in this field because not only does China have a flourishing e-commerce industry, but it is also haunted by a mistrust on the part of the consumers towards China's e-commerce brands.[274] Liu argues that this mistrust can be reduced by sufficient and comprehensive information from manufacturers.[274] Live streaming might be one of the best ways to build consumer's trust because it will allow them to get closer to the manufacturing process.[274]

China lacks copyright and IP protection and has been riddled by counterfeit technology and corporate scandals. There is no FDA per se in Chinese either, so consumers don't feel as completely comfortable purchasing things like food and drinks as they would in Western countries. Liu believes that, in the near future, "live streaming will be a standard feature for all e-commerce platforms in China."[274]

Psychometrics

Social media can also be a wonderful place to capture customer personality traits. As Hannes Grassegger and Mikael Krogerus explain in their *Das Magazin* article *I Just Showed That the Bomb Was There*[275], "Psychologist Michal Kosinski developed a method of analyzing people's behavior down to the minutest detail by looking at their Facebook activity."[275] According to Grassegger and Krogerus[275]:

> *"Psychometrics, sometimes also known as psychography, is a scientific attempt to 'measure' the personality of a person. The so-called Ocean Method has become the standard approach. Two psychologists were able to demonstrate in the 1980s that the character profile of a person can be measured and expressed in five dimensions, the Big Five: Openness (how open are you to new experiences?), Conscientiousness (how much of a perfectionist are you?), Extroversion (how sociable are you?), Agreeableness (how considerate and cooperative are you?), and Neuroticism (how sensitive/vulnerable are you?). With these five dimensions (O.C.E.A.N.), you can determine fairly precisely what kind of person you are dealing with—her needs and fears as well as how she will generally behave. For a long time, however, the problem was data collection, because to produce such a character profile meant asking subjects to fill out a complicated survey asking quite personal questions. Then came the internet. And Facebook. And Kosinski."*

According to Amit Paul Chowdhury, Psychometrics "is a field of study concerned with the theory and technique involved behind psychological measurement. This field is primarily concerned with testing, measurement, assessment, and related activities. The field entails two key aspects for research purposes—a) construction of instruments, b) revolves around the development of procedures for measurement."[276]

In 2008, with a fellow Cambridge student, Kosinski created a small app for Facebook called *MyPersonality* that asked users a handful of questions from the Ocean survey and they would receive a rating, or a "Personality Profile", consisting of traits defined by the Ocean method.[275] The researchers, in turn, got the users' personal data, which soon amounted to millions and millions of reviews.[275] "It was, literally, the then-largest psychological data set ever produced," state Grassegger and Krogerus.[275]

In the ensuing years, Kosinski and his colleagues continued the research; "first surveys are distributed to test subjects—this is the online quiz. From the subjects' responses, their personal Ocean traits are calculated. Then Kosinski's team would compile every other possible online data point of a test subject—what they've liked, shared, or posted on Facebook; gender, age, and location."[275]

Once the researchers dug into the data, they discovered that amazingly reliable conclusions could be drawn about a person by observing their online behavior.[275] For example, "men who 'like' the cosmetics brand MAC are, to a high degree of probability, gay," which isn't that surprising, but there are other interesting findings.[275] For example, one of the best indicators of heterosexuality is liking Wu-Tang Clan.[275] Also, followers Lady Gaga are most probably extroverts, while someone who likes philosophy is probably an introvert.[275]

Kosinski and his team continued their work, tirelessly refining their models. "In 2012, Kosinski demonstrated that from a mere 68 Facebook likes, a lot about a user could be reliably predicted: skin color (95% certainty), sexual orientation (88% certainty), Democrat or Republican (85%)."[275] Level of intellect, religious affiliation, alcohol, cigarette, and drug use could all be calculated as well.[275] For businesses, employee Facebook pages could be scanned by HR to screen out potentially problematic candidates.

As Kosinski continued refining his model, he discovered that with a mere ten likes as input, his model could appraise a person's character better than an average coworker.[275] With seventy, "it could 'know' a subject better than a friend; with 150 likes, better than their parents. With 300 likes, Kosinski's machine could predict a subject's behavior better than their partner. With even more likes it could exceed what a person thinks they know about themselves,"[275] which is a pretty frightening thought in-and-of-itself.

The day Kosinski published his findings, he received two phone calls, both from Facebook; one a threat to sue, the other a job offer.[275]

Since the publication of Kosinski's article, Facebook has introduced a differentiation between public and private posts so the data isn't as easily accessible now.[275] In "private" mode, "only one's own friends can see what one likes. This is still no obstacle for data-collectors: while Kosinski always requests the consent of the Facebook users he tests, many online quizzes these days demand access to private information as a precondition to taking a personality test."[275] Twitter data is completely public so psychometrics tests can also be run using that service as well.

Kosinski and his team are now adding variables beyond Facebook Likes.[275] Offline activity is now traceable and "motion sensors can show, for example, how fast we are moving a smartphone around or how far we are traveling (correlates with emotional instability)."[275]

Flipping this idea on its head, Kosinski speculated his research could become a search engine for people.[275] By using all of this data, psychological profiles could not only be constructed, but they could also be sought and found.[275] For example, if a company, or a politician, wants to find worried fathers, or angry introverts, or undecided Democrats, these profiles could be uncovered in the data.[275]

To Kosinski's chagrin, one company he had been partnered with—Cambridge Analytica—was involved with Donald Trump's 2016 presidential election.[275] Cambridge Analytica has now become infamous and was even shut down in 2018 because of its questionable activities during the U.S. 2016 presidential election. It had bought up extensive personal data on American voters—"What car you drive, what products you purchase in shops, what magazines you read, what clubs you belong to"—and used the data in questionable and highly unethical ways to help elect Donald Trump.[275]

In America, detailed personal consumer data is available for a price and Cambridge Analytica snapped it up and the company crosschecked these data sets with Republican Party voter rolls and online data, such as Facebook likes.[275] Ocean personality profiles were built from this data and, from a selection of digital signatures there suddenly emerged real individual people with real fears, needs, and interests—and home addresses.[275] By the time of the 2016 presidential election, Cambridge Analytica had assembled psychograms for all adult US citizens—220 million people—and they used this data to influence electoral outcomes.[275]

Chowdhury puts it succinctly when he says, the success of the Cambridge Analytica work "can be attributed to the combination of three core techniques, behavioral science using the *OCEAN Model*, Big Data analysis, and ad targeting."[276] Cambridge Analytica bought "personal data from a range of different sources, like land registries, automotive data, shopping data, bonus cards, club memberships, and more." It aggregated "this data with the electoral rolls of the Republican party and online data, to calculate a Big Five personality profile."[276]

According to Chowdhury, Nix showed "how psychographically categorized voters can be differently addressed. The messages differed for the most part only in microscopic details, to target the recipients in the optimal psychological way by including different headings, colors, captions, with a photo or video."[276] Digging down into such granular detail helped Trump reach down to the most granular group-level of customer. "Pretty much every message that Trump put out was data-driven," states Nix.[276]

The return on investment was extraordinary. "The embedded Cambridge Analytica team comprised of only a dozen people. The firm received $100,000 from Trump in July, $250,000 in August, and $5 million in September. According to Nix, the company earned over $15 million overall."[276]

Most importantly, "The decision to focus on Michigan and Wisconsin in the final weeks of the campaign was made on the basis of data analysis done by the organization."[276]

"Trump's conspicuous contradictions and his oft-criticized habit of staking out multiple positions on a single-issue result in a gigantic number of resulting messaging options that creates a huge advantage for a firm like Cambridge Analytica: for every voter, a different message," explains Grassegger and Krogerus.[275]

Mathematician Cathy O'Neil notes that Trump is like a machine learning algorithm that adjusts to public reactions.[275] On the day of the third 2016 presidential debate, "Trump's team blasted out 175,000 distinct variations on his arguments, mostly via Facebook,"[275] which is an astounding number of unique ads. "The messages varied mostly in their microscopic details, in order to communicate optimally with their recipients: different titles, colors, subtitles, with different images or videos" were utilized, explains Grassegger and Krogerus.[275] This is personalization marketing at its finest.

Small towns, city districts, apartment buildings, and even individual people could be targeted, explains Grassegger and Krogerus.[275] Blanket advertising—the idea that a hundred million people will be sent the same piece of marketing collateral, the same television advert, the same digital advert—is over, note Grassegger and Krogerus.[275] Micro and personalization targeting has reached the point where politicians—and regular companies—can advertise highly detailed and personalized messages to a market of one.

Cambridge Analytica separated the entire US population into 32 different personality types, and focused their efforts on only seventeen states.[275] "Just as Kosinski had determined that men who like MAC cosmetics on Facebook are probably gay, Cambridge Analytica found that a predilection for American-produced cars is the best predictor of a possible Trump voter."[275] Among other things, this kind of information helped the Trump campaign focus in on what messages to use, and where to use them, perhaps even what channel to use them on.[275] In effect, the candidate himself became an implementation instrument of the model.[275]

As Grassegger and Krogerus note, the first results seen by *Das Magazin* were amazing: psychological targeting increased the clickthru rate on Facebook ads by more than sixty percent. And the so-called conversion rate (the term for how likely a person is to act upon a personally-tailored ad, i.e., whether they buy a product or, yes, go vote) increases by a staggering 1,400 percent."[275]

Now, what does all of this mean for a marketer? How can a marketer use

Facebook Likes to gain a deeper understanding of its customers? Well, potentially, by analyzing these Likes, a marketer could predict how open, conscientious, outgoing and neurotic an individual user and/or customer is. It could be as simple as doing a Facebook graph search of "Pictures liked" or "Videos liked" and/or "Stories Liked" with the customer's name. In addition to predicting a user's personality, these tests could estimate a user's/customer's age, relationship status, intelligence level, life satisfaction, political and religious beliefs, and education.

A brand's HR department would also find these personality test results interesting as matching a candidate with jobs based on their personality might make more sense than the current scattershot approach HR often takes in hiring—and firing. These personality tests could also reveal troubling traits, like alcohol and/or drug use that should give pause to the hiring of a prospect.

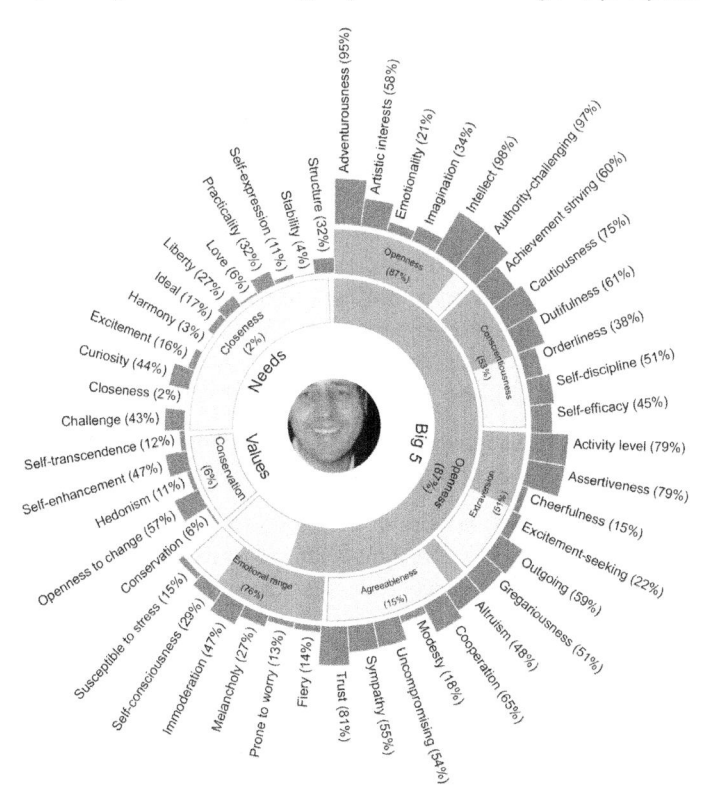

Figure 23: IBM Watson's Personality Insights Sunbrust Chart Visualization on Author's Twitter Feed.
Source: https://personality-insights-demo.ng.bluemix.net/

In its *Artificial Intelligence in Logistics*[16], DHL Customer Solutions & Innovation describe the IBM Watson Personality Insights tool, which allows users to develop a highly specific understanding of a person's character, as seen in figure 23. As per the DHL Customer & Innovation team, "The tool can be used for the creation of novel and personalized services. For example, in the wealth management industry, IBM Watson Investment Advisor can draw correlations between a customer's personality, life situation, and the vast ocean of financial market data."[16] According to the DHL team, "These inputs can be matched with various investment alternatives to recommend an optimal personalized wealth management strategy."[16] In addition, the system "uses deep learning to provide financial advisors with a highly efficient and personalized way to serve clients, while indicating how to deepen relationships through other channels in their firms, such as lending solutions."[16]

(Anyone interested in seeing his or her OCEAN psychometric profile can visit the University of Cambridge's Psychometrics center at www.applymagicsauce.com as well as the IBM Watson personality Insights test at https://personality-insights-demo.ng.bluemix.net/.)

Social Media Analytics

As Melville and Lawrence explain in their article *Social Media Analytics: Channeling the Power of the Blogosphere for Marketing Insight*[277], social media analytics is "the practice of gathering data from blogs and social media websites and analyzing that data to make business decisions. The most common use of social media is to mine customer sentiment." Social media analytics evolved out of the disciplines of social network analysis, machine learning, data mining, information retrieval (IR), and Natural Language Processing (NLP).

According to Melville and Lawrence, the automotive analysis of blogs and other social media sites raise the following intriguing marketing questions[277]:

1. Given the enormous size of the blogosphere, how can we identify the subset of blogs and forums that are discussing not only a specific product, but higher-level concepts that are in some way relevant to this product?
2. Having identified this subset of relevant blogs, how do we identify the most authoritative or influential bloggers in this space?
3. How can we detect and characterize specific sentiment expressed about an entity (e.g., product) mentioned in a blog or a forum?
4. How do we tease apart novel emerging topics of discussion from the constant chatter in the blogosphere?

As Margaret Rouse explains in her article *Social Media Analytics*[278], step one of a social media analytics initiative is "to determine which business goals the data that is gathered and analyzed will benefit. Typical objectives include increasing revenues, reducing customer service costs, getting feedback on products and services and improving public opinion of a particular product or business division." Once these business goals have been identified, "KPIs for objectively evaluating the data should be defined. For example, customer engagement might be measured by the numbers of followers for a Twitter account and number of retweets of a company's name," states Rouse.[278]

Which of the following objectives does your organization seek to achieve by implementing customer analytics technologies and methods with social media data? (Please select all that apply.)

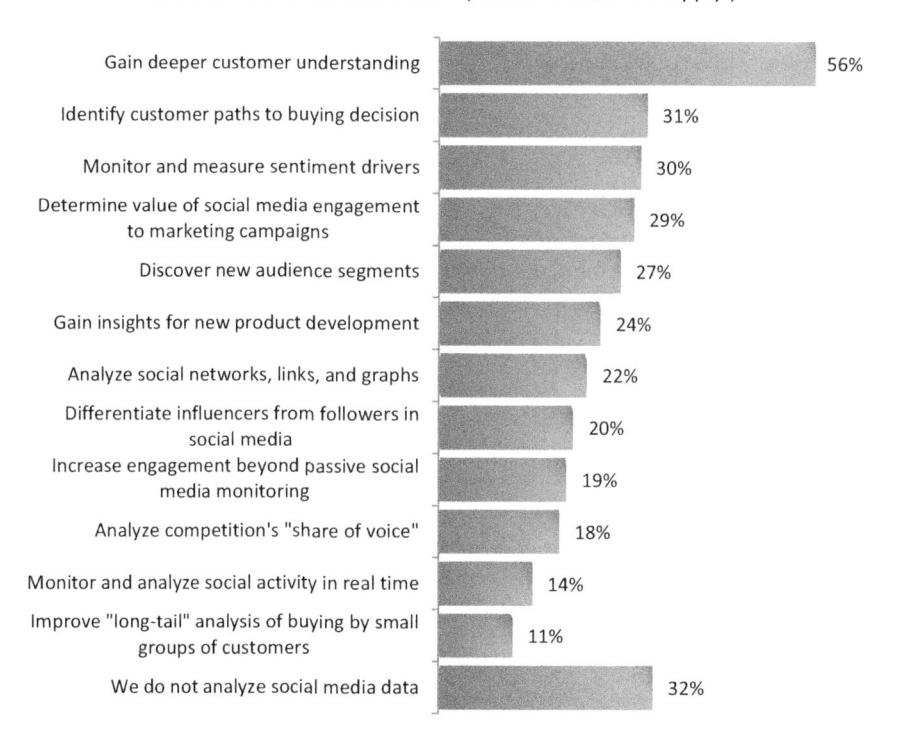

Objective	%
Gain deeper customer understanding	56%
Identify customer paths to buying decision	31%
Monitor and measure sentiment drivers	30%
Determine value of social media engagement to marketing campaigns	29%
Discover new audience segments	27%
Gain insights for new product development	24%
Analyze social networks, links, and graphs	22%
Differentiate influencers from followers in social media	20%
Increase engagement beyond passive social media monitoring	19%
Analyze competition's "share of voice"	18%
Monitor and analyze social activity in real time	14%
Improve "long-tail" analysis of buying by small groups of customers	11%
We do not analyze social media data	32%

Figure 24: Customer Analytics and Social Media Objectives
Based on 1,546 respondents from 418 respondents; a bit more than three responses per respondent, on average.
Source: TDWI Research[118]

Through social networks like Twitter and Weibo, organizations can pick up customer satisfaction in real time.[118] "Social media is enabling companies such as Coca-Cola, Starbucks, and Ford to go beyond standard customer satisfaction data gathering to innovate by setting up and participating in communities to gain feedback from customers."[118] A good example is MyStarbucksIdea.com, which is a website where "Starbucks customers can relate their experiences and offer ideas about how to improve the Starbucks experience, from drinks to foods to ambiance."[118]

When looking at what objectives companies were seeking when implementing customer analytics technologies with social media data (see Figure 24), TDWI Research found that gaining a "deeper customer understanding" topped the list at 56%[118] "Social media listening can provide an unprecedented window into customer sentiment and the reception of an organization's marketing, brands, and services."[118]

Besides the broad objective of gaining deeper customer understanding, nearly one-third (31%) of companies seek to identify attribution, or paths to buying decisions, which can be done on a limited scale with services like Google Analytics as well as other Web site analysis applications.[118] Google's webmaster tools also allow brands to understand the organic search traffic that is linking customers to them.

30% or respondents sought to discover customer sentiment, which is important because it helps companies discover positive and negative comments in social media channels, on customer comment and review sites.[118] "Sentiment analysis often focuses on monitoring and measuring the 'buzz' value, usually through volume and frequency of comments around a topic."[118]

Simply deciding which social media sites' data to analyze can be one of the biggest challenges facing brands going down the analytics path. "Organizations have to research where their customers are most likely to express themselves about products and services. They need to spot influencers who have networks of contacts and take it upon themselves to play an advocacy role."[118] "About 20% of respondents are interested in differentiating influencers from followers in social media.[118]

Link analytic tools can help identify relationships between users in social communities as well as enable organizations to measure a user's influence.[118] "With some tools, data scientists and analysts can test variables to help identify social communities as 'segments'. Then, as they implement segmentation models for other data sources, they can integrate these insights with social media network analysis to sharpen models and test new variables," explains Stodder.[118]

Analytics are critical in helping organizations "make the right decisions about when, where, and how to participate in social media. It isn't enough to just listen; organizations must insert themselves and become part of the conversation."[118] When doing so, however, companies should keep in mind advice from *The Cluetrain Manifesto*[279]—"Conversations among human beings sound human. They are conducted in a human voice." Also, "When delivering information, opinion, perspectives, dissenting arguments or humorous asides, the human voice is typically open, natural, uncontrived."[279]

One interesting strategy is for a brand to start viral campaigns via Twitter, using hashtags for a topic; the campaign could be a part of a larger marketing strategy. Brands can then "monitor social media to see what people say and analyze how the campaign is playing among influencers and across networks."[60]

One example of this type of marketing is Unilever's Dove brand series of web-integrated commercials, which attempted to fundamentally redefine the brand and Unilever's Sunsilk shampoo campaign that, according to the company, placed a "net seed" onto YouTube with the video titled "Bride Has Massive Hair Wig Out."[60] The video, which showed a bride-to-be reacting in horror to her wedding day hair, contained no brand references and quickly accumulated three million hits.[60] Later, Unilever came forward to claim the ad, saying it was intended to plant the term "wig out" in the culture, a term that was to be used in conventional advertising for Sunsilk products at a later date.[60]

Klear, a social media and social data platform that focuses on influencer marketing, offers a product that can help brands understand the effects of their influencer marketing. Klear's campaign reports contain the following summaries[280]:

- How many influencers participated in the campaign?
- Number of updates the influencers posted during the campaign.
- Engagements metrics.
- Number of people who saw the content.

The report also includes a drill-down analysis for every influencer. For each influencer the report will show[280]:

- Who the influencer is?
- The influencer's expertise.
- Fanbase across different social networks.
- Top posts during the campaign.
- Engagements for these updates.
- A direct link to the influencer's profile on Klear.

Klear is a paid service, but most of the information Klear deals with is publicly available and this is something a brand could build up in-house, should they want to create an open source, customized solution.

Influencer marketing taps directly into what Deighton and Kornfeld call the five paradigms of digital interactive marketing[60], i.e., social exchanges—building identities within virtual communities—and cultural exchanges—firms offering culture products that will compete in buzz markets.[60] This peer-to-peer interactivity should motivate the desire to exchange and share information, which should help market any brand event.[60]

As Bifet and Frank explain in their paper *Sentiment Knowledge Discovery in*

Twitter Streaming Data[281], Twitter is a:

> "potentially valuable source of data that can be used to delve into the thoughts of millions of people as they are uttering them. Twitter makes these utterances immediately available in a data stream, which can be mined for information by using appropriate stream mining techniques. In principle, this could make it possible to infer people's opinions, both at an individual level as well as in aggregate, regarding potentially any subject or event."

Services offered by companies like Rival iQ[282] can track a list of brands of one's choosing and monitor their activity on Facebook, Twitter, and Google. Rival IQ could not only provide insight into a marketer's competitor, but also insight into the industry as a whole. For instance, brands could learn from the "Day of the Week" chart when content from the brand's industry is most likely to go viral.

Buzz Sumo[283] also has a search tool that tracks the most popular content on any given topic or website and ranks it according to shares on Facebook, Twitter, LinkedIn, and Google.

As Bifet and Frank note, "There are also a number of interesting tasks that have been tackled using Twitter text mining: sentiment analysis, classification of tweets into categories, clustering of tweets and trending topic detection."[281]

In their article *From tweets to polls: Linking text sentiment to public opinion time series*[284], O'Connor et al. found that surveys of consumer confidence correlate with sentiment word frequencies in tweets, and they proposed text stream mining as a substitute for traditional polling. Free sentiment analysis services like twittersentiment.appspot.com can also be used to analyze a company's sentiment.

Social Media Monitoring

I believe it is high time to revise Wanamaker's oft-made quote that he didn't know which half of his marketing spend was useful, not because it is probably the most overused quote in the history of marketing, but because we now have the ability to figure out which advertisement works for which consumers. We can also extrapolate how that advertising will work on customers similar to the ones we might want to target in lookalike marketing.

In 1999, *The Cluetrain Manifesto*[279] warned, "Reviews are the new advertising." Today, this is truer than ever before. There are a multitude of platforms that allow users to rate or comment on a brand, whether that is a restaurant, a retail establishment, a hotel, or even a local handyman or plumber.

Used properly, reviews can be the new advertising currency for a brand's marketing department. Companies such as Dell, Cisco, Salesforce.com, the American Red Cross, and Gatorade are creating social media command centers that monitor the social conversations about their companies. These social media centers enable company employees to monitor conversations from the social web on channels such as Twitter, Facebook, and YouTube, amongst others, in an attempt to keep track of the health of a company's social brand.

Today, digital advertising should employ a multi-screen strategy that follows its audience throughout his or her digital day. As previously mentioned, successful mobile advertising requires three things—reach, purity and analytics. Analytics "involves matching users' interests—implicit and explicit, context, preferences, network and handset conditions—to ads and promotions in real time."[28] This is very much the terrain that AI works in.

In their *Measuring Social Media Performance and Business Impact (Part 1)*[285], Hamill and Stevenson put forth their '6 Is' of social media monitoring framework that include:

1. Involvement—the number and quality of customers involved in your various online networks.
2. Interaction—the actions taken by online network members—read, post, comment, review, recommend, etc.).
3. Intimacy—the brand sentiments expressed, level of brand "affection" or "aversion".
4. Influence—advocacy, viral forwards, referrals, recommendations, retweets, etc.
5. Insights—the level of customer/actionable insight delivered from monitoring online conversations.
6. Impact—business impact of your social media activities benchmarked against core business goals and objectives.

In December 2010, Dell became one of the first companies to launch a social media command center. Based at company HQ in Round Rock, TX, twelve full-time employees monitor conversations about Dell and its products around the globe, responding via @DellCares or forwarding the post to the right internal Dell team.[286] Through Dell's Social Media Listening and Command Center, Dell aggregates and culls through the 25,000 conversations about Dell every day (more than 6 million every year).[286]

"We're monitoring conversations in 11 languages 24/7, and each one is an opportunity to reinforce our brand," explains Karen Quintos, Dell CMO.[286] Quintos explains that[286]:

> "With the tremendous amount of information being generated, we can track basic demographics, reach, sentiment, subject matter of the discussions, the sites where conversations are happening, and more. We leverage these analytics to

> *identify customer support needs as they happen, influence product development, insert ourselves into conversations with IT decision makers and connect with people having the most impact on these conversations."*

Unlike casual conversations, comments, updates, likes and dislikes uploaded to social networks are collected and, therefore, analyzable and measurable. This results in "a data tsunami: the actions and content generated by participants in social media create 'Big Data' sources that are full of potential for tracking and understanding behavior, trends, and sentiments."[118] Brands should be studying attribution analysis for their social media campaigns on platforms like Facebook, YouTube, Twitter, Weibo, amongst others.

In its *Social Media Analytics: Making Customer Insights Actionable*[287], IBM believes that the "mistake many organizations make is to treat social media as distinct and separate from other customer data and divorced from revenue generating imperatives." IBM recommends companies venturing into the social do the following[287]:

- Integrate company-wide information from different data sources to drive the business through deeper consumer insight.
- Define the real value of the company's brand—its equity, reputation and loyalty—at any moment in time, in any place in the world; and
- Understand emerging consumer trends, both globally and locally and apply predictive models to determine actions with the highest probability of increasing relevance and maximizing marketing campaign ROI.

IBM believes businesses should ask the following questions when devising a social media plan[287]:

- Assess—also referred to as "listening". At this stage a company should monitor social media to uncover sentiment about its products, services, marketing campaigns, employees and partners. The questions that need to be asked at this stage include:
    - What are you company objectives? Are you looking to:
        - Attract customers?
        - Increase the value of existing customer relationships?
        - Retain customers?
    - How do customers interact with you today?
    - What are they interested in?
    - Where and when do they use social media?
    - Are there significant influencers who speak to your brand or products?

- Measure—proactive analytics can uncover hidden patterns that can reveal "unknown unknowns" in the data. Questions that businesses need to ask at this stage include:
    - Who are you targeting with your social media initiatives and why?
    - What will you be measuring:
        - Share of voice.
        - Activation.
        - Brand sentiment.
        - Influencers.
    - Sales over the life of the customer relationship?
- Integrate—social media can give businesses both a broad view of their operations as well as a detailed and intimate view of their individual customers. Questions to ask at this stage include:
    - What is your vision for social media and its integration into the company's operational marketing systems?
    - Do you have a profile of your customer advocates? Can you predict sentiment on products, services, campaigns?
    - How do you measure the effects of social media on brand equity and reputation, pipeline, and sales orders and margins?
    - How will you integrate social analytics into other customer analytics?

Regardless of the sophistication and scope of any social media initiative, the end goal, IBM argues, should be in alignment with corporate imperatives and goals, as well as produce a measurable ROI.[287]

In his article, *Opposition Research: Sentiment Analysis as a Research* Tool, Mullich offers the following tips on how to get the low-down on rivals[179]:

1. Understand that day-to-day online chatter can be misleading, but, over time, a marketer can find directional trends important to its business and industry.
2. The deepest insights often come not from general sources, like Facebook and Twitter, but from blogs and forums that are specific to an industry.
3. Think broadly about the nature of one's "competitors"—sentiment analysis can help a business prepare for unexpected entries that might be preparing to take a piece of its business. Keyword search teams can help.
4. The information you can gain online about competitors is limited, and often must be combined with your own internal data to bring actionable insights.

All-in-all, social media listening can provide a marketer with an ongoing real-time window into customer sentiment, as well as give the business verifiable information about the company's marketing campaigns, brands, and services.

Conclusion

We live in a real-time, 24-7 world, a world where 280-character Tweets foment political revolutions; a world where marketers should fear not the power of the pen, but the destructive force of the critical tweet or the far-reaching viral impact of an inflammatory social media diatribe that can encircle the digital world in seconds, laying waste to a reputation that might have taken decades to develop. Conversely, it is also a world where an advertiser's message can go viral and reach more eyeballs in an hour than a multi-million-dollar television commercial campaign can in a year.

I previously mentioned Paul Greenberg's comment that social CRM was "a philosophy and a business strategy supported by a technology platform, business rules, workflow, processes, and social characteristics, designed to engage and reach accordingly in a collaborative conversation."[105] *The A.I. Marketer* must add social media elements to its CRM systems to give customers a complete personalization experience. Continuous customer engagement can be fostered through a multitude of social channels and they are cheap to use, if not free, in some cases (excluding the brand's staff needed for social media responses, of course).

The beauty of this system is that it can be a real win-win situation when it comes to a brand's marketing plan as customers who are happy with a business's products and/or services will often comment and blog about the products and/or services they like, while those who unhappy with it, can be reached out to and, hopefully, converted into satisfied customers. Often, the simple act of responding to a customer's complaints can stem the tide of negativity and, as long as the remedies are constructive, can turn a hostile customer into a positive one, and, possibly, one who might even tout the company's excellent customer service at a later date.

There are, of course, limits to what competitive sentiment analysis can do. "The challenges you might address, using your company's own customer, product, and transactional data, are far more extensive than those you can tackle via available competitor data," says Seth Grimes, an analyst who runs the annual Social Analysis Symposium.[179] "For instance, you're not going to have access to your competitors' contact-center notes and warranty claims, or to your competitors' customer profiles and transaction records. But with your own company's, you can create some very rich analyses," he adds.[179]

For the above reasons, competitive analysis is usually just one piece of the vast data mosaic a company can tap into.[179] For example, one company that noticed a drop in sales of its flagship product analyzed online chatter and found customers were talking enthusiastically about a new product a competitor had just released.[179] "When the company analyzed its contact-center data, it found that returns correlated to discontent about an attribute its own product lacked, but the new competing product offered."[179] The company was quickly able to identify the problem and by using a combination of competitive sentiment analysis, discovery from its own internal data, it was able to tweak its own product to make it much more competitive.[179]

As Grimes notes, "Sentiment analysis can help you understand how the market perceives you and your competitors' products and services, but keep in mind that sentiment is only an indicator, useful in measuring and projecting market impact, not a substitute for strong human judgment."[179]

The internet has allowed companies to reach consumers in very cheap, easy, and effective ways, but the downside is that it can also give a loud and reverberating voice to unhappy customers, very inexpensively, too. Because humans are, by nature, more attuned to negative messages than positive ones (think about how a raised voice in a crowded restaurant gains instant attention) businesses need to react very quickly to negative stories on social media.

A word of warning here: don't set up fake accounts to try to get your marketing message out. There are people in the blogosphere who would love nothing more than to uncover the latest social media scam, especially in China, and these people probably have access to some of the most sophisticated tools to ferret out dishonest behavior.

Don't pick fights with customers on social media either. Threatening customers with legal action is never a good idea. The old rule that you shouldn't whip out a gun unless you're willing to pull the trigger should be kept in mind when it comes to social media as well.

---

230 Drury, G. (2008). Opinion piece: Social media: Should marketers engage and how can it be done effectively? Journal of Direct, Data and Digital Marketing Practice, Volume 9, pages 274-277.
231 As identified in Claude E. Shannon and Warren Weaver's *The Mathematical Theory of Communication*, the Source-Message-Channel-Receiver model is a basic model of communication; Source is the person who encodes the message and transmits it to the receiver; the Message is the intended meaning the source hopes the receiver will understand; the Channel is the medium through which the message is conveyed and it must tap into the receiver's sensory system; the Receiver is the person at the end of the communication, someone who will decode the message and create their own meaning.

232 Lefebvre, R. C. (2007). The New Technology: The Consumer as Participant Rather Than Target Audience. *Social Marketing Quarterly*, 31-42.
233 Juniper Research. (2008). Mobile User Generated Content: Dating, Social Networking & Personal Content Deliver. Juniper Research.
234 Juniper Research. (2008). Mobile User Generated Content: Dating, Social Networking & Personal Content Deliver. Juniper Research.
235 OECD. (2007). Participative web and user-created content: Web 2.0, wikis, and social networking. Organisation for Economic Co-operation and Development. Paris.
236 Short, J. W. (1976). *The Social Psychology of telecommunication.* Hoboken, NJ: John Wiley & Sons, Ltd.
237 Daft, R. &. (1986). Organization information requirements, media richness, and structural design. *Management Science*, 32(5), 554-571.
238 Goffman, E. (1959). The Presentation of Self In Everyday Life. New York: Doubleday.
239 Divol, R. E. (2012, April). Demystifying social media. Retrieved from Mckinsey.com: http://www.mckinsey.com/insights/marketing_sales/demystifying_social_media (Accessed 25 November 2017).
240 Outing, S. (2007, September). Enabling the Social Company. Enthusiast Group. Retrieved from Steveouting.com: http://www.steveouting.com/files/social_company.pdf (22 November 2017).
241 Business.com. (2010, November 8). Top Tools to measure your social media success. Retrieved from Business.com: http://www.business.com/info/social-media-monitoring-tools (22 November 2017).
[242] Eley, B & Tilley S. *Online Marketing Inside Out: Reach New Buyers Using Modern Marketing Techniques.* May 28, 2009. Sitepoint
[243] Stampler, L. (2013, February 19). *How Maker's Mark turned its watered down whiskey debacle into a social media win.* Retrieved from Business Insider: http://www.businessinsider.com/makers-mark-turns-whiskey-fail-into-win-2013-2 (Accessed 25 November 2017).
[244] Nelson, A. (2013, November 21). *50 ways to drive traffic to your website with social media.* Retrieved from Exact Target Cloud Blog: http://www.exacttarget.com/blog/50-ways-to-drive-traffic-to-your-website-with-social-media/ (Accessed 25 November 2017).
245 Golder, S., & Huberman, B. A. (2006). Usage Patterns of Collaborative Tagging Systems. Journal of Information Science, Volume 32 (2), pages 198-208.
246 Dubois, L. (2010, September 16). *How to Use Social Bookmarking for Business. Inc.* Retrieved from http://www.inc.com/guides/2010/09/how-to-use-social-bookmarking-for-business.html (Accessed 25 November 2017).
247 DuBois, S. (2014, July 4). Google Glass Hits the Operating Room. Retrieved from tennessean.com: http://www.tennessean.com/story/money/industries/health-care/2014/07/05/google-glass-hits-operating-room/12228547/
248 Mathes, A. (2008). Folksonomies – Cooperative Classification and Communication Through Shared Metadata. *Computer Mediated Communication – LIS590CMC.* University of Illinois Urbana-Champaign: Graduate School of Library and Information Science.
249 https://www.merriam-webster.com/dictionary/blog (Accessed 25 November 2017).

250 http://www.webopedia.com/TERM/B/blog.html (Accessed 25 November 2017).
251 Wortham, J. (2007, December 17). After 10 Years of Blogs, the Future's Brighter Than Ever. *Wired Magazine*.
252 Economist, The. (2006, April 20). *It's the links, stupid.* Retrieved from Economist.com: http://www.economist.com/node/6794172 (Accessed 25 November 2017).
253 Baker, J. (2008, April 20). *Origins of "Blog" and "Blogger.* Retrieved from linguistlist.org: http://listserv.linguistlist.org/cgi-bin/wa?A2=ind0804C&L=ADS-L&P=R16795&I=-3 (Accessed 25 November 2017).
254 Lohmann, S. B. (2012). Visual Analysis of Microblog Content Using Time-Varying Co-occurrence Highlighting in Tag Clouds. New York, NY: AVI 2012 Conference.
255 Isaac, Mike. (2017) Twitter to Test Doubling tweet Length to 280 Characters. New York Times. 26 September 2017. https://www.nytimes.com/2017/09/26/technology/twitter-280-characters.html (Accessed October 24, 2017).
256 Twitter.com
257 Bifet, A. a. (2010). *Sentiment knowledge discovery in twitter streaming data.* Retrieved from University of Waikato, Hamilton, New Zealand: http://www.cs.waikato.ac.nz/~ml/publications/2010/Twitter-crc.pdf (Accessed 25 November 2017).
258 www.youtube.com/t/about_youtube (Accessed 5 November 2017).
259 http://www.youtube.com/t/press_statistics (Accessed 5 November 2017).
260 http://www.Slideshare.net/about (Accessed 5 November 2017).
261 https://en.wikipedia.org/wiki/SlideShare (Accessed 21 November 2017).
262 BBC. (2012, April 10). *Facebook buys Instagram photo sharing network for $1bn.* Retrieved from http://www.bbc.co.uk/news/technology-17658264 (Accessed 5 November 2017).
263 Chaykowski, Kathleen. (2016). Instagram, The $50 Billion Grand Slam Driving Facebook's Future: The Forbes Cover Story. Forbes.com. August 1, 2016. https://www.forbes.com/sites/kathleenchaykowski/2016/08/01/instagram-the-50-billion-grand-slam-driving-facebooks-future-the-forbes-cover-story/#5ddd67074a97 (Accessed 5 November 2017).
264 Pinterest Blog. An update on promoted pins. https://blog.pinterest.com/en/update-promoted-pins (Accessed 17 November 17, 2017).
265 https://en.wikipedia.org/wiki/Social_network (Accessed 25 November 2017).
266 Boyd, D. a. (2007). Social Network Sites: Definition, History, and Scholarship. Journal of Computer-Mediated Communication, Vol. 13.
267 Datta, A. J. (2009). Expanding Opportunities in a Shrinking World: A Conceptual Model explicating the Role of Social Networks and Internet-based Virtual Environments in Social Entrepreneurship. International Journal of Virtual Communities and Social Networking, 1 (4), pp. 33-49.
268 Calcano, Reinaldo. The Evolution of Social Media Marketing. Sweetiq.com. January 12, 2017. https://sweetiq.com/blog/the-evolution-of-social-media-marketing-in-retail/ (Accessed 25 November 2017).

269 https://en.wikipedia.org/wiki/WeChat (Accessed 25 November 2017).
270 Segev, L. (2014, March 20). *WeChat is so much more than just Instant Messaging*. Retrieved from Thetechieguy.com: http://thetechieguy.com/2014/03/20/wechat-is-so-much-more-than-just-instant-messaging/ (Accessed 25 November 2017).
271 Baker, C. (2014, May 26). 4 Ways Brands Can Use WeChat for Sales. Retrieved from clickz.com: http://www.clickz.com/clickz/column/2346596/4-ways-brands-can-use-wechat-for-sales (Accessed 25 November 2017).
272 https://en.wikipedia.org/wiki/Virtual_world (Accessed 23 November 2017).
273 Goldenberg, D. (2013, September 5). Virtual roses and the rise of yy.com. Retrieved from Newyorker.com: http://www.newyorker.com/online/blogs/currency/2013/09/virtual-roses-and-the-rise-of-yy-music-china.html (22 November 2017).
274 Liu, Xiaocen. Live streaming in China: boom market, business model and risk regulation. Journal of Residuals Science & Technology, Vol. 13, No. 8, 2016. DEStech Publications, Inc.
275 Grassegger, H., Krogerus, M. December 3, 2016. I Just Showed That the Bomb Was There. Das Magazin https://www.dasmagazin.ch/2016/12/03/ich-habe-nur-gezeigt-dass-es-die-bombe-gibt/ (22 November 2017).
276 Chowdhury, Amit Paul. Analytics India Magazine. Is Machine Learning Key to Psychometrics? May 26, 2017. https://www.analyticsindiamag.com/machine-learning-key-psychometrics/ (2017). Accessed 7 March 2019).
277 Melville, P. &. (2009). Social Media Analytics: Channeling the Power of the Blogosphere for Marketing Insight. Retrieved from citeseerx.ist.psu.edu: http://citeseerx.ist.psu.edu/viewdoc/download?doi=10.1.1.157.3485&rep=rep1&type=pdf (Accessed 22 November 2017).
278 Rouse, M. (n.d.). Social Media Analytics. Retrieved from techtarget.com: http://searchbusinessanalytics.techtarget.com/definition/social-media-analytics (Accessed 22 November 2017).
279 www.cluetrain.com (Accessed 22 November 2017).
280 https://klear.com/ (Accessed 22 November 2017).
281 Bifet, A. a. (2010). Sentiment knowledge discovery in twitter streaming data. Retrieved from University of Waikato, Hamilton, New Zealand: http://www.cs.waikato.ac.nz/~ml/publications/2010/Twitter-crc.pdf (22 November 2017).
282 https://www.rivaliq.com (22 November 2017).
283 http://buzzsumo.com (22 November 2017).
284 O'Connor, B., Balasubramanyan, R., Routledge, B. R. and Smith, N. A. From tweets to polls: Linking text sentiment to public opinion time series. In Proceedings of the International AAAI Conference on Weblogs and Social Media, pages 122–129, 2010.
285 Hamill, J. and Stevenson, A. 2010. Step 3: *Key Performance Indicators (Post 1)*. Available at: www.energise2-0.com/2010/06/27/step-3-key-performance- indicators-post-1/ [accessed: 12 February 2011].

286 Salesforce.com. (2013). 10 Examples of Social Media Command Centers. Retrieved from Salesforce Marketing Cloud: http://www.salesforcemarketingcloud.com/resources/ebooks/10-examples-of-social-media-command-centers/ (Accessed 22 November 2017).

287 IBM. (2013, February). Social Media Analytics: Making Customer Insights Actionable. Retrieved from IBM.com: http://www-01.ibm.com/common/ssi/cgi-bin/ssialias?infotype=SA&subtype=WH&htmlfid=YTW03168USEN (Accessed 22 November 2017).

ANDREW W. PEARSON

CHAPTER SIX: UNIFIED ANALYTICS

"AI and the Internet of Things are inextricably linked. Because we shouldn't be connecting things just because we can—we should be extracting business intelligence from them. Given the immense scale we anticipate for the IoT, AI will be instrumental in allowing us to tap those insights."

~Rose Schooler VP, Data Center Group, Sales, Intel

Overview

To begin with, some words of warning: according to its *Conquer the AI Dilemma by Unifying Data Science and Engineering*, Databricks believes that data-related challenges are hindering 96% of organizations from achieving AI.[10] Nearly all of the respondents (96%) cited multiple data-related challenges when moving projects to production.[10] "According to the survey, 90% of the respondents believe that unified analytics—the approach of unifying data processing with ML frameworks and facilitating data science and engineering collaboration across the ML lifecycle, will conquer the AI dilemma."[10]

Databricks argues that, "Unified Analytics is a new category of solutions that unify data science and engineering, making AI much more achievable for organizations."[10] "Unified Analytics makes it easier for data engineers to build data pipelines across siloed systems and prepare labeled datasets for model building while enabling data scientists to explore and visualize data and build models collaboratively."[10] A unified analytics platform can "unify data science and engineering across the ML lifecycle from data preparation to experimentation and deployment of ML applications—enabling companies to accelerate innovation with AI," Databricks concludes.[10]

The rest of this chapter will focus on how to build the backbone of an IT system that will incorporate a structure that can help a marketer become predictive. General sections on data governance, Hadoop, IoT, Chips, deep learning frameworks, amongst other, will lay out the most common questions that a marketer should ask about an EDW, a data lake and an AI world. The rest of the chapter will detail specific business areas that can be improved with these technologies.

Data Governance

Today, Talend believes that, "Data governance is not only about control and data protection; it is also about enablement and crowdsourcing insights. Data governance is a requirement in today's fast-moving and highly competitive enterprise environment."[29] Ultimately, "Now that organizations have the opportunity to capture massive amounts of diverse internal and external data, they need the discipline to maximize that data's value, manage its risks, and reduce the cost of its management," claims Talend.[29]

Data governance is not optional in today's highly complex and fast-moving IT environment.[29] An effective data governance strategy provides so many crucial benefits to an organization, including[29]:

- A common understanding of data: "Data governance offers a consistent view of, and common terminology for, data, while individual business units retain appropriate flexibility."
- Improved data quality of data.
- A data map.
- A 360-degree view of each customer and other business entities.
- Consistent compliance with government regulations.
- Improved data management because a human dimension is brought into a highly automated, data-driven world.
- Easy accessibility.

To find the right data governance approach for your organization, Talend recommends brands look for "open source, scalable tools that are easy to integrate with the organization's existing environment."[29] Additionally, a cloud-based platform lets brands "quickly plug into robust capabilities that are cost-efficient and easy to use."[29] "Cloud-based solutions also avoid the overhead required for on-premises servers." Talend argues.[29] When comparing and selecting data governance tools, brands needs to focus on choosing ones that will help them realize the business benefits laid out in their data governance strategy.[29] Any chosen tool should help in the following ways:

- Capture and understand data through discovery, profiling, benchmarking and capabilities.[29] For example, the right tools can automatically detect a piece of personal data, like a national ID or social security number, in a new data set and then trigger an alert.[29]
- Improve the quality of a brand's data with validation, data cleansing, and data enrichment.[29]
- Manage a brand's data with metadata-driven ETL and ELT, and data integration applications so data pipelines can be tracked and traced with end-to-end, forward-looking and backward-looking data lineage.[29]
- Control a brand's data with tools that actively review and monitor it.[29]

- Empower the people who know the data best, so they can contribute to the data stewardship tasks with self-service tools.[29]

Modern data governance is about both minimizing data risks and maximizing data usage.[29] There is a need for a more agile, bottom-up approach, which "starts with the raw data, links it to its business context so that it becomes meaningful, takes control of its data quality and security, and thoroughly organizes it for massive consumption."[29] In addition, due to headline-grabbing data scandals and data leaks, government are enacting a proliferation of new regulations and laws that put higher stakes on data protection.[29]

Talend believes that, "New data platforms empower this new discipline, which leverage smart technologies like pattern recognition, data cataloging, data lineage, and machine learning to organize data at scale and turn data governance into a team sport by enabling organization-wide collaboration on data ownership, curation, remediation, and reuse."[29]

With data storage prices plummeting, data is becoming less commoditized.[29] large data repositories such as data lakes are creating vast reservoirs of known and unknown datasets.[29] Although it might take seconds to ingest data into a modern EDW or data lake, it could take weeks for this data to be made available to a business user.[29] At the same time, business users might not even be aware that the data they need is even available for use.[29] Humans are inventive creatures and they often employ data work-arounds, which can create additional governance headaches.[29] When business users add their own rules atop newly created data sources, multiple versions of "the truth" result, which can lead to data governance nightmares.[29]

The challenge "is to overcome these obstacles by bringing clarity, transparency, and accessibility to your data assets."[29] Wherever this data resides, proper data screening must be established so businesses have a holistic view of the data sources and data streams coming into and out of their organization.[29]

In the past, data experts might have manually processed the data using traditional data profiling tools.[29] However, this approach no longer works.[29] "The digital era's data sprawl requires a more automatic and systematic approach," says Talend.[29] Modern data cataloging tools can help schedule the data discovery processes that crawls an EDW or a data lake and intelligently inspects the underlying data, so that it can be understood, documented, and actioned, if necessary.[29] Today's data catalogs "can automatically draw the links between datasets and connect them to a business glossary."[29] Talend argues that, "this allows an organization to automate the data inventory and leverage smart semantics for auto-profiling, relationships discovery and classification thanks to an integrated semantic flow."[29] The benefits are twofold; data owners and providers get an overview of their data and can take actions; data consumers get visibility into the data before consuming it.[29]

Data profiling is the process of discovering in-depth and granular details about a dataset. It helps in accurately assess a company's multiple data sources based on the six dimensions of data quality—accuracy, completeness, consistency, timeliness, uniqueness, and validity.[29] It will help a brand to identify if and how its data could be inaccurate, inconsistent, and, possibly, incomplete.[29]

Oftentimes, the people who know the data best are not the data experts.[29] Sales admins, sales representatives, customer service reps, and field marketing managers will uncover any data quality issues quicker than a company's central IT team.[29] Not only do these people know the data best, but they are also the ones who most keenly feel the pain of data quality issues because it directly impacts upon their day-to-day job.[29]

Of course, these people can't become data quality experts so they must be provided with smart tools that can hide the technical complexity of data profiling. Many vendors provide data preparation tools that have "powerful yet simple built-in profiling capabilities to explore data sets and assess their quality with the help of indicators, trends, and patterns."[29] "While automatic data profiling through both a data catalog and self-service profiling addresses the case for bottom-up data governance, a top-down approach might require a deeper look into the data," says Talend.[29]

With products like Talend Data Quality, users "would start by connecting to data sources to analyze their structure (catalogs, schemas, and tables), and store the description of their metadata in its metadata repository."[29] Users would then "define available data quality analyses including database, content analysis, column analysis, table analysis, redundancy analysis, and correlation analysis," says Talend.[29] "These analyses will carry out data profiling processes that will define the content, structure, and quality of highly complex data structures," adds Talend.[29]

A "trust index" can be created out of all this data discovery and it can be calculated, reported, and tracked on a regular and automated basis.[29] Trigger alerts can be set when an index moves beyond a certain comfortable threshold.[29]

According to Talend, "Data quality is the process of conditioning data to meet the specific needs of business users."[29] However, data quality is not a standalone operation or problem.[29] "To make it successful and deliver trusted data, you need to operate data quality operations upfront and natively from the data sources, along with the data lifecycle to ensure that any data operator or user or app could consume trusted data at the end," argues Talend.[29]

"Successful data governance frameworks require setting accountabilities and then delegating that authority appropriately," argues Talend.[29] For example, Talend says, "a data protection officer in a central organization might want to delegate tasks to data stewards or business users in the operations: a sales engineer might be best positioned to ensure that contact data for his or her accounts are accurate and kept up-to-date. A campaign manager is the one that should ensure that a consent mechanism has been put in place and captured within its marketing database."[29] To support this kind of delegation, organizations need to provide workflow based, self-served apps to different departments, recommends Talend.[29] This provides additional autonomy without putting the data at risk.[29]

"Data preparation is not just a separate discipline to make lines of business more autonomous with data; it's a core element for data quality and integration," says Talend.[29] Not only does it unlock people's data productivity, but it also captures the actions taken on that data, which can help make the data more trustable.[29] In addition to improving personal productivity, the true value of these collaborative and self-service applications is to drive collaboration between business and IT, which is not always an easy thing to do.[29]

Once the incoming data assets are identified, documented and trusted, it is time to organize them for massive consumption by an extended network of data users within an organization.[29]

"This starts by establishing a single point of trust; that is to say, collecting all the data sets together in a single control point that will be the cornerstone of your data governance framework," says Talend.[29] Datasets then need to be identified; roles and responsibilities have to be assigned directly into a single point of control.[29]

"It is one of the advantages of data cataloging: regrouping all the trusted data in one place and giving access to members so that everybody can immediately use it, protect it, curate it and allow a wide range of people and apps to take advantage of it," explains Talend.[29] "The benefit of centralizing trusted data into a shareable environment is that it will save time and resources of your organization once operationalized," they add.[29]

"Within a data catalog, a business glossary is used to define collections of terms and to link them to categories and sub-categories. Building a business glossary can be as simple as dragging in an existing well-documented data model, importing the terms and definitions from other sources (e.g., CSV, Microsoft Excel)," says Talend.[29] Once published, the glossary can be accessed company-wide by anyone who has proper authorizations.[29]

Talend believes that, "As you are about to deliver access to your catalog to others, your dataset will become a living artifact, as you will enable authorized people to edit, validate, or enrich the data directly into data sets."[29] "Doing it automatically through a data catalog will allow you to save lots of time and resources," they contend.[29]

Talend claims that data lineage functionality gives users the ability to track and trace their data flows from source to final destination.[29] Data lineage can dramatically accelerate the speed to resolution of problematic data by helping users spot the specific problem at the right place and ensure that the data is always accurate.[29] Moreover, if new datasets come into an EDW and/or a data lake, data lineage rapidly helps identify these new sources.[29] Errors can quickly be uncovered and accountability understood. A data chain is both forward and backward-looking, their upstream or downstream impact is easily seen and acted upon.

Once the data categories have been defined, a more accurate picture of the data environment sources can be created.[29] "It will also enable you to define better data owners: who is responsible for this particular data domain? Who is responsible for viewing, accessing, editing and curating the data sets?" says Talend.[29]

At this step, using a RACI Model—a model derived from the four key responsibilities most typically used: Responsible, Accountable, Consulted, and Informed—will help users save time defining and assigning roles and responsibilities between stakeholders.[29]

"The next step is to define data owners who are ultimately accountable for one or more data categories and subcategories," says Talend.[29] "These data owners will be responsible for day-to-day operations regarding the data or appoint data stewards for those operational data-centric tasks. They will identify critical datasets and critical data elements (CDEs) as well as establish standards for data collection, data use, and data masking."[29] "A data catalog may also catalog owners and stewards for data categories and sub-categories and assign their related roles and workflows," adds Talend.[29]

For example, a data cataloger "may catalog the data owners for 'customer' as well as 'customer identity', 'customer billing', 'customer contact' and 'customer ship-to information'."[29]

The RACI Model is a good example of a responsibility assignment matrix that is both easy to understand and use.[29] "It's particularly useful if your data governance will involve different departments and divisions in your organization," says Talend.[29]

According to Wikipedia, data curation "is the organization and integration of data collected from various sources. It includes annotation, publication, and presentation of data to make sure it's valid over time."[288] This will be enabled once you put in place an explicit RACI Model that clearly describes who can define, edit, validate, and enrich the data in the systems.[29]

"A data governance project is not just intended to let trusted data be accessible to all," claims Talend.[29] "It's also about promoting data custodians' accountability to the rest of the organization so that they can enrich and curate trusted data and produce valuable, accurate insights out of the data pipelines," they add.[29] "In many cases, data owners realize that they should not manage everything in their data domain, and thus need act as orchestrators rather than doers," notes Talend.[29]

"The data governance team may also delegate responsibilities for data protection," adds Talend.[29] Data masking is a prime example of a responsibility that needs delegation.[29] "In a data lake, for example, IT specialists might not be the ones responsible for data masking and might even not have the authorization privileges to process the data before it has been masked," claims Talend.[29] Data protection tasks can be delegated to people who might not be technical experts with deep expertise in the data masking discipline.[29]

"This is why it is important to empower a large audience to mask the data on their own so that once they identify specific scenarios where sensitive data may be exposed, they can proactively act on it automatically with a user-friendly tool," says Talend.[29] For example, Talend offers the case of a campaign manager who prepares an event with a business partner that doesn't have explicit consent to see the personal data of the customer because of a lack of third party privacy consent.[29] Thankfully, the campaign manager can utilize data prep tools that can mask the data directly on the data so that the data can be easily shared without violating data privacy rules.[29]

Once the data is accessible in a single point of access and reconciled properly, "it is time to extract all its value by delivering at scale to a wide audience of authorized humans and machines," says Talend.[29] Technologies like automation, data integration and machine learning can help enormously with this.[29]

"Advanced analytics and machine learning help democratize data governance and data management because they make things much simpler," argues Talend.[29] "They improve developers' productivity and empower non-data experts to work with data," says Talend.[29] It can also suggest next best actions, while guiding users through their data journey.[29]

"Machine learning also allows the capture of knowledge from business users and data professionals," says Talend.[29] One typical use case is data error resolution and matching.[29] Self-service tools can be used to deduplicate records on a data sample and then machine learning can be applied to a whole data set in a fully automated process, which turns low value and time-consuming tasks into an automated process that can be scaled up to handle millions of records.[29]

Data masking allows a company to selectively share production quality data across their organization for development, analysis and more, without ever disclosing any Personally Identifiable Information (PII) to people not authorized to see it.[29]

Failing to establish strict data privacy controls can leave a company exposed to financial risk, negative reputation, and stiff data privacy regulatory penalties.[29]

To deal with this growing threat, businesses need to find ways to automatically spot sensitive datasets.[29] Data cataloging technologies can help with this.[29]

"A data catalog is the typical starting point for automating the personal data identification process," says Talend.[29] Once data elements have been defined with a PII, data sets that relate to them can automatically be spotted and masked, if necessary.[29] If personal data is not necessary for testing or analytics, why risk exposing it?[29]

In the past, disciplines like data masking were sparingly used, but with the explosion of data privacy scandals and the proliferation of regulations, a much more aggressive approach to data masking is needed.[29] Only then can businesses share production-quality data across their organizations for analysis and business intelligence, without exposing personally identifiable information.[29]

"Many data governance approaches fail because they cannot be applied in a systematic way," claims Talend.[29] Modern data governance controls "need to be embedded into the data chain, so that it can be operationalized and cannot be bypassed."[29] It needs to become part of the process. Data governance can help data engineers orchestrate and automate all of a company's data pipelines, whether they are physical EDWs or cloud-based ones, or even data that surfaces through any company apps.[29] Data governance controls "will act as an orchestrator to operationalize and automate any jobs or flows so that you keep on structuring and cleaning your data along the data lifecycle, all the while putting stewards at work for validation, users for curations or business users for data preparation," says Talend.[29]

A data catalog makes "data more meaningful for data consumers, because of its ability to profile, sample and categorize the data, document the data relationships, and crowdsource comments, tags, likes and annotations."[29] "All this metadata is then easy to consume through full text or faceted search, or through visualization of data flows," explains Talend.[29] Data catalogs make it "possible to locate, use, and access trusted data faster by searching and verifying data's validity before sharing with peers."[29]

Hadoop

Perhaps one of the most interesting data warehouse developments in the last decade has been the introduction of Hadoop and its Hadoop Distributed File System (HDFS). As Grover et al. explain in their book *Hadoop Application Architectures*[289]:

> "At its core, Hadoop is a distributed data store which provides a platform for implementing powerful parallel processing frameworks on it. The reliability of this data store when it comes to storing massive volumes of data coupled with its

flexibility related to running multiple processing frameworks makes it an ideal choice as the hub for all your data. This characteristic of Hadoop means that you can store any type of data as-is, and without placing any constraints on how that data is processed.

Hadoop is a *Schema-on-Read* data warehouse, meaning raw unprocessed data can be loaded into it "with the structure imposed at processing time based on the requirements of the processing application."[289] This differs from a *Schema-on-Write* DW, which is normally used with traditional data management systems.[289] "Such systems require the schema of the data store to be defined before the data can be stored in it. This leads to lengthy cycles of analysis, data modeling, data transformation, loading, testing, etc., before data can be accessed," warns Grover et al.[289] Additionally, if a wrong decision is made, or requirements change, this cycle needs to start anew.[289] "When the application or structure of data is not as well understood, the agility provided by the Schema-on-Read pattern can provide invaluable insights on data not previously accessible," adds Grover et al.[289]

Although the ability to store all of a company's raw data in a Hadoop DW is a powerful option, there are still many factors that should be considered before putting this method into practice.[289] These include:

- How the data is being stored: There are several different file formats and compression formats supported on Hadoop. Each of these have particular strengths and weaknesses, which make them better suited for specific applications.[289] Additionally, although Hadoop provides the HDFS for storing data, there are several other commonly used systems implemented on top of HDFS that do allow additional functionality so these systems should also be taken into consideration.[289]
- Multi-tenancy: It is common for clusters to host multiple users, groups, and application types, so important considerations should be made when planning the management and storage of data.[289]
- Schema design: Despite Hadoop being schema-less, there are still important considerations to consider when devising the structure of data stored in Hadoop, including directory structures for data loaded into HDFS as well as the output of data processing and analysis.[289]
- Metadata: As with any data management system, cataloging and storing the metadata related to the stored data is as important as cataloging and storing the data itself.[289]

As Grover et al. point out, "One of the most fundamental decisions to make when architecting a solution on Hadoop is determining how data will be stored in Hadoop. There is no such thing as a standard data storage format in Hadoop."[289]

"Hadoop allows for storage of data in any format, whether it's text, binary, images, etc. Hadoop also provides built-in support for a number of formats optimized for Hadoop storage and processing," note Grover et al.[289] This gives users complete control over their source data and there are a number of options on how that data can be stored, not just the raw data being ingested, but also the intermediate data generated during data processing, as well as the results of the data processing.[289] Major considerations for Hadoop data storage that need to be made include[289]:

- File format: These include plain text or Hadoop specific formats such as SequenceFile. There are also more complex, but more functionally rich options such as Avro and Parquet; each format comes with its own unique strengths and weaknesses, making it more or less suitable depending on the application and source data types ingested.[289] As Hadoop is customizable, It is also possible to create one's own unique file format.[289]
- Compression: Although this is more straightforward than selecting a file format, compression codecs commonly used with Hadoop have their own unique characteristics, some compress and uncompress faster, but don't compress as aggressively, others create smaller files, but take longer to compress and uncompress, and not surprisingly require more CPU power.[289] The ability to split compressed files is also a very important consideration when working with data stored in Hadoop.
- Data storage: Although Hadoop data is stored in HDFS, there are decisions around what the underlying storage manager should be, i.e. whether you should use HBase or HDFS directly to store the data.[289]

Besides HDFS there are a few alternate file systems available for Hadoop, including open-source file systems such as GlusterFS and the Quantcast File System, and commercial alternatives like Isilon OneFS and Netapp.[289] Amazon's Simple Storage System (S3), a cloud-based storage systems that is gaining converts, includes others.[289] The file system options are growing and this might become yet another architectural consideration in a Hadoop deployment.[289]

For text files like CSV and XML, or binary file types (such as images), it is preferable to use one of the Hadoop specific container formats, but in many cases you'll want to store source data in its rawest form (as that is, after all, one of Hadoop's biggest advantages).[289] "Having online access to data in its raw, source form—'full fidelity' data—means it will always be possible to perform new processing and analytics with the data as requirements change," note Grover et al.[289]

"A primary consideration when storing text data in Hadoop is the organization of the files in the file system," claim Grover et al.[289] Since text files can very quickly consume considerable space on a Hadoop cluster, users should keep in mind that there is an overhead of type conversion associated with the storage of data in text formats.[289] For example, when storing *1234* in a text file and using it as an integer, a String-to-Integer conversion during read, and vice-versa during writing is required, which adds processing time because a lot of such conversions are being done.[289]

The selection of a compression format will depend on how the end user plans to consume the data.[289] For archival purposes the most compact compression method available might be advisable, but if the data is to be used in processing in MapReduce, a splittable format might be preferable, advise Grover et al.[289] "Splittable formats provide the ability for Hadoop to split files into chunks for processing, which is critical to efficient parallel processing."[289]

It should be mentioned that in many, if not all cases, "the use of a container format such as SequenceFiles or Avro will provide advantages which makes it a preferred format for most file types, including text."[289] "Among other things these container formats provide functionality to support splittable compression," state Grover et al.[289]

The structured format text files XML and JSON are especially challenging for Hadoop as splitting XML and JSON files for processing is tricky, and Hadoop does not have a built-in Input-Format for either of these formats.[289] "JSON presents even greater challenges than XML, since there are no tokens to mark the beginning or end of a record." warn Grover et al.[289] When using these formats, there are a couple of options[289]:

- Use a container format such as Avro.
- Use a library designed for processing XML or JSON files; XMLLoader in the PiggyBank library for Pig for XML; the Elephant Bird project provides the LzoJsonInputFormat for JSON.

"Although text is probably the most common source data format stored in Hadoop, Hadoop can also be used to process binary files such as images. For most cases of storing and processing binary files in Hadoop, using a container format such as SequenceFile is preferred," state Grover et al.[289]

MapReduce is a programming model used to process large data sets with a parallel, distributed algorithm on a cluster.[290] The current Apache MapReduce version is built over an Apache YARN Framework, which is a new framework that facilitates writing arbitrary distributed processing frameworks and applications.[290]

According to Wikipedia[291]:

> "MapReduce is a framework for processing parallelizable problems across large datasets using a large number of computers (nodes), collectively referred to as a cluster (if all nodes are on the same local network and use similar hardware) or a grid (if the nodes are shared across geographically and administratively distributed systems and use more

heterogenous hardware). Processing can occur on data stored either in a filesystem (unstructured) or in a database (structured). MapReduce can take advantage of the locality of data, processing it near the place it is stored in order to minimize communication overhead."

There are several Hadoop specific file formats that seamlessly integrate with MapReduce, including "file based data structures such as sequence files, serialization formats like Avro, and columnar formats such as RCFiles and Parquet."[289] These file formats have differing strengths and weaknesses, but having both splittable compression as well as agnostic compression is important for Hadoop applications.[289]

As Grover et al. explain, SequenceFiles store data as binary key-value pairs in the following three formats[289]:

1. Uncompressed, which, for the most part, provide no advantages over their compressed alternatives, since they're less efficient for I/O and take up more space on disk than the same data in compressed form.
2. Record-compressed, which compresses each record as it's added to the file. An inefficient choice compared to block compressed.
3. Block compressed, which waits until data reaches block size to compress, rather than as each record is added. Providing better compression ratios compared to record-compressed SequenceFiles, a *block* in block compression refers to a block of records that are compressed together within a single HDFS block.

"Regardless of format, every SequenceFile uses a common header format containing basic metadata about the file such as the compression codec used, key and value class names, user defined metadata, and a randomly generated sync marker," add Grover et al.[289] "This sync marker is also written into the body of the file to allow for seeking to random points in the file, and is key to facilitating splittability. For example, in the case of block compression, this sync marker will be written after every block in the file," state Grover et al.[289] Although SequenceFiles are well supported within the Hadoop ecosystem, their support outside of the ecosystem is limited and they are commonly used as containers for smaller files.[289] "Since Hadoop is optimized for large files, packing smaller files into a SequenceFile makes the storage and processing of these files much more efficient," note Grover et al.[289]

Serialization refers to "the process of turning data structures into byte streams either for storage or transmission over a network. Conversely, deserialization is the process of converting a byte stream back into data structures," explain Grover et al.[289] "It is core to a distributed processing system such as Hadoop, since it allows data to be converted into a format that can be efficiently stored as well as transferred across a network connection."[289] Serialization is commonly associated with two aspects of data processing in distributed systems: interprocess communication (remote procedure calls, or RPC) and data storage, which is what is focused on here.

The main serialization format utilized by Hadoop is Writables, which is compact and fast, but not easy to extend beyond its natural language, Java.[289] However, Thrift, Protocol Buffers, and Avro are seeing increased use within the Hadoop ecosystem.[289] Avro was specifically created as a replacement for Writables and, of the three, it is the best suited for serialization.[289]

Developed at Facebook, Thrift is sometimes used for data serialization with Hadoop, but it has several drawbacks, including lacking support for the internal compression of records.[289] It is unsplittable and also lacks native MapReduce support.[289] There are externally available libraries to address these drawbacks, but Hadoop does not provide native support for Thrift as a data storage format.[289]

"The Protocol Buffer (protobuf) format was developed at Google to facilitate data exchange between services written in different languages."[289] "Like Thrift, protobuf structures are defined using an IDL, which is used to generate stub code for multiple languages."[289] "Also like Thrift, Protocol Buffers do not support internal compression of records, are not splittable, and have no native MapReduce support," acknowledge Grover et Al.[289]

Apache Avro is a "framework for modeling, serializing and making Remote Procedure Calls (RPC). Avro data is described by a schema, and one interesting feature is that the schema is stored in the same file as the data it describes, so files are self-describing."[290]

Avro was designed to address the major downside of Hadoop Writables: a lack of language portability.[289] "Like Thrift and Protocol Buffers, Avro data is described using a language independent schema," explain Grover et al.[289] Unlike Thrift and Protocol Buffers, however, code generation is optional with Avro.[289] "Since Avro stores the schema in the header of each file, it's self-describing and Avro files can easily be read later, even from a different language than the one used to write the file."[289]

Avro is written in JSON or in Avro IDL, which is a C-like language.[289] It provides better native support for MapReduce, while also supporting schema evolution—the schema used to read a file does not need to match the schema used to write the file—which makes it superior to SequenceFiles for Hadoop applications.[289] This powerful feature makes it possible to add new fields to a schema as requirements change, which can be extremely helpful with constantly updating file systems.[289]

"Until relatively recently, most database systems stored records in a row-oriented fashion. This is efficient for cases where many columns of the record need to be fetched," explain Grover et al.[289] If your analysis relies heavily on fetching all fields for records that belong to a particular time range, row-oriented storage makes sense.[289] "This can also be more efficient when writing data, particularly if all columns of the record are available at write time since the record can be written with a single disk seek."[289] More recently, however, a number of vendors have released columnar storage systems, which provides several benefits over earlier row-oriented systems, including[289]:

- Skips I/O on columns that are not a part of the query.
- Works well for queries that only access a small subset of columns.
- Compression on columns are quite efficient and the column has few distinct values.

"Columnar storage is often well suited for data-warehousing type applications where users want to aggregate certain columns over a large collection of records," explain Grover et al.[289] Unsurprisingly, columnar file formats, such as the RCFile format, are also being utilized for Hadoop applications.[289]

The RCFile format "was developed specifically to provide efficient processing for MapReduce applications, although in practice it's only seen use as a Hive storage format," note Grover et al.[289] Hive is a data warehouse infrastructure that was developed by Facebook to provide SQL-like language for data summarization, query, and analysis.[290] "The RCFile format was developed to provide fast data loading, fast query processing, highly efficient storage space utilization, and strong adaptivity to highly dynamic workload patterns."[289]

Similar to SequenceFiles, except data is stored in a column-oriented fashion, the RCFile format breaks files into row splits, then within each split uses column oriented storage.[289] "Although the RCFile format provides advantages in terms of query and compression performance compared to SequenceFiles, it also has some deficiencies that prevent optimal performance for query times and compression," warn Grover et al.[289] Newer columnar formats such as Parquet and Optimize Row Columnar (ORC), which I will detail next, address many of these deficiencies, and it is replacing RCFile on newer applications.[289]

The ORC format "was created to address some of the short-comings with the RCFile format, specifically around query performance and storage efficiency."[289] The ORC format provides the following features and benefits, over the RCFile format[289]:

- "Light-weight, always-on compression provided by type-specific readers and writers. ORC also supports the use of zlib, LZO, or Snappy to provide further compression."[289]
- "Allows predicates to be pushed down to the storage layer so that only required data is brought back in queries."[289]

- "Supports the Hive type model, including new primitives such as decimal as well as complex types."[289]
- "Is a splittable storage format."[289]

The main drawback of ORC is that it was specifically designed for Hive, and so it "is not a general purpose storage format that can be used with non-Hive MapReduce interfaces such as Pig or Java, or other query engines such as Impala," explain Grover et al.[289] Parquet shares many of the same design goals as ORC, but it is intended to be a general purpose storage format for Hadoop, which attempts to create a format that's suitable for different MapReduce interfaces such as Java, Hive, and Pig, and also suitable for other processing engines like Impala.[289] Parquet provides the following benefits, many of which it shares with ORC[289]:

- Similar to ORC files, allows for returning only required data fields, which reduces I/O and increases performance."[289]
- Provides efficient compression, which can be specified on a per-column level.[289]
- Designed to support complex nested data structure.[289] Parquet stores full metadata at the end of files, so Parquet files are self-documenting.[289]

For its part, the Apache-licensed Impala project brings scalable parallel database technology to Hadoop, enabling users to issue low-latency SQL queries to data stored in HDFS and Apache HBase, without requiring data movement or transformation.[290]

Chips

In his article *5 Artificial Intelligence Trends to Watch Out for in 2019*[292], Janakiram MSV recognizes the unique technological requirements needed for AI. "Unlike other software, AI heavily relies on specialized processors that complement the CPU. Even the fastest and most advanced CPU may not improve the speed of training an AI model. While inferencing, the model needs additional hardware to perform complex mathematical computations to speed up tasks such as object detection and facial recognition."[292,]

Janakiram explains that, "In 2019, chip manufacturers such as Intel, NVIDIA, AMD, ARM and Qualcomm will ship specialized chips that speed up the execution of AI-enabled applications. These chips will be optimized for specific use cases and scenarios related to computer vision, natural language processing and speech recognition."[292]

But, that's not all, claims Janakiram.[292] In 2019, hyperscale infrastructure companies like Amazon, Microsoft, Google, and Facebook will also "increase the investments in custom chips based on field programmable gate arrays (FPGA) and application specific integrated circuits (ASIC).[292] "These chips will be heavily optimized for running modern workloads based on AI and high-performance computing (HPC). Some of these chips will also assist next-generation databases to speed up query processing and predictive analytics," adds Janakiram.[292]

"In 2019, AI meets IoT at the edge computing layer. Most of the models trained in the public cloud will be deployed at the edge," says Janakiram.[292] "Advanced ML models based on deep neural networks will be optimized to run at the edge. They will be capable of dealing with video frames, speech synthesis, time-series data and unstructured data generated by devices such as cameras, microphones, and other sensors."[292]

GPUs

In his article *Accelerating AI with GPUs: A New Computing Model*[293], Jensen Huang claims that, "For as long as we have been designing computers, AI has been the final frontier." "Building intelligent machines that can perceive the world as we do, understand our language, and learn from examples has been the life's work of computer scientists for over five decades," says Huang.[293] It is hard to argue with his assessment. "Yet, it took the combination of Yann LeCun's work in convolutional neural nets[294], Geoff Hinton's back-propagation and Stochastic Gradient Descent approach to training, and Andrew Ng's large-scale use of GPUs to accelerate Deep Neural Networks (DNNs) to ignite the big bang of modern AI—deep learning," Huang notes.[293]

For readers who want to keep up with the latest developments in AI, following the blogs of the companies that produce the chips and the hardware that AI runs on is a good place to start. Nvidia, Advanced Micro Devices (AMD), and Intel are all big players in the AI chip/hardware space, especially the first two. Since AI runs best on high-end processors like chips from Nvidia and AMD, it is a good idea to keep abreast of their latest technological developments. These are all US publicly traded companies and their technological advancement notifications usually coincide with their quarterly earnings reports so keep an eye out for those.

During the time of LeCun's, Hinton's, and Ng's work, NVIDIA was busy advancing GPU-accelerated computing, which was a new computing model that used "massively parallel graphics processors to accelerate applications also parallel in nature."[293] "Scientists and researchers jumped on to GPUs to do molecular-scale simulations to determine the effectiveness of a life-saving drug, to visualize our organs in 3D (reconstructed from light doses of a CT scan), or to do galactic-scale simulations to discover the laws that govern our universe," explains Huang.[293] "NVIDIA GPUs have democratized supercomputing and researchers have now discovered that power," adds Huang.[293]

"By 2011, AI researchers around the world had discovered NVIDIA GPUs," notes Huang.[293] "The Google Brain project had just achieved amazing results—it learned to recognize cats and people by watching movies on YouTube. But it required 2,000 CPUs in servers powered and cooled in one of Google's giant data centers," explains Huang.[293] Obviously, very few companies have computer centers on the scale of Google so this wasn't a viable option for normal companies.[293] So, Nvidia and the GPU rode to the rescue, democratizing the technology for all.[293] "Bryan Catanzaro in NVIDIA Research teamed with Andrew Ng's team at Stanford to use GPUs for deep learning."[293] "As it turned out, 12 NVIDIA GPUs could deliver the deep-learning performance of 2,000 CPUs. Researchers at NYU, the University of Toronto, and the Swiss AI Lab accelerated their DNNs on GPUs. Then, the fireworks started," marvels Huang.[293]

In 2012, Alex Krizhevsky and his team at the University of Toronto won the ImageNet computer image recognition competition.[295] Krizhevsky handily beat out software that was written by several computer vision experts.[293] The innovative thing was Krizhevsky and his team didn't write computer vision code.[293] Instead, using deep learning, Krizhevsy's computer learned to recognize images by itself.[293] Krizhevsky and his team designed a neural network called AlexNet and trained it with a million example images that required trillions of math operations on NVIDIA GPUs that beat the best human-coded software.[293]

At that point, the AI race was on.[293] By 2015, AI hit another major milestone when, using deep learning processes, Google and Microsoft both beat the best human score in the ImageNet challenge.[296][297] Not a human-written program, but an actual human.[293] Soon after, "Microsoft and the China University of Science and Technology announced a DNN that achieved IQ test scores at the college post-graduate level."[298] In 2018, it was Baidu's turn and they "announced that a deep learning system called Deep Speech 2 had learned both English and Mandarin with a single algorithm."[299]

"In 2012, deep learning had beaten human-coded software. By 2015, deep learning had achieved 'superhuman' levels of perception," notes Huang.[293] "Computer programs contain commands that are largely executed sequentially," explains Huang.[293] Deep learning, however, "is a fundamentally new software model where billions of software-neurons and trillions of connections are trained, in parallel. Running DNN algorithms and learning from examples, the computer is essentially writing its own software. This radically different software model needs a new computer platform to run efficiently. Accelerated computing is an ideal approach and the GPU is the ideal processor," says Huang.[293]

Today, AI innovation is happening at breakneck pace.[293] "Ease of programming and developer productivity are paramount," claims Huang.[293] "The programmability and richness of Nvidia's CUDA platform allow researchers to innovate quickly—building new configurations of CNNs, DNNs, deep inception networks, RNNs, LSTMs, and reinforcement learning networks," notes Huang.[293]

Historically, "Baidu, Google, Facebook, Microsoft were the first adopters of NVIDIA GPUs for deep learning," says Huang.[293] This AI technology is how their systems respond to a user's spoken word, how it translates speech or text to another language, how it recognizes and automatically tag images, as well as recommends newsfeeds, entertainment, and products that are tailored to each user's likes.[293]

Today, startups and established companies are "racing to use AI to create new products and services, or improve their operations."[293] In just two years' time, the number of companies Nvidia collaborated with on deep learning exploded nearly 35x, to over 3,400 companies.[293] "Industries such as healthcare, life sciences, energy, financial services, automotive, manufacturing, and entertainment will benefit by inferring insight from mountains of data," claims Huang.[293] "With Facebook, Google, and Microsoft opening their deep-learning platforms for all to use, AI-powered applications will spread fast," concludes Huang.[293]

To be clear, "deep-learning breakthroughs have sparked the AI revolution."[293] "Machines powered by AI deep neural networks solve problems too complex for human coders," claims Huang.[293] "They learn from data and improve with use. The same DNN can be trained by even non-programmers to solve new problems. Progress is exponential. Adoption is exponential. And we believe the impact to society will also be exponential," proselytizes Huang.[293]

"The impact to the computer industry will also be exponential," predicts Huang.[293] "Deep learning is a fundamentally new software model," claims Huang.[293] He also adds that a new computer platform is needed to run it, this needs to have "an architecture that can efficiently execute programmer-coded commands as well as the massively parallel training of deep neural networks."[293] Nvidia is betting that GPU-accelerated computing is the horse to ride. *Popular Science* recently called the GPU "the workhorse of modern A.I.", which is an assessment Huang agrees with completely.[293]

According to Huang[293]:

> *"Convolutional networks are composed of an input layer, an output layer, and one or more hidden layers. A convolutional network is different than a regular neural network in that the neurons in its layers are arranged in three dimensions (width, height, and depth dimensions). This allows the CNN to transform an input volume in three dimensions to an output volume. The hidden layers are a combination of convolution layers, pooling layers, normalization layers, and fully connected layers. CNNs use multiple conv layers to filter input volumes to greater levels of abstraction."*[294]

"Convolutional networks adjust automatically to find the best feature based on the task," explains Nvidia.[294] For instance, when faced with a bird recognition task, "the CNN would filter information about the shape of an object when confronted with a general object recognition task but would extract the color of the bird."[294] "This," explains Nvidia, "is based on the CNN's understanding that different classes of objects have different shapes but that different types of birds are more likely to differ in color than in shape."[294]

Nvidia concludes that the applications for Convolutional Neural Networks "include various image (image recognition, image classification, video labeling, text analysis) and speech (speech recognition, natural language processing, text classification) processing systems, along with state-of-the-art AI systems such as robots, virtual assistants, and self-driving cars."[294]

Deep Learning Frameworks

In their paper *Caffe2 vs. TensorFlow: Which is a Better Deep Learning Framework?*[300], Baige Liu and Xiaoxue Zang focus on the two most used deep learning programs comparing five aspects of the software: the expressiveness, the modeling capability, the performance, help & support, and the scalability.[304] The authors chose "TensorFlow because it is currently the most widely-used deep learning framework."[304] The authors recognize that Caffe was an extremely popular framework before TensorFlow was introduced and the Caffe2 framework can build upon that potential, while gaining a lot of user preference in the near future.[304]

However, as Liu and Zang conclude[300]:

> "in many aspects and as a result we find neither of these two has an [sic] dominating advantages over the other. Therefore, in practice, the choice between these two actually depends on the specific user tasks and the user preferences. Overall if the user need [sic] to pursue speed and has limited space restricted by the device, Caffe2 is a better choice since our experiments' results revealed that Caffe2 has a significant advantage over TensorFlow both in speed and space. Nevertheless, TensorFlow is still powerful and useful because there is a large number official [sic] and third-party resources, services, debugging tools, and a big supportive community that makes it easier to find reference codes."

Readers should be aware that, with software, there often isn't a binary answer, i.e., "*x* piece of software is better for my problem than *y* piece of software?" With software, caveats abound. Always. Deep learning frameworks have a unique problem in that they don't port well, i.e., a deep learning project developed on TensorFlow will not be easily moved onto Caffe2, and vice versa, which means great time should be spent to truly understand a project's goal before a decision on what software to use are made.

TensorFlow

In his article *Google Just Open Sourced TensorFlow, Its Artificial Intelligence Engine*[301], Cade Metz explains that at its 2015 Google I/O conference Google open sourced its deep learning engine known as TensorFlow. In open sourcing TensorFlow, Google is freely sharing the underlying code with the world at large.[301] "In literally giving the technology away, Google believes it can accelerate the evolution of AI. Through open source, outsiders can help improve on Google's technology and, yes, return these improvements back to Google," explains Metz.[301]

"What we're hoping is that the community adopts this as a good way of expressing machine learning algorithms of lots of different types, and also contributes to building and improving [TensorFlow] in lots of different and interesting ways," says Jeff Dean, and a key player in the rise of Google's deep learning technology.[301]

Open sourcing AI has been a common practice over the past few years.[301] Facebook, Microsoft, and Twitter have all made huge strides in AI and some have open sourced software that is similar to TensorFlow, including Torch—a system originally built by researchers in Switzerland—as well as systems like Caffe and Theano.[301] However, Google's move is highly significant because Google's AI engine is considered to be the world's most.[301] Google, however, isn't giving away all its secrets.[301] As Metz explains[301]:

> "At the moment, the company is only open sourcing part of this AI engine. It's sharing only some of the algorithms that run atop the engine. And it's not sharing access to the remarkably advanced hardware infrastructure that drives this engine (that would certainly come with a price tag). But Google is giving away at least some of its most important data center software, and that's not something it has typically done in the past."

Google usually only shares its designs once it has moved onto other designs, and it had never open sourced code.[301] With TensorFlow, however, the "company has changed tack, freely sharing some of its newest—and, indeed, most important—software."[301] Google does open source parts of its Android mobile operating system and several other smaller software projects, but this is far different.[301] With TensorFlow's release, "Google is open sourcing software that sits at the heart of its empire," states Metz.[301]

Deep learning relies on neural networks and Google typically "trains these neural nets using a vast array of machines equipped with GPU chips," says Metx.[301] GPUs are good at processing lots of little bits of data in parallel, and that's what deep learning needs.[301] After they've been trained, these neural nets operate in different ways[301], often running on "traditional computer processors inside the data center, and in some cases, they can run on mobile phones," notes Metz.[301] The *Google Translate* app is a prime example of this. It runs entirely on a mobile device without a data center connection, letting users translate foreign text into native languages.[301]

TensorFlow is a way of building and running neural networks that are required for computations like this, both at the training stage and the execution stage.[301] It is basically a set of software libraries that users "can slip into any application so that it too can learn tasks like image recognition, speech recognition, and language translation."[301]

The underlying TensorFlow software was built in C++[301], but "in developing applications for this AI engine, coders can use either C++ or Python, the most popular language among deep learning researchers," adds Metz.[301] Google hopes that developers "will expand the tool to other languages, including Google Go, Java, and perhaps even Javascript, so that coders have more ways of building apps."[301]

According to Google's Jeff Dean, "TensorFlow is well suited not only to deep learning, but to other forms of AI, including reinforcement learning and logistic regression."[301] TensorFlow is twice as fast as Google's previous system, DistBelief, Dean adds.[301]

In open sourcing the tool, Google provides some sample neural networking models and algorithms, "including models for recognizing photographs, identifying handwritten numbers, and analyzing text."[301] "We'll give you all the algorithms you need to train those models on public data sets," Dean says.[301]

The major caveat to Google's seeming generosity is that the initial open source version of TensorFlow only runs on a single computer, you can't train models across a vast array of machines.[301] "This computer can include many GPUs, but it's a single computer nonetheless," notes Metz.[301] "Google is still keeping an advantage," says Chris Nicholson, Chief Executive of AI startup Skymind.[301] "To build true enterprise applications, you need to analyze data at scale," he adds. "At the execution stage, the open source incarnation of TensorFlow will run on phones as well as desktops and laptops, and Google indicates that the company may eventually open source a version that runs across hundreds of machines," notes Metz.[301]

So why the change of heart at Google? Well, part of it has to do with the very nature of how the machine learning community operates.[301] "Deep learning originated with academics who openly shared their ideas, and many of them now work at Google—including University of Toronto professor Geoff Hinton, the godfather of deep learning," explains Metz.[301]

"TensorFlow was built at a very different time from tools like MapReduce and GFS and BigTable and Dremel and Spanner and Borg," notes Metz.[301] "The open source movement—where Internet companies share so many of their tools in order to accelerate the rate of development—has picked up considerable speed over the past decade. Google now builds software with an eye towards open source," adds Metz.[301] Many of Google's earlier tools were just too closely tied to Google's IT infrastructure to make them easily useful for outside developers.[301]

Unlike its competitors, Google has not handed the open source project to an independent third party, but manages the project itself at Tensorflow.org.[301] The code is shared under an Apache 2 license, meaning anyone can use the code free of copyright.[301]

Any goodwill this generates for Google is less important than the projects it could potentially feed.[301] According to Dean, "you can think of TensorFlow as combining the best of Torch and Caffe and Theano."[301] Like Torch and Theano, Dean says, "it's good for quickly spinning up research projects, and like Caffe, it's good for pushing those research projects into the real world."[301] However, even some people within Google might disagree with this assessment.[301] "According to many in the community, DeepMind, a notable deep learning startup now owned by Google, continues to use Torch—even though it has long had access to TensorFlow and DistBelief," notes Metz.[301] But, the writer concludes, "at the very least, an open source TensorFlow gives the community more options. And that's a good thing."[301]

Even utilizing TensorFlow's powerful AI and ML capabilities, building a deep learning app still requires some serious analytics and coding skills.[301] But this too may change in the years to come, Metz adds.[301] As Dean points out, "a Google deep-learning open source project and a Google deep-learning cloud service aren't mutually exclusive."[301]

For now, Google merely wants to generously share the code.[301] As Dean says, "this will help the company improve this code."[301] At the same time, other benefits will result from this, including improving machine learning as a whole, which will undoubtedly find its way back to the source—Google. The circle of code continues... "Google is five to seven years ahead of the rest of the world," argues Chris Nicholson, adding, "If they open source their tools, this can make everybody else better at machine learning."[301]

According to its article *Comparing Top Deep Learning Frameworks: Deeplearning4J, PyTorch, TensorFlow, Caffe, Kera, MxNet, Gluon & CNTK*[302], TensorFlow's pros and cons include:

- Python + Numpy.
- Computational graph abstraction, like Theano.
- Faster compile times than Theano.

- TensorBoard for visualization.
- Data and model parallelism.
- Slower than other frameworks.
- Much "fatter" than Torch; more magic.
- Not many pretrained models.
- Computational graph is pure Python, therefore slow.
- No commercial support.
- Drops out to Python to load each new training batch.
- Not very toolable.
- Dynamic typing is error-prone on large software projects.

Caffe2

At its F8 developer conference in San Francisco 2018, Facebook announced the launch of Caffe2, an open source framework for deep learning.[303] In his article *Facebook-Open Sources Caffe2, a New Deep Learning Framework,* Jordan Novet explains that the announcement "builds on Facebook's contributions to the Torch open source deep learning framework and more recently the PyTorch framework that the Facebook Artificial Intelligence Research (FAIR) group conceived."[303] However, Caffe2 does have several differences from PyTorch.[303]

"PyTorch is great for research, experimentation and trying out exotic neural networks, while Caffe2 is headed towards supporting more industrial-strength applications with a heavy focus on mobile," explains Yangqing Jia, Facebook's AI Platform engineering lead.[303] "This is not to say that PyTorch doesn't do mobile or doesn't scale or that you can't use Caffe2 with some awesome new paradigm of neural network, we're just highlighting some of the current characteristics and directions for these two projects," notes Jia.[303] "We plan to have plenty of interoperability and methods of converting back and forth so you can experience the best of both worlds," adds Jia.[303]

In their paper *Caffe2 vs. TensorFlow: Which is a Better Deep Learning Framework?*[304], Liu and Zang discovered that, while Caffe2 and TensorFlow do not differ much in expressiveness, modeling capability, and scalability, Caffe2 significantly outperforms TensorFlow in both speed and space aspects, therefore it is a better choice for people who pursue speed or are limited by device restrictions.[304] However, "TensorFlow provides more services and tools, such as Tensorboard, TensorFlow serving, TensorFlow Lite,"[304] and it has a strong advantage in help and support.[304] "It is a better choice if people want to implement new or complicated models and do not know how to implement exactly yet," state Liu and Zang.[304]

Torch

Officially released in October 2002, Torch is an open source machine learning library, computing framework, and a script language based on the Lua programming language. According to its article *Comparing Top Deep Learning Frameworks: Deeplearning4J, PyTorch, TensorFlow, Caffe, Kera, MxNet, Gluon & CNTK*[302], deeplearning4j states that while Torch is powerful, "it was not designed to be widely accessible to the Python-based academic community, nor to corporate software engineers, whose lingua franca is Java."

Keras

Created by Google software engineer Francois Chollet, Keras is a deep-learning library that sits atop TensorFlow and Theano, providing an intuitive API inspired by Torch.[302] According to Deeplearning4j it is "perhaps the best Python API in existence."[302] Deeplearning4j "relies on Keras as its Python API and imports models from Keras and through Keras from Theano and TensorFlow."[302]

According to Martin Heller, "Keras was created to be user friendly, modular, easy to extend, and to work with Python. The API was 'designed for human beings, not machines,' and 'follows best practices for reducing cognitive load.'"[305]

"Neural layers, cost functions, optimizers, initialization schemes, activation functions, and regularization schemes are all standalone modules that you can combine to create new models," explains Heller.[305] "New modules are simple to add, as new classes and functions," he adds.[305]

"The biggest reasons to use Keras stem from its guiding principles, primarily the one about being user friendly," claims Heller.[305] "Beyond ease of learning and ease of model building, Keras offers the advantages of broad adoption, support for a wide range of production deployment options, integration with at least five back-end engines (TensorFlow, CNTK, Theano, MXNet, and PlaidML), and strong support for multiple GPUs and distributed training," says Heller.[305] In addition, "Keras is backed by Google, Microsoft, Amazon, Apple, Nvidia, Uber, and others," adds Heller.[305]

Keras is versatile, its "models can be deployed across a vast range of platforms, perhaps more than any other deep learning framework."[305] These include "iOS, via CoreML (supported by Apple); Android, via the TensorFlow Android runtime; in a browser, via Keras.js and WebDNN; on Google Cloud, via TensorFlow-Serving; in a Python webapp back end; on the JVM, via DL4J model import; and on Raspberry Pi," concludes Heller.[305]

Pytorch

Deeplearning4j states that "A Python version of Torch, known as PyTorch, was open-sourced by Facebook in January 2017. PyTorch offers dynamic computation graphs, which let you process variable-length inputs and outputs, which is useful when working with RNNs, for example."[302] Since its introduction, Deeplearning4J claims that "PyTorch has quickly become the favorite among machine-learning researchers, because it allows certain complex architectures to be built easily."[302]

According to Deeplearning4J, these are the pros and cons of Torch and PyTorch[302]:

- Lots of modular pieces that are easy to combine.
- Easy to write your own layer types and run on GPU.
- Lots of pretrained models.
- You usually write your own training code (Less plug and play).
- No commercial support.
- Spotty documentation.

Deeplearning4j

Deeplearning4j was written in Java to reflect its focus on industry and ease of use.[302] Deeplearning4J believes "usability is the limiting parameter that inhibits more widespread deep-learning implementations."[302] "They believe scalability ought to be automated with open-source distributed run-times like Hadoop and Spark. And we believe that a commercially supported open-source framework is the appropriate solution to ensure working tools and building a community."[302]

Streaming Analytics

As *The Cluetrain Manifesto*[279] points out, "Real-time marketing is the execution of a thoughtful and strategic plan specifically designed to engage customers on their terms via digital social technologies." Adding to that description, Wikipedia notes that real-time marketing is[306]:

> "Marketing performed 'on-the-fly' to determine an appropriate or optimal approach to a particular customer at a particular time and place. It is a form of market research inbound marketing that seeks the most appropriate offer for a given customer sales opportunity, reversing the traditional outbound marketing (or interruption marketing) which aims to acquire appropriate customers for a given 'pre-defined' offer."

Real-time marketing can be inexpensive compared to the cost of traditional paid media. "Expensive research, focus groups, and awareness campaigns can be replaced with online surveys, blog comments, and tweets by anyone or any business," add Macy and Thompson in their book *The Power of Real-Time Social Media Marketing*.[307] Just to be clear, the expense of real-time marketing might be low compared to running through traditional media channels, but setting up an IT operation that can hit a level of personalization that will wow a customer is anything but cheap.

In his article *How Real-time Marketing Technology Can Transform Your Business*[27], Dan Woods' amusing comparison of the differing environments that marketers face today as compared to what their 1980s counterpart faced is highly instructive as today's marketing executives don't have time for a market research study in his sort of figurative first-person-shooter game. "The data arrives too late and isn't connected to the modern weapons of marketing. The world is now bursting with data from social media, web traffic, mobile devices, and tripwires of all kinds," warns Woods.[27]

Today, most large companies have massive amounts of data pertaining to consumer behavior streaming at them constantly, from all channels and angles. The challenge is to make sense of the data in time to make it matter, to understand how consumer attitudes and behaviors are changing and how they are being changed by marketing and advertising efforts; to grab the treasure and avoid the pitfalls of unleashing a Pandora's box full of furies.

The challenge in understanding the modern consumer is in trying to make sense of all of the customer data that is coming in from these vast, unstructured sources.[27] Some of this information might explain the broad fluctuations of mass opinion, while other data might clarifiy what consumers are doing on a company website;[27] Other data might explain what consumers have done, en masse or as individuals.[27] Still other data can be collected after a customer trip in the form of surveys, whether they are mobile or physical surveys.

In his article *When do you need an Event Stream Processing platform?*[308], Roy Schulte states that:

> "An event is anything that happens. An event object (or 'event,' event message, or event tuple) is an object that represents, encodes, or records an event, generally for the purpose of computer processing. Event objects usually include data about the type of activity, when the activity happened (e.g., a time and date stamp), and sometimes the location of the activity, its cause, and other information. An event stream is a sequence of event objects, typically in order by time of arrival."

Large brands typically have three kinds of event streams[308]:

- "Copies of business transactions, such as customer orders, bank deposits or withdrawals, customer address changes, call data records, advance shipping notices, or invoices."[308] These are generated mostly internally, and reflect the operational activities of the company.[308]
- "The second are information reports, such as tweets, news feed articles, market data, weather reports, and social media updates, including Facebook and LinkedIn posts."[308] According to Schulte, "most of these sources are external to the company, but may contain information that is relevant to a decision within the company."[308]

- "The third, and fastest growing, kind of event stream contains sensor data coming from physical assets."[308] Generally known as IoT data, this includes "GPS-based location data from vehicles or smart phones, temperature or accelerometer data from sensors, RFID tag readings, heart beats from patient monitors, and signals from supervisory control and data access (SCADA) systems on machines."[308]

The reason for performing analytics on one or more event streams is to obtain information value from the data.[308] As Schulte explains, "A stream analytics application converts the raw input data (*base* events), into a form, *derived events*, that is better suited for making decisions. The derived events are *complex events*, which means that they are events that are abstracted from one or more other events.[308]

Stream analytics are executed in one of two ways, push-based, continuous intelligence systems, which recalculate as new data arrives without being asked to or pull-based systems that run when a person enters a request, or a timer sends a signal to produce a batch report. Event Stream Processing (ESP) platforms are mostly relevant in highly demanding, push-based systems, but they are occasionally used for pull-based analytics on historical data.[308]

When people think of ESP, they usually think of push-based continuous intelligence systems, which ingests ongoing flows of event data and provide situation awareness, while also supporting near-real-time, sense-and-respond business processes.[308] "Continuous intelligence systems typically refresh dashboards every second or minute, send alerts, or implement hands-free decision automation scenarios," explains Schulte.[308] "They may be used to monitor a data source, such as Twitter, or a business operation, such as a customer contact center, supply chain, water utility, telecommunication network, truck fleet, or payment process," adds Schulte.[308]

Schulte explains that[308]:

> "ESP platforms are software subsystems that process data in motion, as each event arrives. The query is pre-loaded, so the data comes to the query rather than the query coming to the data. ESP platforms retain a relatively small working set of stream data in memory for the duration of a limited time window, typically seconds to hours—just long enough to detect patterns or compute queries. The platforms are more flexible than hardwired applications because the query can be adjusted to handle different kinds of input data, different time windows (e.g., one minute or one hour instead of ten minutes) and different search terms."

According to Schulte, continuous intelligence applications are best implemented on ESP platforms if there is[308]:

- A high volume of data (thousands or millions of events per second).
- Frequently recalculated results (every millisecond or every few seconds).
- Multiple simultaneous queries are applied to the same input event stream.

Schulte gives the example of Twitter's ESP platforms, Storm and Heron.[308] These DWs are "used to monitor Twitter, which averages about 6,000 tweets per second. A simple query might report the number of tweets that included the word 'inflation' in the past ten minutes. However, at any one time, there may be thousands of simultaneous queries in effect against Twitter, each looking for different key words or different time windows."[308]

"In high volume scenarios, ESP platform applications can scale out vertically (multiple engines working in parallel on the same step in a processing flow) and/or horizontally (split the work up in a sequence or pipeline where work is handed from one engine to the next while working on the same multistep event processing query (i.e., an event processing network)," explains Schulte.[308]

Schulte notes that, "On-demand analytics are pull-based applications that support ad hoc data exploration, visualization and analysis of data."[308] On-demand analytics can be used with historical event data to build analytical models.[308] In this context, "historical means stored event streams that are hours, weeks or years old."[308] Schulte adds that the "analytical models can be used for either of two purposes[308]:

1. To design rules and algorithms to be used in real-time continuous intelligence applications (see above), or
2. To make one-time, strategic, tactical and long-term operational decisions.

The most common tool for on-demand analytics with historical data is a data discovery product like Qlik, Tableau, SAS, Tibco, etc., etc. However, "companies occasionally use ESP platforms to run analytics on historical event streams by re-streaming the old event data through the ESP engine," says Schulte.[308] "This is particularly relevant when developing models for subsequent use in real-time, continuous intelligence ESP applications."[308]

ESP platforms are not the only type of software optimized for high performance analytics on event stream data. Some stream analytics products like First Derivatives KDB+, Interana Platform, Logtrust Platform, One Market Data OneTick, Quartet ActivePivot, and Splunk Enterprise combine analytics and longer term data storage in one product.[308] "These products typically provide on-demand, pull-based analytics, but some are also used for continuous, push-based continuous intelligence. They ingest and store high volume event streams very quickly, making the 'at rest' data immediately available for interactive queries, exploration and visualization," explains Schulte.[308]

For a real-time platform to work, data must be gathered from multiple and disparate sources, which can include Enterprise Resource Planning (ERP), Customer Relationship Management (CRM), Social CRM (SCRM) platforms, geofencing applications (like Jiepang and Foursquare), Over-The-Top services (like WhatsApp and WeChat), mobile apps, augmented reality apps, and other mobile and social media systems. This data must be collected and then seamlessly integrated into a data warehouse that can cleanse it and make it ready for consumption.[61] As the authors' state in *Mobile Advertising*[28]:

> "The analytical system must have the capability to digest all the user data, summarize it, and update the master user profile. This functionality is essential to provide the rich user segmentation that is at the heart of recommendations, campaign and offer management, and advertisements. The segmentation engine can cluster users into affinities and different groups based on geographic, demographic or socio-economic, psychographic, and behavioral characteristics."

In his article *Real-Time Stream Processing as Game Changer in a Big Data World with Hadoop and Data Warehouse*[309], Kal Wähner states that:

> "Stream processing is designed to analyze and act on real-time streaming data, using 'continuous queries' (i.e. SQL-type queries that operate over time and buffer windows). Essential to stream processing is Streaming Analytics, or the ability to continuously calculate mathematical or statistical analytics on the fly within the stream. Stream processing solutions are designed to handle high volume in real time with a scalable, highly available and fault tolerant architecture. This enables analysis of data in motion."

As a batch processing framework, Hadoop can't handle the needs of real time analytics. As the first open source distributed computing environment, Hadoop has garnered a lot of attention recently, but it is not necessarily the best platform for real-time analytics of dynamic information.[310]

One recent development in stream processing methods is the invention of the "live data mart", which "provides end-user, ad-hoc continuous query access to this streaming data that's aggregated in memory," explains Wähner.[309] "Business user-oriented analytics tools access the data mart for a continuously live view of streaming data"[309] and a "live analytics front ends slices, dices, and aggregates data dynamically in response to business users' actions, and all in real time," adds Wähner.[309]

For a business, streaming data could be coming in from facial recognition and geo-location software, fraud or anti-money laundering solutions, patron card and campaign management databases, redemption systems, social media feeds,

IoT data, as well as wearables and employee/labor data sets.

Stream processing excels when data must be processed fast and/or continuously. Many different frameworks and products are on the market already, however the number of mature solutions with good tools and commercial support today is quite small.

Apache Storm is a good, open source framework, but it suffers from its open source nature and custom coding is required because of limited developer tools. The typical "commercial solution vs. open source" questions must be answered as well; do I want a pre-built product that will require limited—and sometimes not so limited implementation costs—or do I want to start with a solid solution and be required to customize everything?

As Wähner explains, a stream processing solution has to solve several different challenges, including[309]:

- Processing massive amounts of streaming events (filter, aggregate, rule, automate, predict, act, monitor, alert).
- Real-time responsiveness to changing market conditions.
- Performance and scalability as data volumes increase in size and complexity.
- Rapid integration with existing infrastructure and data sources: Input (e.g. market data, user inputs, files, history data from a DWH) and output (e.g. trades, email alerts, dashboards, automated reactions).
- Fast time-to-market for application development and deployment due to quickly changing landscape and requirements.
- Developer productivity throughout all stages of the application development lifecycle by offering good tool support and agile development.
- Analytics: Live data discovery and monitoring, continuous query processing, automated alerts and reactions.
- Community (component/connector exchange, education/discussion, training/certification).
- End-user ad-hoc continuous query access.
- Alerting.
- Push-based visualization.

Comparison of Stream Processing Services

From a technical perspective, Wähner explains that the following components are required for a stream processing system[309]:

- Server: An ultra-low-latency application server optimized for processing real-time streaming event data at high throughputs and low latency (usually in-memory).

- IDE: A development environment, which ideally offers visual development, debugging and testing of stream processing processes using streaming operators for filtering, aggregation, correlation, time windows, transformation, etc.
- Extendibility, e.g. integration of libraries or building custom operators and connectors, is also important.
- Connectors: Pre-built data connectivity to communicate with data sources such as databases (e.g. MySQL, Oracle, IBM DB2), DWH (e.g. HP Vertica), market data (e.g. Bloomberg, FIX, Reuters), statistics (e.g. R, MATLAB, TERR) or technology (e.g. JMS, Hadoop, Java, .NET).
- Streaming Analytics: A user interface, which allows monitoring, management and real-time analytics for live streaming data. Automated alerts and human reactions should also be possible.
- Live Data Mart and/or Operational Business Intelligence: Aggregates streaming data for ad-hoc, end-user, query access, alerting, dynamic aggregation, and user management.
- Live stream visualization, graphing, charting, slice and dice are also important.

Since these are highly complex systems, there are few market-ready products available and a lot of custom coding is required to implement them.[309] The following products are the leaders of the pack:

Apache Storm is "an open source framework that provides massively scalable event collection. Storm was created by Twitter and is composed of other open source components, especially ZooKeeper for cluster management, ZeroMQ for multicast messaging, and Kafka for queued messaging."[309]

Apache Spark is a "stream processing framework and focuses on continuous computation that can process hundreds of millions of tweets generated every day and now is an open source big data analysis system."[309] Spark is a scalable data analysis platform based on in-memory computing and has a performance advantage over Hadoop's cluster storage method. Spark is written in Scala and offers a single data processing environment. Spark supports iteration tasks of distributed data sets.

Spark is a "general framework for large-scale data processing that supports lots of different programming languages and concepts such as MapReduce, in-memory processing, stream processing, graph processing or machine learning."[309] Although Storm and Spark were not created to run on Hadoop specifically, they can be integrated into Cloudera, Hortonworks, MapR, and used to implement stream processing atop Hadoop.[309]

Amazon's Kinesis is a managed cloud service that was designed for real-time processing of streaming data. Because it is Amazon owned, it integrates seamlessly with other AWS cloud services such as S3, Redshift or DynamoDB.[309]

InfoSphere Streams is "IBM's flagship product for stream processing. It offers a highly scalable event server, integration capabilities, and other typical features required for implementing stream processing use cases. The IDE is based on Eclipse and offers visual development and configuration."[309]

Hitachi's Streaming Data Platform is a real-time streaming software solution that uses CQL, a popular and widely used language similar to SQL for processing and analysis. As per Hitachi Data Systems (HDS)[309]:

> "CQL (Continuous Query Language) is an extension of traditional SQL. CQL executes in memory, designed for high throughput and low latency environments. It has a 'windowing' concept that allows the system to treat each stream, packet and flow individually and allows for 'stateful' analysis unlike open source technologies where this capability has to be custom coded. Hitachi CQL provides the capability to centrally develop and globally deploy applications."[311]

TIBCO StreamBase is "a high-performance system for rapidly building applications that analyze and act on real-time streaming data. The goal of StreamBase is to offer a product that supports developers in rapidly building real-time systems and deploying them easily."[309]

Stream processing solutions can get very complicated very quickly and Wähner warns that[309], "Besides evaluating the core features of stream processing products, you also have to check integration with other products. Can a product work together with messaging, Enterprise Service Bus (ESB), Master Data Management (MDM), in-memory stores, etc., in a loosely coupled, but highly integrated way?"[309] If the answer to these questions is negative, a lot of integration time and considerable costs could be in order, warns Wähner.[309]

In his article *15 "True" Streaming Analytics Platforms For Real-Time Everything*[312], Mike Gualtieri, Vice President and Principal Analyst at *Forrester* argues that "streaming analytics analyzes data right now, when it can be analyzed and put to good use to make applications of all kinds (including IoT) contextual and smarter." Gualtieri then breaks down the offerings as follows:

- Cisco Systems—The acquisitions of ParStream and Truviso give Cisco "the power to collect data as close to the edge as possible and to efficiently parse and pass it back to the center for analysis."[312]
- Data Artisans—Berlin-based data Artisans is the commercial force behind the open source Apache Flink project for distributed stream and batch processing. "While Spark uses micro-batches to enable fast processing, Flink is a true streaming engine that can also do batch processing by treating a stream of events as a data set with a beginning and an end."[312]

- DataTorrent has built a streaming platform to handle the world's biggest and fastest data.[312] "In addition to providing a distributed streaming analytics platform, the vendor also delivers accruements including a visual development tool and a library of over 400 operators. The core of DataTorrent is now open sourced as Apache Apex."[312]
- EsperTech's open source and battle tested "event processing offering provides enterprises with a flexible basis for building applications that require complex pattern matching with sophisticated time windows."[312]
- IBM Streams "can ingest and understand the always-on stream of data from applications and IoT devices needed to make the decisions that underlie cognitive solutions."[312]
- Informatica's streaming capabilities come in the form of a real-time rules engine. "Streaming data is handled by the vendor's rules engine, which includes enterprise capabilities around security, encryption, operational management, and data lineage."[312]
- Oracle's streaming solution "includes two distinct pieces that are critical for the future of analytics: Stream Explorer for ingesting and interrogating data as it lands in the cloud or the enterprise; and Oracle Edge Analytics (OEA) for preprocessing data on IoT devices."[312]
- SAP's Smart data streaming (SDS) engine is available as an integrated add-on to SAP Hana or as stand-alone software. "SAP currently includes two machine learning algorithms—one supervised, one unsupervised—which can incrementally train on data running through the system."[312]
- SAS real time product's architecture "focuses tightly on low-latency, high-throughput complex analytics, so it is well positioned to embed many of SAS's highly regarded advanced analytics algorithms, including text analytics and machine learning."[312]
- Software AG's Apama "powers real-time, digital business transformations. Long-running pattern detection and stream enrichment is also well supported via integration with Software AG's own in-memory data grid, Terracotta, and its integration platform, webMethods."[312]
- SQLstream's Blaze "delivers a solid platform for companies to build real-time applications, especially for customers that have a lot of machine data and prefer a declarative SQL syntax to operate on streaming data."[312]
- Striim's platform "focuses equally on the continuous capture of data at its point of origin and on the upstream real-time analytics. It can ingest streaming data from many sources, including streaming change data capture (CDC) from transactions in databases."[312]
- TIBCO Software "recognizes that ideas come from human insight and domain knowledge. That's why its streaming solution includes LiveView, a real-time view of streaming data."[312]

- WSO2 is "an open source middleware provider that includes a full spectrum of architected-as-one components such as application servers, message brokers, enterprise service bus, and many others."[312]

Internet of Things

In 1982, a modified Coke machine at Carnegie Mellon University became the first connected smart appliance, reporting its inventory and temperature back to Coca Cola.[313] Today, we live in a world where there are more connected devices than human beings.[313] According to *Business Insider Intelligence*, there will be more than 55 billion IoT devices by 2025, up from about 9 billion in 2017.[314] "The rapidly expanding Internet of Things extends connectivity and data exchange across a vast network of portable devices, home appliances, vehicles, manufacturing equipment and other things embedded with electronics, software, sensors, actuators and connectivity."[313]

In their article *The Artificial Intelligence of Things*[313], SAS claims that AI and IoT are "a perfect example of two technologies that complement one another and should be tightly connected." "From consumer wearable devices to industrial machines and heavy machineries, these connected things can signal their environment, be remotely monitored and controlled—and increasingly, make decisions and take actions on their own," says SAS.[313] "In the fast-growing world of IoT, which connects and shares data across a vast network of devices or 'things,' organizations win with analytics," adds SAS.[313] "For its ability to make rapid decisions and uncover deep insights as it 'learns' from massive volumes of IoT data, AI is an essential form of analytics for any organization that wants to expand the value of IoT," SAS concludes.[313]

IoT is omnipresent. SAS claims[313]:

> *"It's a home automation system that detects changing conditions and adjusts the thermostat or lighting. It's production equipment that alerts maintenance technicians to an impending failure. Or an in-vehicle navigation system that detects your location and gives you context-aware directions. Digital personal assistants that use speech recognition to interpret commands. Commercial fleets equipped with dozens of sensors to communicate their status. And much more.*

The opportunity of the IoT, too, is practically endless.

A smart, connected device is made up of four distinct layers[313]:
- Physical elements such as the mechanical and electrical parts.
- Smart elements such as sensors, processors, storage and software.
- Connectivity elements such as ports, antennas and protocols.

- Onboard analytics, in some cases, to train and run AI models at the edge.

The real value of IoT occurs "when devices learn from their specific use or from each other and then automate actions. It happens when they can adapt, change behavior over time, make decisions, take action and tune their responses based on what they learn."[313]

"Deep learning, computer vision, natural language processing, and machine learning in time-tested forecasting or optimization—technologies such as these make AI an essential complement to IoT," says SAS.[313] "AI separates signal from noise, giving rise to advanced IoT devices that can learn from their interactions with users, service providers and other devices in the ecosystem."[313]

As Bernard Marr argues in his article *Will 'Analytics on The Edge' Be The Future Of Big Data?*[315], "Rather than designing centralized systems where all the data is sent back to your data warehouse in a raw state, where it has to be cleaned and analyzed before being of any value, why not do everything at the 'edge' of the system?"

Marr uses the example of a massive scale CCTV security system that is capturing real-time video feeds from tens of thousands of cameras.[315] "It's likely that 99.9% of the footage captured by the cameras will be of no use for the job it's supposed to be doing—e.g. detecting intruders. Hours and hours of still footage is likely to be captured for every second of useful video. So what's the point of all of that data being streamed in real-time across your network, generating expense as well as possible compliance burdens?" he asks.[315]

Marr argues that the solution to this problem is for the images themselves to be analyzed within the cameras at the moment the video is captured.[315] Anything deemed out-of-the-ordinary would trigger alerts, while everything considered to be unimportant will either be discarded or marked as low priority, thereby freeing up centralized resources to work on data of actual value.[315]

Using edge analytics and real-time stream processing engines, companies can "analyze point-of-sales data as it is captured, and enable cross selling or up-selling on-the-fly, while reducing bandwidth overheads of sending all sales data to a centralized analytics server in real time."[315] Edge analytics, of course, goes hand-in-hand with the Internet of Things.

In his seminal 2009 article for the *RFID Journal*, *That 'Internet o Things' Thing*[316], Kevin Ashton made the following assessment:

> Today computers—and, therefore, the Internet—are almost wholly dependent on human beings for information. Nearly all of the roughly 50 petabytes (a petabyte is 1,024 terabytes) of data available on the Internet were first captured and created by human beings—by typing, pressing a record button, taking a digital picture, or scanning a bar code. Conventional diagrams

of the Internet include servers and routers and so on, but leave out the most numerous and important routers of all—people. The problem is, people have limited time, attention and accuracy—all of which means they are not very good at capturing data about things in the real world. And that's a big deal. We're physical, and so is our environment. Our economy, society and survival aren't based on ideas or information—they're based on things. You can't eat bits, burn them to stay warm or put them in your gas tank. Ideas and information are important, but things matter much more. Yet today's information technology is so dependent on data originated by people that our computers know more about ideas than things. If we had computers that knew everything there was to know about things—using data they gathered without any help from us—we would be able to track and count everything, and greatly reduce waste, loss and cost. We would know when things needed replacing, repairing or recalling, and whether they were fresh or past their best. The Internet of Things has the potential to change the world, just as the Internet did. Maybe even more so.

Technology costs are down, broadband's price has dropped, while its availability has increased. There is a proliferation of devices with Wi-Fi capabilities and censors built into them, and smart phone penetration is exploding; all of these individual technological advances were good for the IoT, together they have created a perfect storm for it.[317] Even clothes and footballs are now equipped with censors, as the 2018 World Cup ball given to Donald Trump by Vladimir Putin showed.[318]

With less than 0.1% of all the devices that could be connected to the Internet currently connected[317], there is tremendous growth potential here and those who embrace it now should have the first mover advantage, an advantage that could prove enormously profitable in terms of ROI over the next few years and decades.

Combining IoT data with other structured and unstructured data isn't easy. Previous attempts at broad-based data integration has forced users to build data sets around common predetermined schema, or a unifying data model, but this becomes impossible when unstructured and semi-structured data are added to the mix.

Today, data is coming from everywhere, from business mainframes, from corporate databases, log files, cloud services, APIs, RSS feeds, as well as from social media feeds; most of this information does contain meaning, if one knows what, where, and how to look for it.

According to its *Gartner Says the Internet of Things Installed Base Will Grow to 26 Billion Units By 2020*[319], Gartner claims that, "The Internet of Things (IoT), which excludes PCs, tablets and smartphones, will grow to 26 billion units installed in 2020 representing an almost 30-fold increase from 0.9 billion in 2009."

Gartner believes IoT product and service suppliers will generate incremental revenue exceeding $300 billion in 2020, mostly in services. It will result in $1.9 trillion in global economic value-add through sales into diverse end markets."[319]

Today, it is almost unimaginable how all-encompassing the Internet of Things will be in our daily lives in the not-too-distant future. From such life-changing technology as Google's driverless cars, which could help optimize traffic, thereby reducing traffic congestion, as well as making people more productive, to sensors that can help regulate room temperature thereby saving energy, IoT is unquestionably here to stay.

"The growth in IoT will far exceed that of other connected devices. By 2020, the number of smartphones tablets and PCs in use will reach about 7.3 billion units," said Peter Middleton, research director at *Gartner*.[63] "In contrast, the IoT will have expanded at a much faster rate, resulting in a population of about 26 billion units at that time," Middleton adds.[63]

In terms of marketing, a brand can utilize IoT applications in the following ways:

- NFC payment.
- Intelligent shopping applications.
- Smart product management.
- Smartphone detection.
- Inventory optimization.
- Logistics:
    - Quality of shipment conditions.
    - Item location.
    - Storage incompatibility detection.
    - Fleet tracking.
- Video analytics.

IoT is faced with the typical problems new technologies tend to face—a lack of standards as the big and small players jockey for position. However, there is currently a movement in place to create a vendor-independent protocol that will allow devices to connect with each other under the guise of a common service layer.

Currently, IoT's growing pains are being tackled and security issues are being addressed. The addition of edge analytics, which can reduce network and connectivity costs, is also circumventing the need for cloud integration.

In his article *The Data of Things: How Edge Analytics and IoT Go Hand In Hand*[320], Gadi Lenz explains that, although IoT data has similar characteristics to Big Data, it is much more complicated. IoT data is[320]:

- Messy, noisy, and sometimes intermittent because sensors are often deployed in the field.
- Often highly unstructured and sourced from a variety of sensors (fixed and mobile).
- Dynamic—'data in motion' as opposed to the traditional 'data at rest'.
- Sometimes indirect.

The idea of collecting all of this sensor information and bringing it into one centralized computing station is not viable over the long term, particularly as the volume of IoT devices increases exponentially.[320] "Bringing such a large amount of data into a relatively small number of data centers where it is then analyzed in the cloud, simply [sic] not scale," argues Lenz.[320] The cost, too, would be prohibitive.[320]

"With so many devices producing so much data, a correspondingly large array of analytics, compute, storage and networking power and infrastructure is essential. Though analytics will be necessary to the growth and business value of IoT, the traditional approach to analytics won't be the right fit," Lenz argues.[320]

Edge analytics addresses these problems. Lenz says that a marketer can "harness the smartness of the myriad of smart devices and their low cost computational power to allow them to run valuable analytics on the device itself."[320] As Lenz explains, "Multiple devices are usually connected to a local gateway where potentially more compute power is available (like Cisco's IOx), enabling more complex multi-device analytics close to the edge."[320]

Distributed IoT analytics would work in three ways, "simple" analytics would be done on the smart device itself, more complex multi-device analytics on the IoT gateways, and finally the high computational computing—the "Big Data" analytics, if you will—would connect to and run on the cloud.[320] "This distribution of analytics offloads the network and the data centers by creating a model that scales. Distributing the analytics to the edge is the only way to progress," advises Lenz.[320]

An example of an IoT-edge analytics could be at an airport lounge. The lounge's cameras could pick up a customer once he or she enters. In this case, it makes sense for the analytics to be done inside the camera rather than having the data sent back to a centralized server, which is both inefficient and risks bottlenecking.[320] Lenz adds, "Edge analytics is all about processing and analyzing subsets of all the data collected and then only transmitting the results."[320] So, the systems is essentially discarding some of the raw data and potentially missing some insights, but it should be a calculated loss as analyzing everything is just not productive in most cases.[320]

"Some organizations may never be willing to lose any data, but the vast majority can accept that not everything can be analyzed. This is where we will have to learn by experience as organizations begin to get involved in this new field of IoT analytics and review the results," adds Lenz.[320] This is an exploding field of study and the rules are, literally, been written right now, as the sensors are rolling out.

However, some trade-off must be considered with edge analytics. Lenz notes that, "Edge analytics is all about processing and analyzing subsets of all the data collected and then only transmitting the results."[320] Some of the raw data is discarded and potentially some insights are lost.[320] Lenz states that, "The question is, Can we live with this 'loss' and if so how should we choose which pieces we are willing to 'discard' and which need to be kept and analyzed?"[320]

It is also important to learn the lessons of past distributed systems. "For example, when many devices are analyzing and acting on the edge, it may be important to have somewhere a single 'up-to-date view,' which in turn, may impose various constraints," advises Lenz.[320] "The fact that many of the edge devices are also mobile complicates the situation even more," adds Lenz.[320] Although incredibly powerful devices in their own right, mobile phones and tablets will never reach the capacity and compute technology of EDWs, obviously.

In Tableau's *2018 Top 10 Business Intelligence Trends*[321], one of the leading BI companies coins a new phrase with their "Location of Things" which they believe will drive the Internet of Things. "One positive trend we are seeing is the usage and benefits of leveraging location-based data with IoT devices. This subcategory, termed 'location of things,' provides IoT devices with sensing and communicates their geographic position," argue Tableau.[321] "By knowing where an IoT device is located, it allows us to add context, better understand what is happening and what we predict will happen in a specific location,"[321] which should strengthen personalization marketing.

For companies wishing to capture this data, Tableau is seeing different technologies being used.[321] "For example, hospitals, stores, and hotels have begun to use Bluetooth Low Energy (BLE) technology for indoor location services, which were typically difficult for GPS to provide contextual location," claim Tableau.[321] "The technology can be used to track specific assets, people and even interact with mobile devices like smartwatches, badges or tags in order to provide personalized experiences," note Tableau.[321]

In terms of data analysis, location-based figures can be viewed as an input rather than an output of results, making it much more useful.[321] "If the data is available, analysts can incorporate this information with their analysis to better understand what is happening, where it is happening, and what they should expect to happen in a contextual area," conclude Tableau.[321]

Augmented and Virtual Reality

Not just the stuff of science fiction anymore, Augmented Reality (AR) is now a part of our everyday lives. In his article *CrowdOptic and L'Oreal to make history by demonstrating how augmented reality can be a shared experience*[322], Tarun Wadhwa states that augmented reality works by "displaying layers of computer-generated information on top of a view of the physical world." It is "a technology that alters the perception of reality by distorting it, allowing escape from it, and enhancing it—all at the same time."[322]

Webopedia.com adds that AR is[323]:

> "A type of virtual reality that aims to duplicate the world's environment in a computer. An augmented reality system generates a composite view for the user that is the combination of the real scene viewed by the user and a virtual scene generated by the computer that augments the scene with additional information. The virtual scene generated by the computer is designed to enhance the user's sensory perception of the virtual world they are seeing or interacting with. The goal of Augmented Reality is to create a system in which the user cannot tell the difference between the real world and the virtual augmentation of it. Today Augmented Reality is used in entertainment, military training, engineering design, robotics, manufacturing and other industries."

According to *Gartner's Top 10 Strategic Technology Trends 2017*[324], Augmented reality (AR) and virtual reality (VR) will "transform the way individuals interact with each other and with software systems creating an immersive environment. For example, VR can be used for training scenarios and remote experiences."

AR enables a blending of the real and virtual worlds, which "means businesses can overlay graphics onto real-world objects."[324] Immersive experiences with AR and VR are reaching tipping points in terms of price and capability but will not replace other interface models."[324] In the future, AR and VR are expected to expand beyond visual immersion and they might include all of the human senses[324], although this is a very complicated thing to pull off as smell-o-vision tried and failed to do in the entertainment business in the last century.

According to its press release *Gartner Says Augmented Reality Will Become an Important Workplace Tool*[325], "Augmented reality is the real-time use of information in the form of text, graphics, audio and other virtual enhancements integrated with real-world objects." Tuong Huy Nguyen, principal research analyst at *Gartner*, states that "AR leverages and optimizes the use of other technologies such as mobility, location, 3D content management and imaging and recognition. It is especially useful in the mobile environment because it enhances the user's senses via digital instruments to allow faster responses or decision-making."[325]

Gartner believes "AR technology has matured to a point where organizations can use it as an internal tool to complement and enhance business processes, workflows and employee training."[325] For *Gartner*, "AR facilitates business innovation by enabling real-time decision-making through virtual prototyping and visualization of content."[325]

AR uses location-based data for navigation, overlaying digital maps and directions on real-world environments.[325] Through the lens of an AR device, a user can receive visual guidance based on GPS technology.[325]

So where is AR going? In his article *Augmented reality: expanding the user experience*[326], John Moore claims that "app creators have begun to engage more of a mobile device's sensors—accelerometers and gyroscopes." Augmented reality apps that use detailed animations are also in the works. The objective: inject augmented reality technology in a wider range of apps to boost the user experience."[322]

Pokémon Go was the first location-based augmented reality game that hit it big. Despite mixed reviews, the mobile app quickly became a global phenomenon and it was one of the most used and profitable mobile apps of 2016, having been downloaded more than 500 million times worldwide.[327] It certainly revealed the enormous potential of AR and it proved, without a shadow of a doubt, that the barriers to AR technology were limited and easily scaled by humans seeking out little dueling pocket monsters.

Gartner believes "AR technology has matured to a point where brands can use it as an internal tool to complement and enhance business processes, workflows and employee training."[325] *Gartner* also believes that "AR facilitates business innovation by enabling real-time decision-making through virtual prototyping and visualization of content."[325]

In its article *A Digital Shopping Experience: Coming Soon to a Mall Near You*[328], the Adobe Communications Team describes how augmented reality is being used in the retail industry in ways that also tap into social media. For example, "Neiman Marcus now has a smart MemoryMirror at its cosmetics counter that will record your makeover session in the perfect light and note all the products used."[328] The video can then be sent to the user's phone, allowing it to be used as a tutorial, or it can be shared with friends for their input.[328] This is a clever idea in this day and age of viral marketing because it does much of the hard work of video creation and then provides the content to a person who will market it; seamlessness at its finest.

According to Adobe, "A similar mirror will take video clips of you wearing eyeglasses or sunglasses and then let you compare up to four different styles side by side."[328] "A big benefit here is the ability to see what new frames look like on you, even when it's hard to see because you don't have your own glasses on! This input can lead you to a great purchase—and give Neiman Marcus valuable feedback about your selections."[328]

"A retailer's challenge today is that people are staying at home and shopping online," says Dawn Burrows, senior program manager for the Adobe Innovation Team.[328] "They are trying to get people to come back into the store, and one of the ways they're doing that is to bring digital experiences into the actual physical space."[328]

The real challenge of bringing technology to the store is to ensure it is used in a way that moves beyond the "wow" factor and adds value to a buyer's shopping experience. If retailers get that right, the outcome will also tie back to their goals of getting shoppers to make a purchase, and then keep them coming back for more, and more, and more.

Conclusion

In this chapter, I laid out the various hardware and software products needed to run AI, machine learning and deep learning, as well as some other things to keep in mind when developing an AI system. One of the most important decisions to make regarding deep learning is model framework. As Janakiram warns, "One of the critical challenges in developing neural network models lies in choosing the right framework. Data scientists and developers have to pick the right tool from a plethora of choices that include Caffe2, PyTorch, Apache MXNet, Microsoft Cognitive Toolkit, and TensorFlow. Once a model is trained and evaluated in a specific framework, it is tough to port the trained model to another framework."[292]

To mitigate this integration problem, "AWS, Facebook and Microsoft have collaborated to build Open Neural Network Exchange (ONNX), which makes it possible to reuse trained neural network models across multiple frameworks."[292] However, anyone who has dealt with software applications that cross a manufacturer's or even a version's divide can tell you, some kinks can arise that just can't be ironed out. In general, it is a good idea to think really hard about what platform is best to use.

"In 2019, ONNX will become an essential technology for the industry. From researchers to edge device manufacturers, all the key players of the ecosystem will rely on ONNX as the standard runtime for inferencing," claims Janakiram.[292]

One trend Janakiram thinks will "change the face of ML-based solutions fundamentally is AutoML."[292] It will empower business analysts and developers to evolve machine learning models that can address complex scenarios without going through the typical process of training ML models."[292] "When dealing with an AutoML platform, business analysts stay focused on the business problem instead of getting lost in the process and workflow," explains Janakiram.[292] "AIOps will become mainstream in 2019. Public cloud vendors and enterprises are going to benefit from the convergence of AI and DevOps," concludes Janakiram.[292]

In the next chapter, I bring everything together, explaining how the *A.I. Marketer* can use the theoretical ideas I discussed in chapters one through five into the unified analytics platform of this chapter. I will provide real world examples as well as name platforms that can be used in instances where a brand cannot or should not build them on their own.

---

288 https://en.wikipedia.org/wiki/Data_curation (Accessed 10 April 2019).
289 Grover, Mark, Malaska, Ted, Seidman, Jonathan, Shapira, Gwen. Hadoop Application Architectures: Designing Real-World Big Data Applications. O'Reilly Media. July 2015.
290 https://hadoopecosystemtable.github.io/ (Accessed 27 October 2017).
291 https://en.wikipedia.org/wiki/MapReduce (Accessed 27 October 2017).
[292] MSV, Janakiram. Forbes. 5 Artificial Intelligence Trends to Watch Out for in 2019. December 9, 2019. https://www.forbes.com/sites/janakirammsv/2018/12/09/5-artificial-intelligence-trends-to-watch-out-for-in-2019/#1aa963fc5618 (Accessed 9 March 2019).
293 Huang, Jensen. (2016). Accelerating AI with GPUs: A New Computing Model. Nvidia.com blog. https://blogs.nvidia.com/blog/2016/01/12/accelerating-ai-artificial-intelligence-gpus/ (Accessed 19 September 2018).
294 Components of a Convolutional Neural Network: https://developer.nvidia.com/discover/convolutional-neural-network (Accessed 19 September 2018).
295 Krizhevsky, Alex, Sutskever, Ilya, Hinton, Geoffrey E. (2012). ImageNet Classification with Deep Convolutional Neural Networks. 2012. https://papers.nips.cc/paper/4824-imagenet-classification-with-deep-convolutional-neural-networks.pdf (Accessed 8 October 2018).
296 He, Kaiming, Zhang, Xiangyu, Ren, Shaoqing, Sun, Jian. (2015). Delving deep into rectifiers: Surpassing human-level performance on ImageNet classification. arXiv:1502.01852 [cs] (2015). https://arxiv.org/pdf/1502.01852.pdf (Accessed 8 October 2018).
297 Ioffe, Sergey, Szegedy, Christian. Batch normalization: Accelerating deep network training by reducing internal covariate shift. In International Conference on Machine Learning (ICML) 448–456 (2015). https://arxiv.org/pdf/1502.03167.pdf (Accessed 8 October 2018).

298 Wang, Huazheng, Gao, Bin, Bian, Jiang, Tian, Fei, Liu, Tie-Yan. (2015). Solving Verbal Comprehension Questions in IQ Test by Knowledge-Powered Word Embedding. arXiv:1505.07909 [cs.CL] (2015).

299 Amodei, Dario, Anubhai, Rishita, Battenberg, Eric, Case, Carl, Casper, Jared, Catanzaro, Bryan, Chen, Jingdong, Chrzanowski, Mike, Coates, Adam, Diamos, Greg, Elsen, Erich, Engel, Jesse, Fan, Linxi, Fougner, Christopher, Han, Tony, Hannun, Awni, Jun, Billy, LeGresley, Patrick, Lin, Libby, Narang, Sharan, Ng, Andrew, Ozair, Sherjil, Prenger, Ryan, Raiman, Jonathan, Satheesh, Sanjeev, Seetapun, David, Sengupta, Shubho, Wang, Yi, Wang, Zhijiann, Wang, Chong, Xiao, Bo, Yogatama, Dani, Zhan, Jun, and Zhu, ZHenyao. "Deep speech 2: End-to-end speech recognition in English and Mandarin," arXiv preprint arXiv:1512.02595 (2015). http://proceedings.mlr.press/v48/amodei16.pdf (Accessed 8 October 2018).

300 Liu, Baige, Zang, Xiaoxue. (2017). Caffe2 vs. TensorFlow: Which is a Better Deep Learning Framework? Stanford University. http://cs242.stanford.edu/assets/projects/2017/liubaige-xzang.pdf (Accessed 1 May 2018).

301 Metz, Gade. (2015). Google Just Open Sourced TensorFlow, its Artificial Intelligence Engine. Wired.com. 9 November 2015. https://www.wired.com/2015/11/google-open-sources-its-artificial-intelligence-engine/ (Accessed 1 May 2018).

302 Deeplearning4j.org. Comparing Top Deep LearningFrameworks: Deeplearning4J, PyTorch, TensorFlow, Caffe, Kera, MxNet, Gluon & CNTK. https://deeplearning4j.org/compare-dl4j-tensorflow-pytorch (Accessed 3 May 2018).

303 Novet, Jordan. (2017). Facebook Open Sources Caffe2, a New Deep Learning Framework. Venturebeat. 18 April 2017. https://venturebeat.com/2017/04/18/facebook-open-sources-caffe2-a-new-deep-learning-framework/ (Accessed 1 May 2018).

304 Liu, Baige, Zang, Xiaoxue. (2017). Caffe2 vs. TensorFlow: Which is a Better Deep Learning Framework? Stanford University. http://cs242.stanford.edu/assets/projects/2017/liubaige-xzang.pdf (Accessed 1 May 2018).

305 Heller, Martin. (2019). What is Keras? The Deep Neural Network API Explained. January 28, 2019. https://www.infoworld.com/article/3336192/what-is-keras-the-deep-neural-network-api-explained.html (Accessed 15 April 2019).

306 https://en.wikipedia.org/wiki/Real-time_marketing

307 Macy, B. a. (2011). The Power of Real-Time Social Media Marketing. New York: McGraw Hill, 2011.

308 Schulte, Roy. (May 23, 2017). When do you need an Event Stream Processing Platform? Logtrust.com. https://www.logtrust.com/need-event-stream-processing-platform/ (Accessed 30 August 2017).

309 Wähner, Kai. InfoQ. Real-Time Stream Processing as Game Changer in a Big Data World with Hadoop and Data Warehouse. September 10, 2014. https://www.infoq.com/articles/stream-processing-hadoop (Accessed 14 April 2019).

310 Deng, Lei, Gao, Jerry, Vuppalapati, Chandrasekar. March 2015. Building a Big Data Analytics Service Framework for Mobile Advertising and Marketing. Online: https://www.researchgate.net/profile/Jerry_Gao/publication/273635443_Building_a_Big_Data_Analytics_Service_Framework_for_Mobile Advertising_and_Marketing/links/5508de220cf26ff55f840c31.pdf
311 https://www.hds.com/en-us/pdf/brochure/hitachi-overview-streaming-data-platform.pdf (accessed 30 December 2016)
312 Gualtieri, Mike. April 16, 2016. 15 "True" Streaming Analytics Platforms For Real-Time Everything. Forrester.com. https://go.forrester.com/blogs/16-04-16-15_true_streaming_analytics_platforms_for_real_time_everything/ (accessed 2 September 2017).
313 SAS. The Artificial Intelligence of Things. SAS White Paper. https://www.sas.com/en_us/webinars/artificial-intelligence-of-things.html (Accessed 9 February 2019).
314 Newman, Peter. (2017). IoT Report: How Internet of Things Technology Is Now Reaching Mainstream Companies and Consumers. Business Insider. July 27, 2018. https://www.businessinsider.com/internet-of-things-report (Accessed 9 February 2019).
315 Marr, Bernard. August 23, 2016. Will 'Analytics on The Edge' Be the Future of Big Data? Online: http://www.forbes.com/sites/bernardmarr/2016/08/23/will-analytics-on-the-edge-be-the-future-of-big-data/#124af7ea2b09
316 Ashton, K. (2009, June 22). That 'Internet of Things' Thing. Retrieved from RFID Journal: http://www.rfidjournal.com/articles/view?4986
317 Morgan, J. (2014, May 13). A Simple Explanation of 'the Internet of Things'. Retrieved from Forbes.com: http://www.forbes.com/sites/jacobmorgan/2014/05/13/simple-explanation-internet-things-that-anyone-can-understand/
318 Silver, Vernon. (2018). Putin soccer ball for Trump had transmitter chip, logo indicates. Bloomberg.com. 25 July 2018. https://www.bloomberg.com/news/articles/2018-07-25/putin-soccer-ball-for-trump-had-transmitter-chip-logo-indicates
319 Gartner. (2013, December 12). Gartner Says the Internet of Things Installed Base Will Grow to 26 Billion Units By 2020. Retrieved from Gartner.com: http://www.gartner.com/newsroom/id/2636073 (22 November 2017).
320 Lenz, Gadi. September 22, 2015. Datanami.com The Data of Things: How Edge Analytics and IoT Go Hand in Hand. https://www.datanami.com/2015/09/22/the-data-of-things-how-edge-analytics-and-iot-go-hand-in-hand/ (22 November 2017).
321 Tableau. (2017) 2018 Top 10 Business Intelligence Trends. Tableau. https://www.tableau.com/sites/default/files/pages/838266_2018_bi_trends_whitepaper_1.pdf (Accessed 17 November 2017).
322 Wadhwa, T. (2013, June 3). CrowdOptic and L'Oreal to make history by demonstrating how augmented reality can be a shared experience. Retrieved from Forbes.com: http://www.forbes.com/sites/tarunwadhwa/2013/06/03/crowdoptic-and-loreal-are-about-to-make-history-by-demonstrating-how-augmented-reality-can-be-a-shared-experience/ (22 November 2017).

323 http://www.webopedia.com/TERM/A/Augmented_Reality.html (Accessed 13 November 2017).
324 Gartner. October 18, 2016. Gartner's Top 10 Strategic Technology Trends for 2017. http://www.gartner.com/smarterwithgartner/gartners-top-10-technology-trends-2017/
325 Gartner. 2014, January 14). Gartner believes augmented reality will become an important workplace tool. Retrieved from Gartner.com: http://www.gartner.com/newsroom/id/2649315 (22 November 2017).
326 Moore, J. (2012). Augmented reality: expanding the user experience. Retrieved from Digital Innovation Gazette: http://www.digitalinnovationgazette.com/uiux/augmented_reality_app_development/#axzz2z8tFKN00 (22 November 2017).
327 https://en.wikipedia.org/wiki/Pokémon_Go (22 November 2017).
328 Adobe Communications Team. (2017). Adobe. A Digital Shopping Experience: Coming Soon to a Mall Near You. May 25, 2017. https://theblog.adobe.com/a-digital-shopping-experience-coming-soon-to-a-mall-near-you/ (Accessed 9 March 2019).

CHAPTER SEVEN: THE A.I. MARKETER

"You can't win in the digital era with industrial-age technology."
~Adobe

Overview

One of the first things that the *A.I. Marketer* must do is to build a master marketing record for each of its customer. The *A.I. Marketer* should use Master Data Management (MDM) techniques to communicate important customer preference information to staff that sit at the company's customer interaction points, wherever this information is needed. MDM is the processes, governance, policies, standards and tools that consistently define and manage the critical data of an organization to provide a single point of reference.

One of the benefits of using MDM is that when that single point of reference is a customer profile, the master data can ensure that the treatment of a customer is consistent, and that preference information reaches all customer points of contact. In his Adobe blog *The Expanding Role of Marketing—and Artificial Intelligence—in Experience Business*, David Newman argues that, "Every employee must have the same goal: delivering compelling, personalized, and seamless experiences that enable long-time emotional connections and loyalty to the brand."[56]

As previously mentioned, this allows the brand to test scenarios and options for the website, as well as develop personalized responses for individuals for a multitude of scenarios. The system should include a combination of social listening, analytics, content publication and distribution, and tracking, as well as a workflow and rules engine that is geared around strong governance. All these applications are built to ultimately feed a master marketing profile—a centralized customer record that pulls in all data based on digital activity that can be identified through a single customer ID. Utilizing clickstream analysis and real-time streaming, a marketer can help build a Master Marketing Record for each customer in real-time. This allows the brand to test scenarios and options for the website, as well as develop personalized responses for individuals.

Once a master marketing record has been created, brands can build cognitive styles dimensions on their customers. As previously mentioned, a person's cognitive style is a "preferred way of gathering, processing, and evaluating information."[86] These styles "might include impulsive (makes decisions quickly) versus deliberative (explores options in depth before making a decision), visual (prefers images) versus verbal (prefers text and numbers), or analytic (wants all details) versus holistic (just the bottom line)."[85] The brand should quantify all of its website content and click actions to build functional displays for each customer morph type.

Heller says that one of the keys to personalization at scale is internal structure.[79] He expects companies in 2019 to work on "building agile marketing execution models in which cross-functional teams can experiment, leveraging the data and technology stack to capture value."[79]

All of company's information can be fed into a data lake and a brand's EDW, where it can be utilized by a multitude of operational departments, including security, call center/customer service, HR, marketing, social media marketing, customer management, all the way up to the top executive branch, including individuals in the C-level suite.

One of the main goals of this book is to show brands how to bring more work in-house. If companies can utilize AI to automate many of their current processes, employees can be retrained to work in areas that are more creative and, hopefully, more interesting for them. The workforce of 2025 will be far different from the workforce of today and brands need to prepare themselves for these radical changes today.

In their article *Data-Driven Transformation: Accelerate at Scale Now*[329], Gourévitch et al. argue that, "Data-driven transformation is becoming a question of life or death in most industries." "Most CEOs recognize the power of data-driven transformation. They certainly would like the 20% to 30% EBITDA gains that their peers are racking up by using fresh, granular data in sales, marketing, supply chain, manufacturing, and R&D," claim Gourévitch et al.[329] What's not lost on these CEOs is the fact that today the top five companies with the highest market capitalization worldwide are all data-driven, tech companies—Apple, Alphabet (Google), Microsoft, Amazon, and Facebook.[329] Five years ago, only one of these tech companies was in the top five (Apple), whereas ten years ago only one was in the top ten (Microsoft).[329]

CEOs are correct in worrying about how their organizations are going to handle a tenfold increase in company data when their managers are already complaining about a lack of data skills and overburdened IT systems today.[329] "Transformations should start with pilots that pay off in weeks or months, followed by a plan for tackling high-priority use cases, and finishing with a program for building long-term capabilities," Gourévitch et al. recommend.[329]

"It starts with small-scale, rapid digitization efforts that lay the foundation for the broader transformation and generate returns to help fund later phases of the effort," Gourévitch et al. advocate.[329] "In the second and third phases, companies draw on knowledge from their early wins to create a roadmap for companywide transformation, 'industrialize' data and analytics, and build systems and capabilities to execute new data-driven strategies and processes."[329]

In terms of infrastructure and data transformation, Gourévitch et al. state that companies need to ask the following questions[329]:

> "Can our current infrastructure support our future data value map? Should we make or buy? Should we go to the cloud? Do we need a data lake? What role should our legacy IT systems play in our data transformation? The company should design a data platform (or data lake) that can accommodate its product map and should use that platform to progressively transform its legacy systems."

"To progressively transform its legacy system," is an important concept here because it is imperative that companies don't bite off more than they can chew when they decide to embrace a data-driven culture.

While the company architects the transformation roadmap, it needs to begin industrializing its data and analytics.[329] As Gourévitch et al. explain, "This means setting up a way to standardize the creation and management of data-based systems and processes so that the output is replicable, efficient, and reliable."[329] Digital systems need to have all the attributes of industrial machinery, including reliability and consistency.[329]

For analytics, a flexible open architecture that can be updated continuously and enhanced with emerging technologies works best.[329] "Rather than embracing an end-to-end data architecture, companies should adopt a use-case-driven approach, in which the architecture evolves to meet the requirements of each new initiative," advise Gourévitch et al.[329] "The data governance and analytics functions should collaborate to create a simplified data environment; this will involve defining authorized sources of data and aggressively rationalizing redundant repositories and data flows," recommend Gourévitch at al.[329]

Brands should always keep in mind Adobe's quote that, "You can't win in the digital era with industrial-age technology." To prepare an organization for a digitized future, a company "needs to move on four fronts: creating new roles and governance processes, instilling a data-centric culture, adopting new ways of working, and cultivating the necessary talent and skills."[329]

Change starts at the top and senior leaders need to both buy into and adopt data-driven objectives, as well as instill a data-driven culture in every department throughout the organization.[329] Gourévitch et al. recommend that top management "set up data councils to extend the work to all sectors of the organization and to carry it out more effectively."[329] "The company should promote data awareness by using data champions to disseminate data-driven practices," state Gourévitch et al.[329]

"Not everyone needs to become steeped in data analytics or learn to code in order for digital transformation to work. However, everyone does need to adopt a less risk-averse attitude," recommend Gourévitch et al.[329] The writers believe brands should embrace the software company model that utilizes a test-and-learn philosophy that accepts failure and is constantly changing–and learning.[329] The Japanese have a concept known as *Kaizen*—continuous incremental improvement—and it is an idea that should be kept in mind when a company steps into the data-driven world.

Businesses can also foster the desired cultural change through organizational moves, "such as creating internal startup units where employees can focus on experimentation or co-locating data labs within operating units."[329] "The company can also promote the new culture by using cross-functional teams that share data across silos, thereby encouraging openness and collaboration throughout the organization," advise Gourévitch et al.[329]

For any data-based transformation to succeed, a company needs talent with the right skills to execute data-driven strategies and manage data-based operations.[329]

Brands should be inspired by the idea of using data to make better decisions, to create stronger customer bonds, and to digitize all sorts of processes to improve performance. They should also be motivated "by fear that they won't be able to keep up with competitors who are ahead of them in data-driven digital transformation."[329]

Some caution is due here; sweeping, company-wide change to go digital can easily lead to counterproductive overreaching.[329] In this case, the contest will not necessarily be won by making huge bets.[329] As Gourévitch et al. conclude, "The winners will be agile, pragmatic, and disciplined. They will move fast and capture quick wins, but they will also carefully plan a transformation roadmap to optimize performance in the functions and operations that create the most value, while building the technical capabilities and resources to sustain the transformation."[329]

AI is a problem solver. One of the examples I give in my talks on AI is the idea of giving AI a goal to solve and then setting it off on its own to get an answer. For example, when it comes to marketing, the question for AI to solve might be, "How can I send an offer to a customer to give it the best opportunity of it both being opened and utilized?" Now, the variables to include here would be, what would be the best offer to send, what would be the best time to send, what would be the best channel to send it on, and, who knows, perhaps there is a way to add social activity to increase the odds of the offer being used? Perhaps the customer has a penchant for tweeting and the system notices he tweets in the early evening and the system discovers a strong correlation between tweets and the opening of email offers in the past. The natural conclusion could be that the customer arrives home, sits down at his computer, goes through his email and jumps on his social channels. The system then watches for his tweet and then sends the offer.

Figure 25 lists out a few other business questions that AI or deep learning can be used to solve, as well as particular retail example outputs.

WHAT PROBLEM ARE YOU SOLVING?

Defining the AI/DL task

INPUTS	BUSINESS QUESTIONS	AI / DL TASK	RETAIL EXAMPLE OUTPUTS
Text data	Is "it" present or not?	Detection	Targeted Ads
Images	What type of thing is "it"?	Classification	Basket Analysis
Video	To what extent is "it" present?	Segmentation	Build 360 degree customer view
Audio	What is the likely outcome?	Prediction	Sentiment & Behavior Recognition
	What will likely satisfy the objective?	Recommendations	Recommendation Engine

Figure 25: Defining the AI/Deep Learning task

At the beginning of the book, I broke down the general use cases for AI into five sections—text, image, video, audio, sound, and time series—and, in the next section, I will break down the first four of these as well as explain how the *A.I. Marketer* would use them.

Text

Text use cases break down into several different areas, including chatbots, NLP, sentiment analysis, augmented search, and language translation.

Clothing retailer the North Face has implemented an IBM Watson recommendation engine for customers who want to buy outerwear.[330] This solution, called XPS, uses a chatbot interface to ask a series of questions so that it can match the customers' requirements with the product line.[330] According to North Face, 60% of the users clicks through to the recommended product.[330]

Not to be outdone by IBM, Amazon has several of its own AI text tools. According to Amazon, "Lex is a service for building conversational interfaces into any application using voice and text. Amazon Lex provides the advanced deep learning functionalities of automatic speech recognition (ASR) for converting speech to text, and natural language understanding (NLU) to recognize the intent of the text, to enable you to build applications with highly engaging user experiences and lifelike conversational interactions."[331] Amazon Lex contains the same deep learning technologies that power Amazon Alexa and they are now available to any developer. These will enable users to quickly and easily build sophisticated, natural language, conversational chatbots.[332]

Amazon Transcribe "is an automatic speech recognition (ASR) service that makes it easy for developers to add speech-to-text capability to their applications."[333] Using the Amazon Transcribe API, brands can analyze audio files stored in Amazon S3 and have the service return a text file of the transcribed speech. Brands can also send a live audio stream to Amazon Transcribe and receive a stream of transcripts in real time.

Amazon Transcribe can transcribe customer service calls and generate subtitles on audio and video content. The service can transcribe audio files stored in common formats, like WAV and MP3, with time stamps for every word so that you can easily locate the audio in the original source by searching for the text. Amazon Transcribe is continually learning and improving to keep pace with the evolution of language.

Amazon Comprehend is "a natural language processing (NLP) service that uses machine learning to find insights and relationships in text. No machine learning experience required."[334]

"There is often a treasure trove of potential sitting in a company's unstructured data. Customer emails, support tickets, product reviews, social media, even advertising copy represents insights into customer sentiment that can be put to work for a business," says Amazon.[334] Machine learning is "particularly good at accurately identifying specific items of interest inside vast swathes of text (such as finding company names in analyst reports)."[334] "Amazon Comprehend can learn the sentiment hidden inside language (identifying negative reviews, or positive customer interactions with customer service agents), at almost limitless scale."[334]

Amazon Comprehend "identifies the language of the text; extracts key phrases, places, people, brands, or events; understands how positive or negative the text is; analyzes text using tokenization and parts of speech; and automatically organizes a collection of text files by topic."[334]

In his article *Turning Up Your Brand's Voice to Reach the Most Advanced Customers*[335], Pini Yakuel explains why digital assistants are unique to every other channel when it comes to personalization—they cut through the noise. "Yes, emails can be personalized, just like paid search and social ads, but they share their real estate with thousands of other pieces of content. When there are 20 personalized messages asking for your attention, which one will consumers go for?" ask Yakuel.[335]

"Like any other marketing channel, the key to winning with digital assistants lies in the deep knowledge of the purchase lifecycle customers go through. Delving into the desire to know, go, do and buy that consumers have will deliver success," says Yakuel.[335]

"Micro-moments are defined as intent-rich moments when a person turns to their device to act on a need through the conversational nature of queries to digital assistants. Analyzing these intent-rich moments and acting upon them might be the gate to showing up as the preferred answer," says Yakuel.[335]

Brands should always keep in mind "that retention through digital assistants works so well because consumers want to make life easier for themselves every chance they get."[335] "For example, smart fridges that know when we're running out of food and talk to digital assistants are already out there. Digital assistants will likely broaden their reach across the broad spectrum of consumer needs to anticipate upcoming purchases," says Yakuel.[335]

"Whether by diving into data or by directly speaking with existing and past customers, marketers should always learn what questions and online behavior drives folks toward their brands. Analyze their pain points, and focus on creating content that uses their phrases and makes their lives easier," advises Yakuel.[335] "The better you get at this, the more likely you are to be the digital assistant's chosen option," he concludes.[335]

Chatbots

In its *14 Powerful Chatbot Platforms*[336], Maruti Tech lists some of the best chatbots publishing platform and development platform for brands to use. According to Maruti Tech, a "chatbot publishing platform is a medium through which the chatbot can be accessed and used by the users."[336] "A chat bot development platform, on the other hand is a tool/ application through which one can create a chatbot," says Maruti Tech.[336] These chatbot platforms let users add more functionality to a bot by creating a flow, machine learning capabilities, API integration, etc.[336] These chatbot platforms are simple to use, and users don't need to have deep technical knowledge or programming skills as many come with drag-and-drop functionality.[336] Please note, there aren't 14 platforms here as several have been discontinued or been acquired, which is a testament to how quickly this space changes.

Chatfuel

Calling itself "the leading bot platform for creating AI chatbots for Facebook,"[337] Chatfuel (chatfuel.com) claims that 46% of Messenger bots run on its platform.[337] No coding is required with Chatfuel, which "provides features like adding content cards and sharing it to your followers automatically, gathering information inside Messenger chats with forms."[337] Chatfuel also uses AI to script interactive conversations.[337]

The platform is completely free for anyone to build a bot, but after the bot reaches 100K conversations/month users have to subscribe as a premium customer.[337] Chatfuel's impressive client list includes multinational companies like Adidas, MTV, British Airways, and Volkswagen.

Botsify

"Let your bot chat like a human" is Botsify's (botsify.com) tagline[338] and it is another popular Facebook Messenger chatbot platform that uses a drag and drop template to create bots.[337] Botsify offers features like easy integrations via plugins, smart AI, machine learning and analytics integration.[336] Botsify's platform does allow seamless transition from a bot to a human.[336] First bot is free, but any others are charged for thereafter.[336]

Flow XO

According to its website (flowxo.com)[339], "Flow XO is a powerful automation product that allows you to quickly and simply build incredible chatbots that help you to communicate and engage with your customers across a wide range of different sites, applications and social media platforms." It is the only chatbot platform to provide over 100 integrations.[336] It boasts an easy to use and visual editor.[336] Flow XO's platform allows users to build one bot and implement it across multiple platforms.[336] In terms of pricing, users are limited to a certain number of conversations, surpassing that requires a subscription.[336]

Motion.ai

Recently purchased by Hubspot, Motion.ai was a chatbot platform that helped users to visually build, train, and deploy chatbots on FB Messenger, Slack, Smooch or a company's website.[336] Motion.ai let users diagram a conversation flow like a flowchart to get a visual overview of the outcomes of a bot query.[336] The bot could be connected to a messaging service like Slack and Facebook Messenger. Motion.ai allowed Node.js deployment directly from its interface along with several other integrations.[336] Many of these features are probably still available, but they will done via Hubspot.

Chatty People

This platform has predefined chatbots with templates for e-commerce, customer support, and F&B businesses.[336] When users select the e-commerce chat bot, he or she can simply add products, Q&A information as well as some general settings.[336] The platform even includes PayPal and Stripe API integration.[336]

According to Maruti Tech, "The chatbot platform's simplicity makes it ideal for entrepreneurs and marketers in smaller companies."[336] While its technology makes it suitable for enterprise customers, users can make a simple bot answering customer service questions or integrating it with Shopify to potentially monetize one's Facebook fan pages. Chatty People was acquired by MobileMonkey in 2018 and can now be found at mobilemonkey.com.

QnA bot

Microsoft has created QnA (qnamaker.ai) bot for the same reason as its name suggests, i.e., for answering a series of user questions.[336] The URL FAQ page must be shared with the service and the bot will be created in a few minutes using the information on the FAQ page and the structured data.[336]

Furthermore, the bot can be integrated with Microsoft Cognitive Services to enable the bot to see, hear, interpret and interact in more human ways.[336] QnA Maker also seamlessly integrates with other APIs and can scale to be a know-it-all part of a bigger bot.[336]

Recast.ai

In January 2019, Recast.AI was integrated into the SAP portfolio and renamed SAP Conversational AI.[340] This bot building platform enables users to train, build and run their bots.[336] By creating and managing the conversation logic with Bot Builder, SAP Conversational AI's visual flow management interface and API lets users build bots that understand predefined queries as well as quickly set up responses.[336] Messaging metrics and bot analytics tools are also included.[336]

BotKit

Their rather alliterate tagline is, "Building Blocks for Building Bots" and it is a toolkit that gives users a helping hand to develop bots for FB Messenger, Slack, Twilio, and more.[336] "BotKit can be used to create clever, conversational applications which map out the way that real humans speak," says Maruti Tech.[336] "This essential detail differentiates from some of its other chatbot toolkit counterparts," they add.[336]

"BotKit includes a variety of useful tools, like Botkit Studio, boilerplate app starter kits, a core library, and plugins to extend your bot capabilities. Botkit is community-supported open-source software that is available on GitHub," says Maruti Tech.[336] Online, the company can be found at: botkit.ai.

ChatterOn

On its website (chatteron.io), ChatterOn claims it can help users build a chatbot in five minutes. ChatterOn is a bot development platform which gives users the required tools to build Facebook Messenger chatbots without any coding.[336] ChatterOn's instructions are as follows: "build the bot flow (each interaction with a user has to have a goal that the user has to be taken to the next chat) and setup the AI by entering a few examples of the expected conversation between the user and bot."[336]

India's first full stack chatbot development platform, ChatterOn is, according to the company, "far superior in ease of development and functionalities than its international counterparts."[336] "All the bots on ChatterOn's platform are powered by a proprietary self-learning contextual AI," claims Maruti Tech.[336]

Octane AI

According to its website (octaneai.com), Octane AI "enables Shopify merchants to increase revenue with a Facebook Messenger bot that customers love."[341]

Octane AI has pre-built features that make it easy for users to add content, messages, discussions, showcase merchandise, and much more to their bot.[336] According to Octane AI, convos are conversational stories that can be shared with an audience. It's as easy as writing a blog post and the best way to increase distribution of a company's bot, at least according to Octane AI.[336] The platform also integrates with all of the popular social media channels, as well as provides real-time analytics.[336]

Converse AI

The Converse AI (converse.ai) platform has been built to handle a wide range of use cases and integrates seamlessly with Facebook Messenger and Workplace, Slack, Twilio, and Smooch. Some of its features include[336]:

- A complete UI that allows easy, code-free builds.
- Integration with multiple platforms, including complete user, request and conversation tracking.
- Inbuilt NLP parsing engine, that includes the ability to easily build conversation templates.
- Can converse while using both plain text and rich media.
- Inbuilt query and analytics engine allow for easy tracking and drill down that helps brands understand how users are engaging with the service.

GupShup

The leading smart messaging platform that handles over 4 billion messages per month, GupShup (gupshup.io) has processed over 150 billion messages in total.[336] "It offers APIs for developers to build interactive, programmable, Omni-channel messaging bots and services as well as SDKs to enable in-app and in web messaging," says Maruti Tech.[336] "Unlike plain-text messages, GupShup's innovative smart-messages contain structured data and intelligence, thus enabling advanced messaging workflows and automation," adds Maruti Tech.[336]

In conclusion, chatbot platforms are essential for the development of chatbots.[336] With the availability of such platforms, Maruti Tech argues, anyone can create a chatbot, even if they don't know how to code. However, to make an intelligent chatbot that works seamlessly, AI, machine learning and NLP are required.[336] Chatbots will undoubtedly revolutionize the future of industries by their rich features.[336] They will reduce human errors, "provide round the clock availability, eliminate the need for multiple mobile applications and make it a very seamless experience for the customer."[336]

Sentiment Analysis

In its article *Sentiment Analysis: Types, Tools, and Use Cases*[342], Altexsoft states. that the goal of sentiment analysis is "to know a user or audience opinion on a target object by analyzing a vast amount of text from various sources." "It's not only important to know social opinion about your organization, but also to define who is talking about you," says Altexsoft.[342] Measuring mention tone can also help define whether industry influencers are discussing a brand and, if so, in what context. The power of sentiment analysis software is it can do all of the above in real time and across all channels, thereby making it useful for both sentiment analysis and customer service.[342]

"You can analyze text on different levels of detail, and the detail level depends on your goals," says Altexsoft.[342] "For example, you may define an average emotional tone of a group of reviews to know what percentage of customers liked your new clothing collection," explains Altexsoft.[342] "If you need to know what visitors like or dislike about a specific garment and why, or whether they compare it with similar items by other brands, you'll need to analyze each review sentence with a focus on specific aspects and use or specific keywords," add Altexsoft.[342]

When a brand wants to analyze sentiment, it first needs to gather all relevant brand mentions into one document.[342] Selection criteria must be carefully considered–should mentions be time-limited, should only one language be used, should specific locations be locked in, etc., etc.[342] Data must then be prepared for analysis, read, cleansed, and any irrelevant content should be excluded from the analysis.[342] Once the data has been prepared, full analysis can begin sentiment extracted.[342] Of course, since hundreds of thousands or even millions of mentions may need analysis, the best practice is to automate this tedious work with software and many of the tools I have mentioned throughout this book can help.[342] I have also included a list of social media monitoring tools at the end of this section.

Altexsoft mentions various customer experience software, such as InMoment and Clarabridge that "collect feedback from numerous sources, alert on mentions in real-time, analyze text, and visualize results."[342] "Text analysis platforms (e.g. DiscoverText, IBM Watson Natural Language Understanding, Google Cloud Natural Language, or Microsoft Text Analytics API) have sentiment analysis in their feature set," adds Altexsoft.[342]

"InMoment provides five products that together make a customer experience optimization platform," explains Altexsoft.[342] "One of them, Voice of a Customer, allows businesses to collect and analyze customer feedback in a text, video, and voice form. The number of data sources is sufficient and includes surveys, social media, CRM, etc.," says Altexsoft.[342]

Clarabridge is a CEM platform that "pulls and analyzes text from chats, survey platforms, blogs, forums, and review sites," notes Altexsoft.[342] "Users can also gain insights from emails, employee and agent notes, call recordings and Interactive Voice Response (IVR) surveys: The system can convert them into text."[342] Clarabridge provides social media listening as well.[342] According to Altexsoft, "The system considers industry and source, understanding the meaning and context of every comment. Sentiment analysis results display on an 11-point scale. Users can modify sentiment scores to be more business-specific if needed."[342]

Another useful platform is DiscoverText, "a cloud-based collaborative text analytics system for researchers, entrepreneurs, and governments."[342] "Capterra users note the solution is great for importing/retrieving, filtering, and analyzing data from various sources, including Twitter, SurveyMonkey, emails, and spreadsheets," says Altexsoft.[342]

IBM Watson Natural Language Understanding is a set of advanced text analytics systems that supports analysis in 13 languages.[342] "Analyzing text with this service, users can extract such metadata as concepts, entities, keywords, as well as categories and relationships," says Altexsoft.[342] "It also allows for defining industry and domain to which a text belongs, semantic roles of sentence parts, a writer's emotions and sentiment change along the document," says Altexsoft.[342] Tools for developers to build chatbots and other NLP solutions are provided using IBM Watson services.[342]

"Microsoft Text Analytics API users can extract key phrases, entities (e.g. people, companies, or locations), sentiment, as well as define in which among 120 supported languages their text is written," explains Altexsoft.[342] "The Sentiment Analysis API returns results using a sentiment score from 0 (negative) to 1 (positive)," says Altexsoft.[342] The software can detect sentiment in English, Spanish, German, and French texts.[342] Developers recommend "the analysis be done on the whole document and advise using documents consisting of one or two sentences to achieve a higher accuracy."[342]

Google Cloud Natural Language API can "extract sentiment from emails, text documents, news articles, social media, and blog posts."[342] It can also extract "insights from audio files, scanned documents, and documents in other languages when combined with other cloud services."[342] "The tool assigns a sentiment score and magnitude for every sentence, making it easy to see what a customer liked or disliked most, as well as distinguish sentiment sentences from non-sentiment sentences," notes Altexsoft.[342]

Competitive analysis that involves sentiment analysis can also help brands understand their strengths and weaknesses and maybe assist in finding ways to stand out from the crowd.[342] In times of crisis, sentiment analysis can be instrumental in helping douse social media crisis flames.

Altexsoft believes, "There is one thing for sure you and your competitors have in common—a target audience."[342] Brands can track and research how society evaluates competitors just as they analyze attitudes towards their business. "What do customers value most about other industry players? Is there anything competitors lack or do wrong? Which channels do clients use to engage with other companies?"—these are all important questions that sentiment analysis help answer.[342] Brands can use this knowledge to improve "communication and marketing strategies, overall service, and provide services and products customers would appreciate."[342]

Most brands grapple with the question of how to bring a desired product to market?[342] The best approach, claims Altexsoft, is to ask people what they want.[342] Successful companies build a minimum viable product (MVP), gather early feedback, and continuously try to improve a product, even after its release.[342] "Feedback data comes from surveys, social media, and forums, and interaction with customer support," argues Altexsoft.[342] Sentiment analysis can be extremely handy here.[342] It helps brands learn about product advantages and disadvantages.[342] Armed with strong sentiment analysis results, "a product development team will know exactly how to deliver a product that customers would buy and enjoy."[342]

Using sentiment analysis, marketers can study consumer behavior patterns in real time, which can help to predict future brand trends.[342] "Another benefit of sentiment analysis is that it doesn't require heavy investment and allows for gathering reliable and valid data since its user-generated," explains Altexsoft.[342] Sentiment analysis lets businesses harness an enormous amount of free data to help them understand their customers' attitude towards their brand.[342] This analysis can take customer care to the next level.

Sentiment Analysis Tools

Table 12 lists the Social Media Tools and websites available to business users to track engagement and customer feedback.

Name	Comments
Board Reader	BoardReader allows users to search multiple message boards simultaneously, allowing users to share information in a truly global sense. Boardreader is focused on creating the largest repository of searchable information for our users. Users can find answers to their questions from others who share similar interests. Our goal is to allow our

Name	Comments
	users to search the "human to human" discussions that exist on the Internet.
Buffer	Buffer makes your life easier with a smarter way to schedule the great content you find. Fill up your Buffer at one time in the day and Buffer automagically posts them for you through the day. Simply keep that Buffer topped up to have a consistent social media presence all day round, all week long. Get deeper analytics than if you just post to social networks directly.
Buzzsumo	Analyze what content performs best for any topic or competitor. Find the key influencers to promote your content: • Discover the most shared content across all social networks and run detailed analysis reports. • Find influencers in any topic area, review the content they share and amplify. • Be the first to see content mentioning your keyword; or when an author or competitor publishes new content. • Track your competitor's content performance and do detailed comparisons.
Commun.it	Can help you organize, increase, and manage your followers, and can do so across multiple accounts and profiles. At a glance you can see different aspects of your community management, like the latest tweets from your stream and which new followers might appreciate a welcome message.
Crowdfire	Crowdfire is a powerful phone app and online website that helps you grow your Twitter and Instagram account reach. This tool has a variety of functions designed to understand your social analytics as well as manage your social publishing.
Cyfe	Cyfe is an all-in-one dashboard software that helps you monitor and analyze data scattered across all your online services like Google Analytics, Salesforce, AdSense, MailChimp, Facebook, WordPress and more from one single location in real-time.
Fanpage Karma	Shows a variety of valuable information related to your Facebook page, such as growth, engagement, service and response time, and of course Karma (a weighted engagement value). FanKarma also provides insight into Twitter and YouTube; the latter could be particularly valuable if you're creating a video marketing strategy.
Followerwonk	Followerwonk is a cool social media analytics tool thet lets you explore and grow your social graph. Dig deeper into Twitter analytics: followers, their locations, when do they tweet. Find and connect with influencers in your niche. Use visualizations to compare your social graph to competitors.
Google Alerts	Google Alerts are email updates of the latest relevant Google results (blogs, news, etc.) based on your searches. Enter the topic you wish to monitor, then click preview to see the type of results you'll receive. Some handy uses of Google Alerts include: monitoring a developing news story and keeping current on a competitor or industry.
Google Trends	Trends allows you to compare search terms and websites. With Google Trends you can get insights into the traffic and geographic visitation

THE A.I. MARKETER

Name	Comments
	patterns of websites or keywords. You can compare data for up to five websites and view related sites and top searches for each one.
Hootsuite	Monitor and post to multiple social networks, including Facebook and Twitter. Create custom reports from over 30 individual report modules to share with clients and colleagues. Track brand sentiment, follower growth, plus incorporate Facebook Insights and Google analytics. Draft and schedule messages to send at a time your audience is most likely to be online. HootSuite has the dashboard for your iPhone, iPad, BlackBerry and Android.
HowSocialable	Monitor and post to multiple social networks, including Facebook and Twitter. Create custom reports from over 30 individual report modules to share with clients and colleagues. Track brand sentiment, follower growth, plus incorporate Facebook Insights and Google analytics. Draft and schedule messages to send at a time your audience is most likely to be online. HootSuite has the dashboard for your iPhone, iPad, BlackBerry and Android.
Iconosquare	Key metrics about your Instagram account. Number of likes received, your most liked photos ever, your average number of likes and comments per photo, your follower growth charts and more advanced analytics. Track lead conversations, send private message as on Twitter, and improve communication with your followers.
Klear	Social media monitoring, analytics and reporting. Influencer marketing, find and create relationships with the top influencers in your sector and build your community. Competitive analysis tracks your social media landscape, see what's working for them and develop your strategy.
Klout	Klout's mission is to help every individual understand and leverage their influence. Klout measures influence in Twitter to find the people the world listens to. It analyzes content to identify the top influencers.
Kred	Kred is a social-media scoring system that seeks to measure a person's online influence. Kred, which was created by the San Francisco-based social analytics firm PeopleBrowsr, attempts to also measure a person or company's engagement, or as they call it, outreach. PeopleBrowsr hopes that that combination can offer a more informed metric for non-celebrities like entrepreneurs and those whom they follow and look to for advice.
LikeAlyzer	This Facebook analysis tool comes up with stats and insights into your page and begins every report with a list of recommendations. Keep track of where your Facebook page stands compared to other pages by following the comparison to average page rank, industry-specific page rank, and rank of similar brands.
Mention	Mention prides itself on "going beyond Google Alerts" to track absolutely anywhere your name or your company might be mentioned online. When you subscribe to Mention's daily email you get all these wayward hits right in your inbox, and the Web dashboard even flags certain mentions as high priority.
Mentionmap	Explore your Twitter network. Discover which people interact the most and what they're talking about. It's also a great way to find relevant people to follow. The visualization runs right in your browser and displays data from Twitter. Mentionmap loads user's tweets and finds the people and hashtags they talked about the most. In this data visualization,

Name	Comments
	mentions become connections and discussions between multiple users emerge as clusters.
Must Be Present	Built by the team at Sprout Social, Must Be Present searches your Twitter account to find how quickly you respond to mentions. Their engagement reports place you in a percentile based on other accounts so you can see how you stack up to the speed of others.
NeedTagger	A super-powered Twitter search tool, NeedTagger runs language filters and keyword searches to determine which Twitter users might need your products or services. The tool shows you real-time search results and sends a daily email digest of new finds.
NutshellMail	Collects your activity on Facebook, LinkedIn, and Twitter (and even places like Yelp and Foursquare) to provide an email overview of your accounts. You set how often and when you want to receive the recap emails. Put it to use: If you have a weekly metrics plan you can have NutshellMail send a message once a week with an overview of your accounts. You can then extract the data and insights straight into your weekly report.
Omgili	Omgili helps you find interesting and current discussions, news stories and blog posts. Direct access to live data from hundreds of thousands of forums, news and blogs. Very easy to use, no signup for web interface.
Pinterest Analytics	Find out how many people are pinning from your website, seeing your pins, and clicking your content. Pick a time-frame to see how your numbers trend over time. Get better at creating Pins and boards with metrics from your Pinterest profile. Learn how people use the Pin It button on your site to add Pins. See how people interact with your Pins from whatever device they use. Get a glance at your all-time highest-performing Pins.
Pluggio	Pluggio is a web-based social media tool to help marketers easily grow and manage their social media profiles (Facebook and Twitter). It includes a suite of tools to organize and keep track of multiple accounts, get more followers, and automate the finding and publishing of excellent targeted content.
Postific	The full set of social media tools. Post content to over 10 social networks with one single click of a button. Get real time click-through statistics with your domain name. Measure and analyze the best results from your social posts. Monitor the social media conversations that are important for your business.
Quintly	Quintly is the professional social media monitoring and analytics solution to track and compare the performance of your social media marketing activities. Whether you are using Facebook, Twitter or both, Quintly monitors and visualizes your social media marketing success. Benchmark your numbers against your competitors or best practice examples.
Sentiment	Sentiment was born in 2007 and now boasts a team of bright enthusiastic people dedicated to provide the best social customer service and engagement platform for business.
SocialMention	SocialMention tracks areas such as sentiment, passion, reach, and strength to not just tell you what's being said about your search but how those reactions feel. While you track your brand or yourself, you can also see how your sentiment changes over time.
Social Rank	Identifies your top 10 followers in three specific areas: Best Followers, Most Engaged, and Most Valuable. Your most engaged followers are

Name	Comments
	those who interact with you most often (replies, retweets, and favorites); your most valuable followers are the influential accounts; and your best followers are a combination of the two. Social Rank will run the numbers for free and show you the results today, then follow-up each month with an email report.
Social Oomph	Schedule tweets, track keywords, extended Twitter profiles, save and reuse drafts, view @mentions and retweets, purge your DM inbox, personal status feed — your own tweet engine, unlimited accounts.
This tracking tool	Keeps track of your hashtag campaign or keyword on Twitter, Instagram, or Facebook with a full dashboard of analytics, demographics, and influencers.
Tip Top	TipTop Search is a Twitter-based search engine that helps you discover the best and most current advice, opinions, answers for any search, and also real people to directly engage and share experiences with. A search on any topic reveals people's emotions and experiences about it, as well as other concepts that they are discussing in connection with the original search.
Topsy	A powerful search engine for Twitter content. Want to know how a certain term is being used on Twitter? You can search links, tweets, photos, videos, and influencers.
Twazzup	Offers real-time monitoring and analytics for Twitter on any name, keyword, or hashtag you choose. The Twazzup results page delivers interesting insights like the top influencers for your keyword and which top links are associated with your search.
Tweepi	Has a number of useful Twitter features, many of which fall into a couple categories: managing your followers and supercharging who you're following. For management, you can unfollow in batches those who don't follow you back, and you can bulk follow another account's complete list of followers or who they're following.
Tweetcaster	A Twitter management tool for iOS and Android devices and provides the basics of what you'd expect from a Twitter dashboard plus a few fun extras: enhanced search and lists, hiding unwanted tweets, and photo effects for your images.
Tweetdeck	Lets you track, organize, and engage with your followers through a customizable dashboard where you can see at a glance the activity from different lists, followers, hashtags, and more.
TweetReach	Shows you the reach and exposure of the tweets you send, collecting data on who retweets you and the influence of each. Identify which of your tweets has spread the furthest (and why) and then try to repeat the formula with future tweets.
TwitterCounter	Twitter Counter is the number one site to track your Twitter stats. Twitter Counter provides statistics of Twitter usage and tracks over 14 million users. Twitter Counter also offers a variety of widgets and buttons that people can add to their blogs, websites or social network profiles to show recent Twitter visitors and number of followers.
Twtrland	Provides a snapshot of your Twitter profile and can even track Facebook and Instagram as well. Two of Twtrland's most helpful tools are a live

Name	Comments
	count of how many followers are currently online and advanced search functionality that includes keywords, locations, and companies. Local companies can perform a location search to see which area accounts are most popular and potentially worth following.
SumAll	SumAll is a powerful social media analytics tool that allows our customers to view all of their data in one simple, easy-to-use visualization. Social media, e-commerce, advertising, e-mail, and traffic data all come together to provide a complete view of your activity.
ViralWoot	Pin Alert feature lets you track what are people pinning from your website, who is pinning the most and what images from your website are trending on Pinterest. Thousands of social media marketers and agencies use Viralwoot for their clients. You can manage & grow multiple Pinterest accounts with a single Viralwoot account.
WhosTalkin	WhosTalkin is a social media monitoring tool that lets you search for conversations surrounding the topics that you care about most. Whether it be your favorite sports team, food, celebrity, or brand name; Whostalkin will help you find the conversations that are important to you. WhosTalkin search and sorting algorithms combine data taken from over 60 of the most popular social media sites.

Table 12: Social Media Tools
Source: Dreamgrow.com[343]

Augmented Search

In his article *How to use AI for link building and improve your search rankings*[344], Kevin Rowe claims that "AI's applications in the search engine optimization (SEO) world are continuing to expand to new horizons." Besides the Y Combinator-backed RankScience, which uses thousands of A/B tests to determine how best to positively influence search engine rankings, it is unlikely that a complete handling of SEO by AI will catch on any time soon.[344] While no software exists that leverages AI to build links, brands can still use multiple types of software for various stages of the link building process.[344] These include[344]:

- Data collection. NLP tools can be used to determine if the sites are contextually relevant and keyword relevant.
- Site analysis. AI can determine if a particular site will predictably have an impact on rankings.

This means that AI can be used to augment, automate or automatize processes, claims Rowe.[344] Link building can't specifically be a fully autonomous process, but AI can be leveraged to augment human processes, which can help find bloggers and influencers, as well as improve the quality of sites that are approached for links, says Rowe.[344]

Rowe believes to leverage existing AI in a link-building campaign, brands must first look at websites as a whole, including the multiple contributors or people on staff at these websites.[344] "These can be good link-building opportunities through sponsored or contributed content," says Rowe.[344] Brands should find industry publications or other informative sites that appeal to the brand's target audience.[344] Rowe recommends searching by industry keywords.[344] Brands should look for the following items in these publications[344]:

- Frequent publication: is new content often being published on the site?
- Last publish date: Has there been any new content in the last month?
- User experience and design: Is the design up-to-date and easy to use?

Secondly, brands should identify important industry blogs and influencers.[344] These usually have less people on staff than standard publications, however, they just might have a wider reach.[344]

Rowe believes that, "Text processing analytics like Watson Analytics can be used to find influencers and blog content that hits a brand's target market."[344] "For instance, someone might not always say, 'I am interested in polymer manufacturing,' online, but using AI tools that can predict related text patterns and speech, you might be able to find more influencers who haven't directly used the terms you're looking for," says Rowe.[344]

Things to look for include[344]:

- Comments and social shares on posts: Do the influencer's posts get a lot of engagement?
- Last publish time and frequency: Is content published actively and consistently?
- User experience and design: Is it up-to-date and easy to use?
- Social platform: Does the influencer have a large social media following on the platforms that are preferred by the brand's industry players?
- Reputation: Sometimes, individual influencers or blogs might have a strong opinion about hot topics that you might not want to be associated with for either distinct political and/or religious reasons.

Once a list of publications, influencers and blogs have been compiled, it's time for the hard part, determining if they will have an impact on your target keyword rankings.[344] Rowe calls this "the powerful part of AI—the part that can improve the impact of the links."[344] "AI can process data from multiple sources to identify likely variables or variable clusters that correlate with ranking in Google," claims Rowe.[344]

Image

Gartner predicts that image search will be a lucrative technology in the coming years.[41] Even with visual search still in its early stages, *Gartner* says early adopters will experience a 30 percent increase in e-commerce revenue by

2021.[41] The potential market is huge and brands that sell any type of physical items should utilize AI image technology to simplify the buying process.

To get started with Image search, brands should focus on solving customer problems and getting their own visual assets in order.[41] They shouldn't try to make their visual search workflows all about advertising.[41] Instead, brands should "aim to have solid metadata on products so that searching is easier and more natural."[41] From there, brands should work towards "visual search processes that are real time and increasingly intuitive, creating a positive customer experience that keeps people coming back," Butterfield argues.[41]

Facial Recognition

Facial recognition technology is the capability of identifying or verifying a person from a digital image or a video frame from a video source by comparing the actual facial features of someone on camera against a database of facial images, or faceprints, as they are also known.

Rapid advancements in facial recognition technology have reached the point where a single face can be compared against 36 million others in about one second.[345] A system made by Hitachi Kokusai Electric and reported by DigInfo TV shown at a security trade show recently was able to achieve this blazing speed by not wasting time on image processing.[345]

Using edge analytics, the technology takes visual data directly from the camera to compare the face in real time.[345] The software also groups faces with similar features, so it can narrow down the field of choice very quickly. The usefulness to the company's security enforcement is pretty obvious, but it can be used by multiple departments; facial recognition technology can be set up to send alerts to clerks, managers, or just about anyone needing to identify customers.

As customers enter an area, "security cameras feed video to computers that pick out every face in the crowd and rapidly take many measurements of each one's features, using algorithms to encode the data in strings of numbers,"[346] as explained in the *Consumer Reports* article *Facial Recognition: Who's Tracking Who in Public*.[346] The faceprints are compared against a database, and when there's a match, the system alerts the VIP department or sales people. Faceprints could also be used to allow people to purchase tickets or as part of an airline's boarding system.

Currently, facial recognition technology can be more useful for security departments than customer service.[346] At the 2014 Golden Globe Awards, facial recognition technology was used to scan for known celebrity stalkers.[346] The technology has also been used to bar known criminals from soccer matches in Europe and Latin America.[346] "Police forces and national security agencies in the U.S., the United Kingdom, Singapore, South Korea, and elsewhere are experimenting with facial recognition to combat violent crime and tighten border security."[346]

In some sense, facial recognition technology is becoming second nature to consumers, especially in Asia. Worldwide, consumers are used to tagging themselves in photos on Facebook, Snapchat, Picasa, and/or WeChat. In 2015, Google launched a photo app that helped users organize their pictures by automatically identifying family members and friends.[346] Google, however, suffered a public relations disaster when its system labeled a photo of two black people as gorillas.[346] The search giant quickly apologized profusely and promised to fix its algorithms[346], but this does show that the technology isn't foolproof and sensitivity is important.

Currently, MasterCard is "experimenting with a system that lets users validate purchases by snapping a selfie. Like fingerprint scanners and other biometric technologies, facial recognition has the potential to offer alternatives to passwords and PINs."[346]

This technology is moving so fast that privacy advocates are having trouble keeping up. In this regard, today's facial recognition technology is reminiscent of the World Wide Web of the mid-1990s.[346] Back then, few people would have anticipated that every detail about what we read, watched, and bought online would become a commodity traded and used by big business and sometimes, more sinisterly, hacked and used by nefarious individuals for criminal purposes.[346]

Facial recognition technology "has the potential to move Web-style tracking into the real world, and can erode that sense of control."[346] Experts such as Alvaro Bedoya, the executive director of Georgetown Law's Center on Privacy & Technology, and the former chief counsel to the Senate's subcommittee on privacy, technology, and the law finds this attack on privacy alarming.[346] "People would be outraged if they knew how facial recognition" is being developed and promoted, Bedoya states.[346] "Not only because they weren't told about it, but because there's nothing they can do about it. When you're online, everyone has the idea that they're being tracked. And they also know that there are steps they can take to counter that, like clearing their cookies or installing an ad blocker. But with facial recognition, the tracker is your face. There's no way to easily block the technology," Bedoya warns.[346]

Right now, facial recognition is largely unregulated, and few consumers seem to even be aware of its use. "Companies aren't barred from using the technology to track individuals the moment we set foot outside. No laws prevent marketers from using faceprints to target consumers with ads. And no regulations require faceprint data to be encrypted to prevent hackers from selling it to stalkers or other criminals," Bedoya warns.[346] This is true in the United States, Asia, and in Europe.

Users might be happy to tag their face and the faces of their friends and acquaintances on a Facebook wall, but they might shudder if every mall worker was jacked into a system that used security-cam footage to access their family's shopping habits.[346]

This could, however, be the future of retail, according to Kelly Gates, associate professor in communication and science studies at the University of California, San Diego.[347] In her article *Our Biometric Future: Facial Recognition Technology and the Culture of Surveillance*[347], Gates argues that "Regardless of whether you want to be recognized, you can be sure that you have no right of refusal in public, nor in the myriad private spaces that you enter on a daily basis that are owned by someone other than yourself." Gates concluded that by entering an establishment filled with facial recognition technology, you are tacitly giving your consent to the brands to use it, even if you are unaware of its use.[347]

Facial recognition technology in the offline world is now becoming more and more prevalent, particularly in the hospitality industry. "On Disney's four cruise ships, photographers roam the decks and dining rooms taking pictures of passengers. The images are sorted using facial recognition software so that photos of people registered to the same set of staterooms are grouped together. Passengers can later swipe their Disney ID at an onboard kiosk to easily call up every shot taken of their families throughout the trip."[346]

"In a recent study of 1,085 U.S. consumers by research firm First Insight, 75 percent of respondents said they would not shop in a store that used the technology for marketing purposes. Notably, the number dropped to 55 percent if it was used to offer good discounts."[346] Brands should take this into account if they choose to implement facial recognition technology.

However, consumers may warm to facial recognition technology once it becomes more widespread, especially if brands offer enough incentives to make it worth their customer's time. In some cases, full facial recognition isn't needed, some marketers just want to determine the age, sex, and race of shoppers, although many vendors are now rolling out technology that not only recognizes the face but also the emotion.

In Germany, the Astra beer brand recently created an automated billboard directed solely at women, even to the point of shooing men away.[346] The billboard approximated the women's age, then played one of 80 pre-recorded ads to match.[346] For a marketer, this could help if they want to direct specific advertising towards women, or to men, or to a certain age group.

In 2014, Facebook announced a project it called DeepFace, "a system said to be 97.35 percent accurate in comparing two photos and deciding whether they depicted the same person—even in varied lighting conditions and from different camera angles. In fact, the company's algorithms are now almost as adept as a human being at recognizing people based just on their silhouette and stance."[346]

"Entities like Facebook hold vast collections of facial images," says Gates, the UC, San Diego professor.[346] "People have voluntarily uploaded millions of images, but for their own personal photo-sharing activities, not for Facebook to develop its facial recognition algorithms on a mass scale."[346] Unfortunately for privacy advocates, there is no difference between the two.

Potentially Facebook, Instagram, WeChat, Pinterest, Snapchat, Google, and a whole host of other social media platforms could use their vast databases of faceprints to power real-world facial recognition.[346] "Hypothetically, a tech giant wouldn't need to share the faceprints themselves. It could simply ingest video feeds from a store and let salespeople know when any well-heeled consumer walked through the door."[346] It could also, potentially, do this for a marketer as well, to prevent money laundering.

According to his article *Qantas have seen their Future. It's Facial Recognition*[348], Chris Riddell explains how Qantas is taking facial recognition technology to a the next level. According to Riddell[348]:

> "Qantas have just started a brand-new programme of trialing facial recognition to enable them to monitor passengers from the very moment they check in, all the way through to the gate when they board the plane. They're also going to be monitoring everything in between, including what café you're getting your coffee at, and where you are shopping for that last minute pair of jeans. They'll also know what electrical gadgets you were playing with at the tech shop, and whether you were too busy trying free shots of cognac to buy that gift for your other half that you promised, but then 'forgot'"

Riddell sees this as "a big retail play by the red kangaroo and it is pushing the national airline into very new and unchartered territory. Qantas are exceptionally interested in the movement of people through the terminals, and how they spend their time."[348]

Riddell adds that, "Qantas will want to know what people are doing, how long they are doing it, which shops they are spending the most time, and which shops they spend the least time in. By combining that with the incredible amount of data from frequent flyer programme and passenger information they collect, they'll be catapulting themselves into the world of hyper intelligent retail."[348]

Of course, Qantas are not alone in wanting to capture all this customer data, explains Riddell, every major airline is doing it.[348] "The truth is though, few are using the data they hoard with any level of real sophistication for the customer," claims Riddell.[348]

"All airlines know who you work for, who you book travel through, where you go on holiday, where you travel for work and for how long you are away," says

Riddell.[348] "They also know what food you like, what food you are allergic to, and who you bank with. They also know where you live, and who lives there with you, whether you've got children, and how old they are. The list goes on.... If you've linked other loyalty programmes to your frequent flyer account, they also know a whole lot about your shopping habits," adds Riddell.[348] All of this data helps a business understand its customer down to a micro level, which is more critical than ever.[348] For a business like Qantas this data helps them deliver services and experiences that are relevant, personal and, most importantly, predictive.[348]

Next up, Riddell believes "will be the delivery of experiences in real-time as you are in an airport retail store. Facial Recognition technology will be able to deliver you services based on *how you feel* at the exact moment it matters. *This is the future*, and it's called emotional analytics."[348] It is a step beyond facial recognition technology and the natural next step.

As CB Insights reports in its *What's Next in AI? Artificial Intelligence Trends*[80], "Academic institutions like Carnegie Mellon University are also working on technology to help enhance video surveillance." "The university was granted a patent around 'hallucinating facial features'—a method to help law enforcement agencies identify masked suspects by reconstructing a full face when only periocular region of the face is captured," explains CB Insights. "Facial recognition may then be used to compare 'hallucinated face' to images of actual faces to find ones with a strong correlation."[80]

However, CB Insights warns that the tech is not without glitches. The report stated that, "Amazon was in the news for reportedly misidentifying some Congressmen as criminals"[80]—although perhaps there's a predictive element in the technology that we're unaware of?

"'Smile to unlock' and other such 'liveness detection' methods offer an added layer of authentication," states CB Insight.[80] For example, "Amazon was granted a patent that explores additional layers of security, including asking users to perform certain actions like 'smile, blink, or tilt his or her head.'"[80] These actions can then be combined with 'infrared image information, thermal imaging data, or other such information' for more robust authentication."[80]

In his article *Machine Learning and AI: If Only My Computer Had a Brain Wired for Business*, Michael Klein states that, fifty-nine percent of fashion retailers in the U.K. are using facial recognition to identify V.I.P clients and provide them with special services.[64] "The technology also enables retailers to track customer sentiment and gauge how customers respond to in-store displays, how long they spend in the store and traffic flow in each of their retail locations," says Klein.[64]

"But that's not the only way retailers are taking advantage of facial recognition and its AI technology. They're using the technology, which is typically employed in airports, for added security," notes Klein.[64] For example, Saks "has leveraged facial recognition technology to match the faces of shoppers caught on security cameras with that of past shoplifters. From this perspective, AI can serve the dual purpose of preventing losses while improving the customer experience—and that ultimately helps retailers boost sales."[64]

Image Search

"If a picture is worth a thousand words, visual search—the ability to use an image to search for other identical or related visual assets—is worth thousands of spot-on searches—and thousands of minutes saved on dead-end queries," says Brett Butterfield in his Adobe blog *See It, Search It, Shop It: How AI is Powering Visual Search*.[41] In the article, Butterfield explains how visual search could become a big part of a buyer's shopping future. With visual search, you don't need to try and guess the brand, style, and/or retail outlet where something was purchased, you can simply snap a picture of the item you like, upload the image, and immediately find exactly the same sneakers or ones like them, and then purchase them, all rather seamlessly.[41]

"That spot-it/want-it scene is common, and good for business. It could be a shirt on someone walking down the street, an image on Instagram, or a piece of furniture in a magazine—somewhere, your customer saw something that made them want to buy one, and now they're on a mission to find it," explains Butterfield.[41]

"While it's a seemingly simple task, in many cases the path from seeing to buying is a circuitous and friction-filled route that leads to a subpar purchase—or no purchase at all. Just one in three Google searches, for example, leads to a click—and these people come to the table with at least a sense of what they're searching for," notes Butterfield.[41]

"Visual search is all about focusing your attention toward a target," says Gina Casagrande, senior Adobe Experience Cloud evangelist, "and helping you find what you're looking for that much faster. You also get the added benefit of finding things you didn't even know you were looking for."[41]

"Like text-based search, visual search interprets and understands a user's input—images, in this case—and delivers the most relevant search results possible. However, instead of forcing people to think like computers, which is how the typical text search works, visual search flips the script," adds Butterfield.[41]

"Powered by AI, the machine sees, interprets, and takes the visual cues it learns from people. After applying metadata to the image, AI-powered visual search systems can dig through and retrieve relevant results based on visual similarities, such as color and composition," explains Butterfield.[41] Visual search is another technology that can facilitate better, more frictionless retail experiences that can help buyers find what they want faster.[41]

"One early adopter of visual search is Synthetic, Organic's cognitive technology division, an Omnicom subsidiary," says Butterfield.[41] "Synthetic's Style Intelligence Agent (SIA)—powered by Adobe Sensei—uses AI to help customers not just find specific clothing items, but also find the right accessories to complete their new look."[41]

To use SIA, customers simply upload an image, either from a website, from real life or even from an ad in a magazine and from there, "Adobe Sensei's Auto Tag service extracts attributes from the image based on everything from color, to style, to cut, to patterns."[41] SIA's custom machine-learning model then kicks in, correlating those tags with a massive catalog of products.[41] "SIA then displays visually similar search results as well as relevant recommendations—items with similar styles, cuts, colors, or patterns, for example."[41] Just as importantly, SIA then "uses these visual searches to build a rich profile for that customer's preferences and tastes—a much deeper profile than what could be built from text-based searches alone."[41] Here you are getting customer preferences on steroids, an enormous amount of personalized data that can then be used in customer marketing.

"This is where visual search goes beyond just search and becomes a true shopping consultant," says Casagrande, "and a superior, more sophisticated way to search for what you want and what you didn't know you wanted."[41]

"In delivering such a simple, seamless experience, AI-powered visual search removes the friction from traditional search-and-shop experiences," says Butterfield.[41] "No longer do customers have to visit multiple retailers or sites and strike out. They can now find virtually anything, anywhere, even without knowing exactly where to find it," he adds.[41] This is another important moment for marketers because if brands invest in visual search, they can propel their brand up the Google rankings and get a solid leg up on the competition.

Several retailers currently "use visual search to make the distance between seeing and buying virtually nonexistent—within their own brand experience."[41] "Macy's, for example, offers visual search capabilities on its mobile app, which allows customers to snap a photo, and find similar products on Macys.com. It's 'taking impulse buying to new heights,' one source says."[41]

Frictionless image search is just the beginning.[41] "The value of visual search technology grows as the customer returns to the site," says Casagrande.[41] "On that next visit, it's a more personalized, powerful targeted search. Just being able to pick up where I left off and get to that product that much faster helps reduce friction, and has been shown to increase conversions and order rate."[41]

"Visenze, which builds shopping experiences using AI, is already seeing these benefits," says Butterfield.[41] For example, "the company saw a 50 percent increase in conversion among clients such as Nike and Pinterest that implemented visual search technology."[41]

"In the United States, Amazon and Macy's have been offering this feature for some time," says Visenze CEO Oliver Tan. "Consumers are crying out for a simpler search process," claims Tan.[41] If brands don't have that, their customers will move on to other companies that do.[41]

Though the benefits of visual search are clear, there's still a gap in between customer expectations and delivery.[41] "Our current iteration of visual search gets us maybe 70 percent of the way there," says Casagrande.[41] "Keep in mind, as more data and content become available the algorithms will get smarter, and the visual search experience will only continue to get better," says Casagrande.[41]

Another interesting use of AI is what Pinterest is doing with its visual search technology. According to Lauren Johnson's *Adweek* article *Pinterest Is Offering Brands Its Visual Search Technology to Score Large Ad Deals*[349], "The visual search technology is Pinterest's version of AI and human curation that lets consumers snap a picture of IRL things and find similar items online. Taking a picture of a red dress for example, pulls up posts of red dresses that consumers can browse through and shop," states Johnson.[349]

"The idea is to give people enough ideas that are visually related so that they have a new way to identify and search for things," said Amy Vener, retail vertical strategy lead at Pinterest.[349] "From a visual-discovery perspective, our technology is doing something similar where we're analyzing within the image the colors, the shapes and the textures to bring that to another level of dimension," Vener adds.[349]

Utilizing the technology, someone who points his or her phone's camera at a baby crib will receive recommendations for similar baby products.[349] "Eventually, all of Target's inventory will be equipped with Pinterest's technology to allow anyone to scan items in the real world and shop similar items through Target.com," states Johnson. "Target is the first retailer to build Pinterest's technology into its apps and website, though the site also has a deal to power Bixby, Samsung's AI app that works similarly."[349]

"We're now in a place where we're using Pinterest as a service to power some visual search for other products," Vener said. "I think there's an opportunity for retailers to be a little more of a prominent player when it comes to visual discovery."[349]

Video

In his article *The Future of Video Advertising is Artificial Intelligence*[350], Matt Cimaglia sees a video advertising world that is completely different to the current one. He describes it as such: "Meanwhile, somewhere in another office, in that same year, a different team is creating a different digital video. Except they're not shooting a single video: They're shooting multiple iterations of it. In one, the actor changes shirts. In another, the actor is an actress. In another, the actress is African-American. After finishing the shoot, this agency doesn't pass the footage off to a video editor. They pass it off to an algorithm."[350]

Cimaglia states that, "The algorithm can cut a different video ad in milliseconds. Instead of taking one day to edit one video, it could compile hundreds of videos, each slightly different and tailored to specific viewers based on their user data."[350] "As the video analytics flows in, the algorithm can edit the video in real-time, too—instead of waiting a week to analyze and act on viewer behavior, the algorithm can perform instantaneous A/B tests, optimizing the company's investment in a day," claims Cimaglia.[350]

Cimaglia believes this is what is happening right now.[350] Cimaglia contends, "We are witnessing a moment in video marketing history, like moments experienced across other industries disrupted by the digital revolution, where human editors are becoming obsolete."[350] This is the evolution of advertising—personalized advertising, i.e., tailoring content to individuals rather than the masses[350]; surgically striking relevant offers to a market of one, rather than blasting a shotgun of offerings to the uninterested many.

"Savvy agencies are turning to artificial intelligence for help making those new, specialized creative decisions," says Cimaglia.[350] "It's the same logic that's long overtaken programmatic banner and search advertising, machine learning and chatbots: There are some things computers can do faster, cheaper and more accurately than humans," contends Cimaglia. "In this future of data-driven dynamic content, viewers' information is siphoned to AI that determines aspects of the video based on their data," explains Cimaglia.[350]

Cimaglia sees advertising being tailored towards individuals.[350] "The options for customization extend beyond user data, too. If it's raining outside, it could be raining in the video," easily done by the agency plugging in a geolocating weather script.[350] Similarly, if a user is watching the video at night, the video could mirror reality and be a night scene filled with cricket sounds.[350] For Cimaglia, "This is a logical progression for a society already accustomed to exchanging their privacy for free services."[350] The video could also be in multiple languages thanks to tools like Amazon Polly.

Cimaglia believes that "this customization model of video production is more effective than the current model of creating a single video for the masses."[350] He rightfully questions the current preoccupation of investing tremendous amounts of money in single, groundbreaking commercials.[350] Currently, "It's all about producing a multimillion-dollar, 30-second mini-film that screens during the Super Bowl, gets viewed on YouTube 10 million times and wins a Cannes Lion," claims Cimaglia. "What really does that gain you?" asks Cimaglia, especially in this hyper-personalized world. It's less about the viewer and more about stroking the already inflated egos of a select creative set, who are doing nothing more than delivering a one-size-fits-all product to millions of prospects.[350]

Cimaglia believes there is a place for this in a one-size-fits-all advertising product, but making them "the centerpiece of a multimillion-dollar campaign is foolhardy in an era when companies are sitting on more customer information than ever before."[350] "Personalization is the way of the future, but, unfortunately, most companies simply don't know what to do with their stores of customer data," laments Cimaglia.[350] However, the companies that do will surely reap large financial rewards, he believes.

Audio

In his article *AI's role in next-generation voice recognition*[351], Brian Fuller notes that "speech is a fundamental form of human connection that allows us to communicate, articulate, vocalize, recognize, understand, and interpret. But here's where the complexity comes in: There are thousands of languages and even more dialects." "While English speakers might use upwards of 30,000 words, most embedded speech-recognition systems use a vocabulary of fewer than 10,000 words. Accents and dialects increase the vocabulary size needed for a recognition system to be able to correctly capture and process a wide range of speakers within a single language," states Fuller.[351]

Today, the state of speech-recognition and AI still has a long way to go to match human capability.[351] Fuller claims that, "With the continually improving computing power and compact size of mobile processors, large vocabulary engines that promote the use of natural speech are now available as an embedded option for OEMs."[351]

"The other key to improved voice recognition technology is distributed computing," says Fuller.[351] We've gotten to this amazing point in voice-recognition because of cloud computing, but there are limitations to cloud technology when real-time elements are needed.[351] Things are improving radically but this is a very tricky world to operate in because user privacy, security, and reliable connectivity are difficult to get to work in concert.[351] "The world is moving quickly to a new model of collaborative embedded-cloud operation—called an embedded glue layer—that promotes uninterrupted connectivity and directly addresses emerging cloud challenges for the enterprise," says Fuller.[351]

As Fuller explains it[351]:

> "With an embedded glue layer, capturing and processing user voice or visual data can be performed locally and without complete dependence on the cloud. In its simplest form, the glue layer acts as an embedded service and collaborates with the cloud-based service to provide native on-device processing.

The glue layer allows for mission-critical voice tasks—where user or enterprise security, privacy and protection are required—to be processed natively on the device as well as ensuring continuous availability. Non-mission-critical tasks, such as natural language processing, can be processed in the cloud using low-bandwidth, textual data as the mode of bilateral transmission. The embedded recognition glue layer provides nearly the same level of scope as a cloud-based service, albeit as a native process."

Fuller believes that, "This approach to voice recognition technology will not only revolutionize applications but devices as well."[351]

Voice Activated Internet

In his article *2019 Predictions from 35 voice industry leaders*[352], Bret Kinsella quotes Jason Fields, Chief Strategy Officer of Voicify, who claims that "2019 is going to be the year voice and IVA's are integrated into brands overall CX strategy."

In her article *Voice search isn't the next big disrupter, conversational AI Is*[353], Christi Olson explains the importance of being what she calls 'position zero' in the search rankings. Olson says[353]:

"When you type a query into a search engine, hundreds of options pop up. It's different with voice. When people engage in a voice search using a digital assistant, roughly 40 percent of the spoken responses today (and some say as many as 80%) are derived from 'featured snippet' within the search results. In search speak, that's position zero. When you are that featured snippet in an organic search, that's what the assistant is going to default to as the spoken response. Siri, Google, Cortana and Alexa don't respond with the other ten things that are a possibility on that search page. Just the one."

Understanding this, it's clear why position zero is so important; "while you might be number two in the text-based searches, you're getting little to no traffic if people are engaging with intelligent agents and listening to the spoken response," says Olson.[353]

The opportunity here is for companies to reverse-engineer the process to ensure they get position zero, so they can win the search race and therefore gain the traffic. But how? "It goes back to the best practices of organic search, basic SEO, and having a solid strategy," argues Olson.[353] "It's embracing schema markup and structured data within your website, so you are providing search engines with signals and insights to be included in the knowledge graph. It's claiming your business listings so that the data is up-to-date and correct. It's understanding the questions people are asking and incorporating that question and conversational tone into your content," says Olson.[353] "Simply put: It's understanding the language your customers are using so that you can provide value and answers in their own words and phrases. So, let's conclude with that," Olson adds.[353]

"Conversational AI for voice-assisted search is different from text-based search. If you look at the top 80 percent of queries, text-based searches typically range between one to three words. When we (at Microsoft, my employer) look at our Cortana voice data, the voice searches coming in range from four to six words. That's substantially longer than a text-based search," says Olson.[353]

It means that people are engaging with the digital assistant conversationally, asking questions and engaging in almost full sentences.[353] "Given this insight, there's an opportunity to think about the questions your customers are now asking. Think about what their need is in the way that your customers naturally talk, not in marketer speak or marketing terms. Then, provide value back to them in that manner," recommends Olson.[353]

"With conversational AI, we're going back to being able to create an emotional connection through more meaningful conversations with our customers to build relationships," says Olson.[353] "Brands will be able to differentiate themselves by adding emotional intelligence to IQ through these conversations," concludes Olson.[353]

Amazon Polly is a service that turns text into lifelike speech, allowing users "to create applications that talk, and build entirely new categories of speech-enabled products.[354] Amazon Polly is a text-to-speech service that uses advanced deep learning technologies to synthesize speech that sounds like a human voice."[355]

Amazon Polly contains dozens of lifelike voices across a wide range of languages, allowing users to select the ideal voice and build speech-enabled applications that work in many different countries.[355] At Intelligencia, we use it to quickly create videos in multiple languages. Some of the Polly voices sound a little stilted and machine-like, but there is usually one in the series of specific languages that does a passable job.

In its article *The Next Generation of Search: Voice*[356], seoClarity argues that brands should take voice search very seriously because it is becoming a zero-sum game. seoClarity states that[356]:

> "Because of the rise in voice search, Google has recognized the increasing need to improve the experience for consumers conducting these searches. Instead of simply displaying a list of 10 blue links, Google increasingly provides a single direct answer to queries. This makes sense since voice searches are often conducted when our hands and eyes are otherwise

> occupied (for instance, while driving). A standard SERP result would not be helpful in such situations. Rather, having the answer (which Google believes to be the best answer for the query) read out aloud provides immediate gratification and a much better user experience. Therefore, Google's response of creating the Answer Box is no accident."

"Now, and for the foreseeable future, Google's Answer Box is the golden ticket in the organic search rankings sweepstakes," says seoClarity.[356] "In addition to it being the only answer to voice search queries, it is the result that appears above all other results on the SERP, 'ranking zero,'" notes seoClarity.[356] "Capturing the Google's Answer Box can mean a dramatic increase in traffic to your website, credibility and overall brand awareness," they add.[356]

Google's Answer Box, or "featured snippet block," is the summary of an answer.[356] "Not only is the Google Answer box at the very first spot, above standard organic results, but also has a unique presentation format that immediately sets it apart from the remainder of the page. This instantly increases the credibility and authority of the brand providing the answer to the user's query. Consequently, Google's Answer Box may be the only search result viewed by the user," says seoClarity.[356] Perhaps more importantly, it is the only answer read in response to a voice search.[356] "Not only does Google's Answer Box dominate the SERP, it also boosts organic traffic, leverages mid- to long-range keywords, and focuses on the searcher's intent," notes seoClarity.[356] "Given the great importance of the Answer Box, brands should be focused on delivering the best search experience rather than worrying about any specific tactic to trick the algorithms," argues seoClarity.[356]

"It's valuable to think about the shopper's journey. Shoppers at different stages of their journey are searching for different things. So, it is crucial that brands provide content that meet shoppers' needs wherever they are in their journey. When you are able to capture Google's top result for searches along the shopper's journey, you will maximize your brand's credibility and authority," argues seoClarity.[356]

"Voice search users tend to use specific, long-tail search phrases. Instead of inquiring about a term or phrase, voice searchers typically ask proper questions," says seoClarity.[356] "For example, when looking for places to dine out, desktop users might type 'Italian restaurant.' However, when using voice search, they're more likely to ask, 'where's the nearest Italian restaurant?'"[356] Voice searchers tend to use language that's relevant to them.[356] "When speaking to their device, queries are more conversational, leaving it to the search engine to decipher the actual intent," says seoClarity.[356]

Voice searches are more targeted in the awareness and consideration phase.[356] Many voice searches have local intent—"as much as 22 percent of voice queries inquire about local information such as directions, restaurants, shopping, local services, weather, local events, traffic, etc.," says seoClarity.[356] "The remainder of queries is distributed between non-commercial queries like personal assistant tasks, entertainment, and general searches," notes seoClarity.[356] "This makes local the biggest commercial intent among voice searches. As a result, you should incorporate new strategies to position your business in local voice search," argues seoClarity.[356]

Voice search is still messy and complex.[356] "Google's RankBrain algorithm leverages artificial intelligence to discover contextual connections between searches," says seoClarity.[356] Google "tries to understand 'intent' based on context of the search (such as location, time of day, device used, previous searches, connected data from email and other assistant sources) instead of just plainly matching words from on a page."[356] However, the machine is learning and training, so, "instead of trying to keep up with Google's algorithms, it is essential to understand what your audience needs and focus your optimization to your end user, not on chasing the latest algorithm shifts."[356]

seoClarity recommends brands can "build a more effective content marketing strategy to win the Answer Box by optimizing for topics that reflect the intent of your audience instead of just optimizing for keywords."[356] When brands focus their content strategies on the intent of the audience, it better addresses the real needs of the customer.[356] Additionally, the created content can solve challenges and answer most commonly asked brand questions.[356] By targeting the awareness and consideration phases of the customer journey, brands can capture their audience early in the customer journey.[356]

Brands should optimize to short attention spans as well.[356] It is essential to connect with customers at the right moment.[356] seoClarity says that, "Google outlines the following moments that every marketer should know: I-want-to-know moment; I-want-to-go moment; I-want-to do moment; I want-to-buy moment."[356]

Always create a FAQ page as it can provide answers to common questions that users may have.[356] "By figuring out what questions your customers are asking, you can create the type of content that they are most likely to find useful," says seoClarity.[356]

"Answer the five W's & H—Be sure to answer the essential questions that everyone asks when collecting information or solving a problem: Who, What, Where, When, Why. And don't forget the all-important How," says seoClarity.[356] "The data also showed some other important trigger words including Best, Can, Is, and Top," says seoClarity.[356] Brands should also "Explain steps to complete tasks—Focus on content that details steps and how to complete tasks that relate to your product or service and also other explanations specifically for your product or service. "How to" and "What Is" contain significant lead over other trigger words."[356]

Other things seoClarity recommends are, "Highlight the best options for customers. Create buying guides that help aid the decision making process in list and bullet point type of format to demonstrate the best options for customers."[356]

"Focus on structuring content in a way that matches consumer intent—Use formats that work for your customers and structure the content to intent," recommends seoClarity.[356] "Consider using tables, ordered lists, bullet points, and video. Use schema markup—Always use the best SEO practices by placing your keywords and key phrases in your header, metadata, URL structures, and alt tags," says seoClarity.[356]

One of the most important recommendations seoClarity offers is for brands to produce in-depth content.[356] "In your SEO efforts, you must never forget that content is the most important thing. Be sure to create relevant content that provides in-depth answers to the questions your target audience asks," says seoClarity.[356]

According to seoClarity[357], nearly 20% of all voice search queries are triggered by only 25 keywords, which include "how", "why", or "what", as well as adjectives like "best" or "easy". The top ten are listed below, others included "Why", "Who", "New", "Recipe", "Good", "Homes", "Make", "Does", "Define", "Free", "I", "List", "Home", "Types", and "Do."

Trigger Words	Count	% of Total
How	658,976	8.64%
What	382,224	5.01%
Best	200,206	2.63%
The	75,025	0.98%
Is	53,496	0.70%
Where	43,178	0.57%
Can	42,757	0.56%
Top	42,277	0.55%
Easy	31,178	0.41%
When	27,571	0.36%

Table 13: Voice search words
Search: Dialogtech.com[357]

Programmatic Advertising

"When it comes to advertising," the Adobe Sensei Team believes that, "the promise of AI is that customers will receive the most relevant ads, while allowing brands to drive awareness, engagement, conversions, and loyalty."[5] This should result in happier customers and less wasted ad spend.[5] "With AI, advertisers can budget, plan, and more effectively spend limited ad dollars," claim the Adobe Sensei Team.[5]

The Sensei team provides the following example: "Cynthia is a travel and hospitality media buyer trying to determine the best mix of search advertising for her global hotel brand."[5] "She knows that with millions of keywords, multiple search engines, and different audience segments to consider, coming up with the right bid amount for each combination, as well as determining how to allocate her budget across her campaigns to most efficiently meet her goals is simply too much for her to handle alone."[5] Cynthia "turns to her media buying platform to help her make sense of the data."[5] The Adobe Sensei Team sees the process working as follows for Cynthia[5]:

> *"With AI leading the way, she reviews a forecast simulation to see how an increase or decrease in budget will impact her clicks, revenue, conversions, and other metrics. Once she selects her budget, she reviews AI-powered ad spend recommendations to see how to best allocate her advertising budget. She clicks on her preferred allocation. Later, as her ad campaigns are running, she accesses model accuracy performance reports so she can see how actual performance numbers compare with AI-generated forecasts, allowing her to make any necessary adjustments along the way. Once her campaigns have run, she's thrilled to see that they delivered 99 percent of the clicks that were forecast, and actual revenue was five percent higher than forecasted. Now that Cynthia has a clear picture of what worked during her search ad campaigns, she checks the performance of her display and video campaigns. Again, she calls on AI to report on awareness and performance while letting her demand-side platform (DSP) guide automated budget allocation so she can stay focused on strategic media planning and buying.*

The Adobe Sensei Team believes that with the help of AI, brands "can keep up with changing customer preferences, navigate mountains of data, and make adjustments multiple times per day if needed to make sure"[5] budgets are allocated "most effectively across channels like search, display, and video, or even within a specific channel."[5]

In her article *Experts Weigh in On the Future of Advertising*, Giselle Abramovich believes that AI can help build a media-buying platform that allows a marketer to input goals "and a transparent algorithm does the rest, executing buys and optimizing every millisecond."[191] The ad could dynamically change the tone of the voiceover based on the preferences of the viewer.[191] Abramovich believes that, "The convergence of AI with human creativity and insight will transform advertising, and we're just beginning to see what's possible."[191]

One of the companies delving into AI head-first is Citi, which recently launched its "Welcome What's Next" campaign.[191] "[AI] is allowing us to create custom ads that meet people where they are. For example, if you're looking at the weather, it's serving up the ad in a customized way so it's relevant to what you're looking at," says Jennifer Breithaupt, global consumer CMO at Citi.[191] "It integrates with a consumer's path online and provides a more seamless way to experience the ad."[191]

AI is already helping Citi surpass its advertising benchmarks, Breithaupt adds.[191] "For example, the financial giant has realized a 10%+ lift in video completion rates versus standard, non-customized ads as a result of AI."[191]

"But what's going to be crucial to the success of AI is structuring it in a transparent manner that involves a partnership between parties," Breithaupt says.[191] "In other words, above all as advertisers, it's crucial we're clearly defining the value exchange and providing consumers with the opportunity to make an informed choice about their participation."[191]

In his article *How AI is Driving a New Era of TV Advertising*[358], Varun Batra states that in November 2017, eMarketer reported that 70% of U.S. adults "second screen" while watching TV. Although that sounds pretty discouraging for brands that spend millions on their TV spots, one should consider that this is reported, not observed, behavior.[358] "No doubt we all second screen, but we don't do so all the time. That begs the question: how does a brand know consumers paid attention to its $5 million Super Bowl ad rather than their mobiles?" asks Batra.[358]

"Using AI, data scientists have been able to map multiple devices to the same individual and household, as well as to connect online behavior with offline behavior, such as watching the Super Bowl via a connected TV and engaging with a smartphone during commercials," explains Batra.[358] Brands "can determine when consumers second screen during the commercials by counting the number of bid requests from their devices," says Batra.[358]

"Of course, AI can't tell us if an inactive device meant the consumer watched the ad or went to the kitchen for another beer, but if we track ad requests across millions of household, we can get a lot of insight into a creative's ability to captivate consumers," says Batra.[358]

"AI can also help determine the impact of an ad on consumer behavior, thanks to that same ability to link online and offline behavior. For example, if we know that a particular household was presented with a TV ad for a 'one-day-only sale' on GM pickup trucks, and a mobile device associated that household shows up at the local dealer on sale day, then we can assume the ad had an impact," explains Batra.[358] "The connection becomes more compelling when the behavior is seen across all households that see the ad," he adds.[358]

"Marketers will continue to see new opportunities to improve their campaigns as TV becomes more digitized," argues Batra.[358] He adds that, "As of 2017, there are nearly 133 million connected TV users in the US and will grow to at least 181 million in" 2018.[358] That means the online and offline behavior of 55% of the population can now be tied to ad-views, which is obviously a huge number.[358]

"Many programmatic companies allow marketers to incorporate TV inventory into their multi-channel programmatic campaigns. These connected TVs are targeted using first- and third-party data sets, just as if they were laptops and tablets," says Batra.[358] "Marketers can create surround-sound marketing, hitting consumers with messages on their laptops, mobile devices, and TVs," he adds.[358]

"AI is more precisely transforming the very segments we use to pinpoint consumers who are in the market for a particular product," says Batra. "Machine learning excels at sifting through massive amounts of observed online and offline user behavior to discover distinct signals that indicate purchase intent," explains Batra.[358] AI can also make sub-millisecond decisions to remove a consumer from a targeting segment as soon as he or she stops sending in-market signals.[358] Humans just don't have the capacity to do this, so the models do it completely autonomously and at a scale far beyond human capability.[358]

"Through numerous applications of machine learning, we've learned that there is a host of common—and often non-intuitive—behaviors that people engage in before they exhibit the signals of being in the market," says Batra.[358] For example, "in the classic digital marketing use case, airlines will retarget consumers who search for flights to Las Vegas. In a machine-learning use case, airline marketers would target consumers who look at wedding chapels, an early signal that they'll soon look for a flight to the city."[358] "In other words, the machine predicts who an airline's future customer will be, giving the airline the opportunity to get a jump on its competition," notes Batra.[358]

Batra believes that, "Television has always been a powerful awareness tool, enabling brands to reach millions of consumers quickly and effectively."[358] He concludes that, AI can only enhance "that power by predicting the right people to receive a TV ad, gauging its effectiveness, and assessing its impact on online and offline consumer behavior."[358]

Customer Journey

As I wrote in chapter one, successful marketing is all about reaching a consumer with an interesting offer when he or she is primed to accept it. Knowing what might interest the consumer is half the battle to making the sale and this is where customer analytics and AI come in. Customer analytics have evolved from simply reporting customer behavior to segmenting customers based on their profitability, to predicting that profitability, to improving those predictions (because of the inclusion of new data), to *actually manipulating customer behavior* with target-specific promotional offers and marketing campaigns. AI is central to this process.

As stated before, Disney uses its MagicBand to collect enormous amounts of data on its park patrons.[56] In his Adobe blog, Newman states that, "In today's experience business, every single person—from customer service reps to HR to the designers and developers behind products like the MagicBand—must play a role in creating experiences customers crave."[56] Every brand marketer should have a similar goal today. Newman argues that, "Every employee must have the same goal: delivering compelling, personalized, and seamless experiences that enable long-time emotional connections and loyalty to the brand."[56]

A brand needs to create a single view of the customer so that its marketers can deliver a personalized experience that wows the customer. Data can come from transactional systems, CRM systems, app impressions, operational data, facial recognition software, wearables, iBeacons, clickstream data, etc., etc. Dan Woods explains this in his amusing comparison of the different environments that today's marketers face in comparison to what their 1980's counterparts saw.[27] Today, stealthy marketers are forced to use "email campaigns, events, blogging, tweeting, PR, ebooks, white papers, apps, banner ads, Google Ad Words, social media outreach, search engine optimization."[27] Woods didn't include SMS or OTT, but these are important channels to use as well.

In practice, all these channels should work in concert together; an email campaign can promote a sale at an event, which can be blogged and tweeted about through social media. PR can also promote the event through a brand's typical news channels. Coupons for the event can be disseminated through the brand's mobile app and SMS messaging channel. Banner ads will appear on the brand's website, while Google ads and SEO will drive buyers and potential buyers to the brand's website or its social channels. Hopefully, viral marketing then kicks in, with customers and potential customers sharing on Facebook, Instagram, Pinterest, Weibo, WeChat, etc., etc. Of course, influencer marketing can also help the viral marketing process at some point.

Seen through the lens of the *Engagement and Loyalty Platform*, all these activities can increase personalization to the point where it will be recognized and coveted by the customer. Lovelock and Wirtz's "Wheel of Loyalty"[103] concept and its three sequential steps—building a foundation for loyalty, creating loyalty bonds, and identifying and reducing factors that result in churn should be kept in mind when building up the foundation of The A.I. Marketer's loyalty and CRM systems. The most important part of the second step is the cross-selling and bundling of products and a real-time stream processing recommendation engine will certainly help with that.

Listening

In her article Engage Customers and Gain Advocates Through Social Media and Social Networking[359], Wendy Neuberger argues that: "Social commerce is about making a retailer's brand a destination. Retailers really need to listen to what their customers are saying. Customers can provide valuable input and feedback that can be used to make more informed assortment decisions, changes to website features and enhancements to the shopping experience."

"When customers feel their voice is being heard, they gain a stronger connection to the retailer and are more likely to become advocates."[359] Neuberger claims it is important for brands to identify and engage with the key influencers for several reasons, the two most important being: "to empower their advocacy or capabilities, which helps build and foster a sense of community among brand loyalists, and empowers those loyalists to better advocate on behalf of a brand, product and/or service."[359]

In Bain & Company's Management Tools 2015 An Executive's Guide[108], Darrell K. Rigby claims that CRM requires managers to define strategic 'pain points' in the customer relationship cycle. Pain points can be things like hard-to-navigate customer service channels, providing inaccurate information to customers, poorly designed websites, complicated fee structures, high shipping costs, etc., etc. Pain points can even be problems with data quality that is negatively affecting a CRM system.

Brands should evaluate whether—and what kind of—CRM data can fix those pain points as well as calculate the value that such information would bring the company. As Dan Shewan explains in his article Pain Points: A Guide to Finding & Solving Your Customers' Problems[360], "One of the best ways to learn your customers' biggest problems is by *really* listening to them." The best way to do this is by conducting qualitative research.[360]

"The reason you need to conduct *qualitative* research (which focuses on detailed, individualized responses to open-ended questions) as opposed to *quantitative* research (which favors standardized questions and representative, statistically significant sample sizes) is because your customers' pain points are highly subjective," says Shewan.[360] "Even if two customers have exactly the same problem, the underlying causes of that problem could differ greatly from one customer to another," he adds.[360]

Qualitative research is, of course, a lot harder to quantify, especially without AI and machine learning. With them, it is still difficult because customer complaints can be so subjective—and often wrong. NLP can help with that, as I explained earlier.

"There are two primary sources of the information you need to identify your customers' pain points—your customers themselves, and your sales and support teams," states Shewan.[360] I have listed several ways to listen to your customer throughout this book, but they are just one part of the equation, a brand's sale staff is the other. A brand's sales reps work on the frontlines of the battle for the hearts and minds of the company's customers and prospective customers every single day, which makes them an invaluable source of feedback on your customers' and/or prospects' pain points.[360]

"However," Shewan warns that, "as valuable as your sales team's feedback can be, it's important to distinguish your sales reps' pain points from your prospects' pain points; your sales reps' problems may be very real, but you're not building a product or providing a service to make your sales reps' lives easier."[360]

Rigby recommends that brands select the appropriate technology platform and calculate the cost of implementing it and training employees to use it. He also recommends brands:

1. Assess whether the benefits of the CRM information outweigh the expense involved.
2. Design incentive programs to ensure that personnel are encouraged to participate in the CRM program. Many companies have discovered that realigning the organization away from product groups and toward a customer-centered structure improves the success of CRM.
3. Measure CRM progress and impact. Aggressively monitor participation of key personnel in the CRM program. In addition, put measurement systems in place to track the improvement in customer profitability with the use of CRM. Once the data is collected, share the information widely with employees to encourage further participation in the program."[108]

In his article *Taking Back The Social-Media Command Center* [361], Scott Gulbransen argues that, "To do the command-center model right, a setup has to envision a real-time workflow empowered to take action on all of the relevant content being analyzed, whether it be insights derived from real-time monitoring, opportunities to respond, or great discovered content to feature that elevates you and your fans." Gulbransen recommends breaking down a command center into the following critical functions[361]:

1. Identify trends and insights—track not only the key themes, but also how they evolve over time.
2. Review the content—monitor a wide variety of terms that are meaningful to the brand and assign employees to sort through the responses, deciding which one warrants a response, and what might interest the community at large.
3. Curate the best stuff—leverage the great content that is being said about the company, as well as champion those great content providers.
4. Listen and Respond—this is a two-way conversation, listen and respond quickly and accordingly.

In the *Listening* part, brands should define and look out for triggers, such as photos, hashtags, keywords, likes, video views, etc. Hootsuite's *14 of the Best Social Media Monitoring Tools for Business*[362] lists some of the best tools for brands to use for this step, including Reddit, Streamview, Reputology, and Synthesio, Crowd Analyzer, amongst others (see Table 14).

SERVICE	DESCRIPTION
Streamview for Instagram	With a community of over 700 million users it makes sense to monitor what people are posting on Instagram, especially if your audience falls in the 18 to 29 age range. With the Streamview for Instagram app you can monitor posts by location, hashtag, or username. The app within Hootsuite allows you to monitor and engage with users that are posting in your area, or an area you choose to follow. For example, you can use this tool during events to see what is being posted and to engage with attended.
Hootsuite Syndicator Pro	Manage and monitor all your favorite blogs and websites with Hootsuite Syndicator Pro. This tool provides a quick and easy way to view RSS feeds and quickly share them to your social media channels, as well as rich filtering, monitoring, and tracking tools. You can also track which stories you've shared.
Reputology	Online (and offline) reputation management is extremely important and surprisingly easy. The Reputology app lets you monitor and check major review sites, such as Yelp, Google, Facebook reviews, so that you can engage with reviewers and resolve any issues in a timely manner. You can track activity across multiple storefronts and locations and respond quickly via quick links.
Hootsuite Insights	Hootsuite Insights combines social media listening, analytics, and powerful social media monitoring capabilities. It allows you to gain powerful real-time insights about your brand, track influencers, stories, and trends, and visualize the metrics—all in one place. You can filter and tailor results by sentiment, platform, location, and language, and engage directly from your stream to take action on previously hidden results.

SERVICE	DESCRIPTION
Brandwatch	The name says it all; the Brandwatch app in Hootsuite lets you keep watch over your brand through deep listening. You can identify key insights from more than 70 million traffic sources across the web, including major social channels, blogs, forums, news and review sites, and much more. This tool lets you make real-time, informed decisions and take action on them.
ReviewInc	Whether it's a positive or negative online review, your response should be in the same place as that review. The ReviewInc app for Hootsuite lets you view over 200 popular review sites across over 100 countries. Organize positive reviews for sharing on social media sites and resolve negative issues instantly.
Synthesio	Synthesio is a comprehensive social monitoring tool for finding the information you need to gain deeper insights and better informed business decisions. The tool lets you monitor multiple mention streams at once, so you can listen to the social media conversations most important to you. You can then analyze these conversations and join them.
Crowd Analyzer	If you or your customers are based in the Middle East, Crowd Analyzer is an invaluable analytics and social media monitoring tool. As the first Arabic-focused social media monitoring platform, Crowd Analyzer analyzes "Arabic content in terms of relevancy, dialect and sentiment." It not only monitors major social networks, but also blogs, forums, and news sites.
76Insights	If content marketing is an important aspect of your Facebook marketing strategy, consider 76Insights. This social media monitoring tool measures the resonance of your social media content and breaks down your resonance score, which measures how much social media engagement someone receives after publishing something.
Keyhole	Keyhole lets you see what's being said about you on Twitter and Instagram in real-time. You can monitor keywords, hashtags, URLs, and usernames, and see historical as well as real-time data. One cool feature is the heat maps that show you activity levels around the world.
Digimind	Digimind lets you track keywords in news outlets and social media platforms for mentions of your company in real-time. It also measures sentiment, so you can gauge whether what is being said about you is good, bad, or "meh." You can also compare how your company is perceived online against your competitors.
Google Alerts	Google Alerts lets you monitor the web for mentions of your company, your competitors, or other relevant topics. Just go to the Google Alerts page, type a keyword or phrase in the search box, and provide your email address to receive a notification every time Google finds results relevant to your alert criteria. You can set alerts

SERVICE	DESCRIPTION
	for specific regions and languages.
Hootsuite	On top of all the social media monitoring tools mentioned above, Hootsuite Pro provides social listening capabilities right in the dashboard. Monitor specific keywords, hashtags, regions, and more. Stay on top of what people are saying about your brand and listen to your customers and competitors to gain competitive advantage.

Table 14: Hootsuite's Social Media Monitoring Tools
Source: 14 of the Best Social Media Monitoring Tools for Business[362]

Brands should also be listening to comment boards or short-term blogging sites like Tumblr or social news aggregation sites like Reddit for comments about their company and their services. Customers are often happy to post wonderful reviews about their purchases, and this is gold for word-of-mouth marketing, so brands should do their best to motivate customers to write up reviews on these sites. AI can be utilized to cull these websites for content so brands can be made aware of positive and negative comments that require responses.

Check-ins and geo-posts from sites like Foursquare, WeChat, Instagram, Facebook, WhatsApp, YouTube, as well as a whole host of other social networks can help brands connect with nearby audiences. Underlying these check-ins is a treasure-trove of collected data. As Aaron Gell explains in his *New Yorker* article *The Not-so-Surprising Survival of Foursquare*[363], "Foursquare's stockpile of location-data breadcrumbs has allowed the company to steadily augment its map of the world, and to test the fuzzy signals it receives from users' phones (the service gleans from G.P.S., Wi-Fi, and Bluetooth, and from other markers) against the eleven billion definitive check-ins provided by its users over the past seven years."

"According to Mike Boland, a chief analyst at the market-research firm BIA/Kelsey, Foursquare can now pinpoint a phone's location with an accuracy that matches, and may in some cases surpass, that of much larger rivals," notes Gell.[363] "Facebook has a much larger sample of data points," Boland says, but "Foursquare has more accurate and reliable data."[363] Foursquare claims its map now "includes more than a hundred million locations, many of them in tightly crowded areas, like office buildings and malls, that other services still struggle to identify."[363] "The accuracy of Foursquare's Places database has led more than a hundred thousand other apps and developers—including Snapchat, Twitter, Pinterest, Uber, and Microsoft—to use its application programming interface (A.P.I.) to power their own features," notes Gell.[363]

As the Adobe Sensei Team explains in its article *AI: Your behind-the-scenes marketing companion*, "Analysts spend thousands of hours slicing and dicing data to find insights about what encourages people to purchase, what pushes them away, and which actions they can take to increase conversions. But with the time it takes humans to manually sift through massive amounts of data to find the hidden gems or red flags, you can easily miss opportunities."[5] "This is where AI can act as your personal data analyst to get a holistic view of customers—recognizing patterns, alerting you to unusual activity, and making recommendations," says the Adobe Sensei Team.[5]

The Adobe Sensei Team provides the following example[5]:

> "Daniel is an analyst for a software company that develops project management apps for various industries. After a year of strong sales, his analytics platform alerts him that sales have slowly stalled, and he needs to find out why. Daniel knows that sifting through potentially millions of data points and conducting hours upon hours of flow analysis to find out why people aren't buying is impossible without help, so he turns to his virtual assistant, AI, to run the analysis for him.
>
> "Using his AI-powered analytics platform, in three clicks he's quickly presented with a segment analysis that displays the top 10 indicators that lead people to purchase their software. Surprisingly, more important than a particular feature or low price point, he sees that one of the biggest reasons why people buy their software is access to their online community, which makes it easy for customers to share ideas about how they've successfully used the app. This tells him that the post-sales support his company provides is not only valuable for onboarding and customer retention, but for acquiring new customers, as well."

Knowledge in hand, Daniel can then explain this unexpected development to his boss, as well as provide his fellow marketers with ideas on how they can better promote their online community to address customer needs and increase sales.[5] By relying on predictive analytics tools that use AI, brands can uncover the unexpected and have more time to make strategic decisions that make a huge difference to the company's bottom line.[5]

Rules Engine

The Rules Engine step is a straightforward concept, brands are already creating business rules for their establishments and these rules should be extended to each company's defined rewards program, their reward's economy, and the marketing of the program.

Rewards can be as simple as a 10% off coupon for a store visit, a gift for a points threshold reached or for a birthday or anniversary. Reward rules engine must contain the conditions of the loyalty program, i.e., If the activity of a member fulfills the conditions, the loyalty engine executes the assigned rule actions, which could be giving the member a unique offer based on his or her spend.

Automation

If AI was made for anything it was automation. One of the big benefits of automating campaigns is that offers based on either stated or inferred preferences of customers can be developed. Analysis can identify which customers may be more responsive to a particular offer. The result: more individualized offers are sent out to the brand's customers and, because these offers tap into a customer's wants, desires, needs *and* expectations, they are more likely to be used; more offers used means more successful campaigns; more successful campaigns means a higher ROI.

By understanding what type of customer is using its products and services, brands can individualize marketing campaigns so that they can be more effective, thereby increasing the company's ROI as well. "As customers gravitate towards one-on-one communication, brands should explore the use of social messaging to interact conversationally with customers, providing customer service or support while building relationships," Teeters recommends.[50]

Once a customer leaves a retail store, the marketing cycle begins anew. RFM models can project the time at which a customer is likely to return and social media should be checked for any comments, likes or uploads, left by a customer. All captured customer information can now become part of the master marketing profile that will be the basis for future marketing efforts. Combining the daily, weekly and monthly master marketing profiles will also allow the brand to develop insightful macro views of its customer data, views that could help with labor management, and other brand needs as well.

Moderation

Moderating boards and UGC posts create a double whammy for brands because, as Rachel Perlmutter explains in her article *Why You Need Social Proof on Your Website*[364], "People need to see that others also enjoy that product. It's what we call social proof: the idea that buyers are influenced by the decisions and actions of others around them." Perlmutter offers the following reasons why it is so important to have UGC reviews on your site[364]:

- Testimonials add credibility for the products and services offered.
- People tend to trust online reviews when making purchases.
- Social proof earns better SEO because it adds more favorable language surrounding a brand online.
- When sourcing customer opinions, brands show that they care about the customer experience, thus strengthening the client bond.[364]

Perlmutter states that brands can gather testimonials in a variety of ways, including sending surveys to new clients.[364] Perlmutter also advises brands to encourage buyers to post on social media.[364] Brands should use hashtags to track customers' responses to the company's products and services so they can be easily found and responded to.[364] Instagram should be a big part of a marketer's strategy because testimonials with images usually trump text testimonials alone.[364] Testimonials are powerful examples of social proof as well.[364]

Brands shouldn't be afraid of sending free products to people with large followings on platforms like Instagram, YouTube, Youku, Twitter, etc.[364] "Whether you want to call them social media influencers, bloggers, or local celebrities, consider getting meatier' testimonials from people who have already gained some amount of trust online," states Perlmutter.[364] "Some may ask for a small fee to review your product, but the return you get from their article, video post, Instagram picture, or even just their words and name listed on your site will likely be tremendous," says Perlmutter.[364]

It's important to get instant reactions, too. Perlmutter recommends that "If you host events, then you have the prime opportunity to gather testimonials from attendees right on the spot."[364] Don't be afraid to set up a camera right outside the event space and ask participants to provide their opinions, even livestreaming them on channels like YouTube, Facebook, Snapchat, Youku, Periscope, etc.[364]

Messaging

As I previously stated, the goal here is to surgically strike relevant offers to a market of one, rather than blasting a shotgun of offerings to the uninterested many. The proliferation of marketing channels has made it easier to reach customers and potential customers, but the messaging is still of paramount important. Send the right offer to the right person on the right channel at the right time of day in the wrong context might mean the customer passes on the offer. Everything has to work in concert to give the brand the best possible chance for sales.

In her *Digiday* article *How Facebook is wooing luxury brands*[365], Bethany Biron writes that "Facebook is advocating for 'digitally influenced sales,' that assist consumers with the discovery process while still driving them to e-commerce sites and physical stores. This concept has helped major retailers like Barneys break out of the traditional retail rut and embrace e-commerce."

In his article *How international airlines use WeChat to market to China*[366], Roy Graff explains how four different carriers have tapped into WeChat to market to the Chinese traveler. Currently, "WeChat is used by many international airlines, which have official service accounts, for marketing, ticket sales and more," explains Graff.[366]

As Graff explains, "KLM's mobile website is fully integrated into its WeChat account, so users can book a flight, search their flight status or check-in online all through WeChat."[366] "Once a flight is booked, travelers receive reminders on WeChat when online check-in opens, and can have their boarding pass sent to their WeChat accounts, too, with a QR code to scan at the airport in place of a paper boarding pass."[366] Like many other official airline WeChat accounts, KLM also offers customer service through the app's chat interface.[366]

In 2017, WeChat launched mini-programs—micro apps accessed directly through WeChat—and, as of June 2018, there were 270 million daily active users of mini-programs.[366] "Finnair launched a mini-program in April 2018 where users upload a photo of food, and the mini-program then identifies what kind of food it is (e.g. dessert, noodles) through AI, and plays music to 'pair' with the food."[366] "This all links to an article about Finnair's Chinese in-flight dining options," explains Graff.[366]

The low-cost Singapore airline Scoot uses WeChat for branding. Graff explains that, "Service accounts on WeChat can send out a weekly newsletter with articles to their followers, and airlines' content usually focuses on promotions and sales, as well as practical tips on traveling and destination guides."[366]

"Low-haul low-cost carrier Scoot was one of the most successful international airlines on WeChat in 2017, and the airline used their articles to cultivate a fun, millennial-friendly brand image—appealing to the largest demographic of Chinese outbound tourists," notes Graff.[366] "Scoot also promoted its direct flights from Xi'an to Singapore through a FAM trip to Singapore for young and popular Chinese travel bloggers, which was also featured on WeChat," adds Graff.[366]

"In order to increase brand awareness, follower numbers and interaction with Chinese consumers, Air France launched a competition for Chinese New Year 2018 with an H5 lucky draw landing page on WeChat."[366] "Prizes included airline tickets to France, cosmetics bags and model airplanes, and the campaign encouraged sharing, converting participants into WeChat followers—and thus increasing the number of WeChat users who would be familiar with Air France and exposed to future promotional posts," says Graff.[366] To participate in the lucky draw, "users had to follow and message the Air France WeChat account, and share the campaign with at least one friend. The H5 page got thousands of views, and also spurred WeChat fan growth," notes Graff.[366]

Neuberger recommends that brands use the following social media platforms for messaging[359]:

- Blogs: brands can provide additional product or category information here as well as post how-to information in the form of text, photos and/or videos. Brands should also provide space for customers to add feedback and/or comments about their brand experience.

- Micro-blogging: coupons, sales and promotions can be offered through these channels. Brands can "'tweet press releases, provide exclusive tips and tricks to customers, and ask for customer feedback, suggestions or ideas for improvements. Some forward-thinking brands even use Twitter as a customer service channel."[359]
- Co-Shopping: this is a form of social shopping and it enables two people—a customer and sales associate or two shoppers in different locations—to share a joint shopping experience using live instant messaging such as Skype, WeChat, or any number of other OTT services.
- Widgets: these are tiny applications that can be embedded into a website, blog or social network that are portable and relatively inexpensive to create and use.
- Social Bridging: anyone who has signed into a website using their Facebook, Pinterest or Twitter account knows what social bridging is. "This level of authentication provides enough credentials to participate in the social elements of the site. Additional authentication is required to complete a shopping transaction due to the sensitivity of the content included in a shopper's account. Social bridging can be used to drive traffic and engage existing and new customers. It can access a user's identity, their social graph, and stream activities such as purchases and other social participation on the retailer's site" says Neuberger.[359]
- In-Store Kiosks and Flat Panels can enable customers to use social networking tools from within a store.[359]

In her article *Facebook wants to become the new mobile storefront, unveils new ad tools for brands and airlines*, Tanya Dua states that Facebook is trying again to establish itself as a true shopping outlet. Facebook "believes it can play a unique role in the shopping world–helping people both discover new products and make decisions when they're ready to buy."[49]

"Facebook believes that because people spend so much time on its mobile app, it can lay claim to being able to help marketers pitch their products before people know they even want them (like TV) and then help people find products when they know they're ready to pull the trigger on purchases (like Google and Amazon)," notes Dua.[49]

"Facebook wants to be a solution not just at the very bottom of the marketing funnel for solutions like retargeting, we actually want to create new purchase intent and consideration further up," said Graham Mudd, product marketing director at Facebook.[49] "If you look at 20 to 30 years ago, that was actually done through broadcast media but in a feed-based environment we have the opportunity to do that in a much more relevant way," adds Mudd.[49]

Facebook might be onto something here as its own research has shown that shoppers increasingly rely on Facebook and Instagram to find and purchase products."[49] Facebook claims that, "Mobile-first shoppers in the U.S. are 1.7 times more likely to get inspiration for gifts or shopping ideas on Facebook, and 2.5 times more likely to research gift or shopping ideas on Instagram."[49]

In 2018 and beyond, video will drive more online sales. When Facebook surveyed 20,824 mobiles shoppers across 17 markets, 30% of them said they preferred to discover new products via video.[49] This is why the "company is enhancing its dynamic ads feature, which allows brands and retailers to upload videos to show-off their products catalogues, instead of just static images."[49]

According to Dua, "Dynamic ads automatically promote products to people who have expressed some interest in a brand, whether on its website, in its app or anywhere else on the internet. The new video feature in dynamic ads has already been trailed by retailers like made.com."[49]

"Facebook has also introduced overlays for dynamic ads, a product which enable brands to add price tags and visuals into their dynamic ads, touting discounts and other offers. Among the retailers that have tested the feature include boxed.com," adds Dua.[49]

One other item that should be noted, Facebook now lets brands target consumers on Facebook based on households, rather than just as individuals.[49] According to Dua, "Facebook will allow marketers to create a new 'household audience,' which enables marketers to target to family members in the same household, with the idea being to inspire members of their audience's household to purchase."[49] Facebook believes that advertisers will be able to "measure the impact of these ads, including whether they influence household members who didn't actually see the ads to make purchases."[49]

In his article *Snapchat seeks salvation in long form and "Hands-on" AR ads*[50], Josh Constine states that "Together, these new formats could make Snap's ads less skippable and more memorable, coaxing money out of businesses hoping to make a mark on its premier audience of US teens." "Both Promoted Stories and AR Trial ads go a step beyond what Facebook can offer but could soon be copied like the rest of Snapchat," Constine adds.[50]

In the past, Snapchat's ads were either "single Snap ads inserted between Stories or Discover content that could easily be skipped with a single tap, or sponsored creative tools that let you try on goofy masks or project 3D mascots into the world but that didn't offer much utility."[50] Constine argues that these ads, which, in some cases were quite juvenile, may have left advertisers skeptical about the lasting impact on buying behavior.[50]

"Our advertising partners have been asking for ways to tell deeper stories on mobile," Snap's Director of Revenue Product Peter Sellis told *TechCrunch* in a statement.[50] According to Constine, "HBO is piloting the format with Promoted Stories about why you should stay in and watch Game Of Thrones on Black

Friday, while in Europe clothing brand ASOS highlights 'night-out worthy looks.'"[50]

"These Promoted Stories are labeled 'ad', get their own preview tile, and are purchased on a full-country one-day takeover basis with users having to actively tap to view."[50] Advertisers receive a range of analytics from preview tile impression through to conversions.[50] The numbers are actually quite impressive: "Snap says it can reach 88 million people in the US with Promoted Stories, surpassing the 74 million Instagram Stories users, and approaching half as many as Facebook's 190 million mobile audience members."[50] For the coveted youths 13 to 24 demographic, "Snap reaches 47 million people—supposedly 9 million more than Facebook and 15 million more than Instagram's feed."[50]

"We wanted to insert ourselves in an organic way into the Snapchat environment and its users' world. That is the most meaningful way to address our fans in a style that fits the channel" head of Digital Marketing Jörg Poggenpohl told *TechCrunch*.[50] "A previous BMW sponsored face lens ad in Europe reached 13 million Snapchatters who played with it for an average of 24 seconds," Constine notes.[50]

"That's the magic of these AR ads," Constine says, adding "Even if you never share the content with friends, you still get extended exposure to the brand just playing with the selfie mask or 3D objects."[50] "Actually resizing and walking around a car company's vehicle will probably leave a bigger impact than just scrolling past some Facebook News Feed display ad. If you reshare that content in private messages or Stories, BMW gets bonus exposure to people who see the brand enmeshed with their friends' content, so they don't just skip past it like the banners we've all grown numb to."[50]

In her article *Whatsapp For Business—What Does It Mean?*[367], Holly Turner explains that in August 2017, "WhatsApp announced it was experimenting with verified business accounts on the platform, which would offer brands the opportunity to communicate with its users; a platform the average user checks 23 times a day and which boasts 1.2 billion monthly active users."

"Businesses can gain a verified green checkmark icon to indicate the authenticity of the account, assuring users its legitimacy, alongside opening the door to the platform's previously walled off garden," Turner adds.[367]

"The platform could be following in the footsteps of other messaging apps such as Facebook Messenger and Kik, implementing a chatbot function to enable WhatsApp users to ask businesses questions, make purchases and receive instant bot responses," says Turner.[367]

The opportunity is considerable. WhatsApp business accounts offer up one more channel for brands to send out simple automated messaging to users who opt into their messages.[367] "Whether it be discount codes, new products or brand news, users could stay up to date with businesses they invest in and brands would be presented with the opportunity to reach people on a platform that, sees 6 out of 10 users accessing the app on a daily basis," argues Turner.[367]

WhatsApp's history will work in its favor. Having never allowed any form of advertising previously, WhatsApp currently feels like a very intimate and private environment for its users.[367] Turner believes that "content delivered to users would, therefore, benefit from having an 'organic' feel; providing useful and totally personalised content."[367]

A good example of the potential can be seen in the *Nike On Demand* WhatsApp service.[367] It is a one-to-one messenger-based service that was "created to connect athletes with Nike experts on a regular basis to keep them motivated and on-track with their fitness goals."[367] The campaign delivers "personalised content in the form of images, conversation, playlists, etc. as well as providing expert advice from pacers and trainers all through the WhatsApp platform, akin to a real peer's motivational reminder," explains Turner.[367]

"Whether WhatsApp intends to follow the crowd by implementing a chatbot strategy or go against the grain to offer users something truly useful and personalised will soon become clear," adds Turner.[367] "What is already very clear, however, is the opportunity WhatsApp business accounts presents, regardless of what strategy they choose, to reach inside the walled gardens of messaging apps," Turner concludes.[367]

All-in-all, companies can use social media to manage their brand, enhance brand loyalty, as well as engage both their current customers and their potential customers. The social media world is also the perfect place to harvest customer feedback, provide real-time customer service, build fanbases, and drive traffic to a marketer's website.

Brands should also feel compelled to reward their customers through Facebook, Twitter, WeChat, and Weibo, or any number of blogging and micro-blogging services. The beauty of using these channels is the ability of customers to share these awards or stories of these awards with friends and acquaintances. It wouldn't be that hard to do, either, as a marketer can ask customers for their social media accounts upon sign up, like many already do.

Jones and Sasser warn that, "Extremely dissatisfied customers can turn into 'terrorists,' providing an abundance of negative feedback about the service provider."[117] Through social media channels, negative feedback can reverberate around the world within seconds. Today, more than ever, brands must spot dissatisfied customers and approach them before they do irreparable harm to the company's image and reputation and social media is one of the best channels in which to engage them to diffuse their anger.

In the *zone of indifference*, customers willingly switch if they can find a better alternative, while in the *zone of affection*, satisfaction levels are high and "customers may have such high attitudinal loyalty that they don't look for alternative services."[117] It is within this group that "Apostles"—members who willingly praise the firm in public—reside and this is the group that is responsible for improved future business performance.[107] Brands need to empower their customers to post on Facebook or WeChat or Twitter or comment about their experience and, hopefully, turn these customers into apostles.

Facebook should be a part of every brand's social and mobile media marketing plan, but simply putting up a Facebook page won't cut it these days; creativity and uniqueness are needed to get noticed in today's highly competitive social media world. Gamification is also a good way to stand out from the crowd. Facebook bots can also add a customer service channel that can answer common customer service questions quickly, efficiently and inexpensively.

The best part of being on Twitter or Weibo or any of the other instant messaging services is the ability to interact with a customer in real time. A direct, two-way dialogue can be created, which helps with engagement and, potentially, sales.

In its article *The 5 Different Types of Influencer Marketing Campaigns*[368], Mediakix claims that there are probably a limitless amount of ways for brands to create effective influencer marketing campaigns, but, in general, these campaigns fall within one of the following five subcategories:

1. Product Placement—this involves incorporating a company's product, services, or logo into a digital influencer's content just as it has been done in the film industry for decades. Just like actors in films, social media stars have earned the trust of their followers, so product placements are an excellent opportunity for brands to gain valuable exposure to millions of engaged consumers through the influencer's YouTube, yy.com, Instagram, or Snapchat account.[368]
2. Contests, Giveaways, Sweepstakes—Hosting social media contests like giveaways, sweepstakes, or best-of contests, such as best photograph, video, or blog competitions can generate buzz about a marketer, as well as foster goodwill among consumers. These contests compel social media users to take a specific action (like following the brand's channel or increasing company exposure by using branded hashtags). Aligning with a social media influencer, a marketer can promote a contest that will leverage the social media star's large follower base and ensure that consumers participate in the campaign.[368]
3. Theme/Hashtag Campaign—Hashtags are great ways to build a theme around a campaign. Focusing each influencer marketing campaign around a central theme or hashtag that is leveraged throughout all of the social channels helps build cohesion and encourages consumers to get involved by using the brand's hashtag in their own content. As Mediakix recommends, "Developing and Implementing an influencer

marketing campaign around a memorable branded hashtag is one of the best ways brands can facilitate a genuine social conversation and increase brand exposure, especially if the hashtag happens to go viral."[368]
4. Creative Influencer Campaign–These give the social media star much more freedom to create content and these campaigns usually center around a specific concept or idea. Done right, these campaigns allow the digital influencer to interpret themes to create unique brand-sponsored content, leading to increased levels of engagement from the social media influencer's followers and/or subscribers.[368]
5. Campaign to Build Social Followers—brands can invite social media influencers to expose new audiences to their brand's social media accounts. Snapchat Takeovers—having a social media influencer "take over" a brand's Snapchat account for a set period of time—is one of the most effective ways for businesses to reach thousands or millions of new followers, as well as organically grow their own Snapchat follower fanbase.[368]

In his book *The Executive Guide to Artificial Intelligence: How to Identify and Implement Applications for AI in Your Organization*[369], Andrew Burgess provides another example of AI's use in retail, i.e., Stitchfix's practice of using humans in the AI loop. For those who fear that AI is destined to cause massive human unemployment, Jana Eggers, CEO of Nara Logics, has some comforting words— "We don't talk about the fact that humans and computers together almost always beat computers alone."[5]

Stitchfix's business model is predicated on the recommendation of new clothes to its customers based on a selection of information and data that the customer provides, including measurement, style survey results, Pinterest boards, etc.[369] "All this structured and unstructured data is digested, interpreted and collated by the AI solution, which sends the summary, plus anything that is more nuanced (such as free-form notes written by the customer) to one of the company's 2,800 work-from-home specialist human agents, who then select five pieces of clothing for the customer to try," explains Burgess.[369]

Burgess believes this is a good example of how AI can augment the skills and experience of a human staff, both improving their job and making them more efficient.[369] Having humans in the loop "also makes experimenting easier, as any errors can quickly be corrected by the staff."[369] "To test for this bias, the system varies the amount and type of data that it shows to a stylist—it can then determine how much influence a particular feature, say a picture of the customer or their address, can make on the stylist's decisions. On top of this, the data that they gather about all of their customers can also be used to predict (and influence?) general fashion trends," explains Burgess.[369]

Data & Analytics

In this final stage of the customer journey, brands should acquire social identity tied to customer records. Neuberger argues that it is very important to monitor the market conversation to understand what the marketplace is (or isn't) saying about a brand (its products, services, etc.).[359] Companies "need to understand the tone and impact of the conversation and begin to identify areas of opportunity for helping shape that conversation and gather valuable market intelligence," says Neuberger.[359]

As previously mentioned, ROI is not that difficult to measure with social media, quite the contrary. Today, the endless search for Facebook fans should be replaced by short-term campaign ROI as the main measure for individual campaigns. Brands should look at correlation analysis between activities, engagement and sales, which might be unsettling for some traditional marketers, but the reward should be worth the time and the effort.[48]

As Josh Constine reports in his *Techcrunch* article *How Uber Will Become an Ad Company, Starting with Eats Pool*,[370] Uber plans to help users choose between restaurants that it is promoting through paid ads. Uber could "become the marketing platform through which the physical world vies for your attention," Costine says.[370]

In India, Uber Eats now offers restaurants bonus visibility in a specials section if they offer discounts on meal bundles to Uber's customers.[370] "Knock some rupees off the price of a sandwich, fries and a drink, and a restaurant wins itself some enhanced discoverability. Whether a chef wants to boost orders during slow hours, get rid of surplus food, preference high-margin items or just score new customers, there are plenty of reasons to pay Uber—even if currently only indirectly through discounts instead of a direct ad buy," says Costine.[370]

Uber's senior director and head of its Eats product Stephen Chau confirmed to *Techcrunch* that the company intends to become an ad company.[370] "There's a bunch of different ways we can work with restaurants over time. If we have all the restaurants on the marketplace and we give them tools to help them grow, then this will be a very efficient marketplace. They're going to be spending those ad dollars somewhere," said Chau.[370] "One of the things we've been experimenting with is allowing retailers to create promotions themselves and show them within the product," he added.[370] "To be worthy of ad dollars," Constine states, "Uber has to build leverage over restaurants by accruing sway over how people decide between restaurants."[370] Wanting to show new revenue streams for its upcoming IPO, Uber has created what is effectively an "Uber Eats Pool."[370]

Uber is also now testing a system designed to batch to a single restaurant multiple orders from different customers who are near to each other.[370] "That way, a single delivery driver can pick up all the orders at once and then speedily distribute them to neighbors or co-workers," states Costine.[370] Uber incentivizes customers in the same vicinity to pick the same restaurant in rapid succession by the best method available to it—cash discounts.[370] A countdown timer is attached to the offer that follows users on an eatery's order page, which triggers a sense of urgency to hurriedly buy through Uber Eats rather than shopping around.[370] It also ensures orders "come in close enough together that the first one cooked won't have to wait long for the last before they're all scooped up for delivery."[370]

Some customers have added a gamification element to the process of buying food, "actually playing the Uber Eats Pool discounts like a game they can beat, waiting through several rounds of the timer until they spot one of their favorite restaurants."[370] Amazingly, humans can make even the most mundane of efforts—buying food—a game! "For now, passengers don't ride alongside food orders, though that's certainly a possibility in the future," says Costine.[370] "If Uber Eats can batch your order into a pool with other customers, it will retroactively give you the discount," adds Costine.[370]

"It's similar to what we did with Uber Pool," says Chau.[370] "Generally people are coming in with an intent to eat but there are many, many options available to them. We're giving you a discount on the food delivery by using machine learning to understand these are some restaurants it might make sense to order from. When multiple people order from the same restaurant, delivery drivers can pick up multiple people's food," notes Chau.[370]

Internet companies like Uber "are gaining great influence by becoming marketplaces that connect customers with suppliers when previously customers preemptively chose a particular supplier."[370] "These platforms not only gain enormous amounts of data on customer preferences, but they also hold the power to point customers to certain suppliers that are willing to play ball," says Costine.[370]

"With all the data, the platforms know just who to show the ads to for a maximum conversion rate. And over time, as the aggregator's perks lure in more customers, it can pit suppliers against each other to further drop their prices or pay more for ads," explains Costine.[370]

Spotify showed the power of this type of platform when it "used its own playlists to control which songs became popular, and the artists and record labels became beholden to cutting it sweeter deals to stay visible."[370] "Amazon looks like the best place to shop because it makes merchants fiercely fight to offer the lowest prices and best customer experience," adds Costine.[370] "With Uber Eats Pool, Uber is flexing its ability to influence where you eat, training you to trust where it points you when businesses eventually pay directly to be ranked higher in its app."[370]

"Eats proves the power and potential of the Uber platform, showing how our logistics expertise can create the easiest way to eat," Chau says.[370] "We partner with a wide selection of restaurants and bring our trademark speed and coverage to the food delivery experience. This feature shows how leveraging the Uber network allows us to offer people even more affordable dining options," Chau adds.[370] Uber's logistic network has accrued the power and it creates "leverage over the supplier to benefit customers with the lowest prices."[370]

"We can see on Eats how much more business they're bringing in and how much is incremental new business. Eventually we'll be able to do very precise targeting. 'People who haven't tried my restaurant before, let's give them a discount,'" Chau says.[370] Restaurants are asking Uber how to grow delivery as a percentage of their orders.[370] Uber has "demonstrated the data science it could dangle over restaurants with its review of *Uber Eats 2018 trends*. Uber predicts clean eating, plant-based foods, smoothie bowls, milk alternatives, fermented items like kimchi and Instagrammably dark 'goth food' will rise in popularity next year," predicts Costine. However, now-tired social media clickbait "rainbow-colored foods," Brussels sprouts and seaweed were on the decline.[370]

"It becomes easy to imagine restaurants running Uber Eats software for tracking order trends and predicting spikes to better manage food and staffing resources, with a baked-in option to buy ads or give deeper discounts to get seen by more hungry people," says Constine. "Restaurants can think of Uber Eats as a platform that gives them this intelligence," concludes Chau.[370]

In their article *10 Principles of Modern Marketing*[4], Lewnes and Keller contend that, "The amount of data available today mandates that every brand knows its customers and caters to them at every possible touch point, but at the same time, it is still important to actually meet with customers!" "No dashboard alone can provide the same rich insights as an in-depth conversation with an engaged customer," say Lewnes and Keller.[4] Along with traditional qualitative methods like focus groups and research, Adobe holds live events worldwide because it sees an unprecedented level of engagement from them, something far different to an online connection.[4] "Nothing beats the power of companies and their customers coming together in person to learn, get inspired, and have a little fun," they conclude.[4]

In his *Social CRM as a business strategy*, Woodcock states that, "The explicit use of active and control groups, and experimentation of using different treatments will help marketers understand the impact of specific SM activities."[48] More direct marketing type disciplines will be required, in a world where there is real-time feedback on attitude and behavior and a plethora of data."[48] Because of the enormous proliferation of data, this has become a much more demanding world in terms of capturing and utilizing useful data, but making the effort to turn this data into actionable intelligence will be noticed by fickle consumers, I have no doubt.

Brands should look to assign a percentage value to social media so that a true attribution measurement can be created. Values should be ascribed to social media for being the site of new customer contact or for numbers of positive reviews by current customers. These are all important metrics to know and tracked because a highly followed influencer might not be spending that much with your brand, but their followers might be.

For Neuberger, "Social media metrics include sentiment, activity, share-of-voice, and thematic content of online conversations. Trends and key influencers ('mavens') and the most active sites/blogs are identified and tracked. By understanding the impact, retailers will have a way of identifying measurable progress, quantifying the return on social media investment, and enabling benchmarking against future efforts."[359]

"To be a great technology marketer in today's digital world, it is important to build a culture of testing," argue Lewnes and Keller.[4] The writers work for Adobe and, from "a *product* perspective, Adobe does active beta testing with its customers, releasing versions of its software into the market and actively engaging with customers during the beta period to solicit feedback, add new functionality, and shape product road maps."[4]

"From a *marketing mix* perspective, Adobe applies state-of-the-art econometric modeling, as well as real-time attribution modeling, to test, predict, and ultimately validate the right levels and mix of media investments," explain Lewnes and Keller.[4]

"From a *marketing* perspective, Adobe uses data to build more precise segmentation models based on factors such as the type of content customers create and engage most with and their stage in the customer journey to offer more personalized, relevant experiences—a valuable asset in today's digital world," claim Lewnes and Keller.[4]

Of course, Adobe is not unique in using data analytics to drive marketing experimentation.[4] "Amazon, Capital One, Netflix, and Pandora famously run thousands of tests to optimize their marketing efforts."[4] Facebook can certainly be added to that mix.

"To successfully activate these different insights to improve the customer experience, it is imperative to also work across the organization to integrate data and build real-time data models and decision-driving dashboards," say Lewnes and Keller.[4] "That requires blending marketing inputs like behavioral data (for example, social, PR, web data, and media performance) with inputs from other areas (for example, sales, CRM, in-product, and finance). In today's world, marketing simply can't operate in a silo," conclude Lewnes and Keller.[4]

ANDREW W. PEARSON

The Future

Pretty much everyone working in advertising today agrees that the future will be more intelligent. what McKinsey calls marketing's holy grail: digital personalization at scale[72] is one of the big goals for today's *A.I. Marketer*, who is a marketer that considers how a customer who lands on a company webpage or steps into its brick-and-mortar store affects every facet of the company's business. *The A.I. Marketer* follows a customer before arrival, through his or her entire shopping experience, or potential shopping experience, then keeps tabs on him or her once the purchase is over. The customer experience information is then utilized as part of a predictive model for the brand's entire customer base.

As Kahle puts it, eventually we're going to set a time frame on the sales funnel that never expires.[112] The process starts at the moment of first contact, when the company's system spots the IP address of a web browser, through the capturing of the customer's social ID, to understanding the social activity, all the way through to the loyalty card sign up process. The only thing remaining is to capture post-transaction information if and when it occurs.

Besides Apple and Google, Facebook is now entering the acquisition business full throttle. Along with its Instagram buy, the Oculus Rift purchase further shows that Facebook is obsessed with staying relevant by buying the next big thing argues Paul Berry, founder and CEO of New York City-based social publishing platform RebelMouse.[371] "Through this and other acquisitions, Berry thinks Facebook will become a brand-holding company in the future, similar to Viacom or Hearst."[371] "I see them, better than anyone else, using their market capitalization to create even bigger market cap for the Instagrams or WhatsApps," he says.[371]

The purchase of Oculus Rift should help Facebook grab a large piece of the advertising market.[371] In five years, Arvind Bhatia, managing director of equity research at Sterne Agee, expects Facebook's "graph search to become bigger, and the company to make more inroads in e-commerce."[371] "Then, with its ancillary networks like WhatsApp and Instagram, Facebook will be able to run its own platform, rather than operate through Android and iOS."[371] Currently, Facebook are getting bypassed on the mobile platform, Bhatia says, but that might not last long if Facebook has its way. "They want to be the next Android, and so the only way to do that was to start from scratch, and that's what they're doing with this virtual reality technology."[371]

Just as Facebook might morph into a complex conglomeration of services and brands, Twitter should continue to differentiate itself through its simplicity.[371] First, the network has to focus on monetization, and in "Berry's view, over the next five years Twitter's monetization will be faster than its user adoption."[371] "They are so simple and so public, and it works so much data around what you are interested in—the fact that it's all public is perfect for advertising," Berry says.[371] "I think it achieves being the short, public, status updates of the Internet," Berry adds.[371]

Meanwhile, Twitter's decelerating growth worries Bhatia. "While he thinks the network will continue to grow, he believes it won't equal Facebook's user base."[371] "And already Instagram is catching up," he says.[371] "While Facebook is going to become one of the four horsemen of technology, Twitter will be an interesting, decent-sized company, but not a mainstay, if you will."[371] What really sets Twitter apart is its openness.[371] "As data science continues to boom, this openness will give Twitter increasing utility," says Bhatia.[371] Because of this, there is a long-shot possibility that Twitter gets bought out by a giant organization like the United Nations, for dissemination and collection of data on an almost unimaginable scale.[371]

With their *Cluetrain Manifesto*[279], Rick Levine, Christopher Lock, Doc Searle, and David Weinberger warned that not only are markets conversations but the Internet is revolutionizing the way businesses communicate with their customers and if businesses don't adapt and treat their customers with respect, their customers will desert them. What better way to treat them with respect than to listen to them and respond to them accordingly, which mobile and social media channels do better than any other form of communication. AI, too, greatly assists with this.

In their paper *Marketing Analytics for Data-Rich Environments*[126], Webel and Kannan, argue that there are many promising areas of research that businesses should keep on their radar. The technological developments of tomorrow might just be some of the ones discussed in Table 15.

Technology never sleeps. Breakthroughs in hardware and software technology occur on a daily basis. Kelnar argues that the "effectiveness of AI has been transformed in recent years due to the development of new algorithms, greater availability of data to inform them, better hardware to train them and cloud-based services to catalyse their adoption among developers."[35]

DATA	DETAILS
Structured data	<ul><li>Behavioral targeting with cross-device data; mobile, location-based, and social analytics.</li><li>Fusing data generated within the firm with data generated outside the firm; integrating "small stats.</li><li>Combining machine learning approaches with econometric and theory-based methods for big data applications; computational solutions to marketing models for big data.</li></ul>

Unstructured data	• Development of diagnostic, predictive, and prescriptive approaches for analysis of large-scale unstructured data. • Approaches to analyze unstructured social, geo-spatial, mobile data and combining them with structured data in big data contexts. • Using, evaluating, and extending deep learning methods and cognitive computing to analyze unstructured marketing data.
Marketing-mix modeling	• Aligning analysis of disaggregate data with that of aggregate data and including unstructured data in the analysis of the marketing mix. • New techniques and methods to accurately measure the impact of marketing instruments and their carryover and spillover across media and devices using integrated path-to-purchase data. • Dynamic, multi-time period and cross-category optimization of the marketing mix. • Approaches to incorporate different planning cycles for different marketing instruments in media-mix models.
Personalization	• Automated closed-loop marketing solutions for digital environments; fully automated marketing solutions. • Personalization and customization techniques using cognitive systems, general artificial intelligence, and automated attention analysis; personalization of content. • Mobile, location-based personalization of the marketing mix.
Security and privacy	• Methods to produce and handle data minimization and data anonymization in assessing marketing-mix effectiveness and personalization. • Distributed data solutions to enhance data security and privacy while maximizing personalized marketing opportunities.

Table 15: Area of Focus Promising and Important Issues for Research
Source: Marketing Analytics for Data-Rich Environments[126]

Progress in speech and handwriting recognition "is improving rapidly following the creation of recurrent neural networks (RNNs)," states Kelnar.[35] "RNNs have feedback connections that enable data to flow in a loop, unlike conventional neural networks that 'feed forward' only," explains Kelnar.[35] A powerful new type of RNN is the 'Long Short-Term Memory' (LSTM) model," notes Kelnar. He adds that, "With additional connections and memory cells, RNNs 'remember' the data they saw thousands of steps ago and use this to inform their interpretation of what follows—valuable for speech recognition where interpretation of the next word will be informed by the words that preceded it."[35] "From 2012, Google used LSTMs to power the speech recognition system in Android. In October 2016, "Microsoft engineers reported that their system reached a word error rate of 5.9%—a figure roughly equal to that of human abilities for the first time in history."[35] This is all highly impressive stuff and portends great advances in voice recognition technology are right around the corner.

Today GPUs "are slashing the time required to train the neural networks used for deep learning."[35] "When combined with software development kits tuned for widely used deep learning frameworks, the improvements in training speed can be even greater," notes Kelnar.[35]

Kelnar argues that, "The neural networks used for deep learning typically require large data sets for training—from a few thousand examples to many millions."[35] Fortunately for us all, data creation and availability of this data has grown exponentially.[35] "Today, as we enter the 'third wave' of data, humanity produces 2.2 exabytes (2,300 million gigabytes) of data every day; 90% of all the world's data has been created in the last 24 months," Kelnar notes.[35] All of this data collection will result in vast new reservoirs of information that AI can utilize.

Looking at it historically, while we were busy transferring 100GB of data per day in 1992, by 2020 we will be transferring 61,000GB per second, an increase that is exponential in scale.[35] More data means better models, which mean more accurate predictions, so these are all positive developments for AI and analytics.

"Beyond increases in the availability of general data, specialist data resources have catalysed progress in machine learning," says Kelnar.[35] As previously mentioned, Google, Facebook, and Microsoft have all open sourced their deep learning tools, which is a huge deal not only because the tools are now freely available but because this helps build a community of engineers and available consultants.

Google's Dataset Search is a new search engine built specifically to help users find sets of data useful for analytical modeling. ImageNet "is a freely available database of over 10 million hand-labelled images. Its presence has supported the rapid development of object classification deep learning algorithms," notes Kelnar.[35]

The cloud is also an important part of the analytics and deep learning equation. "Developers' use of machine learning is being catalysed by the provision of cloud-based machine learning infrastructure and services from the industry's leading cloud providers," says Kelnar.[35] "Google, Amazon, Microsoft and IBM all offer cloud-based infrastructure (environments for model-building and iteration, scalable 'GPUs-as-a-service' and related managed services) to reduce the cost and difficulty of developing machine learning capabilities," notes Kelnar.[35]

In China, Alicloud is becoming a major player in the cloud space and their unique "China Connect" service allows companies to upload content outside of China and replicate it on servers inside China, making any brand content easily–and quickly downloadable–by Mainland customers. Fast downloads of mobile content, I'd argue, is a necessary condition for reaching the massive Chinese market, which is probably the most mobilely sophisticated audience in the world, and probably will be for years to come.

In addition, these cloud vendors offer "a burgeoning range of cloud-based machine learning services (from image recognition to language translation) which developers can use directly in their own applications."[35] "Google Machine Learning offers easily accessible services for: vision (object identification, explicit content detection, face detection and image sentiment analysis); speech (speech recognition and speech-to-text); text analysis (entity recognition, sentiment analysis, language detection and translation); and employee job searching (opportunity surfacing and seniority-based matching)."[35] Not to be outdone, Microsoft Cognitive Services offers "more than 21 services within the fields of vision, speech, language, knowledge and search."[35]

All of this open sourcing and sharing of technology by these tech behemoths is perhaps an acknowledgement that the space is too big for one company to contain on its own and assistance will be needed with this profound and incredibly disruptive technology. For-profit companies rarely show this kind of magnanimous behavior, especially on the technological front, where walls of IP are so often constructed to keep competitors at bay. From these actions alone, we can probably conclude that something interesting and highly unique is going on here.

In Greek mythology, once *Pandora's Box* was opened and the evils of the world were let out, the only thing remaining inside was hope. It Is my hope that this book helps brands avoid a *Pandora's Box* full of pain when implementing highly complicated A.I., machine learning and deep learning solutions. It is also my hope that this book helps narrow the gap between what businesses think they are delivering in terms of customer experience and what customers think they are actually delivering. Currently, the chasm is wide, and improvement is needed immediately.

Much of the technology discussed here requires considerable time, energy, and money to implement, but if companies are willing to go down the AI, machine learning, deep learning, and personalization road properly, I have no doubt they will be richly rewarded with highly positive ROI.

As you have reached the end of this book, I'd like to quote Mr. Wilde one last time— "Some cause happiness wherever they go; others whenever they go." Well, it is time for me to go and I hope I am of the former (you probably wouldn't have stuck around this far if I was of the latter, right?). What the reader should ultimately take from this book is that the AI opportunity is here and the time to grab it is right now.

Fin

329 Gourévitch, Antoine, Faeste, Lars, Baltasis, Elias, and Marx, Julien. May 23, 2017. Data-Driven Transformation: Accelerate at Scale Now. Boston Consulting Group. https://www.bcg.com/en-in/publications/2017/digital-transformation-transformation-data-driven-transformation.aspx (Accessed 8 September 2017).
330 Sanz, Luis. Olapic. The North Face & Watson: Bringing the in-store experience online. http://www.olapic.com/resources/the_north_face_ibm_artificial_intelligence/ (Accessed 3 May 2019).
331 https://aws.amazon.com/lex/ (Accessed 11 March 2019).
332 https://aws.amazon.com/lex/ (Accessed 11 March 2019).
333 https://aws.amazon.com/transcribe/ (Accessed 11 March 2019).
334 https://aws.amazon.com/comprehend/ (Accessed 11 March 2019).
335 Yakuel, Pini. Optimove. Turning Up Your Brand's Voice to Reach the Most Advanced Customers. October 25, 2018. https://www.optimove.com/blog/using-digital-assistant-to-help-market-your-brand (Accessed 14 April 2019).
336 Maruti Tech. 14 Powerful Chatbot Platforms. https://www.marutitech.com/14-powerful-chatbot-platforms/ (Accessed 8 April 2019).
337 https://chatfuel.com (Accessed 8 April 2019).
338 https://botsify.com (Accessed 8 April 2019).
339 https://flowxo.com/ (Accessed 8 April 2019).
340 Baron, Justine. SAP.com. Recast.AI will be renamed SAP Conversational AI early 2019! November 15, 2018. https://cai.tools.sap/blog/recast-ai-renaming/ (Accessed 14 April 2019).
341 https://www.octaneai.com/ (Accessed 14 April 2019).
342 Altexsoft. (2018). Sentiment Analysis: Types, Tools, and Use Cases. September 21, 2018. https://www.altexsoft.com/blog/business/sentiment-analysis-types-tools-and-use-cases/ (Accessed 15 April 2019).
343 Dreamgrow.com. https://www.dreamgrow.com/69-free-social-media-monitoring-tools/ (Accessed 22 November 2017).
344 Rowe, Kevin. (2017). Search Engine Land. How to use AI for link building and improve your search rankings. September 26, 2017. https://searchengineland.com/use-ai-link-building-improve-search-rankings-283150 (Accessed 14 April 2019).
345 Bea, Francis. March 25, 2012. Goodbye, anonymity: latest surveillance tech can search up to 36 million faces per second. www.digitaltrends.com http://www.digitaltrends.com/cool-tech/goodbye-anonymity-latest-surveillance-tech-can-search-up-to-36-million-faces-per-second/ (Accessed 25 November 2017).
346 Facial recognition: Who's Tracking You In Public. (December 30, 2015) Consumer Reports. Online: http://www.consumerreports.org/privacy/facial-recognition-who-is-tracking-you-in-public1/ (Accessed 25 November 2017).
347 Gates, Kelly A. January 23, 2011. Our Biometric Future: Facial Recognition Technology and the Culture of Surveillance. NYU Press.

348 Riddell, Chris. Qantas have seen their Future. It's Facial Recognition. 1 August 2017. Chrisriddell.com. http://chrisriddell.com/qantas-future-facial-recognition/ (Accessed 9 October 2018).

349 Johnson, Lauren. 2017. Pinterest Is Offering Brands Its Visual Search Technology To Score Large Ad Deals. Adweek. October 2, 2017. http://www.adweek.com/digital/pinterest-is-offering-brands-its-visual-search-technology-to-score-large-ad-deals/ (Accessed 18 November 2017).

350 Matt Cimaglia, Matt. (2019). Entrepreneur. The Future of Video Advertising is Artificial Intelligence. December 12, 2018. https://www.entrepreneur.com/article/323756 (Accessed 4 January 2019).

351 Fuller, Brian. 2018. Arm Community. AI's role in next-generation voice recognition. IoT Blog. https://community.arm.com/iot/b/blog/posts/artificial-intelligence-is-changing-voice-recognition-technology (Accessed 12 January 2019).

352 Kinsella, Bret. 2019 Predictions from 35 voice industry leaders. January 1, 2019. Voicebot.ai. https://voicebot.ai/2019/01/01/2019-predictions-from-35-voice-industry-leaders/ (Accessed 21 January 2019).

353 Olson, Christi. (2018). Marchtech Today. Voice search isn't the next big disrupter, conversational AI Is. October 11, 2018. https://martechtoday.com/voice-search-isnt-the-next-big-disrupter-conversational-ai-is-226537 (Accessed 3 March 2019).

354 https://aws.amazon.com/polly/ (Accessed 11 March 2019).

355 https://aws.amazon.com/polly/ (Accessed 11 March 2019).

356 SeoClarity. The Next Generation of Search: Voice. https://go.seoClarity.net/hubfs/docs/research/seoClarity_whitepaper_next-generation-search-voice.pdf (Accessed 16 April 2019).

357 https://www.dialogtech.com/blog/search-marketing/voice-search-statistics

358 Batra, Varun. Marchtechseries. How AI is Driving a New Era of TV Advertising. March 29, 2018. https://martechseries.com/mts-insights/guest-authors/how-ai-is-driving-a-new-era-of-tv-advertising/ (Accessed 12 April 2019).

359 Neuberger, W. (n.d.). Engage Customers and gain advocates through social media and social networking. January 24, 2013. ftp://public.dhe.ibm.com/software/solutions/soa/newsletter/2010/newsletter-mar10-article_social_media.pdf (Accessed 13 November 2017).

360 Shewan, Dan. (2018). Wordstream. Pain Points: A Guide to Finding & Solving Your Customers' Problems. November 28, 2019. https://www.wordstream.com/blog/ws/2018/02/28/pain-points (Accessed 7 April 2019).

361 Gulbransen, Scott. January 22, 2014. Taking Back the Social-Media Command Center, Scott Gulbransen. Forbes. http://www.forbes.com/sites/onmarketing/2014/01/22/taking-back-the-social-media-command-center/#3c283a5d6513 (Accessed 22 November 2017).

362 Mathison, Rob. Hootsuite. (2017). 14 of the Best Social Media Monitoring Tools for Business. August 14, 2017. https://blog.hootsuite.com/social-media-monitoring-tools/ (Accessed 23 November 2017).

363 Gell, Aaron. (2017) The Not-so-Surprising Survival of Foursquare. The New Yorker. March 1, 2017. https://www.newyorker.com/business/currency/the-not-so-surprising-survival-of-foursquare (Accessed 23 November 2017).

364 Perlmutter, Rachel. (2016) Why You Need Social Proof on Your Website. Entrepreneur.com. July 6, 2016. https://www.entrepreneur.com/article/296644 (Accessed 23 November 2017).

365 Biron, Bethany. (2017). How Facebook is wooing luxury brands. Digiday. https://digiday.com/media/bringing-retail-speed-feed-facebooks-quest-court-luxury-brands/ (Accessed 24 November 2017).

366 Graff, Roy. (2018). Routes Online. 14 August 2018. https://www.routesonline.com/news/29/breaking-news/280065/how-international-airlines-use-wechat-to-market-to-china/ (Accessed 14 August 2018).

367 Turner, Holly. 2017. Whatsapp For Business—What Does it Mean? M&C Satchi Mobile. http://www.mcsaatchimobile.com/whatsapp-business-mean/ (Accessed 23 November 2017).

368 The 5 Different Types of Influencer Marketing Campaigns. March 30, 2016. Mediakix.com. http://mediakix.com/2016/03/influencer-marketing-campaigns-5-examples/#gs.Lz0k6B4 (Accessed 13 November 2017).

369 Burgess, Andrew. (2017). The Executive Guide to Artificial Intelligence: How to Identify How to Identify and Implement Applications for AI in Your Organization. Springer International Publishing. 29 November 2017.

370 Constine, Josh. (2018). Techcrunch. How Uber Will Become an Ad Company, Starting with Eats Pool. 12 December 2018. https://techcrunch.com/2018/12/10/uber-ads/ (Accessed 1 January 2019).

371 Pullen, J. P. (2014, April 2). What Will Social Media's Giants Look Like in 5 or 10 years? Retrieved from fortune.com: http://fortune.com/2014/04/02/what-will-social-medias-giants-look-like-in-5-or-10-years/ (Accessed 13 November 2017).

ANDREW W. PEARSON

ABOUT THE AUTHOR

ANDREW PEARSON was born in Pakistan, grew up in Singapore, and was educated in both England and America. With a degree in psychology from UCLA, Pearson has had a varied career in IT, marketing, mobile technology, social media, and entertainment.

In 2011, Pearson relocated from Los Angeles to Hong Kong to open Qualex Asia Limited, bringing its parent company's software consulting experience into the ASEAN region.

In 2016, Pearson founded his own consulting company, Intelligencia Limited, and he is currently the managing director overseeing operations throughout the ASEAN region, the Middle East, and North America. Intelligencia is a leading analytics, AI, BI, CI, digital marketing and social media company, implementing complex customer experience and personalization solutions for clients like The Venetian Macau, Galaxy Macau, Genting HK, Tatts Lottery, Tabcorp, Resorts World Casino NY, Mexico's Logrand Group, Junglee Games, and Macau Slot.

In 2010, Pearson published *The Mobile Revolution*, and, in 2013, Pearson was invited to write a chapter in *Global Mobile: Applications and Innovations for the Worldwide Mobile Ecosystem*, a book on mobile technology that was co-authored by several of the mobile industry's leading figures.

The first in the *Predictive* series—*The Predictive Casino*—was published in 2017, while *The Predictive Sports Book, The Predictive Retailer*, and *The Predictive Airliner* followed in 2018. There are plans to tackle several other industries in 2019 and beyond, while *The A.I. Marketer* starts a completely new series.

Pearson is also a noted columnist, authoring articles on such topics such as analytics, AI, smart technology, Chinese social media, esports, and cloud technology. Pearson has written for such publications as *ComputerWorld HK, The Mobile Marketer*, and *The Journal of Mobile and Social Media Marketing*, where he is also a contributing editor. Pearson is the president of the *Advanced Analytics Association of Macau* and one of the founders of *Grow uP eSports*, a Macau association that promotes esports throughout the world.

An avid traveler, Pearson is a sought-after speaker on such disparate topics as AI and Machine Learning, analytics, gaming, social media, and esports. If he's not pounding the pavements of Hollywood, he's probably wandering the labyrinthine streets of Hong Kong's Lang Kwai Fong, or tearing up useless betting slips at Happy Valley (perhaps the most perfectly named racecourse in the world (for some)), or haggling in a Hyderabad street market, or dining at a hawker center in Singapore, or marveling at the historical importance of Moscow's Red Square, or doubling down at the gaming tables in Macau. Basically, Pearson's out there trying to find the next great story that the world doesn't yet know it

ANDREW W. PEARSON

desperately wants to see...

Social Media
LinkedIn: andrew-pearson-96513a3
Amazon Author Central: https://www.amazon.com/Andrew-Pearson/e/B005M5ACG0
Twitter: intelligenciaMD
Academia: PearsonAndrew
Blog: medium.com/@intelligentsiaf

THE A.I. MARKETER

INDEX

A/B Testing, 172
Activity tracing, 231
Adobe, 5, 30, 64, 66, 67, 68, 73, 74, 77, 78, 106, 107, 202, 203, 204, 208, 237, 240, 252, 343
  Auto Crop, 239
  Auto Tag, 368
  Deep Cutout, 239
Adobe Advertising Cloud, 214, 216, 244
Adobe Audience Manager, 195
Adobe Enterprise Content, 240, 241
Adobe Experience Cloud, 74, 75, 77, 238, 367
Adobe Marketing Cloud, 204
Adobe Retail Team, 81
Adobe Sensei, 3, 78, 196, 237, 238, 239, 368
  Auto tagging, 239
Adobe Sensei Team, 377, 385, 386
Advertising
  banner ads, 62
AdWords, 205
Affdex, 92, 93, 94, 95, 97
Affectiva, 91, 92, 93, 94, 95, 96, 97
Affective Computing, 91
AI, 13, 16, 26, 27, 29, 30, 67, 162, 316, 317, 318, 319, 389
AI dilemma, 41, 297
AI-generated content, 119
AI-powered search, 138
Air Canada, 24, 131, 132
Alicloud, 403
AlphaGo, 31, 32
AlphaGo Zero, 31, 32
Alteryx, 163
Amara's Law, 7
Amazon, 6, 8, 26, 30, 67, 70, 138, 164, 232, 274, 327, 344, 369, 390
Amazon Comprehend, 8, 348
Amazon Lex, 8
Amazon Polly, 8
Amazon S3, 306

Amazon Transcribe, 8, 348
Analytics
  descriptive analytics, 73, 160, 161
  diagnostic analytics, 73, 160, 161
  edge analytics, 72, 197, 334, 335
  Market basket analysis, 73
  predictive analytics, 3, 72, 73, 74, 114, 115, 122, 154, 155, 160, 161, 162, 163, 197, 200, 204, 208
  prescriptive analytics, 73, 160, 162, 208
  Propensity models, 121
  Text analytics, 115
Apache Storm, 326, 327
App store, 268
Apple, 6, 48, 127, 400
Artificial General Intelligence, 47
Artificial Intelligence of Things, 330
Artificial Neural Networks, 28
Artificial Super Intelligence, 48
Ashton, Kevin, 331
ASOS, 81, 392
Astra beer, 364
Attribution analysis, 79, 116, 155, 256, 288
Augmented reality, 4, 12, 67, 325, 336, 337
Augmented search, 360
Avro, 306, 307, 308, 309
Backlinks, 233
Backpropagation, 33, 34, 35, 37
Baidu, 6, 28, 50, 232, 263, 313, 314
Bain & Company, 102, 103, 381
Bebo, 251
Behavioral information, 164
Behavioral patterns, 163
Big Data, 24, 54, 105, 166, 206, 288, 331, 334
Blogging, 251, 265
Blogosphere, 264
Blogroll, 263
Blogs, 46, 251, 257
Bookmarking, 251

Bookmarking websites
  Delicious.com, 251
Brand management
  Apostles, 102, 110, 394
BT Group, 87
Caesars, 105, 106, 202, 203
Caffe2, 125, 315, 319, 338, 340
Cambridge Analytica, 40, 69, 245, 279, 280
Campaign management, 155, 164
Casino Engagement and Loyalty Platform, 123
Chatbots, 26, 82, 121, 157, 347, 348, 349, 350, 351, 352, 354, 370
Chauhan, Alok S., 28
China's AI Awakening, 48
Cialdini, Robert, 226, 227
Cisco, 129, 287, 328, 334
Classification of Social Media, 254
Clickstream, 85, 114, 141, 154, 161, 201, 231, 343
Clickstream analysis, 79, 201
Click-thrus, 62
Cloud computing, 62
Cluetrain Manifesto, The, 286, 321
Collaborative projects, 46, 233, 255
Concept of self-presentation, 254
Consumer-Generated Media, 252
  blogs, 252
  digital video, 252
  mobile phone photography, 252
  news, 252
  online encyclopedias, 252
  podcasting, 252
  user reviews, 252
Content communities, 46
Content management, 251
Convolutional Neural Networks, 29, 30, 314, 315
CRISP-DM, 150, 151
CRM, 72, 77, 79, 97, 98, 99, 100, 101, 102, 103, 107, 109, 117, 122, 123, 162, 257, 273, 290, 325, 381, 382
CrowdOptic, 336
Cultural exchanges, 231
Customer acquisition, 79
Customer Acquisition Model, 185
Customer analytics, 23, 63, 110, 111, 113, 114, 115, 154, 155, 156, 157, 158, 159, 198, 245, 283, 380
Customer behavior, 23, 63, 97, 159, 380
Customer Centric Relationship Management, 102
Customer churn, 79, 102, 110, 111, 114, 123, 154, 192, 198, 208
Customer Churn Model, 191
Customer Conversion Model, 189
Customer dissatisfaction, 110, 123
Customer journey, 118
Customer Loyalty, 101, 108, 113, 115, 187
Customer satisfaction, 110, 123
Customer segmentation, 154, 181
  Segmentation→ Targeting → Positioning, 183
Customer's Psychological Profile, 277
Das Magazin, 277, 280
Data catalog, 300, 301, 302, 304
Data cataloging, 299, 301
Data governance, 8, 22, 153, 297, 298, 299, 300, 301, 302, 303, 304, 345
Data lake, 344
Data profiling, 300
Databricks, 7, 42, 43, 297
Decision tree, 165
  construction of, 166
Deep learning, 7, 15, 16, 18, 29, 33, 37, 38, 39, 43, 55, 313, 314, 315, 316, 317, 318, 319, 320, 331
Deep Neural Networks, 312, 313, 314
Deeplearning4j, 320, 321
DeepMind, 31, 32, 48, 318
Deighton, John A., 63, 230, 231, 232
Delicious.com, 261
Dell, 287
  social media command center, 287
Digital ecosystem, 22
Digital Interactive Marketing
  The Five Paradigms, 230
Discriminant Analysis, 178
Disney, 52, 364
  MagicBand, 52, 53, 54, 380
Drury, Glen, 251
eBay, 135
Eckerson, Wayne, 165
Economist, The, 263
Emarsys, 76

Engagement and Loyalty Platform, 124
Facebook, 1, 6, 21, 28, 34, 40, 41, 44, 46, 47, 51, 63, 69, 72, 78, 81, 82, 97, 98, 100, 101, 102, 105, 106, 109, 114, 115, 116, 121, 125, 128, 129, 138, 157, 175, 195, 200, 213, 214, 215, 229, 230, 232, 244, 245, 251, 253, 257, 258, 259, 263, 265, 268, 269, 270, 272, 277, 278, 279, 280, 281, 286, 287, 288, 289, 309, 310, 311, 314, 316, 319, 320, 322, 338, 344, 349, 350, 351, 352, 363, 364, 365, 380, 383, 384, 385, 388, 390, 391, 392, 393, 394, 396, 399, 400, 401, 403, 407
Facial Action Coding System, 92
Facial recognition, 362, 363, 364
Fitbit, 5, 97
Flickr, 251
folksonomy, 261
Forrester Research, 75
Four Steps of Social Media, The, 257
　create, 260
　join, 259
　listening, 258
　participating, 259
Foursquare, 124, 128, 129, 270, 325, 385
Gamification, 24, 131, 132, 133, 394
Gartner, 333, 336, 337, 361
Geofencing, 22, 126, 127, 128
Global Challenges Foundation, 50
Global Trust in Advertising, 109
GlusterFS, 306
Google, 6, 21, 29, 30, 40, 48, 51, 63, 67, 72, 129, 138, 205, 213, 231, 232, 233, 234, 256, 265, 268, 286, 309, 314, 316, 317, 318, 320, 344, 363, 365, 380, 383, 384, 390, 400, 403
　driverless cars, 333
Google Analytics, 205, 284
Google Answer Box, 374
Google Assistant, 67
Google Attribution, 205
Google Cloud Natural Language, 354
Google Dataset Search, 403
Google Home, 19
Google search, 233
GPUs, 39, 312, 313, 314, 316, 317, 320, 403
Greenberg, Paul, 100
Gulbransen, Scott, 382
Hadoop, 43, 114, 115, 116, 125, 297, 304, 305, 306, 307, 308, 309, 310, 311, 321, 325, 327, 340
　HDFS, 304, 305, 306, 308, 311
Having humans in the loop, 395
Hinton, Geoffrey, 33, 34, 36, 312, 317
Hitachi, 328, 362
Hive, 40, 310, 311
iBeacon, 126, 127
IBM, 1, 24, 48, 51, 96, 107, 110, 113, 116, 125, 154, 158, 162, 204, 288, 289, 327, 329, 353, 403
IBM InfoSphere, 328
IBM social media plan
　Assess, Measure, Integrate, 288
IBM Watson, 354
IBM Watson Analytics, 361
Image search, 30, 361, 367, 368
ImageNet, 57, 313, 403
InfiniteInsights, 116
Influence
　The Psychology of Persuasion, 226
Influencer marketing, 394
Instagram, 47, 72, 78, 100, 109, 124, 129, 225, 244, 268, 270, 365, 367, 380, 383, 384, 385, 388, 390, 392, 394, 400, 401
Internet, 231
Intromercials, 62
IoT, 67, 72, 95, 198, 297, 331, 332, 333, 334, 335
IoT, 330
Jiepang, 128
Jones, Thomas, 110
Juniper Research, 252
Kaliouby, Rana el, 91, 92, 93, 94, 95, 97
Keras, 154, 320
k-Means cluster, 167
k-Means Cluster Regression, 167
k-nearest neighbors, 169
Knowing What to Sell, When, and to Whom, 163
Kornfeld, Leora, 63, 230, 231
Kosinski, Michal, 277, 278, 279, 280
Kumar, R., 163
LeCun, Yann, 312

Lift and gains charts, 165
Lighthouse Signal Systems, 128, 129
Link building process, 360
LinkedIn, 44, 100, 114, 115, 253, 259, 260, 270, 286
Location analytics, 206, 207
Location-aware advertising, 126
Logistic regression, 39, 162, 170, 171, 172, 193, 317
Long Short-Term Memory' (LSTM) model, 402
Lovelock, Christopher, 99
Loyalty, 23, 98, 99, 102, 103, 104, 106, 108, 109, 110, 111, 114, 115, 122, 123, 128, 157, 158, 201, 203, 207, 245, 273, 288, 393, 394
Machine learning, 1, 3, 7, 8, 10, 12, 14, 15, 16, 17, 25, 26, 28, 37, 38, 39, 40, 41, 42, 43, 49, 51, 54, 56, 67, 72, 74, 77, 81, 91, 93, 119, 120, 121, 122, 135, 138, 139, 161, 162, 174, 175, 178, 194, 196, 205, 234, 235, 237, 238, 240, 241, 280, 282, 299, 303, 316, 317,318, 319, 327, 329, 331, 338, 339, 348, 349, 350, 353, 370, 379, 382, 397, 403, 404
Macy's, 369
Made in China 2025, 6
Maker's Mark, 258
MapReduce, 43, 116, 307, 308, 309, 310, 311, 318, 327
Market segmentation, 104, 105, 178, 184
Marketing Analytics Implementation
   Chronological view, 196
Marketing campaigns, 23, 63, 155, 165, 380
   automating campaigns, 163, 387
Marketing promotions, 97
Marketo, 204
Marr, Bernard, 331
Master Data Management, 149, 328, 343
MasterCard, 363
Media Richness Theory, 254
Message boards, 251
Messenger, 392
Micro-blog, 46, 265
Micro-blogging, 251

Microsoft, 3, 51, 67, 107, 204, 314, 316, 344, 385
Microsoft Text Analytics, 354
Millward Brown, 93, 94
MIT Technology Review, 7
MMS, 129
Mobile
   digital advertising, 62
Mobile advertising
   broad-based brand advertising campaign, 62
   campaigns, 62
   Interactive, direct response campaign, 63
   targeted search advertising, 63
Mobile Advertising, the book, 61, 62, 63, 325
Mobile analytics, 155
Mobile commerce
   personalization, 61
Mobile Marketing, 233
Mobile search, 233
Mobile value chain, 62
MyPersonality, 277
MySpace, 63, 114, 251, 259
Napster, 232
Natural Language Processing, 19, 134, 137
Net seed, 285
Netflix, 6, 26, 70, 164
Neural networks
   types of training, 29
Neural Networks in Data Mining, 28
NFC, 126, 333
Ng, Andrew, 312, 313
Nielsen, 109, 268, 270
Nike FuelBand, 97
Nvidia, 311, 312, 313, 314, 315, 320
Ocean Method, 277, 278, 279
Oculus Rift, 400
Omni-commerce, 75
Optimizing Offers, 193
Oracle, 3, 107, 204, 327
OTT, 22, 129, 390
Pandora, 26, 50, 70, 119, 164, 399
Patron Worth Model, 190
Periscope, 125, 129, 388
Personalization, 1, 13, 26, 27, 51, 54, 61, 64, 67, 68, 69, 70, 71, 72, 73, 74,

75, 76, 77, 80, 81, 82, 85, 90, 99,
102, 120, 121, 123, 124, 139, 140,
141, 164, 182, 202, 204, 213, 217,
225, 235, 236, 240, 245, 246, 280,
290, 321, 335, 344, 348, 371, 380,
400, 404, 409
Pinterest, 270, 358, 365, 385, 390
Podcasts, 251
Pokémon Go, 337
Post-roll video, 62
Predictive asset maintenance, 13
Predictive modeling, 163
  predictive models, 165
  segmentation methods, 164
  six steps of creating them, 165
Procter & Gamble, 61
Programmatic advertising, 10, 27, 119,
  120, 213, 214, 216, 377
Programmatic Media buying, 119
Propensity to Respond Model, 188
Property exchanges, 231
Proximity marketing, 126
Psychographics, 69
Psychology of personalization
  acquiescence effect, 218
  availability heuristic, 218, 223
  buffer effect, 218, 223
  conformity and social influence, 218, 221
  consistency principle, 218, 219
  decoy effect, 218, 222
  endowment effect, 217, 219
  foot-in-the-door technique, 218
  framing effect, 218, 220
  informational social influence, 218
  loss aversion, 218, 220
  mere exposure effect, 218, 221
  propinquity effect, 218, 223
  reciprocity, 24, 218, 227
  scarcity principle, 218, 224
Psychometrics, 277, 282
Push technology, 77
Pyra Labs, 263
Python, 116, 149, 154
PyTorch, 318, 319, 320, 321, 338
Qantas, 365, 366
Qlik, 163, 324
QlikView, 154
QQ Bookmarks, 263

QR codes, 22, 62
RACE framework, 121
RACI Model, 302
Real-time marketing, 24, 321
Reichheld, Frederick, 108
Reinartz, V.K., 163
Reinforcement learning, 13
RetailNext, 206
RFID, 52, 127, 323, 331
RFM Models, 186
Roku, 214, 247
Salesforce.com, 107
Samsung, 77, 97, 369
SAP, 3, 107, 116, 149, 154, 162, 200,
  329, 351
SAS, 1, 10, 11, 15, 51, 107, 116, 149,
  152, 153, 154, 162, 204, 324, 329,
  330, 331
Sasser, W. Earl, 102, 108, 110, 393
SCRM, 100, 122
Search engine, 21, 213, 232, 233, 234,
  255, 262, 279, 380
Second Life, 253
SEMMA, 152, 153
Sentiment analysis, 198, 199, 353
SEO, 236, 360
SEOMoz's, 262
Sharma, Chetan, 61, 62
Silicon Valley, 34
Singh, Dr. Yashpal, 28
Six Types of Social Media, 260
  Blogs, 263
  Collaborative Projects, 261, 262
  Content Communities, 267
  Social Networks, 270
  Virtual Game Worlds, 274
  Virtual Social Worlds, 274
Slideshare, 260, 268
Smith, P.R., 204
SMS, 77, 127, 129
Snapchat, 47, 363, 365, 385, 388, 391
  Promoted Stories, 392
Social bookmarking, 251, 261, 262
Social exchanges, 231
Social media, 251
  collaborative and dynamic communication model, 251
  The six types of, 46
  two-way dialogue, 251

Social media analytics, 282, 288
Social media monitoring, 100
Social Media Monitoring Tools, 355
Social media uses
  Discover Important Brand Trends, 61
  Social Media Monitoring, 286
Social network analysis, 282
Social Network Sites
  Definition, 270
Social networking, 251, 265
Social networking sites, 46
Social networks, 251
Social presence, 253
Social proof, 225, 387
  wisdom of the Crowds, 229
Source-Message-Channel-Receiver model, 251
Spark, 327
SPSS, 116
Starbucks, 46, 128, 283
Stodder, David, 155, 158, 159, 200
Stream Processing, 325
  comparison of services, 326
Streaming Analytics, 321, 325, 327, 328
Stumbleupon, 262
SugarCRM, 107
Supervised learning, 13
Survival or Duration Analysis, 179
Sutton, Scott, 172, 189, 191, 193
Swarm Intelligence, 181
Swiss AI Lab, 313
Tableau, 163, 324
  2018 Top 10 Business Intelligence Trends, 335
Talend, 22, 298, 299, 300, 301, 302, 303, 304
Taobao, 45, 134, 136, 137
  Rebate-for-Feedback, 137
TDWI research, 199
TDWI Research, 112, 158, 198, 284
Techcrunch, 37, 396
TensorFlow, 42, 43, 125, 154, 315, 316, 317, 318, 319, 320, 338
Text analytics, 198
Thought tracing, 231
TIBCO, 329
TIBCO StreamBase, 328
Time Series Model, 176
Tracinski, Rob, 55

Trust index, 300
Twitch, 72, 98, 125
Twitter, 44, 45, 72, 98, 100, 101, 114, 115, 125, 128, 129, 200, 229, 256, 257, 259, 263, 265, 266, 267, 269, 272, 283, 285, 286, 287, 288, 289, 316, 384, 385, 388, 390, 393, 394, 400, 401, 410
  Promoted Trends, 267
  Tweets, 265
  what is it?, 265
Twitter Revolution, 45
Uber, 24, 41, 247, 320, 385, 396, 397, 398
Uber Eats, 396
  Pool discounts, 397
Unilever, 285
Unsupervised learning, 13
User Generated Content, 252
  categories, 252
  mobile dating, 252
  personal content distribution, 252
  social networking, 253
Venkatesan, Rajkumar, 163
Verizon, 96
Video advertising, 369
Video pre-rolls, 62
Videocasting, 251
Virtual game worlds, 46
Virtual Reality, 336
Virtual social worlds, 46
Virtual worlds, 251
Virtual worlds websites
  worldofwarcraft.com, 251
Vlogs, 251, 257
Voice Activated Internet, 372
Voice recognition, 13, 241, 371, 372, 403
Voice Search, 233
Wähner, Kai, 325, 326, 328
Walmart, 82
Webopedia, 263
Website Morphing, 85
WeChat, 21, 24, 40, 44, 45, 53, 66, 72, 77, 78, 98, 101, 102, 114, 124, 128, 129, 244, 270, 271, 272, 273, 274, 325, 363, 365, 380, 385, 388, 389, 390, 393, 394
Weibo, 45, 72, 98, 100, 101, 102, 114,

253, 259, 265, 272, 283, 288, 393, 394
WhatsApp, 44, 53, 78, 98, 325, 392, 393, 400
Wheel of Loyalty, 109, 381
Wikipedia, 63, 251, 253, 254, 261, 262, 270, 271, 274, 321
Wirtz, Jochen, 99, 109, 381
Woods, Dan, 21, 213, 322, 380
Xbox One, 96
Yahoo!, 61
Youku, 44, 98, 125, 388
YouTube, 44, 63, 98, 129, 130, 232, 259, 267, 285, 287, 288, 388, 394
Youtube Live, 125
YY.com, 46, 275, 394
Zone of affection, 102, 110, 394
Zone of defection, 110
Zone of indifference, 110, 393